Κοινὴ Γραμματική

KOINE GREEK GRAMMAR

A Beginning-Intermediate Exegetical and Pragmatic Handbook

Κοινὴ Γραμματική

KOINE GREEK GRAMMAR

A BEGINNING-INTERMEDIATE EXEGETICAL AND PRAGMATIC HANDBOOK

FREDRICK J. LONG

GLOSSAHOUSE
WILMORE, KY
www.glossahouse.com

Κοινὴ Γραμματική

KOINE GREEK GRAMMAR: A BEGINNING-INTERMEDIATE EXEGETICAL AND PRAGMATIC HANDBOOK

© 2015 by GlossaHouse

GlossaHouse, LLC
110 Callis Circle
Wilmore, KY 40390

Publisher's Cataloging-in-Publication Data

Long, Fredrick J., 1966-
  Koine Greek grammar : a beginning-intermediate exegetical and pragmatic handbook / Fredrick J. Long. – Wilmore, KY : GlossaHouse, ©2015.

  xx, 605, [1] pages : illustrations ; 28 cm. – (Accessible Greek resources and online studies series. Tiers 1-3)

  Includes bibliographical references.
  ISBN 9781942697084 (hardback)
  ISBN 9781942697008 (paperback) (corrected version 21)

1. Greek language, Biblical – Grammar. 2. Greek language, Hellenistic (300 B.C.-600 A.D.) – Grammar. 3. Bible. – New Testament – Language, style – Problems, exercises, etc. I. Title. II. Series

Library of Congress Control Number: 2015909907
PA817.L66 2015   487/.4

The fonts used to create this work are available from www.linguistsoftware.com/lgku.htm.

Book Design and Typesetting by Fredrick J. Long.

Cover Design by T. Michael W. Halcomb. Cover image is "Man with a Wax Tablet." Original is from Douris (ca. 500 BCE). Image is public domain and is accessed at http://tiny.cc/ivi42x. The image has been slightly modified.

I dedicate KOINE GREEK GRAMMAR: A BEGINNING-INTERMEDIATE EXEGETICAL AND PRAGMATIC HANDBOOK *and its* WORKBOOK AND ANSWER KEY & GUIDE *to my Greek instructors. First, my beginning Greek instructor, now Dr. Richard Boone, whose kindness and constant encouragement provided the best environment for learning Greek. Second, to my Greek exegesis professors, Dr. Joseph Wang, for teaching me how to gather and weigh biblical evidence and illustrating the important exegetical principle CAP—Consider All Possibilities—and, in fond memory, Dr. Robert Lyon, for conveying to me his love for textual-criticism (which still inspires me) and the important exegetical principle CIE—Context Is Everything—Indeed!*

CONTENTS

AGROS

ACCESSIBLE GREEK RESOURCES AND ONLINE STUDIES

SERIES EDITORS

T. Michael W. Halcomb   Fredrick J. Long

GlossaHouse
Wilmore, KY

AGROS

The Greek term ἀγρός is a field where seeds are planted and growth occurs. It also can denote a small village or community that forms around such a field. The type of community envisioned here is one that attends to Holy Scripture, particularly one that encourages the use of biblical Greek. Accessible Greek Resources and Online Studies (AGROS) is a tiered curriculum suite featuring innovative readers, grammars, specialized studies, and other exegetical resources to encourage and foster the exegetical use of biblical Greek. The goal of AGROS is to facilitate the creation and publication of innovative, accessible, and affordable print and digital resources for the exposition of Scripture within the context of the global church. The AGROS curriculum includes five tiers, and each tier is indicated on the book's cover: Tier 1 (Beginning I), Tier 2 (Beginning II), Tier 3 (Intermediate I), Tier 4 (Intermediate II), and Tier 5 (Advanced). There are also two resource tracks: Conversational and Translational. Both involve intensive study of morphology, grammar, syntax, and discourse features. The conversational track specifically values the spoken word, and the enhanced learning associated with speaking a language in actual conversation. The translational track values the written word, and encourages analytical study to aide in understanding and translating biblical Greek and other Greek literature. The two resource tracks complement one another and can be pursued independently or together.

ACKNOWLEDGEMENTS

This grammar and workbook have been in the making for over two decades. It was first a small manual *Kairos Greek Grammar*; then it grew into a fully integrated and hyperlinked CD that has been published by Logos Bible Software (2005). Now, in this current form, *KOINE GREEK GRAMMAR: A BEGINNING-INTERMEDIATE EXEGETICAL AND PRAGMATIC HANDBOOK* has been thoroughly expanded to include a more explicit description of emphatic and pragmatic features of Greek, ideas that were nascent in *KAIROS*, but now grounded in a communication theory informed by relevance theory (Dan Sperber and Deirdre Wilson), prominence theory with reference to translation (Kathleen Callow), and discourse grammar and pragmatics (Stephen Levinsohn, Stanley Porter, and Steven Runge). To see this approach to Greek discourse in action, please refer to my *2 CORINTHIANS: A HANDBOOK ON THE GREEK TEXT*, Baylor Handbook on the Greek New Testament (Waco, TX: Baylor University Press, 2015), for which many thanks are due to Marty Culy, the series editor, for assisting me with that project that has greatly informed this current one.

There are many people to thank for their participation in this present undertaking. First and foremost would be the hundreds of Greek students over the years—first the seminary students at Asbury Theological Seminary, then one year at Trinity Evangelical Divinity School's extension campus in Milwaukee, WI, and then with undergraduate and graduate students at Bethel College in Mishawaka, IN. Since returning back to Asbury, I have had the privilege of teaching and learning from dozens more students in my classes on Greek Exegesis, Intermediate Greek, Advanced Greek, Textual Criticism of the NT, Independent Studies on Verbal Aspect and on Classic Greek, and informally in Greek reading groups. At Asbury 2013, we began *Gamma Rho Kappa*, the first ever (International) Greek Honor Society to promote and encourage Greek language and cultural study. In all, these students knew that they were and continue to be affectionately my "guinea pigs" and fellow disciples; a handful solicited and unsolicited were ever so helpful to point out dozens of typos. Thank you. It is the students who have inspired me to continue to improve this handbook and ultimately to publish it in print. Special thanks go to Gregory Neumayer, who was an excellent beginning student at Bethel College, who produced a fine word study that he generously allowed me to include as an example of what can be done in such word studies (see CH. 27).

Then there are the people who actually worked on the project because they needed to. (God bless their souls!) First is Bethel College's Religion and Philosophy School's office assistant, Mrs. Renee Kaufman, who helped retype the whole grammar portion of the manuscript when it only existed in a word processing format run from MS-DOS. This took her a good portion of a summer in early 2000s. Also, Matt Eaton as a research assistant during the summer 2004 helped me to correlate grammatical topics with Daniel Wallace's grammar among other things. Thanks to each of them. Also, I am extremely grateful for Dr. Jim Stump, then VP of Academic Services at Bethel College, for awarding me a Bethel Summer Research Grant over the summer 2004 to cover expenses in the final preparation of the manuscript for electronic publishing. Since then, there have been many graduate and post-graduate students who have helped discuss and look over chapters in various degrees of completion: Kei Hiramatsu, Na Lim Heo, Benson Goh, Shawn

Craigmilles, Jake Neal, Klay Harrison, Isaiah Allen, Caleb Wang, Cliff Winters, Andrew Coutras, Ryan Giffin, Lindsay Arthur, Sue Liubinskas, Adesola Akala, Matt Spangler, Daniel Johnson, David McAbee, Kevin Southerland, Jesse Moffitt, Mark Porterfield, Taylor Zimmerman, Jerry Breen, Anita Davis, Marshall Johns, and many others. Forgive me for forgetting to mention you! Jenny Read-Heimerdinger also read through two portions of my grammar attempting to summarize her and Stephen Levinsohn's work regarding the discourse pragmatic use of the article; I greatly appreciate her timely feedback. Then there is my colleague at GlossaHouse, Michael Halcomb, who has urged me to finish this project on a number of occasions and who has helped form ideas and to edit portions. We learn much from each other. I am particularly indebted to him for helping to identify Koine Greek grammatical terms (in Greek) for inclusion throughout this grammar, although I could not include all such terms. In addition to Robertson's magisterial grammar that has many of these, I also directly consulted Halcomb's *Handbook of Ancient Greek Grammatical Terms: Greek-English and English-Greek*, AGROS (Wilmore, KY: GlossaHouse, 2013).

The last group to thank include those who have encouraged and inspired me. Here my wife, Shannon, and our five children have urged me on in the project at different points, although it has not come without some cost for certain intense weeks here and there affecting our family time (okay, maybe more than a few weeks). Also, I would mention my first instructors of Greek, Dr. Richard Boone, Dr. Joseph Wang, Dr. David Bauer (who led weekly lunch reading groups), and Dr. Robert Lyon, all at Asbury Theological Seminary. Each played such inspiring roles as instructors and mentors of Greek. Dr. Julian Hills at Marquette University was a great help to me personally, helping me to obtain teaching assistantships there in my doctoral studies, largely on the merit of my abilities in Greek (which were invisible on the application forms). I attribute my electing to take his exegetical seminar on *The Psalms of Solomon* my first semester at Marquette as indeed providential. His excellent understanding of Greek inspired and spurred me on. Thanks to all of you!

To God be the glory! I can honestly say that His strength and grace have and motivated and sustained me.

ABOUT THIS GRAMMAR

Let me briefly explain about the what, how, and the why of *KOINE GREEK GRAMMAR: A BEGINNING-INTERMEDIATE EXEGETICAL AND PRAGMATIC HANDBOOK*. I once told a fellow seminary friend that I would never write a Greek textbook because of the vast numbers of them and, if I did, that he should shoot me. (We have met since then after having written one, and he has not done so!) However, when I became a Greek Teaching Fellow at Asbury Theological Seminary (1993-1995), I soon began to realize that no beginning textbook was completely "adequate." Each had their strengths, but also their corresponding weaknesses. Some explained English grammar; some assumed it. Some taught diagramming methods; some ignored them. Some explained too much; some explained too little. Some had adequate exercises; most very scanty. Some presented the material in a systematic and logical fashion; some appeared scattered. Some were deductive; some inductive. I could go on. Then, in 1994, I took an intensive Latin class in fulfillment of a Master's degree in Classics from the University of Kentucky. The textbook used was Floyd L. Moreland and Rita M. Fleischer's *LATIN: AN INTENSIVE COURSE* (1990). In this textbook I found a model for a *KOINE GREEK GRAMMAR* that would span two semesters (27 chapters). It is possible to work through one chapter a week and still have time for reviewing and testing during the semester. These are some of the special features that are built into *KOINE GREEK GRAMMAR*:

- ❖ An overview of a English grammar is provided in CHAPTER 1 that is set within a broader understanding of discourse as a Communicative Act. Also, the learning of newly presented Greek grammatical constructions is often accompanied by brief discussions of English grammar.
- ❖ Three methods for diagramming and analyzing sentences are introduced: first, a Constituent Marking Method, then the Reed-Kellogg diagramming approach, and finally Semantic Diagramming and Analysis
- ❖ A systematic presentation of grammar:
  - ➢ beginning with the Verb, the building block of Greek sentences;
  - ➢ followed immediately by First and Second Declensions Nouns along with the Article;
  - ➢ Prepositions and Compound verbs (verbs with affixed prepositions);
  - ➢ the more frequent Pronouns, such as Personal, Demonstrative, and Relative;
  - ➢ by the end of the first half of the *KOINE GREEK GRAMMAR*, all the tenses of the Indicative Mood are presented, all the proper prepositions covered, and the consonant-stem Third Declension nouns introduced.
  - ➢ In the second half, we cover the non-Indicative moods, vowel-stem Third Declension nouns, Mι Verbs, conditional sentences, and then generally, the least frequent points of grammar which have an occurrence of roughly 50 times or more.
- ❖ A strategic presentation of exegetically significant points of syntax and the use of language (i.e., pragmatics) occurs throughout *KOINE GREEK GRAMMAR*, including the following:
  - ➢ conjunctions and their constraints and point/counterpoint sets
  - ➢ fronted modifiers for nuance and emphasis (genitive, demonstrative, quantitative)
  - ➢ vocatives as thematic address and appositional statements
  - ➢ the historic present and the verb tense options in narrative
  - ➢ metacomments and interjections as attention getting devices
  - ➢ quantitative, qualitative, interrogative, negative, and comparative types of emphasis
  - ➢ polysyndeton, asyndeton, correlative emphasis, and lists

- ➢ special uses of the noun cases
- ➢ participle uses, including periphrastic and genitive absolutes, and special uses of the Moods
- ➢ left (dis)locations
- ➢ discourse pragmatic uses of the article
- ➢ conditional and exception clauses

❖ An overall vocabulary of words occurring 50 times or more (plus a dozen or so others)

❖ In each chapter the VOCABULARY is laid out in a simple, organized fashion:

- ➢ The most frequently occurring vocabulary words are included towards the beginning of the Grammar with few exceptions.
- ➢ Since the chapters are arranged by grammar, the corresponding parts of speech are presented then; for example, many adjectives are provided when the grammar of adjectives is introduced.
- ➢ Also, the parts of speech and special groups of Greek words within a Chapter Vocabulary are grouped together; for example, all the verbs are listed together, all the prepositions, all the nouns, etc. This makes memorization easier.
- ➢ A special section after each Chapter's VOCABULARY is included called NOTES ON VOCABULARY. This section contains a discussion of word meanings, English cognates to assist in memorization, common Greek idioms using the vocabulary words, and other important information.

❖ CHECK POINTS are often found in each chapter, sometimes two or three. These CHECK POINTS give students a chance to practice what is being learned then and there, and (SUGGESTED) ANSWERS immediately follow. If need be, cover up these answers as you work on these CHECK POINTS.

❖ A significant upgrade to this grammar has been my inclusion of intermediate level material, which is reflected in the above list of exegetically significant aspects of syntax and pragmatics; some material may approach advanced levels of analysis. Such intermediate material will be placed within greyed sections that often extend one or more pages. Beginning students are encouraged to skim or skip over this material, and then to return to it when they are able to digest it. In this respect, *KOINE GREEK GRAMMAR* is intended (in part) to be a reference work, to be referred to again. In the (near) future, I plan on collecting and expanding these discussions for a separate volume. Admittedly, in this HANDBOOK, there may be places, particularly in the latter chapters, where my discussions should have been placed within greyed sections and are not; yet, I thought that students advancing further and further through *KOINE GREEK GRAMMAR* would be more able to engage this material.

❖ A CASE IN POINT is included at the end of each chapter that briefly describes how a particular point of Greek grammar just presented helps us when interpreting the NT. In other words, the CASE IN POINT illustrates how Greek grammar and pragmatics are valuable for the study of the NT.

❖ Chapters will usually have one or more images of ancient *realia*, i.e., remnants of Mediterranean material culture including biblical and non-biblical papyri fragments, writing materials, vase paintings, coins, bas-reliefs, an imperial seal, inscriptions, funerary stele, statues, gems, temples, maps, and reconstructed scenes of life in the *polis*. The language and syntax of the Greek NT is contextually located in these worlds at some level.

❖ The final chapter describes perspectives and best practices for performing word studies.

❖ A well-organized and comprehensive APPENDIX is provided which includes a summary of all grammatical forms, accent rules, and pronunciation conventions.

❖ A master VOCABULARY [OF WORDS OCCURRING] 20 TIMES OR MORE is included at the end.

❖ Finally, *KOINE GREEK GRAMMAR* has a separate and extensive accompanying *WORKBOOK* that has been carefully crafted and also has within it an *ANSWER KEY & GUIDE*.

The content and approach of *KOINE GREEK GRAMMAR* is eclectic; I have learned Greek from many sources, first from J. Gresham Machen's classic text. Also, I have taught from and tutored students using the beginning Greek grammars of James Hewitt, J. W. Wenham, and William Mounce. I have consulted dozens of beginning Greek textbooks and most of the standard intermediate and advanced Greek grammars. I have especially appreciated the NT grammar of A. T. Robertson and the classical Greek grammar by Herbert Weir Smyth. I have also taught intermediate and advanced Greek classes using the grammars by Daniel B. Wallace, Stephen Levinsohn, Stanley Porter, and Steven Runge, whose works I am obviously indebted to, as my footnotes and citations duly indicate. The following works I have not provided full bibliographic citation in each instance, but rather I have indicated their last name or an abbreviated title (as given below =) and page or section numbers when used:

Blass, Friedrich, Albert Debrunner, and Robert Walter Funk (=BDF) *A Greek Grammar of the New Testament and Other Early Christian Literature*. Chicago: The University of Chicago Press, 1961.

Danker, Frederick W., Walter Bauer, and William Arndt, eds. (=BDAG) *A Greek-English Lexicon of the New Testament and Other Early Christian Literature*. 3rd ed. Chicago: University of Chicago Press, 2000.

Levinsohn, Stephen H. *Discourse Features of New Testament Greek: A Coursebook on the Information Structure of New Testament Greek*. 2nd ed. Dallas: Summer Institute of Linguistics, 2000.

Liddell, Henry George, Robert Scott, Henry Stuart Jones, and Roderick McKenzie. (=LSJ) *A Greek-English Lexicon*. Oxford: Clarendon Press, 1996.

Louw, Johannes P., and Eugene Albert Nida. (=L&N) *Greek-English Lexicon of the New Testament: Based on Semantic Domains*. New York: United Bible Societies, 1996.

Porter, Stanley E. *Idioms of the Greek New Testament*. 2nd ed. Sheffield: Sheffield Academic Press, 1994.

Robertson, A. T. *A Grammar of the Greek New Testament in the Light of Historical Research*. Nashville: Broadman, 1934.

Runge, Steven E. *Discourse Grammar of the Greek New Testament: A Practical Introduction for Teaching and Exegesis*. Peabody, MA: Hendrickson, 2010.

_____. *The Lexham Discourse Greek New Testament* (=LDGNT). Bellingham, WA: Logos Bible Software, 2008.

Smyth, Herbert Weir. *A Greek Grammar for Colleges*. New York: American Book Company, 1920.

Wallace, Daniel B. *Greek Grammar Beyond the Basics: An Exegetical Syntax of the New Testament*. Grand Rapids: Zondervan, 1996.

Finally, I must express my gratitude and indebtedness to my former Greek professors at Asbury Theological Seminary, Dr. Robert Lyon, Dr. Joseph Wang, Dr. David Bauer (who regularly held Greek reading groups at lunchtime), and particularly, Dr. Richard Boone, my first Greek instructor.

It is my hope that you will come to love the NT in Greek through using this Grammar and Workbook. Furthermore, I pray that you will become fruitful interpreters of God's Word and ultimately more effective pastors and teachers.

Fredrick J. Long
Ordinary Time, July 2015

CHAPTER 1

1.0 THE COMMUNICATIVE EVENT OF DISCOURSE

Faithful and insightful interpretation of Koine Greek is the purpose of this grammar; it has been written to help you read, understand, and faithfully interpret/exegete the Greek NT (GNT).

I want to begin by describing a foundational idea—that when one looks at a book as a whole, one is observing a **discourse**. Discourses are written to address the situation that exists between authors and their audiences. Authors **conceive** of the purposes of the discourse with **arguments** and **themes** in mind that will run throughout the discourse, involving **repetition**, which is the most basic and essential way to stress agents, actions, and attendant purposes and results. *In fact*, the discourse will be intentionally organized around agents, actions, and attendant purposes and results into **units**, **sections**, **paragraphs**, **sentences, clauses,** and **phrases**; notice that these organizational units range from larger size to smaller size. Many factors are at play why an author would develop this or that theme, using this or that organization, literary form, or genre. But the communicative goal is the maximum **reception** by the audience(s). At the smallest scale are **words** and word component parts that are called **morphemes**. Words are the foundational building blocks of discourse that can be understood within a hierarchal **discourse pyramid** set within **The Communicative Event** (see DIAGRAM 1).

The initial idea for this basic pyramid structure came from Stanley Porter.[1] However, I have added three more layers to it—morpheme, section, and unit. Each of these levels helps to describe discourse organization more completely, since even morphemes may be affixed to words for thematic purposes and since sections and units are observable within discourses to develop **themes** of topical focus for the sake of contributing to **conversations** or exchanges (real or imagined) between persons.[2] Some words, phrases, clauses, paragraphs, etc. will be distinguished from other words, phrases, clauses, paragraphs in that they will be **naturally prominent** in their con-

---

[1] Stanley E. Porter, *Idioms of the Greek New Testament*, 2nd. ed. (Sheffield: JSOT, 1994), 299 (Fig. 21).

[2] For example, between paragraph and discourse levels, one observes sections and units; e.g., the Corinthian Correspondence contains thematic summaries that relate back to consolidate whole sections and units (see 1 Cor 10:31-11:1; 14:37-40; 15:58; 2 Cor 12:11–13:10).

tent or form. Death, judgment, salvation, sex, strife, injustice, and suffering are naturally prominent content or themes. Commands, purpose statements, and questions are naturally more prominent forms, since our attention is given to them. But, authors may also grammatically mark or
emphasize words, phrases, clauses, paragraphs through special constructions to give them more
prominence. It is our work as interpreters to seek to understand the exact nature of specially emphasized discourse elements or constituents within their complete communicative context.

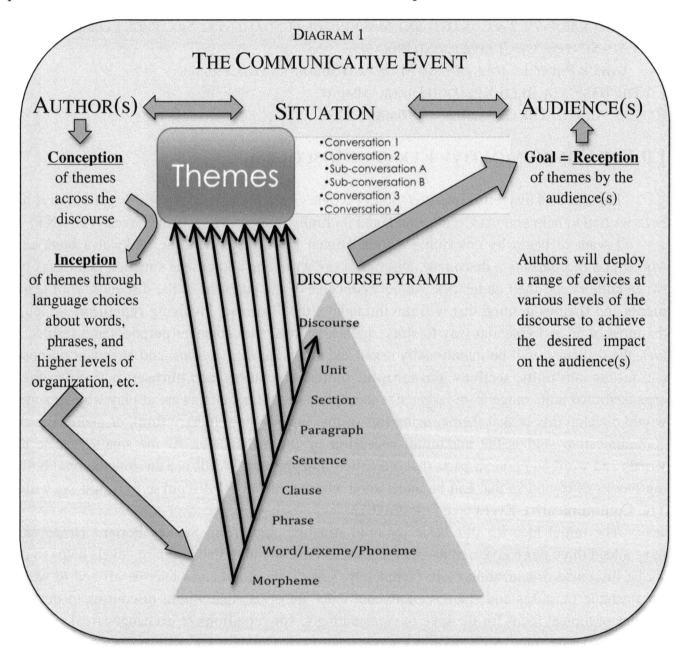

DIAGRAM 1

THE COMMUNICATIVE EVENT

AUTHOR(S)   SITUATION   AUDIENCE(S)

Conception
of themes
across the
discourse

Themes

•Conversation 1
•Conversation 2
 •Sub-conversation A
 •Sub-conversation B
•Conversation 3
•Conversation 4

Goal = Reception
of themes by the
audience(s)

Inception
of themes through
language choices
about words,
phrases, and
higher levels of
organization, etc.

DISCOURSE PYRAMID

Discourse

Unit

Section

Paragraph

Sentence

Clause

Phrase

Word/Lexeme/Phoneme

Morpheme

Authors will deploy
a range of devices at
various levels of the
discourse to achieve
the desired impact
on the audience(s)

For example, consider what Jesus said in Matt 5:17: *Do not think that I have come to destroy the Law or the Prophets; I did not come to destroy but to fulfill!* Naturally prominent words
and notions involve the actions of destroying/fulfilling and the entities of the Law or the Prophets.
Moreover, people hearing these words in tandem would especially pay careful attention. Also, the
negative command is rather prominent: *Do not think…* since it involves opposition and the call to

stop some activity. Taken together, all these notions are attention getting; their combination here together only would have augmented their prominence. However, these naturally prominent items are also grammatically marked in relation to each other in three ways. First, the activities of destroying and fulfilling are connected in what is called a "point-counterpoint" statement (*not this … but* this) that creates an explicit contrast. Second, these same notions are communicated as purpose statements by the protagonist in the discourse, namely, Jesus. Third, these purpose state-ments of Jesus are nestled within what is called a "meta-statement"—a statement that stands above those surrounding it to provide perspective and an awareness of the communicative event. Here Jesus explicitly calls the audience not to hold a certain view of him, to let go of some nega-tive assessment of him—an assessment that he denied: *Do not think this other thing of me, but rather think this of me about my purpose!* Meta-statements rise above what is happening to ex-press evaluation, attitude, or feeling about what is happening in communication. As such, meta-statements disclose important information about people's awareness and intentions in the situation of the communicative event.

This meta-statement leads us to consider the broader significance of 5:17 in the context of the Sermon of the Mount (Matthew 5-7). This verse expresses the purpose of the protagonist Jesus to fulfill the Law and the Prophets in view of a real or potential misunderstanding about his purpose. The importance of 5:17 is further seen in its shift to first person singular ("I") from the second person plural ("you") in the previous paragraph of 5:12-16. This previous paragraph culminated with its own purpose statement in 5:16: "(You) let your light shine, in order that…people would glorify God…!"). So, Jesus' purpose immediately follows his admonition to his audience to let their light shine in order that people would glorify God. We should consider why this would be. What relationship exists between these two purposes? In 5:18, Jesus further comments about the Law (5:18) and having a righteousness that surpasses that of the preeminent religious leaders of Jesus' day (Scribes and Pharisees); this statement is followed by a warning that if a person does not have a surpassing righteousness to that of these religious leaders, he or she will not ever enter into the Kingdom of Heaven (5:19-20). We should also consider the broader discursive signifi-cance of 5:17 across Matthew's Gospel. Jesus' statement of *fulfillment* relates to the Gospel of Matthew's fulfillment theme centered on Jesus (see, e.g., 1:22; 2:15, 17, 23; 3:15; 4:14, etc.). What other connections exist?? Well, I think you get the point! (This exclamation is a meta-statement from me to you to encourage you in this task of learning language.)

Thus, what I present above in Diagram 1 is a reconstruction of the workflow of discourse formation, starting with a **shared situation** and moving to the **authorial conception of themes** to contribute to **conversations**, then to the **inception of those themes** within the discourse, and fi-nally to the goal of **maximum reception by the audience**. If this model is an accurate portrayal, then the implication is that *all textual phenomena that can be observed in a discourse must be in-vestigated to determine their respective contribution to thematic development as contributing to conversations for meaningful, receptive, and successful communication.* What we are doing, then, when interpreting discourses such as we have in the NT is reverse engineering the process; we are unpacking what was communicated to arrive at the communicative intentions of the authors. But first we must learn some rules before we can play safely on this enjoyable playground.

1.1 GRAMMAR: THE FINAL FRONTIER

It is true that we speak every day unaware of the grammatical and syntactical rules, even the communicative conventions that govern our language. Many of us may not remember the *parts of speech* that English uses (noun, verb, adjective, etc.). When one learns a new language, it may be helpful to review basic grammatical terminology. To do so, additionally, has many benefits. Not only will we obtain a better command of our own language use, but we will also grow in our awareness of communication processes and how meaning is conveyed through word choice, modifying relationships among sentence elements, sentence structures, arrangement of materials, and conventions of discourse. Thus, relearning English grammar alongside Koine Greek grammar will aid our interpretation of the Bible or any discourse, whether we are working with Hebrew, Greek, or English.

Throughout this textbook, I will set English grammar alongside Greek grammar as an aide to learning Koine Greek grammar. Additionally, you may want to consult an introductory English grammar textbook. The ultimate goal, however, is not to become "grammatical geniuses" but to learn Greek *effectively* so as to gain a confident and productive use of Greek in your handling of the Word of God as given in the GNT.

This present chapter will provide a basic review of English grammar. This will begin foundationally with reviewing **the parts of speech: noun, pronoun, adjective, preposition, verb, adverb, conjunction**, and **interjection** (§1.2). Next, the basic constituents of the English sentence—namely, **subject, verb, direct object, indirect object**, and **modifiers**—will be explained (§1.3) in addition to the important function of **conjunctions** (§1.4). This information will allow one to recognize different types of **clauses** and phrases (§1.5). During these explanations, you will be introduced to **Constituent Marking** that will **help** you navigate sentences; this method will eventually be applied to Greek sentences (see §4.6 CONSTITUENT MARKING FOR NAVIGATING A GREEK SENTENCE). Then the **Reed-Kellogg procedure** for diagramming simple English sentences will be explained. Finally, a set of examples will conclude the chapter.

1.2 THE PARTS OF SPEECH

A. **Introduction:** The *parts of speech* are the basic building blocks of sentences. Greek, like English, has many parts of speech. The English language belongs to the larger family of languages called Indo-European (see §2.1 GREEK LANGUAGE TREE that contains a family chart of these languages). As such, it has been greatly influenced by many languages, including Greek. Although this influence is seen especially with vocabulary words built from Greek words (such words are called cognates), the two languages are also very similar with regard to their parts of speech.

B. **Noun:** a person, place or thing; e.g. *house, woman*, or *Jesus* (a proper noun). Another name for a noun is ***substantive***. This word *substantive* helps to identify certain words that are "converted into" and function like nouns, even though these words technically are another part of speech. For example, consider the adjectives in the title, *The Good, the Bad, and the Ugly*, that function like nouns. As we will see, Greek adjectives and other words not uncommonly function as *substantives* (i.e. as nouns).

C. **Pronoun:** stands in the place of a noun; e.g., *he*, *she*, *it*, *they*, *we*, *you*. The noun to which the pronoun refers is called the "antecedent" (lit. *going before*), because often the pronoun comes sometimes after the noun antecedent, which is located before it. For example, "Jesus healed the blind man next. He said, ..." The *He* refers back to *Jesus*. Often it is clear for what noun a pronoun stands in place. Yet sometimes the exact antecedent is debatable. When working with sentences, you need to consider whether it is clear what the pronoun refers to. I recommend drawing a dashed line with arrow from the pronoun to its antecedent; if more than one possibility exists, put a question mark over the various options to alert that more work is needed to consider the options. For example, consider the verse below (NASB95):[3]

1 Cor 1:18 [18] *For the word of the cross is foolishness to those who are perishing,*

but to us who are being saved it is the power of God.

The pronoun *it* refers back to *the word of the cross*.[4] Sometimes the English is unclear, as is the case with the first *them* in Luke 18:16 (using the NASB95). However, in Greek *them* is not unclear in its referent (for which see NIV).

English has many types of pronouns:

personal: *I, my, me, we; you, your; he, she, it, they, his, hers, their*
reflexive: *myself, yourself, herself, themselves* (note: relates back to subject)
demonstrative: *this, these; that, those* (note: a pointer)
interrogative: *Who? What? Why? Where?*
indefinite: *someone, anyone, a certain one*
relative: *who, which, what* (note: starts a subordinate clause)

The Greek language adds several other types of pronouns that are very significant for interpretation (see, e.g., §19.1 REFLEXIVE PRONOUNS, §19.2 RECIPROCAL PRONOUNS, §19.3 POSSESSIVE PRONOUNS, §19.4 INDEFINITE RELATIVE PRONOUNS).

---

[3] Most Scripture quotations are either from the NASB95 or slightly altered from it in order to illustrate a point of grammar, unless otherwise noted.

[4] In English, one could argue that *it* refers to *the cross*; however, the primary idea is *the word*, because it is the subject of the first *is*; thus it is more likely to be the subject of the second *is*. Also, the Greek places emphasis on *of the cross* as a modifier of *the word*, so that one must understand *the word of the cross* as a unit (Ὁ λόγος ... ὁ τοῦ σταυροῦ).

D. **Adjective:** modifies a noun or acts alone like a noun (i.e. becomes a substantive). Adjectives ascribe qualities or attributes to nouns; e.g. *noisy* cat, *good* woman, *righteous* man. Or, consider this title once again: *The Good, the Bad, and the Ugly.* Here the adjectives function like nouns, standing alone. Alternatively, we might understand that these adjectives modify implied nouns: *The Good Guy, the Bad Guy, and the Ugly Guy.* Notice that we might assume and supply the noun "Guy" to indicate what the adjectives modify.

E. **Preposition:** a word that governs a noun or pronoun or substantive to form a phrase that modifies either the verb (adverbial use) or a substantive (adjectival use). A preposition begins a prepositional phrase (abbreviated PP), which can be marked off easily by placing it within parentheses: (*into the house*). Common English prepositions include the following: *in, into, out, of, from, through, for, alongside, up (to), with, over, at, to.* There are many others, however! Prepositions express important relationships between agents, objects, and entities in general (cause, purpose, location, means, etc.).

Consider this sentence: *The woman (in the house) walked (into the garage) (with the stroller).* Which prepositional phrase is modifying a noun (adjectival use) or the verb (adverbial use)? Sometimes, the decision between them is not easy (as is the case with the last PP in this sentence). Consider also the prepositional phrases in this verse:

Rom 5:2 *(Through Christ) we have also obtained (by faith) our introduction (into this grace).*

Can you identify which prepositional phrases are adjectival and which are adverbial in function? Such is the stuff of interpretation and theology. The first two are adverbial.

F. **Verb:** explains the action or state of being of the grammatical subject within a sentence. In English, the verb will often be made up of several elements: a helping or auxiliary verb and the main verb. For example, *She has learned* contains the auxiliary verb "has" and the main verb "learned." Critical concepts for verbs in English include "tense" (time of action: present, past, progressive past, perfect, pluperfect, and future), "voice" (whether the subject is the "active" actor, acts upon himself/herself, or is acted upon and "passive"), and "modality" (whether the action is a simple statement, command, or potential action). To <u>identify</u> the verb in sentences, we <u>will use</u> a single underline. Consider the verbs in the verses below:

Gal 3:11-12 [11] *Moreover, that no one <u>is justified</u> by the Law before God <u>is</u> evident; for, "The righteous man <u>shall live</u> by faith." [12] However, the Law <u>is</u> not of faith; on the contrary, "He who <u>practices</u> them <u>shall live</u> by them."*

The first verb "is justified" is passive in voice—that is, the subject "no one" is receiving the action of "being justified." The second and fourth verbs (both, "is") are indicating states of being. The third and sixth verbs are active in voice—that is, the subject performs the action of the verb) and are also in the future tense ("shall live"). As you can see, verbs are very dynamic and will deserve (and will take!) much of your focus when learning Greek.

G. **Adverb:** often modifies the action of the verb but may also modify adjectives or other adverbs. To mark an ⌐adverb⌐, place it in a dashed box. For example, consider Rom 5:7:

Rom 5:7 *For one will* ⌐hardly⌐ *die for a righteous man, although* ⌐perhaps⌐ *for the good man someone would dare* ⌐even⌐ *to die.* Notice that the adverbs are placed in immediate proximity to the verb they modify, sometimes in the middle of the verb.

H. **Conjunction:** connects sentences, clauses, or phrases in some formal or logical relationship. Some conjunctions will connect equal parts, as in compound subjects in this sentence: *Dogs and cats fight.* Some conjunctions will subordinate one clause to another: *Dogs fight cats, because dogs are guarding their territories.* Common conjunctions in English include *and*, *but*, *however*, *therefore*, *for*, *because*, *if*. To mark a [conjunction], place a solid box around it. For example, in Gal 3:11-12 below, the English boxed words function as conjunctions and are translated from the underlying Greek conjunctions:

Gal 3:11-12 [11] [Moreover], [that] *no one is justified by the Law before God is evident;* [for], *"The righteous man shall live by faith."* [12] [However], *the Law is not of faith;* [on the contrary], *"He who practices them shall live by them."*

The English translation attempts to accurately convey the formal relation and logic conveyed by the conjunctions. Conjunctions are very dynamic and sometimes difficult to translate. In fact, we are still learning how best to understand their function. In this textbook, I will be including the most current research on conjunctions and their function.

I. **Interjection:** are exclamations like *Wow! Alas! Behold! Truly.* These words are not extremely common, but when present, they are very important. Interjections function as "attention-getters" pointing forward and highlighting what immediately follows.[5] As such, the use of interjections often occurs at the beginning of a sentence (somewhat like a conjunction) and highlights what follows. As far as marking, [interjections] can be placed within a box, although one could make a case that interjections should be marked like ⌐adverbs⌐. For example, consider 2 Cor 6:2b:

2 Cor 6:2b [Behold], *now is "the acceptable time,"* [behold], *now is "the day of salvation."*

Also consider Jesus' teaching in John 14:12:

John 14:11-12 [11] *Believe me that I myself am in the Father and the Father is in me, but if you don't believe, believe because of the works themselves.* [12] [Amen! Amen!] *I say to you, he who believes in Me, the works that I do, he will do also; and greater works than these he will do; because I go to the Father.*

---

[5] See particularly Runge §5.4.2.

1.3 THE BASIC CONSTITUENTS OF THE ENGLISH SENTENCE

A. **The Simplest English Sentence must have both a Subject and a Verb:** For example, *Jesus wept*. Even the command *Go!* has an understood subject *(You) Go!* The subject may be a noun or a pronoun or a substantive (any word that acts like a noun). Sometimes in English, and especially in Greek, substantives can be made from certain parts of speech: adjectives, prepositional phrases, verbals (i.e. infinitives and participles) and, therefore, can function as the subject. When marking a sentence, both the <u>verb</u> and the <u>subject</u> receive a single underline. Why? Because they work so intimately together. For example, consider John 3:17:

> **John 3:17** *For <u>God</u> <u>did</u> not <u>send</u> the Son into the world <u>to judge</u> the world, but that <u>the world</u> <u>would be saved</u> through Him.*

One observes three verbs with the first and the last having an expressed subject: *God did send* and *the world would be saved*. The second verb *to judge* (an infinitive in English) implies the subject *he* (either referring to God or the Son), and when placed with the implied subject would need to be rendered *in order that he would judge…*, which formally represents the underlying Greek. It is important to notice that the second and third verbs are not part of the main sentence; they are subordinate clauses, yet each verb has its own subject.

B. **Transitive and Intransitive Verbs:** Some verbs transfer action from the subject to another noun. These are called **transitive verbs**. Verbs that do not transfer action from the subject to another noun are called **intransitive verbs**. From the example above, the verb *wept* is intransitive. Some examples of transitive and intransitive verbs are given below.

> <u>transitive</u>: *to hit, to put, to send, to heal*

> Here are some examples: *He hit <u>the ball</u>. She put <u>the pencil</u> on the table. He sent <u>the apostles</u>. Jesus healed <u>them</u>. Peter walked <u>the dogs</u>.*

The underlined words are affected by the verb. Notice how the subjects *act* upon the other nouns. The verbs above describe this transference of action.

> <u>intransitive</u>: *to walk, to sit, to laugh, to be.*

> Here are examples: *Peter walked (across the street). Julie sat (quietly). We laughed (together). He is good (good is an adjective).*

Some verbs may act either transitively or intransitively depending on the sentence: For example, in the sentence *He walked*, the verb is intransitive; and yet in the sentence *He walked the dog*, the verb is used transitively.

C. **Direct Object:** Transitive verbs, as stated above, involve the subject performing some activity involving or creating another noun or substantive. This other noun is called a **direct object** (DO). In marking, the DO receives a <u>double underline</u>. The direct object is acted upon by the subject. For example, *Peter healed <u>the man</u>*, and *He called <u>the woman</u> <u>a disciple</u>*. The direct objects are *the man* in the first sentence and *the woman* and *a disciple* in the second sentence. The *man* receives the action; he was healed. The *woman* was ascribed a status, *a disciple*. It should be noted that transitive verbs may have two direct objects: one an **external object** to the action (here *the woman*) and one an **internal object** produced by the action (the name *disciple*). Another example of an internal direct object would be *She sang <u>a song</u>* where the *song* is produced by the action of singing. In this case the direct object would also be a **cognate object** that is derived from the same word root ("sang" and "song").

D. **Indirect Objects:** Occasionally the action done by the subject is done *to* or *for someone* or *something*. The substantive or noun *to whom* and *for whom* an action is done is called the **indirect object** (IO). In marking, the IO receives a <u>dashed underline</u>. For example,

> *The man brought a bone <u>to the dog</u>* and *She gave the speech <u>to them</u>*.

E. **The Basic Sentence "Slots" of Subject, Verb, DO, and IO:** Thus far we have learned that the essential sentence is built around a <u>verb</u> with a <u>subject</u> (present or implied). In addition, one may observe at times a <u>direct object</u> and sometimes an <u>indirect object</u>, although these elements are strictly optional depending on the verb used and the intended meaning. These basic sentence components are the backbone, so to speak, and provide basic information about persons and objects involved in the action or statement made by the verb. Importantly—pay attention!—every other element in the sentence may be considered a "modifier" (see immediately below)—something that Eugene Nida (visiting lecturer) taught during an exegesis class when I was a graduate student at Asbury Theological Seminary.

F. **Modifiers:** All the parts of speech—but especially adjectives, adverbs, prepositional phrases, pronouns, direct address, and verbals (participles and infinitives)—might function in the sentence to modify the <u>subject</u>, <u>verb</u>, <u>direct object</u> or the <u>indirect object</u> **by providing more information about them**. This is what modifiers do: to qualify and to describe other sentence constituents. In fact, modifiers may modify other modifiers. Therefore, modifiers are *extremely important* in interpretation because they involve authorial decisions to provide further delimitation and description to any particular element or word in the sentence. Additionally, a word may have multiple modifiers. In Rom 5:11 below, consider all the modifiers and modifying clauses that are placed in bold. The motherload of meaning is born by the modifiers.

> **Rom 5:11** ⬚And⬚ **not only this,** ⬚but⬚ <u>we</u> **also** <u>exult</u> **in God through our Lord Jesus Christ, through whom we have now received the reconciliation**…

1.4 Conjunctions: Lexical Meanings, Constraints, And Pragmatic Effects

A. **Conjunctions Interlink Sentences and Sentence Constituents:** Thus far we have learned terms that describe the basics of the English sentence: subject (S), verb (V), direct object (DO), indirect object (IO), and modifiers (M). But how do conjunctions function? Basically, I like thinking of *conjunctions* as glue that links and relates words, phrases, clauses, sentences, and paragraphs together. These "linkages" conveyed involve semantic constraints and functional-pragmatic uses that may not be adequately described by a brief gloss definition and that are context dependent.

1. Gloss Word Definitions. A basic meaning for a word is called a "gloss." A gloss is a brief definition of the word. It is simplified. Throughout this textbook, you will be given word definitions that are glosses.

2. Lexical Semantics is Context Dependent. Simply put, **lexical semantics** refers to the **inherent** or **dictionary meaning(s) of a word** or **language unit**. Any particular word may carry meanings that are fairly stable, although these meanings will always be context dependent; words will be used within a given context or will begin to create their own context that will delimit their meanings. For instance, the word *well* alone can signify an adverb, adjective, exclamation, noun, or verb with ten basic meanings.[6] However, under these ten basic meanings, *well* can be used with thirty-three different sub-uses and nuances. These various uses emerge through careful study of the context; when *well* is added with other words in an emerging discursive context, its semantics become fairly obvious to the native speaker, as in "Well, I disagree!" (exclamation of emotion) or "The well is deep" (noun indicating a hole, although possibly used poetically, since we don't know if this refers to an actual physical hole or a metaphorical hole). Although the exact meaning of a word must be determined by studying its use in context, the semantics or meaning of a word is still normally constrained (*well*, after all, is still delimited to ten basic meanings!); in other words, words are not empty, meaning anything, but have limited meanings in contextual use.

3. Constraints. Recently, Stephen Levinsohn describes Greek conjunctions as providing **contextual constraints** that help readers or hearers properly *process the information conveyed in the interlinked clauses, sentences, and even paragraphs or sections*.[7] I find his work particularly helpful. So, when introducing this or that Greek conjunction in this handbook, I will describe their functional constraints as marked in actual usage.

---

[6] Data is based on Apple's *Dictionary* Version 2.2.1 (156).

[7] See especially Stephen H. Levinsohn, *Discourse Features of New Testament Greek* and "'Therefore' or 'Wherefore': What's the Difference?" (Paper presented at the SBL Greek Language and Linguistics Section, San Francisco, Calif., November, 20, 2011).

4. <u>Functional-Pragmatic Use and Effects</u>. The **meaning of words in contextual use** *transcends* or *is more than their inherent semantic constraint of meaning*.[8] For example, the Greek conjunction ἀλλά (pronounced *ahl-lah*) is normally glossed as meaning "but, yet, rather." Yet, Levinsohn describes the constraint of ἀλλά to be **correction**; it is marked +correction. In other words, ἀλλά introduces a correction in contextual use. Pragmatically, however, ἀλλά is very often conjoined with negative words like οὐκ (*ouk*) or equivalents that mean *no(t)*; when combined, οὐκ ... ἀλλά produce corrective statements, "*Not* this ... *but* this ...". Further intensive study is being conducted on this pragmatic corrective function of οὐκ ... ἀλλά and similar constructions.[9] What else might we learn about the contexts of correction where these constructions occur? Are the corrections based upon real or perceived problems? What kinds of problems are these; thinking, practical matters, or social realities? Are there other dimensions signified in such corrections? Does the οὐκ ... ἀλλά construction mark intensity of correction? What variations are allowed? Are their alternative constructions? What might these variations mean? The bottom line is this: We need to understand that words occur in context with other words in specific uses and that their sum total may often be greater than their individual contributions. In other words, the significance of words will extend beyond their singular dictionary glosses and meanings, because they work with other words around them for broader communicative effect. Word usage is strategic within discourses.

5. <u>Constituent Marking Conjunctions</u>. For now, we need to consider some basics of how to understand conjunctions. When constituent marking a sentence, I recommend placing con-junctions in a box. Below are the two major categories of conjunctions according to their broadest functions.

B. **Two Functional Categories of Conjunctions:** Conjunctions may be classified into two categories: coordinating and subordinating. **Coordinating conjunctions** connect two or more equal components or sentences. **Subordinating conjunctions** place a subordinate clause into relationship with the main clause. A sentence that has a subordinate clause in it is called a **complex sentence**. A few examples of each are given below:

<u>coordinating</u>: *and, but, however, therefore*

<u>subordinating</u>: *if, that, because, while, after, (al)though, in order that, so that*. When marking a sentence, if you see one of these or other subordinating conjunctions, place an opening bracket [... in front of it and then consider where the subordinate clause ends in order to place a closing bracket ...]

---

[8] Jef Verschueren indicates, "Pragmatics does not deal with language *as such* but with *language use* and the relationships between language form and language use" ("Introduction: The Pragmatic Perspective," pages 1-27 in Jef Verschueren and Jan-Ola Östman, eds., *Key Notions for Pragmatics* [Handbook of Pragmatics Highlights 1; Amsterdam: John Benjamins, 2009], 1, emphasis original).

[9] Shawn Craigmiles, *The Pragmatic Constraints of Ἀλλά in the Synoptic Gospels* (Wilmore, KY: GlossaHouse, 2015).

1. <u>Coordinating Function</u>. Sometimes conjunctions coordinate two more or less **equal** parts; e.g., *Peter* and *John went to the tomb*. Here two subjects are joined by *and*; thus we have what is called a **compound subject**. It is also possible to connect two sentences together, thus forming a **compound sentence**. For example, *They went to the tomb,* but *Mary left it*. The *but* signals a contrast of expectation: we might have expected Mary to stay, *but* she left. In English, compound sentences reflect poor style, but in Greek these are quite common.

2. <u>Subordinating Function</u>. A conjunction may be used to connect two or more **unequal** parts, thus signaling that one clause is **subordinate** to another. What makes a clause subordinate is that it cannot stand alone as an independent statement and make "sense." Thus, an **independent clause** is one that can be said alone and be relatively complete, whereas a **dependent clause** typically cannot be said alone and make sense.[10] Instead, the dependent clause depends on the main, independent clause. A sentence containing a subordinate clause is said to be complex. Consider these examples that begin with a capitalized word but otherwise have no punctuation. Which clauses can be spoken alone and be understood independently without assuming something else, and which clauses need another clause to make them complete?

    a. *When the Son of Man comes in his glory*
    b. *Although Jesus himself was not baptizing*
    c. *God has spoken to us through his son*
    d. *Because you did not believe my words*
    e. *If anyone wants to come after me*
    f. *Whoever hears the word of God and believes*
    g. *In order that you would be filled with joy*
    h. *that John came home*

The only certain independent clause above is the third one (c.). If you found this a difficult exercise, don't fret too much. If punctuation is provided (like commas and quotation marks, etc.), as is sometimes the case, they would help you identify dependent/subordinate clauses, which will occur in the beginning or end of the dependent clause. In this previous sentence, which of the four clauses is the main clause?[11]

3. <u>Marking Subordinate Clauses</u>. When marking sentences, subordinate clauses are placed within brackets, [since this sets them apart from the main clause]. Notice that I placed this

---

[10] The only exceptions are indirect and direct statements. For example, *John came home* could be an independent clause (as is), or a subordinate direct statement, *She said, 'John came home.',* or a subordinate indirect statement, *She said that John came home.* These later two sentences would each have *John came home* as a subordinate clause.

[11] The main clause is this statement: "they would help you identify dependent/subordinate clauses."

last clause in brackets […]; I did so because it is a subordinate clause. Consider this example:

John 3:23a *John also was baptizing in Aenon near Salim*, [because *there was much water there*];

In this example, the subordinate clause *because there was much water there* is initiated with the conjunction *because* linking the idea of *much water* with the main clause *John also was baptizing* (providing the "reason"). This sentence is a **complex sentence**, because it contains one or more subordinate clauses.

CHECK POINT 1.2-4
CONSTITUENT MARKING OF FUNDAMENTAL SENTENCE ELEMENTS

In our discussion to this point, we have described the eight parts of speech and how these might function as constituents to form the backbone of a Greek sentence: Subject, Verb, Direct Object (DO), and Indirect Object (IO). Additionally, one finds modifiers (M).

Some parts of speech may always be marked a certain way, because of their relative stability of function within the sentence. Thus, adverbs receive a dashed box or circle and conjunctions and interjections are placed within a solid box. Verbs are always single-underlined, and (prepositions and their phrases) are placed within parentheses (…). For pronouns, draw a dashed arrow from them to their antecedent (i.e. what they stand in for). Additionally, the basic sentence components are marked in special ways. On the one hand, the subject is underlined to correspond to the verb; on the other hand, direct objects receive a double underline and indirect objects receive a dashed underline. So, to summarize, these markings are:

adverbs

conjunctions and interjections

subjects and verbs

direct objects

indirect objects

(prepositions and their phrases)

pronoun and its antecedent or postcedent

Below are Scripture verses that have been used as examples above. Further below are the answers; cover them up. First, mark these constituents in the verses accordingly. Then compare your work with the answers. You will have more opportunity to practice in the workbook exercises for this chapter.

EXERCISES

Gal 3:11-12: [11] Moreover, that no one is justified by the Law before God is evident; for, "The righteous man shall live by faith." [12] However, the Law is not of faith; on the contrary, "He who practices them shall live by them."

Rom 5:2: Through Christ we have also obtained by faith our introduction into this grace.

Rom 5:7: For one will hardly die for a righteous man, although perhaps for the good man someone would dare even to die.

2 Cor 6:2b: Behold, now is "the acceptable time," behold, now is "the day of salvation."

John 3:17: For God did not send the Son into the world in order that he would judge the world, but in order that the world might be saved through Him.

ANSWERS AND NOTES

Gal 3:11-12: [11] Moreover, that no one is justified (by the Law) (before God) is evident; for, "The righteous man shall live (by faith)." [12] However, the Law is not (of faith); ((on the contrary) , "He who practices them shall live (by them)."

NOTE: "On the contrary" is technically a prepositional phrase (…) in English, but here functions as a conjunction to connect two clauses together. In fact, in the Greek the English prepositional phrase is a conjunction, so it is boxed above.

Rom 5:2: (Through Christ) we have also obtained (by faith) our introduction (into this grace).

Rom 5:7: For one will hardly die (for a righteous man), although perhaps (for the good man) someone would dare even to die.

NOTE: "To die" is a complementary infinitive completing the meaning of "dare"—so it is functioning with the main verb and single-underlined.

2 Cor 6:2b: Behold, now is "the acceptable time," behold, now is "the day (of salvation)."

NOTE: "The acceptable time" and "the day" are really subjects, but are placed last in the sentence for English emphasis. One can easily rearrange the sentences as follow: "The acceptable time is now…the day of salvation is now."

John 3:17: For God did not send the Son (into the world) in order that he(?) would judge the

world, but * in order that the world might be saved (through Him).

NOTE: Between "but" and "in order that" is an implied sentence * "he sent the Son…" Also, it is unclear precisely who the "he" (?) is who would be judging: Is it God or the Son? The underlying Greek does not definitively resolve this; so, one would need to study the theme of "judgment" in John's gospel, and whether it is God or the Son who is presented as judge or who will eventually judge.

1.5 MAIN SENTENCES, CLAUSES, AND PHRASES

Once we understand how the parts of speech (1.2) function within a basic sentence (1.3) and how conjunctions can function to connect equal elements within a sentence or to subordinate elements to other elements (1.4), then we can continue to expand our understanding of types of clauses (main/independent and dependent) and to understand types of phrases as modifying expressions.

A. **Review: The Main Clause and Dependent Clauses:** A clause is any group of words having or implying a verb in it, usually with a subject. The **main sentence**, which may be comprised of a subject, verb, modifiers, and objects, is called the **main clause.** The main clause is able to be stated alone and be grammatically correct. It can be spoken by itself and make sense. A **dependent clause** (also called a **subordinate clause**) cannot be stated on its own and make sense; it requires connection to another clause, the main sentence. In the two sentences below from Rom 5:6-7, try to identify the main sentence and dependent clause.

> **Rom 5:6-7** [6] *For while we were still helpless, at the right time Christ died for the ungodly.* [7] *For one will hardly die for a righteous man, although perhaps for the good man someone would dare even to die.*

There are four clauses. The first and the fourth are dependent or subordinate clauses. The second and the third are the main sentences.

First Clause= *For while we were still helpless,*
Second Clause= *at the right time Christ died for the ungodly.*
Third Clause= **For one will hardly die for a righteous man;* [*For is a conjunction]
Fourth Clause= *although perhaps for the good man someone would dare even to die.*

Thus, there are two types of clauses: main clauses and dependent clauses. It is helpful to mark off dependent clauses using brackets [...].

B. **Phrases:** A *phrase* is any group of words that belong together but have no verb. A very common type of phrase is a prepositional phrase. When marking a sentence, prepositional phrases are placed within parentheses (...). From Rom 5:6-7 above, there are several phrases: *at the right time, for the ungodly, for a righteous man, for the good man.*

CHECK POINT 1.5
IDENTIFYING MAIN AND SUBORDINATE CLAUSES

Below are two Scripture passages; one was used as an example immediately above. Further below are the answers. Cover them up.

First, place boxes around all the conjunctions. Second, place brackets [...] around all the subordinate clauses. Be sure you are able to identify the main clause and differentiate it from the subordinate clause(s). You may number subordinate clauses on their brackets [¹...¹], [²...²], etc. Finally, compare your work with the answers. You will have more opportunity to practice in the Workbook exercises.

EXERCISES

Rom 5:6-7: [6] For while we were still helpless, at the right time Christ died for the ungodly.

[7] For one will hardly die for a righteous man, although perhaps for the good man someone would dare even to die.

John 3:16-17: [16] For God so loved the world, that He gave His only begotten Son, that he who believes in Him shall not perish, but have eternal life. [17] For God did not send the Son into the world in order that he judge the world, but in order that the world might be saved through Him.

ANSWERS AND NOTES

Rom 5:6-7: [6] For [while we were still helpless], at the right time Christ died for the ungodly.

[7] For one will hardly die for a righteous man, [although perhaps for the good man someone would dare even to die.]

John 3:16-17: [16] For God so loved the world, [¹ that He gave His only begotten Son, [² that he [³ who believes in Him³] shall not perish, but have eternal life ²] ¹].* [17] For God did not send the Son into the world [in order that he judge the world], but [in order that the world might be saved through Him].

* **NOTE**: Sometimes subordinate clauses will occur within a subordinate clause; in such cases it is helpful to number the successive subordinate clauses [¹ [² [³ ... and then consider where they properly end, sometimes all "crashing closed" at the end of the sentence ³] ²] ¹]. This will take some careful observation, consideration, and skill.

To the left is a depiction of a Greek Hoplite or heavy soldier (to be distinguished from slingers and archers).[12] The Greeks were adept at warfare, being disciplined and well-organized. There are several ancient accounts of their prowess and tactics. One of my favorites is Xenophon's *Anabasis* (Ἀνάβασις; "The Expedition Up"), which recounts 10,000 Greek Hoplites as mercenaries hired by Cyrus the Younger to help settle the dispute between him and his brother Artaxerxes II. After fighting their way deep up into the Persian empire, Cyrus died; then all the Persian troops united and fought against the Greek Hoplites, who had to march back to Greece greatly outnumbered. However, at one point they stopped to hold athletic contests. Paul's discussion in Romans 5 draws upon military imagery of a hero dying on behalf of many, although the current Emperor Nero was reminded by his court philosopher Seneca that thousands of soldiers are ready to die for him (Seneca, *On Mercy*).

---

[12] William Carey Morey, *Outlines of Greek History: With a Survey of Ancient Oriental Nations* (New York: American Book Company, 1903), 223.

1.6 THE BASICS OF REED-KELLOGG DIAGRAMMING

A. **Introduction:** The use of sentence diagramming methods may help students unpack and understand the semantic relationships among constituents in the Greek sentence. Throughout this handbook, I will present three methods of marking or diagramming English and Greek sentences. First, **Constituent Marking** has already been demonstrated in part above and will be introduced in relation to the Greek sentence in §4.6. Second, immediately below, I will present a basic approach to **Reed-Kellogg Diagramming**. Both Constituent Marking and Reed-Kellogg Diagramming will be explained further in this handbook at strategic points. Third, a description of **Semantic Diagramming** and **Semantic Analysis** is given in §16.4 and §16.5 respectively. Semantic diagramming complements Constituent Marking quite well and may be very profitably used after many kinds of modifiers and subordinate clauses are learned.

B. **Which Diagramming Approach to Use?** Each method may have a place in the analysis of a Greek sentence. However, for beginners, I strongly encourage **Constituent Marking** for three reasons. First, it is fairly easy. Second, it requires no manipulation of the Greek text, that is, there is no copying and pasting in or typing in of the Greek text. Third, and most importantly, constituent marking preserves Greek word order, which is very significant for indicating nuance, emphasis, and thematic focus. After working with constituent marking, students should be able to move into Semantic Diagramming and Analysis fairly easily. The principles below are applicable for any of the diagramming methods.

C. **Word Order:** The word order in the typical English sentence is relatively standard: subject (S), verb (V), direct object (DO), indirect object (IO). Modifiers (M)—such as adverbs, adjectives, possessives, prepositional phrases and the like—may be found anywhere in the sentence close to the word they modify.

	S	**V**	**DO**	**IO**	**M**
An example:	*The man*	*sent*	*the letter*	*to the parents*	*of his wife.*

This word order is very important. To change the word order is to change the meaning of the sentence altogether: *The letter sent the man of his wife to the parents.* In fact, this sentence is virtually nonsensical. Although word order is very important to carry the basic idea in English, in Greek it is somewhat less important to communicate the *basic* idea. It must be said, however, that the variation in word order in Greek is *often quite significant* for conveying thematic focus, emphasis, and structural patterning. **NOTE:** *The variable word order in the Greek sentence is often troublesome for the beginning Greek student.*

D. **English Word Order Variations:** English does sometimes vary word order slightly. These variations can be seen occasionally in questions, poetry, and proverbs.

	DO	**V and S**	**IO**
An example:	*All*	*have I given*	*to you.*

I recall singing this hymn by Henry F. Lyle, "Jesus, I My Cross Have Taken." Notice how out of place *My Cross* is as the DO. This variation abuts the *I* with *My Cross* for rhetorical impact.

E. **Basic Sentence Functions:** Before diagramming a sentence, one must first understand the sentence grammar and be able to identify all the sentence components. The most essential parts have been described above: **subject** (S), **verb** (V), **direct object** (DO), **indirect object** (IO), and **modifiers** (M). After finding these components, one puts them into this type of format:

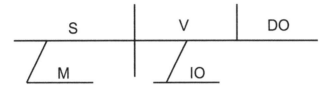

Modifiers (M) are placed directly below whatever they modify:

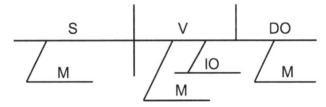

<u>**Example 1:**</u> Matt 8:23b *His disciples followed Him.*

<u>**Step one:**</u> Identify each component in the sentence:

M	**S**	**V**	**DO**
His	*disciples*	*followed*	*Him.*

<u>**Step two:**</u> Place the components in their appropriate place within the diagram.

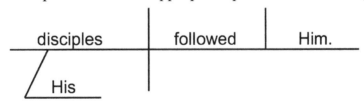

<u>**Example 2:**</u> Matt 9:2a *They brought to Him a paralytic.*

<u>**Step one:**</u> Identify each component in the sentence:

S	**V**	**IO**	**DO**
They	*brought*	*to Him*	*a paralytic*

Step two: Place the components in their appropriate place within the diagram.

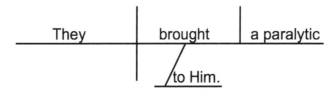

F. **Compound Components:** Diagramming two or more subjects, verbs, or direct objects that are compounded (connected with *and* or equivalent) is easy. First, identify how each word is functioning in the sentence. Then diagram it as shown in the example below.

Example: Mark 4:39 *He got up and rebuked the wind.*

Step one:

S	V	Compound V	DO
He	*got up*	*and rebuked*	*the wind*

Step two: The subject "He" is placed far left. Since there are two closely connected verbs that are compound, they are placed one atop the other with the conjunction in between. Since the second verb "rebuked" has a DO, this is placed after "rebuked."

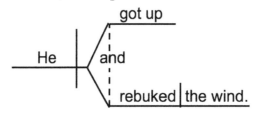

G. **Conjunctions, Interjections, and Direct Address:** Currently it would be valuable to learn how to diagram initial **coordinating conjunctions** (*And, Therefore, For*, etc.), **interjections** (*Behold!*), and statements of **direct address** (usually set off by commas such as *Brethren,…*). These are elevated on platforms. The platform for the initial coordinating conjunction or interjection is placed upon the subject line at the beginning of the clause.

Example: Matt 10:26a *Therefore, do not fear them.* [Note, there is no expressed subject since this is a command: *(You) do not fear!*]

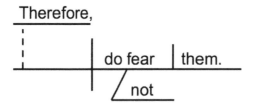

The direct address platform is placed upon whatever part of the sentence grammar the direct address relates. Here are two examples, with the first having direct address "*Lord, …*".

Matt 14:30b *"Lord, save me!"*

NOTE: The direct address "Lord," is placed on a platform above the implied subject "you."

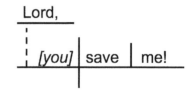

2 Thess 2:13 *But we should always give thanks to God for you, brethren…*

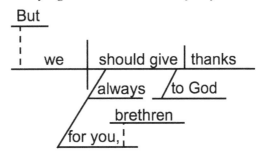

Complete WORKBOOK EXERCISES 1 and consult the ANSWER KEY & GUIDE as needed.

CASE IN POINT 1: THE GRAMMAR OF ROMANS 5:8-11

Simply knowing the grammatical and syntactical functions of words, phrases, and clauses will go a long way in the analysis and interpretation of any given biblical passage. To illustrate this, let's look at Rom 5:8-11 (NASB95), which will be shown having some constituent marking applied (as explained above) in stages or "scans" overlaid on the text.

In this first scan, I will identify both the main sentences by underlining the main verbs and their subjects and the subordinate clauses by placing them [¹ in numbered brackets ²].

[8] But <u>God demonstrates</u> His own love toward us, [¹ in that [² while *we were* yet *sinners²*], *Christ died* for us ¹].

[9] Much more then, [³ *having* now *been justified* by His blood ³], <u>we shall be saved</u> from the wrath of God through Him.

[10] For [⁴ if [⁵ while *we were enemies* ⁵] *we were reconciled* to God through the death of His Son ⁴], much more, [⁶ *having been reconciled* ⁶], <u>we shall be saved</u> by His life.

[11] And not only this, but <u>we</u> also <u>exult</u> in God through our Lord Jesus Christ, [⁷ through whom *we have* now *received* the reconciliation ⁷].

Essentially there are four <u>main sentences</u> with corresponding <u>subject and verb</u>. In the display below, I have included the connectors—mainly conjunctions and adverbs—at the front of each:

[8] But <u>God demonstrates</u>

[9] Much more then, <u>we shall be saved</u>

[10] For…much more, <u>we shall be saved</u>

[11] And not only this, but <u>we</u> also <u>exult</u>

The first main sentence in 5:8 indicates that God is the active subject. In the next three main sentences *we* is the subject; however, in the second and third sentences *we* is subject of future tense passive voice verbs—*we shall be saved*. The passive voice indicates that we shall be saved

through the action of another—that is the meaning of the passive voice. It would seem that our response to receiving so much is to *exult in God*.

We have received much! In 5:8 <u>God demonstrates</u> his own love (toward us), [¹ in that *Christ died* (for us) ¹]. This latter clause is one of seven subordinate clauses, all placed in numbered brackets (their subjects and verbs are *italicized*).

8 [¹ in that … *Christ died* for us ¹], [² while *we were* yet *sinners* ²]

9 [³ *having* now *been justified* by His blood ³]

10 [⁴ if … *we were reconciled* to God through the death of His Son ⁴], [⁵ while *we were enemies* ⁵], [⁶ *having been reconciled* ⁶]

11 [⁷ through whom *we have* now *received* the reconciliation.⁷]

After the first active verb in the first subordinate clause (*Christ* died for us), all the remaining verbs in the subordinate clauses relate to humans; these either describe our past time prior poor state of being ([² while *we were* yet *sinners* ²]; [⁵ while *we were enemies*⁵]) or are passive in voice ([³ *having* now *been justified* ³], [⁴ *we were reconciled* ⁴], [⁶ *having been reconciled* ⁶], [⁷ *we have* now *received* ⁷]).

Now, I would like to run another scan over what I have already done, a preposition scan. I will place all the prepositional phrases in parentheses (…) and within these indicate the repeated references to Jesus in **bold**.

8 But <u>God demonstrates</u> His own love (toward us), [¹ in that [² while *we were* yet *sinners* ²], *Christ died* (for us) ¹].

9 Much more then, [³ *having* now *been justified* (**by His blood**) ³], <u>we shall be saved</u> (from the wrath of God) (**through Him**).

10 For [⁴ if [⁵ while *we were enemies* ⁵] *we were reconciled* (to God) (**through the death of His Son**) ⁴], much more, [⁶ *having been reconciled* ⁶], <u>we shall be saved</u> (**by His life**).

11 And not only this, but <u>we also exult</u> (in God) (**through our Lord Jesus Christ**), [⁷ (**through whom**) *we have* now *received* the reconciliation ⁷].

The active agent demonstrating God's own love for us throughout is Christ Jesus. **Christ's agency** (in bold) is emphasized throughout the paragraph especially with the prepositional phrases beginning with *through* and *by*. These prepositions indicate "means" and "agency" (i.e. by what means or whose action of agency things get accomplished), and in this context, the phrases describe the means/agency behind God's purposes for humanity. What has Christ done and accomplished for us? Well, first and foremost, Paul affirms that Jesus demonstrates God's love for us by dying for us. Next, Jesus' blood brings us justification saving us from God's wrath. But more than this, Jesus' death reconciles us to God and His resurrected life will save us. Finally, it is through our Lord Jesus Christ that we "exult" (i.e., "boast" or "glory") in God. This is our reasonable response to what God has done in Christ (see Rom 12:1-2).

Another angle by which to look at this passage is through the seven subordinate clauses, which involve the time words "while," "yet," and "now." A contrast exists between *what we were* when God demonstrated his love for us and *what we now are*. We were sinners and enemies of God. But, through the agency of Christ, we now are justified and have now received reconciliation with God. We also await a final, future salvation. Here Paul emphasized how important and necessary this work of Christ is: We were sinners and thus enemies of God, deserving wrath (5:9). We had a desperate need to be reconciled with God; now through our Lord Jesus Christ we have this reconciliation and a future hope (5:9-10; cf. Rom 8:18-39). And all this leads us to *exult in God* **through our Lord Jesus Christ**. This verb translated *exult* in 5:11 is worthy of careful study; this verb also occurs in Rom 5:3. I demonstrate how to do a word study by looking at this verb in CH.27 (see CASE IN POINT 27: WORD STUDY ON Καυχάομαι *I BOAST* FROM ROM 5:3).

As you learn Greek, your analysis of the structure of English translated sentences will be greatly enhanced, since you will be able to double-check the underlying Greek words and constructions, which sometimes are not often fully or even accurately translated. You will more readily understand the semantics (word, phrase, and clause meanings) and the pragmatic function or use of language in context.

Below is the first leaf of a wooden wax tablet from the 2nd century AD found in Egypt.[13] It contains a portion of the Athenian comedy dramatist Menander (342-291 BC). The teacher has first written out the text and then provided lines within which the student was to rewrite the text. The verb ΠΙΣΤΕΥΕΤΑΙ at the end of the second line has been misspelled by the teacher (and pupil) and should be ΠΙΣΤΕΥΕΤΕ. (Oops!) These endings sounded the same in the Koine Era.

---

[13] BM Add MS 34186 (1); this photo, slightly edited, is in public domain. For the type of stylus used to write on such a tablet, see p. 108.

CHAPTER 2

2.0 PUNCTUATION—DOES IT MATTER?

Images speak loudly to people, because "[w]e prize and value our sight over our other senses."[1]   The writing of language initially was "pictorial" as seen in the Egyptian hieroglyphs. The very common Greek verb "I write" (γράφω) originally meant to "scratch" and hence "represent by lines, draw, or paint" (LSJ 360.I). Eventually the verb γράφω meant to "express by written characters, write" (LSJ 360.II). In English, this visual dimension is often seen in words derived from γράφω, like "graphic," "geo-graphy" (depiction of land/earth), etc.

At the same time, the ancient practice of writing represented an innovation to preserve oral communication, where often there was "power" in preserving a written word: Laws, the proclamation of military victory in praise of a god and a king (or a god-king), epic poetry, or a speech against a political rival. The first libraries were associated with royalty and temples (e.g., at Alexandria). Some texts were canonized; consequently, ancient textual production, especially of canonized texts, was often intended to encourage seeing and living in the world differently by later learners/disciples. One problem with the transmission of texts is that subsequent learners are farther and farther removed from the ancient "real world" that authors assumed in creating their discourse. Learning New Testament Greek is a major avenue to reenter the ancient world.

This chapter will introduce the student to the history of the **Greek language** and its **alphabet**—how to write it (orthography), pronounce it (orthoepy), and understand accents and other marks seen in the Greek NT, including punctuation conventions. Finally, the distinction between **Greek** and **non-Greek** or **foreign** "loan words" is discussed.

---

[1] Benjamin K. Bergen, *Louder Than Words: The New Science of How the Mind Makes Meaning* (New York: Basic Books, 2012), 49.

2.1 THE GREEK LANGUAGE (ἡ Ἑλληνικὴ Γλῶσσα)

A. **Greek Language Family:** All languages belong to a larger family of related languages. Related languages share characteristics, such as grammatical features and word roots, which are usually preserved in the consonants, because vowels show greater variation in pronunciation. Several different language families govern the thousands of languages spoken on earth. **Greek** is a part of the **Indo-European language family**. It would appear that in the distant past, a Proto-Indo-European language existed from which all Indo-European languages descended. CHART 2.1 depicts relationships among the Indo-European languages.

CHART 2.1 INDO-EUROPEAN LANGUAGE TREE

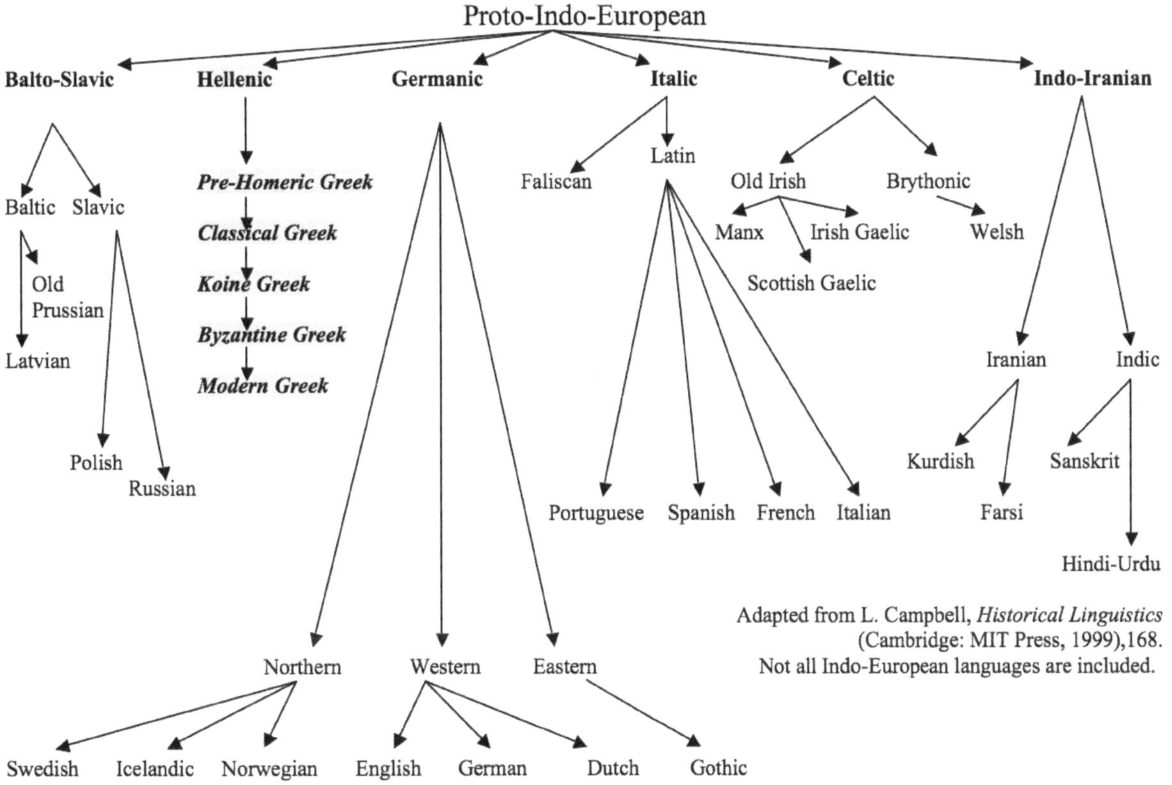

Proto-Indo-European

Balto-Slavic | Hellenic | Germanic | Italic | Celtic | Indo-Iranian

Baltic   Slavic

Pre-Homeric Greek

Classical Greek

Koine Greek

Byzantine Greek

Modern Greek

Old Prussian

Latvian

Polish

Russian

Latin

Faliscan

Old Irish   Brythonic

Manx   Irish Gaelic   Welsh

Scottish Gaelic

Iranian   Indic

Kurdish   Sanskrit

Farsi

Hindi-Urdu

Portuguese   Spanish   French   Italian

Adapted from L. Campbell, *Historical Linguistics* (Cambridge: MIT Press, 1999),168. Not all Indo-European languages are included.

Northern   Western   Eastern

Swedish   Icelandic   Norwegian   English   German   Dutch   Gothic

These languages (including English) share similar grammatical features and even in some cases vocabulary roots. Yet, how each language was written using symbols varied considerably according to the available writing systems. As we will see in §2.2 below, the Greek alphabet system derived from a Phoenician script that was originally written from right to left.

B. **Developmental Stages of the Greek Language:** Typically, the Greek language is described according to significant developmental phases throughout its history.[2] You can see above that Koine Greek is sandwiched in the middle of these developments.

---

[2] See Wallace (12-30) for a brief history of the language and its developments

1. Pre-Homeric Greek refers to the Greek language and its dialects used from its inception until about 1000 BC. This includes Linear A, Linear B, Cypriotic, etc.

2. Classical Greek refers to the regional dialects of Greek used from about 1000 to 330 BC. Attic Greek, named after the region Attica, is the best-known type from this period; many literary works have been preserved in this dialect, e.g. Plato and Aristotle. Other dialects include Doric, Ionic, Aeolic, which were spoken in Greece, the islands, and the western coast of Asia Minor (modern day Turkey).

3. Koine (or Hellenistic Greek) is the predominant style of Greek from approximately 330 BC to AD 330. You will be learning Koine Greek in this textbook, since it is the Greek of the NT period. Koine Greek became the *lingua franca* because of the conquests of Alexander the Great and the subsequent proliferation of Hellenistic culture throughout the Mediterranean world.

4. Byzantine (or Medieval Greek) refers to the use of the language from approximately AD 330 to 1453. In AD 330, the emperor Constantine relocated the seat of the Roman Empire to Byzantium or Constantinople (modern Istanbul). The latter date corresponds to the fall of the Byzantine Empire, which was conquered by the Turks.

5. Modern Greek is that used from AD 1453 to the present.

2.2 THE GREEK ALPHABET (ὁ Ἑλληνικός Ἀλφάβητος)

A. **Early Alphabet:** Greek was first written down using characters from the Phoenician alphabet. Significantly, the Greek Alphabet *was the first alphabet to represent vowels as letters*. CHART 2.2 contains the script used on inscriptions found at Crete dating to around 800 BC.[3] The Phoenicians wrote from right to left like Hebrew.

CHART 2.2a THE PHOENICIAN LETTERS

---

[3] This non-techincal basic description and CHART 2.2a is summarized from Simon Ager, "Greek language, alphabets and pronunciation" at http://www.omniglot.com/writing/greek.htm accessed 2-20-2014 and used by permission.

B. **The Greek Alphabet Standardized:** Around 500 BC, the Greeks established writing from left to right. Then officially in 403/2 BC, the Athenians standardized the Greek alphabet for writing with 24 characters that continued in use in the *Koine* era.[4] In CHART 2.2b the Greek letter names are given, first in Greek and then in an English pronunciation approximation (the $\bar{o}$ is a long "oh" sound). The additional marks are accents and breathing marks (see §2.5 ACCENTS, BREATHING, AND OTHER MARKS). The Greek characters have **uncial forms** (capital letters) and **minuscule forms** (lower case). Although the minuscule characters were developed in the 10th century, it is standard for modern Greek Bible editions to use them along with uncials.

CHART 2.2B THE GREEK ALPHABET			
Letter Names		**Uncials**	**Minuscules**
Greek	**Pronunciation**	**(capital letters)**	**(small letters)**
ἄλφα	*ahl-phah*	A	α
βῆτα	*vāy-tah*	B	β
γάμμα	*ghahm-mah*	Γ	γ
δέλτα	*dhehl-tah (≈thehl-tah)*	Δ	δ
ἒ ψιλόν	*eh-psee-lōn*	E	ε
ζῆτα	*zāy-tah*	Z	ζ
ἦτα	*āy-tah*	H	η
θῆτα	*thāy-tah*	Θ	ϑ
ἰῶτα	*yō-tah* or *ee-ō-tah*	I	ι
κάππα	*kahp-pah*	K	κ
λάμβδα	*lahmv-thah*	Λ	λ
μῦ	*meew*	M	μ
νῦ	*neew*	N	ν
ξῖ	*ksee*	Ξ	ξ
ὂ μικρόν	*ō-mee-krōn*	O	o
πῖ	*pee*	Π	π
ῥῶ	*rhō*	P	ρ
σίγμα	*seeg-mah*	Σ	σ, ς
ταῦ	*tahv*	T	τ
ὖ ψιλόν	*eew-psee-lōn*	Υ	υ
φῖ	*phee*	Φ	φ
χῖ	*khee*	X	χ
ψῖ	*psee*	Ψ	ψ
ὦ μέγα	*ō-meh-gah*	Ω	ω

---

[4] See the discussion of J. H. W. Penney "63. Writing Systems," in Edward Bispham, Thomas Harrison, and Brian A. Sparkes eds., *The Edinburgh Companion to Ancient Greece and Rome* (Edinburgh: Edinburgh University Press, 2010), 477-84 at 479-81.

The vowel names ἒ ψιλόν, ὂ μικρόν, ῦ ψιλόν, and ὦ μέγα developed later, but are used in this grammar for the the sake of consistent convention. In addition to these letters used in writing, some older letters like *digamma* (F ϝ), *kōppa* (Ϙ ϙ), and *sampi* (ϡ ϡ) were still used to signify numbers (see §12.4 GREEK ALPHABET AND NUMERIC VALUES). Kevin Robb summarizes the significance of this alphabet concisely:

> [T]he Greek alphabet, the first complete or true alphabet, was a recording instrument for human speech of unique precision and simplicity, permitting, in time, the emergence of the first fully literate—by which I mean alphabetically dependent—society. With fewer than thirty symbols to burden the memory of its learners, the Greek alphabet permitted a reader familiar with an underlying language to read with understanding any text, however unfamiliar. It also permitted a reader not familiar with an underlying language to know approximately how any written words ought to be sounded. No earlier script, including Old Phoenician and Old Hebrew, had achieved this.[5]

2.3 WRITING GREEK CHARACTERS: ORTHOGRAPHY (Ὀρθογραφία)

A. Writing Greek Letters takes Practice: Below are suggested ways to write out the Greek letters for minuscules (lower case) and uncials (upper case).[6] The arrows indicate pen strokes that may involve doubling back, bends, or circles. Ignore reproducing the tiniest serifs at the end of the strokes (as seen, e.g., in K). If more than one stroke is needed, the asterisk (*) indicates which stroke to begin with. Notice that some letters will extend slightly below the bottom (imaginary) line. At CHECK POINT 2.2-3 below, you will be asked to practice writing these letters.

---

[5] Kevin Robb, *Literacy and Paideia in Ancient Greece* (New York: Oxford University Press, 1994), 252.
[6] See also Eugene Van Ness Goetchius, *The Language of the New Testament* (New York: Charles Scribner's Sons, 1965).

B. **Paleography of Ancient Scripts:** The study of ancient writing style is called **paleography**. At the time the NT was written, scribes and secretaries wrote in uncial characters in a continuous script (*scriptum continuum*) with no formal punctuation system. Manuscripts reflecting such handwriting are called **uncials**. The conventions of writing characters—style, shape, size, form, and abbreviations—remained fairly consistent at any given point in time (over decades), because of the uniformity expected of scribes in their writing profession. In other words, writing style was conservative. However, one observes development in how these characters were written over time when comparing datable scribal hands, where the reconstructed script uses datable manuscripts found in Egypt.[7]

2nd BC from *Louvre j. d'e.* 7172	A B Γ Δ E Z H Θ I K Λ M N Ξ O Π P Σ T Y Φ X Ψ Ω
1st BC from *P. Oxy. xxxiii* 2654	A B Γ Δ E Z H Θ I K Λ M N Ξ O Π P Σ T Y Φ X Ψ Ω
1st AD from *P. Fouad* 266	A B Γ Δ E Z H Θ I K Λ M N O Π P Σ T Y Φ X Ψ Ω
2nd AD from the *Hawara Homer, Bodl. MS Gr Class a.I (P)*	A B Γ Δ E H Θ I K Λ M N Ξ O Π P Σ T Y Φ X Ψ Ω
3rd AD from *Cairo Mus. Inv.* 47426	A B Γ Δ E H I K Λ M N Ξ O Π P Σ T Y Φ X Ω

Eventually in the 10th century, the handwriting style began switching to cursive minuscules, and actual manuscripts are labeled as "**minuscules**" on this basis. Below is a depiction of the scribal hands of some major NT manuscripts in roughly chronological order in comparison to the Rosetta Stone (c. 196 BC).[8]

---

[7] These summaries of paleographic scripts are from http://users.ipa.net/~tanker/grkpal.htm accessed 2-22-2014 from the Bellum Catilinae Home Page. The creator stresses, "These examples are for those who are curious about what Greek letters looked like at certain periods in history. They are not useful for dating documents. For that, you need to consider the aspect of the entire document; letter shapes alone will not guide you. Letter sizes have been changed to enhance legibility. **This page is experimental**" (emphasis original).

[8] Image is from http://www.skypoint.com/~waltzmn/UncialScript.html, accessed 2-26-08 from *A Site Inspired by* "The Encyclopedia of New Testament Textual Criticism" conceived by Rich Elliott at Simon Greenleaf University.

As Found In:

Letter	Rosetta Stone	$\mathfrak{P}^{66}$	ℵ	B	A	D^ea	N	L^e	E^e	Θ	S
Α											
Β											
Γ											
Δ											
Ε											
Ζ											
Η											
Θ											
Ι											
Κ											
Λ											
Μ											
Ν											
Ξ											
Ο											
Π											
Ρ											
Σ											
Τ											
Υ											
Φ											
Χ											
Ψ											
Ω											

Of particular note is the σίγμα (Σ) that is written as a *lunar* σίγμα (ϲ). Many other particularities of ancient script and scribal practices are not represented above (e.g., the use of raised horizontal line [...¯] at the end of a line to represent a final νῦ).[9]

CHECK POINT 2.2-3					
PRACTICE WRITING GREEK CHARACTERS					
Letter	Minuscule	Uncial	Letter	Minuscule	Uncial
ἄλφα	- - - - - - - - -	- - - - - - - - -	νῦ	- - - - - - - - -	- - - - - - - - -
βῆτα	- - - - - - - - -	- - - - - - - - -	ξῖ	- - - - - - - - -	- - - - - - - - -
γάμμα	- - - - - - - - -	- - - - - - - - -	ὂ μικρόν	- - - - - - - - -	- - - - - - - - -
δέλτα	- - - - - - - - -	- - - - - - - - -	πῖ	- - - - - - - - -	- - - - - - - - -
ἒ ψιλόν	- - - - - - - - -	- - - - - - - - -	ῥῶ	- - - - - - - - -	- - - - - - - - -
ζῆτα	- - - - - - - - -	- - - - - - - - -	σίγμα	- - - - - - - - -	- - - - - - - - -

[9] For an excellent discussion, see Philip Wesley Comfort, *Encountering the Manuscripts: An Introduction to New Testament Paleography & Textual Criticism* (Nashville: Broadman & Holman, 2005).

ἦτα	- - - - - - - - -	- - - - - - - - -	ταῦ	- - - - - - - - -	- - - - - - - - -
θῆτα	- - - - - - - - -	- - - - - - - - -	ῦ ψιλόν	- - - - - - - - -	- - - - - - - - -
ἰῶτα	- - - - - - - - -	- - - - - - - - -	φῖ	- - - - - - - - -	- - - - - - - - -
κάππα	- - - - - - - - -	- - - - - - - - -	χῖ	- - - - - - - - -	- - - - - - - - -
λάμβδα	- - - - - - - - -	- - - - - - - - -	ψῖ	- - - - - - - - -	- - - - - - - - -
μῦ	- - - - - - - - -	- - - - - - - - -	ὦ μέγα	- - - - - - - - -	- - - - - - - - -

2.4 PRONUNCIATION AND SYLLABLES

A. **Pronunciation Systems:** Although there is no consensus which convention of Greek pronunciation should be followed, in this handbook I follow what T. Michael W. Halcomb has called Koine Era Pronunciation (KEP)[10] rather than the available Erasmian pronunciation conventions. If one wants to learn the Erasmian pronunciation, they can see APPENDIX §28. However, several substantial reasons exist for learning the KEP.

1. *Historical Study.* Since the study of NT Greek is an historical enterprise, students should utilize the best data for reconstructing Koine era pronunciation as possible.

2. *Euphony and Aural Impact.* NT authors constructed sentences and phrases naturally using sounds of actual speech; since there was no "silent reading," there was likewise no silent writing. So, NT authors spoke and wrote not just for semantic effect, but also with aural or auditory impact in mind. Writing replicated actual speech that contains alliteration, rhyming, and cadence; such features of the text support more formal aspects of discourse, such as repetition, parallelism, alternation, and chiasms. Thus, the ability to hear these features of Greek discourse will improve one's observation and recognition of patterning and emphasis.

3. *Tonal Stress and Emphasis.* My research to identify and describe emphatic features of Greek language has resulted in recognizing the aural impact of such constructions—e.g. isolated or "hanging" words, pauses, rhyming, repetition of sounds. So, this or that word or

---

[10] T. Michael W. Halcomb of the Conversational Koine Institute (ConversationalKoine.com) has kindly allowed me to use his research. See additionally, T. Michael W. Halcomb, "Never Trust a Greek…Professor: Revisiting the Question of How Koine Was Pronounced" (paper presented at the annual Stone-Campbell Journal Conference, Johnson City, TN, March 14, 2014); idem, "Pronouncing Koine Greek, A Dead Language: Issues Concerning Orality, Morality, and the Pronunciation of Koine Greek" (paper presented at the annual Theological Educators Forum on Orality, Wilmore, KY, April 14, 2014); T. Michael W. Halcomb and Fredrick J. Long, *Mark: GlossaHouse Illustrated Greek-English New Testament*, Accessible Greek Resources and Online Studies (Wilmore, KY: GlossaHouse, 2014), viii-ix.

this or that construction may often have been chosen for more than purely lexical-semantic reasons, i.e. for tonal stress and emphasis. Thus, our careful attention to the aural dynamics of utterance will bring us closer to the complete original communicative impact intended for audiences, both semantically and aurally. Additionally, the aural dimension will assist one to ascertain the atmosphere, mood, and tone of a pericope.

4. *More Natural Phonetic Language Acquisition.* I have personally found working with the Koine Era Pronunciation more natural and intuitive, in all likelihood simply because it represents a language actually spoken by living people, rather than an artificial academic convention. For additional reasons for following KEP, see APPENDIX §30.

B. **Koine Era Pronunciation:**

GREEK LETTER & PRONUNCIATION		PRONUNCIATION VALUE IN ENGLISH	EXAMPLES
ἄλφα	*ahl-phah*	*ah* – tor*ah*	λαμβάνω = *lahm-vahnō*
βῆτα	*vāy-tah*	*v* – *v*et	λαμβάνω = *lahm-vahnō*
γάμμα	*ghahm-mah*	*y* – *y*et (before ε and ι) *gh* – *gh*ost (before other vowels) *n* – before γ, κ, χ, or ξ	ἅγιος = *ah-yee-ōs* ἀγαθός = *ah-ghah-thōs* ἄγγελος = *ahn-gheh-lōs*
δέλτα	*dhehl-tah*	*dh* or *th* – *th*e	διά = *dhi-ah* or *thi-ah*
ἒ ψιλόν	*eh-psee-lōn*	*eh* – mikv*eh*	σέ = *seh*
ζῆτα	*zāy-tah*	*z* – *z*oo	ζῷον = *zō-ōn*
ἦτα	*āy-tah*	*āy* – p*ay*	μή = *māy*
θῆτα	*thāy-tah*	*th* – *th*ink	θεός = *theh-ōs*
ἰῶτα	*yō-tah* or *ee-ō-tah*	*y* – *y*es (at beginning of a word) *ee* – b*ee*t	νίκη = *nee-kāy* Ἰακώβ = *Yāh-kōv*
κάππα	*kahp-pah*	*k* – *k*eep	καπνός = *kahp-nōs*
λάμβδα	*lahmv-thah*	*l* – *l*eg	λέγω = *leh-ghō*
μῦ	*meew*	*m* – *m*ad	μέν = *mehn*
νῦ	*neew*	*n* – *n*o	νῦν = *neewn*
ξῖ	*ksee*	*ks* – boo*ks*	ξένος = *kseh-nōs*
ὂ μικρόν	*ō-mee-krōn*	*ō* – *go*	πρός = *prōs*
πῖ	*pee*	*p* – *p*eek	πρόσωπον = *prō-sō-pōn*
ῥῶ	*rhō*	*r* – *r*im (trill/roll)	ῥίζα = *ree-zah*
σίγμα	*seeg-mah*	*s* – *s*it	σάρξ = *sahrks*
ταῦ	*tahv*	*t* – *t*ip	τίς = *tis*

ὖ ψιλόν	*eew-psee-lōn*	*eew* – ewe or *au jus* (cf. οι) *v* – in diphthongs with α, ε, η	κύριος= *keew-ree-ōs* See diphthongs below.
φῖ	*phee*	*ph*– <u>ph</u>one	φάγε = *phah-geh*
χῖ	*chee*	*kh* – ba<u>ckh</u>oe (slight guttural)	χάρις = *khah-rees*
ψῖ	*psee*	*ps* – <u>ps</u>alm	ψώρα = *psō-rah*
ὦ μέγα	*ō-meh-gah*	*ō* – <u>go</u>	ὡσαννά = *ō-sahn-nah*

C. Vowels (**Φωνήεντα**), Monophthongs (**Μονόφθογγοι**), and Diphthongs (**Δίφθογγοι**):

1. <u>Vowels</u>. The Greek vowels are α, ε, η, ι, ο, υ, and ω. Vowels are either short or long in weight or stress. Ἔ ψιλόν (ε) and ὂ μικρόν (ο) are always short. Ἦτα (η) and ὦ μέγα (ω) are always long. Ἄλφα (α), ἰῶτα (ι), and ὖ ψιλόν (υ) can be either short or long.

2. <u>Monophthongs and Diphthongs</u>. A **monophthong** involves a combination of two vowels producing one sound whereas a **diphthong** involves two vowels where one sound glides into the other sound. Below are the **proper monophthongs and diphthongs** with pronunciation equivalents:

		PRONUNCIATION VALUE IN ENGLISH	**EXAMPLES**
MONOPHTHONGS	αι	*eh* – s<u>ai</u>d	δικαιοσύνη = *dee-<u>keh</u>-ō-seew-nāy*
	ει	*ee* – b<u>ee</u>t	βασιλεία = *vah-see-<u>lee</u>-ah*
	οι	*eew* – in ewe or *au jus* (French)	μακάριοι = *mah-kah-ree-<u>eew</u>*
	ου	*ou* – s<u>ou</u>p	τοὺς ὄχλους = *t<u>ous</u> ō-khl<u>ous</u>*
	υι	*eey*– ter<u>iy</u>-aki	υἱός = *eey-ōs*
DIPHTHONGS	αυ	*av* – <u>av</u>ocado *af*– w<u>af</u>t (before β, δ, γ, ζ, λ, μ, ν, ρ)	<u>αὐ</u>τοῦ= *<u>ahv</u>-tou* κραυγή = *kr<u>af</u>-gāy*
	ευ	*ev* – <u>ev</u>ery *ef* – l<u>ef</u>t (before β, δ, γ, ζ, λ, μ, ν, ρ)	πιστ<u>ευ</u>ω = *pee-st<u>ev</u>-ō* πν<u>ευ</u>μα = *pn<u>ef</u>-mah*
	ηυ	*āyv* – <u>āv</u>iary *āyf* – s<u>af</u>e (before β, δ, γ, ζ, λ, μ, ν, ρ)	προσ<u>ηύ</u>χετο = *prō-s<u>āyv</u>-cheh-tō* ηὕρισκον = *<u>āyf</u>-ree-skōn*

3. <u>Improper Monophthongs</u>. The **improper monophthongs** are ᾳ, ῃ, and ῳ. Notice the small ἰῶτα **subscript** (called ἰῶτα ὑπογεγραμμένον *written under*). Only these three vowels may have an ἰῶτα subscript. On the one hand, the ἰῶτα subscript *does not change* the pronunciation of ἄλφα (α), ἦτα (η), and ὦ μέγα (ω); thus, they are called **improper monophthongs**. On the other hand, the presence or absence of the ἰῶτα subscript is *always* important grammatically and lexically to distinguish forms and words. In ancient documents and inscriptions, when the ἰῶτα is not subscripted, it is found as an **adscript** written beside the ἄλφα, ἦτα, or ὦ μέγα.

D. **Syllabification:** To pronounce Greek words properly, one must be able to divide them into syllables. A **syllable** (συλλαβή) is a distinct pronunciation unit with a natural pause.

1. *A Greek word has as many syllables as it has vowels, monophthongs, and diphthongs.* Also, a vowel or diphthong normally ends a syllable when it is in the middle of a word.

GREEK WORD		SYLLABIFIED	PRONUNCIATION	ENGLISH MEANING
θέος	→	θέ ος	*theh-ōs*	*God*
γραφή	→	γρα φή	*ghrah-phāy*	*writing; Scripture*
οἶκος	→	οἶ κος	*eew-kōs*	*house*
βασιλεία	→	βα σι λεί α	*vah-see-lee-ah*	*kingdom*
θρόνος	→	θρό νος	*thrō-nōs*	*throne*
κλητός	→	κλη τός	*klāy-tōs*	*called*

2. *Consonant Clusters.* Two or three consonants in succession are called a **consonant cluster**. Sometimes you will find two or three consonants together in the middle of a word and you may not know immediately if they are a consonant cluster or not. So, here is a rule: When two or three consonants occur together in the middle of a word, *if they can begin a word,* then pronounce them together as a consonant cluster starting a new syllable. Otherwise, split up the consonants into two different syllables so that the first consonant ends the previous syllable. One exception to this rule are the consonant clusters γγ, γκ, γξ, and γχ which never begin a word. Here is a list of the most common consonant clusters beginning a word and therefore beginning a syllable:

			βλ					βρ	
			γλ					γρ	
			θλ					θρ	
			κλ					κρ	
			πλ		πν			πρ	ππ
	σκ			σμ			σπ		σχ
			τλ	τμ				τρ	στ(ρ)
	φθ		φλ					φρ	
	χθ		χλ					χρ	

Thus, consider these examples:

	SYLLABIFIED	PRONUNCIATION	EXPLANATION	MEANING
ἄνθρωπος	ἄν θρω πος	*ahn-thrō-pos*	(θρ- can begin a word)	*person*
ἐκκλησία	ἐκ κλη σί α	*ehk-klāy-see-ah*	(κλ- can begin a word)	*church*
λαμβάνω	λαμ βά νω	*lahm-vah-nō*	(μβ never begins a word)	*I take*
ἄγγελος	ἄγ γε λος	*ahn-ghehl-ōs*	(γγ never begins a word)	*angel*

2.5 ACCENT (Τόνος), BREATHING (Πνεῦμα), & OTHER MARKS (Στίχοι)

A. Greek has three accent marks: acute (´), grave (`), and circumflex (˜): In Greek, these accent names were respectively, ὀξύς (*high pitched*), βαρύς (*low pitched*), and ὀξύβαρις (*high-low pitch*). Normally a word will have only one accent. Accents may have originally indicated tone: acute rising ("no?"), grave falling ("No!"), and circumflex rising and falling ("ahhh."). But this was not the case in the Koine Era. In pronunciation, one should stress the syllable upon which the accent falls; this will be indicated by an accent mark in the transliteration value. The rather complex accent rules are presented in §24 SYNOPSIS OF GREEK ACCENT RULES. In this handbook, only in those cases where accent differentiates two otherwise identical words will they be discussed.

B. Greek has Smooth (᾿) and Rough (῾) Breathing Marks (τὸ Ψιλὸν καὶ τὸ Δασὺ Πνευμάτα): In common printing conventions, breathing marks *always* are found over initial vowels, monophthongs, diphthongs, and the Greek letter ῥῶ that begins a word. The smooth breathing mark is not pronounced, and the rough breathing mark originally added some aspiration, but hardly noticeable. By the Koine Era, the breathing marks were not relevant for pronunciation. However, when learning vocabulary, certain Greek words are differentiated on the basis of having a smooth or rough breathing mark. So, pay attention primarily to rough breathing marks. Consider the following words:

ῥῆμα (*rhāy-mah*). At the beginning of a word, the Greek letter ῥῶ will always have a rough breathing mark that does not change the pronunciation of the ῥῶ .

Ἰησοῦς (*Yāy-soús*). Breathing marks come before initial capital vowels.

αἱρέω (*eh-réh-ō*). Breathing marks fall on the second vowel of an initial monophthong or diphthong.

οἶκος (*eéw-kōs*). The circumflex accent goes above a breathing mark.

To the right is a papyrus plant from which paper was made as early as 3000 BC.[11] The plant grows abundantly in Egypt. To make paper, cut strips were layered one direction and then the other on top. Somewhat expensive to manufacture, papyrus was yet broadly used in the Medi-

---

[11] Image slightly adapted from Victor Duruy, *History of Greece, and of the Greek People: From the Earliest Times to the Roman Conquest*, trans. M. M. Ripley, Vol. 2, Sect. 1 (London: Kegan Paul, Trench, Trübner & Co., 1898), 172.

terranean world until vellum (leather) gained currency, which is more durable and less expensive to make (c. 4th century AD). Scholars are still finding old fragments of the GNT. Approximately 130 GNT papyri have been documented, but seven or more have recently been found inside cartonnage (mummy mask material) and are not yet catalogued.

C. Some other Marks will be encountered in the Text:

1. <u>Punctuation and Textual Conventions</u>. Within various editions of the Greek NT, you will encounter conventional punctuation marks. For an extended comparison of recent scholarly editions, see §5.6 NT GREEK CRITICAL EDITIONS AND PUNCTUATION. Note that these punctuation marks are somewhat interpretive; they derive from later manuscripts, printing practices, and exegetical decisions.
    a. A *period* (.) corresponds to an English period (.).
    b. A *comma* (,) corresponds to our comma (,).
    c. A *semi-colon* (;) corresponds to an English question mark (?).
    d. A *raised dot* (·) corresponds to either colon (:) or semicolon (;).
    e. *Parentheses* (…) corresponds to English parentheses (…).
    f. Not infrequent are *brackets* […]. These indicate that the words within are questionable and may reflect a scribal addition.

2. <u>Apostrophe</u>. An apostrophe (') is commonly seen. It looks like BUT it is NOT a breathing mark. An apostrophe will stand in the place of a vowel when this vowel has dropped from the end of a word due to the fact that the next word begins with a vowel. This is called **elision**. Thus, one finds μετ' ἐμοῦ (*with me*) when the ἄλφα in μετά is **elided** (i.e. dropped off). The few instances where elision may occur are noted in the NOTES ON VOCABULARY found in each chapter of this grammar.

3. <u>Dieresis</u>. A dieresis (¨) is rare. It will occur over the second of two consecutive vowels to indicate that they do not form a monophthong. Thus, the two vowels should be pronounced separately. For example, προΐστημι is προ-ΐ-στη-μι (pronounced *pro-eé-stāy-mee*).

<table><tr><td colspan="3" align="center">**CHECK POINT 2.3-5**
SYLLABIFICATION AND PRONUNCIATION

First, syllabify and write out the pronunciation for the following words.</td></tr>
<tr><td>**Greek Word**</td><td>**Syllabified**</td><td>**Pronunciation Value**</td></tr>
<tr><td>συγγένεια</td><td></td><td></td></tr>
<tr><td>ἁγιάζω</td><td></td><td></td></tr></table>

ἀσχημοσύνη		
πλημμέλεια		
Καϊάφα		
φυλάσσω		

Second, be able to identify all the non-alphabetical marks in **John 18:26-30.**

[26] λέγει εἷς ἐκ τῶν δούλων τοῦ ἀρχιερέως, συγγενὴς ὢν οὗ ἀπέκοψεν Πέτρος τὸ ὠτίον· οὐκ ἐγώ σε εἶδον ἐν τῷ κήπῳ μετ' αὐτοῦ; [27] πάλιν οὖν ἠρνήσατο Πέτρος, καὶ εὐθέως ἀλέκτωρ ἐφώνησεν. [28] Ἄγουσιν οὖν τὸν Ἰησοῦν ἀπὸ τοῦ Καϊάφα εἰς τὸ πραιτώριον· ἦν δὲ πρωΐ· καὶ αὐτοὶ οὐκ εἰσῆλθον εἰς τὸ πραιτώριον, ἵνα μὴ μιανθῶσιν ἀλλὰ φάγωσιν τὸ πάσχα. [29] ἐξῆλθεν οὖν ὁ Πιλᾶτος ἔξω πρὸς αὐτοὺς καὶ φησίν· τίνα κατηγορίαν φέρετε [κατὰ] τοῦ ἀνθρώπου τούτου; [30] ἀπεκρίθησαν καὶ εἶπαν αὐτῷ· εἰ μὴ ἦν οὗτος κακὸν ποιῶν, οὐκ ἄν σοι παρεδώκαμεν αὐτόν.

ANSWERS

Greek Word	Syllabified	Pronunciation Value
συγγένεια	συγ-γέ-νει-α	*seewn-yéh-nee-ah*
ἁγιάζω	ἁ-γι-ά-ζω	*ah-yee-áh-zō*
ἀσχημοσύνη	ἀ-σχη-μο-σύ-νη	*ah-skhāy-mō-seéw-nāy*
πλημμέλεια	πλημ-μέ-λει-α	*plāym-méh-lee-ah*
Καϊάφα	Κα-ϊ-ά-φα	*Kah-ee-áh-phah*
φυλάσσω	φυ-λάσ-σω	*pheew-láhs-sō*

[26] λέγει εἷς ἐκ τῶν δούλων τοῦ ἀρχιερέως, συγγενὴς ὢν οὗ ἀπέκοψεν Πέτρος τὸ ὠτίον· οὐκ ἐγώ σε εἶδον ἐν τῷ κήπῳ μετ' αὐτοῦ; [27] πάλιν οὖν ἠρνήσατο Πέτρος, καὶ εὐθέως ἀλέκτωρ ἐφώνησεν. [28] Ἄγουσιν οὖν τὸν Ἰησοῦν ἀπὸ τοῦ Καϊάφα εἰς τὸ πραιτώριον· ἦν δὲ πρωΐ· καὶ αὐτοὶ οὐκ εἰσῆλθον εἰς τὸ πραιτώριον, ἵνα μὴ μιανθῶσιν ἀλλὰ φάγωσιν τὸ πάσχα. [29] ἐξῆλθεν οὖν ὁ Πιλᾶτος ἔξω πρὸς αὐτοὺς καὶ φησίν· τίνα κατηγορίαν φέρετε [κατὰ] τοῦ ἀνθρώπου τούτου; [30] ἀπεκρίθησαν καὶ εἶπαν αὐτῷ· εἰ μὴ ἦν οὗτος κακὸν ποιῶν, οὐκ ἄν σοι παρεδώκαμεν αὐτόν.

NOTES:
1. The underlined characters (only marked in 18:26) have breathing and accent marks.
2. The grey highlights represent pronunciation marks, with the semi-colon (;) indicating question

marks (?) and the raised dot (·) representing either a colon (:) or semi-colon (;) in English. The commas and periods are the same as in English.

3. The three words (μετ' in 18:26; and Καϊάφα and πρωΐ in 18:28) show instances of apostrophe (') and dieresis (¨). Notice the presence of ἰῶτα subscripts in the word τῷ κήπῳ in 18:26.

4. Notice the brackets in 18:29, indicating that there is some question whether [κατὰ] is original to the manuscript (i.e., it may reflect a scribal addition).

2.6 PROPER NOUNS AND BORROWED NON-GREEK WORDS

A. **Proper Names:** Greek has proper nouns—formal names of people, places, and things. These will be capitalized. This capitalization will usually help you as you translate sentences. NOTE: *Be careful not to confuse initial capitalized words that begin paragraphs or direct quotations.*

B. **The Endings of Greek Words:** Greek is an **inflectional language**. That is to say, different endings are placed at the end of a word to tell the reader or hearer *how* that word functions in the sentence (as subject, direct object, the main verb, etc.). Every vowel can be found at the very end of a Greek word. However, not every consonant can end a Greek word. In fact, only these consonants can end a Greek word: ν, ξ, ρ, ς, ψ. See below.

C. **Loan Words:** Occasionally, you will run across a word in the Greek NT that ends in some other consonant than ν, ξ, ρ, ς, ψ. Such a word is borrowed from another language and did not accept the normal Greek endings. Most of these words are proper nouns (names of places or persons) that were transliterated into Greek. However, a good number of foreign names that entered the Greek culture were incorporated into the language, and thus, have Greek endings. The names Jesus (Ἰησοῦς) and John (Ἰωάννης) are two such names.

CHECK POINT 2.6
PROPER NAMES AND LOAN WORDS

Given below is Luke 2:1-5. First, single underline all the proper nouns. Second, place an asterisk (*) at the end of the proper noun, if it is a loan word that is transliterated into Greek characters from another language (like Hebrew).

¹ Ἐγένετο δὲ ἐν ταῖς ἡμέραις ἐκείναις ἐξῆλθεν δόγμα παρὰ Καίσαρος Αὐγούστου ἀπογράφεσθαι πᾶσαν τὴν οἰκουμένην. ² αὕτη ἀπογραφὴ πρώτη ἐγένετο ἡγεμονεύοντος τῆς Συρίας Κυρηνίου. ³ καὶ ἐπορεύοντο πάντες ἀπογράφεσθαι, ἕκαστος εἰς τὴν ἑαυτοῦ πόλιν. ⁴ Ἀνέβη δὲ καὶ Ἰωσὴφ ἀπὸ τῆς Γαλιλαίας ἐκ πόλεως Ναζαρὲθ εἰς τὴν Ἰουδαίαν εἰς πόλιν Δαυὶδ ἥτις καλεῖται Βηθλέεμ, διὰ τὸ εἶναι αὐτὸν ἐξ οἴκου καὶ πατριᾶς Δαυίδ, ⁵ ἀπογράψασθαι σὺν Μαριὰμ τῇ ἐμνηστευμένῃ αὐτῷ, οὔσῃ ἐγκύῳ.

ANSWER

¹ Ἐγένετο δὲ ἐν ταῖς ἡμέραις ἐκείναις ἐξῆλθεν δόγμα παρὰ <u>Καίσαρος Αὐγούστου</u> ἀπογράφεσθαι πᾶσαν τὴν οἰκουμένην. ² αὕτη ἀπογραφὴ πρώτη ἐγένετο ἡγεμονεύοντος τῆς <u>Συρίας Κυρηνίου</u>. ³ καὶ ἐπορεύοντο πάντες ἀπογράφεσθαι, ἕκαστος εἰς τὴν ἑαυτοῦ πόλιν. ⁴ Ἀνέβη δὲ καὶ <u>Ἰωσὴφ</u>* ἀπὸ τῆς <u>Γαλιλαίας</u> ἐκ πόλεως <u>Ναζαρὲθ</u>* εἰς τὴν <u>Ἰουδαίαν</u> εἰς πόλιν <u>Δαυὶδ</u>* ἥτις καλεῖται <u>Βηθλέεμ</u>*, διὰ τὸ εἶναι αὐτὸν ἐξ οἴκου καὶ πατριᾶς <u>Δαυίδ</u>*, ⁵ ἀπογράψασθαι σὺν <u>Μαριὰμ</u>* τῇ ἐμνηστευμένη αὐτῷ, οὔσῃ ἐγκύῳ. **NOTE**: Ἐγένετο in 2:1 is capitalized because it begins a new paragraph.

2.7 VOCABULARY

VOCABULARY 2	GREEK AND NON-GREEK NAMES

Ἰάκωβος [42]	James (Jacob)	<u>Non-Greek Names</u>	
Παῦλος [158]	Paul	Ἀβραάμ [73]	Abraham
Πέτρος [156]	Peter	Δαυίδ [59]	David
Πιλᾶτος [55]	Pilate	Ἰερουσαλήμ [77]	Jerusalem
Φαρισαῖος [98]	Pharisee	Ἰεροσόλυμα [63]	Jerusalem
Χριστός [529]	Christ, Messiah, Anointed One	Ἰσραήλ [68]	Israel

The superscripts give word frequencies in the Greek NT. After learning these words, you will know about 1% of the words used in the GNT. If you are able, listen to audio recordings of VOCABULARY 2 and complete the CROSSWORD PUZZLE in the WORKBOOK Exercises. Then, complete the rest of EXERCISES and consult the ANSWER KEY & GUIDE as needed.

CASE IN POINT 2: EARLY CHRISTIAN WORDS-LETTERS-SYMBOLS

I began to experience some understanding of God's saving work in the world (i.e. salvation history) as a young boy contemplating the stained glass windows and murals in the sanctuary of the First United Methodist Church of Libertyville, IL. I remember gazing intently at the huge gnarly wooden cross that is suspended in the sanctuary. Copies of Scripture sometimes included elaborate pictures. For instance, a scene depicted in the *Codex Aureus* of Echternach, the "Golden Co-

dex," dated AD 1240 shows the progression of the parable of Lazarus (Luke 16:19-31) on Folio 78 (recto).[12]

But well before this, our earliest Christian symbols merged written text, confession, and image. The earliest Christian datable surviving symbol is the Ταῦ 'Ρῶ (*Tahv Rhō*) circled above, known as the *staurogram* (lit. "cross-letter"). The word "cross" σταυρόν is abbreviated **CTPON** (starting with a lunar σίγμα), but the letters ταῦ and ῥῶ are overlaid before the Greek **ON** to look like a person on a "cross" (σταυρός). This occurs in Papyrus 75 (c. AD 200) at Luke 14:27 when Jesus says, "Whoever does not carry his own cross [σταυρόν] and come after me, cannot be my disciple."[13]

Perhaps the most common Christian symbol (apart from the Cross) is the "fish," which is the Greek word ἰχθύς (pronounced *eekh-theéws*). These Greek letters are an acronym for the words Ἰησοῦς Χριστός Θεοῦ Υἱὸς Σωτῆρ that translate "Jesus Christ, God's Son, Savior." The earliest attestation of this symbol is the funerary stele of Licinia Amias dated c. AD 300, which reads in Greek at the top:

ΙΧΘΥC ΖΩΝΤΩΝ

"Fish of the Living Ones"[14]

Finally, a well-known symbol is the Χῖ 'Ρῶ (*khee-rhō*), representing the first two letters of "Christ" (Χριστός). The image was popularized in the reign of the Emperor Constantine. The Χῖ may, too, represent the cross. The symbol is seen below on a bronze coin dated c. AD 350 during the brief rule of Magnentius who was a self-proclaimed emperor (or usurper) opposed and at war against those

faithful to Constantine.[15] Here the symbol for the Christ became a useful political tool.

These earliest Christian images tell a story of the conversion of what it meant to be "Christian" or somehow identified with Jesus Christ, from taking up one's own cross and belonging to Christ in resurrection hope to a symbolic tool of empire.

---

[12] Located at http://en.wikipedia.org/wiki/File:Meister_des_Codex_Aureus_Epternacensis_001.jpg accessed April 21, 2014. This codex is located at the German National Museum at Nuremberg.

[13] Image from http://www.biblicalarchaeology.org/daily/biblical-topics/crucifixion/the-staurogram/ accessed 3-6-2014.

[14] Image from http://en.wikipedia.org/wiki/File:Stele_Licinia_Amias_Terme_67646.jpg, accessed 3-6-2014.

[15] Image is from http://en.wikipedia.org/wiki/File:Double_Centenionalis_Magnentius-XR-s4017.jpg, accessed 4-21-2014; attribution Classical Numismatic Group, Inc. http://www.cngcoins.com.

CHAPTER 3

At the end of the Good Samaritan parable, Jesus issues a command "Go and do likewise!" (Luke 10:37b). Is this in the singular (*you*) or plural (*y'all*)? In 1 Cor 6:18 Paul admonishes, "Flee sexual immorality!" Then in 6:20 he exhorts, "Glorify God in your body!" Are these commands singular or plural? What difference might this make in our interpretation?

This chapter first familiarizes students with the concepts of **word roots**, **stems**, and **endings**. Endings will often indicate **number** (singular or plural); these would help one resolve the questions posed above. Also, you will learn what a **lexicon** is and a word's **lexical meaning**.

Then students are introduced to the **Present Tense** of the Greek verb in the **Indicative Mood**. At this point, a few **Middle-Formed Verbs** are introduced. Finally, students are shown **how to negate a verb, how to parse a verb,** and the **basic rules of verb accentuation.**

VOCABULARY 3	REGULAR AND MIDDLE-FORMED VERBS

βαπτίζω [77]	I soak, submerge, wash; I baptize	λέγω [2352]	I say, speak
βλέπω [133]	I see, observe	πέμπω [79]	I send, dispatch
γράφω [192]	I write	σώζω [106]	I save, rescue; I preserve
διδάσκω [97]	I teach, instruct	Middle-Formed Verbs:	
δοξάζω [61]	I glorify, honor, esteem	ἔρχομαι [633]	I come, go
εὐαγγελίζω [54]	I announce the good news	πορεύομαι [153]	I go, walk
εὐαγγελίζομαι		προσεύχομαι [85]	I pray, offer prayer
εὑρίσκω [176]	I find, discover	Negative Adverb:	
ἔχω [707]	I have; I am	οὐ, οὐκ, οὐχ [1621]	no, not

After learning vocabulary to this point, you will know 5.7% of the words used in the GNT. If you are able, listen to audio recordings of VOCABULARY 3 and complete the CROSSWORD PUZZLE in the WORKBOOK EXERCISES.

NOTES ON VOCABULARY 3:

Sometimes, students may need to read the whole chapter first before they can fully grasp the Notes on Vocabulary. This is probably the case now. The form of the words given above is called the **lexical form** because these are the forms the student would look up in a **Greek *lexicon*** (= Greek *dictionary*). The form of a Greek verb in a lexicon will almost always show the 1st person singular endings: –ω, –ομαι, or –μι. This format is followed throughout this handbook.

Most of the verbs above are chosen for their regularity of formation; however, εὑρίσκω, ἔχω, and λέγω are included because of their high frequency in the Greek NT. Also, many of these verbs have English **derivatives** (or **cognates**): baptize, graphics, didactic, doxology, evangelize (announce the good news), heuristics. To the extent that students may already know these English words, this should help in memorizing the basic meaning of the Greek word.

The verb εὐαγγελίζομαι uses the middle voice endings 90% of the time, but it carries some truly passive senses on several occasions (Matt 11:5; Luke 7:22; 16:16; Gal 1:11; Heb 4:2, 6; 1 Pet 1:25; 4:6) and is even found twice with active forms (Rev 10:7; 14:6). This kind of behavior in verbs—switching from middle-active to passive endings and meanings—is not very common, but can be confusing to beginning students.

There are two Greek words meaning *no* or *not*. The first we will learn is οὐ, οὐκ, οὐχ. (The other word μή is presented in CHAPTER 14.) As an adverb, οὐ will immediately precede the word or idea that it negates. Οὐ has two other forms: οὐκ and οὐχ. These forms are found when the word it is negating (that is, the word that immediately follows it) begins with a vowel. When that word begins with a rough breathing mark (ʽ), then οὐχ is used; if the next word has a smooth breathing mark (ʼ), then οὐκ is used. For example, οὐ βλέπω. οὐκ ἔρχομαι. οὐχ εὑρίσκω. The reason for this phenomenon is that generally Greek speakers/writers avoided having a word ending in a vowel followed by the next word beginning with another vowel (this situation is called **hiatus**). It simply sounds better to add a consonant in between the two words and vowel sounds. Greek speakers were interested in **euphony** (from the Greek, εὐ- *good* and φωνή *sound*)—simplifying and improving sound for ease of pronunciation. Indeed, the choice of words in combination will often include conscious or unconscious decisions to maximize aural impact on sounds and thus in the hearing. So, pay attention to repeated sounds.

3.1 GREEK WORDS (αἱ Λέξεις) AND LEXICAL MEANINGS

A. **The Root (ἡ ʽΡίζα) and the Parts of Speech (τὰ Μέρη τοῦ Λόγου):** A Greek word is composed of a **stem**, produced from a **root**, plus **endings**. A **root** may be used to form different stems to form different parts of speech. For example, the root διδαχ* is the base of the words below, which are called cognates. **Cognates** are words derived from the same root. Notice how the same root forms stems with endings that may form different parts of speech:

Root	Stem + ending	Basic Meaning	Part of Speech
διδαχ*	διδακ τός	*instructed*	adjective (*one who is taught*)
	διδάσκαλ ος	*teacher*	noun

Stem + ending	Basic Meaning	Part of Speech
διδάσκ ω	*I teach*	verb
διδαχ ή	*doctrine*	noun (*that which is taught*)

The addition of asterisk [*] to a word indicates that it is a Greek form that does not occur in actual usage; one never finds the Greek word διδαχ.

B. **Root vs. Stem:** A helpful distinction can be made between a root and a **stem** from the above examples. Each word above shares the same root διδαχ*. However, each word slightly changes the root *into its particular stem* depending on the part of speech or particular class of noun each word is. Each stem then is slightly different, yet shares the same root. Thus, their meanings are similar. In this example, each word built off of the root διδαχ* carries a meaning that is related to the idea of *teach*. For an extensive discussion of Greek work roots, stems, and suffixes, see Smyth §§822-37. What is presented here is simplification of Smyth's detailed discussion.

C. **Affixes (τὰ Μόρια) and Endings (αἰ Τελευταί):** These different stems are created by adding suffixes and endings to the root. The type of ending depends on the part of speech (verb, noun, adjective, adverb, etc.). Greek's use of such endings (or inflections) make Greek an *inflectional language*. Endings are very important: They can help identify the part of speech and how that word functions within the sentence. Together, understanding a word's root, stem, and ending will help me understand a word's lexical meaning and grammatical function within a sentence.

For example, before I can understand the meaning and function of the word δικαίως, I must be able to recognize *both the ending and the stem-root*. The ending will tell me what part of speech it is, as well as how it functions in the sentence. The stem-root will narrow its lexical meaning. In this example, the –ως ending helps signify to me that it is an adverb. Thus, as an adverb the word would probably be modifying the verb. The stem δικ* has meaning *right(eous)* or *just*, and so this word has the sense of *justly* or *righteously*. Of course, scholars have already done this work for me in the creation of dictionaries or lexicons. Thus, I would simply look up the adverb δικαίως in the lexicon to find its possible range of meanings.

To illustrate further the importance of root, stems, and endings, consider this slightly adapted material from William D. Chamberlain.[1] He explains that the Sanskrit root δικ* carried the meaning of *show*, and then was further adapted to form the verb δείκνυμι *I show*. From δικ-, *to show, point out,* is derived δίκ-η, *the way pointed out,* i.e. *the thing which is right, justice*. From there, several different words are created using suffixes (endings) that carry certain senses. For example, masculine nouns with a –της ending are personal agents of an occupation (three instances occur below); feminine nouns with –σις endings indicate active processes (two are below):

---

[1] William D. Chamberlain, *An Exegetical Grammar of the Greek New Testament* (New York: Macmillan, 1941), 10.

δίκ-η, *right, justice.*
δικ-άζω, *I render justice.*
δικ-ασ-τής, *a judge.*
δικ-ασ-μός, *a giving of justice.*
δικ-άσ-ι-μος, *judicial.*
δικ-ασ-τικός, *pertaining to the courts, the juror's fee.*
δίκ-αι-ος, *one observant of the rules, righteous.*
δικ-αι-όω, *I declare righteous.*
δικ-αί-ω-μα, *a righteous act, an ordinance, a decree.*
δικ-αί-ω-σις, *the act of setting right, doing justice.*
δικ-αι-ω-τής, *a judge.*
δικ-ασ-τήριον, *a place of justice, a house of correction.*

Taking the longer root δεικ*, several other words are formed:

δείκ-νυ-μι, *I show, point out.*
δεῖγ-μα, *a thing shown, a pattern, a sample.*
δειγ-ματ-ίζω, *I make a show of.*
δειγ-ματ-ισ-μός, *an exhibition, a public show.*
δεικ-τήριον, *a place for showing.*
δείκ-της, *an exhibitor.*
δεικ-τικός, *able to show.*
δεῖξ-ις, *a showing, displaying.*

This demonstrates how far one's learning of roots, stems, and endings may help with understanding word meanings, especially if one learns the basic significance of types of endings.

D. **Prefixes (αἱ Προτάξεις):** Greek also allows for the addition of a **prefix** to the front of a word to modify and affect its meaning. So, we will observe words like ἀ-<u>δίδακτος</u> *untaught, ignorant* or εὐ-<u>δίδακτος</u> *well-taught, receptive to teaching.* These words do not occur in the GNT or LXX, but illustrate the use of prefixes. Once you become familiar with Greek, you can begin to recognize the component parts of Greek words, which will aid your learning of vocabulary.

E. **The Lexical Meaning (ἡ Δύναμις τῆς Λέξεως) and Standard NT Lexicons:** The lexical meaning of a word is its definition as given in dictionaries or lexicons. The field of lexicography concerns how best to discover and describe word meanings in lexicons. Definitions given in lexicons vary, and this can confuse beginning students. So, typically beginning students are given **gloss definitions**, which are brief definitions that represent a basic range of meanings. However, students need to recognize that they are initially learning merely glosses. As you progress, you will need to learn more about how to determine word meanings and how to study words. See the following chapter discussions:

§6.7 A FIRST LOOK AT MAJOR LEXICONS: BDAG, L&N, AND LSJ
§12.6 NAVIGATING MAJOR LEXICONS
§14.7 LEXICAL INFORMATION ON THE CASE OF VERBAL OBJECTS
§27.1 HOW TO DO A WORD STUDY

For now, here is a list of lexical resources for students studying Koine Greek:

1. Resources to assist learning NT vocabulary.
    a. *Books.*
        Halcomb, T. Michael W. *800 Words and Images: A New Testament Greek Vocabulary Builder.* AGROS. Wilmore, KY: GlossaHouse, 2013.
        Metzger, Bruce M. *Lexical Aids for Students of New Testament Greek.* Grand Rapids: Baker, 1997.
        Trenchard, Warren C. *The Complete Vocabulary Guide to the Greek New Testament.* Revised. Zondervan, 1998.
        Van Voorst, Robert E. *Building Your New Testament Greek Vocabulary.* Grand Rapids: Eerdmans, 1990.
    b. *Apps.*
        Halcomb, T. Michael W. "Getting Greek: Word Roots App." http://blog.michael halcomb. com/2011/08/getting-greek-word-roots-app.html
        Perkins, Casey. "Greekkit" at http://appsto.re/us/q6102.i
    c. *Computer Programs.* All the major Bible softwares will offer tools to help learn vocabulary by frequency.

2. Standard lexicons recommended for interpreting the GNT.
    Bauer, Walter and F. W. Danker, W. F. Arndt, and F. W. Gingrich (BDAG). *Greek-English Lexicon of the New Testament and Other Early Christian Literature.* 3rd ed. Revised. Chicago: The University of Chicago Press, 2000. This is the standard scholarly Greek NT Lexicon.
    Liddell, H. G., R. Scott and H. S. Jones (LSJ). *A Greek-English Lexicon.* 9th ed., revised. Oxford: Clarendon, 1996. This is the standard Classical Greek lexicon, including coverage of the NT. The previous edition, missing only a supplement, can be accessed on the web at http://www.perseus.tufts.edu/cgi-bin/resolveform.
    Liddell, H. G. *A Lexicon: Abridged from Liddell and Scott's Greek-English Lexicon.* Oxford: Clarendon, 1963. An abridgment of the 7th edition that importantly still contains word derivation information in parentheses.
    Louw, Johannes and Eugene Nida (L&N). *Greek-English Lexicon of the New Testament Based on Semantic Domains.* 2 Vols. 2nd ed. New York: United Bible Societies, 1988. A very valuable lexicon which allows one to find synonyms and antonyms; has its own numbering system based upon semantic domains.

Swanson, James. *Dictionary of Biblical Languages With Semantic Domains: Greek (New Testament)*. electronic ed. Oak Harbor, WA: Logos Research Systems, 1997. Very accessible lexicon using Strong's numbering and referencing other lexicons and theological dictionaries.

Thayer, Joseph Henry. *Thayer's Greek-English Lexicon of the New Testament*. Electronic ed. International Bible Translators (IBT), Inc., 1998-2000. Prior to BDAG, Thayer's was the standard GNT lexicon. It is dated, but still contains some insightful information, e.g., the underlying roots are sometimes given in the formation of the word.

Zodhiates, Spiros. *The Complete Word Study Dictionary: New Testament*. Chattanooga, TN: AMG, 1992. Not recognized as an academic lexicon, but this is still helpful to provide a perspective on the possible meanings of a word, as well as listing synonyms and antonyms and often the roots used in the formation of the word.

F. **A Word of Caution is in Order:** A word's meaning is derived from its use in context within a sentence, within a paragraph, within a literary unit, within a book, and within a culture. It is difficult for lexicographers (those who study and compile word meanings into lexicons) to study each occurrence of a word in *each* context *thoroughly*. This is the task of interpreters of those particular passages. Each individual occurrence of a word must be carefully studied in its own unique literary context. Lexicons are helpful in that they provide guidelines or boundaries for a word's meaning. In this handbook, the word meanings provided are glosses. This simplification of a word's meaning is necessary as a starting point for the beginning student; but this gloss should in no way be considered the final authority on a word's meaning.

CHECK POINT 3.1
GREEK WORDS, ROOTS, STEMS, AND MEANINGS

Given this word, ἀγράμματος, match the following statements with the answers on the right.

1. The basic definition is *uneducated*.	a. ending
2. To get a more complete definition you would consult this.	b. stem
3. The ἀ- affixed to ἀ-γράμματος is this.	c. gloss
4. The -ος affixed to ἀγράμματ-ος is this.	d. lexicon
5. In ἀγράμματος, the component γράμματ- would be this.	e. root
6. Behind ἀγράμματος and γράμματ- is γράφ*.	f. cognate
7. The word γραμματεύς, also derived from γράφ*, would be this.	g. prefix
8. Trenchard's book would provide a definitive understanding of the lexical definition of the word.	h. true
9. A lexicon gives a range of possible word meanings; however, it is often beneficial to perform a more intensive study of individual occurrences of a word in each context.	i. false

ANSWERS: 1.c., 2.d., 3.g., 4.a., 5.b., 6.e., 7.f., 8.i., 9.h.

3.2 THE GREEK VERB (τὸ Ῥῆμα)

A. **The Central Item of the Greek Sentence: The Verb:** The Greek verb is the most important and dynamic component of the sentence. Even when it must be implied from context, its importance still governs sentence elements: The verb or implied verb dictates how the words around it are formed. A single verb can represent a complete sentence. Why is this? Because the endings used on a verb tell the reader generically who is the subject. No noun is needed as the subject. The ending provides what might be called a **default subject**. This default subject corresponds to the various personal pronouns in English, some of which are given below.

διδάσκ ει.　→ "He, she, or it teaches."
διδάσκ ομεν. → "We teach."
διδάσκ ετε.　→ "You (pl.) teach."
διδάσκ εις.　→ "You (sg.) teach."

Notice how each Greek ending underlined above corresponds to a distinct English personal pronoun as the default subject.

B. **Person (ἡ Πρόσωπον) and Number (ὁ Ἀριθμός):** **Person** refers to whether the subject involves me (*I* or *we*), you (*you*), or someone else (*he*, *she*, *it*, or *they*). If *I* or *we* is involved, this is called **first (1st) person**. If *you* (singular or plural) is involved, this is called **second (2nd) person**. If the subject is *he*, *she*, *it*, or *they*, this is called **third (3rd) person**. **Number** is easily enough understood: **singular** and **plural**. Thus we have the following chart for the default subjects for Greek verbs:

	Singular	Plural
First	I	we
Second	you	you
Third	he, she, it	they

Thus, **Greek verbs generally have six endings to correspond to each combination of person and number**. And, after looking at any verb in context, someone can identify what person (first, second, or third) and number (singular or plural) are represented by that particular ending. (For a discussion of person, see Wallace 391-99; for number, see Wallace 399-406.)

C. **Mood (ἡ Ἔγκλισις):** The Greek verb has five characteristics; we have just learned person and number. What are the other three? Mood, Tense, and Voice. The **mood** of the verb expresses how a writer describes the action of a verb in terms of its certainty or the likelihood of its actually happening. (See Wallace 442-48.) English has the following moods:

> Indicative: *You are running.*
> Imperative: *Run!*
> Subjunctive: *You should run.*

In English one also finds **infinitives** (*to run*, *to hide*, *to preach*) as well as **participles** (*running*, *hiding*, *preaching*). Greek shares these moods and has an additional one, called the **Optative**. Technically, participles and infinitives behave more like adjectives and nouns, respectively. However, since they show tense and voice in Greek, they are included as moods. The Optative Mood will briefly covered in this handbook since at this time in the history of the Greek language it is being replaced by the Subjunctive Mood (see Wallace 480-84). This is evidenced by the fact that the Optative Mood occurs only 68 times in the GNT, and 15 times (mainly in Paul's letters) as the conventional expression Μὴ γένοιτο *May it not be!* For the endings of the Optative Mood, see APPENDIX §19. Simply stated, the Greek Moods can be explained as follows:

> **Indicative Mood** = statements of fact (see §3.3 below)
> **Imperative Mood** = commands or requests (see CHAPTER 25)
> **Subjunctive Mood** = statements of possibility or potentiality (see CHAPTER 22)
> **Optative Mood** = statements of wish (CHAPTER 24.5)
> **Infinitive** = verbal noun (see CHAPTER 23)
> **Participle** = verbal adjectives (see CHAPTER 17 and CHAPTER 18)

This brief presentation of moods will suffice for now. For more specific details on each particular mood, see the chapters in which they are first introduced. More will be said concerning the Indicative Mood in §3.3 below.

D. **Tense (ὁ Χρόνος):** Greek Verbs have **tense**; but what exactly is conveyed grammatically by Greek verb tense? Grammarians have discussed, are still debating, and will continue to wrestle with **time of action**, **type of action** (*Aktionsart*), and **verbal aspect**.

1. Greek Tenses. The Greek tenses presented in this handbook are Aorist, Present, Imperfect, Future, Perfect, and Pluperfect. There is another called the Future Perfect that is very rare. There has been considerable debate about the proper understanding of Greek Tense. On verb tense generally, see Wallace 494-512.

GREEK TENSES FROM HIGHEST TO LOWEST FREQUENCY					
Aorist	Present	Imperfect	Future	Perfect	Pluperfect
(11,606)	(11,583)	(1,682)	(1,623)	(1,571)	(86)

2. <u>Traditional View of "Time of Action"</u>. Traditionally, the Greek Tenses were thought to convey *action in time* in the Indicative Mood. Greek Tenses, then, would be comparable to English Tenses as follow:

GREEK TENSE	TRADITIONAL TRANSLATION	ENGLISH TENSE NAME
Aorist	*You taught*	Past Simple
Present	*He teaches*	Present Simple
	He is teaching	Present Progressive
Imperfect	*I was teaching*	Past Progressive
Future	*She will teach*	Future
Perfect	*They have taught*	Present Perfect
Pluperfect	*They had taught*	Pluperfect

Importantly, the Greek Tenses differ from English Tense in that English connects tense with time of the action. However, *in Greek past time is only marked in the Indicative Mood* (for a review of arguments, see Wallace 505-12). To help explain the complexity of the Greek Verb, grammarians have described two further ideas: Verbal Aspect and *Aktionsart*.

3. <u>*Aktionsart* and "Kind of Action" in Time</u>. The concept of *Aktionsart* (German: "action type") describes a particular use of a verb *as kind of action in time*. Summarized succinctly, the kinds of action are "punctiliar (Aorist), durative/linear (Present/Imperfect), or resultative (Perfect/Pluperfect), with the addition of durativity or punctiliarity in future time for the Future form."[2] Often within the *Aktionsart* system, grammarians will categorize types of tense usage, which may be understood as ways in English to translate the tense in certain contexts. In other words, **these uses are context dependent.** Throughout this handbook, I have summarized the "Common Uses" or "Special Uses," even though these uses or categories are not intrinsic to the verb form itself. Rather, evidence from the context must guide how best to render the verb. See also further below under 5.

4. <u>Verbal Aspect</u>. "Verbal aspect is, in general, the portrayal of the action (or state) as to its *progress*, *results*, or *simple occurrence*" (Wallace 499, emphasis original). Grammarians have described **verbal aspect** in relation to Greek verbs as follows:

<u>Aspect</u> <u>Greek Tenses</u>

a. **Imperfective**: action as viewed internally as in progress or incomplete — **Present, Imperfect**

b. **Perfective**: action as viewed as a whole externally or as complete (but not necessarily completed) — **Aorist**

---

[2] Wally V. Cirafesi, *Verbal Aspect in Synoptic Parallels: On the Method and Meaning of Divergent Tense-Form Usage in the Synoptic Passion Narratives*, Linguistic Biblical Studies 7 (Leiden: Brill, 2013),17.

c. **Resultative-stative**: action reflects "a given (often complex)   **Perfect, Pluperfect**
state of affairs"[3]

d. **Future**: action reflects expectation or intention of occurrence   **Future**
in the future[4]

A scholarly consensus is beginning to emerge around these categories and definitions. However, debate continues whether the augment marks past time in the Indicative Mood. See §8.1 IMPERFECT TENSE: TENSE MARKERS AND FORMATION. B. AUGMENTATION.

5. <u>Semantics, Verbal Aspect, and Pragmatics</u>. In the end, we must ask, What is meant by using one tense form over another? And, What is inherently conveyed semantically in the grammatical forms that distinguish the Greek Tenses from one another? In addition to this question, we must ask, How much should *language use for communicative impact or effect* (i.e. pragmatics) govern our understanding of Greek Verb Tenses?

Aspect Theory as summarized above represents a basic emerging consensus. However, a major voice continues to be Wallace (499), who while discussing verb tense, attempts to differentiate, while still correlating, Verbal Aspect and *Aktionsart*:

It is important to distinguish aspect from Aktionsart. In general, we can say that *aspect is the unaffected meaning while **Aktionsart** is aspect in combination with lexical, grammatical, or contextual features*. Thus, the present tense views the action from within, without respect to beginning or end (aspect), while some uses of the present tense can be iterative, historical, futuristic, etc. (all of these belong to Aktionsart and are meanings of the verb affected by other features of the language).

Wallace is quite comfortable summarizing multiple "Specific Uses" for each verb Tense such as iterative, historical, futuristic, gnomic, etc.. But in so doing, he and grammarians generally may be ascribing "too much" for the tense forms. In other words, we may be mistaken to think that Greek authors intended these Specific Uses of the Present Tense (Wallace essentially identifies ten of them) to be marked grammatically in the Greek verb

---

[3] Porter 21–22; cf. Stanley E. Porter, *Verbal Aspect in the Greek of the New Testament: With Reference to Tense and Mood*, Studies in Biblical Greek 1 (New York: Peter Lang, 1989), 258–59 and Stanley E. Porter, Jeffrey T. Reed, and Matthew Brook O'Donnell, *Fundamentals of New Testament Greek* (Grand Rapids: Eerdmans, 2010), 319.

[4] The development of future aspect was an innovation and derives from the Present tense (Michael Weiss, "Morphology and Word Formation," in *A Companion to the Ancient Greek Language*, ed. Egbert J. Bakker; Blackwell Companions to the Ancient World [Malden, MA: Wiley-Blackwell, 2010], 104–19 at 110). The description here merges the views of Weiss, McKay, and Porter-Reed-O'Donnell; see Wally V. Cirafesi, *Verbal Aspect in Synoptic Parallels: On the Method and Meaning of Divergent Tense-Form Usage in the Synoptic Passion Narratives*, Linguistic Biblical Studies 7 (Leiden: Brill, 2013), 45-46. McKay sees the Future Tense as a Fourth Aspect (K. L. McKay, *A New Syntax of the Verb in New Testament Greek: An Aspectual Approach*, Studies in Biblical Greek 5 [New York: Peter Lang, 1994], 34). Alternatively, Porter-Reed-O'Donnell do not view the Future Tense as having verbal aspect, but rather as somewhat like the Subjunctive Mood (*Fundamentals*, 86).

forms. Indeed, Wallace posits the influence of "contextual features" (and rightly so) that must be taken into account to discern these special uses. However, to the extent that one must appeal to explicit external contextual indicators (i.e. other words in the context) to support the identification of this or that specific use of the Present Tense, *the more unlikely it is that the specific uses are actually indicated by the grammatical form of the Present Tense*. Additionally, beyond meaning/semantics and beyond contextual indicators, very importantly *pragmatic constraints* govern an author's choice to use one verb tense instead of another, which may include, e.g., rhyming, style, tone, sentence arrangement, and prominence effect.[5] These pragmatic constraints have not consistently been taken into account.

For now, this introductory summary of the complex matter of Verb Tense and Verbal Aspect will need to suffice. We shall return to these topics several more times when discussing particular Greek tenses and their pragmatic use throughout this handbook.

E. **Voice (ἡ Διάθεσις):** The concept of voice may be tricky for the beginning student, although not too difficult to master quickly. *Voice has to do with the subject's relationship to the action of the verb.* (On voice generally, see Wallace 407-10.)

1. The Active Voice (ἡ Διάθεσις Ἐνεργετική). *The **Active Voice** is when the subject is doing or performing the action.* See examples below (see also Wallace 410-14).

2. The Middle Voice (ἡ Διάθεσις Μέση). Greek has a voice called the middle voice. The **middle voice** *marks the subject's own involvement in the action of the verb and/or in the resultant benefits arising from the action of the verb.* A clear instance where Greek would employ the middle voice is seen in **Mark 7:4** "They washed *themselves.*" Here the ones performing the action of washing are affecting themselves. Formally, English has no such voice, but uses pronouns and different verb glosses to convey the subject's involvement. Grammarians sub-categorize many types of uses of the middle voice in the Greek NT, with the second use below being the most common (see Wallace 414-30).

   a. The **Reflexive** or **Reciprocal (direct) Middle** or "direct middle" can describe a situation where *the action performed by the subject(s) is actually **reflected back** to the subject* (Wallace 416-18) or *performed **reciprocally** among subjects of a group* (Wallace 427). In an attempt to translate this idea into English we could use the English reflexive pronouns: myself, ourselves, yourself, yourselves, himself, herself, itself, themselves. This use is rare in the Greek NT, but here are two examples.

   Matt 27:5b *He [Judas] hanged **himself.***

---

[5] For example, consider in Luke 7:8 when the Present Tense form ἔρχου is used before the Present Tense ἔρχεται in order to preserve the same sound (aural pragmatic effect), when the surrounding verbs have first an Aorist Tense and then a Present Tense. If the Aorist Tense/Present Tense pattern had been followed, then the aural impact of rhyming would have been lost by thus using the Aorist Tense form ἐλθέ followed by the Present Tense form ἔρχεται, which do not sound similar.

b. The **Middle of Personal Interest** or "indirect middle" expresses that the subject is acting out of some **personal interest.** This is related to the **causative middle**, in which the subject causes the action to take place back upon himself or herself (Wallace 419-23).

> **2 Tim 4:15a** *You guard **yourself** against him….*

One way to translate this usage is adding the words *with one's own interest in mind.*

c. The **Permissive Middle** is used to indicate that the subject allows something to be done for himself or herself (Wallace 425-27). This use is also relatively rare in the GNT.

> **1 Cor 6:7** *Why not rather (**let yourselves**) be wronged?*

Finally, it should be said that the middle voice in Koine Greek is sometimes quite significant for interpretation. Some exegetical debates concern whether one should understand a form as having middle voice sense or a passive voice sense. Is Acts 13:48b *"they were appointed"* (passive) or *"they appointed **themselves**"* (middle) *for everlasting life?*

3. The Passive Voice (ἡ Διάθεσις Παθητική). *The **Passive Voice** is when the subject is being acted upon.* This is called the passive voice because the subject does "nothing" but be acted upon. The subject is passive. In the development of the Greek language, the Passive Voice meaning was initially included in the Middle Voice forms; but over time, the passive voice forms were differentiated in the Aorist and Future Tenses. However, for the Present, Imperfect, Perfect, and Pluperfect Tenses the Middle-Passive forms are identical.

The notions of active and passive voice (illustrated below) are relatively easy to comprehend and correspond well to English usage:

Active Voice:	a) Jesus healed the paralytic.
	b) Peter preached the gospel to the people.
	c) Jesus wept.
Passive Voice:	a) The paralytic was healed by Jesus.
	b) The gospel was being preached by Peter.
	c) Jesus was taken away.

As can be seen above, the same idea can be expressed either actively or passively. Thus, in a) and b) under Active Voice, *Jesus* and *Peter* are subjects. However, in a) and b) under Passive Voice, *Jesus* and *Peter* are not subjects, but rather are in prepositional phrases. In the passive voice, the action is being performed on the subjects; *the paralytic, the gospel,* and *Jesus* respectively are passive, doing nothing (see Wallace 431-41).

4. Verb Entries in Lexicons. It may be helpful to compare lexical glosses for verbs that show active, passive, and middle forms. CHART 3.2 below showing **the Semantics of Verbal Voice** has been adapted from Wallace (416) by adding passive voice senses. If the passive

form is not attested in BDAG, I have specified the source from LSJ as =LSJ. If glosses from BDAG are supplemented, I have noted where by simply adding LSJ. Some passive forms are not attested. Notice that *for the middle voice glosses one can often perceive personal participation or interest in the action of the verb.*

CHART 3.2 THE SEMANTICS OF VERBAL VOICE		
Active	**Passive**	**Middle**
αἱρέω *I take*	αἱρέομαι *I am taken or I am chosen* = LSJ	αἱρέομαι *I choose, prefer*
ἀναμιμνήσκω *I remind*	ἀναμιμνήσκομαι *I am reminded, I remember; I recall to mind* (LSJ)	ἀναμιμνήσκομαι *I remember*
ἀποδίδωμι *I give away*	ἀποδίδομαι *I am evacuated* = LSJ	ἀποδίδομαι *I make an exchange, I sell*
ἀπόλλυμι *I destroy*	(see middle meaning →)	ἀπόλλυμαι *I perish*[6]
δανείζω *I lend*	δανείζομαι *I am lent out* = LSJ	δανείζομαι *I borrow*
ἐνεργέω *I work*	ἐνεργέομαι *I am actively carried out* (only impersonal) = LSJ	ἐνεργέομαι *I work* (only impersonal)
ἐπικαλέω *I call upon, name*	ἐπικαλέομαι *I am called; I am called by surname* (LSJ)	ἐπικαλέομαι *I appeal*
ἔχω *I have, hold*	ἔχομαι *I am possessed by, belong to* = LSJ	ἔχομαι *I cling to*
κληρόω *I appoint, choose*	κληρόομαι *I am appointed by lot*	κληρόομαι *I obtain, possess, receive*
κομίζω *I bring*	κομίζομαι *I am conveyed; I journey, travel; I come back* = LSJ	κομίζομαι *I get, receive*
κρίνω *I judge*	κρίνομαι *I am on trial; I am judged*	κρίνομαι *I bring a lawsuit*
παύω *I stop* (transitive)	παύομαι *I am (forced) to cease* (intransitive); *I am deposed from* = LSJ	παύομαι *I cease* (intransitive)
πείθω *I persuade, convince*	πείθομαι *I am won over as the result of persuasion, I am persuaded; I am convinced, certain* (in the perfect tense)	πείθομαι *I obey, trust*
φυλάσσω *I guard*	φυλάσσομαι *I am held in reserve, kept, reserved; I am watched, kept under guard* (LSJ)	φυλάσσομαι *I am on my guard*

3.3 MEANING OF THE INDICATIVE MOOD (ἡ Ὁριστικὴ Ἔγκλισις)

A. **Statements of Presumed Fact:** The Indicative Mood is used to convey basic information of fact. In short, by using the Indicative Mood an author portrays something as true. This does not mean that an author necessarily believes in the truthfulness of the statement, but only that he/she is portraying an occurrence or statement as real or true (see Wallace 448-61). Here are some examples of sentences that reflect the Indicative Mood:

---

[6] Wallace notes (416 n.18): "With ἀπόλλυμι the change from active to middle is more pronounced: the middle now has the force of a passive (which form does not occur in the NT)."

1) *I arrived home late for dinner yesterday.*
2) *Jesus healed the blind man.*
3) *Who will win the Superbowl? San Francisco?*

These notions could be similarly expressed using different Moods:

1) *...in order that I would arrive home late for dinner yesterday*
   = a purpose statement made with the **Subjunctive** Mood or an Infinitive

2) *Oh, that Jesus would heal the blind man!*
   = a wish using the **Optative** Mood, which is rare in the GNT

3) *Should we win the Superbowl, or let San Francisco win?*
   = a deliberative question using the **Subjunctive** Mood

Only the Indicative Mood is presented in the first half of this handbook, CHS. 3-16.

B. **Primary and Secondary Endings and Coupling Vowels:** The Indicative Mood endings are formed by placing coupling vowels with endings onto the end of the verb stem. There are two sets of coupling vowels: o/ε and α/ε. There are two sets of endings: primary and secondary. The primary endings, both active voice and middle/passive voice, are given below. The secondary endings will be presented in §8.1 IMPERFECT TENSE: TENSE INDICATORS AND FORMATION.

3.4 PRESENT TENSE (Ἐνεστὼς Χρόνος): FORMATION AND TRANSLATION

A. **Primary Active Voice Endings:** Remember that Greek is an inflectional language; that is, various endings are added to the end of words to communicate the function and meaning of words. The endings below are formed with an ε/o coupling vowel with the primary tense endings. Learn this set of endings well:

	Singular	Plural
First	-ω	-ομεν
Second	-εις	-ετε
Third	-ει	-ουσι(ν)

These endings are then added to the stem of the verb. Take the verb πιστεύω *I trust*:

πιστεύ-ω   πιστεύ-ομεν
πιστεύ-εις   πιστεύ-ετε
πιστεύ-ει   πιστεύ-ουσι(ν)

Notice: (1) Remember that the Lexical form of a verb is its 1st person singular form: in this case πιστεύ-ω. Thus you would find βλέπω, σῴζω, πέμπω, etc. (2) The 3rd person plural form may end with a νῦ or not. This is called a **movable νῦ**. This depends normally on whether the next word begins with a vowel or not in order to prevent hiatus (two vowels in a row).

B. **Translating the Present Active Indicative:** Remember that these endings have a default subject. They are translated into English as either a Simple or Progressive Present as follows:

Singular		Simple Present		Progressive Present
1	πιστεύω	*I trust.*	or	*I am trusting.*
2	πιστεύεις	*You (sg.) trust.*	or	*You (sg.) are trusting.*
3	πιστεύει	*He, She, or It trusts.*	or	*He, She, or It is trusting.*
Plural				
1	πιστεύομεν	*We trust.*	or	*We are trusting.*
2	πιστεύετε	*You (pl.) trust.*	or	*You (pl.) are trusting.*
3	πιστεύουσι(ν)	*They trust.*	or	*They are trusting.*

Notice: Throughout the handbook and its exercises, translate the verb tenses as indicated in the grammar. However, this grammar only introduces basic ways in which each tense may be translated. There are numerous exegetically significant nuances and exceptions to a typical translation of each tense. Other issues in the text of the NT such as context and word definition may affect a tense's general meaning. (For other special uses of the present tense, see Wallace 513-39.)

C. **The Middle/Passive Endings:** The endings for the passive and the middle voice happen to be <u>identical</u> in the Present Tense. Once again, the endings below are formed with a ε/o coupling vowel with the primary tense endings. This is the second set of endings the student needs to learn to master the Indicative Mood.

	Singular	**Plural**
First	-ομαι	-όμεθα
Second	-η	-εσθε
Third	-εται	-ονται

These endings are added to the stem of the verb. For example,

$$\text{πιστεύ}\underline{\text{ομαι}} \quad \text{πιστευ}\underline{\text{ό}}\text{μεθα}$$
$$\text{πιστεύ}\underline{\text{η}} \quad \text{πιστεύεσθε}$$
$$\text{πιστεύ}\underline{\text{εται}} \quad \text{πιστεύ}\underline{\text{ονται}}$$

D. **Translating the Present Passive Indicative is slightly more Difficult:** First, one must decide, after they have recognized this set of endings, whether they are to be translated in the middle voice <u>or</u> the passive voice. In the GNT this choice is dependent on context. Indeed, the relevance of whether or not one takes a verb form as a middle or passive can have tremendous implications for interpretation. Again, is the verb in Acts 13:48b to be translated as *"were appointed"* (passive) or *"appointed **themselves**"* (middle)? In the context, personal agency of response is stressed, as seen in 13:46 "you judged ***yourselves*** unworthy...." Therefore, in 13:48 the middle voice is most naturally in use.

In general, follow this rule: ***Try first to translate the verb as a passive.*** The reasons for this are twofold: First, relatively speaking, the middle voice is not very frequent in the NT compared to the passive voice. Second, if once you try, you *cannot* render the Greek verb as a passive, then you can be more confident that it is indeed to be translated as a middle voice. The Passive voice is translated as follows:

			Simple Present		Progressive Present
sg.	1	πιστεύομαι	*I am trusted.*	or	*I am being trusted.*
	2	πιστεύῃ	*You (sg.) are trusted.*	or	*You (sg.) are being trusted.*
	3	πιστεύεται	*He, She, or It is trusted.*	or	*He, She, or It is being trusted.*
pl.	1	πιστευόμεθα	*We are trusted.*	or	*We are being trusted.*
	2	πιστεύεσθε	*You (pl.) are trusted.*	or	*You (pl.) are being trusted.*
	3	πιστεύονται	*They are trusted.*	or	*They are being trusted.*

E. **Translating the Present Middle Indicative may be even more Difficult:** The middle voice is more *nuanced* than the passive voice. When used, if the active voice was possible, the middle voice draws special attention to the subject's participation in the action and/or outcomes. As explained above in §3.2.E, it may indicate reflexive or reciprocal action, personal interest, or permission. The middle, however, *is often translated simply as the active voice.* Below are some examples of how to translate an indirect middle of personal interest:

sg.	1	πιστεύομαι	I trust *with my own interest in mind.*
	2	πιστεύῃ	You trust *with your own interest in mind.*
	3	πιστεύεται	He trusts *with his own interest in mind.*
pl.	1	πιστευόμεθα	We trust *with our own interest in mind.*
	2	πιστεύεσθε	You trust *with your own interest in mind.*
	3	πιστεύονται	They trust *with their own interest in mind.*

The lexical entry in BDAG does not show any instances of middle uses of πιστεύω in the NT; but the LSJ offers a middle-voice gloss of "I have entrusted" to someone; and the LSJ intermediate offers a middle voice gloss of "to believe mutually" (a reflexive or reciprocal middle).

3.5 MIDDLE-FORMED VERBS

Like most languages, Greek has "irregular" verbs. One type in Greek has been traditionally called "deponent" or "defective" because these verbs only are found with middle or passive endings, but yet they seem adequately to be translated by the active voice (see Wallace 428-30). However, already in 1934 Robertson, while discussing the "So-called 'Deponent' Verbs," indicates that the term "should not be used at all" (332). *I would agree; these verbs are not defective nor should they be considered deponent.* Instead, verbs that show only (or primarily) middle endings do so because they are representing the subject's involvement in the action in some way. Robertson's description is helpful (804):

> The only difference between the active and middle voices is that the middle calls especial attention to the subject. In the active voice the subject is merely acting; in the middle the subject is acting in relation to himself somehow. What this precise relation is the middle voice does not say. That must come out of the context or from the significance of the verb itself…. Sometimes the variation from the active is too minute for translation into English.

Currently, then, grammarians are moving away from the category of Deponent Verb.[7]

In this handbook, such verbs that primarily show middle endings will be called **Middle-Formed Verbs**. These verbs are never (or very rarely) found with active endings; they have either middle or passive endings. However, despite the middle or passive endings, these verbs may often be translated actively with the understanding that *some stress is being placed on the subject's involvement with the action*. Students will be introduced to ten or so such middle-formed verbs. In the vocabularies, their lexical form will typically end in -ομαι. Incidentally, some middle-formed verbs generally are very difficult to put into a passive sense, like ἔρχομαι *I come, I go*, πορεύομαι *I go, travel*, and προσεύχομαι *I pray*. If one attempts to put these into a passive sense, one arrives at nonsensical translations: *I am come* or *I am being come*; *I am being gone* or *I am being travelled*; *I am being prayed*. Each attempt is fairly meaningless in English, and so this fact should assist students to remember that such verbs are middle-formed verbs.

3.6 NEGATING A VERB: SOME HELP IN TRANSLATION

To negate a verb, the negative adverb is placed in front. For the Indicative mood, οὐ is used to negate the verb. It may be helpful to use the English helping verb *do/does*. Here are some examples of translating a verb that is negated.

---

[7] See Marty Culy's "Series Introduction" in the Baylor Handbooks in, e.g., Fredrick J. Long, *2 Corinthians: A Handbook on the Greek Text*, Baylor Handbook on the Greek New Testament (Waco, TX: Baylor University Press, 2015), ix-xi. Culy cites (among others) Jonathan T. Pennington, "Deponency in Koine Greek: The Grammatical Question and the Lexicographical Dilemma," *Trinity Journal* 24 (2003): 55–76. However, see also a dissertation with a dissenting view under the direction of Daniel Wallace by Stratton L. Ladewig, "Defining Deponency: An Investigation into Greek Deponency of the Middle and Passive Voices in the Koine Period" (Ph.D., Dallas Theological Seminary, 2010).

οὐ βλέπομεν	*We do not see.* Or, *We are not seeing.*
οὐχ εὑρίσκουσιν	*They do not find.* Or, *They are not finding.*
οὐ λέγει	*He does not say.* Or, *She is not saying*

As you will learn, there are several ways to create negation within a Greek sentence. Also, Greek can pile on several negative words for the sake of emphasis, because the negative words do not cancel each other out as they do in English. See §22.4 NEGATIVE EMPHASIS.

3.7 HOW "TO PARSE" (Κανονίζειν) A VERB

A. **Introduction to Parsing:** We have seen that there are five characteristics to a verb: Tense, Voice, Mood, Person, and Number. To parse a verb is to give all five characteristics of a verb *along with that verb's lexical form* and *meaning*. When parsing, Tense, Voice, Mood (TVM) are placed together, then, person, number (P #). Thus, consider these examples of some verbs parsed:

Verb to be parsed	Tense	Voice	Mood	Person	#	Lexical Form & Meaning
δοξάζομεν	P	A	I	1	P	δοξάζω *I glorify*
βλέπουσιν	P	A	I	3	P	βλέπω *I see*
διδάσκεται	P	M/P	I	3	S	διδάσκω *I teach*
ἔρχῃ	P	M/P-D	I	2	S	ἔρχομαι *I come*

Notice: (1) Try to parse verbs in the same order as given above TVM P#. (2) If a verb could be either Passive or Middle *in form*, both Middle and Passive should be indicated (M/P). Note also that -*D* is added to the voice of middle-formed verbs. (Traditionally, the D represented "deponent.") This clarifies that, although their endings are middle, passive, or middle-passive, such verbs *still* carry some active sense that will be seen in translation.

B. **Parsing Legend:** For simplicity's sake, one can use the following guide:

Tense	Voice	Mood	Person	Number
P=Present	**A**=Active	**I**= Indicative	**1**= First	**S**= Singular
I=Imperfect	**P**=Passive	**S**= Subjunctive	**2**= Second	**P**= Plural
F=Future	**M**=Middle	**P**= Participle	**3**= Third	
A=Aorist	**M/P**=Middle/Passive	**M**= Imperative		
R=Perfect	**D**= MiDDle-formed (formerly	**N**= Infinitive		
L=Pluperfect	called "Deponent" verbs)			

You are not expected to know all of these forms or endings yet! However, by the end of CHAPTER 15, you will have been introduced to all the Indicative Mood forms.

CHECK POINT 3.2-7
PARSE AND TRANSLATE THESE VERBS

Verb to be parsed	Tense	Voice	Mood	Person	#	Lexical Form & Meaning
εὐαγγελίζεσθε						
προσεύχονται						
βλέπουσιν						
διδάσκονται						
ἔρχεται						
λέγει						

Translate these sentences that use the same verb forms above.

εὐαγγελίζεσθε.	
οὐ προσεύχονται.	
βλέπουσιν.	
διδάσκονται.	
οὐκ ἔρχεται;	
λέγει ὁ Ἰησοῦς·	

ANSWERS

Verb to be parsed	Tense	Voice	Mood	Person	#	Lexical Form & Meaning
εὐαγγελίζεσθε	P	M/P-D	I	2	P	εὐαγγελίζομαι *I announce good news*
προσεύχονται	P	M/P-D	I	3	P	προσεύχομαι *I pray*
βλέπουσιν	P	A	I	3	P	βλέπω *I see*
διδάσκονται	P	M/P	I	3	P	διδάσκω *I teach*
ἔρχεται	P	M/P-D	I	3	S	ἔρχομαι *I come/go*
λέγει	P	A	I	3	S	λέγω *I say*

Translate these sentences that use the same verb forms above.

εὐαγγελίζεσθε.	*You are announcing the good news.*
οὐ προσεύχονται.	*They are not praying.*
βλέπουσιν.	*They are seeing.* (or, *They see.*)
διδάσκονται.	*They are being taught* (passive voice). Or, *They are teaching themselves* (direct middle)
οὐκ ἔρχεται;	*Is she/he not coming?*
λέγει ὁ Ἰησοῦς·	*Jesus says:* Or, *Jesus is saying:*

3.8 THE ACCENT (ὁ Τόνος) ON VERBS

A. **Introduction:** You may (or may not!) want to learn how to properly place accents on Greek words. If you want to understand how verb accents work, below are basic rules that will help you. At key points throughout this grammar, more brief explanations of accents will be given. For a more detailed accounting, see APPENDIX §24.

B. **There are three accents:** acute (´), grave (`), and circumflex (˜), respectively, ὀξύς, βαρύς, and ὀξύβαρις. These accents are placed on one of the last three syllables.

C. **Syllable Names:** Since accents may only fall on one of the last three syllables, these syllables have been given special names. The last syllable is called the *ultima* (ὀξύτονος), the one just before the ultima is the *penult* (παροξύτονος), and the one before the penult is the *antepenult* (προπαροξύτονος).

	antepenult	penult	ultima
πιστεύω	πι	στεύ	ω

D. **Locations of Accents**: The acute accent (´) may be found on any of these syllables. The circumflex (˜) may be found <u>only</u> on heavy vowels, monophthongs, and diphthongs and <u>only</u> in the last two syllables (penult and ultima). The grave (`) may be found <u>only</u> on the last syllable (ultima).

E. **Syllable Weight:** Since the placement of accents on verbs generally depends on the respective weight of syllables (particularly the ultima), it is important to understand the "weight" of the vowels, monophthongs, and diphthongs.

Always Light
1. <u>Vowels</u> ε and o
2. <u>Monophthongs</u> αι and οι *except* dative pl. forms –αις and –οις)

Always Heavy
1. <u>Vowels</u> η and ω
2. *All other monophthongs and diphthongs*
3. <u>Endings</u> in –αις and –οις

Light or Heavy
<u>Vowels</u> α, ι, and υ

F. **Verbs Generally have Recessive Accents:** Verb accents are generally *recessive*; that is, *they move as far away from the end of the verb ending as possible*. Put another way, the verb accent moves as close to the front of the verb as possible.

G. **Recessive Accent Rules:** Given the statements in A.–E. above, here are the general verb recessive accent rules:

1. A verb form with a **heavy ultima** will generally be accented on the penult with an acute accent (πιστεύω).

2. A verb form with a **light ultima** will generally be accented on the antepenult with an acute accent (πιστεύομεν); or if the verb only has only two syllables, a light ultima and a heavy

penult, it will be accented with a circumflex on the penult (ἦλθον).

3. Special exceptions to these rules of verb accenting are discussed in APPENDIX §24.

H. **Examples:** Can you understand why these verb forms are accented where they are?

πιστεύω	πιστεύομεν	πιστεύομαι	πιστευόμεθα
πιστεύεις	πιστεύετε	πιστεύῃ	πιστεύεσθε
πιστεύει	πιστεύουσι(ν)	πιστεύεται	πιστεύονται

Complete WORKBOOK EXERCISES 3 and consult the ANSWER KEY & GUIDE as needed.

CASE IN POINT 3: THE LARGER CONVERSATION IN JOHN 4

The Greek language allows for less ambiguity than English in some cases. This is especially true with regard to the use of pronoun *you*. Is the word *you* singular or plural? In older English usage, a distinction was made: *Thee* was singular and *Ye* was plural. In our modern English translations, a *you* remains ambiguous. However, both the Greek and Hebrew languages specify whether the *you* is singular or plural.

Consider Jesus' conversation with the Samaritan woman. In John 4:20 she says to Jesus, "<u>You</u> say that there is a place in Jerusalem where it is necessary to worship." When did Jesus say that? Did she say λέγεις (you singular) or λέγετε (you plural)? Jesus answers her and addresses her as *you* in 4:21-22. Likewise, one should ask, Is Jesus saying *you* singular or *you* plural?

Not unless you check the Greek text do you discover for certain that Jesus and the Samaritan woman are engaged in a larger conversation beyond the two of them; in fact, they are engaged in an ethno-religious discussion. Both instances of *you* above are plural! The Samaritan woman is a representative of the Samaritans (plural) and Jesus, from the perspective of the woman, is a representative of the Jews (plural). She initiates this larger conversation with Jesus just when He mentions the fact of her having had five husbands. She changed topics on Jesus to discuss a contemporary issue of dispute between Jews and Samaritans. Much hinges on a proper understanding of *you* in John 4. Thus, when encountering a *you*, check it out. If it is not entirely clear from the context whether or not it is singular or plural, it is worth taking a closer look.

Some further examples, see also Isaiah 42:6 (in Greek or Hebrew) and 1 Cor 3:16. Are these singular or plural? Also, when Jesus gives the commands "Go and do likewise!" at the end of the parable of the Good Samaritan in Luke 10:37, these are singular; additionally, the second command ("[you] do likewise!") has the subject further emphasized by adding an unnecessary subject pronoun σύ *you* (see §9.2 PERSONAL PRONOUNS).

Paul, on the other hand, uses plural verb forms when issuing his commands in 1 Cor 6:18 "Flee [pl.] sexual immorality!" and 6:20 "Glorify [pl.] God in your [pl.] body [sg.]!" This reminds us that even though sexual immorality may be performed individually, it has social implications for the *singular* body of believers.

CHAPTER 4

What is eternal life? How does a person obtain it? John's Gospel has a lot to say about "everlasting life" (αἰώνιος ζωή)—the phrase occurs seventeen times. But it is not until its last occurrence in 17:3 that it is given an article and a definition.

    This chapter introduces the Greek noun and article. The important concepts **gender**, **number**, and **case** are covered. Then, the endings are given for the first group of nouns, the **First Declension** or **"a" Class Declension**. This group of nouns is primarily feminine in gender. After this, the forms of the **feminine article** (*the*) are given. Students are then shown **Constituent Marking for Navigating a Greek Sentence**. Finally, some very important and frequent **coordinating conjunctions** are introduced.

VOCABULARY 4   FIRST DECLENSION NOUNS AND SOME CONJUNCTIONS

Feminine Nouns in the First Declension

ἡ ἀλήθεια [109]	truth, reality
ἡ βασιλεία [162]	kingdom, reign
ἡ δικαιοσύνη [91]	righteousness, justice
ἡ εἰρήνη [91]	peace; well-being
ἡ ἐκκλησία [114]	assembly, church
ἡ ἐντολή [66]	commandment, order
ἡ ζωή [135]	life; existence
ἡ ἡμέρα [389]	day
ἡ Ἰουδαία [43]	Judea
ἡ παραβολή [50]	parable, illustration

Coordinating Conjunctions:

ἀλλά [638]	but (*denoting correction*); yet, rather
οὐ ... ἀλλά	not ... but (*a point/counter point set*)
δέ [2777]	and, but, moreover, additionally (*postpositive*); signifies a new development
καί [8984]	and (*connective*)
καί ... καί	both ... and
καί	also, even (*additive emphasis*)
οὖν [495]	therefore (*postpositive*)

Masculine Nouns in the First Declension:

ὁ Ἡρῴδης, -ου [43]   Herod   ὁ μαθητής, -οῦ [262]   disciple, student
ὁ Ἰωάννης, -ου [135]   John   ὁ προφήτης, -ου [144]   prophet

After learning vocabulary to this point, you will know 16.4% of the words in the Greek NT. This is nearly one in every six words! This is a great accomplishment. If you are able, listen to audio recordings of VOCABULARY 4 and complete the CROSSWORD PUZZLE in the WORKBOOK.

NOTES ON VOCABULARY 4:

In the vocabulary lists, nouns will always be presented with the article in front to indicate the gender of that noun. Knowing the gender of a Greek noun is very important grammatically. When other Greek parts of speech—such as adjectives, pronouns, and participles—are modifying nouns, they must agree in gender.

English nouns have no gender, but Greek nouns do. There are patterns in Greek with respect to the gender of any particular noun. Generally, nouns denoting male persons are masculine; nouns denoting female persons are feminine; but there are many exceptions to this. Below are a few more general rules.

Many feminine nouns are abstract nouns; that is, they communicate a non-tangible quality or condition. Thus, most feminine nouns presented above (and in the rest of the textbook) fit this description: ἡ ἐκκλησία (*church*), ἡ ἡμέρα (*day*), ἡ ζωή (*life*), ἡ δόξα (*glory*), ἡ ἐντολή (*commandment*), ἡ παραβολή (*parable*), ἡ ἀλήθεια (*truth*), ἡ δικαιοσύνη (*righteousness*), and ἡ εἰρήνη (*peace*). Some of these concepts were so important that deities were identified with them, in the Greek and Roman cultures as seen represented on statuary and coins. See GRAPHIC 4A: THE GODDESS PEACE. A good number of these vocabulary words have English cognates: ecclesio-logy, zoo-logy (from ζῷον, animal), dox-ology, parable, and irenic.

GRAPHIC 4A: THE GODDESS PEACE

Obverse: ΝΙΚΟΜΗΔΕΩΝ (*"of/from the Nicomedians"*)—Bare head to right. Augustus. Νικομήδεια was a major city of the Roman region Bithynia, located in northern Turkey.
Reverse: ΕΙΡΗΝΗ—The goddess *Peace* standing to left, holding caduceus, monogram in inner right field and monogram or letter in outer right field.

Date Range: From 27 BC to AD 14. Very Rare.

Reference: RPC 2062. Photo courtesy of Classical Numismatic Group www.cngcoins.com at http://www.asiaminorcoins.com/gallery/displayimage.php?pid=4791 accessed 4-30-2014.

Words denoting countries, cities, and regions are often feminine as well, such as ἡ Ἰουδαία (*Judea*) and ἡ Γαλιλαία (*Galilee*). Such entities may be seen personified on coins, statues, and reliefs. See GRAPHIC 4B: *JUDEA CAPTA*.

GRAPHIC 4B: *JUDEA CAPTA* "JUDEA CAPTURED"

Obverse: VESPASIAN. 69-79 AD. Æ Sestertius (26.30 gm). IMP CAES VESPASIAN AVG P M TR P P P COS III, laureate head right. Most of these are abbreviated Latin words that name (as was common practice) Vespasian's titles: "Imperator [emperor] Caesar Vespasian Augustus, Pontifex Maximus [high priest], Tribunicia Protestate [tribune], Pater Patriae [father of the fatherland], Consul [chief magistrate] 3 three times."

Reverse: IVDEA CAPTA, S C [Sentatus Consultus] in exergue, Jewess in attitude of mourning, seated right beneath palm tree; to left, captive Jew with hands tied behind back standing left; captured weapons behind.

Date Range: Struck AD 71.

Reference: RIC II 426; BMCRE 542; BN 494; Cohen 238. Image and information was obtained from http://en.wikipedia.org/wiki/File:Sestertius_-_Vespasiano_-_Iudaea_Capta-RIC_0424.jpg accessed 4-29-2014, courtesy of Classical Numismatic Group http://www.cngcoins.com.

There are four masculine nouns indicated by ὁ (the masculine article formally introduced in CH. 5.2) yet have mostly feminine endings. These are the only four you will learn in this textbook. They are included here because they share basically the same feminine endings. Two of these are proper nouns: ὁ Ἰωάννης, -ου (*John*) and ὁ Ἡρῴδης, -ου (*Herod*). The other two actually represent a larger group of nouns pertaining to occupations or "The person concerned or occupied with anything" (Smyth, §843): ὁ μαθητής, -οῦ (*disciple*) and ὁ προφήτης, -οῦ (*prophet*).

Can you guess the profession of these nouns: ὁ ναύτης or ὁ κλέπτης? (Think "the seas" and shoplifting.)

The conjunction καί is very common. When it begins a clause or connects two or more words, it means *and*. Sometimes two instances (καί ... καί) will work together and should be translated *both ... and*. Additionally, καί can also function like an adverb to indicate an "additive emphasis" (see "καί" BDAG, 496.2.c-i). In such cases, it is usually best translated *also* (cf. Runge ch.16 "Thematic Addition"). When καί functions this way, it will immediately precede the sentence elements to add them emphatically to the discussion. Such a location (often in the middle of a sentence) will often distinguish this additive emphatic use of καί.

Δέ and οὖν are called **postpositive** because they are placed after the first word(s) of the clause where they are found. Thus, they are often the second word in a sentence. The conjunction δέ is marked +new development in the narrative or argument, sometimes minor sometimes major (Levinsohn 112-18). When the sentence it introduces stands in a clear contrastive relationship (ideas are contrasted), then *But* is a good translation. But such a clear contrast is not always present. In such cases it can be difficult to translate, and some translations don't always translate a δέ (see NASB95 on John 17:3). Yet, let me encourage you to try using the English conjunctions *Moreover, Additionally*, or if in a transition, *"Well (this is what happened next)…."* The conjunction οὖν is marked +continuity and +development (Runge 43-48, 57). It is generally safe to translate οὖν as *therefore*, especially if one perceives that οὖν shows continuity and development in such a way leading to an inference or conclusion.

Ἀλλά is marked +correction and found often in the form of a contrast translated as *but*. The Louw-Nida *Greek-English Lexicon Based on Semantic Domains* describes ἀλλά as "a marker of more emphatic contrast" than δέ (§89.125) or "a marker of contrastive emphasis" (§91.11). Very commonly, ἀλλά follows a negative statement made with a negative adverb like οὐ or οὐκ to form what Runge calls a "point/counter point set" (92-100).

Much more extensive discussion of these conjunctions is provided below in §4.8 SOME COORDINATING CONJUNCTIONS.

4.1 GREEK WORD ORDER AND INITIAL CONJUNCTIONS

A. Default Word Order in Sentences:

1. <u>The Verb is the Anchor.</u> So far you should understand that the Greek sentence is constructed around the verb. See again, if needed, §3.2 THE GREEK VERB. The verb is the anchor of the sentence. Even if the verb is not present (see §9.4 ELLIPSIS: SUPPLYING AN IMPLIED WORD), it will be implied and will still dictate the required grammatical forms and so govern the surrounding sentence elements!

2. <u>Subjects, Objects, and Adjunct Modifiers.</u> In addition to the verb (V), one may typically find an initial Coordinating Conjunction (CC), and possibly the expressed subject (S), object complements (O; direct objects = DO and indirect objects = IO), and/or various kinds

of modifiers (M). Optional sentence elements are commonly called adjuncts in linguistic nomenclature, and would include many types of modifiers. These types of constituents are true of English and other languages.

3. <u>Greek and VSO Word Order</u>. In Greek, after the initial conjunction (=C), the default word order has been debated.[1] But I agree with Levinsohn (17), who maintains that Verb-Subject-Object (VSO) is the unmarked or default Greek sentence order. In contrast, for English the standard word order is Subject (=S) + Verb (=V) + Object (=O), which is expressed briefly as SVO.

God (S) *gave* (V) *the Holy Spirit* (DO) *to us* (IO) *in Christ Jesus* (M).

So, for English students, it may take some adjustment to work with Greek word order and the flexibility it robustly demonstrates.

4. <u>Variations from VSO Indicate Framing, Focus, and/or Special Emphasis</u>. Sentence constituents—i.e., expressed subjects, objects, and modifiers—that are preposed before the verb are in a **marked position** (Levinsohn 37–40), and may indicate framing, focus, or emphasis. **Framing** involves the orientation of audiences to what they are hearing/reading by providing a segue from previous material to new material or by providing logical sequences of action. **Focus** refers to special attention on the topic of the sentence; typically, this would be the verbal subject. **Emphasis** refers to important sentence information that is contextually stressed. Consider this verse translated literally preserving sentence order:

Luke 4:40a *And <u>while the sun was setting</u>, **all**, as many as were having sick people with various kinds of illnesses, led them to Him.*

The preposed temporal clause *while the sun was setting* provides a segue from one scene to the next. The preposed subject *all* has focus, and is further emphasized by repeated reference to quantity in the word *all* and the clause begun with *as many as*. Sometimes, the prepositioning of a constituent will place it within a structural relation with another constituent, either inside the sentence or outside it (with an adjoining sentence) to form patterns, like parallelism (ABABABAB, where the A and B represent repeated topics), bracket or inclusio (A … A), or chiasm (ABC-CBA). For example, the central elements of 2 Cor 9:8 involve three abutted words built from the word πᾶς *all* (*... in everyway, always, all ...*) prepositioned before the verb of its clause to produce a chiasm in that verse, as follows:

---

[1] See my treatment in "Word Order and Preposed Sentence Elements" in Fredrick J. Long, *2 Corinthians: A Handbook on the Greek Text*, Baylor Handbook on the Greek Text (Waco, TX: Baylor University Press, 2015), xxxix-xliii.

9:8 A δυνατεῖ δὲ ὁ θεὸς **πᾶσαν** χάριν   *God empowers **all** grace*
       B   περισσεῦσαι   *to abound*
MEANS C   εἰς ὑμᾶς,   *to you*
  ↓   D   ἵνα ἐν **παντὶ**   *in order that in **everyway***
TO   E   **πάντοτε**   ***always***
          D   **πᾶσαν** αὐτάρκειαν ***all** (self-)sufficiency*
  ↓   C   ἔχοντες   *having*
END B   περισσεύητε   *you would abound*
     A   εἰς **πᾶν** ἔργον ἀγαθόν,   *in **every** good work.*

The central abutted elements help reinforce Paul's understanding of **all** God's grace to help believers *abound to **every** good work*; the same root πᾶς *all* modifies *grace* and *good work*. This elaborate patterned emphasis supports Paul's larger communicative goals in 2 Corinthians, to encourage the Corinthians to complete their portion of the collection for the saints of Jerusalem. So, prepositioning of constituents may produce patterned emphasis. Thus, one should carefully consider contextually why a variation from the standard word order of VSO exists.

B. **Polysyndeton (Πολυσύνδετον):** When initial conjunctions link one sentence to others, this is called polysyndeton. Polysyndeton, in fact, is the default sentence structure in Greek. So, most commonly students will observe an initial coordinating conjunction (CC). Thus, one should think of the unmarked or typical Greek sentence to have this structure: CC+VSO. This conjunction importantly delimits a certain relationship between its sentence and those coming before it and (sometimes) after it. Thus, it is standard to have a series of Greek sentences connected together by a series of conjunctions, as in this example below from Romans 2:1–6 (NASB95). The CCs are underlined:

Rom 2:1-6 ¹ <u>Therefore</u> you have no excuse, everyone of you who passes judgment, <u>for</u> in that which you judge another, you condemn yourself; <u>for</u> you who judge practice the same things. ² <u>And</u> we know that the judgment of God rightly falls upon those who practice such things. ³ <u>But</u> do you suppose this, O man, when you pass judgment on those who practice such things and do the same *yourself,* that you will escape the judgment of God? ⁴ <u>Or</u> do you think lightly of the riches of His kindness and tolerance and patience, not knowing that the kindness of God leads you to repentance? ⁵ <u>But</u> because of your stubbornness and unrepentant heart you are storing up wrath for yourself in the day of wrath and revelation of the righteous judgment of God, ⁶ who will render to each person according to his deeds:

Notice several things. <u>First</u>, not all numbered verses contain a single complete sentence; some will have several (as 2:1), or none, because the sentence will continue and be completed in later verses (as in 2:5-6). <u>Second</u>, in the English above the initial CCs will typically begin the sentence. However, the "for" in 2:1b immediately follows a comma, which obscures its status as an initial CC in the Greek. The other instance of "for" in 2:1 is the same conjunction γάρ. This itself is important to see; the English translations may or may not translate CCs consistently; nor do they clearly indicate the beginning of a new sentence, as in Rom 2:1b above. Too often conjunctions are not translated at all. For example, an "and" (καί) is untranslated in Luke 18:18 NASB95; the NIV84 leaves an important resumptive "therefore" (οὖν) untranslated in Matt 5:19 (but corrected in NIV2011). Third, there are several other conjunctions present in this paragraph, but they are not CCs. This can be tricky for students. For example, the conjunction καί is very often translated *and*, and can begin a sentence (Luke 18:18); but καί can also connect equal sentence elements, as in 2:4 (*kindness _and_ tolerance _and_ patience*), and thus καί is not functioning in 2:4 as an initial CC. And, fourth, Rom 2:1-6 contains seven sentences using four different initial CCs. Indeed, Greek shows tremendous variety of conjunctions; major monographs have been written dedicated to explicating the significance of them.[2]

C. **Asyndeton ('Ασύνδετον):** The absence of an initial CC is called **Asyndeton**. Perhaps surprisingly, asyndeton is not that uncommon, and this varies depending on the NT author. For example, asyndeton is quite common in the Johannine Writings. In general, you should take notice of asyndeton, since it breaks the default pattern. Grammarians have concluded that asyndeton either marks +high emotion by creating a staccato effect of sentence after sentence after sentence, or marks a major discourse break.[3] See the extensive discussion of both polysyndeton and asyndeton in §15.5 Asyndeton and Polysyndeton.

4.2 Greek Nouns (Ὀνόματα): Three Characteristics

A. **Number (Ἀριθμός):** Greek nouns are like and unlike English nouns. As in English, Greek nouns distinguish between singular and plural forms. English usually adds an *-s* to the end of a word to make it plural; for example, *dog → dogs* or *form → forms*. **Singular** (sg.) and **plural** (pl.) refer to a noun's number. In Classical Greek, there was also a **dual** form, which by the NT era, had fallen out of use.

B. **Gender (Γένος):** Greek nouns also have **gender**. If you have learned a foreign language, you are probably already familiar with this concept. Greek has three genders: **feminine, masculine**, and **neuter**. Each Greek noun has only one gender. In general, nouns that refer to female persons would be feminine in Greek and nouns referring to male persons would be masculine. Gender can usually be identified by the endings of a noun. However, this is a bit more compli-

---

[2] The classical and standard treatment is by J. D. Denniston, *The Greek Particles*, 2nd ed., revised by K. J. Dover (London: Bristol Classical, 1996). Focused on NT usage, see Margaret E. Thrall, *Greek Particles in the New Testament: Linguistic and Exegetical Studies* (Leiden: Brill, 1962).

[3] See the extensive discussion of Asyndeton in the Appendix of Long, *2 Corinthians*. This basic explanation excludes the high frequency in the Johannine Literature, where the asyndeton may simply keep the discourse moving along.

cated with the nouns in the Third Declension (see CHAPTER 12.1 and CHAPTER 16.1). *But if an article is with a noun, gender can generally be determined*, since the article endings will help indicate the gender. One exception is the genitive plural article τῶν, which is the same for all three genders! Therefore, memorize the article endings well.

C. Case (Πτῶσις):

1. <u>Importance and Definition</u>. This is the single most important feature to learn about a Greek noun. **Case** indicates to the reader how a noun functions in the sentence. Some of the most important functions are as subject, direct object, indirect object, and modifier. In contrast, English nouns largely do not express the notion of "case." The closest instance is with possessives; for example, to make the word *boy* a possessive modifier one would add an – *'s*. Thus, *the boy's hat*. This represents one central use of the Greek genitive case. Some commonly learned languages also show case endings; Latin has a full array of comparable case endings. French and German show case endings in pronouns.

2. <u>Greek has Five Case Forms</u>. The basic sense of the cases is provided in the chart below. *Nouns in the Vocative Case are always set off by comma(s)*, as in English; thus, they are easy to identify. Moreover, often the Vocative Case endings are identical to the Nominative Case endings. Notice that the Genitive and Dative cases are fairly dynamic. Each can convey multiple notions, although most commonly possession and indirect objects, respectively. The additional significances are the remnants of an eight case system: The Greek genitive form is used for *ablative* functions (i.e. *separation*); the Greek dative form is used also for *locative* and *instrumental* (i.e. cause and means) functions (see Wallace 31-35).

THE GREEK FIVE CASE SYSTEM			
NAME	**GREEK CASE NAME**	**CASE SIGNIFICANCE**	**EXAMPLE**
vocative case	κλητική πτῶσις	direct address	*Saul, Saul, why are you persecuting me?* <u>Σαοὺλ Σαούλ</u>, τί με διώκεις; See §5.5 VOCATIVES AS THEMATIC ADDRESS.
nominative case	ὀνομαστική πτῶσις	naming or designation, often as subject	*Magi from the east arrived…* <u>μάγοι</u> ἀπὸ ἀνατολῶν παρεγένοντο… See §21.2 COMMON USES OF THE NOMINATIVE CASE.
genitive case	γενική πτῶσις	description (often possession) and separation	*We are coworkers <u>of the joy</u> <u>of you</u>.* συνεργοί ἐσμεν <u>τῆς χαρᾶς</u> <u>ὑμῶν</u>· See §11.6 COMMON USES OF THE GENITIVE CASE.

| dative case | δοτική πτῶσις (also τοπική & χρηστική) | indirect object, personal interest, location, and instrumentation | *Truly I say to you…* ἀμὴν γὰρ λέγω ὑμῖν…

 See §14.4 COMMON USES OF THE DATIVE CASE. |
| accusative case | αἰτιατική πτῶσις | direct object & extension | *A person had two sons.* ἄνθρωπος εἶχεν τέκνα δύο.

 See §23.6 SPECIAL USES OF THE ACCUSATIVE CASE. |

3. <u>Oblique Cases</u> (πλάγιαι πτώσεις). The term "oblique cases" is applied to the genitive, dative, and accusative cases. Students will often encounter this expression in grammar books.

4.3 NOUNS OF THE FIRST OR "A" CLASS DECLENSION (Πρῶτη Κλίσις)

A. **The First Declension is Mostly Feminine:** As has already been indicated, the vast majority of nouns in the first declension are feminine in gender.

B. **Some Masculine Nouns are Found:** The four masculine nouns of the First Declension provided here have the same endings as the feminine nouns except when singular (see below). As you will find out in CHAPTER 5.1, this odd ending is actually a regular Second Declension masculine ending.

C. **The Long "a" Class Declension:** The endings of the First Declension are constructed with a long "a" class vowel, either an ἄλφα (α) or an ἦτα (η). These endings are added to the noun stem. Regular stems use an ἦτα (η) in the singular endings. Stems ending in ε, ι, or ρ use an ἄλφα (α) in the singular endings. Stems ending in σ, ξ, ζ, or ψ are mixed, using ἄλφα (α) for nominative and accusative and ἦτα (η) for the genitive and dative singular (see δόξα, θάλασσα, and γλῶσσα in CHS. 15 and 17). However, all the plural endings are the same regardless of how the noun stem ends.

	Regular Stem	ε, ι, ρ Stems	σ, ξ, ζ, ψ Stems	Masculine Stems	Regular Stems	ε, ι, ρ Stems	σ, ξ, ζ, ψ Stems	Masculine Stems
sg. nom.	-η	-α	-α	-ης	ἐντολή	ἡμέρα	δόξα	μαθητής
gen.	-ης	-ας*	-ης	-ου	ἐντολῆς	ἡμέρας	δόξης	μαθητοῦ
dat.	-ῃ	-ᾳ	-ῃ	-ῃ	ἐντολῇ	ἡμέρᾳ	δόξῃ	μαθητῇ
acc.	-ην	-αν	-αν	-ην	ἐντολήν	ἡμέραν	δόξαν	μαθητήν
	all stems have same plural endings							
pl. nom.	-αι				ἐντολαί	ἡμέραι	δόξαι	μαθηταί
gen.	-ων				ἐντολῶν	ἡμέρων	δόξων	μαθητῶν
dat.	-αις				ἐντολαῖς	ἡμέραις	δόξαις	μαθηταῖς
acc.	-ας*				ἐντολάς	ἡμέρας	δόξας	μαθητάς

Notice: (1) Two endings marked with (*) are identical in form. But their meaning and significance are different. These two identical forms can only be distinguished in context by an article, if present (see why in 4.3 below). (2) There are Masculine ε, ι, ρ stem First Declension nouns (e.g. νεανίας, νεανίου, νεανία, νεανίαν... "young man"), but none of them occur frequently enough to be included in this textbook.

CHECK POINT 4.2-3 Parse these nouns providing gender, case, number, and lexical form				
Noun to be parsed	**Gender**	**Case**	**Number**	**Lexical Form & Meaning**
ἐκκλησίας				
ἐντολῶν				
δικαιοσύνης				
εἰρήνην				
μαθητοῦ				
προφήτης				
ἀληθείᾳ				
βασιλείαις				
ANSWERS				
Noun to be parsed	**Gender**	**Case**	**Number**	**Lexical Form & Meaning**
ἐκκλησίας	F	gen. sg. or acc. pl.		ἐκκλησία *church assembly*
ἐντολῶν	F	gen.	pl.	ἐντολή *commandment*
δικαιοσύνης	F	gen.	sg.	δικαιοσύνη *justice*
εἰρήνην	F	acc.	sg.	εἰρήνη *peace*
μαθητοῦ	M	gen.	sg.	μαθητῆς *disciple*
προφήτης	M	nom.	sg.	προφήτης *prophet*
ἀληθείᾳ	F	dat.	sg	ἀλήθεια *truth*
βασιλείαις	F	dat.	pl.	βασιλεία *kingdom*

4.4 FEMININE ARTICLE FORMS

The Feminine Article is used only with Feminine nouns. The complete Article forms, including Masculine and Neuter, will be learned in CHAPTER 5 (see §5.2 MASCULINE AND NEUTER ARTICLE ENDINGS). The Article is the most frequently used word in the GNT. You had better learn these forms! We begin with the Feminine forms since they are most relevant now:

	sg.	pl.
nom.	ἡ	αἱ
gen.	τῆς*	τῶν
dat.	τῇ	ταῖς
acc.	τήν	τάς*

Notice the following:
1. The endings look exactly like the First Declension regular stem endings.
2. The nominative singular and plural forms both have rough breathing marks.
3. The genitive singular and accusative plural forms (*) are different. If the article is present, this will help distinguish between the identical forms noted immediately above.

4.5 THE ARTICLE (τὸ Ἄρθρον) AND LACK OF AN ARTICLE (Ἄναρθρος)

A. **Definitions:** In English, the word *the* is called the definite article. The words *a, an* are indefinite articles. In Greek, there is no indefinite article; thus, when we talk about the "article" we have in mind something closer to the English definite article, although the functions of the Greek article are quite nuanced. A noun or word having the article (τὸ ἄρθρον) is called **arthrous** or **articular** (ἀρθριτικός). A noun without an article is called **anarthrous** (ἀναρθριτικός).

B. **Agreement:** The article must agree in **gender**, **number**, and **case** with its word. Thus, a masculine Greek noun takes the masculine article; a feminine Greek noun takes the feminine article. If the noun is singular, so must the article be. If the noun is in the genitive case, so must the article be.

C. **Nouns of Unique Referential Identity, or Not:** A critical distinction must be made at the outset between nouns that have unique referential identity because they refer to entities (people, places, or things) that are known and clearly identifiable to the author and audience, and nouns that are not (assumed as) known. For example, in the United States, one could refer to *the White House*, and most people would probably understand this referent. However, most people would probably not know what is meant by *the Arch*, unless they lived in the St. Louis area. In conversation, nouns can achieve unique referential identity through their introduction. Thus, if I said, *There is an arch in St. Louis that is worth seeing, the Gateway Arch*, I would be introducing and giving unique referential identity to *the arch*. These distinctions are important as we consider the presence or lack of the Greek article.

D. **Basic Functions of Arthrous and Anarthrous Nouns:** The NT writers did not use the article randomly. They tended to use it when they wanted to refer to a well-known entity (*the White House*), to refer to a specific entity previously introduced in the discourse (*the specific entity I just referred to*), to conceptualize an idea ([*the*] *living* vs. [*the*] *dying*), or to refer to a category of type of items (*the worker is worth his or her wages*). Conversely, the lack of article may indicate indefiniteness (*an apple*) or stress the unique quality/essence of the noun (*it was a banana, not an orange, that caused his allergic reaction*).[4] In the information flow of a Greek discourse, there are many factors to consider in order to understand the presence or absence of the article (see E. below).

1. <u>A Noun **without** the Article is called an Anarthrous (Ἀναρθριτιχος) Substantive.</u>

   a. *Indefiniteness.* A noun may be signaled as **indefinite** (as in <u>*an*</u> *apple* or <u>*a*</u> *book*) when it lacks an article.

      i. For example, in John 4, the Greek noun γυνή is anarthrous and is translated as *a woman* when Jesus first meets her; we as the audience also meet her for the first time in John 4:7. However, the woman gains unique referential identity, and is subsequently found with the article as <u>*the*</u> *woman* (4:9, 11, 15, 17, 19, 25, 28, 39, 42). However, in the story flow, when the disciples return to Jesus and see him with her (4:27), their perception is that *he is speaking with <u>a</u> women* (no article). From their vantage point, the woman is only <u>*a*</u> *woman* and not *the* woman. Interestingly, in Christian circles today she is referred to as <u>*the Samaritan woman*</u>.

      ii. Similarly, the noun ἄνθρωπος is *a person* when encountered for the first time, as often happens to Jesus when he travels about (see, e.g., Matt 9:9, 32; 12:10; 17:14; 27:32, 57). However, in the case of 12:10, when *the person* is mentioned again in 12:13, he has the article. Additionally, an anarthrous ἄνθρωπος is found when introducing parables: *The Kingdom of God is like <u>a</u> person...* (Matt 13:24, 31, 44, 45, 52; 18:23; 20:1; 21:28; 22:2, 11; 25:14).

   b. *Qualitative.* However, another significance of the lack of the article may be to emphasize the **quality** or **essence** of what that noun signifies (see Wallace 244). In 1 John 4:8b, what is stressed is the quality/essence of love that God is.

      1 John 4:8b ὁ θεὸς <u>ἀγάπη</u> ἐστίν. = *God is <u>love</u>.*

---

[4] For extended discussions of the article or its absence, see Wallace 207-43 and Porter 103-114.

c. *Definite because of Unique Reference*. As puzzling as this may seem, some nouns that have unique reference are anarthrous, yet still refer to "definite" entities. Such include proper names (Jesus, Peter, and Paul), but occasionally other nouns. See Wallace (245-53), who provides a list of ten situations when "definite nouns" have no article.

d. *Summary Chart of Anarthrous Nouns*. Wallace's Chart 21 (243) helpfully summarizes the semantics of anarthrous nouns, which overlap in potential uses.

What has remained unexplained is why certain nouns that are definite in their unique referential identity *sometimes do* and *sometimes do not have an article*. See **E. Preliminary Discourse Considerations** below.

2. <u>A Noun **with** the Article is called an Arthrous (Ἀρθριτικός) Substantive.</u>

a. *Determiner* or *Pointer*. The Greek article essentially functions as a **determiner** or **pointer**. It specifies any particular Greek word, but especially nouns. Here are the two broad classifications that interpreters have used to subcategorize this function of the article.

i. **Broad Categorical Use.** The article may help identify one class of things as opposed to another class; e.g., *(the) Humankind* [ὁ ἄνθρωπος] *shall not live on bread alone* (Luke 4:4, quoting Deut 8:3).

ii. **Particular Identification Use**. In distinction from the broad categorical use, the article will specify a particular, specific entity as opposed to a class of entities. Within this use, the article may identify a person, place, event, or thing as a known or assumed as a **well-known entity** (e.g., *the* big game). Or, if the entity is one of a kind, the article use may be called **monadic** (*the* United Nations; *the* God of Israel).

b. *Anaphoric Use to Indicate Previous Referent*. Often subcategorized under the Particular Identification Use immediately above, the anaphoric use occurs within a discourse when the article refers back to a noun previously mentioned. (An **anaphor** is a word or phrase referring back to that which was previously spoken.) Thus, when the article helps identify or to refer back to an earlier referent, this use is considered the **anaphoric use**. See more at §7.4.B.

c. *Substantivizer (or Nominalizer)*. Additionally, the article can convert adjectives, adverbs, prepositional phrases, verbs—really almost any unit of Greek grammar—into nouns or what are called **substantives**. This transformation **nominalizes** such words; thus, the article can function as a **substantivizer** or **nominalizer**. Students will encounter this at different points in the textbook; for adverbs, see §7.1.B. and for adjectives, see §7.3.B., and more generally see more at §7.4.C. etc.

d. *Marker of Grammatical Construction.* The article may be used to show the case of nouns that are foreign words that show no case endings. So, in Acts 7:8 at the first mention of Isaac, we find τὸν Ἰσαάκ *(the) Isaac*, even though a rule for introducing new persons is to do so without the article (Levinsohn 151). In this case, the accusative article may help to indicate that Isaac is not the subject, but the direct object of the verb. (Alternatively, Isaac is well-known in this context, and so this may explain the article.) In Heb 11:20, we see εὐλόγησεν Ἰσαὰκ τὸν Ἰακὼβ καὶ τὸν Ἡσαῦ *Isaac blessed [the] Jacob and [the] Esau.* Once again, the accusative article may help to identify more readily each direct object. Additionally, as you continue learning Greek, you will see that the article must be present to demarcate certain special constructions.

E. **Preliminary Discourse Considerations:** From a discourse perspective, the article with proper names that have unique referential identity is unmarked or default; conversely, the lack of article is marked.[5] The presence of the article may function to identify participants that have already been "activated" and "placed on stage." Conversely, the absence of the article is "marked" and draws attention to introduce or reintroduce participants onto the stage. Additionally, if a participant has already been introduced and is on stage, then emphasis attends to them when they should normally have an article but are not given one and are anarthrous; in these cases, the participants/entities are often highlighted as performing some important action (in word or deed) or as having special focus. Below are some basic principles; more discussion is provided in §21.4 DISCOURSE PRAGMATIC USE OF THE ARTICLE OR ITS ABSENCE.

1. Anarthrous Names of Persons or Participants.

   a. *Introduce a Participant into the Discourse.* **Participants** can be introduced or activated ("placed on stage") by their introduction as anarthrous. This occurs with nouns of unique referential identity (like persons), but not usually with common nouns.[6]

   b. *Reintroduce a Participant back on Stage.* Unless the participant is a Global Very Important Participant (VIP), they normally will need to be reintroduced without the article.[7]

---

[5] Jenny Read-Heimerdinger, *The Bezan Text of Acts: A Contribution of Discourse Analysis to Textual Criticism,* JSNTSS 236 (London: Sheffield Academic Press, 2002), 119.

[6] In email correspondence with Jenny Read-Heimerdinger, she related variance in proper nouns: "names of cities, for example, are usually (but not always) anarthrous at first mention whereas names of regions/provinces/countries are arthrous."

[7] Levinsohn (153) notes, however, some exceptions in Acts, when a reintroduced participant who has been off-stage comes back in, but with the article; he suggests that the article signals the audience to recall the participant's previous involvements.

    c. *Emphasize Purposeful Action of an Active Participant.* The lack of article **highlights** or **emphasizes participants' activity** if occurring after they have been formally introduced and remain activated in the episode. Why? In such cases, the typical pattern is for the participant to have an article (see 2. below). So, the lack of article is noticeable (!) and attracts attention to the participant. It may be that the lack of article signals the essence or quality of that participant as agent about to do or say something significant.

2. <u>Arthrous Persons as Activated Participants</u>. For Proper nouns that have unique referential identity (i.e. persons), the article marks them as "actively on stage." The proper noun may be known either as "commonly known" outside the discourse or as "having become known" within the discourse. If previous mention has been made, the continued use of the article functions essentially anaphorically, referring back to the previous reference(s).

3. <u>Textual Variants</u>. Ancient scribes, when copying NT manuscripts, might add or subtract articles to assist their audiences based upon their knowledge of (un)known entities. There are a considerable number of textual variants concerning the Greek article.

F. **Translation Help:** Although one must consider the discourse functions of the presence and absence of articles on nouns, for now here are some initial guidelines to help you translate them.

1. <u>Arthrous Nouns or Substantives</u>. One should avoid the simple notion that the article should always be translated as *the*. For example, ἡ ἐντολή is *the commandment*; ἡ παραβολή is *the parable*. In fact, with abstract nouns (e.g. *faith, hope, love*), if present, the article is often *NOT* translated in English. For example, ἡ δικαιοσύνη is sometimes translated simply as *righteousness* (Rom 5:17). See also *grace* in Eph 2:8, which in the Greek is literally *saved by <u>the</u> grace* (it is anaphoric). Additionally, certain words like God (sg.) and personal names may have an article, but these are not translated (ὁ Πέτρος is simply *Peter*).

2. <u>Anarthrous Nouns</u>. One should avoid the simple notion that the lack of article should always be translated as *a* or *an*, as if the absence of the article means it is indefinite. It is true that a Greek writer could leave off the article to indicate indefiniteness, which approximates our English *a, an* (e.g., ἐντολή is *a commandment*; παραβολή is *a parable*). The lack of article may help indicate the quality or essence of that noun. However, more often then these possibilities, one needs to consider the discourse flow and activation status of participants of unique identity—the lack of article may activate a participant or, if already activated, may emphasize that agent's or entity's activity or speech.

4.6 TRANSLATING THE CASES

A. **The Default Greek Word Order:** Below are basic instructions and guidelines for translating the Greek noun cases. But you should always remember the default word order for Greek sentences and clauses: begin with a Conjunction, then the Verb, then Subject, and then any Objects; Modifiers will be near what they modify. However, Greek shows great flexibility of word order, which helps indicate various types of information status and emphasis.

B. **Location is not so Important:** English has a fairly fixed word order, and changes from that order are often significant. Greek word order is more flexible, but nuances and emphasis are often achieved through strategic variations allowed by such flexibility, e.g., whether a sentence constituent is placed before the verb (**preposed**) or at a clause end or **final position**. Additionally, some modifiers are **fronted** or **placed before** what they modify.

By now you know that noun cases reflect different noun function in the sentence. Since the ending delimits the noun's function (and not so much its location), *the order of Greek words in sentences can vary*. At the same time, *the Greek sentence is arranged more or less in terms of clusters of related elements or constituents*. For example, the negative adverb οὐ *no* is always placed before what it negates, a prepositional phrase remains together, nouns are found with their modifiers typically, and subordinate clauses cohere together. Exceptions to this rule normally indicate some sort of emphasis, as in the case of **discontinuous constituent elements**.

C. **Discontinuous Constituent Elements Possible:** Occasionally, modifiers will be separated from what they modify and be found on different sides of the verb. This can be troublesome for beginning students. Such separation is for effect; emphasis may fall on either element, or on both. Such must be determined in context. Elements placed before the verb are called **preposed** and elements placed after the verb are called **postposed**.[8]

1 John 5:13c ζωὴν ἔχετε αἰώνιον = *You have life everlasting.*

In 1 John 5:13c, the accusative direct object ζωὴν *life* is **prepositioned** and separated from its adjectival modifier αἰώνιον *everlasting*, which is **postpositioned** to the verb ἔχετε.

Consider this example that shows a **fronted** genitive form and discontinuous elements:

2 Cor 1:24a οὐχ ὅτι κυριεύομεν ὑμῶν τῆς πίστεως
It is not that we lord over YOUR faith

ἀλλὰ συνεργοί ἐσμεν τῆς χαρᾶς ὑμῶν·
*but we are **coworkers** of your JOY.*

---

[8] For an intermediate-advanced discussion, see Levinsohn 57-62.

The word συνεργοί *coworkers* has been **preposed** before the verb ἐσμεν *we are* and is discontinuous with (or, separated from) its genitive modifier τῆς χαρᾶς *of (the) JOY*, in order to clarify and emphasize that Paul and his fellow ministry companions are not lording over the Corinthians' *faith*, but rather are *coworkers* of their *JOY*. Incidentally, this example illustrates nicely two other emphatic features: the use of a point/counter point set (οὐχ ... ἀλλὰ; see §4.8.D. below) and **genitival emphasis, in which the genitive modifier is fronted before what it modifies to draw more attention to its modification** (ὑμῶν τῆς πίστεως *YOUR faith*). The default genitive position is placement *after* what the genitive word modifies, as in τῆς χαρᾶς ὑμῶν *of your joy*. As you can see from this one sentence, only the first half of one verse (2 Cor 1:24a), there is much to be appreciated about word order and special constructions! It may seem like a lot to take in, but with time and practice, you will get it.

D. **Some Order within Constituents:** Amidst this flexibility, there are some generally true and reliable rules about the order of elements within a constituent grouping. Here are three general rules:

1. <u>The article will be placed before the word to which it belongs, often immediately so.</u> You need to think of an article and its noun as a team unit; article comes first, then its noun. For example, one would find τὴν ἐντολὴν and not ἐντολὴν... τήν. *An important exception to this is when that noun has a modifier such as an adjective or prepositional phrase inserted in between it and its article.* In this particular situation, the article and noun will then make a team "sandwich" around the modifier, as in <u>τὴν</u> δικαίαν <u>ἐντολήν</u> = *the righteous law*. I call this the **sandwich technique**, and some sandwiches are thin and small (as above) and some are "big macs" or "triple stacks." You will encounter this kind of sandwiching often in the GNT. Have a feast!

2. <u>A noun in the genitive case is regularly placed after the noun it modifies. If the genitive noun is preposed, there is **genitival emphasis**.</u> For example, one would see as a default αἱ ἐντολαὶ τῶν προφητῶν = *the commandments of the prophets. Any exception to this normally indicates emphasis on the genitive word and its modification*, as the example of 2 Cor 1:24 above illustrates. Consider also this example from Eph 2:10a.

   2:10 **αὐτοῦ** γάρ ἐσμεν ποίημα,
         *For we are **HIS** workmanship,*

   The genitive αὐτοῦ *his* (a pronoun) is **discontinuous** with what it modifies, namely, ποίημα *workmanship*. Additionally, αὐτοῦ *his* is **preposed**, greatly emphasizing that we are *HIS* (God's!) workmanship (and not *our own*; see 2:8-9).

3. <u>Generally, the word emphasized will be placed in the front of the clause, although occasionally it is placed last in a final position.</u>

John 1:1c θεός ἦν ὁ λόγος = *the Word was* **God.**

Here the prepositioning of and lack of article on θεός *God* helps to stress the divinity of the Word. See again 2 Cor 1:24 and Eph 2:10a above.

E. **There are <u>two important steps</u> to translate Greek nouns into proper English:**

1. <u>Step One: Translate the Cases suitably into English</u>. Although there are special uses of the noun cases that will require special translation, here is how to try to understand and translate the cases when you encounter nouns in a sentence. Obviously, as you learn more Greek and specialized constructions, you will need to make adjustments.

		Greek	**English Translation**	**English Grammar**
<u>sg.</u>				
	nom.	ἀληθεί-α	*truth*	subject
	gen.	ἀληθεί-ας	*...of truth* or *truth's ...*	modifier or possessor
	dat.	ἀληθεί-ᾳ	*to/for truth*	indirect object
	acc.	ἀληθεί-αν	*truth*	direct object
<u>pl.</u>				
	nom.	ἀληθεί-αι	*truths*	subject
	gen.	ἀληθεί-ων	*... of truths* or *truths' ...*	modifier or possessor
	dat.	ἀληθεί-αις	*to/for truths*	indirect object
	acc.	ἀληθεί-ας	*truths*	direct object

<u>Notice</u>: (1) If an article accompanies a noun, you should consider translating it with the noun: ... τῆς ἀληθείας is ... *of (the) truth*. (2) A choice must be made for the genitive and dative cases. These two cases are the most dynamic. Each can be rendered two basic ways. You must determine which makes the best sense in English. Special uses of the Genitive, Dative, and Accusative cases will be learned later.

Now, consider this example:

οἱ <u>προφηταὶ</u> <u>τῆς δικαιοσύνης</u> διδάσκουσιν τὴν ἀληθείαν <u>ταὶς ἐκκλσίαις</u>.

<u>Translation A</u>: *The prophets of (the) righteousness are teaching the truth to the churches.*

<u>Translation B</u>: *The righteousness's prophets are teaching the truth to the churches.*

Which translation sounds right, A or B? One must consider how best to translate the Genitives and datives. Translation B is no good. Usually the genitive is safely translated using *of*; here, the better translation is *the prophets <u>of</u> (the) righteousness*. In fact, we probably are seeing a specialized use of the Genitive case here, called the **attributive genitive** where the genitive word functions like an attributive adjective: *the righteous prophets*. However, as beginning students, it is sufficient to use *of* to translate the genitive in many cases, including this one.

2. <u>Step Two: Put the Greek sentence into good English sentence order</u>. Greek sentences show variation in word order. The subject may come at the end of the sentence. How would we know it was the subject? By its ending! But when it comes time to translate Greek into English, we would need to set the Greek word meanings into proper English word order. Consider this example with marking:

<u>τὴν ζώην καὶ εἰρήνην</u>   διδάσκ|ει   ὁ Ἰωάννης   τῇ Ἰουδαίᾳ.
    compound DOs   V   S   IO

Word for word translation: *The life and peace teaches the John to the Judea.*
Proper translation: *John teaches (the) life and peace to Judea.*

<u>Notice</u>: (1) Articles need not always be translated, yet their significance should not be ignored. *The life* mentioned may be the theologically specific *life* that Jesus offers. (2) Remember Greek endings help one to determine how that word is functioning in the sentence.

F. **A Final Note on Dynamism of Cases:** Greek noun cases are very dynamic, especially the Genitive and Dative. This textbook will provide an essential introduction. At this point in learning Greek, it is not important that you know all the other uses. However, you should understand that eventually you will be introduced to the main functions of the Genitive (§11.6), Dative (§14.5), Nominative (§21.2) and the Accusative cases (§23.6). More information can be found in Wallace's discussion of the cases: Nominative (36-67), Genitive (72-136), Dative (137-75), and Accusative (176-205).

4.7 CONSTITUENT MARKING FOR NAVIGATING A GREEK SENTENCE

Here is a procedure that you will find most helpful. It allows one to mark up the sentence in such a way as to visualize the function of the words and *thus to navigate the sentence*. I recommend that you use it for all your exercises and translations from this point on.

GRAMMAR AND TYPE OF CONSTITUENT MARKING	COMMENT
<u>Verb</u>|s and <u>subjects</u>	Both subject and its verb are <u>single underlined</u>; also "chop off" verb endings.
[Conjunctions] and [Interjections]	Place a box around conjunctions and interjections.

Adverbs	Place a dashed box or circle around adverbs.
Direct Objects	Direct objects receive a <u>double underline</u>, which are often in the accusative case, but some verbs use the dative or genitive case.
Indirect Objects	Indirect object receives a <u>dashed</u> underline.
Noun ⟵ Genitive Modifier	Draw an arrow to what is modified. One can also apply this rule to all modifiers that may be ambiguous (adverbs, prepositional phrases)
Noun = Appositional Phrase	Place an equal sign (=) to indicate apposition. First covered in CHAPTER 5.5.
(Prepositional Phrases)	Place prepositional phrases within parentheses (…). First introduced in CHAPTER 6.1.
{Special uses of Cases} including {Vocatives}	Place curly braces around special case functions, including the vocative. See more on the genitive (CHAPTER 11.6), dative (CHAPTER 14.4), nominative (CHAPTER 21.2) and accusative cases (CHAPTER 21.3). If present, draw arrows to what is modified.
[Subordinate Clause] [¹… [²… [³…³] …²] …¹]	Put brackets around subordinate clauses. First covered in CHAPTER 8.5 and CHAPTER 9.4. Add superscript numbers for more than one clause and close off the clause with the same number.
antecedent ? ambiguous ? postcedent pronoun	Draw a dotted line to the antecedent or the postcedent of an ambiguous pronoun. If you are uncertain, put a question mark. First covered in CHAPTER 9.
unobvious [relative antecedent pronoun clause]	Place relative pronoun clauses within brackets […], since it is a subordinate clause. Draw a dotted line to its antecedent, if unclear. Covered in CHAPTER 9.
Adjectival Modifiers	Mark these with whatever noun they are linked grammatically or logically. Adjectives are first introduced in CHAPTER 7.1.

Example from Matt 4:7: You will not recognize all these endings or words yet, but a "word-for-word" interlinear translation is provided below the Greek.

ἔφη   αὐτῷ ὁ Ἰησοῦς· πάλιν γέγραπται· οὐκ ἐκπειράσεις κύριον τὸν θεόν σου.
was saying to him the Jesus: "Again it has been written: 'Not shall you tempt Lord the God
of you.'"

Sentence Marked Up:

ἔφη αὐτῷ ὁ Ἰησοῦς·[¹πάλιν γέγραπ|ται·[² οὐκ ἐκπειρά|σεις κύριον = τὸν θεόν σου.²]¹]

Notice that there are two subordinate clauses, each direct speech, one within the other.

Properly Translated:

Jesus was saying to him: "Again it has been written: 'You shall not tempt the Lord, your God'."

4.8 SOME COORDINATING CONJUNCTIONS (Σύνδεσμοι Παρατακτικοί)

A. **The Importance of Conjunctions and Particles:** In this lesson are a number of special Greek conjunctions that connect words and sentences together. The importance of understanding how such words function is indicated by Robert Funk:

> Negatives, conjunctions, sentence connectors, and subordinators may be termed underline{function words} or underline{structure signaling words}. The point of these labels is that such words are nearly lexically empty, i.e. they have little or no dictionary meaning of their own. underline{However, they are grammatically significant in indicating the structure of sentences and parts of sentences.} Some of them are so common as to require acquaintance at the grossest level of the language. This simply means that one must learn how they function early in the process. One may guess at the meaning of lexically full words, or leave them blank when reading, but one must know the grammatical "meaning" of function words to be able to proceed at all [underline{underlining} added].[9]

So, take heed to these most common conjunctions. Other conjunctions and particles will be discussed in subsequent chapters, but see especially § 8.5 and §16.2.

B. **Καί is very common with nearly 9,000 occurrences in the GNT:** When used to directly link two words, clauses, or sentences, καί means *and*. Καί is occasionally used with another καί to link two words or clauses together. In this case, the construction καί ... καί is to be translated as *both ... and*. For example, καὶ Ἰωάννης καὶ Ἡρῴδης ... is translated *Both John and Herod ....*

C. **Καί *also* is used as an Adverb for Additive Emphasis:** An important and fairly common construction is when καί functions as an adverb **additively** to emphasize the following sen-

---

[9] Robert Walter Funk, *A Beginning-Intermediate Grammar of Hellenistic Greek*, 2nd ed. (Missoula, MT: Scholars Press, 1973), 475; as quoted by Rick Brannan, "The Discourse Function of Ἀλλά in Non-Negative Contexts," in *Discourse Studies & Biblical Interpretation: A Festschrift in Honor of Stephen H. Levinsohn*, ed. Steven E. Runge (Bellingham, WA: Lexham Press, 2011), 263-88 at 264.

tence element. This use of καί is grammarians call "ascensive." In this case, καί is usually best translated *also*. This special usage can be recognized when καί is <u>not</u> at the start of a clause (i.e. not clause initial) or when καί is <u>not</u> coordinating equal grammatical elements. Typically, when καί begins a clause or coordinates two equal grammatical elements, it is functioning as a conjunction and is best translated *and*. **Note**: But there are a few clause initial instances of καί where the καί can be readily determined to be additive because of the presence of another conjunction (usually a postpositive one). See, e.g., 1 John 1:4a **καὶ ἡ κοινωνία** δὲ ἡ ἡμετέρα μετὰ τοῦ πατρὸς ... *Moreover [δέ] also [καί] our fellowship is with the Father....* In context, John is emphasizing the importance and the nature of our **fellowship** as involving fellowship with God the Father.

D. **Ἀλλά is marked +Correction and is used in Point/Counterpoint Sets:** Ἀλλά is a conjunction that can often be translated *but*. Such would indicate a **contrast** between two or more ideas. However, behind this contrast is a more basic processing function of **correction.** Ἀλλά is commonly found following a negative statement with the negative adverb οὐ or οὐκ to form οὐ ... ἀλλά in what Runge calls a "point/counter point set" (92-100). Fortunately, translating ἀλλά simply as *but* often will carry this sense of correction. However, the recognition of the οὐ ... ἀλλά point/counter point construction is important for exegesis. Consider this example:

2 Cor 1:24 οὐχ ὅτι κυριεύομεν ὑμῶν τῆς πίστεως ἀλλὰ <u>συνεργοί</u> ἐσμεν τῆς χαρᾶς ὑμῶν·
*(It is) not that we lord over **your** faith, but we are **<u>coworkers</u>** of your joy.*

To conclude this discussion, Rick Brannan helpfully summarizes the essential function of ἀλλά and what questions interpreters should ask:[10]

Function of ἀλλά	Interpretive Questions
o ἀλλά involves enhancing the contrast between two things. o ἀλλά involves correction or replacement.	1. What items (words, phrases, clauses) are being contrasted? 2. What is the correction or replacement that is taking place?

To answer these questions, Annemieke Drummen provides some guidance: "The corrected (substituted) element is either **an explicitly stated element, a presupposed element, an implication,** or **the discourse topic**" (bolding added).[11]

E. **Δέ is Marked +New Development and is Postpositive:** Δέ is a postpositive conjunction, meaning that it is often second (sometimes even third or fourth) in the clause. But rendering postpositive conjunctions in English often translates them first. The conjunction δέ is marked

---

[10] Rick Brannan, "Discourse Function of Ἀλλά," 278. For analysis of the construction's use, see Shawn Craigmiles, *The Pragmatic Constraints of Ἀλλά in the Synoptic Gospels* (Ph.D. Asbury Theological Seminary, Wilmore, KY, 2015).

[11] Annemieke Drummen, "Discourse Cohesion in Dialogue Turn-Initial ἀλλά in Greek Drama," in *Discourse Cohesion in Ancient Greek*, ed. Stéphanie Bakker and Gerry Wakker, Amsterdam Studies in Classical Philosophy 16 (Leiden: Brill, 2009), 135-54 quoted by Brannan, "Discourse Function of Ἀλλά," 278.

+new development in the discourse, sometimes minor sometimes major. Levinsohn explains the information processing indicated by δέ: "[T]he information it introduces builds on what has gone before and makes a distinct contribution to the argument.... It also introduces background material" (112). When used in clearly contrastive setting (usually in argumentative discourse) with two or more opposing elements, then the δέ should be translated *but*. In narrative contexts and otherwise, δέ is often difficult to translate, sometimes functioning as a transition: "*Now (this is what happened next)...*" Consider using *Moreover* or *Additionally*, which may help indicate a new development in English.

F. **Οὖν is marked +Continuity and +Development and is Postpositive:** Although commonly treated simply as an inferential conjunction "therefore" (see Wallace, 673), this may obscure the sense of continuity and development conveyed by οὖν.[12] In truth, οὖν may often be safely translated "therefore," yet this logical connection will vary in scale within the discourse. Οὖν may signal a concluding inference of a smaller argument unit stressing more "continuity" (cf. Matt 5:48); at other times, however, οὖν may signal a new section of discourse stressing more "development" (Rom 12:1). However, in other places οὖν signals "resumption" of the main argument line (Matt 5:19), which equally reflects continuity and development. For an extended discussion of this and other conjunctions, see Wallace 666-78.

CHECK POINT 4.6-8
NOUN CASES AND TRANSLATION

First, match the Noun Cases to basic sentence function or significance. **Second**, mark up the verse and provide a basic translation.

1. indirect object ___	N) Nominative
2. subject ___	Γ) Genitive
3. direct address ___	Δ) Dative
4. direct object ___	A) Accusative
5. possession ___	Φ) Vocative

τὴν δὲ ἀλήθειαν διδάσκει ὁ προφήτης ταῖς ἐκκλησίαις τῆς Ἰουδαίας.

ANSWERS

1. Δ, 2. N, 3. Φ, 4. A, 5. Γ, 6. Δ, 7. Γ, 8. Δ, 9. Γ, 10. N

τὴν δὲ ἀλήθειαν διδάσκει ὁ προφήτης ταῖς ἐκκλησίαις τῆς Ἰουδαίας.

Moreover, the prophet teaches the truth to the churches of Judea.

---

[12] On the significance of this conjunction as marked +development and +continuity, see Runge 43-48, 57.

4.9 Noun and Adjective Accents

A. **Noun and Adjective Accents are *Retentive*:** That is, the accents will resist moving; they will try to retain their initial position on the lexical form of the word. When adding different case endings, however, the accent may need to shift depending on the weight of the last syllable (i.e. the *ultima*). You may need to review the weight of the vowels, monophthongs, and diphthongs provided in Ch. 3.8 or Appendix §24.

B. **Some Relevant Rules on Accents:** Here are some additional rules and examples with explanations. Additional exceptions to the retentive rule are treated in Appendix §24.

  1. For First and Second Declension words that have an acute on the ultima, all genitives and datives receive a circumflex. (παραβολή → παραβολῶν, παραβολῇ)

  2. The genitive plural of First Declension words has a circumflex on the ultima: -ῶν.

C. **Examples:** Here are some examples with explanations. Some involve endings that you have not yet learned.

Lexical Form	Other Case Form	Explanation
ὁδός	ὁδοῦ or ὁδῷ	A. above applies here.
πονηρότερος	πονηρότερα	In this comparative adjective form (covered in §25.5), the acute accent is able to be retained since this ἄλφα ending is light in weight.
γράμμα	γράμματι	In this Third Declension noun (covered in §12.1), the ἰῶτα ending is light in weight thus allowing the acute accent to be retained.
γράμμα	γραμμάτων	In this Third Declension noun (covered in §12.1), the acute accent is pulled from its position due to the change in the ultima from light to heavy weight.
βασιλεία	βασιλεῖαι	The diphthong –αι is light in weight and this allows the accent to be retained, but also to be changed into a circumflex. But notice that the acute accent remains on the form βασιλείαις, because –αις is considered heavy in weight.

Complete the Workbook Exercises 4 and consult the Answer Key & Guide as needed.

CASE IN POINT 4: WHAT IS (*THE*) *ETERNAL LIFE*?

The article, ὁ, ἡ, τό is a specifier. It identifies a known entity/noun. This is especially important with abstract nouns like *truth*, *righteousness*, and *love*. The identification and definition of such words are important. To specify one "life" or "righteousness" as opposed to another "life" or "righteousness" requires qualification and specification. In such cases, the article can assist to point to "*the* life" (ἡ ζωή) or "*the* righteousness" (ἡ δικαιοσύνη).

However, an author could leave a noun anarthrous (i.e. with no article) to indicate an unspecified thing (*a god*; *a* light) or to emphasize the quality, essence, or character of that noun (*truly God*; *light in essence!*). This latter qualitative significance is especially possible with nouns that are normally concrete like *God*, *road*, and *teacher*. Within discourses, when emphasized in this way by lack of the article, authors may introduce an entity or participant into the scene. In general, then, a noun with an article is specified; conversely, an anarthrous noun should be understood either as indefinite, as being emphasized regarding the essence of what the noun signifies (e.g. *humanity* as opposed to *divinity*), and/or as possibly being introduced into a scene for significant action or participation. So, one must consider the presence or lack of the article within the larger discursive development.

This principle can be seen in John's Gospel. Here the phrase αἰώνιος ζωή *eternal life* occurs seventeen times.[13] In each case except one, no article accompanies the expression. *Life* is sometimes articular, referring to Jesus himself (11:25; 14:6; cf. 6:35, 48) or to the Light that is in Jesus (1:4; 8:12). However, *eternal life* remains anarthrous until 17:3. Since an indefinite meaning (*an eternal life*) does not fit well with what John is conveying, it is more likely that the qualitative meaning is what John had in mind. According to this understanding, what John is emphasizing is the essence or quality of what the noun signifies, i.e. *eternal life in essence*. Anyone hearing John's Gospel and hearing again and again references made to this *eternal life* would be not simply curious but especially desirous to experience this eternal life. But, what is this *eternal life*?

Critically, towards the end of John's Gospel, at the most intimate moment when Jesus is praying to God the Father at 17:3, specificity and definition is given to *eternal life*:

17:3 αὕτη δέ ἐστιν ἡ αἰώνιος ζωή
   Moreover this is (the) eternal life

ἵνα γινώσκωσιν	σὲ τὸν μόνον ἀληθινὸν θεὸν
that they know	*You, the only true God,*
	καὶ ὃν ἀπέστειλας Ἰησοῦν Χριστόν.
	and Him whom you sent, Jesus Christ.

Here eternal life is found for the first and only time with the article, and a demonstrative pronoun αὕτη—which is an even stronger "pointer" word (see §12.3 DEMONSTRATIVE PRO-

---

[13] The adjective modifier αἰώνιος, in fact, agrees with ζωή: feminine, nominative, singular. This adjective belongs to a type of adjective that shows no distinct feminine endings, but uses the masculine endings for such.

NOUNS). Moreover, this demonstrative pronoun is preposed and discontinuous with what it modifies, ἡ αἰώνιος ζωὴ, drawing even more attention to its function as a pointer specifying just what is *the eternal life*. There is no doubt that *the eternal life* is here finally fully defined in John's Gospel: "*This* is *(the)* eternal life *that they know You, the only true God, and Him whom You sent, Jesus Christ.*" What is affirmed here is that eternal life entails knowing God the Father and Jesus Christ, God's Son. "Knowing" involves intimate relationship, which in John's Gospel involves having the authority (legally?) to become God's children (1:12). Jesus told the disciples that he was departing but would prepare a place for them within the Father's house, which has Many rooms" (14:2). John's affirmation in 17:3 leaves audiences something to think about. This example illustrates the importance of observing and pondering the presence of the article or its absence. Of course, each case must be carefully considered in context.

Below is a rendition of a Greek house interior.[14] Morey explains: "In its plan the house was simply a series of rooms surrounding a court, which was open to the sky.... Sometimes there might be a second court in the rear, surrounded by the women's apartments; and often the house might be constructed with a second story." One wonders what house structure Jesus had in mind when making the statement that he did. What would ancient audiences have imagined?

---

[14] Image is sightly enhanced from William Carey Morey, *Outlines of Greek History: With a Survey of Ancient Oriental Nations* (New York: American Book Company, 1903), 255. The quotation is from 254-55.

CHAPTER 5

"In the beginning was the Word, and the Word was God...." Or, is it "a god" as endorsed by Jehovah's Witnesses in their New World Translation? This famous text is found at the beginning of John's Gospel. At issue is the lack of article on θεός. One might ask, Doesn't the lack of article automatically mean that the noun is indefinite (*a god*)!? No! See CASE IN POINT.

This chapter introduces the student to the **Second Declension of Nouns** or the **"o" Class Declension**, mainly masculine and neuter nouns but with a few feminine nouns. Also, students are presented the **masculine** and **neuter article**. Next, two very important verbs are introduced which do not take a direct object, but rather take a **predicate nominative**. Lastly, short, yet important, discussions of **proper nouns, vocatives,** and **apposition** are provided, before an extended discussion of **modern critical editions of the Greek NT**.

VOCABULARY 5	THE SECOND DECLENSION AND THE VERB "TO BE"

Masculine Second Declension Nouns:

ὁ ἄγγελος [175]	messenger; angel
ὁ ἀδελφός [342]	brother
ὁ ἄνθρωπος [550]	person, human; people
ὁ ἀπόστολος [79]	delegate, apostle
ὁ διδάσκαλος [59]	teacher, master
ὁ θεός [1307]	God; god
ὁ Ἰησοῦς [911]	Jesus; Joshua
ὁ κόσμος [185]	world
ὁ κύριος [714]	Lord; master, owner
ὁ λόγος [330]	word, speech; matter
ὁ νόμος [194]	law; the Law
ὁ οὐρανός [273]	heaven; sky
ὁ υἱός [375]	son
ὁ Χριστός [(529)]	Christ, Messiah

Article:

ὁ, ἡ, τό [19796]	the (*and other significations*)

Neuter Second Declension Nouns:

τὸ δαιμόνιον [63]	demon, spirit, inferior deity
τὸ εὐαγγέλιον [75]	good news, gospel
τὸ τέκνον [99]	child

A Feminine Second Declension Noun:

ἡ ὁδός [101]	road, way, path

Special Verb that takes a Predicate Nominative:

εἰμί [2458]	I am, exist

After learning vocabulary to this point, you will know 36.7% of the words in the GNT. If you are able, listen to audio recordings of VOCABULARY 5 and complete the CROSSWORD PUZZLE in the WORKBOOK EXERCISES.

NOTES ON VOCABULARY 5:

Many of these nouns have English cognates: angel, Phil-<u>adelphia</u> (*city of brotherly love*), <u>anthropo</u>-logy, apostle, didactic, <u>theo</u>-<u>logy</u>, <u>cosmo</u>-logy, auto-<u>nomy</u> (*self-rule/law*), Christ, demon. Memorizing these words should not be too difficult. Notice that the neuter nouns have the neuter singular nominative article. Also, ἡ ὁδός is a feminine noun; thus it has a feminine article, even though its endings look masculine. For εἰμί see the discussion below.

5.1 NOUNS OF THE SECOND OR "O" CLASS DECLENSION (Δευτέρη Κλίσις)

A. **Gender, Case**, and **Number:** As always, nouns have these three characteristics.

B. **The nouns of the Second Declension are mainly masculine and neuter in gender:** However, there are a handful of feminine nouns using these same endings, *but they use feminine articles and adjectives*. Only one such word is presented in this textbook: ἡ ὁδός *road, way*.

C. **The endings of the Second Declension use "o" class vowels to form their endings:** ὁ μικρόν (o) and ὦ μέγα (ω) are used to form these endings. Notice that masculine and neuter nouns use the exact same endings in the genitive and dative cases (→).

		Masculine Stems		Neuter Stems	Examples:	Masculine Stems	Neuter Stems
sg.	nom.	-ος		-ον*		λόγος	τέκνον
	gen.	-ου	→	-ου		λόγου	τέκνου
	dat.	-ῳ	→	-ῳ		λόγῳ	τέκνῳ
	acc.	-ον		-ον*		λόγον	τέκνον
pl.	nom.	-οι		-α*		λόγοι	τέκνα
	gen.	-ων	→	-ων		λόγων	τέκνων
	dat.	-οις	→	-οις		λόγοις	τέκνοις
	acc.	-ους		-α*		λόγους	τέκνα

Notice: (1) The neuter nominative and accusative endings (marked with *) will always be the same for singular and plural. (2) In the plural, the neuter endings will always end in *alpha* (-α). (3) ἡ ὁδός *road* (a feminine noun) has the same endings as the masculine nouns in the Second Declension.

5.2 MASCULINE AND NEUTER ARTICLE ENDINGS

The masculine article is used only with masculine nouns.

	MASCULINE			NEUTER	
	singular	plural		singular	plural
nom.	ὁ	οἱ	nom.	τό	τά
gen.	τοῦ	τῶν	gen.	τοῦ	τῶν
dat.	τῷ	τοῖς	dat.	τῷ	τοῖς
acc.	τόν	τούς	acc.	τό	τά

Notice: (1) These ending are very similar to the Second Declension endings. (2) The masculine nominative forms for the singular and plural each have a rough breathing mark. (3) The neuter nominative forms are the same as the accusative forms.

<table>
<tr><td colspan="5" align="center">CHECK POINT 5.1-2
Parse these Nouns by providing Gender, Case, Number, and Lexical Form</td></tr>
<tr><td>Noun to be parsed</td><td>Gender</td><td>Case</td><td>Number</td><td>Lexical Form & Meaning</td></tr>
<tr><td>ἀπόστολοι</td><td></td><td></td><td></td><td></td></tr>
<tr><td>κόσμος</td><td></td><td></td><td></td><td></td></tr>
<tr><td>δαιμονίοις</td><td></td><td></td><td></td><td></td></tr>
<tr><td>διδασκάλῳ</td><td></td><td></td><td></td><td></td></tr>
<tr><td>ὁδοῦ</td><td></td><td></td><td></td><td></td></tr>
<tr><td>τέκνα</td><td></td><td></td><td></td><td></td></tr>
<tr><td>τῷ Ἰησοῦ</td><td></td><td></td><td></td><td></td></tr>
<tr><td>κυρίων</td><td></td><td></td><td></td><td></td></tr>
<tr><td colspan="5" align="center">ANSWERS</td></tr>
<tr><td>Noun to be parsed</td><td>Gender</td><td>Case</td><td>Number</td><td>Lexical Form & Meaning</td></tr>
<tr><td>ἀπόστολοι</td><td>M</td><td>nom.</td><td>pl.</td><td>ἀπόστολος apostle</td></tr>
<tr><td>κόσμος</td><td>M</td><td>nom.</td><td>sg.</td><td>κόσμος world</td></tr>
<tr><td>δαιμονίοις</td><td>N</td><td>dat.</td><td>pl.</td><td>δαιμόνιον demon</td></tr>
<tr><td>διδασκάλῳ</td><td>M</td><td>dat.</td><td>sg.</td><td>διδάσκαλος teacher</td></tr>
<tr><td>ὁδοῦ</td><td>F</td><td>gen.</td><td>sg.</td><td>ὁδός road, way</td></tr>
<tr><td>τέκνα</td><td>N</td><td>nom./acc.</td><td>pl.</td><td>τέκνον child</td></tr>
<tr><td>τῷ Ἰησοῦ</td><td>M</td><td>dat.</td><td>sg</td><td>Ἰησοῦς Jesus</td></tr>
<tr><td>κυρίων</td><td>M</td><td>gen.</td><td>pl.</td><td>κύριος Lord, master</td></tr>
</table>

5.3 VERBS THAT CAN TAKE PREDICATE NOMINATIVES: Εἰμί AND Γίνομαι

A. **Predicate Defined:** The **predicate** is that part of the sentence that includes the verb and whatever else is said about the subject. Thus, a sentence could be broken down into two simple components: the subject and the predicate. For example, *Jesus healed the man with the touch of his finger*. The subject is *Jesus*. The predicate is everything else in the sentence: *healed the man with the touch of his finger*.

B. **Predicate Nominatives and Predicate Adjectives Defined:** Verbs of "being" (*to be* or *to become*) are commonly used to make statements about identity (using another noun) or an attribute (using an adjective—see CHAPTER 7).

   The teacher is (a) pastor. The teacher became (a) pastor.

   Teacher is the subject. The other noun, *pastor*, is called the **predicate nominative.** *Pastor* is a part of the verbal statement (the predicate) that is telling the reader more about the subject *teacher* (see Wallace 40-49). In the next sentence, *good* is a **predicate adjective** (covered in CHAPTER 7): *The teacher is good.*

C. **Verbs that take Predicate Nominatives:** The most common by far are εἰμί *I am* and γίνομαι *I become* (presented in CHAPTER 11). Εἰμί belongs to the less frequently occurring Μι-conjugation of verbs that will be covered in CHAPTER 24. However, εἰμί occurs so frequently that students need to learn it early; so learn it well! Below are the Present Tense endings. The verb εἰμί technically has no voice, but when parsing εἰμί, one commonly identifies it as active (A), although one may encounter a dash (-).

	singular		plural	
First	εἰμί	*I am*	ἐσμέν	*we are*
Second	εἶ	*you are*	ἐστέ	*you are*
Third	ἐστίν	*he/she/it is;* *there is*	εἰσίν	*they are;* *there are*

D. **Εἰμί may be implied from the Context:** This is called "ellipsis," which is discussed more fully in §9.4 ELLIPSIS. For example, ἀπόστολος ὁ Παῦλος. = *Paul [is] an apostle.*

E. **Subject or Predicate Nominative?** With predicate constructions, one must distinguish the subject from the predicate nominative.

   1. <u>Subject is Articular, the Predicate Nominative is Not</u>. In Greek, one must decide which nominative noun is the subject and which is the predicate nominative. In English we translate the subject first. The presence of the article with one nominative and the absence on the second will distinguish the subject from the predicate nominative, respectively:

Mar 2:28 ὥστε <u>κύριός</u> ἐστιν <u>ὁ υἱὸς</u> τοῦ ἀνθρώπου καὶ τοῦ σαββάτου.
Therefore, <u>the Son</u> of Humanity is <u>Lord</u> even of the Sabbath.

Now consider this sentence:

1 John 4:8b ὁ θεὸς ἀγάπη ἐστίν.

Translated in the same word order one arrives at *God love is*. But is *God* the subject (God is love) or is *Love* (Love is God)? The rule in Greek is that the subject is differentiated from the predicate nominative by adding the article to the subject. Thus, 1 John 4:8b is to be translated *God is Love*. The article with θεός prevents the translation *Love is God*.

2. <u>Equative Statements</u>. When both the subject and predicate nominative have an article, the sentence affirms the co-identity of subject with the predicate nominative. Consider this exchange:

> *John said, "The teacher is the pastor."*
> *Jane retorted, "That is what I said! The pastor is the teacher."*
> *John agreed, "Okay, yes, that is what I meant! He taught my class."*

What this exchange illustrates is that, in English, when the definite article is present, the subject and the predicate are interchangeable, although the word order may vary, and likely signals emphasis/priority (in this case John's primary point of reference was having the pastor as his *teacher*). This same rule applies in Greek. Thus, one will find this, adapted from John 14:6:

> ὁ Ἰησοῦς ἐστίν <u>ἡ ὁδὸς</u> καὶ <u>ἡ ἀλήθεια</u> καὶ <u>ἡ ζωή</u>·
> *Jesus is <u>the Way</u>, and <u>the Truth</u>, and <u>the Life</u>.*

In such a case, Jesus is co-identified with "the Way, the Truth, and the Life" since each has the article.

3. <u>Pronouns and Proper Names</u>. In addition to the article, the presence of either a pronoun or proper name will assist your proper translation of the predicate nominative.

   a. First, an explicit pronoun (*he, she, they, you, this one*, etc.) in a predicate nominative construction will be considered the subject. (Pronouns are covered in CHAPTER 9.) Consider Mark 3:35b just after Jesus says, *Whoever does the will of God, ...*

   Mark 3:35b ...<u>οὗτος</u> ἀδελφός μου καὶ ἀδελφὴ καὶ μήτηρ ἐστίν.
   ...<u>this one</u> is my brother and sister and mother.

b. Second, a proper name (see below in 5.4) also signifies the subject in a predicate nominative construction.

Luke 2:36 Καὶ ἦν Ἄννα προφῆτις = *And <u>Anna</u> was a prophetess.*

c. In the case that both nominatives include one of these elements—an articular noun, a pronoun, or a proper name—the following rules can be applied (see Wallace 42-46):

i. A pronoun trumps everything, becoming the subject in English translation.

Matt 14:2b <u>οὗτός</u> ἐστιν <u>Ἰωάννης</u> ὁ βαπτιστής
<u>This one</u> is <u>John</u> the Baptist

ii. Articular nouns and proper names are equivalent in identity and grammatically; however, if a proper name is anarthrous, it may signal its introduction into the discourse (see §21.4 Discourse Pragmatic Use of the Article or its Absence). In this case, translate the first (and often articular) noun as the subject.

John 8:39b <u>ὁ πατὴρ ἡμῶν</u> Ἀβραάμ ἐστιν. = *Our <u>father</u> is <u>Abraham</u>.*

E. **Constituent Marking and Sentence Diagramming Predicate Nominatives:**

1. <u>Constituent Marking</u>. The subject and predicate nominative are single underlined, since these are equated at some level. Also, the verb is single underlined.

1 John 4:8b <u>ὁ θεὸς</u> <u>ἀγάπη</u> <u>ἐστίν</u>. *<u>God</u> <u>is</u> <u>Love</u>.*

The single underline distinguishes the predicate nominative from a direct object:

Rom 4:6b <u>ὁ θεὸς</u> <u>λογίζεται</u> <u>δικαιοσύνην</u> (χωρὶς ἔργων).

<u>God</u> <u>accounts</u> <u>righteousness</u> (without works).

2. <u>Reed-Kellogg Diagramming</u>.

1 John 4:8b ὁ θεὸς ἀγάπη ἐστίν.

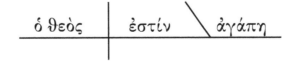

5.4 Proper Nouns

A. **We have already learned some proper nouns in Chapter 2:** Return to Vocabulary 2 and place the masculine nominative article in front of each noun except for Ἰερουσαλήμ, which is feminine. Give it a feminine article.

B. **Non-Greek Names may be Non-Declinable:** Since these names have only one form and show no case endings, they are called **non-declinable**. But, how does one know how these nouns are functioning in the sentence since they have no case endings?! *The key is the article, if present.* If an article is present and modifying one of these nouns, then *it will help to reveal the noun's function in the sentence.* If there is no article present to provide this information, then the context of the sentence must determine the word's function, as in the following cases:

Luke 19:9 υἱὸς Ἀβραάμ *a son of Abraham*

Luke 20:37 τὸν θεὸν Ἀβραὰμ καὶ θεὸν Ἰσαὰκ καὶ θεὸν Ἰακώβ.
    the God of Abraham and the God of Isaac and the God of Jacob.

Matt 1:20 υἱὸς Δαυίδ *a son of David*

In these examples, the proper nouns are genitives modifying the head noun.

C. **Definiteness:** Proper nouns are always considered **definite,** even if they do not have an article. Thus, if a choice exists between two nouns as to which of the two is the subject and which is the predicate nominative, then the proper noun is the subject even though it may not have a article. For example,

διδάσκαλός ἐστιν Παῦλος. = *Paul is a teacher.*

D. **The Name of Jesus:** Jesus' name is slightly irregular. It is declined as follows:

nom.	ὁ	Ἰησοῦς
gen.	τοῦ	Ἰησοῦ
dat.	τῷ	Ἰησοῦ
acc.	τόν	Ἰησοῦν

Notice that the genitive and dative forms are identical. How would you be able to distinguish them?

5.5 VOCATIVES (Κλητικαί) OF DIRECT ADDRESS

A. **The Vocative Case is Significant for Interpretation:** The use of the vocative case serves an important function in communication: It semantically identifies the addressee of the discourse, i.e. the one(s) receiving the communication. See discussion and examples of uses further below (cf. Wallace 65-71).

B. **Endings:**

1. <u>Plural</u>. The vocative case endings in the plural for all genders of nouns are the same as the nominative endings.

2. <u>Singular</u>. In the singular, however, the vocative form is different. Here are the basic rules for First and Second Declension Nouns.

Feminine		Masculine		Neuter
1st decl.	2nd decl.	1st decl.	2nd decl.	2nd decl.
-α or -η	-ος	-η or -α	-ε	-ον
Example:		Example:		Example:
ὦ γενεὰ ἄπιστ<u>ος</u>,... *Oh unbelieving generation, ...*		κύριε,... *Lord, ...*		Τέκν<u>ον</u>, *Child, ...*
Notice in this first example that vocatives may take adjectival modifiers. In this case, the adjective vocative form ἄπιστ-<u>ος</u> shows a 2nd declension feminine/masculine vocative ending, because the adjective ἄπιστος, -ον is a "dual termination" adjective, i.e. it shows only two endings, the neuter and the masculine that serves also as the feminine form.				

C. **Set off by Commas or Other Punctuation:** Commas or other punctuation will always set apart vocative case nouns and substantives, isolating them from the rest of the sentence. Thus, they are easy to identify.

D. **The Semantics and Pragmatics of Direct Address:** Smyth indicates that a vocative will never be followed by conjunctions like δέ or γάρ, and "is usually found in the interior of a sentence. At the beginning it is emphatic" (312; §1283a, §1285). So, inherent in the semantics of the vocative is both identifying the addressee and drawing attention to the statement that follows. Pragmatically, then, vocatives may function in various ways, and these need not be mutually exclusive:

1. To signal a ***change of address***. It is reported that 31% of the vocative usage in NT epistles simply signals a change of address (Runge 117). So, when Paul identifies different addressees, it is because he is providing material appropriate to each group. Consider how the vocatives in Eph 5:25–6:9 identify the addressees:

5:25 Οἱ ἄνδρες,... *Husbands, ...*
6:1 Τὰ τέκνα, ... *Children, ...*
6:4 Καὶ οἱ πατέρες,... *And fathers, ...*
6:5 Οἱ δοῦλοι, ... *Servants, ...*
6:9 Καὶ οἱ κύριοι, ... *And masters, ...*

2. To provide ***thematic address***. The deployment of vocatives may serve to characterize "the addressee(s), based upon how the speaker conceives of them" (Runge in the LDGNT); Runge calls this "thematic address" (Runge 117-18). Attending to such details contextually is often important for interpretation. One clue to this usage is that the vocative occurs at the end of the sentence. Consider these examples.

Phlm 7b τὰ σπλάγχνα τῶν ἁγίων ἀναπέπαυται διὰ σοῦ, <u>ἀδελφέ</u>.
   The compassions of the saints have been refreshed through you, <u>brother</u>.

2 Cor 6:11a Τὸ στόμα ἡμῶν ἀνέῳγεν πρὸς ὑμᾶς, <u>Κορίνθιοι</u>,...
   Our mouth has opened wide to you, <u>Corinthians</u>, ...

In this second example, we should consider why Paul identifies the "Corinthians" as such. In fact, Paul was preparing to launch into a full-scale confrontation of their idolatrous relationships in 6:14–7:1. Very likely the "Corinthian" believers were affected by the larger civic-pride of the city of Corinth, which was a Roman Colony founded by Julius Caesar and committed to the imperial family. Just before Paul's writing, Corinth had been awarded the official seat of the Provincial Imperial Cult in Achaia (AD 54) in coordination with the new Emperor Nero's accession to the throne.[1]

3. To serve as ***forward pointing devices***. "They [Vocatives] prototypically create a break in the discourse just before something surprising or important" (Runge 118).

1 Thess 2:14a Ὑμεῖς γὰρ μιμηταὶ ἐγενήθητε, <u>ἀδελφοί</u>, τῶν ἐκκλησιῶν τοῦ θεοῦ τῶν οὐσῶν ἐν τῇ Ἰουδαίᾳ ἐν Χριστῷ Ἰησοῦ,
   For you became imitators, <u>brethren</u>, of the church assemblies of God being in Judea in Christ Jesus,

---

[1] See A. J. S. Spawforth, "The Achaean Federal Cult Part I: Pseudo-Julian, Letters 198," *TynBul* 46 (1995): 151-68.

Here in 1 Thess 2:14, the vocative ἀδελφοί *brethren* is located five words inside the clause and helps to emphasize *the church assemblies of God*, which is a genitive modifier that is discontinuous (or separated) from *imitators* (μιμηταὶ) for effect. Paul wants these new believers to see themselves within the broader fellowship of believers, even as they (all) are being persecuted, each respectively, by their own fellow country men and women. Paul's placement of the vocative ἀδελφοί *brethren* helps to emphasize the object of imitation and the relationship of co-identification.

4. To help signal a *__unit boundary__*. Many paragraph and section level boundaries in epistolary material have vocatives that attend them.[2] However, every vocative does not signal a new paragraph or section unit; furthermore, there are sectional breaks that do not contain vocatives. For example, consider widely acknowledged major sectional breaks found at Rom 12:1a and Eph 4:1a.

> **Rom 12:1a** Παρακαλῶ οὖν ὑμᾶς, ἀδελφοί, διὰ τῶν οἰκτιρμῶν τοῦ θεοῦ παραστῆσαι τὰ σώματα ὑμῶν...
> *Therefore, I exhort you, brethren, to offer your bodies through the compassions of God...*

> **Eph 4:1** Παρακαλῶ οὖν ὑμᾶς ἐγὼ ὁ δέσμιος ἐν κυρίῳ...
> *Therefore, I exhort you—I, the prisoner in the Lord, ...*

In the first example, a vocative ἀδελφοί *brethren* is used. In the second, no vocative is found, although there is an extensive appositional statement concerning Paul (*I, the prisoner in the Lord*). Other factors contribute to determining paragraph or sectional breaks; in these two instances, the formula Παρακαλῶ *I exhort* and the presence of οὖν *therefore* are two such indicators. So, although a vocative expression may help signal such a break, it need not be present for such a break.

E. **Sometimes with the Interjection ὦ that is Marked +Emotion (Negative or Positive):** Moreover, sometimes an interjection ὦ *oh!* will precede the vocative form as in, e.g. Rom 2:1, ὦ ἄνθρωπε... *Oh Person...*! The significance of the inclusion of the interjection ὦ to mark +emotion is worth consideration in context. Zerwick summarizes the historical development of the use of ὦ:

In classical usage, the vocative is regularly introduced by the particle ὦ, whose omission constitutes an exception into whose reasons one may profitably inquire. In Hellenistic usage the contrary is the case: the omission of the particle has become the rule (and hence has

---

[2] Stephen H. Levinsohn, *Self-Instruction Materials on Non-Narrative Discourse Analysis* (Dallas: SIL International, 2011), §8.9.

no special significance), so that where ὦ is exceptionally used in the NT one is justified in supposing that there is some reason for its use. In fact ὦ, apart from the Acts [i.e., Luke-Acts], occurs in contexts suggesting deep emotion on the part of the speaker.[3]

An example of positive feeling is Jesus' acknowledgement of the faith of *the Syrophoenician Woman*.

Matt 15:28 ὦ γύναι, μεγάλη σου ἡ πίστις.

> *O woman, great is your faith!* [Notice also the forward position of σου "your."]

An example of the negative feeling of exasperation is seen in Galatians:

Gal 3:1a ὦ ἀνόητοι Γαλάται, τίς ὑμᾶς ἐβάσκανεν...;

> *O Foolish Galatians, who has bewitched you...?!*

Zerwick's exclusion of Luke-Acts, however, is due to what he recognizes as a more formal style there, which is a constraint of the social context and the literary-form or genre of Luke-Acts. So, the interjection ὦ would be marked +formal address in Luke-Acts. Zerwick surmises:

> On the other hand, it is not without a certain pleasure that we find the learned writer Luke in the first chapter of the Acts addressing his friend and patron ὦ Θεόφιλε, obviously without any special emphasis, but in conformity with the elegance of style which he has adopted as suitable to a dedicatory formula (note also the position of the vocative, fairly late in the sentence). This Attic unemphatic use of ὦ is to be found only in the Acts. Thus Gallio addresses the Jews ὦ Ἰουδαῖοι, likewise, in completely classical manner, not at the beginning of the phrase, but after several words, Acts 18:14.[4]

F. Constituent Marking and Diagramming Vocatives:

1. <u>Constituent Marking</u>. Use curly braces to mark vocatives: {ἀδελφοί,}.... Why? Because curly braces are used to indicate special uses of the cases, of which the vocative is a very important one.

   Rom 12:1a Παρακαλῶ ⌐οὖν¬ ὑμᾶς, {ἀδελφοί,}

   > *Therefore, I exhort you, brothers,...*

---

[3] Maximilian Zerwick, *Biblical Greek: Illustrated by Examples*, trans. Joseph Smith; 4th ed.; Scripta Pontificii Instituti Biblici 114 (Rome: Editrice Pontificio Istitutio Biblico, 1963), 11–12.

[4] Zerwick, *Biblical Greek*, 12.

2. <u>Sentence Diagramming</u>. The Reed-Kellogg method places vocatives on floating line detached from the rest of the diagram. I would suggest placing such floating vocatives in the diagram where they occur in the sentence word order.

Rom 12:1a *Therefore, I exhort you, brethren,...*

Rom 12:1a

$$\begin{array}{c}
\overset{\text{οὖν}}{} \qquad \qquad \qquad \overset{\text{ἀδελφοί}}{} \\
\hline
[\text{ø I}] \mid \text{Παρακαλῶ} \mid \text{ὑμᾶς} \\
\end{array}$$

5.6 APPOSITION (Παράθεσις)

A. **Apposition Defined:** The Greek Language has many special grammatical constructions. Apposition is but one. A (second) noun placed after another prior noun giving it further description or explanation is said to be *in apposition* to the first noun. Normally the noun in apposition immediately follows the noun that it is describing. In English, the noun in apposition may be set off by commas. This is not usually the case in Greek. Here are some examples:

2 Cor 1:1 Παῦλος ἀπόστολος Χριστοῦ Ἰησοῦ...καὶ Τιμόθεος ὁ ἀδελφὸς
    Paul, an apostle of Christ Jesus,...and Timothy, the brother,

Both *an apostle* and the *brother* are in apposition to the nouns immediately before them. Each further explains just who Paul and Timothy are: an apostle and a brother.

Col 2:2b ...εἰς ἐπίγνωσιν τοῦ μυστηρίου τοῦ θεοῦ, Χριστοῦ,
    ...into a knowledge of the mystery of God, [that is,] Christ,

B. **Vocatives Given Apposition Take Articular Nominatives:** Zerwick helpfully summarizes a rule: "the nominative with the article is always used in appositions added to a vocative."[5] The key is the article: since the article does not have a vocative form, the nominative suffices.

Rev 15:3b Μεγάλα τὰ ἔργα σου, Κύριε <u>ὁ Θεὸς ὁ παντοκράτωρ</u>...
    Great are your works, Lord, The God Almighty...

Rom 8:15b κράζομεν· αββα <u>ὁ πατήρ</u>.
    We Cry out: Abba <u>(the) Father</u>.

---

[5] Zerwick, *Biblical Greek*, 11.

C. **Pragmatic Discourse Significance:** It may be helpful to use the expression, *that is*, to translate apposition. Apposition is a fairly common construction and is exegetically significant because the appositional phrase further defines or qualifies the lead noun, which is usually an important person or concept in context to receive such modification. From the perspective of information processing, hearers/readers are asked to spend more time thinking about this noun or substantive with the broadened description, explanation, or definition provided in the appositional phrase. Unless this information is necessary to disambiguate the referent, more attention is given to the substantive than would otherwise be necessary. *Such additional information and processing is often for communicative effect or* **elaborative emphasis.** So, we should pay careful attention to appositional statements as possibly signifying such, asking how such elaboration contributes to key themes.

Consider the significance of apposition in this obelisk on the right that dates to AD 55-59 at the beginning of Nero's reign as emperor.[6] It was located in front of the Great Sphinx. After the dedicatory statement ἀγαθῇ τύχηι "To Good Fortune" (the first straight line of text), we see a subordinate clause that begins identifying and praising Nero through appositional statements. An English translation and the underlying Greek are given below with the appositional equal sign (=):

Since Nero Claudius Caesar Augustus Germanicus, = Emperor, = the good deity of the inhabited world, ...

line 2: ΕΠΕΙ ΝΕΡΩΝ ΚΛΑΥΔΙΟΣ ΚΑΙΣΑΡ ΣΕΒΑΣΤΟΣ
line 3: ΓΕΡΜΑΝΙΚΟΣ = ΑΥΤΟΚΡΑΤΩΡ, = Ο ΑΓΑΘΟΣ ΔΑΙΜΩΝ ΤΗΣ
line 4: ΟΙΚΟΥΜΕΝΗΣ, ...

Here, the appositional statements are significant to express political and religious devotion.

---

[6] The image is slightly adapted and enhanced from George Long, *The British Museum: Egyptian Antiquities*, vol. 2 The Library of Entertaining Knowledge (London: C. Knight, 1836), 380. The Greek text is from the same source, but can also be found at PHI inscription database at http://epigraphy.packhum.org/inscriptions/main, identified as *OGIS* 2.666.

D. **Constituent Marking and Diagramming Apposition:** Appositives can be found attached to any noun or noun-like substantive.

1. <u>Constituent Marking</u>. Appositives are indicated by the equal sign (=).

> **2 Cor 1:1** Παῦλος = ἀπόστολος ←Χριστοῦ Ἰησοῦ...καὶ Τιμόθεος = ὁ ἀδελφὸς
> *Paul, an apostle of Christ Jesus, … and Timothy, the brother,*

2. <u>Sentence Diagramming</u>. Like Constituent Marking, appositives are indicated with an equal sign and are placed in the diagram according to their sentence function. Below are shown appositives on the direct and indirect objects.

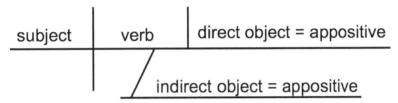

CHECK POINT 5.3-6

Identify the <u>Subject</u>, <u>Predicate Nominatives</u>, =Appositional Nouns, and {Vocatives} with Constituent Marking. In the answers, additional Constituent Marking is provided. For example,

John 4:19b κύριε, θεωρῶ ὅτι προφήτης εἶ σύ.

> *Lord, I see that you are a prophet.*

John 4:19b {κύριε,} <u>θεωρῶ</u> [|ὅτι| προφήτης εἶ <u>σύ</u>.]

> *{Lord,} <u>I see</u> [|that| <u>you</u> <u>are</u> a prophet.]*

John 1:49b ῥαββί, σὺ εἶ ὁ υἱὸς τοῦ θεοῦ, σὺ βασιλεὺς εἶ τοῦ Ἰσραήλ.

> *Lord, you are the Son of God, you are King of Israel.*

Acts 9:17b Σαοὺλ ἀδελφέ, ὁ κύριος ἀπέσταλκέν με, Ἰησοῦς ...,

> *Saul Brother, the Lord, Jesus, has sent me ...,*

ANSWERS

John 1:49b {ῥαββί,} <u>σὺ</u> <u>εἶ</u> <u>ὁ υἱὸς</u> ← τοῦ θεοῦ, <u>σὺ</u> <u>βασιλεὺς</u> <u>εἶ</u> τοῦ Ἰσραήλ.

{Lord,} <u>you</u> <u>are</u> <u>the Son</u> ← of God, <u>you</u> <u>are</u> <u>King</u> ← of Israel.

Notice that the genitive modifier τοῦ Ἰσραήλ *of Israel* is discontinuous with its head noun βασιλεὺς *King*, and so an arrow is drawn to indicate this.

Acts 9:17b {Σαοὺλ = ἀδελφέ}, <u>ὁ κύριος</u> <u>ἀπέσταλκέν</u> <u>με</u>, = <u>Ἰησοῦς</u> ...,

{Saul = Brother}, <u>the Lord</u>, = <u>Jesus</u>, <u>has sent</u> <u>me</u> ...,

Notice that the proper name Σαοὺλ *Saul* is a vocative that is modified by an appositional noun ἀδελφέ *Brother*. Also, ὁ κύριος *the Lord* (the subject) is further modified by an appositional descriptor Ἰησοῦς *Jesus,* which is discontinuous with ὁ κύριος and so an arrow is needed in Greek to specify with what *Jesus* is in apposition. Nouns in apposition are given an equal sign (=) and also marked liked the noun they modify. So, here, ὁ κύριος and = Ἰησοῦς are single underlined because ὁ κύριος is subject. Incidentally, if you look at Acts 9:17 in context, *the Lord* is given a much fuller appositional elaboration: *Jesus, the One that appeared to you on the road by which you were coming.* At this critical juncture in Saul's life, he was being told exactly who the Lord Jesus is.

5.7 NT Greek Critical Editions and Punctuation

A. **Original Manuscripts:** Although we have no original manuscripts of the Greek NT, in comparison with other ancient Greek texts, we know that they would not have shown any punctuation. At most, whole words may have wrapped across lines, showing some demarcation; possibly, too, major units may have begun with an indentation. Manuscripts will show spacing and other markings, but it is difficult to know when these were added. We just don't know. What we do know is that documents were written in capital letters (uncials) and ran together, as in the two examples below. On the left is "a letter from Harmiysis, a small Egyptian farmer, to Papiscus, an official, and others" on papyrus found at Oxyrhynchus, Egypt, dated to AD July 24, 66. On the right is the beginning portion of an honorary inscription (British Museum No. 193) to Tiberius Claudius Balbillus, an educated man and a renowned astrologer, newly appointed Prefect over Egypt by Nero in AD 56. The Greek is likely a translation of the Egyptian "sacred characters" (hieroglyphs) probably originally on the same slab. In both one can see select word wrapping and some (re)sizing of letters. On the stone slab, one can detect irregularities likely caused by the medium and considering word wrapping (see especially the first full line).

The Image on the right is from G. Adolf Deissmann, *Licht Vom Osten: Das Neue Testament und die Neuentdeckten Texte der Hellenistisch-römischen Welt*, 1st ed. (Tübingen: Mohr, 1908), 112.

B. **Standard Editions of the Greek NT:** The most popular standard editions of the Greek NT, which are identical in wording but not necessarily in punctuation, are the Nestle-Aland 26th, 27th, and 28th Editions (NA[26], NA[27], or NA[28]) and the United Bible Society 3rd, 4th, or 5th Editions (UBS[3], UBS[4], UBS[5]). The NA[28] has been released in 2013; although the text is nearly the same, about thirty differences in readings are indicated in the Catholic Epistles. Michael Holmes has also edited the Society of Biblical Literature Greek New Testament (SBL GNT), which is much like the NA and UBS texts, but with notable differences here and there. Besides these more recent critical editions, there are very helpful older editions, e.g., Westcott-Hort text (WH), which is now in public domain. Then there are Greek editions based upon the Byzantine (Byz) or Majority (Maj or 𝔐) text traditions; but these editions are based upon later manuscripts that are additive to the text to the NT. For example, in the NA[27] text there are 138,020 total words; but there are 140,196 total words in the Majority text edition of William G. Pierpont and Maurice A. Robinson.[7]

---

[7] *The New Testament in the Original Greek: According to the Byzantine/Majority Textform* (Roswell, GA: The Original Word Publishers, 1995), based upon statistics in BibleWorks 9.

C. Punctuation Conventions:

1. There are several conventional punctuation marks found within editions of the Greek NT.

> A period (.) corresponds exactly to an English period (.).
> A comma (,) corresponds exactly to our comma (,).
> A semi-colon (;) corresponds to an English question mark (?).
> A raised dot (·) corresponds to either colon (:) or semicolon (;).
> Parentheses (…) corresponds to English parentheses (…).

Capitalized first letters at the beginning of a quotation correspond to quotation marks (UBS text only). Notice that the student must determine where the quotation ends. Additionally, modern editors of the Greek NT have taken the liberty to include capital letters sometimes to designate either a beginning of a new chapter, a proper noun.

2. An interesting and early example of a gap in an early manuscript is seen in Papyrus 46 (dated c. AD 100-200, recreated below). One sees a slight gap in 2 Cor 1:12 at a natural pause (where the comma is placed below), which costs the Scribe critical space who then needs to extend a word into a margin and write the characters smaller (only partially seen).

EN ΧΑΡΙΤΙ Θ[ΕΟ]Υ, ΑΝΕΣΤΡΑΦΗΜΕΝ ΕΝ

ΤΩ ΚΟΣΜΩ, ΠΕΡΙΣΣΟΤΕΡΩΣ ΔΕ ΠΡΟΣ ΥΜΑΣ.

"IN THE GRACE OF GOD, WE ACTED IN
THE WORLD, AND ESPECIALLY TOWARDS YOU."

D. Other Marks Found in the Greek Editions of the NT:

1. Brackets […]. Critical editions of the GNT will indicate in brackets textual doubtful words—that is, words that have conflicted attestation in the earliest manuscripts. These brackets are not punctuation marks. Thus, one will find the opening line of Mark 1:1 in the UBS and NA texts to read: Ἀρχὴ τοῦ εὐαγγελίου Ἰησοῦ Χριστοῦ [υἱοῦ θεοῦ]. However, in the SBL GNT the questionable text υἱοῦ θεοῦ is not included at all.

2. **Bold** or *Italics*. The critical editions will place direct quotations from the Old Testament Greek (i.e. the Septuagint or LXX) either in bold (UBS) or italics (NA), or not at all (SBL GNT).

3. Capitalization. Each of the critical editions will use capitalized words to indicate proper nouns, as well as the start of a new paragraph or section. Unfortunately, the editions will disagree on which break is significant enough to begin with a capitalized word (cf. Luke 2:1, where all editions have the first word capitalized; but see Luke 2:6, where the NA has an initial capitalized word, but the UBS and the SBL GNT do not).

4. A Comparison of Conventions in Critical Editions in 2 Cor 9:8-9. Below students can see how the UBS[4-5], NA[27-28], and SBL GNT punctuate and mark 2 Cor 9:8-9, which includes a quotation from Ps 112:9 (LXX). I include my English translation below each, reflecting the difference of punctuation.

a. The UBS[4-5] uses capitalization, **bold**, indentation, and parallel alignment to show a direct quotation. Also, καθὼς γέγραπται ends with a comma.

8 δυνατεῖ δὲ ὁ θεὸς πᾶσαν χάριν περισσεῦσαι εἰς ὑμᾶς, ἵνα ἐν παντὶ πάντοτε πᾶσαν αὐτάρκειαν ἔχοντες περισσεύητε εἰς πᾶν ἔργον ἀγαθόν, **9** καθὼς γέγραπται,
Ἐσκόρπισεν, ἔδωκεν τοῖς πένησιν,
ἡ δικαιοσύνη αὐτοῦ μένει εἰς τὸν αἰῶνα.

8 "Moreover, God is powerful to increase all grace to you, in order that, in all ways always all self-sufficiency having, you would increase in every good work, [9] just as it is written,
"He scattered abroad, he gave to the poor;
his righteousness remains forever."

b. The NA[27-28] uses no capitalization to introduce quotations, but uses italics, indentation, and parallel alignment. Also, καθὼς γέγραπται ends with a raised dot (·) like the SBL GNT.

8 δυνατεῖ δὲ ὁ θεὸς πᾶσαν χάριν περισσεῦσαι εἰς ὑμᾶς, ἵνα ἐν παντὶ πάντοτε πᾶσαν αὐτάρκειαν ἔχοντες περισσεύητε εἰς πᾶν ἔργον ἀγαθόν, **9** καθὼς γέγραπται·
ἐσκόρπισεν, ἔδωκεν τοῖς πένησιν,
ἡ δικαιοσύνη αὐτοῦ μένει εἰς τὸν αἰῶνα.

8 "Moreover, God is powerful to increase all grace to you, in order that, in all ways always all self-sufficiency having, you would increase in every good work, [9] just as it is written:
"He scattered abroad, he gave to the poor;
his righteousness remains forever."

c. The SBL GNT uses neither italics, bold, indentation, nor parallel alignment. Additionally, the editor Michael Holmes has placed 2 Cor 9:9 into parentheses (which ends in 9:10) and concludes both 9:8 and 9:9 with a raised dot (·) rather than a common and period, respectively. These editorial decisions involve interpretation. Holmes presumably judged 9:9-10 to be an aside.

^{8}δυνατεῖ δὲ ὁ θεὸς πᾶσαν χάριν περισσεῦσαι εἰς ὑμᾶς, ἵνα ἐν παντὶ πάντοτε πᾶσαν αὐτάρκειαν ἔχοντες περισσεύητε εἰς πᾶν ἔργον ἀγαθόν· ^{9}(καθὼς γέγραπται· Ἐσκόρπισεν, ἔδωκεν τοῖς πένησιν, ἡ δικαιοσύνη αὐτοῦ μένει εἰς τὸν αἰῶνα·

^{8} "Moreover, God is powerful to increase all grace to you, in order that, in all ways always all self-sufficiency having, you would increase in every good work; ^{9}(just as it is written: "He scattered abroad, he gave to the poor; his righteousness remains forever;" … $^{9:10}$….)

These examples indicate the need to understand the conventions of each edition and also the possible benefit of comparing editions to consider interpretive options.

Complete WORKBOOK EXERCISES 5 and consult the ANSWER KEY & GUIDE as needed.

CASE IN POINT 5: MORE ABOUT PREDICATE NOMINATIVES IN JOHN 1

A particularly intriguing verse is John 1:1, which has tremendous implications for understanding the nature of Jesus' divinity in relation to God. The whole verse is given below.

Ἐν ἀρχῇ ἦν ὁ λόγος, καὶ ὁ λόγος ἦν πρὸς τὸν θεόν, <u>καὶ θεὸς ἦν ὁ λόγος.</u>
In the beginning was the Word, and the Word was with God, <u>and the Word was God</u>.

One issue is whether the last statement affirms the equal divine status of Jesus (as the Word) with God the Father. Although there are other passages that can be brought to bear on this theological point (e.g. John 5:18; 10:33; 14:28; Rom 9:5; Phil 2:6; Titus 2:13), John 1:1 is commonly cited in such discussions.

Grammatically, John 1:1 contains the verb εἰμί (here in the imperfect "past" tense form ἦν *was*) and a predicate nominative having no article (i.e., anarthrous). E. C. Colwell early last century investigated the NT use of predicate nominatives.[8] His study revealed an interesting phenomenon that became known as Colwell's rule: "Definite predicate nouns which precede the verb usu-

---

[8] E. C. Colwell, "A Definite Rule for the Use of the Article in the Greek New Testament," *Journal of Biblical Literature* 52 (1933): 12-21.

ally lack the article ... a predicate nominative which precedes the verb cannot be translated as an indefinite or a 'qualitative' noun solely because of the absence of the article; if the context suggests that the predicate is definite, it should be translated as a definite noun..."[9] Much further refinement of the rule was necessary.[10] One important qualification was that preverbal predicate nominatives are usually qualitative, not definitive or indefinite. In fact, Philip B. Harner found that in such cases of preverbal anarthrous predicate nominatives, approximately 80% were qualitative in significance and 20% remained definite. Importantly, none are indefinite.[11]

At this point, students should recall the discussion in the previous chapter at §4.5 THE ARTICLE AND LACK OF AN ARTICLE. Specifically, remember that the lack of the article may carry a range of significance:

This research and discussion shows that sentence placement in preverbal position helps delimit the significance of why a noun, and particularly a predicate nominative, is anarthrous: it is most often qualitative or it remains definite by unique referent. What is likely happening is that prepositioning is a rather prominent sentence location and would help the audience recognize that an anarthrous predicate nominative likely carries a qualitative meaning.

It may be helpful to look at few examples of predicate nominatives that Colwell discussed. At the end of John 1, Nathanael confesses who Jesus is:

John 1:49 σὺ εἶ ὁ υἱὸς τοῦ θεοῦ, σὺ <u>βασιλεὺς</u> εἶ τοῦ Ἰσραήλ.
You are the son of God, you are (the) King of Israel.

Notice how the noun for *king* (βασιλεύς) is anarthrous and preverbal (before the verb εἰμί); yet clearly *king* is not "a king" but either carries a qualitative sense ("*KING* indeed") or is definite (*The King of Israel*). There was only to be one king for Israel. For Nathanael to be affirming Jesus as simply *a king* is quite absurd. Just as important is the fact that the equivalent title *The King of the Jews* is found after the verb εἰμί <u>always</u> with the article:

σὺ εἶ ὁ βασιλεὺς τῶν Ἰουδαίων; (Matt 27:11//Mark 15:2//Luke 23:3//John 18:33)
Are you <u>the</u> King of the Jews? (Pilate's question to Jesus)

---

[9] As quoted by Wallace 257.

[10] For a discussion of the subsequent research and qualification of Colwell's Rule, see Wallace 256-69, on whom I am dependent here.

[11] Philip B. Harner, "Qualitative Anarthrous Predicate Nouns: Mark 15:39 and John 1:1," *Journal of Biblical Literature* 92 (1973): 75–87; cited and summarized by Wallace.

εἰ σὺ εἶ ὁ βασιλεὺς τῶν Ἰουδαίων, σῶσον σεαυτόν. (Luke 23:37)
If you are <u>the</u> king of the Jews, save yourself! (This is the mocking by the soldiers.)

Yet, when this same title is placed before the verb εἰμί, it has no article:

βασιλεὺς Ἰσραήλ ἐστιν. (Matt 27:42)
He is (the) King of Israel. (Jesus is being mocked by the religious leaders.)

Returning to John 1:1, we must determine the significance of the anarthrous θεός: Does it mean *a god* (indefinite meaning) or does it mean *God in essence* (qualitative meaning)? The consideration of preverbal predicate nominatives and the book context of John allows us to conclude that the anarthrous θεός in John 1:1 is *qualitative* emphasizing the divine status of the Word, *God in essence* (so Wallace 269). In the context of 1:1, the Word is affirmed as existing before creation: "in the beginning <u>was</u> the Word." Thus, we have little doubt as to what John wanted to affirm about the identity of the Word: The Word was not created, but was *God in essence* from before the beginning with God the Father.

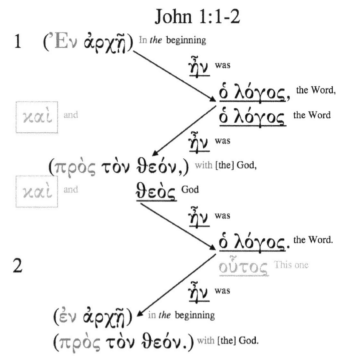

This interpretation is also supported by the rhetorical and chiastic structure of the Greek text (ABC-CBA) twice that interweaves the Word (ὁ λόγος) and God (ὁ θεός), thus affirming the full deity of the Word, Jesus, in the beginning in eternal fellowship with God, the Father, ***before*** creation. The graphical depiction helps one see the beautiful intricacy and logic of John's thought.

Below is an image of a Roman metal stylus (Greek γραφίς; Latin *stilus*) used to write on wax tablets that could be rubbed off and reused.[12] The rounded knob at the right end was used to smooth out the wax after making a mistake and needing to re-write something. (See the 2nd century AD wax tablet on p.23 above upon which such a stylus as this would have been used.)

---

[12] Image, slightly edited, is from James P. Maginnis, "Cantor Lectures. Reservoir, Fountain, and Stylographic Pens: Lecture I. Ancient Writing Implements," *Journal of the Society of Arts* 53 (1905): 1125–39 at 1126 fig.2.

CHAPTER 6

6.0 VOCABULARY

6.1 PREPOSITIONS (Προθέσεις)

6.2 PREPOSITIONAL COMPOUND VERBS AND WORDS

6.3 AGENCY, MEANS, SOURCE, AND DIVINE PASSIVE

 CHECK POINT 6.1-3 PREPOSITIONS AND CASE USAGE

6.4 PREPOSITIONAL PHRASES WITH Πρός MAY MARK INDIRECT OBJECTS

6.5 SPECIAL USES OF THE PRESENT TENSE

6.6 HISTORIC PRESENT (HP) AND DISCOURSE PRAGMATICS

6.7 A FIRST LOOK AT MAJOR LEXICONS: BDAG, L&N, AND LSJ

CASE IN POINT 6: DIVINE AGENCY AND HUMAN RESPONSE IN EPH 2:8-10

An excellent passage to memorize is Eph 2:8-10 (NASB95, underlining added):

> [8] For <u>by grace</u> you have been saved <u>through faith</u>; and that not <u>of yourselves</u>, *it is* <u>the gift of God</u>; [9] not <u>as a result of works</u>, so that no one may boast. [10] For we are His workmanship, created <u>in Christ Jesus</u> <u>for good works</u>, which God prepared beforehand so that we would walk <u>in them.</u>

The underlined portions indicate underlying Greek prepositional phrases or special uses of the noun cases. You can see that much hangs on understanding these phrases. In Eph 2:8-10, what is the significance of such phrases? What do we learn about God's purposes for us as revealed in Jesus Christ? Check out CASE IN POINT 6 further below.

 This chapter introduces **prepositions** and **prepositional phrases**. Nine Greek prepositions are presented in the vocabulary. Also, the student is introduced to **compound verbs and words**, i.e., words that have prepositions added to the front of a basic stem to form a different word with its own lexical form. Next we look at several types of constructions that may be found when translating passive voice constructions, to express **means**, **agency**, and **source**. Next students are guided through a discussion of **non-routine indirect and direct verbal objects**. Then, we discuss some **further uses of the Present Tense**. Finally, we look at how **Greek lexicons provide data** concisely for our interpretive work.

VOCABULARY 6	PREPOSITIONS AND COMPOUND VERBS

Compound Verbs:

ἀποκρίνομαι [232]	I answer back, respond	εἰσέρχομαι [193]	I go into, enter
ἀπολύω [67]	I release, send away; I pardon	ἐξέρχομαι [217]	I go out, exit
ἀπέρχομαι [117]	I go away, depart	προσέρχομαι [85]	I come/go to (+ dat.)
διέρχομαι [43]	I pass through/over		

Prepositions with One Case: ἐν [2737]   dat. in, among, with

ἀπό, ἀφ᾿, ἀπ᾿ [645]   gen. from   ἐνώπιον [94]   gen. before, face-to-face, in view of

εἰς [1857]   acc. into, to; for   πρός [698]   acc. towards, to; with
                                    (*may express purpose*)   (*may express purpose*)

ἐκ, ἐξ [913]   gen. from, out of   σύν [129]   dat. with, along with

Prepositions with Two Cases:

διά, δι᾿ [666]   gen. through   ὑπό, ὑφ᾿, ὑπ᾿ [221]   gen. by (means of), with
                          acc. on account of, because of   acc. under

After learning vocabulary to this point, you will know 43.2% of the words in the GNT. If you are able, listen to audio recordings of VOCABULARY 6 and complete the CROSSWORD PUZZLE in the WORKBOOK EXERCISES.

NOTES ON VOCABULARY 6:

Above are seven compound verbs, which are verbs formed with a preposition permanently added to the front, e.g., ἀπό + λύω= ἀπολύω. The verb δι-έρχομαι has the preposition διά added to ἔρχομαι. The ἄλφα is dropped before another vowel. Five compound verbs above are from ἔρχομαι. Notice how the meanings of these compounded verbs are derived from the basic meaning of ἔρχομαι and the respective prepositions. However, this will not always be the case with compound verbs. For example, ἀποκρίνομαι is a compound from ἀπό (*from*) and the verb κρίνω (*I judge*). Most of these compound verbs happen to be middle-formed (-ομαι). But, this is not always the case with compound verbs (see VOCABULARY 8). The verb ἀποκρίνομαι has a rather interesting discourse function of some speaker taking back or taking over a conversation or event. See §18.5 TAKING CONTROL OR "ANSWERING BACK" IN CONVERSATION.

Nine prepositions are presented here. Ἀπό has two other forms, ἀφ᾿ and ἀπ᾿ that occur when the word that follows begins with a vowel. The ὄ μικρόν is dropped (or **elided**) before another vowel. Thus, the same thing happens in the compound verb ἀπ-έρχομαι. If the word following has a rough breathing mark, then ἀπό becomes ἀφ᾿. The πῖ (π) changes to φῖ (φ), which is an **aspirated** *p*. ("Aspirated" indicates that the sound is formed with air moving out of the mouth.) Similar changes occur with ὑπό when it becomes ὑπ᾿ or ὑφ᾿. In a similar fashion, ἐκ becomes ἐξ when followed by a vowel.

Robertson (577) provides a succinct statement of the slight nuance of meaning between ἐκ and ἀπό: " Ἐκ means 'from within' while ἀπό is merely the general starting-point. Ἀπό does not deny the "within-ness"; it simply does not assert it as ἐκ does."

Most of the prepositions introduced in this lesson use only one case; that is, the noun they govern (i.e., the object of the preposition) is found in the genitive, dative, or accusative case. However, the meaning of ὑπό and διά depends on whether its object is in the genitive or accusative case. Finally, some of these prepositions have more than one meaning: πρός *towards, with*; ἐν *in, among, with*; ἐκ, ἐξ *from, out of*. One must determine from the context which meaning makes the best sense.

6.1 PREPOSITIONS (προθέσεις)

A. **Defined: Prepositions** are words that often form noun phrases that modify either verbs or nouns, depending on the context. The basic components of a **prepositional phrase** are the preposition itself and a noun or substantive (word functioning like a noun). One frequently finds additional modifiers (articles, genitive modifiers, adjectives, etc.). For example, these are prepositional phrases: *in the boat, on a house, into rain, out of their jail*. In their most common usage, Greek prepositions function very much like English prepositions. See further below F. and G. and Wallace 355-63.

B. **The Object of the Preposition:** The noun that a preposition uses in its phrase is called the *object of the preposition*. In the above examples *boat, house, rain* and *jail* are the objects of their respective prepositions.

C. **The Case of the Object:** Since Greek nouns have *case*, the object of the preposition will occur with nouns having a case ending. Most of the time, the genitive, dative, or accusative cases are used. *About half of the prepositions you will learn in this textbook will always have the same case for their object.* That is, these prepositions occur with only one case. However, there are a good number of prepositions that are found with two or three cases. *With these prepositions, the case of the object will determine the meaning of the preposition.* For example, ὑπό occurs with two cases. When its object is in the genitive case, ὑπό is to be translated *by (means of)*; but when in the accusative case, ὑπό should be translated *under*.

ὑπὸ τοῦ κυρίου = *by the Lord* (the object in genitive case)

ὑπὸ τὸν νόμον = *under the Law* (the object in accusative case)

Thus, when learning prepositions that have more than one case, you must memorize the meaning of that preposition when it is found with each particular case. In a sense, it is like learning two different words.

D. **Location and Use in the Sentence:** Prepositions are modifying expressions that modify either nouns (**adjectival use**) or verbs (**adverbial use**). The adverbial use is more common. Technically, prepositional phrases can be located just about anywhere in the sentence. Thus, one needs to consider exactly which word the prepositional phrase is modifying. *However, typically the prepositional phrase will be located near to whichever word it is modifying.*

E. **Improper Prepositions:** Grammars will identify a class of prepositions called "improper" that are typically not compounded onto verbs. This label is a misnomer, since prepositions initially did not get compounded (a later development), and so there is nothing improper for them not to be compounded. These improper prepositions also typically use only the genitive case for their object. In this handbook, one improper preposition is presented: ἕως (Ch.11). There are about two-dozen such words. Here is a list of those that occur twenty times or more. You do **not** need to memorize these now.

ἕως (in Ch.11)	*until, as far as, up to; while (conj.)*
ἀντί (compounded)	*instead of, for*
ἕνεκα or ἕνεκεν	*on account of*
πέραν	*beyond*
χωρίς	*without, apart from*

F. **History of Prepositions:** It may be helpful for students to understand that in the history of the Greek language, prepositions were stand-alone adverbs that assisted in the "locking in" of special case meaning; thus they helped to indicate special uses of the noun case functions. (See also §22.5 Adverbs: More on Formation and Function.)

G. **Common Semantic Relations Conveyed by Prepositions and Adverbs:** It may be helpful for you to begin to conceptualize the dynamism of prepositions and some of the semantic relations they can convey. Their entries in the Lexicons are often very detailed and complex, in large part because of this dynamism. The chart below provides semantic categories that describe general modifying relations appropriate to adverbs and prepositional phrases.[1]

General Modifying Relations with basic English Gloss	
Location ("in, out, at…")	**Agency** ("through, by…")
Temporal ("at, before…")	**Cause** ("because, on acc. of…")
Direction ("towards, away…")	**Origin** or **Source** ("from…")
Purpose ("for…")	**Manner** (describing "how")
Beneficiary ("on behalf of, for")	**Association** ("with…")
Reference ("concerning…")	**Substitution** ("in place of…")
Instrumental ("by, through…")	

6.2 Prepositional Compound Verbs and Words

A. **Prepositional Compound Words Defined:** Greek words may be formed that have one or more prepositions affixed to or compounded onto the front. In English, these may be permanently affixed (*to undertake, undertaking*) or separable (*to build up, up building*). In Greek, these are always affixed to the front of the word. For example, the verb ἐξ-απο-στέλλω *I send forth* is formed with two prefixed prepositions. Why an author would use this particular verb rather than the simpler, less marked, ἀπο-στέλλω *I send forth* with the same English gloss, is

---

[1] From David Alan Black, *Linguistics for Students of New Testament Greek: A Survey of Basic Concepts and Applications,* 2nd ed. (Grand Rapids: Baker, 1995), 111-12.

[2] Although acknowledging this, H. P. V. Nunn attempts a gloss "I give a decision from myself" (*The Elements of New*

worth considering contextually in virtually every case. Such a morphological addition of the preposition reflects a trend in Koine Greek towards "greater explicitness" (Wallace 20). *Often such authorial decisions reflect morphological emphasis.*

B. **The Preposition's Influence:** Here we find the epitome of the preposition as a modifier: It joins directly to a word stem and alters that stem's meaning—sometimes slightly, sometimes entirely. If the student can find a way to understand the individual combination of the word and the preposition compounded onto it, then fine. Each compound verb, however, should be memorized with its own particular meaning. Not all compound words will be as easy to derive meanings as are the compounded forms of ἔρχομαι (see C.2. below).

C. **Meaning:** The basic significances of compounded words include the following, which may overlap with one another in certain cases. Here the discussion is limited to the large category of Compound Verbs, although this material may be applied to other parts of speech to which prepositions are commonly compounded (nouns, adjectives, and adverbs).

1. Unapparent. The force of the preposition on the verb may be "unapparent" (from our modern perspective) and/or may so alter the sense of the verb stem so as to give the verb stem a unique sense. This may be the case with ἀποκρίνομαι *I answer*, in which the component parts could be rendered as "I distinguish/judge from."[2]

2. Additive. The meaning of the preposition is added to the meaning of the verb in translation. For example, from our vocabulary are the following compound verbs:

ἀπέρχομαι	*I go away (from)*	εἰσέρχομαι	*I go into*
διέρχομαι	*I go through*	ἐξέρχομαι	*I go out of*

3. Perfective and/or Intensive. Smyth indicates, "The addition of a preposition (especially διά, κατά, σύν) to a verbal form may mark the completion of the action of the verbal idea (perfective action)" (366). In such cases, greater attention is drawn to the final effect of the action and one should consider why. Additionally, Dana and Mantey state, "A very frequent use of prepositions is in composition with words for the purpose of expressing emphasis or intensity."[3] Such use of the preposition is one type of *morphological emphasis.*

ἀποκόπτω *I cut off* (cf. κόπτω *I cut*)
ἐκκόπτω   *I cut off/down* (κόπτω *I cut*)
κατεσθίω *I eat up* (or *I gobble down*) (from ἐσθίω *I eat*)

---

[2] Although acknowledging this, H. P. V. Nunn attempts a gloss "I give a decision from myself" (*The Elements of New Testament Greek* [Cambridge: Cambridge University Press, 1923], 161).

[3] H. E. Dana and Julius R. Mantey, *A Manual Grammar of the Greek New Testament* (New York: Macmillan, 1927), 98. See the many examples they provide in 99-112.

A fine example of morphological emphasis through the intensive compounded preposition ἐκ occurs within Paul's list of hardships in 2 Cor 4:8:

2 Cor 4:8 ἀπορούμενοι ἀλλ᾽ οὐκ <u>ἐξ</u>-απορούμενοι,
       being perplexed but not <u>utterly</u> perplexed

The LSJ lexical entry indicates that ἐξαπορέω is "strengthened for ἀπορέω."

This chart provides other examples of Perfective or Intensive use of a compounded preposition.[4] The list is representative, not exhaustive.

ἀπό	ἀπέχω, *I have fully, have received*; also in sense (I), *I am away, distant*; (middle), *I hold myself off from, abstain* ἀπόλλυμι, *I destroy utterly*; middle, *I perish completely* ἀπολούομαι, *I wash myself thoroughly*
διά	διαβεβαιόομαι, *I assert confidently, emphatically* διακαθαρίζω, *I cleanse thoroughly* διαφυλάσσω, *I guard carefully*
ἐκ	ἐκπληρόω, *I fill completely* ἐξαπορέομαι, *I am utterly at a loss*
ἐπί	ἐπιγινώσκω *I understand* (distinguished from γινώσκω *I know*)
κατά	κατεργάζομαι, *I work out thoroughly* κατεσθίω, *I eat up, devour*
παρά	παροξύνω, *I provoke, irritate* (compare to the adj. ὀξύς, *sharp*) παραπικραίνω, *I embitter, provoke* (compare to πικραίνω *I make bitter*) παρατηρέω, *I watch closely*
περί	περιαιρέω, *I take away altogether* περικαλύπτω, *I cover all round,* περικρύβω, *I cover up*
πρός	προσκαρτερέω *I am attached to, faithful to* "with dative of person and emphasis on continuity" (BDAG s.v.)
σύν	συναρπάζω *I snatch away* (perfective of ἁρπάζω, *I snatch*) συνθρύπτω, *I break in pieces, crush utterly* συνκαλύπτω, *I veil (cover) completely* συντηρέω, *I keep safe*

---

[4] This chart has been collected from several sources: Bruce M. Metzger, *Lexical Aids for Students of New Testament Greek* (3rd ed.; Grand Rapids, Mich.: Baker Academic, 1998), 79-85; Robertson (passim); and J. H. Moulton, *A Grammar of New Testament Greek, Vol. I, Prolegomena*, 3rd ed. (Edinburgh, 1908), 111-18.

Two other extreme examples of intensive morphological emphasis are found in the modifying expressions in **Eph 3:20** (ὑπὲρ πάντα ... ὑπερ-εκ-περισσοῦ, *beyond all things ... far more abundantly*) and **2 Cor 9:15** (ἐπὶ τῇ ἀν-εκ-δι-ηγήτῳ αὐτοῦ δωρεᾷ, *for his indescribable gift*), praising God at climactic moments for what God can do and has given.

4. Creates Redundancy. The use of compound verbs may produce redundancy and extra stress on the prepositional idea when attended by a prepositional phrase with the same preposition.[5] Often the choice to use the compound verb form is optional; "Often the preposition with the verb may be followed by the case that is usual with the preposition without much regard to the verb itself" (Robertson 562). Thus, to choose a verb form that repeats the prepositional morpheme produces repetitive, aural effect for emphasis. Consider the following examples:

Matt 15:18a τὰ δὲ ἐκπορευόμενα ἐκ τοῦ στόματος ἐκ τῆς καρδίας ἐξέρχεται,
      So, the things coming [from] out of the mouth come [from] out of the heart,...

Heb 4:3a Εἰσερχόμεθα γὰρ εἰς [τὴν] κατάπαυσιν οἱ πιστεύσαντες,
      For the ones of us believing are entering into [the] rest,

Notice how repetitive the prepositions ἐκ and εἰς are. In the translation of Matt 15:18a, the redundant preposition "from" may be added to help stress the notion of "origin": [*from*] *out of...* .

5. A Different Prepositional Phrase after a Compound Verb. The use of a different preposition in the compounded verb and in the prepositional phrase is often significant. Robertson (560-61) indicates, while providing numerous examples afterwards, "a different preposition may be used other than the one in composition.... In general the varying of the preposition is pertinent and is to be noted." So, the bottom line is to pay attention to prepositions since they play a significant role in sentences by further qualifying and elaborating meanings and relationships.

E. **Semantic and Pragmatic Discourse Function:** Since the presence of compounded prepositions may be optional and their presence often adds distinctive semantic and pragmatic weight, one must consider how their presence serves the larger discursive purpose. Thus, the addition of prepositional compound may heighten and intensify the meaning of a word. Furthermore, in the case of redundancy, hearers/readers would have been impacted by the repeated sounds as well as the additional semantic force of the preposition itself, as in the example of Matt 15:18a

---

[5] Smyth acknowledges such for prepositions with dative case indicating location; but it is reasonable to extend this the other cases. He says, "When the idea of place is emphatic, the preposition may be repeated" (§1549).

above. Only occasionally will English translations capture the force of these repeated prepositions. Let's look at a several more examples.

1. In **2 Tim 4:1**, Paul "solemnly testifies" (δια-μαρτύρομαι) to Timothy before God and Jesus Christ who judges the living and the dead. This verb διαμαρτύρομαι (occurs 15x in
   the Greek NT) is formed with the preposition διά and the verb μαρτύρομαι. It is given
   these gloss definitions in BDAG:

   a. to make a solemn declaration about the truth of something *testify of, bear witness to*
   b. to exhort with authority in matters of extraordinary importance, frequently with refer-
      ence to higher powers and/or suggestion of peril, *solemnly urge, exhort, warn*

   Very similar gloss definitions are given for the uncompounded form μαρτύρομαι (occurs
   6x in the Greek NT).

   a. to affirm something with solemnity, *testify, bear witness*;
   b. to urge something as a matter of great importance, *affirm, insist, implore*.

   However, a study of the contexts where διαμαρτύρομαι is used reveals greater intensity
   and/or that God's ultimate judgment is directly stated as in view; i.e., one's solemn testimony pertains to the eternal fate or the judgment of individuals who proclaim the gospel.
   Although such eternal accountability can also be present with μαρτύρομαι (e.g., Acts
   20:26; 26:22), the intensified compound form διαμαρτύρομαι helps convey the solemnity
   of the testimony before God even more (e.g. Acts 2:40; 10:42; 1 Thess 4:6; 2 Tim 4:1).

2. In **Mark 12:17**, the Pharisees and Herodians' reaction to Jesus's statement to render to Caesar what is Caesar's and to God what is God's is explained using the verb ἐκ-θαυμάζω, *to
   be utterly amazed* (BDAG). The verb occurs only here in the critical editions of the NT. It
   is what is called ἅπαξ λεγόμενον (*ahpahx lehgōmehnōn*) "once spoken." The shorter, uncompounded, more common verb θαυμάζω (43x) could have been used, which BDAG
   glosses as 1. *to be extraordinarily impressed or disturbed by something* or 2. *to wonder, be
   amazed* (BDAG). It is interesting that in the text-critical manuscript traditions, one finds
   later scribes upgrading the simpler θαυμάζω to the intensive form ἐκ-θαυμάζω (Luke
   2:33; 4:22; 20:26; Acts 3:12).[6] Relying on BDAG, one would get the impression that
   θαυμάζω is roughly equivalent in meaning, or perhaps even intensified in sense because of
   the added gloss "extraordinarily"! However, both impressions would be mistaken. The lexical entry for this compound verb in LSJ rightly indicates that ἐκθαυμάζω is "*strengthened
   for θαυμάζω.*" (In fact, LSJ also identifies ἀνα-θαυμάζω as a strengthened form.) So also

---

[6] As reported by Spiros Zodhiates, *The Complete Word Study Dictionary: New Testament* (Chattanooga, TN: AMG,
2000), θαυμάζω #2296.

Zodhiates notes that ἐκθαυμάζω is an intensified compound. However, our major English versions often do not convey the intense response: "they were amazed/marveled at him" (KJV; RSV; NASB95; NIV84; ESV); compare, "His reply completely amazed them" (NLT, which changes the subject "they" to be the direct object "them"); the use of *amazed* and *marveled* is typical for θαυμάζω (cf. Matt 8:10; Luke 20:26, etc.).

3. In **2 Cor 10:14**, Murray J. Harris has described succinctly the use of the preposition ὑπέρ:

> In verbs compounded with ὑπέρ (there are fourteen in the NT), the prefix may be intensive (e.g., ὑπερπλεονάζω, 'abound exceedingly,' 1 Tim. 1:14) or may indicate excess, as in ὑπερεκτείνω here [2 Cor 10:14], 'stretch out (ἐκτείνω) beyond (ὑπέρ) [the measure assigned].' This notion of excess is regularly rendered in English by the prefix 'over,' so that ὑπερεκτείνω may be translated 'overstretch,' 'overextend,' or 'overreach.'[7]

6.3 AGENCY, MEANS, SOURCE, AND DIVINE PASSIVE

A. **Modification and the Passive Voice:** It is almost always significant who is acting as agent, or what is used as the means, or the source of activities. These relations of agency, means, and source are common with active verbs, but especially with passive voice verbs. We have already learned that the passive voice derived from the middle voice forms to signify when the subject is not performing the action of the verb, but rather is being acted upon by someone or something else. Just *who* or *what* is performing this action may be indicated in Greek by several grammatical constructions (see also Wallace 431-38).

B. **Agency, Means, and Source:** If the action is accomplished by a specified person, this is called **agency**; if it is accomplished by an impersonal entity, this is called **means** (or **instrumentation**). Another relevant category is **source**, in which the origin of the action is identified and stressed. A note on the difference between agency, means, and source is in order. An agent is a *person* who is responsible for accomplishing an act. Means, on the other hand, expresses *something* that is *used by an agent*. So, *means* is more of an instrument for accomplishing a task than the actual *source* of the cause of something. Also, when we say that *means* is "impersonal," the stress is more on the instrument than on the entity as a means is not a person. So then, *means* may be expressed with personal nouns (i.e., nouns that refer to persons). These nouns, while they are persons, are being used as instruments to accomplish something. Their personhood is not taken away by using the construction of "means"; but so also the focus of the construction is **not** on their personhood as agents. Thus, *means* may imply some further personal *agency*. See Wallace 433-35.

---

[7] Murray J. Harris, *The Second Epistle to the Corinthians: A Commentary on the Greek Text*, New International Greek Testament Commentary (Grand Rapids: Eerdmans, 2005), 717.

C. **Constructions to convey Means, Agency, and Source:** Not surprisingly, Greek shows a robust understanding of agency, means, and source—as well as a variety of constructions to convey such notions. I will not venture to discuss *cause*, which would expand this section even more, although *cause* is implied with *agency* and *means*, and *source* can approach *cause*.

1. <u>Personal Agency</u>: The preposition ὑπό with the genitive case (translated *by*) is used to indicate the person who is performing the action upon a passive subject (Wallace 433; cf. 125-27 and 389). Somewhat rare—the Genitive Case may be used to indicate either means or agency with adjectives formed with –τος (see Wallace 125-27). Prepositional phrases are placed within parentheses and special uses of the Noun cases are placed within curly braces.

a. οἱ ἄνθρωποι βαπτίζονται (<u>ὑπὸ</u> τοῦ Ἰωάννου).
   The persons are being baptized (<u>by</u> John).

- *The persons* are the passive subject. *John* is the person performing the action of baptizing on them.

b. ἡ ἐκκλησία σῴζεται (<u>ὑπὸ</u> τοῦ θεοῦ).
   The church is being saved (<u>by</u> God).

- In this example, *the church* is passive and the person performing the action is *God*.

c. ἐκλεκτῶν {<u>θεοῦ</u>} [**Rom 8:33**]
   called {<u>of/by God</u>}

- Note that this construction occurs with specialized adjectives that are formed with –τος endings that have a passive meaning.

2. <u>Impersonal Means</u>: The Dative Case alone, or with the preposition ἐν, can be used to indicate impersonal means by which some action was accomplished (on the use of ἐν, see Wallace 372-75). When the dative alone occurs in this sense, the construction is called the **dative of means** (see Wallace 162-66, 434-35). Otherwise, ἐν + the dative can express means when in reference to a person, "though they are conceived of as impersonal (i.e., used as an instrument by someone else)" (Wallace 373).

a. βαπτίζονται (<u>ἐν</u> τῷ ὕδατι καὶ τῷ λόγῳ).
   They are being baptized (<u>with</u> the water and the word).

b. σῴζεται {<u>τῇ ἀληθείᾳ</u> τοῦ εὐαγγελίου}.
   She/he is being saved {<u>by the truth</u> of the gospel.}

c. κτιζόμεθα (<u>ὑπὸ</u> θεοῦ) (<u>ἐν</u> Χριστῷ Ἰησοῦ)
   We are founded (<u>by</u> God) (<u>by way of</u> Christ Jesus).

- Notice that an interpretive decision has to be made whether ἐν means *in* (specifying location) or *with* (indicating means).
- Christ Jesus is God's instrument to form the body of believers.

3. <u>Intermediate Means or Intermediate Agency</u>: Occasionally the **means** (entity) or the **agent** (person) is indicated through the use of διά in the genitive case translated *through*. It has often been noted that in this construction διά points to the secondary or intermediate means or agency (see Wallace 433-34; cf. 368-69).

a. δοξάζεται ὁ θεὸς (<u>διὰ τῶν μαθητῶν</u>). *God is glorified (<u>through the disciples</u>).*	▪ The disciples are the secondary agents through whom God is glorified. We might consider who the primary agent is in the biblical context.
b. ἁγιάζεται <u>διὰ λόγου</u> θεοῦ. *He is being sanctified (<u>through the Word</u> of God).*	▪ The *word* is the sanctifying means. Notice that the parentheses includes *of God*, since it belongs with these constituents.

4. <u>Source with possible sense of Agency or Means</u>: In this discussion, it is worth mentioning that the prepositions ἐκ and ἀπό and παρά (in CH. 10) can signify source that may at times converge into the sense of agency or means (on ἐκ, see Smyth §1688.c).

a. Ἰωσὴφ... ὁ ἐπικληθεὶς Βαρναβᾶς (<u>ἀπὸ τῶν ἀποστόλων</u>) [**Acts 4:36a**] *Joseph... the one called Barnabas (<u>from/by the apostles</u>).*	▪ The apostles are the source and agency for the name Barnabas applied to Joseph. It is not surprising there is a textual variant that has ὑπό instead. See Robertson 579-80.
b. (<u>ἐκ τοῦ εὐαγγελίου</u>) ζῆν [**1 Cor 9:14**] *to live (<u>from/by means of the Gospel</u>)*	▪ The gospel is the source and means of sustaining a livelihood (see in context).

5. <u>Divine Passive</u>: Just exactly *who* is acting on the subject is not always indicated in a sentence. However, depending on the context, it may be determined that God is the One *who* is acting. If it is determined that God is the assumed agent, this may be called a **Divine Passive** (see Wallace 435-38). For example, the sentence in C.1.b above would not need the phrase ὑπὸ τοῦ θεοῦ. In an ultimate sense, only God "saves." An important rule is, *when there is a passive voice verb and no agent or means is specified, then it may be that God is to be assumed as the One who is agent.*

CHECK POINT 6.1-3

Consider the influence of the Preposition or Special Noun Case. Given Romans 3:24-26, first, identify the function of each underlined preposition (prepositional phrase or compounded) or noun case; and, second, consider the semantic contribution or possible influence of the preposition or noun case. If needed, ask questions, since additional research would be necessary to determine such properly. Not all noun endings will be familiar to you, but use the article endings to guide you.

Romans 3:24-26 being justified freely <u>by his grace</u> (τῇ αὐτοῦ χάριτι)[1] <u>through the redemption</u> (διὰ τῆς ἀπολυτρώσεως[2])[3] <u>in Christ Jesus</u> (ἐν Χριστῷ Ἰησοῦ)[4], 25 whom God put forward as a sacrifice of atonement <u>through faith</u> (διὰ τῆς πίστεως)[5] <u>by his blood</u> (ἐν τῷ αὐτοῦ αἵματι)[6] <u>for a demonstration</u> (εἰς ἔνδειξιν[7])[8] of his righteousness, <u>on account of the passing over</u> (διὰ τὴν πάρεσιν)[9] of sins occurring <u>before</u> (προγεγονότων)[10] 26 <u>in</u> the <u>forbearance of God</u> (ἐν τῇ ἀνοχῇ τοῦ θεοῦ)[11], <u>towards the demonstration</u> (πρὸς τὴν ἔνδειξιν)[12] of his justice <u>in the present time</u> (ἐν τῷ νῦν καιρῷ)[13] in order that he would be just and the one justifying the one <u>from the faith of Jesus</u> (ἐκ πίστεως Ἰησοῦ)[14].

	Function	**Semantics or Possible Influence**
1. <u>by</u> his grace (τῇ αὐτοῦ χάριτι)		
2. redemption (ἀπολυτρώσεως)		
3. <u>through</u> the redemption (διὰ τῆς ἀπολυτρώσεως)		
4. <u>in</u> Christ Jesus (ἐν Χριστῷ Ἰησοῦ),		
5. <u>through</u> faith (διὰ τῆς πίστεως)		
6. <u>by</u> his blood (ἐν τῷ αὐτοῦ αἵματι)		
7. demonstration (ἔνδειξιν)		
8. <u>for</u> a demonstration (εἰς ἔνδειξιν)		
9. <u>on account of</u> the passing over (διὰ τὴν πάρεσιν)		
10. occurring <u>before</u> (προγεγονότων)		
11. <u>in</u> the forbearance of God (ἐν τῇ ἀνοχῇ τοῦ θεοῦ)		
12. <u>towards</u> the demonstration (πρὸς τὴν ἔνδειξιν)		
13. <u>in</u> the present time (ἐν τῷ νῦν καιρῷ)		
14. <u>from</u> the faith of Jesus (ἐκ πίστεως Ἰησοῦ)		

SUGGESTED ANSWERS		
	Function	**Semantics or Possible Influence**
1. <u>by</u> his grace (τῇ αὐτοῦ χάριτι)	special case usage; a dative of means	impersonal means (in distinction from agency) for some end
2. redemption (ἀπο̲λυτρώσεως)	prepositional compound	intensive; strengthens the meaning? (There is a shortened form of the word: λύτρωσις)
3. <u>through</u> the redemption (δι̲ὰ τῆς ἀπολυτρώσεως)	prepositional phrase	intermediate means
4. <u>in</u> Christ Jesus (ἐ̲ν Χριστῷ Ἰησοῦ),	prepositional phrase	ἐν with a person as instrument
5. <u>through</u> faith (δι̲ὰ τῆς πίστεως)	prepositional phrase	intermediate means
6. <u>by</u> his blood (ἐ̲ν τῷ αὐτοῦ αἵματι)	prepositional phrase	ἐν with a thing as instrument
7. demonstration (ἔ̲νδειξιν)	prepositional compound	unapparent or additive
8. <u>for</u> a demonstration (εἰ̲ς ἔνδειξιν)	prepositional phrase	purpose
9. <u>on account of</u> the passing over (δι̲ὰ τὴν πάρεσιν)	prepositional phrase	"because of" διά with the accusative
10. occurring <u>before</u> (προ̲γεγονότων)	prepositional compound	additive; the meaning "before" is added to the basic meaning
11. <u>in</u> the forbearance of God (ἐ̲ν τῇ ἀνοχῇ τοῦ θεοῦ)	prepositional phrase	"in" describing circumstance or is this "cause" (because of God's forbearance)?
12. <u>towards</u> the demonstration (πρὸ̲ς τὴν ἔνδειξιν)	prepositional phrase	purpose
13. <u>in</u> the present time (ἐ̲ν τῷ νῦν καιρῷ)	prepositional phrase	"in"–indicating location of time
14. <u>from</u> the faith of Jesus (ἐ̲κ πίστεως Ἰησοῦ)	prepositional phrase	source with possible agency? Much attention has been given to this and related phrases; it is called the πίστις Χριστοῦ debate ("faith of/in Christ")

6.4 PREPOSITIONAL PHRASES WITH Πρός MAY MARK INDIRECT OBJECTS

A. **Introduction:** We have learned that the accusative case is normally the case of the direct object (that which is transferred in the verbal action) and that the dative case is used for the indirect object (the entity specified as receiving the action of the verb). However, an alternative way to mark the indirect object is via the preposition πρός *to*.

B. **Πρός with the Accusative is Marked +Nearness in Conversation:** In narrative dialogue, one will find the prepositional phrase πρός (with its accusative object) functioning like an indirect object. This usage will occur next to the simple dative case that may indicate the indirect object. Although both constructions are translated the same way in English, πρός with the accusative requires more space and cognitive processing when the simpler dative case noun would have sufficed. So, πρός with the accusative is a more marked construction.

C. **Explanation:** I began noticing this use of πρός in Luke's Gospel within "intense" conversational settings: John the Baptist talking to the crowds about repentance (3:12-13), Jesus being tempted by Satan (4:4), Jesus talking to his hometown folks who want to kill him (4:21, 23). I began speculating that such exchanges were marked +intensity: e.g., *he said back at them....* A broader explanation is preferred. Although πρός can be used in contexts to mean "against" (e.g., Eph 6:11-12), the more essential meaning of πρός is "nearness (towards)" (Robertson, 622-23). So, πρός marks +nearness, which may indicate either "heated intensity" (i.e., engaged, argumentative conversation) or "closeness" (i.e., personal, engaging conversation). I think each of us can recall conversations were the closeness or nearness of the conversation partners signaled either heated exchange (even fighting) or more friendly discourse leaning towards one another. So, the setting and other contextual indicators must be observed to determine the difference.

    Robertson, commenting on πρός with the accusative case, noticed, "There seems to be something almost intimate, as well as personal, in some of the examples of πρός. The examples of πρός with persons are very numerous, as in ἐξεπορεύετο πρὸς αὐτόν (Mt. 3:5), δεῦτε πρός με (Mt. 11:28), etc. But one must not think that the notion of motion is essential to the use of πρός and the accusative (cf. εἰς and ἐν)" (624–25). Continuing on, Robertson considers why NT authors did not use other prepositions: "Certainly the more common Greek idiom would have been παρά, while μετά and σύν might have been employed. Abbott,[8] however, rightly calls attention to the frequent use of πρός with verbs of speaking like λέγω, λαλέω, etc., and Demosthenes has it with ζάω [*I live*]. So then it is a natural step to find πρός employed for living relationship, intimate converse" (625).

D. **Examples:** Robertson directs readers to consider Luke 24:14, 17. So let's look at the uses of πρός in this context with a fairly literal translation:

---

[8] Edwin A. Abbott, *Johannine Grammar* (London: Adam and Charles Black, 1906), 275.

Luke 24:14-18 [14] And they themselves were conversing with [πρός] one another about all these things that had taken place. [15] And it happened while they were talking and discussing, Jesus also Himself, drawing near, began traveling with them. [16] But their eyes were being restrained not to recognize Him. [17] Then He said to [πρός] them, "What are these words, which you are casting back and forth to [πρός] one another as you are walking?" And they stood [there] sad. [18] So, one by the name of Cleopas, answering back, said to [πρός] Him, "Are You yourself alone visiting Jerusalem and did not know the things that happened here in these days?!"

There are several indicators in the Greek text that indicate the conversation was intense and intimate: "they themselves" as agents are stressed (24:14), the reciprocal pronoun "one another" is used (24:14), the unusual verbs used for "talking" ("conversing," "discussing," "casting back and forth"), and the tense aspect of these verbs of speaking is imperfective, indicating "ongoing-ness." So, the use of πρός helps convey engaging nearness and intensity of the conversations.

Another example where πρός signals a radical nearness is when Paul commands masters to treat their slaves in the same way that he has directed the slaves to treat their masters (Eph 6:5-8). So, at Eph 6:9, Paul turns to address the masters.

Eph 6:9a Καὶ οἱ κύριοι, τὰ αὐτὰ ποιεῖτε πρὸς αὐτούς, ...
And masters, do the same things to them,...

In the NT, this verb "to do" never takes πρός to indicate an indirect object; but its use here helps communicate the "nearness" and "friendly posture" that Paul wanted believing Masters to show towards their slaves by doing "the same things" that Paul has commanded the slaves to do for their masters. This is revolutionary without inciting revolution. Although it is clear that Paul elsewhere urges a slave to be free if they can (1 Cor 7:21), nevertheless some persons preferred to stay in the slave-master relationship for a variety of reasons. But it is important to observe here that Paul calls for a transformation of the masters' relationships towards their slaves.

6.5 SPECIAL USES OF THE PRESENT TENSE

A. **Imperfective Aspect:** In §3.2 THE GREEK VERB, we learned that along with Greek Tense one must consider Verbal Aspect. Most grammarians acknowledge that the Present Tense has a imperfective aspect in its meaning, viewing the action internally as progressive. Most basically this is translated into English as, e.g., *We are teaching, you are learning, they are hearing.* Yet, the Present Tense is a fairly dynamic and flexible tense, probably due to its being the most commonly used tense, and beginning students should be aware of special uses.

B. **Categorical Uses:** Grammarians have given "labels" to various discerned uses of the Present Tense, which are provided below under five basic headings. See Wallace 513-39 for further explanations and examples.

1. Repeated Action of Some Sort.
   a. *Progressive Present.* Continuous action in the present. See Wallace 518-19.
   b. *Iterative Present.* Action done instance-by-instance over time. See Wallace 520-21.
   c. *Customary Present.* Action regularly or habitually done. See Wallace 521-22.
   d. *Extending-from-the-Past Present.* Action begun in the past and still ongoing in the present. See Wallace 519-20.
   e. *Gnomic Present.* This is used for general, timeless truths. [Since the timeless truth may repeat in circumstances, this subcategory is placed here.] See Wallace 523-25.

2. Instantaneous Present. The action is completed at the moment of speaking; it is relatively common and only occurs in the Indicative Mood. See Wallace 517-18.

3. Historic Present (HP). One important use of the Present Tense Indicative occurs in the narratives of the Gospels and Acts when referring to past events; in most translations, the verb is translated as a past tense verb in English. Traditionally grammarians have thought this usage adds vividness in the historical account (see Wallace 526-32). However, from an information processing and discourse pragmatic perspective, Historic Present verbs highlight the descriptions or events that follow them (Levinsohn §12.2). See the discussion immediately below in §6.6 HISTORIC PRESENT (HP) AND DISCOURSE PRAGMATICS.

4. Futuristic Present. This involves an action that takes place in the Future. A common verb that has this sense in the present tense is ἔρχομαι. See Wallace 535-37.

5. Attempted, but Failed Actions (i.e., Conative Present). This involves an action that is attempted but never realized; it is relatively rare and more common with the Imperfect Tense. See Wallace 534-35.

C. **Words of Caution:**
1. Too Many Options or Information Overload. This list may be daunting for a beginning student. However, *these specific uses reflect more the sense required by the surrounding context or the particular verb used than the intrinsic meaning of the present tense itself.* So, as a beginning student, it is not necessary to learn these subcategories.

2. "Labeling" Danger. There is also a danger of such labels for intermediate students (and instructors!) because they may be treated *as equal options to choose from when interpreting any passage. Additionally, one or another label may be chosen (if not even created!) on the basis of a particular doctrine rather than evidence.* In other words, one may be tempted to

"slap" a label onto this or that instance of the Present Tense to explain, interpret, or resolve an exegetical issue. However, such labels are not exegetically decisive in and of themselves. Instead, the labels provide a *possible* range of usage that can contribute to interpretive explanation that must attend carefully to other words in context.

3. <u>Keep it Simple</u>. You will do well simply to remember the basic verbal aspect of the Present Tense, which is *imperfective: action as viewed internally as in progress or incomplete.*

6.6 HISTORIC PRESENT (HP) AND DISCOURSE PRAGMATICS

A. **Introduction:** As indicated above, one important use of the Present Tense in the Indicative Mood is the Historic Present (HP), i.e. the use of the Present Indicative in past time narrative description. Grammarians have conceived of the HP as making actions or speech more vivid; specifically, they have thought the HP lends prominence to events, scenes, or actors[9] and marks boundaries within discourse.[10]

B. **Discourse Pragmatic Explanation:** Levinsohn (§12.2) summarizes these views and then explains that the HP usage points beyond the HP verb to subsequent events or speech. So, it just happens that HPs may begin a unit, but they may not. Instead, the imperfective verbal aspect of +incompleteness with regard to the HP has a *forward referencing function*, i.e., it is *kataphoric* (Levinsohn 203 n.6). In other words, by using the HP, an author "opens up" the action *marked as incomplete* thus creating anticipation and pointing forward to the unfolding of events or an actor's action/speech that will take place. In the end, one needs to pay careful attention to the use of the HP and consider its pragmatic discursive function to point forward to important events and speech, which may often, but not always, occur at the beginning of a discourse unit or paragraph.

---

[9] Buist M. Fanning, when reviewing and discussing the topic, summarizes the common view: "One adjustment to the vivid approach is the observation that this portrayal often works its way out by *drawing attention to crucial events* or *highlighting new scenes or actors* in the narrative" (*Verbal Aspect in New Testament Greek*, Oxford Theological Monographs [New York: Clarendon Press□1990], 231, emphasis original). Fanning then summarizes the instances of HP in Mark (except those instances with a verb of saying) as follows: "the other occurrences of the historical present display a clear pattern of discourse-structuring functions, such as to highlight the beginning of a paragraph, to introduce new participants into an existing paragraph, to show participants moving to new locations, or to portray key events in lively fashion" (232; he then catalogs instances in Mark according to these four uses).

[10] E.g., see Rodney J. Decker, who calls the HP rather a "narrative present" that functions to introduce a new character and/or to indicate the beginning of a new paragraph (*Mark 1-8: A Handbook on the Greek Text*, Baylor Handbook on the Greek New Testament [Waco, TX: Baylor University Press, 2014], 24). As indicated in his index, Decker identifies forty-nine narrative presents at Mark 1:12, 21, 40; 2:3, 4, 8; 3:13, 20, 31; 4:36; 5:15, 35, 38, 40[3]; 6:7, 30, 45, 48; 7:1; 8:22; 9:2, 35; 10:1, 23, 35[2], 46; 11:1, 15, 27[2], 33[2]; 12:13, 18; 14:12, 13, 17, 27, 32, 43, 51, 66; 15:24, 27; 16:2, 4.

C. **Examples:** Consider these first instances of HPs in Matthew, which I have underlined in the NASB95 and ESV. Note that the NASB95 adds asterisks to alert readers to their presence along with a traditional explanation of "vividness."[11]

Matthew 2:13 (see also 2:19)

[13] Now when they had gone, behold, an angel of the Lord *appeared to Joseph in a dream and said, "Get up! Take the Child and His mother and flee to Egypt, and remain there until I tell you; for Herod is going to search for the Child to destroy Him." (NASB95)

[13] Now when they had departed, behold, an angel of the Lord appeared to Joseph in a dream and said, "Rise, take the child and his mother, and flee to Egypt, and remain there until I tell you, for Herod is about to search for the child, to destroy him."

Matthew 3:1

[1] Now in those days John the Baptist *came, preaching in the wilderness of Judea, saying, (NASB95)

[1] In those days John the Baptist came preaching in the wilderness of Judea, (ESV)

Matthew 3:13 (see also 3:15)

[13] Then Jesus *arrived from Galilee at the Jordan *coming* to John, to be baptized by him. (NASB95)

[13] Then Jesus came from Galilee to the Jordan to John, to be baptized by him. (ESV)

Matthew 4:5 (see also 4:6, 8[2], 10, 11)

[5] Then the devil *took Him into the holy city and had Him stand on the pinnacle of the temple, (NASB95)

[5] Then the devil took him to the holy city and set him on the pinnacle of the temple (ESV)

Matthew 4:19

[19] And He *said to them, "Follow Me, and I will make you fishers of men." (NASB95)

[19] And he said to them, "Follow me, and I will make you fishers of men." (ESV)

In each case, one can discern important events (actions and speech) that the Historic Present verb introduces. In Matt 2:13 and 2:19, it is the angel's warning and the subsequent actions. In

---

[11] The NASB95 translators explain: "**A star** (*) is used to mark verbs that are historical presents in the Greek which have been translated with an English past tense in order to conform to modern usage. The translators recognized that in some contexts the present tense seems more unexpected and unjustified to the English reader than a past tense would have been. But Greek authors frequently used the present tense for the sake of heightened vividness, thereby transporting their readers in imagination to the actual scene at the time of occurrence. However, the translators felt that it would be wise to change these historical presents to English past tenses."

Matt 3:1, it is the initiation of John's ministry and his proclamation. In Matt 3:13 and 3:15, it is Jesus's baptism by John, which initiates Jesus's ministry. In Matt 4:5, the Historic Present highlights the *second* temptation of the Devil (not the first!); in fact, the Historical Present also highlights the third temptation (4:8[2]), and then Jesus's final response to the Devil (4:10) and the Devil's departure (4:11). In 4:19, the Historic Present verb λέγει highlights Jesus's call of his first disciples.

D. **Occurrences:** At this point, students need to recognize this common occurrence. How common? In the discussions, interpreters will distinguish HPs involving verbs of speech (e.g. λέγει *he says*) or verbs of action (e.g. προσεύχεται *he prays*). Buist M. Fanning provides this summary of occurrences:

> Matthew 93 (inclusive of 68 speech verbs)
> Mark 151 (inclusive of 72 speech verbs)
> Luke 11 (inclusive of 8 speech verbs)
> Acts 13 (inclusive of 11 speech verbs)
> John 162 (inclusive of 127 speech verbs).[12]

This basic accounting will help orient students when studying one of these books and prepare them to consider the use of the HP.

6.7 A FIRST LOOK AT MAJOR LEXICONS: BDAG, L&N, AND LSJ

One of the basic tools for students learning and studying a language is a dictionary, or, what is more technically called, a lexicon. In §3.1 GREEK WORDS AND LEXICAL MEANINGS, students were given a basic description of types of lexicons. For a detailed explanation of full entries of BDAG, L&N, and LSJ, see §12.6 NAVIGATING MAJOR LEXICONS. For a discussion of verbal objects with BDAG and LSJ, see §14.7 LEXICAL INFORMATION ON THE CASE OF VERBAL OBJECTS. Here I would like to compare the basic lexical entries for the verb κτίζω, since this verb plays prominently in Eph 2:10, which is discussed below in CASE IN POINT 6. To compare lexical entries will be instructive.

A. **BDAG:** The following extended definition and gloss, followed by an explanatory comment, is given in BDAG: "**to bring something into existence,** *create,* in our literature of God's creative activity." The singular basic gloss is to *create.*

> Bauer, Walter and F. W. Danker, W. F. Arndt, and F. W. Gingrich (BDAG). *Greek-English Lexicon of the New Testament and Other Early Christian Literature.* 3rd ed. Revised.

---

[12] Fanning, *Verbal Aspect*, 231-38; citing John C. Hawkins, *Horae Synopticae: Contributions to the Study of the Synoptic Problem*, 2nd ed. (Oxford: Clarendon Press, 1909), 143-49.

Chicago: The University of Chicago Press, 2000. This is the standard scholarly Greek NT Lexicon.

B. **L&N:** The basic gloss given is *create*. The fuller description explains: "to make or create something which has not existed before—'to create, creation' (in the NT, used exclusively of God's activity in creation)."

> Louw, Johannes and Eugene Nida (L&N). *Greek-English Lexicon of the New Testament Based on Semantic Domains*. 2 Vols. 2nd ed. New York: United Bible Societies, 1988. A very valuable lexicon which allows one to find synonyms and antonyms; has its own numbering system based upon semantic domains.

C. **LSJ:** The classical lexicon provides rather lengthy entry:

1. *to people* a country, *build houses and cities* in it, *colonise,*
2. of a city, *to found, plant, build*—Passive *to be founded*
3. *to plant, to set up, to establish*
4. *to create, bring into being, bring about*
5. *to make* so and so
6. *to perpetuate* a deed

> Liddell, H. G., R. Scott and H. S. Jones (LSJ). *A Greek-English Lexicon*. 9th ed., revised. Oxford: Clarendon, 1996. This is the standard Classical Greek lexicon, including coverage of the NT. The previous edition, missing only a supplement, can be accessed on the web at http://www.perseus.tufts.edu/cgi-bin/resolveform.

D. **Discussion:** Considerable discrepancy exists between the standard NT lexicons (BDAG and L&N) and LSJ. Within LSJ, the meaning *to create* is the fourth entry! Lexical entries are typically given with the most basic or common meanings first. We must also consider that LSJ covers classical Greek literature from its earliest attestation—Homer, which was still used foundationally in education in the NT era—through the NT era and past it. So, the LSJ represents a broader linguistic base for lexical entries and should be taken seriously. In this case, the first three entries for κτίζω reveal that the verb (not to mention cognate nouns) had broader social usage. So, we must ask, how would the original readers/hearers of the NT documents have understood the term κτίζω in use? By default, unless there were clear contextual indicators that would restrict meaning to God's creation of the world, the original audiences would have envisioned the formation of peoples, colonization, the founding of cities, and establishment of institutions. Literally, across the Mediterranean basin, there were hundreds and hundreds of colonies from mother cities and people groups including Athens and other Greek cities, Rome and other Italian peoples, Carthage, etc. Indeed, the available inscription data aptly bears this out, in which κτίζω and its cognate noun κτίστης *founder* occur over 1,000 times over a broad span of time and location—this excludes coins and literary references, which would greatly increase this number. In the *TLG* database, one finds 9500 + instances of κτίζω.

E. **Conclusion:** While there are good reasons to place relative confidence in the major NT lexicons, we still need to exercise caution. Students are well-advised to consult several lexicons for comparison. Furthermore, consulting lexicons is only the first step in careful lexical study; see §27.1 HOW TO PERFORM A WORD STUDY.

Complete WORKBOOK EXERCISES 6 and consult the ANSWER KEY & GUIDE as needed.

CASE IN POINT 6: DIVINE AGENCY AND HUMAN RESPONSE IN EPH 2:8-10

A passage to study carefully is Eph 2:8-10 (NASB95—with my formatting and notes, and one important change "for good works" is changed to "upon good works").

8a For <u>by grace</u>[1] you **have been saved** <u>through faith</u>[2];
Τῇ γὰρ χάριτι[1] **ἐστε σεσῳσμένοι** <u>διὰ πίστεως</u>[2].

[1] τῇ χάριτι	Dative of Means
[2] διὰ πίστεως	Intermediate Means

8b and that not <u>of yourselves</u>[3] it is <u>the gift of God</u>[4];
καὶ τοῦτο οὐκ <u>ἐξ ὑμῶν</u>[3], <u>θεοῦ τὸ δῶρον</u>[4].

[3] ἐξ ὑμῶν	Source
[4] θεοῦ τὸ δῶρον	Possession/Originator

9 not <u>as a result of works</u>[5] so that no one may boast.
οὐκ <u>ἐξ ἔργων</u>[5], ἵνα μή τις καυχήσηται.

[5] ἐξ ἔργων	Source with Means

10a For we are <u>His</u> workmanship,
<u>αὐτοῦ</u>[6] γάρ ἐσμεν ποίημα,

[6] αὐτοῦ	Possession/Originator

10b created <u>in Christ Jesus</u>[7] <u>upon good works</u>[8],
κτισθέντες <u>ἐν Χριστῷ Ἰησοῦ</u>[8] <u>ἐπὶ ἔργοις ἀγαθοῖς</u>[9]

[7] ἐν Χριστῷ Ἰησοῦ	Means
[8] ἐπὶ ἔργοις ἀγαθοῖς	Location (*not* Purpose)

10c which God prepared beforehand, so that we would walk <u>in them</u>[9].
οἷς προητοίμασεν ὁ θεός, ἵνα <u>ἐν αὐτοῖς</u>[9] περιπατήσωμεν.

[9] ἐν αὐτοῖς	Spatial/Manner

This passage demonstrates the use of prepositional and noun phrases to convey the truth of the salvation offered to us from God, the Source. First, we might notice that in 2:8a *you* is the subject of the passive voice verb "**have been saved.**" Who is the real actor here? This is a good example of the **divine passive.** Indeed, Paul specifies in 2:8b that what is given is *the gift of God*, with God as the genitive modifier preposed for emphasis, θεοῦ τὸ δῶρον (see §4.6.D.2).

However, there are several other critical facets to this gift of salvation. Through a dative of means construction (τῇ χάριτι), Paul emphasizes *the means by which* God saves. Our salvation is attributed to *the* grace. Notice the anaphoric article referring to previous references in 1:2 (anarthrous), 1:6-7 (arthrous) and 2:5 (anarthrous). However, there is an adverbial prepositional phrase *through faith* (διὰ πίστεως) that also provides more information about this salvation. The preposition διά with the genitive case indicates secondary or intermediate means for obtaining this salvation. Essentially Paul explains that we, *through placing our faith in Christ*, play a necessary part in the reception and experience of salvation. Our faith, however, is certainly secondary to the primary gift of God's grace. This point is driven home forcefully at 2:8b when the matter of source or origin is described. However, both our faith and the grace of God are needed in our experience of salvation.

Looking more closely at 2:8-9, we understand that Paul denies two possible misunderstandings about salvation through the use of the preposition ἐκ: its origin and its means. Paul first asserts of this salvation that it *is not of ourselves* (ἐξ ὑμῶν). The origin of salvation is rather *from God*—it is *God's* gift (θεοῦ τὸ δῶρον)—with genitival emphasis on *God*. Next in 2:9 Paul denies the misunderstanding that God's salvation might somehow be achieved through *our works* (ἐξ ἔργων). The kind of works denied as efficacious for salvation is elaborated in 2:11-18; in Paul's mind, these would have included Jewish boundary markers such as circumcision, Sabbath observance, and dietary restrictions (cf. Rom 2:14-29; 3:1; Gal 3:1-5; Col 2:16-17).

In 2:10 Paul describes in positive terms the nature of our salvation. First, we are *God's workmanship*, with emphasis on *His* via the preposed and discontinuous genitive modifier (αὐτοῦ γάρ ἐσμεν ποίημα). Second, our salvation consists in being *created* or better *founded* (like a *colony* or *people group*—cf. the verb κτίζω in LSJ versus what is found in BDAG). The prepositional phrase *in Christ Jesus* indicates the means by which God directly acts to *create* or *found* his people. The foundational location or possibly basis (but **not** purpose) is *upon good works* (ἐπὶ ἔργοις ἀγαθοῖς). I conclude against the typical view that ἐπί here with the dative conveys the notion of purpose (as all translations and BDAG 366 **defn. 16**). Rather, ἐπί most essentially conveys location *upon* (BDAG 362 **defn.1**), and so the meaning *upon good works* seems quite appropriate. In context, whose good works are these? The works would include God's in Christ, i.e., Christ's own good deeds. Also possibly included would be God's deeds of salvation as revealed in Hebrew Scripture. Importantly, in the Greco-Roman world, the concept of "founding" a colony or people group occurs with this verb κτίζω; its noun cognate κτίστης ("founder") was integrally connected to the good works of the founder, the political leader, under the purview of the gods (cf. Romulus for the Romans, or Moses for the Israelites). Paul envisions the formation of the body of believers under the headship of Jesus Christ in God's master plan of salvation.

The notion of purpose is present at the end of 2:10—"in order that we would walk *in them* [i.e. good works]." Although such good works are not the means of our salvation, Paul makes it clear that they are God's desired end for us to walk in them.

In conclusion, attending to notions of means, agency, source, etc. is critical in interpretation. In Eph 2:8-10, Paul wanted to make clear the *means*, the *agency*, the *source*, the *foundation*, and the *purpose* of our salvation. God plays a central role by supplying grace and we respond to this grace in faith. God also supplies Jesus as Messiah King, who performed good works as a foundation in order that we would walk in good works. We might describe this as God's gracious offer which is received in turn by our faithful response in living a fruitful life of good works to the praise of God (see Matt 5:16-17), and we do so out of God's abundantly given grace (2 Cor 9:8).

CHAPTER 7

7.0 VOCABULARY
7.1 ADVERBS (Ἐπιρρήματα): A FIRST LOOK
7.2 ADJECTIVES (Ἐπίθετα): AGREEMENT AND FORMATION
7.3 ADJECTIVAL FUNCTIONS AND CONSTRUCTIONS
      CHECK POINT 7.2-3 ADJECTIVE CONSTRUCTIONS
7.4 COMMON USES OF THE ARTICLE
7.5 NON-ROUTINE DIRECT AND INDIRECT VERBAL OBJECTS
7.6 OTHERWISE IDENTICAL FORMS BUT FOR THE DIFFERENT ACCENT
CASE IN POINT 7: ADVERBIAL INSIGHTS FROM GAL 4:6-9

The Apostle Paul was a master in using modification. In Galatians 4:6-9, he used eleven adverbs to help convey his point. These seemingly innocent (often little) words are important modifiers.

      Two parts of speech are introduced here: **adverbs** and **adjectives**. Fortunately, there are no new endings to be learned! Both can function as modifiers. Four uses of the adjective will be presented: **adverbial, attributive, substantive,** and **predicative**. Next, very common uses of the article are described. After this, two more verbs are introduced that use other cases besides the accusative case for their direct object. Lastly, the CASE IN POINT 7 concerning Galatians 4:6-9 demonstrates the importance of paying attention to modifiers like adverbs.

VOCABULARY 7   ADVERBS; FIRST & SECOND DECLENSION ADJECTIVES

Adverbs:

ἔτι [93]	yet, still
νῦν [145]	now, currently
πάλιν [141]	again

Adjectives: Regular Stems

ἀγαθός, -ή, -όν [101]	good, beneficial
ἄλλος, -η, -ον [154]	other; another
ἕκαστος, -η, -ον [82]	each
καλός, -ή, -όν [101]	good; beautiful; noble
πιστός, -ή, -όν [67]	faithful, believing; certain
πρῶτος, -η, -ον [155]	first; prominent

Verbs:

ἀκούω [428]	I hear; I obey (+ *acc. or gen.*)
πιστεύω [241]	I trust; I believe (+ *dat.*)

Adjectives: ε, ι, ρ Stems

ἅγιος, -α, -ον [233]	holy; devout; οἱ ἅγιοι = *saints*
δίκαιος, -α, -ον [79]	righteous, just, fair
ἕτερος, -α, -ον [97]	different; another
ἴδιος, -α, -ον [114]	one's own
Ἰουδαῖος, -α, -ον [195]	Judean, Jewish; Jew
μακάριος, -α, -ον [50]	blessed, happy, favored
νεκρός, -ά, -όν [128]	dead
πονηρός, ά, όν [78]	wicked, evil; sick

After learning vocabulary to this point, you will know 45.1% of the words in the GNT. If you are able, listen to audio recordings of VOCABULARY 7 and complete the CROSSWORD PUZZLE in the WORKBOOK EXERCISES.

NOTES ON VOCABULARY 7:

Ἀκούω can take either the accusative or genitive case for its direct object. Πιστεύω takes the dative case. Often, however, it is found with the preposition εἰς with the accusative case to mean *trust in someone*. See the extended discussion below in §7.5 NON-ROUTINE DIRECT AND INDIRECT VERBAL OBJECTS.

Adjectives are modifiers. They modify nouns. When an adjective modifies a noun, it must share that noun's gender, case, and number. Thus, in the above vocabulary, you will see three endings corresponding to masculine, feminine, and neuter endings. Adjectives will always be presented in this fashion. Notice that there are ε, ι, ρ stems among the adjectives. Will these take an ἄλφα or ἦτα in their singular endings?! Need a refresher? See §4.3 NOUNS OF THE FIRST OR "A" CLASS DECLENSION under subsection C.

Ἀγαθός *good* is to be generally distinguished from καλός *good; beautiful* in that ἀγαθός more often pertains to moral goodness in the Greek NT. However, καλός can also refer to moral goodness. Context must determine the exact nuance of each word.

Ἄλλος *other; another* and ἕτερος *different; another* can both mean *another*. Some interpreters have understood that the difference between the two lies in this subtlety: ἄλλος refers to that which is numerically distinct, whereas ἕτερος refers to that which is simply different in kind. This distinction, however, has been questioned. These adjectives may function like pronouns, and may be classed, together with ἕκαστος, as alternative or distributive pronouns (ἀντωνυμίαι δατηρίαι) (Robertson 744). Pronouns are introduced in CHAPTER 9. Ἕκαστος *each* specifies and focuses upon the individual as opposed to the whole group and may be strengthened with other adjectives; e.g. εἷς ἕκαστος *each single one* (εἷς means *one*).

Ἅγιος and δίκαιος both come from stems that form a large family of words. Each stem has a corresponding verb form (ἁγιάζω *I sanctify*; δικαιόω *I justify*) and several noun forms. The adjective is commonly made into a substantive (noun) in the expression οἱ ἅγιοι *the saints*.

Ἴδιος has the generic meaning *one's own*. Ἴδιος is marked +unique possession (as opposed to belonging to others). Thus, ἴδιος signifies one option among many to indicate possession. The pronoun supplied will depend on the subject of the clause within which it occurs; ἴδιος may be translated *my own; her own; their own*. Thus, πιστεύουσι τὸν ἴδιον θεόν is translated *They are believing their own god*.

Finally, several of these adjectives have Greek and/or English cognates that should make learning their meaning much easier: πιστός (πιστεύω *I believe*), πρῶτος (English: *proto*-logy, the study of first things), Ἰουδαῖος (*Judean*), and νεκρός (English: *necro-mancer*, one who speaks with the dead; or, *necro-sis*, death of body tissue). Importantly, the adjective Ἰουδαῖος *Jewish* often is used as a substantive in John's Gospel meaning *Jewish Officials* and not all *Jews*.

7.1 ADVERBS (Ἐπιρρήματα): A FIRST LOOK

A. **Introduction:** Adverbs mainly modify verbs. However, they can modify other adverbs. They provide more information about the time, nature, location, or any thing else pertinent to the action of the verb. In this chapter, only three adverbs are presented. These adverbs give more information about the *time* or *repetition* of the action:

ἔτι *still, yet*   νῦν *now*   πάλιν *again*

B. **Adverbs may be Substantized (Nominalized) by the Article:** A particularly interesting phenomenon in Greek is that the article can be added to an adverb to make it into a substantive or noun. Articles do that to Greek words! It also can happen with adjectives (see 7.3.B. below). Consider these examples:

ἕως τοῦ νῦν = *until the present (time)*
τὸ ἔξωθεν τοῦ ποτηρίου = *the outside of the cup*

C. **More Adverbs to Come:** Throughout the textbook, more adverbs will be presented in the vocabularies of CHAPTER 8, CHAPTER 14, and CHAPTER 15 and will be discussed at greater length in CHAPTER 22.

7.2 ADJECTIVES (Ἐπίθετα): AGREEMENT AND FORMATION

A. **Modifiers and Agreement:** Adjectives are modifiers. They modify nouns (or substantives) and verbs. *When an adjective modifies a noun, it must share all the characteristics of that noun: gender, number, case.* That is, an adjective must agree with the noun it modifies in gender, number, and case. For example,

τῷ <u>δικαίω</u> υἱῷ = *to/for the <u>righteous</u> son*
ἡ <u>ἑτέρα</u> παραβολή = *the <u>different</u> parable*

Notice that it is possible to have slightly different endings on words that still agree in gender, number, and case when an ε, ι, ρ stem adjective or noun is present. The difference is whether the noun or adjective ends in ἄλφα or ἦτα. Both are feminine.

B. **Degrees:** Adjectives show three formations of degrees: the **positive**/normal meaning (*cold*), the **comparative** (*colder*), and the **superlative** (*coldest*). These degrees show different modifying descriptions and relations. The comparative typically entails two groups with the comparative degree distinguishing some attribute on one group in relation to another: *This water is <u>colder</u> than that water*. The superlative degree typically distinguishes one group from all others as the *most* distinguished in the attribute: *This is the <u>coldest</u> water (from all other water)*. The formation and function of the comparative and superlative adjectives is given in §25.5 COMPARATIVE AND SUPERLATIVE ADJECTIVES AND ADVERBS. For now you will learn the positive degree of the 1st and 2nd Declension adjective.

C. **Positive Degree Endings:** You already know the first and second declension adjective endings. The Vocabulary gives you the nominative singular forms for the masculine, feminine, and neuter endings. This grouping of adjectives display all the masculine, feminine, and neuter endings that you have already learned depending on which noun(s) that adjective is modifying or how that adjective is being used in the sentence. There is another grouping of adjectives of the third declension that show different endings (see CHAPTER 22 VOCABULARY). For now, however, here are the first and second declension adjective endings placed onto the adjective ἀγαθός, -ή, -όν:

		Masculine	Feminine	Neuter
sg.	N	ἀγαθός	ἀγαθή	ἀγαθόν
	G	ἀγαθοῦ	ἀγαθῆς	ἀγαθοῦ
	D	ἀγαθῷ	ἀγαθῇ	ἀγαθῷ
	A	ἀγαθόν	ἀγαθήν	ἀγαθόν
pl.	N	ἀγαθοί	ἀγαθαί	ἀγαθά
	G	ἀγαθῶν	ἀγαθῶν	ἀγαθῶν
	D	ἀγαθοῖς	ἀγαθαῖς	ἀγαθοῖς
	A	ἀγαθούς	ἀγαθάς	ἀγαθά

Notice: (1) The only difference from the above endings is in the ε, ι, ρ stems in the feminine singular. Thus, the feminine singular for δίκαιος, -α, -ον is: δικαία, δικαίας, δικαίᾳ, δικαίαν. (2) The feminine forms of all adjectives are found less often than the masculine and neuter forms, with masculine and neuter forms being found four times more often.

7.3 ADJECTIVAL FUNCTIONS AND CONSTRUCTIONS

There are five major uses of the Adjective. Let's look at four of these from the simplest (acting alone like an adverb) to the most complex (forming sentences). A fifth use entails the comparative and superlative forms of the adjective that is presented in §25.5 COMPARATIVE AND SUPERLATIVE ADJECTIVES AND ADVERBS. For adjective uses, see Wallace 291-314.

A. **Adverbial Adjectives:** It might seem odd to begin with the adverbial use of adjectives, but this use is the simplest. An adjective may function like an adverb by being placed in the neuter singular form, with or without an article (but more often without). The relative position of an adverb is typically next to the verb or at the beginning at the clause in initial position; but there are exceptions (as in John 2:10 below). In VOCABULARY 7, πρῶτος, -η, -ον is the only adjective that occurs as an adverb (some 63 times). Consider these select examples:

Rom 1:8a <u>Πρῶτον</u> μὲν εὐχαριστῶ τῷ θεῷ μου διὰ Ἰησοῦ Χριστοῦ
   First indeed I give thanks to my God through Jesus Christ...

John 2:10b πᾶς ἄνθρωπος <u>πρῶτον</u> τὸν καλὸν οἶνον τίθησιν
   every person   first   the good wine   sets out [literal word order]

Some of the most common adverbial adjectives are βραχύ (*briefly*), λοιπόν (*finally*), μίκρον (*little*), μόνον (*only*), πολύ (*much*), πρῶτον (*first*), ὕστερον (*last, afterward*). See Wallace 293 and §22.5 ADVERBS: MORE ON FORMATION AND FUNCTION.

B. **Substantive Adjective:** This usage is so-called because the adjective functions like a noun, i.e. a **substantive**. Remember that a substantive is any word or phrase functioning like a noun. In the **substantive position** the adjective stands alone; that is, it does not accompany any noun. My favorite English example of substantive adjectives is the movie featuring the young Clint Eastwood, *The Good, the Bad, and the Ugly*, which are substantives *The Good (Guy), the Bad (Guy), and the Ugly (Guy)*.

1. <u>A Generic Noun to be Supplied</u>. As is suggested by the movie title, normally the adjective must be given a **generic noun** such as *one, man, guy, woman, thing* in its English translation. Just which generic noun should be used depends on the context and gender of the adjective. For example, the feminine adjective, ἡ ἀγαθή standing alone, if allowed by the context, should normally be translated *the good <u>woman</u>*. The generic *woman* is added in English since in Greek this adjective is feminine; the context would need to confirm this.

2. <u>Neuter Substantive Adjectives as Abstract Nouns</u>. Substantive adjectives that are neuter are normally to be supplied with the generic noun *thing(s)*. In fact, the neuter singular substantive adjective often suggests an abstract notion, as in 1 Cor 1:25: "The foolishness [τὸ μωρὸν] of God is wiser than people and the weakness [τὸ ἀσθενὲς] of God is stronger than people." Both "the foolishness" and "the weakness" are substantive adjectives. Although semantically the nouns ἡ μωρία *foolishness* and ἡ ἀσθένια *weakness* are roughly equivalent and used in context (μωρία in 1 Cor 1:18, 21, 23; 2:14; 3:19; ἀσθένια in 2:3), Paul's use of the substantive adjectives *generalizes the notions* of foolishness and weakness. The noun forms are more concrete and specific (see references above) and substantive adjectives more generalized. This principle is worth remembering when considering in other instances of substantive adjectives.

3. <u>Formation</u>. The substantive adjective needs no article, although it commonly has one. The two ways this use of the adjective will be found are (see Wallace 294-95):

a. article + adjective   *the...*
b. adjective   *[a]...*

4. <u>Examples</u>.

a. τὰ δίκαια	*the righteous <u>things</u>* [both are neuter]	
b. δίκαια	*righteous <u>things</u>*	
c. ἡ καλή	*the beautiful <u>woman</u>* [both are feminine]	
d. καλή	*[a] beautiful <u>woman</u>*	
e. τοῦ πονηροῦ	*of the evil <u>man</u>, <u>thing</u>,* or <u>*one*</u> [either neuter or masculine]	
f. πονηροῦ	*of an evil <u>man</u>, <u>thing</u>,* or <u>*one*</u>	

Notice: Whenever a substantive adjective is feminine, it should normally be translated in such a way to reflect this, usually with the word *woman*. This is particularly important because the default gender for a Greek writer was masculine. An author who refers to a group comprised of both males and females would have used a masculine adjective. Thus, οἱ δίκαιοι is to be translated *the righteous ones* instead of *the righteous men*, since women would have been normally assumed included by such a designation. Of course, context is critical.

IMAGE 7.3 AN INSCRIPTION WITH A SUBSTANTIVE ADJECTIVE

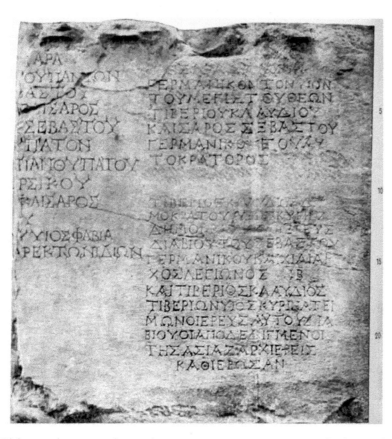

```
1   Ν[έρωνα Κλαύ]διο[ν]
    [Κα]ίσαρα Δροῦσον
    Γερμανικὸν τὸν υἱὸν
    τοῦ μεγίστου θεῶν
5   Τιβερίου Κλαυδίου
    Καίσαρος Σεβαστοῦ
    Γερμανικοῦ τοῦ αὐ-
    τοκράτορος [—]
    [—]
10  [—]
    Τιβέριος Κλαύδιος Δη-
    μοκράτου υἱὸς Κυρίνα
    Δημοκράτης ὁ ἱερεὺς
    διὰ βίου τοῦ Σεβαστοῦ
15  Γερμανικοῦ καὶ χιλίαρ-
    χος λεγιῶνος ιβ'
    καὶ Τιβέριος Κλαύδιος
    Τιβερίων υἱὸς Κυρίνα Τεί-
    μων ὁ ἱερεὺς αὐτοῦ διὰ
20  βίου οἱ ἀποδεδιγμένοι
    τῆς Ἀσίας ἀρχιερεῖς
    καθιέρωσαν.
```

This votive proclamation commemorates Nero being adopted by the emperor Claudius and heralds him as "'¹Nero Claudius ²Caesar Drusus ³Germanicus, the son ⁴of the greatest of the gods, ⁵Tiberius Claudius ⁶Caesar Augustus ⁷Germanicus, the ⁸Emperor....'"[1] In order to understand the "referents" in this (incomplete) inscription, one has to track the noun cases as well as know the imperial family names. At the start is Nero in the accusative case; but then Claudius is first introduced in the genitive case in the phrase τὸν υἱὸν τοῦ μεγίστου θεῶν *the son of the greatest of the gods*. The word τοῦ μεγίστου is a substantive adjective (in the superlative degree) meaning "the greatest one" referring to the deceased but divinized Claudius, which then expressed that the new emperor, Nero, was "the son" of such a wonderful god.

[1] The Greek text is from PHI inscriptions database at http://epigraphy.packhum.org/inscriptions/main under regions Asia Minor, Caria, Magnesia 198. The image is from G. Adolf Deissmann, *Light from the Ancient East: The New Testament Illustrated by Recently Discovered Texts of the Graeco-Roman World*, trans. L. R. M. Strachan; 2nd ed. (London: Hodder & Stoughton, 1910), 351 fig. 54.

C. **Attributive Adjective:** This **attributive use** occurs when an adjective (or equivalent modifier) ascribes an attribute to the noun it is with, as for example, *the evil man*, *the first parable*, *the whole truth*. In very common usage, the adjective is placed into the **attributive position**. In this position, the adjective usually must have an article directly in front of it and **must agree with its noun in gender, case, and number**. Both the noun and its adjective can be found in any case (voc., nom., gen., dat., and, acc.) depending on how the noun is functioning in the sentence. See Wallace 309-14. This attributive use can be observed in four constructions:

1. First Attributive Position: [article +] adjective + noun.
                              [the article is optional in this construction]

   John 20:25a οἱ ἄλλοι μαθηταί *The other disciples*

   Matt 2:12b δι ἄλλης ὁδοῦ *through another way* [without the article]

   When this construction occurs with the article and noun, I like to refer to it as involving a **Sandwich Technique, in which the article and noun are like buns surrounding the modifier inside.** This sandwich technique occurs not only with adjectives, but also adverbs, genitive case nouns, prepositional phrases, participles, or any other modifier to a noun. Sometimes there are multiple middle modifiers. Here are three examples:

   John 9:13b τόν ποτε τυφλόν *the formerly blind man* (with an adverb)

   Rom 10:3 τὴν τοῦ θεοῦ δικαιοσύνην *the righteousness of God* (with a genitive modifier)

   Phil 3:9 τὴν ἐκ θεοῦ δικαιοσύνην *the righteousness from God* (with a prep. phrase)

2. Second Attributive Position: article + noun + article + adjective.

   Of these attributive constructions, this second is **the most emphatic, since the article is repeated**, thus setting off the adjectival modifier. The type of **attributive emphasis** should be investigated in context. Wallace, commenting on the 2nd attributive construction, states, "This difference in the placement of the adjective is not one of relation, but of position and emphasis" (306). Here are some examples:

   Matt 13:8a ἄλλα δὲ ἔπεσεν ἐπὶ τὴν γῆν τὴν καλὴν
                  But other ones fell upon the good soil.

   Note also that ἄλλα *other ones* is a substantive adjective from ἄλλος,-η,-ον.

John 1:41a εὑρίσκει οὗτος πρῶτον <u>τὸν ἀδελφὸν τὸν ἴδιον</u> Σίμωνα
This one finds first <u>his own brother</u>, Simon...

Note too that πρῶτον is an adverbial adjective. Σίμωνα is appositional to *his own brother*.

3. <u>Third Attributive Position</u>: noun + article + adjective.

This position is relatively rare (about two dozen instances). Again, because the article is placed before the adjective, there is also some attributive emphasis, since the article highlights the adjectival modification.

Acts 2:20 (=LXX Joel 3:4) ... ἡμέραν κυρίου <u>τὴν μεγάλην καὶ ἐπιφανῆ</u>.
                         ... <u>the great and manifest</u> day of the Lord.

4. <u>Fourth Attributive Position</u>: noun + adjective

This position is very common. However, when the noun and adjective occur in the nominative case, it is possible that the adjective functions predicatively (see D.2. below). See Wallace 309-14.

Luke 8:15b ἐν καρδίᾳ <u>καλῇ καὶ ἀγαθῇ</u>   *in <u>a beautiful and good</u> heart*

Acts 10:22b ὑπὸ ἀγγέλου <u>ἁγίου</u>   *by a <u>holy</u> angel*

5. Finally, to illustrate rough equivalency of expressions, here are all the attributive positions as simple phrases as examples:

a. τὰς ἄλλας ἐκκλησίας	*the other churches*	[pl. accusative case]
b. τὰς ἐκκλησιας τὰς ἄλλας	*the other churches*	
c. ἐκκλησιας τὰς ἄλλας	*the other churches*	
d. ἄλλας ἐκκλησίας	*other churches*	

a. τοῦ ἑτέρου κόσμου	*of the different world*	[sg. genitive case]
b. τοῦ κόσμου τοῦ ἑτέρου	*of the different world*	
c. κόσμου τοῦ ἑτέρου	*of the different world*	
d. ἑτέρου κόσμου	*of the/a different world*	

a. ὁ δίκαιος θεός	*The righteous God*	[sg. nominative case]
b. ὁ θεός ὁ δίκαιος	*The righteous God*	
c. θεός ὁ δίκαιος	*The righteous God*	
d. δίκαιος θεός	*The/A righteous God*	

D. **Predicative Adjective:** You have already learned what a predicate nominative is in CHAPTER 5.3. In like fashion, the **predicative adjective** is put into the nominative case and is a part of the verbal assertion being made about the subject. For example, *God is good*, *The disciple is beloved*, or, *The church is holy*. Here the predicate adjectives are in a **predicate position** and are part of the verbal assertions made about the subjects. Like all adjectives, the predicate adjective must agree in gender, case, and number with the subject it describes. It is found in two situations, the first of which is much more common (see also Wallace 307-9):

1. With the Verb εἰμί.

> **Rom 7:14** ὁ νόμος πνευματικός ἐστιν· ἐγὼ δὲ σάρκινός εἰμι.
>   *The Law is spiritual; but I myself am carnal.*

> **1 Cor 3:17** ὁ γὰρ ναὸς τοῦ θεοῦ ἅγιός ἐστιν, οἵτινές ἐστε.
>   *For the temple of God is holy, which you are.*

> **1 Cor 7:14** τὰ τέκνα ὑμῶν νῦν ἐστιν ἅγια.
>   *Your children are now holy.*

2. Without εἰμί. This is also common. The appropriate form of εἰμί is lacking in the text and must be supplied by the reader. This "missing" sentence component, which can easily be supplied, is common in Greek. It's formally called **ellipsis** (see §9.4 ELLIPSIS: SUPPLYING AN IMPLIED WORD).

> **1 Cor 1:9** πιστὸς ὁ θεός. *God is faithful.*

> **2 Cor 1:3** εὐλογητὸς ὁ θεός. *God is blessed.*

> **1 Tim 1:8** καλὸς ὁ νόμος. *The Law is good.*

Pay attention to the presence of a punctuation mark (here, a period) that will alert you to the fact that a sentence is made.

3. Predicative Positions. Although it is more helpful to understand the predicate use of the adjective in relation to the presence or absence of the verb εἰμί, interpreters will often describe predicate positions. Look for the presence of the period to denote a sentence.
   a. *First Predicate Position.* Adjective + Article + Noun
   b. *Second Predicate Position.* Article + Noun + Adjective

E. **Attributive or Predicative Positions?** There are two situations, both with no article present, where both attributive and predicative possibilities exist:

   1. Adjective + Noun
   2. Noun + Adjective

In order for these to be predicate position, one would require them to be in the nominative case. Also, the presence of a major punctuation mark (period, question mark, etc.) will indicate predicative use. Finally, the sense of context will help one determine whether the adjective is attributive or predicative. For some exegetically significant passages where debate exists, see Wallace 312-14.

CHECK POINT 7.2-3	
Identify the Adjective Functions and Constructions and then provide a translation.	
τὰ <u>ἀγαθά</u>	<u>ἀγαθά</u>
<u>δίκαιός</u> ἐστιν·	<u>δίκαιος</u>
τὴν <u>καλὴν</u> γῆν (γῆ = *ground, land*)	<u>καλὴν</u>
τὴν γῆν τὴν <u>καλὴν</u> (γῆ = *ground, land*)	<u>καλὴν</u>
<u>πιστὸς</u> ὁ λόγος.	<u>πιστὸς</u>
ζητεῖτε[1] <u>πρῶτον</u> τὴν βασιλείαν τοῦ θεοῦ ([1]ζητεῖτε = *seek!*)	<u>πρῶτον</u>
οἱ δὲ <u>δίκαιοι</u> ἔρχονται εἰς ζωὴν <u>αἰώνιον</u>. (αἰώνιον is a feminine adjective = *eternal*)	<u>δίκαιοι</u> <u>αἰώνιον</u>
<u>ἕκαστος</u> <u>ἴδιον</u> ἔχει νόμον ἐκ θεοῦ	<u>ἕκαστος</u> <u>ἴδιον</u>
ANSWERS	
τὰ <u>ἀγαθά</u>	<u>ἀγαθά</u> is a substantive adjective = *the <u>good</u> <u>things</u>*
<u>δίκαιός</u> ἐστιν·	<u>δίκαιος</u> is predicative adjective with a form of εἰμί = *He is righteous/just;*
τὴν <u>καλὴν</u> γῆν (γῆ = *ground, land*)	<u>καλὴν</u> is an attributive adjective in the 1st position = *the good ground*
τὴν γῆν τὴν <u>καλὴν</u> (γῆ = *ground, land*)	<u>καλὴν</u> is an attributive adjective in the 2nd position = *the <u>good</u> ground*
<u>πιστὸς</u> ὁ λόγος.	<u>πιστὸς</u> is a predicative adjective with an implied form of εἰμί = *The word is <u>faithful</u>.*

ζητεῖτε¹ πρῶτον τὴν βασιλείαν τοῦ θεοῦ (¹ζητεῖτε = seek!)	πρῶτον is an adverbial use = *Seek first the kingdom of God!*
οἱ δὲ δίκαιοι ἔρχονται εἰς ζωὴν αἰώνιον. (αἰώνιον is a feminine adjective = *eternal*)	δίκαιοι is a substantive adjective. αἰώνιον is an attributive adjective in the 4th position = *But the righteous ones are coming into eternal life.*
ἕκαστος ἴδιον ἔχει νόμον ἐκ θεοῦ	ἕκαστος is a substantive adjective. ἴδιον is an attributive adjective modifying νόμον; it is discontinuous = *Each one has his own law from God.*

7.4 COMMON USES OF THE ARTICLE

A. **Substantival Use:** The article may be added to words to make them into nouns, or to substantize them. When this happens, the words are **conceptualized** as an entity and are thus transformed into a substantive/noun. See Wallace 231-38.

1. Adjectives. οἱ ἀγαθοί   *the good ones*

2. Prepositional Phrases. τοὺς σὺν αὐτῷ   *the ones with him*
                          τὸν ἀπ᾽ οὐρανῶν   *the One from (the) heaven(s)*

3. Genitive Modifiers. τὰ τοῦ θεοῦ   *the things of God*
                       τὰ Ἰησοῦ Χριστοῦ   *the things of Jesus Christ*

4. Adverbs. οἱ νῦν   *the present times*

5. Other Constituents, Statements, or Sentences. This may appear very odd to beginning students, but other constituents (like verbs), statements, or sentences may be grammaticalized by the article. **The article will be neuter.** Consider these examples. Just after Paul quoted Ps 68:18 that describes the Lord's *going up*, he asks this question on the meaning of the verb in the quotation:

Eph 4:9 τὸ δὲ ἀνέβη τί ἐστιν ... ;   *But, what is the "he went up" ... ?*

Later in the textbook, you will learn that infinitives can substantized, as in this example:

Phil 1:21 ἐμοὶ γὰρ <u>τὸ ζῆν</u> Χριστὸς καὶ <u>τὸ ἀποθανεῖν</u> κέρδος.
For for me <u>to live</u> [living] is Christ and <u>to die</u> [dying] is gain.

Finally, whole sentences may be identified as an grammatical entity.

Luke 19:48 καὶ οὐχ εὕρισκον <u>τὸ</u> τί ποιήσωσιν
And they were not finding <u>the</u> "what should they do"

In this example, the indirect deliberative question (*"what should they do"*) is given an article that marks it as functioning as the direct object of the verb *were not finding*.

B. **Anaphoric (Previous Reference) Use:** If in the course of a discussion a noun is referred to again, the reader may be alerted to this by the use of the article on that noun. The anaphoric use was briefly explained in §4.5.D.2.b. (See Wallace 217-20.) Thus, notice how *life* is first introduced and then immediately given an article.

John 1:4 ἐν αὐτῷ ζωὴ ἦν, καὶ <u>ἡ ζωὴ</u> ἦν τὸ φῶς τῶν ἀνθρώπων·
In him was life, and <u>this</u> life was the light of humanity.

Also, in John 2:1-2 consider how the wedding is first introduced (NASB95):

John 2:1 Καὶ τῇ ἡμέρᾳ τῇ τρίτῃ <u>γάμος</u> ἐγένετο ἐν Κανὰ τῆς Γαλιλαίας, καὶ ἦν ἡ μήτηρ τοῦ Ἰησοῦ ἐκεῖ· ² ἐκλήθη δὲ καὶ ὁ Ἰησοῦς καὶ οἱ μαθηταὶ αὐτοῦ εἰς **<u>τὸν γάμον</u>**.

John 2:1 *On the third day there was <u>a wedding</u> in Cana of Galilee, and the mother of Jesus was there; ² and both Jesus and His disciples were invited to **<u>the</u> wedding**.*

C. **Implied Family Relative:** One may observe, on occasion, the article as a place marker of family relationship, like a *son, wife,* or *mother*, in relation to a named father, husband, or son that follows in the genitive case. This genitive use is called the genitive of relationship (see §11.6 COMMON USES OF THE GENITIVE CASE).

Mark 15:47 Μαρία ἡ Ἰωσῆτος   *Mary, <u>the [mother]</u> of Justus*

Matt 1:6b Δαυὶδ δὲ ἐγέννησεν τὸν Σολομῶνα ἐκ <u>τῆς</u> τοῦ Οὐρίου
And David begat Solomon from <u>the (wife)</u> of Uriah

D. **The So-Called "Pronominal Uses":** Occasionally, the article is placed where we might expect a personal, possessive, or relative pronoun (see Wallace 211-12). However, it would be wrong to think that the article functions like a pronoun; rather, in these cases we might recognize the article as anaphoric marker, or marker of grammatical construction.

1. <u>Alternating Subjects in Narrative</u>. As an anaphoric marker in narrative material, the article with δέ indicates the alternation between two different grammatical subjects. The construction will involve the conjunction δέ (*and, but; moreover, then*) and the nominative article:

ὁ δὲ εἶπεν... = *Moreover, he said...*
οἱ δὲ εἶπον... = *Then, they said...*

For example,

Matt 27:23a <u>ὁ δὲ</u> ἔφη, Τί γαρ κακον ἐποίησεν;
But <u>he</u> said, 'Indeed, what bad thing did he do?'

Matt 27:23b <u>οἱ δὲ</u> περισσῶς ἔκραζον λέγοντες, Σταυρωθήτω.
Then louder <u>they</u> were crying out saying, 'Let him be crucified!'

Notice that ὁ δέ and οἱ δέ indicate a switch in grammatical subject in the context. In Matt 27:23a there is first a switch from crowd to Pilate (ὁ δέ = *But he*) and then there is a switch back in Matt 27:23b to the crowd (οἱ δέ = *Then ... they*).

2. <u>"Relative Pronoun-Like."</u> In English translations, sometimes the article appears to approach the meaning of a relative pronoun (*who, which, that*), as in these examples:

John 5:44b <u>τὴν</u> δόξαν <u>τὴν</u> παρὰ τοῦ μόνου θεοῦ
the glory (<u>that is</u>) from the only God [Preferred Translation]
Or, *the glory <u>which</u> is from the only God*

John 6:50a <u>ὁ</u> ἄρτος <u>ὁ</u> ἐκ τοῦ οὐρανοῦ καταβαίνων,
the bread <u>that is</u> coming down from heaven [Preferred Translation]
Or, *the bread <u>which</u> is coming down from heaven*

However, these articles are instances of the more emphatic 2nd Attributive Position using here prepositional phrases instead an adjective. In such cases, the second article is unnecessary; the article could be removed and the same meaning attend. However, the article marks **attributive emphasis** in its modification, and may be translated with *that is*.

7.5 NON-ROUTINE DIRECT AND INDIRECT VERBAL OBJECTS

A. **Introduction:** We have learned that the accusative case is normally the case of the direct object (that which is transferred in the verbal action) and that the dative case is used for the indirect object (the entity specified as receiving the action of the verb). However, specific verbs in Greek may use either the genitive or dative cases for their direct object. In this Chapter, Students are introduced to two such verbs: ἀκούω and πιστεύω. For more information on verbs that take Genitive and Dative objects, see §14.6 VERBS THAT TAKE GENITIVE, ACCUSATIVE, AND DATIVE OBJECTS. For a discussion of how to access this information in lexicons, see §14.7 LEXICAL INFORMATION ON THE CASE OF VERBAL OBJECTS.

B. **Ἀκούω:** The verb ἀκούω *I hear* may take either the accusative case or the genitive case for its direct object under specific rules. At issue is whether the object is a person or a thing. The rule is succinctly stated by BDF §173 (p.95): "The classical rule for ἀκούειν is: the person whose words are heard stands in the genitive, the thing (or person: E[ph] 4:21 αὐτὸν ἠκούσατε) about which (or whom) one hears in the accusative." However, in NT usage, the thing may be placed in the accusative or genitive. Also, the person *from* whom something is heard may be provided by the prepositions παρά, ἀπό, ἐκ, or διά. Also, the thing *about* which something is heard may be provided by the preposition περί. These rules are explained below.

1. "Thing" in Accusative or Genitive. With the verb ἀκούω, the object can be placed into either the genitive or accusative if the object is a thing. For example, Matt 7:24 uses the accusative but Luke 6:47 the genitive. Also, in Acts, the same event is recounted once with the accusative and once with the genitive.

> **Matt 7:24a** ἀκούει μου <u>τοὺς λόγους</u> *she/he hears my <u>words</u>*
> **Luke 6:47b** ἀκούων μου <u>τῶν λόγων</u> *the one hearing my <u>words</u>*

> **Acts 9:4** ἤκουσεν <u>φωνὴν</u> *he heard <u>a voice</u>* (so also Acts 26:14)
> **Acts 22:7** ἤκουσα <u>φωνῆς</u> *I heard <u>a voice</u>*

2. Person as *Direct Source* in Genitive. A person or group of persons, if understood as the *direct source* of what is heard, is placed in the genitive case.

> **Mark 7:14** ἀκούσατέ <u>μου</u> πάντες... *You all hear <u>me</u>...!*
> **Mark 14:58** ἠκούσαμεν <u>αὐτοῦ</u> λέγοντος... *we have heard <u>him</u> saying...*

3. Person *about whom one hears* in Accusative. If a person is placed into the accusative, it renders that person the object about which something is heard, not the source of the hearing.

> **Eph 4:21** εἴ γε <u>αὐτὸν</u> ἠκούσατε... *If indeed you heard <u>about Him</u> [Jesus]...*

Notice that Paul writes to Gentile believes in Asia Minor who have not "heard Him" directly (NASB95), but "heard about Him" (ESV, NLT; NIV84 "of him").

C. **Πιστεύω:** The Verb πιστεύω *I believe* takes the dative case for its direct object. In addition to this, NT authors will use πιστεύω with prepositional phrases, especially εἰς (45x, 37 in John and 1 John) and ἐπί (13x) that is translated similarly as the dative case: *I trust in (or up-on) someone.*

> πιστεύετε τῷ κυρίῳ. *You are trusting the Lord.*
> πιστεύετε εἰς τὸν κύριον. *You are trusting in the Lord.*

However, from a discourse pragmatic perspective, the use of the prepositions represents more compositional effort (space) and cognitive processing on the part of the audiences; thus these instances are more marked and emphasize the person/object that is trusted. In support of this, Robertson (540) summarizes research on πιστεύω: "What he [Moulton] does properly accent is the use of these two prepositions by the Christian writers to show the difference between mere belief (dative with πιστεύω) and personal trust (εἰς and ἐπί)."

7.6 OTHERWISE IDENTICAL FORMS BUT FOR THE DIFFERENT ACCENT

A. **E, ι, ρ Stems:** With feminine nouns whose stem ends in ε, ι, or ρ, there might be some confusion between the feminine singular nominative and the neuter plural nominative accusative forms:

<u>Feminine sg. nom.</u>	δικαία
<u>Neuter pl. nom./acc.</u>	δίκαια

Notice the location of the acute accent. In the feminine form, the accent is held from going to the front of the word because the ἄλφα is long (ᾱ). However, the neuter plural uses a short ἄλφα, thus allowing the accent to move to the front of the word. In addition to careful attention to the accent, the context will certainly make clear whether the adjective is feminine or neuter.

B. **Identical, BUT for the Different Accent:** The two forms ἄλλα and ἀλλά look the same except for the accent. But, the first word is a form of the adjective ἄλλος *other*; the second word ἀλλά is a conjunction historically derived from ἄλλος *other*. The conjunction ἀλλά always begins the clause it is in. Also, context should leave only one viable option. Here is one place that has both forms; can you discern the difference?

> **2 Cor 1:13** οὐ γὰρ <u>ἄλλα</u> γράφομεν ὑμῖν <u>ἀλλ'</u> ἢ ἃ ἀναγινώσκετε ἢ καὶ ἐπιγινώσκετε·
> *For we do not write <u>other things</u> to you, but either what you read or also know.*

Complete WORKBOOK EXERCISES 7 and consult the ANSWER KEY & GUIDE as needed.

CASE IN POINT 7: ADVERBIAL INSIGHTS FROM GAL 4:6-9

What would you do if someone entered your church and began preaching a different gospel message, but one close to the truth? Paul found himself in this rather complicated situation; his letter to the Galatians is his impassioned response. Essentially Paul must persuade the new Galatian converts to stick with the initial gospel message that he had preached. The new message presented to them was that circumcision (i.e. removal of the male foreskin) and coming under the Jewish Law was required for new Gentile converts. Given this new message and the great disdain for circumcision among Gentiles, it is not surprising that probably many of the new Galatian Christ-followers were turning away from the Gospel and back to their pagan religion, renouncing Christ altogether!

Consider how Paul uses adverbs to describe this situation in Gal 4:6-9 (my translation):

[6] And because you are sons, God sent the Spirit of his Son into your hearts, crying "Abba, Father." [7] Therefore, **no longer** [οὐκέτι] are you a slave but a son. And if a son, then **also** [καί] an heir through God. [8] But **at that time** [τότε] **indeed** [μέν], when you did not know God, you were enslaved to the ones by nature not being gods. [9] But **now** [νῦν], after having known God, or **rather** [μᾶλλον] having been known by God, **how** [πῶς] is it that you are turning **again** [πάλιν] to the weak and destitute principles to which you want to serve **again** [πάλιν] **anew** [ἄνωθεν]? [10] You observe days, months, seasons, and years! [11] I am afraid that **perhaps** [πως] I have labored for you in vain.

Amazingly Paul uses eleven adverbs in the course of six verses. These adverbs accentuate Paul's point and serve to draw a contrast between what the Galatians are *with God* and what they are *without God*. With God they are sons, heirs, possessors of God's Spirit, and have God as Αββα *Father*, knowing God and being known by Him. However, due to the influence of this ἕτερον εὐαγγέλιον *other gospel* (1:6-7), the Galatians were reverting back to their prior state: enslaved to phony gods and attached to powerless and beggarly principles (4:9). An interesting substantive adjectival construction occurs in 4:8: *to the ones by nature not being gods* (τοῖς φύσει μὴ οὖσιν θεοῖς). Who are these ones? Paul may have in mind the pagan pantheon of deities like Zeus, Hera, Poseidon, etc. (see 1 Thess 1:9; 1 Cor 8:4-6). However, more likely in my view is that Paul makes reference to human beings masquerading as gods, preeminently in Paul's day the Roman Caesars and their deceased imperial family members.[2] On the next page, the marble pedestal with inscription (upon which was placed some statuary) illustrates this reality.[3]

---

[2] See the fascinating description of imperial cults set up honoring imperial family members as divine gods (after having died or while living) in Fernando Lozano, "*Divi Augusti* and *Theoi Sebastoi*: Roman Initiatives and Greek Answers," *The Classical Quarterly* 57 (2007): 139-52.

[3] This Image is based upon G. Adolf Deissmann, *Light from the Ancient East the New Testament Illustrated by Recently Discovered Texts of the Graeco-Roman World*, trans. L. R. M. Strachan (London: Hodder & Stoughton, 1910), 350, fig. 53. The inscription reference is *IvP* II 381 and the physical pedestal is at the Berlin Museum. The image has been enhanced.

A MARBLE PEDESTAL FROM PERGAMUM WITH "THE GOD AUGUSTUS"

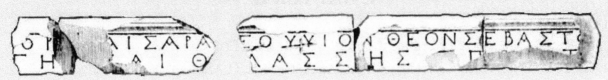

Αὐτοκράτορα Καίσαρα θεοῦ υἱὸν θεὸν Σεβαστὸν
πάσης γῆς καὶ θαλάσσης ἐπόπτην

*The Emperor, Caesar, <u>son of a god, the god Augustus</u>,
the overseer of every land and sea.*

Particularly at the end of Gal 4:9, through the repetition of adverbs, Paul emphasizes that the Galatians have returned **again** to their prior miserable state of paganism.[4] Paul was indeed "perplexed" about them (4:10-11). However, Paul's addition of the adverb πως *perhaps* in v. 11, even in the midst of depicting the potential futility of his preaching the good news to them, indicated that he believed there was still hope for the Galatians. This is why he sends the letter in the first place, in order to try to persuade them to continue adhering to "the truth of the Gospel" (ἡ ἀλήθεια τοῦ εὐαγγελίου, 2:5), just as he had himself remained true despite controversy.

Margaret L. Laird has reconstructed what the statue "consecrated to the divine-god Augustus" (*DIVO AVGVSTO SACRVM*) located at the center of the Forum in Corinth may have looked like at the time of Paul (image at the right).[5] Estimates are that as many as 25,000 to 50,000 portraits [not including coin images!] of Augustus were spread across the Roman empire, one per 1,000 to 2,000 persons; thus, Michael Peppard ventures, "it does not seem an exaggeration to call the emperor—especially Augustus—the only Empire-wide god in the Roman pantheon."[6]

---

[4] To read more about this possible reconstruction of the events, see Troy Martin, "Apostasy to Paganism: The Rhetorical Stasis of the Galatians Controversy," *Journal of Biblical Literature* 114 (1995): 437-61.

[5] Margaret L. Laird, "The Emperor in a Roman Town: The Base of the *Augustales* in the Forum at Corinth," in *Corinth in Context: Comparative Studies on Religion and Society*, ed. Steven J. Friesen *et al.*, NovTSup 134 (Boston: Brill, 2010), 67-116 at 89. Image used by permission of the author.

[6] Michael Peppard, *The Son of God in the Roman World: Divine Sonship in its Social and Political Context* (New York: Oxford University Press, 2011), 91.

CHAPTER 8

8.0 VOCABULARY

8.1 IMPERFECT TENSE (Παρατατικός): TENSE MARKERS & FORMATION

8.2 IMPERFECT TENSE (Παρατατικός): VERBAL ASPECT & TRANSLATION

8.3 AUGMENTATION: SPECIFICS RULES AND EXAMPLES

8.4 IMPERFECT TENSE FORMS OF Εἰμί

    CHECK POINT 8.1-4 PARSING IMPERFECT VERBS

8.5 CONJUNCTIONS: Γάρ, Ὅτι, AND Εἰ

CASE IN POINT 8: INSIGHTS FROM JESUS' "IMPERFECT" MINISTRY

The use of the Present and Aorist Tenses in the Indicative Mood is fairly common. We have already learned that the historic Present is discursively significant to highlight events, actions, or speech. When you see an Imperfect or Perfect Tense verb in the Greek NT, you need to take special notice. Something significant is being communicated about the verbal action. A study of the use of the Imperfect Tense in the Gospels reveals how important certain activities were in Jesus' ministry, particularly *praying* and *teaching*.

    Focal in this chapter are the endings and formation of **Imperfect Tense**. One indication of the Imperfect Tense is the addition of an ἒ ψιλόν (ε) directly to the front of the verb stem. This added ἒ ψιλόν is called an **augment** and the phenomenon is called **augmentation**. The copula εἰμί also shows Imperfect forms. Additionally, three conjunctions are presented: γάρ, ὅτι, and εἰ. The introduction of the subordinating conjunction ὅτι requires an explanation of concepts such as **direct** and **indirect discourse**, **substantiation**, and **noun clauses**. Lastly, the Vocabulary contains modifiers: time-oriented adverbs and prepositions found with the genitive or accusative cases.

VOCABULARY 8   VERBS, ADVERBS, PREPOSITIONS, AND CONJUNCTIONS

Verbs:

ἄγω [69]	I lead; I bring, carry
συνάγω [59]	I gather together
ὑπάγω [79]	I depart, go away
βάλλω [122]	I cast, throw; I place
ἐκβάλλω [81]	I throw out, expel
πάσχω [42]	I suffer
φέρω [66]	I bear, carry; I bring
προσφέρω [47]	I bring to; I offer

Adverbs:

ἤδη [60]	already; now
πρῶτον [(155)]	first; before
τότε [159]	then, at that time

Prepositions taking two cases:

κατά, κατ᾽, καθ᾽ [470]	<u>gen.</u> against; down from
	<u>acc.</u> according to
μετά, μετ᾽, μεθ᾽ [470]	<u>gen.</u> with
	<u>acc.</u> after, behind
περί [332]	<u>gen.</u> concerning; about
	<u>acc.</u> around; about
ὑπέρ [150]	<u>gen.</u> on behalf of, for
	<u>acc.</u> above; over; superior to

Conjunctions:

γάρ [1039]	For, because (*postpositive*)
ὅτι [1294]	that; because
εἰ [502]	if, whether

After learning vocabulary to this point, you will know 48.8% of the words in the GNT. This is nearly 50%! If you are able, listen to audio recordings of VOCABULARY 8 and complete the CROSSWORD PUZZLE in the WORKBOOK EXERCISES.

NOTES ON VOCABULARY 8:

Notice the compounded verb forms from ἄγω, βάλλω, and φέρω. For each of these except the compounded verb ὑπάγω, the prepositional impact is additive. See §6.2 PREPOSITIONAL COMPOUND VERBS AND WORDS.

The adverb πρῶτον is simply the neuter nominative/accusative singular form of the adjective πρῶτος, -η, -ον introduced in the previous chapter. Due to the rather high frequency of the form πρῶτον as an adverb in the Greek NT, it is presented as a separate word to be memorized.

All these prepositions share the pattern of having their object either in the genitive or accusative case. Notice that the meanings may vary considerably from one case to the next. Thus each preposition needs to be memorized with the case for the object. The two prepositions κατά and μετά may experience elision (see §2.5.C and NOTES ON VOCABULARY 6), thus sometimes having the forms κατ' or καθ' and μετ' or μεθ'.

Γάρ is postpositive, which means that it will often be found second at the beginning of a sentence. Γάρ is an extremely important independent conjunction because it is marked +continuity and +strengthening/support in relation to the preceding sentence or sentences (to be determined). Thus, the English gloss given is *For* which is nearly equivalent in meaning to *because*. Don't confuse this conjunction meaning with various English meanings of the word *for* when indicating benefit (e.g., *the boy spoke for the dog*), direction (*she headed for the house*), or purpose (*Gifts were given for the building up of the body of Christ*). Ὅτι similarly can indicate +support and be translated *because*. Whereas γάρ connects one sentence or paragraph to another, ὅτι usually functions to link clauses within a single sentence. Thus ὅτι is a **subordinating conjunction** whereas γάρ is not. Ὅτι, however, has several additional uses that are context dependent. It can also demarcate +content and have the meaning *that* when it is used to form a noun clause (i.e. I know *that...*) and when it introduces an indirect quotation (She said *that...*). Ὅτι may also need to be left untranslated in English when used to introduce a direct quotation (She said, "...."). Finally, εἰ *if, whether* is a conjunction marked +situational contingency that begins a subordinate clause or signifies an indirect question.

8.1 IMPERFECT TENSE (Παρατατικός): TENSE MARKERS & FORMATION

A. **Verb Tense Markers:** There are five possible ways to show verb tense: (1) affixing a **prefix** to the front of a verb stem; (2) **changing** the verb stem; (3) supplying a **tense indicator**; (4) supplying a **coupling vowel**; and (5) adding types of **endings**.

Prefix + Stem Change + Tense Indicator + Coupling Vowel + Endings

   (1)   (2)   (3)   (4)   (5)

Some of these elements are optional: there may not be a prefix, stem change, tense indicator, or coupling vowel, *but there will always be endings*. We have already learned that the Present Tense in the Indicative Mood is indicated by its primary endings formed with the o/ε coupling vowels. The Imperfect Tense affixes an ἒ ψιλόν augment prefix (ε) and uses its own set of endings, called the secondary endings. Otherwise, the Imperfect has the same verb stem as the Present (thus, no stem change), has no tense indicator, and uses the same o/ε coupling vowels.

B. Augmentation (adding ἐ-) on the Front of the Verb Stem:

1. <u>Tenses Augmented in the Indicative Mood</u>: One characteristic of the Imperfect Tense is pre-fixing an ἒ ψιλόν (ἐ-) directly to the front of the verb stem. The Aorist and Pluperfect Indicative also show augmentation. These tenses use the secondary tense endings. Also, augmentation does not occur outside the Indicative Mood.

2. <u>Semantics of the Augment</u>. Just what is conveyed by the augment? Traditionally, it has been thought that the augment marked verb tenses (Imperfect, Aorist, and Pluperfect) *with past time*. In this view, the augment indicated past time reference. When understood with verbal aspect, augmentation resulted in the following basic schema of translation:

Aspect	Augmented Tenses	Translation
perfective (external; complete)	**Aorist**	*I ate*
imperfective (internal; incomplete)	**Imperfect**	*I was eating*
resultative-stative (complex action/resultant state)	**Pluperfect**	*I had eaten*

More recently, some have argued that the augment marks "remoteness" or "there-ness" and thus does not primarily mark past time.[1] If the augment marks +*remoteness*, this often would refer to remote time (but not always). However, the traditional view has strong support, despite the view that originally Homer used the augment as a concrete pointer to an event to make it more salient-prominent without necessarily referring to time.[2]

3. <u>Augmentation Rules</u>. Unfortunately, augmenting the verb stem with an ἒ ψιλόν (ἐ) is not always simple. The complexities of augmentation are explained further below in §8.3 AUGMENTATION: SPECIFICS RULES AND EXAMPLES.

---

[1] On the remoteness understanding, see Constantine R. Campbell, *Verbal Aspect, the Indicative Mood, and Narrative: Soundings in the Greek of the New Testament* (Studies in Biblical Greek 13; New York: Peter Lang, 2007), 77-102; on "there-ness," see Wally V. Cirafesi, *Verbal Aspect in Synoptic Parallels: On the Method and Meaning of Divergent Tense-Form Usage in the Synoptic Passion Narratives*, Linguistic Biblical Studies 7 (Leiden: Brill, 2013), 28-37.

[2] See Egbert J. Bakker, "Similes, Augment, and the Language of Immediacy," in *Speaking Volumes: Orality and Literacy in the Greek and Roman World*, ed. Janet Watson; Mnemosyne Bibliotheca Classica Batava 218 (Leiden: Brill, 2001), 1–23 and Olav Hackstein, "The Greek of Epic," in *A Companion to the Ancient Greek Language*, ed. Egbert J. Bakker; Blackwell Companions to the Ancient World (Malden, MA: Wiley-Blackwell, 2010), 400–23 at 405. Cirafesi (*Verbal Aspect*, 35) quotes and affirms Bakker's work in support of his own non-time "there-ness" view of the augment, yet Bakker clearly understands the augment's development in Classical Greek to denote past time ("Similes," 19).

C. **The Secondary Endings and o/ε Coupling Vowels of the Imperfect Tense:** After affixing the augment to the front of the verb stem, one simply adds the Imperfect endings that are formed with the o/ε coupling vowels and the Secondary endings, which have both active and middle/passive forms.

   1. <u>Imperfect Active Endings.</u>

	sg.	pl.
First	-ο-ν*	-ο-μεν
Second	-ε-ς	-ε-τε
Third	-ε(ν)	-ο-ν*

* <u>Notice</u> that the 1st singular ending is the same as the 3rd plural ending. Context must determine how to translate a verb with this ending.

These endings are added to the stem of the verb. Imperfect Active forms for πιστεύω are:

ἐπίστευ<u>ον</u>   ἐπιστεύ<u>ομεν</u>

ἐπίστευ<u>ες</u>   ἐπιστεύ<u>ετε</u>

ἐπίστευ<u>ε</u>(ν)   ἐπίστευ<u>ον</u>

   2. <u>The Imperfect Middle/Passive Endings.</u> The middle and passive endings are identical:

	sg.	pl.
First	-ό-μην	-ό-μεθα
Second	-ου (ε-σο)*	-ε-σθε
Third	-ε-το	-ο-ντο

* <u>Notice</u> that originally the 2nd sg. ending was –σο, but for the sake of euphony (*good sound*) the σίγμα dropped, leaving the two vowels ε and o to combine into –ου.

These endings are added to the augmented stem of the verb. Here are the Imperfect Middle/Passive forms on πιστεύω.

ἐπιστευ<u>όμην</u>   ἐπιστευ<u>όμεθα</u>

ἐπιστεύ<u>ου</u>   ἐπιστεύ<u>εσθε</u>

ἐπιστεύ<u>ετο</u>   ἐπιστεύ<u>οντο</u>

<u>8.2 IMPERFECT TENSE (Παρατατικός): VERBAL ASPECT & TRANSLATION</u>

A. **Verbal Aspect:** Like the Present Tense, the Imperfect Tense expresses **imperfective** aspect: The action of the verb is viewed as internally in progress and incomplete. This tense is only found in the Indicative Mood. The augment of Imperfect Tense formation marks it for past time (or possibly simply "remoteness"). It is not surprising, then, that 90% of the occurrences of the Imperfect are in narrative. Most basically, one can translate the Imperfect Tense with the past progressive English: e.g., *I was teaching*.

B. **Translating the Imperfect Active Indicative:** Once you recognize that you have an Imperfect Tense verb, you must consider if the context of the sentence or paragraph is sufficient to determine whether or not a particular type of action (above) is involved. The past progressive may be used as an initial translation, although such a translation may not capture a particular nuance behind the Imperfect.

			Progressive Past
sg.	1	ἐπίστευον	*I was trusting.*
	2	ἐπίστευες	*You* (sg.) *were trusting.*
	3	ἐπίστευε(ν)	*He, She, or It was trusting.*
pl.	1	ἐπιστεύομεν	*We were trusting.*
	2	ἐπιστεύετε	*You* (pl.) *were trusting.*
	3	ἐπίστευον	*They were trusting.*

A more specific translation may be necessary if the context demands it. For example, the imperfect verb may carry a continuative sense (*I kept trusting*); or, more rarely a conative or attempted action (*I tried believing*), the realization being incomplete.

C. **Translating the Imperfect Middle or Passive Indicative:** First one must decide, after they have recognized this set of endings, whether they are to be translated in the middle voice or the passive voice. In the Greek NT, this choice is dependent on context. But follow this rule: *Always first try to translate the verb as a passive, if the form is the same for both.* The passive and middle voices are translated below. For considerations involved in translating the middle voice see §3.4.E.

			Progressive Past Passive	Progressive Past Middle
sg.	1	ἐπιοτευόμην	*I was being trusted.*	*I was trusting for myself.*
	2	ἐπιστεύου	*You were being trusted.*	*You were trusting for yourself.*
	3	ἐπιστεύετο	*He/she/it was being trusted.*	*She was trusting for herself.*
pl.	1	ἐπιστευόμεθα	*We were being trusted.*	*We were trusting for ourselves.*
	2	ἐπιστεύεσθε	*You were being trusted.*	*You were trusting for yourselves.*
	3	ἐπιστεύοντο	*They were being trusted.*	*They were trusting for themselves.*

D. **Common Uses of the Imperfect Tense:** Greek grammarians have described particular uses of the Imperfect Tense. Below are the most frequent uses (see Wallace 543-52):

1. Progressive. Ongoing action in the past.
>   *I was teaching them (over a period of time)....*

2. Ingressive or Inceptive. An action is begun and continued for a while.
>   *He began (and continued) teaching them....*

3. <u>Continuative</u>. An action continues.

> *He kept teaching them….*

4. <u>Customary</u>. A particular action is done regularly

> *He (customarily) taught them.…*

5. <u>Conative</u>. A particular action was desired or attempted, ***but not fulfilled***

> *He tried teaching them* or *He was attempting to teach them.*

When translating the Imperfect Tense, first try a progressive meaning in a past time frame. But, if this does not seem to fit the context, you may have a specialized, nuanced usage such as may be described above. For a thorough discussion of possible uses, see Wallace 540-53.

E. **Discourse Pragmatic Function of the Imperfect Tense:**

1. <u>One Tense Among Others</u>. As you will learn, Greek has four past tense verb formations for the Indicative Mood: the Imperfect, Aorist, Perfect, and Pluperfect. This contrasts with only one tense for Present time and one for Future time (excluding the rather rare Future Perfect). Obviously, an author had many options for how to represent past events in narrative, especially if one throws in the Historic Present, which, remember, is used to highlight subsequent unfolding significant action or speech (see §6.6 HISTORIC PRESENT (HP) AND DISCOURSE PRAGMATICS).

2. <u>Verbal Aspect, Augmentation, and Pragmatic Functions</u>. What can be said here is that, since the Imperfect Tense uniquely represents the verbal action as *imperfective*, i.e. as internal and in progress without view of beginning and ending, and is marked for past time through augmentation, its use alerts audiences to envision such *ongoing past action* performed by narrative participants. Thus, Imperfect Tense verbs may be used to slow down narrative events through more vivid, internal representation, which may serve to introduce a new scene and/or to highlight significant events. See further §13.5 DISCOURSE PRAGMATIC FUNCTIONS OF THE INDICATIVE PAST TENSES.

8.3 AUGMENTATION: SPECIFICS RULES AND EXAMPLES

A. **Complexities of Augmentation:** Augmentation (putting the ἒ ψιλόν prefix ἐ- directly to the front of the verb stem) is usually very simple. A slight problem exists, however, when the verb stem begins with a vowel. Often, when an augment (ἐ-) is added to this initial vowel, the two vowels combine and form a lengthened vowel, usually an ἦτα or ὦ μέγα (η or ω). Another tricky situation is with compound verbs. The augment sneaks behind the prepositional compound and attaches directly to the verb stem. Thus, the augment is not always easily seen. Study these possible scenarios below.

1. <u>Simple Augmentation.</u>

Augment	Verb Stem		Augmented Stem
ἐ +	πιστευ...	→	ἐπιστυε...
ἐ +	λυ...	→	ἐλυ...
ἐ +	βλεπ...	→	ἐβλεπ...
ἐ +	πάσχ...	→	ἐπάσχ...

2. <u>Augmenting Verb Stems Beginning with a Vowel.</u> If the verb stem begins with ἄλφα, ἐ ψιλόν, or ὂ μικρόν (α, ε, ο), the augment joins and causes a lengthening of the vowel. If the verb stem begins with ι, υ, η, or ω, **no visible change is seen**.

Augment	Initial Vowel		Result	Example		Imperfect Form
ἐ +	α	→	ἠ	ἄγω	→	ἦγ-ον
ἐ +	ε	→	ἠ	ἔρχομαι	→	ἠρχ-όμην
ἐ +	ο	→	ὠ	ὀφείλω	→	ὤφειλ-ον

3. <u>Augmenting Verb Stems Beginning with Monophthongs or Diphthongs.</u> These vowel combinations are also affected by augmentation. An ἰῶτα becomes an ἰῶτα subscript.

Augment	Initial vowels		Augmented	Example		Augmented Imperfect
ἐ +	αι	→	η	αἴρω	→	ἦρ-ον
ἐ +	αυ	→	ηυ	αὐξάνω	→	ηὔξαν-ον
ἐ +	ευ	→	ηυ or ευ	εὑρίσκω	→	ηὕρισκ-ον
						εὕρισκ-ον
ἐ +	οι	→	ῳ or οι	οἰκοδομέω	→	ᾠκοδόμ-ουν
						οἰκοδόμ-ουν

<u>Notice</u>: Frequently with ευ and οι, no change occurs with augmentation.

4. <u>Augmentation of Compound Verbs.</u> As indicated previously, the augment needs to "sneak" behind the preposition to join directly with the verb stem.

a. With prepositions that end with a consonant such as σύν, ἐκ, ἐξ, εἰς, and πρός the ἐ ψιλόν augment simply squeezes between the preposition and the stem. The preposition περί and the pseudo-preposition ευ- (meaning *good*) also belong in this category. For example, ἐκβάλλω is given an augment as follows:

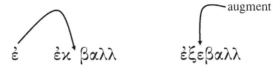

$$\dot{ε} \quad \dot{εκ} \; βαλλ \qquad \dot{εξ}εβαλλ$$

Notice that ἐκ converts to ἐξ when followed by a vowel, which is typical.

Here are some other examples:

$$\dot{ε} \;+\; προσ\text{-}φέρ\text{-}ω \qquad \rightarrow \quad προσέφερ\text{-}ον$$
$$\dot{ε} \;+\; περι\text{-}πατέ\text{-}ω \qquad \rightarrow \quad περιεπάτ\text{-}ουν$$

Here are some examples when the compounded verb stem begins with a vowel:

$$\dot{ε} \;+\; εὐ\text{-}αγγελίζω \qquad \rightarrow \quad εὐηγγέλιζ\text{-}ον$$
$$\dot{ε} \;+\; προσ\text{-}εύχομαι \qquad \rightarrow \quad προσηυχ\text{-}όμην$$
$$\dot{ε} \;+\; συν\text{-}άγω \qquad \rightarrow \quad συνῆγ\text{-}ον$$
$$\dot{ε} \;+\; εισ\text{-}έρχομαι \qquad \rightarrow \quad εἰσηρχ\text{-}όμην$$

b. When prepositions end in vowels (except for περί), it is normal for the augment to bump off these vowels. Such prepositions are ὑπό, ἀπό, ἀνά, κατά, παρά, ἐπί and διά. Then, if the verb stem begins with a vowel, the rules apply from §8.3.A.2 above. Here are several examples:

$$\dot{ε} \;+\; ἀπο\text{-}κρίνομαι \qquad \rightarrow \quad ἀπεκριν\text{-}όμην$$
$$\dot{ε} \;+\; ἐπι\text{-}γινώσκω \qquad \rightarrow \quad ἐπεγίνωσκ\text{-}ον$$
$$\dot{ε} \;+\; ἀπο\text{-}λύω \qquad \rightarrow \quad ἀπέλυ\text{-}ον$$
$$\dot{ε} \;+\; κατα\text{-}βαίνω \qquad \rightarrow \quad κατέβαιν\text{-}ον$$

Examples with verb stems beginning with a vowel augment:

$$\dot{ε} \;+\; ἀπέρχομαι \qquad \rightarrow \quad ἀπηρχ\text{-}όμην$$
$$\dot{ε} \;+\; διέρχομαι \qquad \rightarrow \quad διηρχ\text{-}όμην$$
$$\dot{ε} \;+\; ὑπάγω \qquad \rightarrow \quad ὑπῆγ\text{-}ον$$

B. Two Oddities of Augmentation to Mention Now:

1. One must not confuse the εὐ- attached to εὐαγγελίζω, which is an adverbial prefix (not unlike a preposition), and the εὐ- that is a part of the verb stem εὑρίσκω, which is not. In the first case, the augment sneaks behind ευ- and lengthens the ἄλφα as in εὐ-ηγγέλιζον. However, in the second case, the augment is added directly to the verb stem, which just happens to begin with the diphthong ευ: ηὕρισκον.

2. The augmentation of ἔχω results in εἶχον (not ἦχον).

8.4 IMPERFECT TENSE FORMS OF Εἰμί

These forms conform somewhat to the Imperfect endings just learned. Do you see the pattern? Also, remember that the verb εἰμί has no voice.

	Singular		**Plural**	
First	ἤμην	*I was*	ἦμεν or ἤμεθα	*we were*
Second	ἦς	*you were*	ἦτε	*you were*
Third	ἦν	*he/she/it was*	ἦσαν	*they were*

CHECK POINT 8.1-4

Given these verbs, first, create 3rd sg. Imperfect Tense forms, properly including the augment. Second, provide a translation.

1.	συνάγω	
2.	προσφέρω	
3.	προσεύχομαι	
4.	λέγω	
5.	ὑπάγω	
6.	ἀποκρίνομαι	
7.	εἰμί	
8.	πάσχω	
9.	ἀπολύω	
10.	ἐκβάλλω	

ANSWERS

1.	συνάγω	→ συνῆγεν *s/he was gathering together*
2.	προσφέρω	→ προσέφερεν *s/he was offering*
3.	προσεύχομαι	→ προσηύχετο *s/he was praying*
4.	λέγω	→ ἔλεγεν *s/he was saying*
5.	ὑπάγω	→ ὑπῆγεν *s/he was departing*
6.	ἀποκρίνομαι	→ ἀπεκρινέτο *s/he was answering back*
7.	εἰμί	→ ἦν *s/he was, it was,* or *there was*
8.	πάσχω	→ ἔπασχεν *s/he was suffering*
9.	ἀπολύω	→ ἀπέλυεν *s/he was releasing*
10.	ἐκβάλλω	→ ἐξέβαλλεν *s/he was casting out*

8.5 CONJUNCTIONS: Γάρ, Ὅτι, AND Εἰ

A. **Γάρ is a Postpositive Conjunction Marked +Continuity and +Support:** This postpositive conjunction is often found second in its clause although in English it is to be translated first.

1. <u>Marked +Continuity and +Support</u>. Most fundamentally, the conjunction γάρ communicates **continuity** with the previous context along with the semantic constraint of **strength** and **support**. The strengthening may take the form of explanation or logical cause, as Levinsohn (69) explains: "γάρ constrains the reader to interpret the material it introduces as *strengthening* an assertion or assumption that has been presented in or implied by the immediate context. . . . The *nature* of that strengthening, viz., explanation versus inference or cause, is deduced from the content of the material, not from the presence of γάρ" (emphasis original). Drawing on Levinsohn, Runge (54) summarizes his understanding:

   > Γάρ introduces explanatory material that strengthens or supports what precedes. This may consist of a single clause, or it may be a longer digression. Although the strengthening material is important to the discourse, it does not advance the argument or story. Instead, it supports what precedes by providing background or detail that is needed to understand what follows. Plots or arguments that are resumed after the supporting material are typically introduced using οὖν, whereas new lines of argument are signaled by δέ.

   Thus, the statement with γάρ strengthens the preceding material by providing background explanation or logical ground or support. See Wallace 673-74.

2. <u>Tracking the Support in the Argument</u>. To illustrate points above, let us look at Paul's argument in **Rom 2:1-2:**

   2:1a *Wherefore (διό) you are defenseless, O every person who judges;*
   2:1b *For (γάρ) by that which you judge others, you condemn yourself,*
   2:1c *For (γάρ) you, the one who judges, are doing the same things.*
   2:2 *Moreover (δέ), we know that the judgment of God is according to truth upon those doing such things as these.*

   Here in Rom 2:1 two clauses introduced with γάρ are used to provide support for the preceding statement. In fact, they build upon one another adding strength to the initial statement. The first γάρ substantiates the claim of 2:1a that everyone who judges is defenseless. Why? Because they are self-condemned. The second γάρ provides the basis for the first substantiation. They are self-condemned. Why? Because they do the same things. The next development of the argument is indicated in 2:2 by the use of δέ, here translated "Moreover." Thus, one must pay careful attention to the use of γάρ.

B. **Ὅτι:** This conjunction begins a subordinate clause and is generally the first word in the clause. It has five main uses (for these and other uses, see Wallace 453-61):

1. <u>Substantiation or Support</u>. Like γάρ the conjunction ὅτι can be used to indicate support for the previous statement. In this usage, the ὅτι clause may be set off by a comma and is best translated *because*. For example,

> οἱ ἄνθρωποι προσήρχοντο τῷ Ἰησοῦ, <u>ὅτι</u> ἔλεγε τὴν ἀλήθειαν.

> *The people were coming to Jesus, <u>because</u> he was speaking the truth.*
> **[statement]**   **[support** or **reason]**

2. <u>Direct Discourse with Verbs of Saying/Writing</u>.

   a. *Verbs of Saying/Writing.* Ὅτι may or may not be found after verbs of saying or writing: (*I speak, I teach*, I write, etc.) to mark the beginning of a direct quote, i.e. what was actually said by someone. This is often called **direct discourse**. However, ὅτι is not translated into English, since this is not English idiom: *He said, "I am sick."* or *You said, "There he is!"* In Greek the ὅτι would be located after *said,* but would be left untranslated into English. Consider this Greek sentence:

   > λέγει ὅτι Ἡ βασιλεία τοῦ οὐρανοῦ ἐγγίζει.
   > *He is saying, "The kingdom of heaven is near."*

   The ὅτι begins the direct discourse. When so used, this is called ὅτι *recitativum* or recitative ὅτι.

   b. *Recitative ὅτι: Semantics and Pragmatics.* Levinsohn (ch.16) has been interested in describing the discourse pragmatic function of ὅτι in narrative with verbs of saying. His conclusions are that in John and Luke-Acts such explicit use of ὅτι occurs at the culmination of a unit or sub-unit, i.e., the ὅτι will "signal that the quotation it introduces culminates an argument" (269). He also notes that in Luke's and John's Gospel the statement Ἀμὴν ἀμὴν λέγω ὑμῖν/σοι *truly, truly I say to you*, when followed by ὅτι, is used to explicate previous teaching.[3] From a semantic and marked prominence perspective, I would maintain that recitative ὅτι is a more marked construction than not having ὅτι; thus fittingly and pragmatically, ὅτι may be used to highlight previous teaching or direct quotation that would culminate argumentation or (sub-)units. However, these pragmatic, contextual functions are not inherent to the semantics of the

---

[3] See also Stephen H. Levinsohn, "Ὅτι Recitativum in John's Gospel: A Stylistic or a Pragmatic Device?," *Work Papers of the Summer Institute of Linguistics, University of North Dakota Session 43* (1999): 1-14. Online: http://www.und.edu/dept/linguistics/wp/1999Levinsohn.PDF.

construction. *Rather, it is simply enough to say that recitative* ὅτι *is marked* +prominence *for introducing direct speech.* I would tentatively suggest a translation of *this:* prior to the start of the speech quotation, since *this:* sets off and anticipates what follows formally in English. For example, Mark 3:11-12 occurs near the end of a unit (which ends formally in 3:12; NASB95; ESV, NIV, etc.) in a generalizing statement.

Mark 3:11-12 καὶ τὰ πνεύματα τὰ ἀκάθαρτα, ὅταν αὐτὸν ἐθεώρουν, προσ-έπιπτον αὐτῷ καὶ ἔκραζον λέγοντα <u>ὅτι</u> Σὺ εἶ ὁ υἱὸς τοῦ θεοῦ. ¹² καὶ πολλὰ ἐπετίμα αὐτοῖς ἵνα μὴ αὐτὸν φανερὸν ποιήσωσιν.

> *¹¹ And the unclean spirits, whenever they were seeing him, were falling down before him and were crying out saying* <u>this:</u> *"You yourself are the Son of God!" ¹² And many times he was rebuking them, in order that they would not make him known.*

c. *Direct Quotation Conventions.* In this textbook direct quotations will normally begin with a capital letter (as in the Greek NT UBS 3/4 eds.). Thus, when you see this combination—a verb of saying + ὅτι + a capitalized letter—then you will know not to translate ὅτι and to provide quotation marks to indicate direct discourse; but then also you know to consider what is the contextual significance of ὅτι.

3. <u>Indirect Discourse with Verbs of Saying.</u> When what someone said is not quoted directly, but told indirectly, this is called **Indirect Discourse** or **Indirect Statement**. In this usage ὅτι is translated as *that*. For example, "He said *that* he was going to the temple." What was the man's actual statement? "I am going to the temple." Consider this example:

ὁ Ἰησοῦς ἔλεγε ὅτι ὁ Πέτρος <u>προσεύχεται</u>.
Jesus was saying that Peter <u>was praying</u>.

What was actually said by Jesus was *Peter is praying*, using the Present Tense. Notice that Greek differs at this point from English: Greek retains the <u>original verb tense</u> of what was said. Thus, προσεύχεται (Present Tense) retains the tense of what was originally said, namely, *Peter is praying*. However, when translating Greek indirect discourse into English idiom, we need to convert the tense to past time, "Peter was praying." Admittedly, this may be a little confusing. However, after some drills and practice, this will become easier.

4. <u>Verbal Complements or Content Clauses with Verbs of hearing, knowing, believing, hoping, etc..</u> This construction is very similar to Indirect Discourse, except that, instead of a verb of saying, one finds verbs of knowing, thinking, believing, etc. or their equivalents. **Here ὅτι functions to give the actual *content* to what was thought, believed, etc.** This is also called a **noun clause**. For example, *Jesus knew <u>that</u> [ὅτι] the Pharisees were plot-*

ting to arrest him. The key is to look for verbs of knowing, believing in conjunction with ὅτι where the "content" is given.

5. <u>Appositional Clauses or the Target of Forward Pointing Demonstrative Pronouns.</u> This usage is very similar to indirect discourse and noun clauses in that ὅτι is used as the *content* of a previous noun or demonstrative pronoun (e.g., "*(in) this...*" or "*that...*") that prepares for and highlights what follows, which is introduced by the ὅτι. The initial noun or demonstrative pronoun effectively introduces and sets off the actual content target to which it points (Runge, §3.3.2). One can translate the ὅτι as *that (is)* or *namely*. The example below illustrates the similarity of the appositional ὅτι and the complementary ὅτι, since in Luke 10:20, the each construction effectively provides the content of the same verb (*rejoice*)

Luke 10:20a πλὴν <u>ἐν τούτῳ</u> μὴ χαίρετε <u>ὅτι</u> τὰ πνεύματα ὑμῖν ὑποτάσσεται,
  However, <u>in this</u> do not rejoice, <u>namely that</u> the spirits obey you,

Luke 10:20b χαίρετε δὲ <u>ὅτι</u> τὰ ὀνόματα ὑμῶν ἐγγέγραπται ἐν τοῖς οὐρανοῖς.
  but rejoice <u>that</u> your names have been written in the heavens.

It must be stated that the appositional target introduced by the ὅτι is emphasized. In the example above, the emphasis is one of contrast. Since this usage features demonstrative pronouns introduced in Ch.12, it will be more fully explained in §12.5 Demonstrative Pronouns.

6. <u>Summary of ὅτι.</u> These are the following ways that ὅτι is used:

   a. *Substantiation.* When ὅτι does not come after a verb of saying and is not followed by a capital letter, and when the translation *because* fits best, you are probably looking at substantiation. See Wallace 460-61.

   b. *Direct Statement.* Ὅτι, after a verb of saying and followed by a capital letter, indicates direct discourse and <u>should not be translated</u>. See Wallace 454-55.

   c. *Indirect Statement.* Ὅτι, after a verb of saying with no capital letter, indicates indirect discourse and should be translated as *that*. Watch out for the tense when translating this clause into proper English. See Wallace 456-58.

   d. *Verbal Complement or Content Clause.* Ὅτι after a verb of hearing, knowing, believing, etc. is translated as *that* and provides the actual content of what was known or believed. See Wallace 458-60.

   e. *Recitative ὅτι.* Since ὅτι is not required for direct quotation, its presence indicates a more marked construction, thus setting off and highlighting the direct quotation. Students should consider the broader discursive significance of such to further explicate or to bring to culmination argumentation in (sub-)units.

f. *Appositional Clause or the Target of Forward Pointing Demonstrative Pronouns*. In this usage, the student will see a noun or a demonstrative pronoun (see §12.5 DEMONSTRATIVE PRONOUNS) that will initially introduce and point forward to the clause begun by the ὅτι. This ὅτι clause is emphasized.

C. **Εἰ:** This conjunction begins a subordinate clause and is the first word in the clause. It is marked +situational contingency. It has two main functions: to state the supposition in a conditional sentence and to mark an indirect question. NOTE: Don't confuse εἰ with the verb form εἶ (2nd sg. form of εἰμί).

1. <u>Conditional Sentences</u>. It is the "if" part or supposition (i.e. the protasis) of a conditional sentence. Conditional sentences contain a supposition ("if") and a conclusion that stands in causal relationship with the supposition. For example,

Mark 14:29 ὁ δὲ Πέτρος ἔφη αὐτῷ· <u>εἰ</u> καὶ πάντες σκανδαλισθήσονται, ἀλλ᾽ οὐκ ἐγώ.
Additionally, Peter was saying to him, "Even <u>if</u> they all fall away, I, on the contrary, won't!"

This verse is interesting at many levels grammatically and pragmatically—the use of the imperfect verb (*was saying*), the adverbial-additive use of καί *even*, the inclusive scope *they all*, the contrast-corrective ἀλλ᾽ *on the contrary*, and the final word ἐγώ *I* all contribute to the rhetorical impact of the verse. But the condition or supposition that Peter vividly and emphatically describes is introduced with εἰ. To read more on conditional sentences and their rich complexity, see CHAPTER 26.

2. <u>Indirect Questions</u>. When the context would indicate, εἰ introduces an indirect question. For example, *I asked <u>whether</u> he would give an extension on this assignment*. The original or direct question was, *Would you give me an extension on this assignment?* Consider also this example that contains two instances of this meaning:

Mark 15:44: ὁ δὲ Πιλᾶτος ἐθαύμασεν <u>εἰ</u> ἤδη τέθνηκεν καὶ προσκαλεσάμενος τὸν κεντυρίωνα ἐπηρώτησεν αὐτὸν <u>εἰ</u> πάλαι ἀπέθανεν·
But Pilate wondered <u>whether</u> he had already died and, after calling the centurian, he asked him <u>if</u> he died just now.

The original questions were *Has he died already?* and *Did he die just now?*

Complete WORKBOOK EXERCISES 8 and consult the ANSWER KEY & GUIDE as needed.

CASE IN POINT 8: INSIGHTS FROM JESUS' "IMPERFECT" MINISTRY

Observing the Imperfect Tense in the Gospels reveals how important certain activities were in Jesus' ministry, particularly *praying* and *teaching*. For descriptions of Jesus' teaching, see especially Mark 2:13; 4:2; 5:2, Matt 13:54, and John 7:14. Let's take a closer look at some examples of Jesus' praying from the Gospels of Mark and Luke (NASB95, underlining and insertions mine).

Mark 1:35 In the early morning, while it was still dark, Jesus got up, left *the house*, and went away to a secluded place, and was praying [προσηύχετο] there.

Mark 14:35 And He went a little beyond *them*, and fell [ἔπιπτεν—imperfect] to the ground and *began* to pray [προσηύχετο] that if it were possible, the hour might pass Him by.

Luke 22:44 And being in agony He was praying [προσηύχετο] very fervently; and His sweat became like drops of blood, falling down upon the ground.

In Mark 1:35 the progressive nature of Jesus' prayer is emphasized: He was praying at that location for some time. Does the Imperfect tell us exactly how long? Not specifically, but we can surmise that it was longer than 5 minutes (!). Notice also the time of day (early morning; still dark) and the setting (a secluded spot). Also, we need to consider that Jesus did this regularly. Mark has not told us every time Jesus prayed. However, we should notice that this occurs early in the Gospel of Mark, as if Mark wants us to understand that *this is the sort of thing that Jesus did on a regular basis* (hence, *customary*). We can learn from Jesus, despite or in view of our busy and hectic schedules, to value prayerful fellowship with our Heavenly Father as much as He did.

With regard to Mark 14:35, notice that Mark records the event vividly, from an imperfective, internal perspective by placing the verbs "fall" and "pray" in the Imperfect Tense. By doing this, he foregrounds the event (see the discussion at §13.5 DISCOURSE PRAGMATIC FUNCTIONS OF THE INDICATIVE PAST TENSES). The NASB95 does not properly translate these verbs to reflect the imperfective aspect. First, rather than "fell," perhaps a better translation would be to preserve a progressive sense, "He was falling on his knees…." Second, for the second verb, notice that the NASB95 renders the Imperfect Tense as an ingressive imperfect "He *began* to pray…." However, better translation options would be, "He began praying…." or simply to retain a progressive sense: "He was praying…." We should not miss the sense that Jesus is repeatedly praying over this matter of his impending death.

It is worth comparing Mark 14:35 with the parallel passage in Luke 22:44. Interestingly, Luke records Jesus praying much more often than in the other Gospels; to learn more, simply perform a word search on the verb προσεύχομαι *I pray*. Here, Luke makes the agonizing nature of Jesus' praying more evident by prefacing his praying with "being in agony." Also, Luke adds afterwards the adverbial statement "very fervently." Next Luke provides details of Jesus' physical state with his sweat becoming as blood dropping on the ground. Such vivid description corresponds to a virtue of narrative referred to in the ancient rhetorical handbooks, ἔκφρασις *description*. One ancient rhetorical educator, Aelius Theon, who lived in the first century AD, describes rhetorical exercises or *progymnasmata* (προγυμνάσματα). One of these exercises was ἔκφρασις, which he defines as "a descriptive composition that brings what is being disclosed vividly before the eyes" (Theon, *Prog.* 11). Both Mark and Luke accomplish this in their descriptions; Mark by relating Jesus' falling and praying (Imperfect Tense) and Luke likewise also by additional comments concerning Jesus' agony, fervency, and sweating. So, at this occasion, we vividly see Jesus' struggle to remain faithful to His calling as the Messiah King of the Jews.

As the King of a subjugated people, Jesus was about to be paraded through the crowds with his crime written on a placard and eventually placed on the cross. John's Gospel indicates that the charge was written in three languages: Hebrew, Latin, and Greek (19:19-20). The penalty was crucifixion. Ida Östenberg, in her treatment of the Roman Triumphal parade, connects Jesus' receiving the title of his crime (Grk. τίτλον; Lat. *titulus*) with Roman practice:

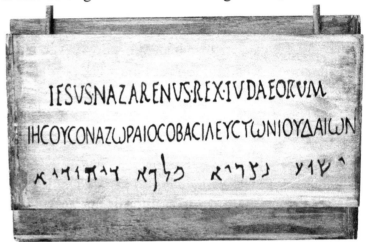

> Crime and penalty were closely linked and both were on display. The public announcement of the crimes that justified the punishment formed an important part of the processional exhibition and added to the humiliation of the captives. The crimes were announced by way of written placards or they were shown by imagery, closely attached to the prisoners. Outside the triumphal context too, placards stating their crimes preceded criminals led to their execution [Suet. *Cal.* 32.2, *Dom.* 10.1; Dio Cass. 54.3.6–7; John 19:19]. This practice forms a clear parallel to the emphatic announcement of the captives' misdeeds in the triumph that further strengthens the interpretation of the leading and killing of captives as a public punishment.[4]

The Apostle Paul did not miss this connection, since he understood that God was triumphing in Christ (2 Cor 2:14-16) and that Christ has actually triumphed over the rulers and authorities by his cross, disarming and making a public display of them (Col 2:14-15). Such is the nature of Jesus' imperfect ministry.

---

[4] Ida Östenberg, *Staging the World: Spoils, Captives, and Representations in the Roman Triumphal Procession*, Oxford Studies in Ancient Culture and Representation (Oxford; New York: Oxford University Press, 2009), 163. This titulus is based upon Paul L. Maier's reconstruction of the hand writing in first century Israel ("The Inscription of the Cross of Jesus of Nazareth," *Hermes* 124 (1996): 58-75 at 70.

CHAPTER 9

9.0 VOCABULARY
9.1 INTRODUCTION TO PRONOUNS (Ἀντωνυμίαι)
9.2 PERSONAL PRONOUNS (Πρωτότυποι ἢ Προσωπικαὶ Ἀντωνυμίαι)
9.3 RELATIVE PRONOUNS (Ἀναφορικαὶ Ἀντωνυμίαι)
9.4 ELLIPSIS (Ἔλλειψις): SUPPLYING AN IMPLIED WORD
9.5 MARKING OR DIAGRAMMING SUBORDINATE CLAUSES AND IMPLIED ITEMS
CASE IN POINT 9: THE DIMENSIONS OF HUMAN SINFULNESS IN EPH 2:1-3

What are the causes of human sin? How have we all been affected by it? How has God rectified the situation? A careful look at Paul's use of relative and personal pronouns in Eph 2:1-3 will help us answer these questions.

This chapter introduces the student to **pronouns**. Two very important types of pronouns are covered: **Personal** and **Relative**. The relative pronoun endings mimic the article and adjective endings you already know. The personal pronoun endings are also familiar. Next, the common grammatical phenomenon **ellipsis** is explained. The chapter ends with a description of how to **diagram subordinate clauses**, **apposition**, and **ellipsis**. The vocabulary list includes more Second Declension nouns.

VOCABULARY 9 PERSONAL & RELATIVE PRONOUNS SECOND DECLENSION NOUNS

Personal Pronouns:

ἐγώ [1805]	I	
ἡμεῖς [865]	we	
κἀγώ [83]	and I; *or* I also	
σύ [1067]	you (sg.)	
ὑμεῖς [1840]	you (pl.)	
αὐτός, -ή, -ό [5569]	he, she, it	
αὐτοί, -αί, -ά	they	

Relative Pronoun:

ὅς, ἥ, ὅ [1407]	who, which	

More Second Declension Nouns:

ὁ ὄχλος [174]	crowd, multitude (of people)
τὸ ἔργον [169]	work, activity; accomplishment
ὁ λαός [142]	people, populace
ὁ δοῦλος [126]	slave; servant
ὁ θάνατος [120]	death
ὁ οἶκος [113]	house, dwelling; family
ὁ ὀφθαλμός [100]	eye
ὁ ἄρτος [174]	bread, loaf; food
ὁ τόπος [174]	place, position
ὁ καιρός [174]	season, time; opportunity

After learning vocabulary to this point, you will know 59% of the words in the GNT. If you are able, listen to audio recordings of VOCABULARY 9 and complete the CROSSWORD PUZZLE in the WORKBOOK EXERCISES.

NOTES ON VOCABULARY 9:

A few words should sound familiar to you based on English words: Sigmund Freud's *ego* from which we have <u>ego</u>-maniac; but also <u>ergo</u>-nomics or en-<u>ergy</u>, <u>ophthalmo</u>-logist, <u>topo</u>-graphy.

Κἀγώ (*And I...* or *I also*) is a **crasis** (i.e. two words joined together) of καί and ἐγώ. The apostrophe mark (’) is called a *coronis* and signifies the loss of one or more letters.

One must be careful to distinguish between the two pronouns ἡμεῖς (*we*) and ὑμεῖς (*you*). One easy way to remember the difference is to think of the initial ὖ ψιλόν as a "u" standing for *you*. Early copyists of the GNT regularly confused or switched these two pronouns. We observe many textual variants within the NT epistles (e.g. 1 John 1:4).

9.1 INTRODUCTION TO PRONOUNS (Ἀντωνυμίαι)

A. **Pronouns in General:** Pronouns are words that are used in the place of nouns. Greek and English have many different types of pronouns! Of course, not all of these types are commonly used. Robertson helpfully explains, "As a matter of fact all pronouns fall into two classes, Deictic (δεικτικαί) and Anaphoric (ἀναφορικαί). They either 'point out' or they 'refer to' a substantive" (676). More pronouns are covered in §12.5 DEMONSTRATIVE PRONOUNS, §14.1 INTERROGATIVE AND INDEFINITE PRONOUNS, and §19.1-4. But in this chapter, we cover two very common pronouns: Personal and Relative. Consider these sentences that place subordinate clauses within brackets:

    1. Jesus healed the blind man, [<u>whom</u> *he* brought to the temple.]
    2. [¹After John, [²<u>who</u> was at the Jordan²], baptized *him*,¹] Jesus went into the desert.

In the example, there are four pronouns: *he, him* are personal pronouns and <u>whom</u>, <u>who</u> are relative pronouns, which are placed within brackets […], since they form subordinate clauses.

B. **Antecedent, Postcedent,** or **Implied Referents:** To which person does each pronoun refer? Sometimes one must disambiguate (i.e., determine among options) pronominal referents. There are three possibilities: a referent may 1) come before the pronoun, i.e. be **antecedent** (Latin *antecedens*, "that which comes before"); 2) come after the pronoun, i.e. be **postcedent** (Latin *postcedens*, "that which comes after"); or, 3) be **implied** from the context. Given the examples above, we can disambiguate the referents by using arrows.

    1. Jesus healed the blind man, [<u>whom</u> *he* brought to the temple.]

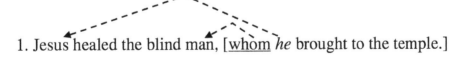

    2. After John, [<u>who</u> was at the Jordan], baptized *him*, Jesus went into the desert.

The pronouns *whom, he*, and *whom* have antecedents. The pronoun *him*, however, has a postcedent *Jesus*, i.e. *him* points forward to the referent *Jesus*.

C. **Agreement in Gender and Number:** In Greek, *a pronoun and its antecedent must agree in gender and number.* Thus, if a noun is feminine singular, a pronoun used in its place would also have to be feminine singular in form. English would do the same if it had gender. However, English pronouns only show agreement in number. Consider this example:

> 3. Tom and I went fishing. *We* caught nothing.

Here, the pronoun *we* agrees in number with the nouns it refers to, *Tom and I* (a compound subject—thus plural). Since Greek nouns have both gender and number, a pronoun and its antecedent must agree in both gender and number.

D. **Case is Context Dependent:** *The case of the pronoun is typically determined by how the pronoun is functioning within its own sentence or clause.* (But see on "attraction" in §9.3.D. below.) For example, in sentence 2. above, *him* is the direct object (accusative case), but the pronoun's referent *Jesus* is subject (nominative case). Not infrequently, however, especially with relative pronouns, a pronoun and its referent happen to be in the same case, as would be true with the other pronouns in sentences 1-3 above. However, this is context dependent.

E. **Anaphora (Ἀναφορά) and Kataphora (Καταφορά):** Students may encounter these terms. Anaphora can be used generally as the phenomenon of one element referencing another, as in pronouns to their referents, as is found in the quotation above. More specifically, anaphora identifies the previous (lit. upward born) referent, i.e., the **antecedent**. Kataphora, conversely, specifies the subsequent (lit. down born) referent, i.e., the **postcedent**.

9.2 PERSONAL PRONOUNS (Πρωτότυποι ἢ Προσωπικαὶ Ἀντωνυμίαι)

A. **English Personal Pronouns:** English personal pronouns are broken down into person, number, case and gender (only in the 3rd person):

	sg.	pl.
1st:	I, my, me	we, our, us
2nd:	you, your(s)	you, your(s)
3rd:	he, his, him	they, their, them
	she, hers, her	
	it, its	

<u>Notice</u>: (1) Case function is most easily discerned in the English language in its pronouns. *My, our, your(s), his, hers, its* are all in the possessive (genitive) case. This parallels Greek usage. (2) Gender distinction in English is made in the 3rd person singular *only*; in Greek gender distinction applies also to the plural forms.

B. Greek Forms of the 1st and 2nd Person Personal Pronouns:

a. 1st Person

	sg.				pl.	
nom.	ἐγώ	*I*		nom.	ἡμεῖς	*we*
gen.	ἐμού (μου)	*my*		gen.	ἡμῶν	*our*
dat.	ἐμοί (μοι)	*to me /for me*		dat.	ἡμῖν	*to us /for us*
acc.	ἐμέ (με)	*me*		acc.	ἡμᾶς	*us*

b. 2nd Person

	sg.				pl.	
nom.	σύ	*you*		nom.	ὑμεῖς	*you*
gen.	σού (σου)	*your*		gen.	ὑμῶν	*your*
dat.	σοί (σοι)	*to you /for you*		dat.	ὑμῖν	*to you /for you*
acc.	σέ (σε)	*you*		acc.	ὑμᾶς	*you*

Notice: (1) Two forms exist in the singular genitive, dative, and accusative. **The first accented forms indicate emphasis or contrast** (see σύ BDAG 950.b.α.). However, this emphatic form is the normal form used in prepositional phrases, which may indicate that the pronoun is made prominent due to the modification with which it participates. (2) The plural forms all begin with a rough breathing mark.

C. Greek Forms of the 3rd Person Personal Pronoun αὐτός, -ή, -ό: These forms basically use the 1st and 2nd Second declension endings or article endings:

	Masc.	Fem.	Neut.	Translations		
sg. nom.	αὐτός	αὐτή	αὐτό	*he*	*she*	*it*
gen.	αὐτοῦ	αὐτῆς	αὐτοῦ	*his*	*hers*	*its*
dat.	αὐτῷ	αὐτῇ	αὐτῷ	*to him*	*to her*	*to it*
acc.	αὐτόν	αὐτήν	αὐτό	*him*	*her*	*it*
pl. nom.	αὐτοί	αὐταί	αὐτά	*they*	*they*	*they*
gen.	αὐτῶν	αὐτῶν	αὐτῶν	*their*	*their*	*their*
dat.	αὐτοῖς	αὐταῖς	αὐτοῖς	*to them*	*to them*	*to them*
acc.	αὐτούς	αὐτάς	αὐτά	*them*	*them*	*them*

Notice that the breathing mark is smooth over the first syllable.

D. **Uses of the Personal Pronouns in a Sentence:** In general, the personal pronoun functions the same as our English personal pronoun. Below are provided the basic noun functions in the sentence (subject, possessive, indirect and direct object). *When provided as the subject with a verb the personal pronoun is emphatic.* Additional special functions of the 3rd person personal pronoun are covered in §20.3 INTENSIVE AND IDENTICAL USES OF Αὐτός.

1. As Emphatic Subject:

 a. The nominative pronoun forms are unnecessary since the verb supplies a default subject. **Therefore, the nominative forms are emphatic when with a verb.** In terms of emphatic pronouns, the first definition for αὐτός, ἡ, ὁ is as an "intensive marker, setting an item off fr. everything else through emphasis and contrast, self." Richard A. Young is correct to state: "Personal pronouns functioning as the subject are always somewhat emphatic since the information is already carried by the verb ending. It is the redundancy, not the placement of the pronoun, that triggers emphasis."[1] Stephen Levinsohn also indicates, "So-called 'emphatic' pronouns are often used to give thematic prominence to their referent (see Lowe 1998:36)."[2] Just what kind of emphasis must be determined from the context. It may involve contrast: *You did this! But, he did not!* It may involve topical prominence given to persons as acting/responsible agents.

 Mark 5:40a καὶ κατεγέλων αὐτοῦ. <u>αὐτὸς</u> δὲ ἐκβαλὼν πάντας παραλαμβάνει τὸν πατέρα τοῦ παιδίου καὶ τὴν μητέρα...

   And they began laughing at Him. But, <u>he himself</u>, after putting them all out, took along the child's father and mother….

 Here one detects contrastive as well as a focus on Jesus' agency.

 Mark 3:13a Καὶ ἀναβαίνει εἰς τὸ ὄρος καὶ προσκαλεῖται οὓς ἤθελεν <u>αὐτός</u>,...

   And He goes up into the mountain and summons those whom <u>He Himself</u> wanted,….

---

[1] Richard A. Young. *Intermediate New Testament Greek: A Linguistic and Exegetical Approach* (Nashville, TN: Broadman & Holman, 1994), 215. Cynthia Long Westfall likewise argues, "The use of pronouns in the nominative often is not necessary. When a pronoun is not needed to disambiguate the participants, it is emphatic…. The use of third person pronouns is often more necessary to disambiguate. However, the use of αὐτός as an intensive pronoun, and the unnecessary use of the third person pronoun are also emphatic" ("A Method for the Analysis of Prominence in Hellenistic Greek," in *The Linguist as Pedagogue: Trends in the Teaching and Linguistic Analysis of the Greek New Testament*, ed. Stanley E. Porter and Matthew Brook O'Donnell, New Testament Monographs 11 (Sheffield: Sheffield Phoenix, 2009), 75–94 at 89. Cf. Stanley E. Porter, *Idioms of the Greek New Testament*, 2nd ed. (Sheffield: Sheffield Academic Press, 1994), 295-97.

[2] Stephen H. Levinsohn, *Self-Instruction Materials on Narrative Discourse Analysis* (Dallas: SIL International, 2012).

Here Jesus' agency is highlighted at this significant moment in the discourse where he calls the Twelve disciples.

b. How to translate this emphasis is difficult: the student can <u>underline</u> the emphatic pronoun in their translation or emphasize the English subject in translation by adding the reflexive pronoun (*myself*, *yourself*, etc.) For example,

<u>ἐγὼ</u> βλέπω τὸν κύριον. = <u>*I*</u> *see the Lord.* Or, <u>*I myself*</u> *see the Lord.*

c. The 3rd person nominative forms αὐτός and αὐτοί are occasionally found with 1st or 2nd person verbs **to add emphasis.** If the verb is singular, then αὐτός is used; if the verb plural, then αὐτοί. For example,

αὐτός βλέπω τὸν κύριον. = <u>*I myself*</u> *see the Lord.*
αὐτοί ἀκούομεν... = <u>*We ourselves*</u> *hear...*

d. The most emphatic way to express the subject is to have a verb, expressed subject, the 1st or 2nd person personal pronoun, and the 3rd person personal pronoun. For example,

2 Cor 10:1a <u>Αὐτὸς</u> δὲ <u>ἐγὼ</u> Παῦλος παρακαλῶ ὑμᾶς...
Additionally, <u>*I myself*</u> *Paul exhort you...*

It is difficult to translate adequately the prominence that Paul gave to himself as subject and agent here. Paul's change in tone is marked by his use of emphatic indicators.

2. <u>As Possessive Modifier</u>: βλέπω τὸν κύριον <u>ἡμῶν</u>. = *I see* <u>*our*</u> *Lord.*

3. <u>As Indirect Object</u>: ὁ κύριος λέγει <u>αὐτοῖς</u>. = *The Lord speaks* <u>*to them*</u>.

4. <u>As Direct Object</u>: ὁ μαθητὴς βλέπει <u>αὐτόν</u>. = *The disciple sees* <u>*him*</u>.

5. <u>As Object of Preposition</u>: πιστεύω <u>εἰς αὐτόν</u>. = *I believe* <u>*in him*</u>.

9.3 RELATIVE PRONOUNS (Ἀναφορικαὶ Ἀντωνυμίαι)

A. English and Greek Relative Pronouns:

1. <u>Basic Function</u>. Relative pronouns function much the same way in Greek as in English: they point, refer, and modify. Historically, the relative pronoun was more a pointer, but then became a "bond of connection between clauses" (Robertson 711). The relative pronoun can

technically function in any capacity that a noun can, but refer to and modify nouns; hence, they function adjectivally to modify nouns.

2. <u>Types of Relative Pronouns</u>. In addition to ὅς, ἥ, ὅ *who, which* that is presented here, there are a number of other types of relative pronouns, some found elsewhere in the textbook but others not due to lower frequency: ὅστις *who(soever)* (ch.19), οἷος *what sort of, what quality of* (13x), ὁποῖος *of what sort* or *quality* (5x), ὅσος *how many, as much as* (Ch.26), and ἡλίκος *how great* (3x). In the historical development of Greek, certain conjunctions and adverbial particles derive from relative pronouns: ὡς, ὅπως, ὅτε, ἕως, ὅπου, etc. What one observes in these forms is the rough breathing mark.

3. <u>Case Depends on Function</u>. Remember that *how a pronoun functions in its respective clause determines its case (nom., gen., dat., and acc.)*. Since the relative pronouns refer to nouns, the forms show gender, case, and number.

B. **Greek Relative Pronoun Forms:** The endings correspond to the 1st and 2nd declension endings or article endings. Most notable about the Relative Pronoun forms are the rough breathing marks **and** accents. This will distinguish the feminine singular nominative form ἥ from the corresponding article form ἡ.

	Masculine	Feminine	Neuter	Masculine	Feminine	Neuter
				Translations		
sg. nom.	ὅς	ἥ	ὅ	*who/which*	*who/which*	*which/who*
gen.	οὗ	ἧς	οὗ	*whose*	*whose*	*of which*
dat.	ᾧ	ᾗ	ᾧ	*to whom*	*to whom*	*to which*
acc.	ὅν	ἥν	ὅ	*whom*	*whom*	*which*
pl. nom.	οἵ	αἵ	ἅ	*who/which*	*who/which*	*which/that*
gen.	ὧν	ὧν	ὧν	*whose*	*whose*	*of which*
dat.	οἷς	αἷς	οἷς	*to whom*	*to whom*	*to which*
acc.	οὕς	ἅς	ἅ	*whom*	*whom*	*which*

C. **Subordinate Clause Formation:**

1. <u>Relative Clauses</u>. Relative pronouns always initiate a subordinate or dependent clause called **relative clauses**. A good way to recognize a subordinate clause is by saying the clause all by itself and considering if it makes "sense." Subordinate clauses by themselves don't make sense.

2. <u>Word Order</u>. Relative Pronouns may be found anywhere in the sentence, but typically follow immediately upon their antecedent referent. Typically the relative pronoun will begin

their subordinate clause. Also, this relative clause is a tight unit. The tricky part is to determine how far to the right this relative clause extends into the main sentence.

3. <u>Constituent Marking Method</u>. Relative clauses are marked using brackets [...], since the relative pronoun forms a subordinate clause. When you see a relative pronoun, place a bracket at the beginning and look to see where the relative clause ends. Relative clauses may have all the components of a regular sentence: verb, subject, direct object, indirect object, prepositional phrases, etc.

4. <u>Examples</u>. Study these examples of relative pronouns and the relative clauses that they create.

   a. ἔλεγεν ὁ Ἰησοῦς πρὸς τὸν ἄνθρωπον ὃν ἐδίδασκεν περὶ τοῦ Θεοῦ.
    Jesus was speaking to the man whom he was teaching about God.

Where does the relative clause begin and end? Which noun is the antecedent? Remember, the antecedent agrees in gender and number. Below is the sentence partially marked to answer these questions.

   ἔλεγεν ὁ Ἰησοῦς πρὸς τὸν ἄνθρωπον [ὃν ἐδίδασκεν περὶ τοῦ Θεοῦ.]

What is the main sentence or main clause? It is ἔλεγεν ὁ Ἰησοῦς πρὸς τὸν ἄνθρωπον = *Jesus was speaking to the man*. The subordinate clause is ὃν ἐδίδασκεν περὶ τοῦ θεου = *whom he was teaching about God*. Notice that this clause is not complete; it cannot be said in isolation and make sense.

   b. ἀπέλυον τὸν ἀδελφὸν <u>οὗ</u> λόγον ἀκούετε.
    They were releasing the brother <u>whose</u> word/speech you are hearing.

What is the main sentence? Why is the relative pronoun in the genitive case?

   c. δοξάζομεν Ἰησοῦν εἰς <u>ὃν</u> πιστεύομεν.
    We glorify Jesus in <u>whom</u> we believe.

Notice that the relative clause can begin within a prepositional phrase. Why is this prepositional phrase used here? (<u>Hint</u>: consider the verb πιστεύω.)

   d. ἡ ζωὴ <u>ἣν</u> ἔχομεν ἐν τῷ υἱῷ αὐτοῦ ἐστιν ἐκ θεοῦ.
                   or
   ἡ ζωή ἐστιν ἐκ θεοῦ <u>ἣν</u> ἔχομεν ἐν τῷ υἱῷ αὐτοῦ.
   The life, <u>which</u> we have in his son, is from God.

In the first sentence, notice that one must decide how far the relative clause extends. It extends through αὐτοῦ. Here also one observes that the relative pronoun may be separated from its antecedent. Notice also that abstract ideas or impersonal realities like *life* are best translated *which* when represented by a relative pronoun.

D. **Attraction and Incorporation:** Two strange phenomena may occur with relative clauses that might confuse students.

1. <u>Attraction</u>. The case of the relative pronoun can be attracted to the case of its antecedent. This is good classical idiom and occurs most often in Luke's writings. Such attraction occurs mainly when the relative pronoun is in the oblique cases (i.e., genitive, dative, and accusative) and functions as the direct object in its own clause. When the pronoun should be accusative, it is attracted to the genitive or dative (Robertson 715-18). For example,

> **John 15:20a** μνημονεύετε τοῦ λόγου [οὗ ἐγὼ εἶπον ὑμῖν]
> *Remember the word <u>which</u> I spoke to you*

Strictly speaking, the relative pronoun οὗ should be accusative as the direct object of εἶπον. Instead, it is genitive, matching the case of its antecedent, which is genitive going with the verb μνημονεύω that takes a genitive direct object.

2. <u>Incorporation</u>. Sometimes the antecedent is placed within the relative pronoun clause (Robertson 718-19). For example, think about the subordinate clause […]:

> **Rom 6:17b** ὑπηκούσατε δὲ ἐκ καρδίας [εἰς ὃν παρεδόθητε τύπον διδαχῆς,]
> *Moreover, obey from the heart, [to <u>which</u> type of teaching you were committed.]*

The technically correct grammar would be ὑπηκούσατε ... τύπῳ διδαχῆς εἰς ὃν παρεδόθητε. *Obey ... the type of teaching to which you were committed.* We should consider what is achieved instead? Zerwick (§17) indicates that such was done "[f]or the sake of greater elegance."[3]

E. **Semantics and Pragmatic Function of Relative Pronouns:** Semantically, the relative pronoun simply connects clauses together at the point of a noun or substantive, which receives further specification or elaboration introduced by the relative pronoun. One could think of the noun or substantive and its corresponding relative pronoun as a hinge point, connecting two closely linked clauses. However, unlike a hinge, which is typically in the middle of equally swinging parts, the relative clause varies in size and shows more flexibility of location–and

---

[3] Maximilian Zerwick, *Biblical Greek: Illustrated by Examples*, trans. Joseph Smith, 4th ed., Scripta Pontificii Instituti Biblici 114 (Rome: Editrice Pontificio Istitutio Biblico, 1963).

both size and location are for the sake of optimal, strategic information flow. Burton helpfully summarizes the two basic functions of relative pronoun clauses: restrictive and explanatory (non-restrictive): "All relative clauses … may be distinguished as either restrictive or explanatory. A restrictive clause defines its antecedent, indicating what person, thing, place, or manner is signified. An explanatory clause adds a description to what is already known or sufficiently defined. The former *identifies*, the latter *describes*."[4]

1. Restrictive Use. A relative pronoun can function to **disambiguate**, that is, **distinguish one entity (person, thing) from others**. Such use of the relative pronoun clause restricts the referential identity of the entity. For example,

> **Luke 2:11** ὅτι ἐτέχθη ὑμῖν σήμερον σωτὴρ <u>ὅς</u> ἐστιν χριστὸς κύριος ἐν πόλει Δαυίδ
> *because a Savior was born to us today, <u>who</u> is Christ the Lord, in the city of David.*

In the Mediterranean world, there were many acclaimed as "savior" (see the inscriptions!). So, in Luke 2:11 the relative clause restricts the title "savior" to "Christ the Lord." It would seem that even the location of the prepositional phrase "in the city of David," abutted to this relative clause, provides further specificity and identity in relation to King David, from whom the Messiah would come.

2. Explanatory or Non-Restrictive Use. If the relative pronoun is not needed to restrict and disambiguate the reference, then it has an explanatory function. Levinsohn (190-96) further delineates here two further sub-uses: **appositional** or **continuative-descriptive**.

a. *Continuative-Descriptive Use.* "Continuative relative clauses … typically describe an event that involves the referent of the relative pronoun and occurs subsequent to the previous event or situation in which the referent featured." And, "Continuative relative clauses are most common in narrative, linking events in chronological sequence, though they are found in non-narrative. Characteristically, the information preceding the relative pronoun is *backgrounded* vis-à-vis what follows [in the relative clause]" (Levinsohn 191, emphasis original). Then, Levinsohn concludes: "The rhetorical effect of using a continuative relative clause in narrative is apparently to move the story forward quickly by combining background and foreground information in a single sentence" (192).

b. *Appositional Use.* Relative pronouns may further elaborate an entity in such a way as to bring it or its circumstances into more prominence. In other words, relative pronouns can contribute **elaborative emphasis** to an entity that strategically contributes to the

---

[4] Ernest De Witt Burton, *Syntax of the Moods and Tenses in New Testament Greek*, 3rd ed. (Edinburgh: T&T Clark, 1898), 119.

identity or the importance of entities for discursive thematic development. Just what sort of emphasis must be studied in the literary and socio-ideological context.

3. Extended Example from **Gal 2:1-5**. This passage will help illustrate and clarify the use of the relative pronoun to highlight sentence elements. I will identify relative pronouns within my literal translation and categorize their use:

Gal 2:1-5 [1] Then after within fourteen years I again went up into Jerusalem with Barnabas, taking along also Titus. [2] Moreover, I went up because of a revelation and I submitted to them the gospel that [**appositional**] I preach among the Gentiles. Additionally, this was in private to those who were of reputation, lest somehow I were running, or had run, in vain. [3] But not even Titus who was with me, although he was a Greek, was compelled to be circumcised. [4] So *I went up* because of the false brethren secretly brought in, who [**continuative-descriptive**] slipped in to spy on our liberty, which [**appositional**] we have in Christ Jesus, in order to enslave us,[5] to whom [**continuative-descriptive**] neither for even an hour did we yield in subjection, in order that the truth of the gospel would remain with you.

The two appositional relative clauses (2:2, 4) further elaborate the nouns *gospel* and *freedom*, and by such, advance Paul's argument that his gospel is *for all the nations* and that the *freedom* is gained *in Christ Jesus*. Extra prominence is afforded these concepts, which contributes to discourse wide thematic development: Paul had earlier frammed the entire discourse around different *gospels* and the distortion of *the gospel* of Christ (1:6-12) and Paul will argue pointedly later for the *freedom* that Christ brings (4:21-31; 5:1, 13). The two **continuative-descriptive** relative clauses (2:4, 5) are foregrounded events—what do they add to the situation Paul describes? They strategically characterize agency, manner, and purpose. Each continuative relative clause describes significant actions of the false brethren and their purposes (*to enslave us*) and Paul's significant action of not submitting and his purpse (*in order that the truth of the gospel would remain with you*). Thus, by attending to the elaborative descriptive and appositional contribution of relative pronouns, one can discern larger discursive purposes. This example demonstrates the importance of attending to relative clauses and how they serve to highlight important information.

9.4 ELLIPSIS (Ἔλλειψις): SUPPLYING AN IMPLIED WORD

At this point it will be helpful to formally introduce a particular feature of Greek (and English) sentences. Occasionally, for purposes of style, efficiency, and/or pragmatic effect, a Greek author would not include a word in the sentence that can be easily supplied from the context. This is called ellipsis, and it is fairly common. Consider the following English sentence.

I went to the grocery store, then to the bank, and after that to the post office.

Which word is implied? The verb *went*. Any word may be used in ellipsis, but verbs are especially common. To diagram ellipsis, see below. Here are some Greek examples with the elliptical word in brackets in the English translation:

1 Cor 1:12b ἐγὼ μέν εἰμι Παύλου, ἐγὼ δὲ Ἀπολλῶ, ἐγὼ δὲ Κηφᾶ, ἐγὼ δὲ Χριστοῦ.

I indeed am of Paul, and I [am] of Apollos, and I [am] of Cephas, and I [am] of Christ.

1 John 4:3a καὶ πᾶν πνεῦμα ὃ μὴ ὁμολογεῖ τὸν Ἰησοῦν ἐκ τοῦ θεοῦ οὐκ ἔστιν· καὶ τοῦτό ἐστιν τὸ τοῦ ἀντιχρίστου,

And every spirit that does not confess Jesus is not from God; and this is the [spirit] of the antichrist.

9.5 MARKING OR DIAGRAMMING SUBORDINATE CLAUSES & IMPLIED ITEMS

A. **What types of Subordinate Clauses have we learned thus far?** We have encountered essentially many types of subordinate clauses: direct/indirect discourse and content clauses (ὅτι), substantiation clauses (ὅτι), conditional suppositional clause (εἰ), and relative clauses (ὅς, ἥ, ὅ). We already know how to diagram the standard sentence. But when adding subordinate clauses, we are dealing with a **complex sentence**. A complex sentence has a main sentence and one or more subordinate clauses. Knowing how to diagram complex sentences will help your understanding of them. Here is how to diagram these types of complex sentences using the traditional diagramming method. For the Constituent Marking Method, simply place the subordinate clause within brackets [...]. To review constituent marking, see §4.7 CONSTITUENT MARKING FOR NAVIGATING A GREEK SENTENCE).

1. Direct/Indirect Discourse and Noun Clauses. These clauses can begin with ὅτι. Since they are so similar, they are diagrammed in the same fashion: an erected terrace where the direct object would normally go. Also, when the conjunction εἰ introduces an indirect question (*whether*), it is diagrammed and marked similarly.

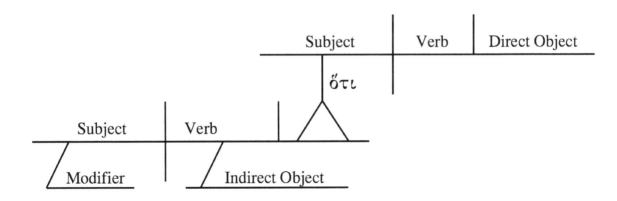

For example, here is a simple sentence with **direct discourse**. Remember that the ὅτι is optional:

λέγει αὐτοῖς ὅτι, Ἡ βασιλεία τοῦ οὐρανοῦ ἐγγίζει.
He is saying to them, 'The kingdom of heaven is near.'

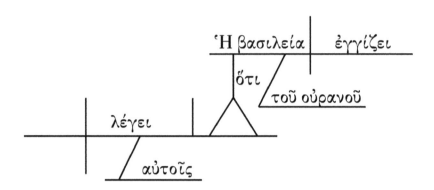

2. <u>Adverbial Clauses: Substantiation and Conditional.</u> Thus far we have encountered two types of adverbial clauses: Ὅτι when meaning *because* and εἰ introducing a conditional clause (*if...*). There are many types of **adverbial clauses**. These clauses deal with manner, time, cause, purpose, condition, concession, means, location, and comparison. Why are these called adverbial? Because they somehow tell us more about the action of the main verb (thus, adverbial). **Adverbial clauses tell us when, how, why, and where in relation to the verb of the sentence.** However, all adverbial clauses are diagrammed in the same fashion: a slanted line to right underneath the verb. Notice that adverbial clauses often are introduced with subordinating conjunctions.

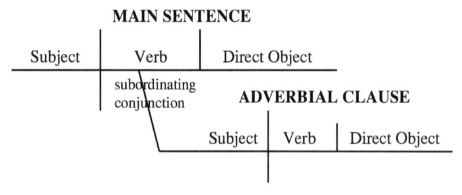

For example, consider this complex adverbial sentence:

οἱ ἄνθρωποι προσήρχοντο τῷ Ἰησοῦ, ὅτι ἔλεγε τὴν ἀλήθειαν.
The people were coming to Jesus, because he was speaking the truth.

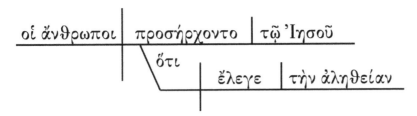

Remember that προσέρχομαι takes the dative case to indicate the destination.

3. Relative Clauses. Since relative pronouns are both directly linked to their antecedent and yet can function in any capacity in their own dependent clause, their diagramming is a bit tricky. It requires two separate diagrams joined by a dotted line connecting the relative pronoun to its antecedent.

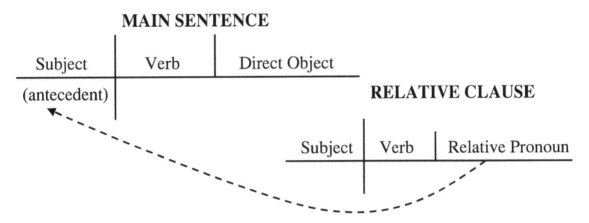

Of course this schema could vary depending on whether the referent is antecedent or postcedent and depending how its relative pronoun is functioning. Two examples will be given below to demonstrate the flexibility of such sentences and their diagrams.

δοξάζομεν Ἰησοῦν εἰς ὃν πιστεύομεν.
We glorify Jesus in whom we believe.

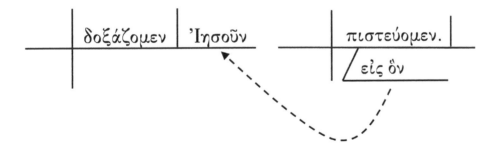

ἡ ζωή ἐστιν ἐκ θεοῦ ἣν ἔχομεν ἐν τῷ υἱῷ αὐτοῦ.
Life, which we have in his son, is from God.

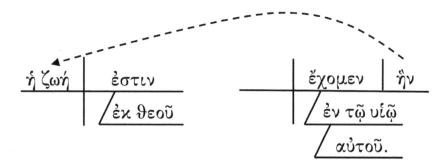

B. **Other Types of Subordinate Clauses Yet to Be Covered:** As already indicated above, there are other types of subordinate clauses. Understanding how subordinate clauses work at this point in the textbook will prevent frustration later. It also will help in your translation of the exercises and better equip you for interpretation and exegesis. So, learn well these concepts in this chapter!

C. **Ellipsis or Implied Elements:** Elliptical sentence elements that can be supplied from the context; they are implied from the context. Within the Constituent Marking Method and the Reed-Kellogg Diagramming, implied essential sentence elements should be included in English and placed in brackets [...]. Why in English? Because in our critical Greek editions the words that are questionable are placed in brackets. So, to avoid confusion, place your additions in English; otherwise, you risk creating a textual variant, if someone comes after you and thinks you have recorded what was in the Greek text.

1 John 1:3b καὶ ἡ κοινωνία δὲ ἡ ἡμετέρα μετὰ τοῦ πατρὸς καὶ μετὰ τοῦ υἱοῦ αὐτοῦ
        Ἰησοῦ Χριστοῦ.
    And also our fellowship is with the Father and with His Son, Jesus Christ.

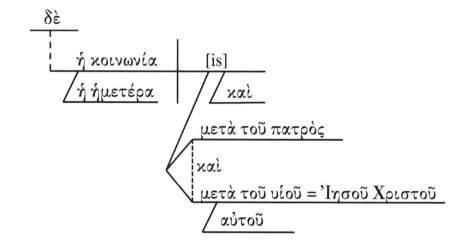

Complete WORKBOOK EXERCISES 9 and consult the ANSWER KEY & GUIDE as needed.

CASE IN POINT 9: THE DIMENSIONS OF HUMAN SINFULNESS IN EPH 2:1-3

Ephesians is a masterfully constructed discourse. At almost every turn, its elaborate grammatical structure supports the particular thematic point. Paul's discussion of the reality of "death" resulting from sinfulness in 2:1-3 is no exception. The sentence syntax here involves a grammatically incomplete and suspended clause in 2:1-3 (no main verb!), which is not properly given a main verb until 2:5, when God's loving mercy describes what God has given to humanity in and with Christ. In 2:5 the syntax picks up almost verbatim to 2:1, "and, you being dead in trespasses, God made you alive with Christ...." To answer the disjointed reality of death through sin, God makes us alive in Christ.

The opening disjunctive statement in 2:1 is followed by two elaborative relative pronoun clauses in 2:2 and 2:3. Let's look at how these relative pronouns function. Here is a literal rendering of the Greek text with the relative pronouns in bold:

> [1] And you being dead in your trespasses and sins, [2] **in which** you formerly walked according to the age of this world, according to the ruler of the authority of the air, of the spirit that is now working in the sons of disobedience, [3] **in which/among whom** we too all formerly lived in the lusts of our flesh, doing the wills of the flesh and of the thoughts, and were by nature children of wrath, even as the rest...

> [1] Καὶ ὑμᾶς ὄντας νεκροὺς <u>τοῖς παραπτώμασιν</u> καὶ <u>ταῖς ἁμαρτίαις</u> ὑμῶν, [2] **ἐν αἷς** ποτε περιεπατήσατε κατὰ τὸν αἰῶνα τοῦ κόσμου τούτου, κατὰ τὸν ἄρχοντα τῆς ἐξουσίας τοῦ ἀέρος, τοῦ πνεύματος τοῦ νῦν ἐνεργοῦντος ἐν τοῖς υἱοῖς τῆς ἀπειθείας· [3] **ἐν οἷς** καὶ ἡμεῖς πάντες ἀνεστράφημέν ποτε ἐν ταῖς ἐπιθυμίαις τῆς σαρκὸς ἡμῶν ποιοῦντες τὰ θελήματα τῆς σαρκὸς καὶ τῶν διανοιῶν, καὶ ἤμεθα τέκνα φύσει ὀργῆς ὡς καὶ οἱ λοιποί·

One important issue for interpretation is to determine the antecedent of the relative pronouns, which typically agrees in gender and number with the relative pronoun. In 2:2, the relative pronoun in the phrase *in which* **ἐν αἷς** is feminine plural and its antecedent appears to be the immediately preceding feminine plural noun at the end of 2:1, namely, ταῖς ἁμαρτίαις *sins*. In 2:3, **ἐν οἷς** is masculine or neuter plural and its antecedent should agree in gender and number. In the immediately preceding context, there is one masculine plural noun, namely, ἐν τοῖς υἱοῖς *among the sons of disobedience*. Most translations and interpreters take *sons* as the antecedent to **ἐν οἷς**, thus translating it *among whom* in reference to the *sons*. However, there is another exegetical possibility that I would like to explore.

One important exegetical principle is *to consider all the possibilities* (CAP). What else could be the antecedent? Earlier a neuter plural noun occurs in 2:1: τοῖς παραπτώμασιν *the trespasses*. So, we should consider whether *sons* or *trespasses* is the antecedent. Well, *sons* in 2:2

is the closest, which is an important piece of evidence in its favor. However, there are other considerations that point us to consider the grammatical possibility that **ἐν οἷς** refers back to *the trespasses* (τοῖς παραπτώμασιν). Let me explain.

I start with word definitions and the structure of the passage. If in 2:3 **ἐν οἷς** refers to *the trespasses* of the more distant verse 2:1, then we have two relative clauses in 2:2 and 2:3 that each elaborate two different dimensions of human sinfulness introduced in 2:1. Paul may be using these words to make an important distinction. The first word παράπτωμα *trespass* involves the "imagery of one making a false step so as to lose footing"; it is "a violation of moral standards, offense, wrongdoing, sin" ("παράπτωμα" BDAG). The other word ἁμαρτία *sin* is a more generic term given two basic glosses in BDAG, "sin" and sinfulness"; in the LSJ lexicon, the word is glossed as "a failure, fault, sin" or "generally, guilt, sin." The first word παράπτωμα *trespass* presupposes a given moral standard that is broken; the second word ἁμαρτία *sin* appears to be more general.

Next, let's consider the pronouns and personal reference. Paul emphatically switches from second person plural (*you*) in 2:1-2 to first person plural (*us; we*) in 2:3. This may indicate that in 2:1-2 Paul was singularly describing the Gentiles (the *you*) but then in 2:3 switches to first person ("*also we all*") to include Jews particularly (but not exclusively) under the notion of *trespassing*. As has been noted by many interpreters, in Ephesians 1-3, Paul acknowledges that a distinction exists between Jews and Gentiles, which distinction is, however, overcome by God in Christ: He forms "one body" from the two groups (1:12-13; 2:11-22; 3:1, 6). So, in 2:1-3 Paul may have described how Gentiles have committed *sins* ἁμαρτίαι more generally (2:2), and then how Jews and Gentiles, who were attempting to live under the law, have committed *trespasses* παραπτώματα more specifically (2:3).

In terms of structure, working with this possibility, Paul appears to have designed a rhetorical pattern consisting of a chiasmus (ABBA) in 2:1-3 and then a parallelism in 2:2-3.

2:1 You were dead...	A	in (your) **trespasses** [τοῖς **παραπτώμασιν**]
	B	and in your **sins** [καὶ **ταῖς ἁμαρτίαις** ὑμῶν,]
2:2	B	in **which** (sins) you once walked/lived [ἐν **αἷς** ποτε περιεπατήσατε...] according to the age of this world, according to the ruler of the authority of the air, the spirit that is now working in the sons of disobedience.
2:3 (move to WE)	A	in **which** (transgressions) <u>also we all</u> once lived [ἐν **οἷς** καὶ ἡμεῖς πάντες ἀνεστράφημέν ποτε] in the lusts of our flesh, doing the wills of the flesh and of the thoughts,

In Paul's elaboration in 2:2 and 2:3, we observe a grammatical parallelism in three ways: (1) each begins with a relative pronoun in a prepositional phrase with ἐν; (2) each has the adverb ποτε *once*; and (3) each involves a verb of *living* or *behaving* (περιεπατήσατε and ἀνεστράφημέν).

Apart from these three parallels, 2:2 and 2:3 contain two fundamental differences. The first is the emphatic subject change to "we" (ἡμεῖς), which includes both Gentiles and Jews together as trespassers. Notice the inclusive scope of "all" (πάντες). Moreover, this emphatic pronoun and quantitative "all" is preceded by an adverbial or additive καί, which further underscores the inclusive nature and subject change to "we."

Second, the context in which the sin/trespass is described in each verse is different, but still complement one another. In 2:2, the cosmic and spiritual dimension to sin is described as far as the Gentile world was concerned: Gentiles were walking *according the age of this world* and were under the influence of *the ruler of the authority of the air, the spirit that is now working among the sons of disobedience* (cf. 4:27; 6:11). Most interpreters identify this "ruler" (accusative case) and the "spirit" (genitive case) as the same entity, the Devil. However, grammatically this does not work, since "spirit" (genitive) is in apposition to "the authority of the air" (both "authority" and "air" are genitive). So, the ruler and the spirit are two different entities. We must ask how the Ephesians would have understood Paul's language. I have argued that the *ruler* (ἄρχων) refers to the Roman emperor, since the word commonly has a human referent elsewhere in the NT.[5] Then, "the authority of the air," which is the spirit behind the ruler, would have been understood as the "divinity" Jupiter-Zeus, whom Greeks and Romans understood to control what happens in the "air" (rain, thunder, lightning); in ancient pagan commentators of Homer, Hesiod, and other works, Zeus was identified with *air* ἀήρ; then, too, it was a commonly held belief that Jupiter-Zeus gave complete rule to the Roman emperor. Paul does not explicitly name these entities, but uses understandable language. Certainly also, we can recognize Satan's disguise to deceive and lead people astray, using human rulers and so-called divinities to deceive and mislead, as Paul understood (2 Cor 11:14). So, Eph 2:2 describes the fallen Gentile world; this description does not apply to Israel as God's people, which belonged uniquely to God and was directly under God's influence (Deut 26:17-19) in distinction from the nations around them who had false gods. Only the Gentiles were under foreign rule of the Roman emperor, Satan's domain (cf. Acts 26:17-18).

But turning to what is common to all people, the *also we all* in 2:3, Paul switches to discuss the matters of embodied sin that affect **_all_** people—the thoughts, the will (i.e. volition), and the flesh. All people (Jews and Gentiles) have succumbed to *the lusts of the flesh, doing the wills of the flesh and of the thoughts*. Notice how *wills* is plural; people controlled by their flesh and their thoughts are pulled in multiple directions, as opposed to being under the will of God. It is simply not possible for people to blame human rulers or the devil for their sinfulness—it arises from within our own fleshly desires, which corrupt one's thoughts and subsequent behavior (cf. James 1:13-15). We are all responsible for our trespasses and sins, because we have all followed our own lusts and poor thinking leading us into sinful thoughts, attitudes, and behaviors.

However, Paul's point was not only to "equalize" the playing field by arguing that "we all"— Jews and Gentiles—"are *children of wrath*" (cf. Rom 11:30-32). Rather, the disjointed grammar of 2:1-3 is finally resolved when Paul supplies grammatically the main verb in 2:4-5.

---

[5] Fredrick J. Long, "Roman Imperial Rule under the Authority of Jupiter-Zeus: Political-Religious Contexts and the Interpretation of 'the Ruler of the Authority of the Air' in Ephesians 2:2," in *The Language of the New Testament: Context, History and Development*, ed. S. E. Porter and A. W. Pitts; Linguistic Biblical Studies 6; Early Christianity in its Hellenistic Environment 3 (Leiden; Boston: Brill, 2013), 113–54.

Paul moves the audience to the good news of the Gospel through God's mercy and loving initiative to save us when **_we all_** were spiritually dead: He made us alive, raised us with Christ, and has seated us with Christ in the heavenly realms (2:5-7). We are saved by God's grace through faith in order to walk in good deeds (2:8-10). It is important to understand that, just as our sinful problem is one that is socially alienating, politically modeled and encouraged, and bodily embedded in death, so too God's mercy and love deals with sin by providing social unity (one unified body of believers), a political Lord and Savior (Jesus the Messiah, our exemplar), and renewed life to walk in good goods as holy people.

So, in this Case in Point, I wanted to illustrate the importance of pronouns and in particular relative pronouns to elaborate critical points. Whether you are convinced or not by my evidence, and particularly the Chiasm in 2:1-3 that I have identified, Paul certainly has created a parallelism in 2:2 and 2:3; moreover, he describes general bad influences upon people (the age of this world, the ruler, and the spirit) before then explaining how sinfulness is embodied such that it affects mind, will, and flesh—causing all of us to be children of wrath and dead before God. Careful attention to details makes God's mercy and love even more amazing! In contrast, consider a prevailing alternative worldview at the time of Jesus, as seen in the *Gemma Augustea*.

The *Gemma Augustea*

Dating to AD 10, the *Gemma Augustea* is sculpted onyx (7.5 x 9 inches). Here Augustus is enthroned on the right as Jupiter (with Jupiter's Eagle below), being crowned by goddess Οἰκουμένη ("the inhabited world") with the goddess *Roma* sitting beside him (on his right). Below him is a scene of humiliating conquest of defeated Barbarian foes. Accessed Dec 7, 2009 From http://upload.wikimedia.org/wikipedia/commons/4/45/Kunsthistorisches_Museum_Vienna_June_2006_031.png

CHAPTER 10

In this lesson two tenses are presented: the **Future** and the **Aorist**. These tenses are included together due to similarities of formation, specifically, the addition of a σίγμα to the end of the verb stem. Then the important concept of **Principal Parts** is explained. Also, an oddly formed yet common verb, οἶδα, is introduced. This verb often participates in the creation of **metacomments**, which are discursively significant. Finally, two more prepositions are in the vocabulary, each taking three cases.

VOCABULARY 10   MORE VERBS AND PREPOSITIONS; ALSO Οἶδα

Verbs:			
ἀνοίγω [77]	I open	λύω [42]	I loosen, untie; I destroy
διώκω [45]	I pursue; I persecute	πείθω [52]	I persuade; I trust (+ *dat.*); I obey (*middle*)
ἐγγίζω [42]	I draw near, approach	Prepositions:	
ἑτοιμάζω [40]	I make ready, prepare	ἐπί, ἐπ᾽, ἐφ᾽ [887]	gen. on, over
θαυμάζω [43]	I wonder, am amazed		dat. on, near
θεραπεύω [43]	I heal; I serve		acc. on, to, toward
καθίζω [46]	I sit; I seat; I stay	παρά, παρ᾽ [193]	gen. from, alongside
κηρύσσω [61]	I proclaim, announce, preach		dat. beside, near
κλαίω [40]	I weep (for), lament		acc. at, by; out from
κράζω [55]	I cry out, call out	Special Verb:	
		οἶδα [320]	I know, understand

After learning vocabulary to this point, you will know 60.4% of the words in the GNT. If you are able, listen to audio recordings of VOCABULARY 10 and complete the CROSSWORD PUZZLE in the WORKBOOK EXERCISES.

NOTES ON VOCABULARY 10:

Only one verb has a recognizable English cognate: therap-y. But θεραπεύω can also mean *serve*. Notice that several verbs have a secondary meaning that is significantly different than the first: διώκω, θεραπεύω, and λύω. For διώκω and λύω, the second meaning is an intensification of the first meaning. For example, λύω means *to loosen* or *untie*. However, for many objects, such as tents, walls, etc., to loosen them would amount to destroying them.

The two prepositions in this vocabulary each take three cases. Notice that it appears that the meaning of ἐπί is possibly the same regardless of the case of its object. However, remember that these are glosses for beginning students. BDAG has eighteen separate definition entries with many having multiple parts depending on the case of the object, etc. Ἐπί has two other forms, ἐπ' and ἐφ' that occur when its object begins with a vowel. The ἰῶτα is dropped (or elided) before another vowel. If the word following has a rough breathing mark, then ἐπί is aspirated to become ἐφ'. In a similar fashion, παρά often becomes παρ' when followed by a word beginning with a vowel (although see, e.g. John 1:40; 5:41).

10.1 AORIST TENSE (Ἀόριστος) AND FUTURE TENSE (Μέλλων): TENSE MARKERS AND VERBAL ASPECT

A. **Tense Markers:** We have already learned that tense in the Greek verb can be signaled in five ways: (1) affixing a **prefix** to the front of a verb stem; (2) **changing** the verb stem; (3) supplying a **tense indicator**; (4) supplying a **coupling vowel**; and (5) adding types of **endings**.

Prefix + Stem Change + Tense Indicator + Coupling Vowel + Endings

(1)   (2)   (3)   (4)   (5)

We have seen how the Present and Imperfect Tenses show no stem change and no tense indicator, but use the ε/ο coupling vowel with their endings. The Imperfect tense, however, uses secondary endings and has an augment prefix. As we move outside of the Present and Imperfect Tenses, **verb stem changes sometimes occur** and help to indicate a particular tense. Additionally, we often see **tense indicators**.

1. Tense Indicator. Within the tense presented in this chapter, the tense indicator is a σίγμα.

2. A Stem Change in this Chapter. One verb in this chapter exhibits a slight stem change from the Present to the Future Tense: κλαί-ω (Present) to κλαύ-σω (Future). Admittedly, this stem change is minor, but it is important to remember. See §10.2 below.

3. Second Aorist Verbs. A special classification of verbs called the Second Aorists show drastic stem changes. You have learned some of these verbs as vocabulary and in the Present and Imperfect Tenses: εὑρίσκω, ἔχω, λέγω, ἔρχομαι (and its compounds), and all the

verbs presented in VOCABULARY 8. However, since these verbs constitute a special group, their formation of the Future and Aorist Tenses are presented in CHAPTER 11.

B. Verbal Aspect:

1. <u>Future Tense Aspect</u>. The Future Tense entails action that is intended and expected to occur. Stated again, the future tense reflects expectation or intention of occurrence in the future.[1]

2. <u>Aorist Tense Aspect</u>. The Greek word for the Aorist Tense is ἀόριστος meaning *without boundaries*.

   a. *Perfective*. The Aorist tense expresses perfective aspect in that the verbal action is viewed as a whole externally or as complete, but not necessarily completed. When augmented (marked for past time), the Aorist tense generally indicates an action viewed as a whole that happened sometime in the past.

   b. *Within Narratives*. The Aorist Tense is the default past tense in the Indicative Mood. No further view or perspective is given about this action or event; it is viewed externally and as complete(d). It is not presented internally as in progress and incomplete, as would be indicated by using the Imperfect Tense (see CHAPTER 8); nor is the action represented as complex with continuing results/effects (as stative), as would be indicated by using the Perfect Tense (see CHAPTER 13). The unique semantics of the Aorist Indicative makes it suitable for storyline narrative—the Aorist Indicative moves the narrative forward. All the other tenses are unmarked for storyline and are rather marked for some sort of prominence in the narrative.

10.2 PRIMARY AND SECONDARY TENSE ENDINGS

A. **Introduction:** Thus far, two sets of endings have been learned: Present Active and Middle/Passive and Imperfect Active and Middle/Passive.

---

[1] The development of the future aspect is an innovation of Greek, and derives from the Present tense (Michael Weiss, "Morphology and Word Formation," in *A Companion to the Ancient Greek Language*, ed. Egbert J. Bakker; Blackwell Companions to the Ancient World [Malden, MA: Wiley-Blackwell, 2010], 104–19 at 110). The description of the fourth Verbal Aspect converges the views of Weiss, McKay and Porter-Reed-O'Donnell; see Wally V. Cirafesi, *Verbal Aspect in Synoptic Parallels: On the Method and Meaning of Divergent Tense-Form Usage in the Synoptic Passion Narratives*, Linguistic Biblical Studies 7 (Leiden: Brill, 2013), 45-46. K. L. McKay sees the Future Tense as a Fourth Aspect (*A New Syntax of the Verb in New Testament Greek: An Aspectual Approach*, Studies in Biblical Greek 5 [New York: Peter Lang, 1994], 34). Alternatively, Porter, Reed, and O'Donnell do not view the Greek Future Tense as having verbal aspect, but rather is somewhat like the Subjunctive Mood (*Fundamentals of New Testament Greek* [Grand Rapids: Eerdmans, 2010], 86).

PRESENT ACTIVE

	sg.	pl.
First	-ω	-ομεν
Second	-εις	-ετε
Third	-ει	-ουσι(ν)

PRESENT MIDDLE/PASSIVE

	sg.	pl.
First	-ομαι	-όμεθα
Second	-η	-εσθε
Third	-εται	-ονται

IMPERFECT ACTIVE

	sg.	pl.
First	-ον	-ομεν
Second	-ες	-ετε
Third	-ε(ν)	-ον

IMPERFECT MIDDLE/PASSIVE

	sg.	pl.
First	-όμην	-όμεθα
Second	-ου	-εσθε
Third	-ετο	-οντο

B. Primary and Secondary Tense Endings:

1. <u>Primary Tense Endings</u>. The Present Tense is formed with the primary tense endings. With the addition of the ο/ε coupling vowel, many of the endings (*) change considerably. Compare with the Present Tense endings above.

ACTIVE

	sg.	pl.
First	-μι*	-μεν
Second	-σι*	-τε
Third	-τι*	-ντι*

MIDDLE OR PASSIVE

	sg.	pl.
First	-μαι	-μεθα
Second	-σαι*	-σθε
Third	-ται	-νται

Hence, the following is good advice: "Because of the radical nature of the phonetic changes and because several of the endings... do not appear in any tense, it is best to disregard the primitive endings μι, σι, τι, μεν, τε, ντι and to learn the resultant endings: ω, εις, ει, ομεν, ετε, ουσι...."[2]

2. <u>Secondary Tense Endings</u>. The Imperfect Tense is formed with the secondary tense endings. In actuality, one must remove the ο/ε coupling vowel that begins the Imperfect endings to see the **secondary tense endings**.

ACTIVE

	sg.	pl.
First	-ν	-μεν
Second	-ς	-τε
Third	-(ν)	-ν

MIDDLE OR PASSIVE

	sg.	pl.
First	-μην	-μεθα
Second	-σο	-σθε
Third	-το	-ντο

---

[2] James A. Brooks and Carlton L. Winbery, *A Morphology of New Testament Greek: A Review and Reference Grammar* (New York: University Press of America, 1994), 182.

3. <u>Discussion.</u>

    a. To form the tenses, typically a **coupling vowel** is added before these endings. For the Present, Imperfect, and Future Tenses the coupling vowels are ο/ε. Both the Aorist and Perfect Tenses use α/ε for their coupling vowels. For the pluperfect -ει is added; the Future Passive and Aorist Passive have -η.

    b. Some of these endings are "abstract" (*) in that one rarely, if ever, observes them, since they are changed for phonetic reasons and also contract with coupling vowels in their formation. For example, the secondary tense 2nd singular Middle ending -σο drops its σίγμα and then the coupling vowel -ε- combines with -ο to form –ου.

    c. The active endings of the 3rd person singular sometimes end with a νῦ (ν) and sometimes not. This is called **movable νῦ**.

    d. For the secondary endings, one might think that many active endings will look alike, since many end in νῦ. However, the coupling vowel placed in front of the endings is different for the 3rd singular (-ε) and 3rd plural (-α). Also, νῦ is absent from the 1st singular forms of the Aorist Active and Perfect Active.

C. **Primary and Secondary Tenses:** Most grammarians will break all the tenses into two groups: Primary and Secondary Tenses. The Primary Tenses are the Present, Future, and Perfect M/P and are built from the primary tense endings. The Secondary Tenses are Imperfect, Aorist, Perfect Active, and Pluperfect and are built from the Secondary tense endings.

10.3 FUTURE ACTIVE AND MIDDLE TENSE: FORMATION AND TRANSLATION

A. **Formation:** The Future Tense is easy to form. Simply add the **tense indicator** (a σίγμα) to the stem and then add the ο/ε coupling vowel with the primary endings:

    <u>verb stem</u> + σ + ο/ε with <u>primary endings</u>

The Future of πιστεύω looks like this:

ACTIVE		**MIDDLE**	
πιστεύ-σ-ω	πιστεύ-σ-ομεν	πιστεύ-σ-ομαι	πιστευ-σ-όμεθα
πιστεύ-σ-εις	πιστεύ-σ-ετε	πιστεύ-σ-η	πιστεύ-σ-εσθε
πιστεύ-σ-ει	πιστεύ-σ-ουσι(ν)	πιστεύ-σ-εται	πιστεύ-σ-ονται

Thus, one can isolate the Future Active and Middle Endings as follows:

	FUTURE ACTIVE				**FUTURE MIDDLE**	
	sg.	pl.			sg.	pl.
First	-σω	-σομεν		First	-σομαι	-σόμεθα
Second	-σεις	-σετε		Second	-ση	-σεσθε
Third	-σει	-σουσι(ν)		Third	-σεται	-σονται

B. **Translating the Future Indicative:** The Future Tense corresponds to our English. See Wallace 566-71 for more details on how the Future Tense may be translated.

1. <u>Active Voice.</u>

			English Simple Future
<u>sg.</u>	1	πιστεύσω	I will trust
	2	πιστεύσεις	you will trust
	3	πιστεύσει	he/she/it will trust
<u>pl.</u>	1	πιστεύσομεν	we will trust
	2	πιστεύσετε	you will trust
	3	πιστεύσουσι(ν)	they will trust

2. <u>Middle Voice.</u> The significance of a Future Middle would be the same as that for the Present Tense, except that it is in future tense aspect. See §3.2.E.3.

3. <u>Where's the Future Passive Endings?</u> In the Present and Imperfect Tenses, the middle and passive endings are one and the same. However, this is not the case with the Future and Aorist Tenses. The reason for this is that the verb stem used to form the Future Passive voice <u>can be slightly different</u> from the stem used to form the Future middle. Thus, the Future Passive (and Aorist Passive) Tense is treated separately (see CHAPTER 15). See also the discussion below under **Principal Parts**.

C. **Common and Special Uses of the Future Tense:** The Future Tense is generally used for statements about anticipated events, often set within a future time frame. This is called Predictive. It can rarely be used in general, gnomic statements. However, the use of the Future Tense impinges upon two other moods: the Imperative and the Subjunctive. Hence, one will find Imperatival Futures and Future Tense verbs in Deliberative Questions and Purpose Statements (typically the mode of the Subjunctive). See Wallace 569-71.

1. <u>Predictive (most common).</u>
   Matt 1:21 <u>τέξεται</u> δὲ υἱόν, καὶ <u>καλέσεις</u> τὸ ὄνομα αὐτοῦ Ἰησοῦν· αὐτὸς γὰρ <u>σώσει</u> τὸν λαὸν αὐτοῦ ἀπὸ τῶν ἁμαρτιῶν αὐτῶν.
   And she <u>will bear</u> a son, and you <u>will call</u> his name Jesus. For he himself <u>will save</u> his people from their sins.

2. <u>Gnomic (very rare).</u>
   Rom 5:7 μόλις γὰρ ὑπὲρ δικαίου τις ἀποθανεῖται.
   For scarcely <u>would</u> someone <u>die</u> for a righteous person.

3. <u>Impinging on the Imperative Mood (rare)</u>. The examples are almost limited to quotations from the Septuagint (LXX) or influence of the LXX and from Matthew's Gospel, as Matt 5:48 below:

Matt 5:48 ἔσεσθε οὖν ὑμεῖς τέλειοι ὡς ὁ πατὴρ ὑμῶν ὁ οὐράνιος τέλειός ἐστιν.
Therefore, you <u>be perfect</u> as your heavenly Father is perfect.

4. <u>Impinging on the Subjunctive Mood (rare)</u>. Used in deliberative questions and statements of purpose.

Mark 6:37b ἀγοράσωμεν δηναρίων διακοσίων ἄρτους καὶ <u>δώσομεν</u> αὐτοῖς φαγεῖν;
Should we buy two-hundred denarii of bread and <u>will we give</u> to them to eat?

10.4 AORIST ACTIVE AND MIDDLE TENSE: FORMATION AND TRANSLATION

A. **Formation:** The Aorist Tense in the Indicative Mood is formed by 1) adding an augment to the front of the verb stem, 2) adding a σίγμα tense indicator to the end of the verb stem, 3) using the α/ε coupling vowel along with the secondary endings:

$$ἐ + \underline{verb\ stem} + σα/ε + \underline{secondary\ endings}$$

Thus, the Aorist Active and Middle of πιστεύω looks like this:

ACTIVE		MIDDLE	
ἐπιστεύ<u>σα</u>	ἐπιστεύ<u>σαμεν</u>	ἐπιστευ<u>σάμην</u>	ἐπιστευ<u>σάμεθα</u>
ἐπίστευ<u>σας</u>	ἐπιστεύ<u>σατε</u>	ἐπιστεύ<u>σω</u>	ἐπιστεύ<u>σασθε</u>
ἐπίστευ<u>σε(ν)</u>	ἐπιστεύ<u>σαν</u>	ἐπιστεύ<u>σατο</u>	ἐπιστεύ<u>σαντο</u>

Thus, the endings for the Aorist Active and Middle Tense are as follows:

	AORIST ACTIVE			**AORIST MIDDLE**	
	sg.	pl.		sg.	pl.
First	-σα	-σαμεν	First	-σαμην	-σάμεθα
Second	-σας	-σατε	Second	-σω	-σασθε
Third	-σε(ν)	-σαν	Third	-σατο	-σαντο

<u>Notice</u>: (1) In the active endings the 1st singular has no νῦ but is simply -σα. This is distinguished from the 3rd singular -σε(ν) and the 3rd plural -σαν. (2) In the Middle endings, the 2nd singular is -σω. This results from a contraction (i.e. combining) of ἄλφα with an ὂ μικρόν: α + ο → ω.

B. **Translating the Aorist Indicative:** The Aorist Tense in the Indicative Mood is marked for past time due to the augment and represents perfective aspect. In translation, this corresponds to our English simple past tense.

   1. <u>Active Voice.</u>

			English Simple Past
sg.	1	ἐπίστευσα	I trusted
	2	ἐπίστευσας	you trusted
	3	ἐπίστευσε(ν)	he/she/it trusted
pl.	1	ἐπιστεύσαμεν	we trusted
	2	ἐπιστεύσατε	you trusted
	3	ἐπίστευσαν	they trusted

   2. <u>Middle Voice.</u> The significance of the Aorist Middle Indicative is the same as that for the Present or Imperfect.

   3. <u>Where are the Aorist Passive Endings?</u> The Aorist Passive, like the Future Passive, occasionally shows slight stem changes. Thus, the Aorist and Future Passive Tenses are presented in CHAPTER 15. See the discussion of Principal Parts below.

C. **Common and Special Uses of the Aorist Tense:** The Aorist Tense is used with certain verb stems and in certain contexts in which it may be translated variously. See Wallace 554-65.

   1. <u>Constantive.</u> The basic use of the Aorist tense is called the Constantive use. Other uses include the following:
   2. <u>Ingressive or Inceptive.</u> Beginning of action or entrance into a state of being
   3. <u>Consummative.</u> Action that has come to a conclusion
   4. <u>Gnomic.</u> A general event true at any time (rare)
   5. <u>Epistolary.</u> An action written as if from the readers' perspective (rare)
   6. <u>Proleptic.</u> A future event (rare)
   7. <u>Immediate/dramatic.</u> An event that just happened (rare)

10.5 ADDING Σίγμα TO VERB STEMS: RULES AND EXAMPLES

Both the Future and Aorist Tenses add a σίγμα to the verb stem. This σίγμα is a **tense indicator** and helps the reader to know what tense a particular verb is. However, the addition of a σίγμα to the end of a verb is not always a simple matter. The σίγμα may combine with other consonants or simply disappear. Before students can understand when and why this happens, further sub-classification of the consonants is needed.

A. **Further Consonant Classification:** The vowels were already sub-classified into long and short vowels. Now it is time to understand how consonants are further classified. These classifications are important for adding σίγμα to verb stems. Not all of this information will be immediately pertinent, but *it will be eventually*. The consonant sub-classification **mutes** is most important for this chapter.

1. <u>The Mutes</u>. This subclass of consonants includes sounds produced from the lips, teeth or palate. Also, they are classified from hard sounds to soft sound—the difference being in pronunciation, caused by how much air is used to make the sound:

	hard sounds	soft sound (**aspirates**)
Labial (lip sounds)	π β	φ
Dental (teeth sounds)	τ δ	ϑ
Palatal (palate sounds)	κ γ	χ

Note also that from left to right, the consonants proceed from smooth to rough breathing in pronunciation. In the last column of consonants (φ, ϑ, χ), each is pronounced with an *h* sound. These mutes are called **aspirates**.

2. <u>The Spirant</u>. Greek has only one spirant: σίγμα σ, ς.

3. <u>Double Consonants</u>. Three consonants are really composed of two consonant sounds:

> Ζῆτα (ζ) is the combination of a δσ sound (δέλτα-σίγμα).
> Ξῖ (ξ) is the combination of κσ, γσ, or χσ sounds.
> Ψῖ (ψ) is the combination of πσ, βσ, or φσ sounds.

The double consonants ξ and ψ are formed at the end of a verb stem when a σίγμα is added to their respective mute consonants. However, a σίγμα added to a τ, δ, ϑ, or ζ will completely replace it. (See B. below.)

4. <u>Liquid Consonants</u>. Greek has four liquid consonants: λ, μ, ν, and ρ. Liquid consonants do not combine with an added σίγμα. This results in the total disappearance of the σίγμα as a tense indicator. **Liquid Verbs,** whose stem ends in a liquid consonant, are covered in CHAPTER 21.

B. **How to Add Σίγμα to Various Verb Stems:**

1. <u>For Verb Stems that End in a Vowel</u>. To add a σίγμα to these verbs is simple:

ἀπολύω	ἀπολυ-	+ σ	→ ἀπολυσ-
ἀκούω	ἀκου-	+ σ	→ ἀκουσ-
θεραπεύω	θεραπευ-	+ σ	→ θεραπευσ-
κλαίω	κλαι-	+ σ	→ κλαυσ- (κλαίω has a slight stem change)

2. <u>For Verb Stems Ending in a Consonant</u>. When a σίγμα is added to a consonant either 1) the σίγμα wins out and totally replaces the consonant, 2) the σίγμα combines with the consonant to form ξ or ψ, or 3) the σίγμα is rejected by the consonant and simply is not added. This last scenario occurs when the consonant is liquid and is covered in **CHAPTER 21** (Liquid Verbs). The first two scenarios involve mutes:

Labial (lip sounds)	π	β	φ	+ σ	→ ψ
Dental (teeth sounds)	τ	δ	ϑ or ζ	+ σ	→ σ
Palatal (palate sounds)	κ	γ	χ	+ σ	→ ξ

Note that the dental mutes and ζ are simply replaced by the σίγμα. Examples of these are as follow:

Labials:	βλεπ	+ σ	→ βλεψ-
	γραφ	+ σ	→ γραψ-
Dentals and ζ:	πειϑ	+ σ	→ πεισ-
	βαπτιζ	+ σ	→ βαπτισ-
	δοξαζ	+ σ	→ δοξασ-
	εὐαγγελιζ	+ σ	→ εὐαγγελισ-
Palatals:	ἀνοιγ	+ σ	→ ἀνοιξ-
	διωκ	+ σ	→ διωξ-

Two verbs already learned also fit into the category of palatal, namely διδάσκω and κηρύσσω. Both verbs come from roots that actually end in Χῖ (χ): διδαχ- and κηρυχ-:

$$\text{διδασκ} + \sigma \quad → \text{διδαξ-}$$
$$\text{κηρυσσ} + \sigma \quad → \text{κηρυξ-}$$

C. **Actual Forms of Future and Aorist Tense Verbs:**

1. <u>Future Tense Forms</u>. A σίγμα added to a verb stem that ends in a consonant will cause some predictable changes. Here are the Future Active 1st singular forms of some verbs:

	<u>Pres. Ind.</u>		<u>Fut. Ind.</u>
labial	γράφω	→	γράψω
dental	πείϑω	→	πείσω
ζ stem	βαπτίζω	→	βαπτίσω
palatal	ἀνοίγω	→	ἀνοίξω
hidden	διδάσκω	→	διδάξω
stem -χ	κηρύσσω	→	κηρύξω

2. <u>Aorist Tense Forms</u>. A σίγμα added to a verb stem that ends in a consonant will cause some predictable changes. Here are the Aorist Active 1st singular forms of some verbs:

		Pres. Ind.		Aor. Ind.
labial		γράφω	→	ἔγραψα
dental		πείθω	→	ἔπεισα
ζ stem		βαπτίζω	→	ἐβάπτισα
palatal		ἀνοίγω	→	ἤνοιξα
hidden		διδάσκω	→	ἐδίδαξα
stem -χ		κηρύσσω	→	ἐκήρυξα

CHECK POINT 10.1-5

Given these verbs, first, create 3rd pl. Aorist Active and Future Active Tense forms, properly including the augment. Second, provide a translation.

		Aorist 3rd pl.	Future 3rd Pl.
1.	ἀνοίγω		
2.	πείθω		
3.	γράφω		
4.	ἀκούω		
5.	διδάσκω		
6.	κηρύσσω		
7.	διώκω		
8.	βαπτίζω		
9.	βλέπω		
10.	θεραπεύω		

ANSWERS

		Aorist 3rd pl.	Future 3rd Pl.
1.	ἀνοίγω	ἤνοιξαν *they opened*	ἀνοίξουσιν *they will open*
2.	πείθω	ἔπεισαν *they persuaded*	πείσουσιν *they will persuade*
3.	γράφω	ἔγραψαν *they wrote*	γράψουσιν *they will write*
4.	ἀκούω	ἤκουσαν *they heard*	ἀκούσουσιν *they will hear*
5.	διδάσκω	ἐδίδαξαν *they taught*	διδάξουσιν *they will teach*
6.	κηρύσσω	ἐκήρυξαν *they preached*	κηρύξουσιν *they will preach*
7.	διώκω	ἐδίωξαν *they persecuted*	διώξουσιν *they will persecute*
8.	βαπτίζω	ἐβάπτισαν *they baptized*	βαπτίσουσιν *they will baptize*
9.	βλέπω	ἔβλεψαν *they saw*	βλέψουσιν *they will see*
10.	θεραπεύω	ἐθεράπευσαν *they healed*	θεραπεύσουσιν *they will heal*

10.6 PRINCIPAL PARTS: AN EXPLANATION

A. **Stem Changes:** It has been repeated several times that tense can be indicated by a stem change in the verb. To keep track of these stem changes (which can be relatively small or extreme), the Greek verb has been divided up by grammarians into six Principal Parts. Within a Principal Part, the verb stem never changes, but across Principal Parts a verb's stem <u>may</u> undergo changes.

B. **Tense and Voice:** Fortunately, each Principal Part roughly corresponds to Tense and Voice. The six Principal Parts correspond to the tenses and voices given below:

First	Second	Third	Fourth	Fifth	Sixth
Present A M/P	Future A M	Aorist A M	Perfect A	Perfect M/P	Aorist P
Imperfect A M/P			Pluperfect A	Pluperfect M/P	Future P

Thus far, we have learned the first three Principal Parts of the verb. Note three things:

1. Always the Present and Imperfect Tense of any particular verb *will share exactly the same verb stem*. This is because they are both formed using the same Principal Part, i.e., the First Principal Part.

2. The Second and Third Principal Parts have no passive voice. To form the passive voice of these two tenses, one must look at the Sixth Principal Part.

3. The Fourth Principal Part is used to make the active voice of the Perfect and Pluperfect Tenses. To make the middle or passive voice of these two tenses, one must build it from the Fifth Principal Part.

C. **Verbs presented thus far in the Textbook:** *Most of the verbs presented so far experience no change in verb stem from one Principal Part to another.* However, probably half of all Greek verbs do have a slight (or great) stem change. One example is seen in our vocabulary: κλαίω. Here are the Principal Parts of κλαίω found in the Greek NT:

First	Second	Third	Fourth	Fifth	Sixth
κλαίω	κλαύσω	ἔκλαυσα	-	-	-

This verb is illustrative of several points:

1. This is the standard format for presenting verbs, i.e., in order of their Principal Parts.

2. Not every verb will show each Principal Part. This is true for κλαίω with regard to the last three Principal Parts in the Greek NT. A dash (-) is commonly used to show that no such form occurs in the Greek NT. "In the Greek NT" is an important qualifier, since the Perfect Middle (and Future Perfect Middle) occurs for κλαίω in classical poetry (Smyth, *College Grammar*, p. 702, §359). This is another reminder to us that the Greek of the NT is only one slice through the Greek language, a language that had undergone change and was in flux during the NT era.

3. A slight stem change occurs from the First Principal Part to the Second or Third Principal Parts (κλαι- to κλαυ-). There is no guarantee that any two Principal Parts of any given verb will be identical: One must simply learn the Principal Parts of each verb in order to see if this is the case. Thus far in the textbook, mostly regular verbs have been presented. Our paradigm verb πιστεύω is regular throughout all six Principal Parts. Its verb stem never changes. Unfortunately, not every Greek verb is like πιστεύω.

4. For now, try to become familiar with the concept of Principal Part, while not worrying about the tenses not yet covered or the more irregular verbs. The order of presentation and arrangement of chapters has been designed to make each student's mastery of the Greek verb as easy as possible.

10.7 An Oddly Formed Verb: Οἶδα

A. **Formation:** The verb οἶδα is irregular. In form it is actually in the Perfect Tense. However, *in translation* it is equivalent to the Present Tense. Although we have not covered the Perfect Tense, and since οἶδα occurs frequently and basically uses the Aorist endings (with no σίγμα), it is presented in this chapter.

	sg.			pl.
First	οἶδα	*I know.*	οἴδαμεν	We know.
Second	οἶδας	*You know.*	οἴδατε	You know.
Third	οἶδε(ν)	*He/She/It knows.*	οἴδαν	They know.

B. **Semantic and Pragmatics Uses:** Although in translation οἶδα is often translated by a simple present, its semantic and pragmatic use is often marked and important to observe. In its use, it often forms content clauses; also, it may create a metacomment.

1. <u>Content Clauses.</u> Semantically, οἶδα is a verb of thought; thus, it will often, although not always, use ὅτι to form a content clause (or indirect thought):

John 8:37a οἶδα ὅτι σπέρμα Ἀβραάμ ἐστε·
       I know that you are the seed of Abraham;

2. <u>Metacomments</u>. Pragmatically, οἶδα draws attention to the "knowing" of participants. Knowledge is power. Consider this scenario of children playing tag: John says, "I'm not it!" Susie responds, "You were tagged!" John retorts, "I was not!" Susie says, "I *know* that you were tagged." What difference does the claim make when appeal to firsthand knowledge (I *know*) is made? Such attention is one way that speakers and authors can prioritize information in the discourse, by letting audiences be privy to it. Such comments have been described as metacomments. See immediately below.

10.8 METACOMMENTS AND PRAGMATICS

A. **Definition:** Metacomments involve any explicit, self-reflective statements about information and communicative processes, outcomes, or warnings using verbs of saying, knowing, believing, hoping, etc. With speaking, a metacomment exists "When speakers stop saying what they are saying in order to comment on what is going to be said, speaking abstractly about it" (Runge, 101). For example, consider the prominence afforded to "Truly, truly I say to you, X…." when all that was needed to be said was simply "X…." But we all experience that metacomments are not limited to simply statements of speech. (I could have just said, "Metacomments are not limited to speech.")

B. **Pragmatics:** Metacomments slow down the discourse and point forward to statements for pragmatic effect (Runge, 101-24). Jeffrey Reed indicates, "Words of beseeching and saying (mental processes) often signal upcoming, thematically prominent material (e.g. 'I beseech you …')."[3] In short, the statements help reveal authorial intent by highlighting what is important. According to Paul Ricoeur (13), one advantage of "paying attention to these grammatical devices of the self-reference of discourse" is to understand that "The utterance meaning points back to the utterer's meaning thanks to the self-reference of discourse to itself as an event." The comments, then, point to the rhetorical situation, that is, the broader environment of the communicative event. (Read again §1.0 THE COMMUNICATIVE EVENT OF DISCOURSE.) Luming Mao describes the implications:

> ….if metadiscourse is a full-fledged rhetorical activity to be realized through metadiscourse markers, it has to be studied in connection to its rhetorical context. This rhetorical context provides a stage, as it were, on which various discourse activities, including metadiscourse, are to be 'enacted.' To try to make sense of metadiscourse without even alluding to such a context amounts to trying to present an incomplete, abstracted construct.[4]

---

[3] Jeffrey T. Reed, *A Discourse Analysis of Philippians: Method and Rhetoric in the Debate Over Literary Integrity*, Journal for the Study of the New Testament Supplement Series 136 (Sheffield: Sheffield Academic Press, 1997), 112.

[4] Luming R. Mao, "I Conclude Not: Toward a Pragmatic Account of Metadiscourse," *Rhetoric Review* 11 (1993): 265–89 at 270.

C. **Example:** The example given above from John 8:37a illustrates the strategic use of meta-comment that should be considered within the broader rhetorical context.

John 8:37a <u>οἶδα</u> ὅτι σπέρμα Ἀβραάμ ἐστε· ἀλλὰ ζητεῖτέ με ἀποκτεῖναι, ὅτι ὁ λόγος ὁ ἐμὸς οὐ χωρεῖ ἐν ὑμῖν.
<u>I know</u> that you are the seed of Abraham; but you are seeking to kill me, because my word does not occupy you!

Jesus's use of οἶδα marks off the declaration "You are Abraham's offspring" by recalling the earlier statement in 8:33 that was made by the religious authorities of themselves, "We are Abraham's offspring and have been enslaved to not one ever!" But notice how Jesus corrects their assertion immediately with the conjunction ἀλλὰ "But…!" The metacomment contrasts the self-affirmation (*we are Abraham's descendants*) with the reality (*you are seeking to kill me*). Jesus immediately introduces a further contrast by affirming his relationship with his Father, in contrast to their father, a discussion that builds to Jesus's statement that their father is the devil (8:44). So, the metacomment in 8:37 strategically functions to bring our attention to an important topic in a highly rhetorical context.

Complete WORKBOOK EXERCISES 10 and consult the ANSWER KEY & GUIDE as needed.

CASE IN POINT 10: AORIST AND FUTURE AMONGST THE TENSES

This chapter has introduced two new tenses and the concept of metacomment. It would be valuable to analyze the distinctiveness of the tenses in a context where several different tenses are found. If a metacomment is present, then all the better. Let's look at a few examples. Below is given the NASB95 translation with the verbs in bold and the Greek tenses identified in brackets.

John 16:19-20 [19] Jesus **knew** [*Aorist*] that they **wished** [*Imperfect*] to question Him, and He **said** [*Aorist*] to them, "**Are** you **deliberating** [*Present*] together about this, that I **said** [*Aorist*], 'A little while, and you **will** not **see** [*Present*] Me, and again a little while, and you **will see** [*Future*] Me'? [20] Truly, truly, I **say** [*Present*] to you, that you **will weep** and **lament** [*Future*], but the world **will rejoice** [*Future*]; you **will grieve** [*Future*], but your grief **will be turned** [*Future*] into joy.

These verses contain four different tenses. The context is the Farewell Discourse of John's Gospel (chs.13-17) in which Jesus discloses to the disciples the nature of his departure and what will befall them in the future. The disciples are indeed puzzled, which is indicated by the Imperfect verb *wished*, which would probably better translated *were wishing* or *were wanting*, meaning that they had hitherto not asked; this is a conative imperfect (see §8.2.D and Wallace 550-52). Jesus *knew* (Aorist) that they were puzzled. This is an indirect metacomment, since it is narrated about Jesus. A direct metacomment would be if Jesus made the claim himself, "I know that…." Still, however,

John is highlighting Jesus's awareness of the disciples' wanting to do something. The Aorist Tense with *knew* represents mainline narrative. In reality *Jesus was likely knowing all along* (an imperfective verbal aspect) that the disciples were puzzling about his statements; but, the grammar of John's Gospel does not stress Jesus's knowledge as imperfective. Instead, we have a constantive use of the Aorist Tense, found also with the verb **said**. The actions of Jesus *knowing* and *saying* are perfective in aspect and are translated using the English simple past tense. The first present tense verb ("**are you deliberating**") reflects imperfective action that is ongoing. The second Present Tense verb (*you **will** not **see***) shows a special use called the Futuristic Present (see Wallace 535-37). All the instances of the Future Tenses here reflect the predictive use. Finally, 16:20 begins with a very marked metacomment that indicates Jesus' subsequent statements are certain: Jesus foretells certain events, especially the disciples' grieving using an emphatic subject (ὑμεῖς λυπηθήσεσθε), but then also predictes their greif turning into joy. Thus, the metacomment underscores the hardship that will come, but more importantly the eventual reversal of circumstance.

Here is another verse to illustrate the use of tenses:

Matt 4:11 Then the devil **left** [*Present*] Him; and behold, angels **came** [*Aorist*] and **began to minister** [*Imperfect*] to Him.

The Present Tense verb is an Historic Present (HP) and is thus translated as a past tense in English. Remember that HPs highlight significant actions or speech (see §6.6 HISTORIC PRESENT (HP) AND DISCOURSE PRAGMATICS). Here, the Devil finally leaves Jesus after a series of temptations. The Aorist Tense for the verb translated **came** is constantive. Of particular interest is the Imperfect Tense verb. The NASB95 translates it as an Inceptive or Ingressive Imperfect (starting an action), **began to minister**. However, the verb may simply be a Progressive Imperfect, with emphasis being on the description of the angels serving Jesus repeatedly for a time; in other words, *it was not a brief assistance*. Finally, consider this verse.

James 2:22 You **see** [*Present*] that faith **was working** [*Imperfect*] with his works, and as a result of the works, faith **was perfected** [*Aorist*];

The use of the Present Tense is timeless or gnomic; James wanted them to have before their eyes the general truth on faith and works. This is, moreover, a metacomment that makes explicit the audiences' "sight" of seeing how faith works. The metacomment highlights what follows as important. It is not surprising, then, that we find an imperfect tense verb form with imperfective aspect, to help convey either a progressive act (faith and works continuously working together in the one example of Abraham offering up Isaac) or a customary action (that on each occasion of faith Abraham displayed works/action). The final verb is in the Aorist Tense, in which the aspect conveys that the action is viewed as a whole, complete or completed. This instance can be classified as a consummative aorist—faith is perfected (brought to its goal) through actions as it is lived out.

One can see from these examples that the Greek Tenses are dynamic. The choice of tense is contextually constrained, but also reveals authorial perspectives on the actions. Errors of interpretation have occurred from neglect of tense, from using outdated or wrongly stated grammatical information, and from assigning "labels" of possible uses without proper consideration of lexical choice and context. So, my recommendation: Rely on updated grammars for current and balanced descriptions of the tense and exercise caution and restraint when interpreting the significance of Greek verb tenses. Let the verb choice and context guide you.

Returning to John's Gospel, something significant happened earlier when Andrew (Ἀνδρέας) and Philip (Φίλιππος), both Greek names meaning *manly* and *horse-lover* respectively, are sought out by Greeks and this is reported to Jesus (12:20-22). At this, Jesus stated, "The hour has come for the Son of Humanity to be glorified" (12:23). Earlier in John, when Jesus spoke of his departure, the Jewish Officials were confused and wondered, "He isn't about to go into the diaspora of the Greeks and to teach the Greeks, is he?" (7:35). Below is a map of Greece showing major travel routes by sea that Paul and other missionaries would have taken.[5]

HELLAS: THE ÆGEAN LANDS

Routes across the Ægean Sea

---

[5] Map (slightly edited) is from William Carey Morey, *Outlines of Greek History: With a Survey of Ancient Oriental Nations* (New York: American Book Company, 1903), 72

CHAPTER 11

How versatile is the Greek language to convey the truth of the Gospel! Wallace has said, "Learning the genitive uses well pays big dividends. It has a great deal of exegetical significance, far more so than any of the other cases, because it is capable of a wide variety of interpretations" (74). The genitive case as used in Col 2:16-23 illustrates such versatility as the Apostle Paul warns believers not to be judged or defrauded by people issuing "religious" rules that do not draw people to Christ. A close look at the use of the genitive case will raise important questions and provide helpful data to consider Paul's points in this passage.

This chapter covers the **2nd Aorist Verbs**. These verbs show their tense by their stem change. There are seventeen such verbs (some have already been learned). A complete listing of Principal Parts for these 2nd Aorist Verbs is given below. The **Future of εἰμί** is presented. Lastly, further common uses of the **Genitive Case** are described.

VOCABULARY 11 2ND AORIST VERBS

ἀναβαίνω [81]	I go up, ascend	ἐσθίω [158]	I eat, consume
κ αταβαίνω [80]	I go down, descend	λαμβάνω [258]	I take; I receive
ἀποθνῄσκω [111]	I die	παραλαμβάνω [49]	I take along
γίνομαι [667]	I become, am; I come; I happen	ὁράω [453]	I see; I perceive; I understand
γινώσκω [221]	I know, understand	πίνω [72]	I drink
ἐπιγινώσκω [44]	I know about; I understand	πίπτω [90]	I fall, collapse
	Special Preposition:	ἕως [145] gen. until; as far as; as long as	
		ἕως while (as a conjunction)	

After learning vocabulary to this point, you will know 62.1% of the words in the GNT. If you are able, listen to audio recordings of VOCABULARY 11 and complete the CROSSWORD PUZZLE in the WORKBOOK EXERCISES.

NOTES ON VOCABULARY 11:

You should notice that several of the verbs above are compound forms of other verbs. The verb βαίνω (I walk; I go) does not occur in the GNT, yet it has two compounded forms that are clearly related in meaning. Κατά carries the sense of *down* and ἀνά (an improper preposition and more like an adverb) means *again; upwards*. Ἀποθνῄσκω is related to ὁ θάνατος *death*. Are you able to see the condensed Greek root after the compounded preposition?

The next two verbs are very common and important. Γίνομαι is involved in various idioms. It carries a wide range of meanings and sometimes takes a predicate nominative like εἰμί. Ἐπιγνώσκω is an intensified compounded verb form. This compound verb might denote more of an intimate or complete knowledge than γινώσκω.

Two common verbs are λαμβάνω and ὁράω. The former has many compounded forms and a high frequency inclusive of these compounded forms. It may seem odd that this verb can mean both *take* and *receive*. We normally perceive these two actions to be quite opposite, but in a gift-giving reciprocating society, this is not so strange. Below is a common Greek drinking cup, called a κύλιξ, which dates to 500 BC.[1] This depicts a woman dancing. Such a cup would be used in re-lation to several verbs in the vocabulary: eating (ἐσθίω), drinking (πίνω), and falling down (πίπτω).

Ἕως is an improper preposition that takes the genitive case when it has an object. Sometimes it functions as a conjunction meaning *while*.

---

[1] "Dancing woman krotala BM 1920,0613.1" by Euergides Painter - ChrisO, Own work, 2007. Licensed under CC BY-SA 3.0 via Wikimedia Commons; http://commons.wikimedia.org/wiki/File:Dancing_ woman_ krotala_BM_1920, 0613.1.jpg. In the original image, the dancer and light colors are sandy tan.

11.1 2ND AORIST VERBS: GENERAL INFORMATION

A. General Information:

1. <u>Same Aorist Meaning</u>. Some verbs show a special formation of the Aorist Tense that is called a 2nd Aorist. These 2nd Aorist verbs also belong to the Third Principal Part <u>and</u> *have the exact same Aorist meaning of perfective aspect—action viewed as a whole and complete(d)*. However, 2nd Aorist verbs are formed differently than the 1st Aorist verbs. A verb is *typically* formed *either* as a 1st Aorist *or* as a 2nd Aorist. The 1st Aorist form, re-member, adds a σίγμα with α/ε coupling vowels to the end of the verb stem with the sec-ondary tense endings. The 2nd Aorists usually do not (yet –σα endings sometimes occur).

2. <u>Stem Changes, Sometimes originally a different Verb Stem</u>. People use different "forms" for the same verb in different tenses: I *go*, I *went*, I *had gone*. In Greek, this is also true. In fact, sometimes these **different tense forms are the roots of different verbs**. For the com-mon verb λέγω *I say*, the future tense form ἐρῶ *I will say* and aorist tense form εἶπον *I said* are from two different verb roots! But in actual usage and in grammar conventions, these different verb forms are often treated together as if from the same verb λέγω (or sometimes εἶπον is acknowledged).

B. In Principal Parts:
The 2nd Aorist forms belong to the Third Principal Part. Thus, the verb stem used to form the 2nd Aorist is seen primarily under the Third Principal Part column. Oc-casionally, however, the same or a very similar stem is used in other Principal Parts.

11.2 2ND AORIST VERBS: FORMATION AND TRANSLATION

A. Formation:
Typically the 2nd Aorist Verbs use the Imperfect Tense endings (o/ε coupling vowels and the secondary endings). *So, one differentiates the Imperfect Tense form and the Aorist Tense form in 2nd Aorist Verbs by the difference of the changed verb stem in the aorist formation.* Thus, the 2nd Aorists are formed as follows:

augment + changed stem + o/ε coupling vowels + secondary endings.

1. For example, here are the 2nd Aorist forms for ἄγω (2nd Aorist stem → ἀγαγ):

ἐ + αγαγ + 2nd Aorist Tense Endings (here active)

ἤγαγον	ἠγάγομεν	Remember that augments combine
ἤγαγες	ἠγάγετε	with initial vowel on verb stems:
ἤγαγε(ν)	ἤγαγον	ἐ + α → ἠ

2. Here is another example with γίνομαι (2nd Aorist stem → γεν):

<table>
<tr><td>ἐγενόμην</td><td>ἐγενόμεθα</td><td rowspan="3">Notice that the endings are middle
in form. This is because γίνομαι is
a middle-formed verb.</td></tr>
<tr><td>ἐγένου</td><td>ἐγένεσθε</td></tr>
<tr><td>ἐγένετο</td><td>ἐγένοντο</td></tr>
</table>

3. Ἀναβαίνω and γινώσκω have forms in which the long vowel of their 2nd Aorist Verb stems (βη- and γνω-) absorb the coupling vowel of the ending. So, here are there full endings:

<table>
<tr><td>ἀνέβην</td><td>ἀνέβημεν</td><td></td><td>ἔγνων</td><td>ἔγνωμεν</td></tr>
<tr><td>ἀνέβης</td><td>ἀνέβητε</td><td></td><td>ἔγνως</td><td>ἔγνωτε</td></tr>
<tr><td>ἀνέβη</td><td>ἀνέβησαν</td><td></td><td>ἔγνω</td><td>ἔγνωσαν</td></tr>
</table>

4. Occasionally, 2nd Aorist Verbs will show 1st Aorist Verb endings (–σα etc.), often with the σίγμα missing. Although this might sound confusing, it actually will aid your parsing and translation. See the listing of forms in §11.4 below for which verbs occasionally show –(σ)α endings.

B. **Translation:** The 2nd Aorist Verbs are translated *just like other Aorist Tense Verbs*. For the translation of Aorist Tense Verbs, see §10.4 and Wallace 554-65.) Here is the translation of the 2nd Aorist forms from ἄγω.

<table>
<tr><td>ἤγαγον</td><td>I led.</td><td>ἠγάγομεν</td><td>We led.</td></tr>
<tr><td>ἤγαγες</td><td>You led.</td><td>ἠγάγετε</td><td>You led.</td></tr>
<tr><td>ἤγαγε(ν)</td><td>He/She led.</td><td>ἤγαγον</td><td>They led.</td></tr>
</table>

11.3 COMMON 2ND AORIST STEMS

We have already learned that tense in the Greek verb can be signaled in five ways: (1) affixing a **prefix** to the front of a verb stem; (2) **changing** the verb stem; (3) supplying a **tense indicator**; (4) supplying a **coupling vowel**; and (5) adding types of **endings**.

Prefix + Stem Change + Tense Indicator + Coupling Vowel + Endings

   (1)   (2)   (3)   (4)   (5)

For 2nd Aorist verbs, the stem change is paramount. Below is a comprehensive listing of the 2nd Aorist stems. Notice that compound verbs, since they share the same stem, also have the 2nd Aorist stem change. The student will need to memorize these 2nd Aorist stems to recognize and parse them in context. The most frequent stems in the Greek NT are given an asterisk (*). **Focus first on these.** Some are very similar to their lexical form; some are *very different*. For example, the 2nd Aorist stem for βάλλω (βαλ) is very similar to the Imperfect stem (βαλλ). This can create parsing problems. Thus, one λάμβδα is the difference between the Imperfect ἔβαλλον and the 2nd Aorist ἔβαλον.

Lexical Form	Compound Forms	2nd Aorist Stem
ἄγω	συνάγω, ὑπάγω	ἀγαγ
[βαίνω]	ἀναβαίνω, καταβαίνω	ἀνα-βη
ἀποθνῄσκω		ἀποθαν
βάλλω	ἐκβάλλω	βαλ*
γίνομαι		γεν*
γινώσκω	ἐπιγινώσκω	γνω*
ἔρχομαι	ἀπέρχομαι, διέρχομαι, εἰσέρχομαι, ἐξέρχομαι, προσέρχομαι	ἐλθ*
ἐσθίω		φαγ
εὑρίσκω		εὑρ
ἔχω		σχ
λαμβάνω	παραλαμβάνω	λαβ*
λέγω		εἰπ*
ὁράω		ἰδ*
πάσκω		παθ
πίνω		πι
πίπτω		πεσ
φέρω	προσφέρω	ἐνεγκ

11.4 COMPLETE LIST OF PRINCIPAL PARTS FOR THE 2ND AORIST VERBS

This list is provided to ease your mind about which tenses and forms you should be learning. These will be reviewed in this Chapter's exercises. Over half of the 2nd Aorist verbs will show a middle-formed Future Tense. What this means is that, when formed in the Future, the verb will take Future Middle endings, yet with an active meaning. A few verb forms (marked with †) involve special matters of formation to be treated later in the textbook; ignore these for now. The arrow (→) indicates that the compounded forms also display that Principal Part in the Greek NT. A dash (–) means no Principal Part of that verb is found in the GNT.

2ND AORIST VERBS BY PRINCIPAL PART COVERED THROUGH CH.11			
First	Second	Third	Important Notes
ἄγω	ἄξω	ἤγαγον	
συνάγω	→	→	
ὑπάγω	–	–	
βάλλω	βαλῶ †	ἔβαλον	
ἐκβάλλω	→	→	

εὑρίσκω	εὑρήσω	εὗρον	εὗρα is an alternative form
ἔχω	ἔξω	ἔσχον	
λέγω	ἐρῶ †	εἶπον	εἶπα is an alternative form
πάσχω	–	ἔπαθον	Has no Future form in NT
φέρω	οἴσω	ἤνεγκα	Has endings like οἶδα;
προσφέρω	–	→	ἤνεγκον sometimes occurs

2ND AORIST VERBS WITH A MIDDLE-FORMED FUTURE TENSE

ἀναβαίνω	ἀναβήσομαι	ἀνέβην	The stem vowel η in αναβη rejects the coupling vowels ο or ε.
καταβαίνω	→	→	
ἀποθνήσκω	ἀποθανοῦμαι †	ἀπέθανον	
γίνομαι	γενήσομαι	ἐγενόμην	
γινώσκω	γνώσομαι	ἔγνων	The stem vowel ω in γνω rejects the coupling vowels ο or ε. Also, ἔγνωσα is an alternative form.
ἐπιγινώσκω	→	→	
ἔρχομαι	ἐλεύσομαι	ἦλθον	ἦλθα is an alternative form
ἀπέρχομαι	→	→	
διέρχομαι	→	→	
εἰσέρχομαι	→	→	
ἐξέρχομαι	→	→	
προσέρχομαι	–	→	
ἐσθίω	φάγομαι	ἔφαγον	
λαμβάνω	λήμψομαι	ἔλαβον	
παραλαμβάνω	→	→	
ὁράω †	ὄψομαι	εἶδον	εἶδα or ὤψησα as alternatives
πίνω	πίομαι	ἔπιον	
πίπτω	πέσομαι	ἔπεσον	ἔπεσα is an alternative form.

11.5 FUTURE FORMS OF Εἰμί

Remember that the verb εἰμί has no voice. The Future Tense forms are built from the Future Middle endings:

	sg.		pl.	
1	ἔσομαι	I will be	ἐσόμεθα	we will be
2	ἔσῃ	you will be	ἔσεσθε	you will be
3	ἔσται	s/he will be	ἔσονται	they will be
		it will be		

CHECK POINT 11.1-5

Parse these verb forms, identify the 2nd Aorist Stem, and provide a basic translation.

1. κατέβη			
2. ἦλθον			
3. ἀπῆλθεν			
4. ἀπέθανον			
5. ἐγένετο			
6. ἔσται			
7. ἤνεγκαν			
8. ἔσεσθε			
9. ἐξέβαλεν			
10. ἦλθεν			
11. συνήγαγον			
12. ἔσῃ			
13. ἔγνωσαν			
14. ἔσχεν			

ANSWERS

1. κατέβη	A-A-I 3 S	βη	*he went down*
2. ἦλθον	A-A-I 1 S or 3 P	ἐλθ	*I (or they) came*
3. ἀπῆλθεν	A-A-I 3 S	ἐλθ	*s/he departed*
4. ἀπέθανον	A-A-I 1 S or 3 P	ἀποθαν	*I (or they) died*
5. ἐγένετο	A-D-I 3 S	γεν	*it happened (or s/he became)*
6. ἔσται	F-A-I 3 S	from εἰμί	*s/he will be*
7. ἤνεγκαν	A-A-I 3 P	ἐνεγκ	*they brought*
8. ἔσεσθε	F-A-I 2 P	from εἰμί	*you (pl.) will be*
9. ἐξέβαλεν	A-A-I 3 S	βαλ	*s/he cast out*
10. ἦλθεν	A-A-I 3 S	ἐλθ	*s/he came*
11. συνήγαγον	A-A-I 1 S or 3 P	ἀγαγ	*I (or they) gathered together*
12. ἔσῃ	F-A-I 2 S	from εἰμί	*you (sg.) will be*
13. ἔγνωσαν	A-A-I 3 P	γνω	*they knew*
14. ἔσχεν	A-A-I 3 S	σχ	*s/he had*

11.6 COMMON USES OF THE GENITIVE CASE

A. Introduction:

1. <u>Analogous to the Dative Having Other Uses</u>. In §6.3.C.3, we learned that the dative case, in addition to signifying the indirect object, may be used to indicate the means by which some action is accomplished. Grammarians regularly call this special usage the Dative of Means. For each of the Greek noun cases, there are other special uses with which beginning students should become acquainted. In §14.5 the common uses of the dative case will be treated. Here is a suitable location to introduce students to the more common uses of the genitive case.

2. <u>Genitive Categories</u>. Most essentially, the Genitive case is the case of **description** or **separation (ablative senses)**. Wallace (72-136) will subdivide specific uses of the Genitive into five broad categories: Adjectival, Ablative (source/separation), Verbal, Adverbial, and "After Certain Words." Prepositions will help delimit the sense of genitive nouns; for instance, the prepositions ἐκ *out of/from* and ἀπό *from* help demarcate the ablative senses of source or separation, which rarely occur with the genitive by itself. In earlier Greek, such was not the case.

B. **Major Uses:** Included below are the most common genitive functions in the GNT based upon Wallace's estimations of "quite common" to "fairly common."

1. <u>Possessive Genitive</u>. This use is quite common (Wallace 81-83). The noun in the genitive case possesses the noun it modifies. Closely related to this is the **Genitive of Relationship** (see Wallace 83-84) in which the genitive case is used to indicate formal family relationship. <u>How to translate:</u> *belonging to*, or *of*.

   Acts 20:28 τὴν ἐκκλησίαν τοῦ θεοῦ *the church of God*

   Matt 14:3 Ἡρῳδιάδα τὴν γυναῖκα Φιλίππου *Herodia, the wife of Philip*

2. <u>Attributive Genitive</u>. This use is very common (Wallace 86-88). The noun in the genitive case ascribes an attribute to the noun it modifies. How to translate: *characterized by*.

   Rom 6:6 τὸ σῶμα τῆς ἁμαρτίας *the body characterized by sin* or *the sinful body*

   2 Cor 1:3 ὁ πατὴρ τῶν οἰκτιρμῶν *the Father characterized by compassions* or *the compassionate Father*

3. <u>Subjective Genitive</u>. This use is common (Wallace 113-16). This construction is more difficult to identify and translate. The idea is that the noun in the genitive case functions as the subject of the verbal idea implicit in the noun it modifies. <u>How to translate</u>: Convert the verbal noun to which the genitive is related into a verbal form and turn the genitive into its subject.

Rom 8:35a τίς ἡμᾶς χωρίσει <u>ἀπὸ τῆς ἀγάπης τοῦ Χριστοῦ</u>;
Who will separate us <u>from the love of Christ</u>? (i.e. *Christ's love for us*)
Thus, *Who will separate us from <u>Christ's</u> love?*

2 Cor 7:15 τὴν πάντων ὑμῶν ὑπακοήν *the obedience of you all* (i.e. *your obedient action*)

4. <u>Objective Genitive</u>. This use is common (Wallace 116-19). This construction is the converse of the subjective genitive. Here the genitive case noun functions as the direct object of the verbal idea implicit in the noun it modifies. <u>How to translate</u>: Instead of using *of*, supply words like *for*, *toward*, *about*, *concerning*, or sometimes *against*.

Rom 2:23b <u>διὰ τῆς παραβάσεως τοῦ νόμου</u> τὸν θεὸν ἀτιμάζεις.
You dishonor God <u>through transgression of the law</u>.
(i.e., *your transgressing the law*)

Acts 2:42 τῇ κλάσει τοῦ ἄρτου = *the breaking of bread*

Here are two examples. See if you can determine which one is more likely a subjective genitive or which one is more likely an objective genitive.

ἡ παρουσία τοῦ κυρίου = *The coming of the Lord (or [when] the Lord comes)*

ἡ βλασφημία τοῦ πνεύματος = *The blasphemy of the Spirit (or blaspheming the Spirit).*

5. <u>Attributed Genitive</u>. This use is relatively common (Wallace 89-91). It is the opposite of the attributive genitive. The noun being governed by the genitive noun is acting like an attributive adjective. <u>How to translate</u>: Either translate with *of* or simply convert the noun being modified into an adjective.

Rom 6:4 οὕτως καὶ ἡμεῖς <u>ἐν καινότητι ζωῆς</u> περιπατήσωμεν.
so that we may walk <u>in newness of life</u> (i.e. *in a new life*)

1 Pet 1:7 τὸ δοκίμιον ὑμῶν τῆς πίστεως *the genuineness of your faith*

6. Genitive of Direct Object. This use is relatively common (Wallace 131-34). Here particular verbs take the genitive case for their direct objects. These verbs typically involve the notions of sensation, emotion/volition, sharing, or ruling.

Luke 22:25 οἱ βασιλεῖς τῶν ἐθνῶν <u>κυριεύουσιν αὐτῶν</u>
The Kings of the gentiles <u>rule over them</u>.

7. Partitive Genitive. This use is relatively common (Wallace 84-86). It occurs when one member or smaller group is identified as belonging to a larger group indicated by the genitive noun. How to translate: *which is a part of* or *who is a member of*, etc.

εἷς τῶν διδασκάλων *one [who is a member] of the teachers*
πολλοὶ (ἐκ) τῶν Ἰουδαίων *many [who are members] of the Jews*

8. Genitive of Comparison. This use is relatively common (Wallace 110-12). It is used after comparative adjective constructions that are covered in §25.5. How to translate: *than*.

9. Appositional Genitive. This use is fairly common (Wallace 94-100). "The genitive of apposition typically states a specific example that is a part of the larger category named by the head noun" (95). How to translate: *which is; who is.*

Rom 4:11a καὶ σημεῖον ἔλαβεν <u>περιτομῆς</u> *He received the sign of circumcision*

2 Cor 1:22b τὸν ἀρραβῶνα <u>τοῦ πνεύματος</u> *the advanced payment <u>of the Spirit</u>*

This appositional genitive is different than the "simple apposition" in which one substantive agrees with another in number and case (not just the genitive case) and the two substantives are essentially equivalent:

John 8:44 ὑμεῖς ἐκ τοῦ πατρὸς <u>τοῦ διαβόλου</u> ἐστὲ
You are from the <u>father</u>, <u>the devil</u>.

10. Genitive of Content. This use is fairly common with certain words (Wallace 92-94). The genitive noun is the "content" of the noun it modifies. How to translate: *full of; containing*.

John 21:8b τὸ δίκτυον τῶν ἰχθύων *net full of fish*

Col 2:3 πάντες οἱ θησαυροὶ τῆς σοφίας καὶ γνώσεως...
All the treasures of wisdom and knowledge...

Complete WORKBOOK EXERCISES 11 and consult the ANSWER KEY & GUIDE as needed.

CASE IN POINT 11: THE GENITIVE NOUNS OF COL 2:16-23

The genitive case may convey a variety of nuances. A consideration of possible meanings of the genitive case will raise important questions for exegesis. An investigation of how genitive case nouns function in Col 2:16-23 will provide us an opportunity to consider important interpretive options. The genitive case nouns are underlined in English translation of the NASB95.

[16] Therefore no one is to act as your judge in regard to food or drink or in respect <u>to a festival</u> or <u>a new moon</u> or <u>a Sabbath day</u>– [17] things which are a *mere* shadow of what is to come; but the substance <u>belongs to Christ</u>. [18] Let no one keep defrauding you of your prize by delighting in self-abasement and the worship <u>of the angels</u>, taking his stand on *visions* he has seen, inflated without cause by his <u>fleshly</u> mind, [19] and not holding fast to the head, from whom the entire body, being supplied and held together by the joints and ligaments, grows with a growth <u>which is from God</u>. [20] If you have died with Christ to the elementary principles <u>of the world</u>, why, as if you were living in the world, do you submit yourself to decrees, such as, [21] "Do not handle, do not taste, do not touch!" [22] (which all *refer to* things destined to perish with use)-- in accordance with the commandments and teachings <u>of men</u>? [23] These are matters which have, to be sure, the appearance <u>of wisdom in</u> self-made religion and self-abasement and severe treatment <u>of the body</u>, *but are* of no value against <u>fleshly</u> indulgence.

[16] Μὴ οὖν τις ὑμᾶς κρινέτω ἐν βρώσει καὶ ἐν πόσει ἢ ἐν μέρει <u>ἑορτῆς</u> ἢ <u>νεομηνίας</u> ἢ <u>σαββάτων</u>· [17] ἅ ἐστιν σκιὰ τῶν μελλόντων, τὸ δὲ σῶμα τοῦ <u>Χριστοῦ</u>. [18] μηδεὶς ὑμᾶς καταβραβευέτω θέλων ἐν ταπεινοφροσύνῃ καὶ θρησκείᾳ τῶν <u>ἀγγέλων</u>, ἃ ἑόρακεν ἐμβατεύων, εἰκῇ φυσιούμενος ὑπὸ τοῦ νοὸς τῆς <u>σαρκὸς</u> αὐτοῦ, [19] καὶ οὐ κρατῶν τὴν κεφαλήν, ἐξ οὗ πᾶν τὸ σῶμα διὰ τῶν ἁφῶν καὶ συνδέσμων ἐπιχορηγούμενον καὶ συμβιβαζόμενον αὔξει τὴν αὔξησιν τοῦ <u>θεοῦ</u>. [20] Εἰ ἀπεθάνετε σὺν Χριστῷ ἀπὸ τῶν στοιχείων τοῦ <u>κόσμου</u>, τί ὡς ζῶντες ἐν κόσμῳ δογματίζεσθε; [21] μὴ ἅψῃ μηδὲ γεύσῃ μηδὲ θίγῃς, [22] ἅ ἐστιν πάντα εἰς φθορὰν τῇ ἀποχρήσει, κατὰ τὰ ἐντάλματα καὶ διδασκαλίας τῶν <u>ἀνθρώπων</u>, [23] ἅτινά ἐστιν λόγον μὲν ἔχοντα <u>σοφίας</u> ἐν ἐθελοθρησκίᾳ καὶ ταπεινοφροσύνῃ [καὶ] ἀφειδίᾳ <u>σώματος</u>, οὐκ ἐν τιμῇ τινι πρὸς πλησμονὴν τῆς <u>σαρκός</u>.

The first three Genitive nouns are modifying a word meaning *portion* or *matter* (μέρος). It is hard to determine whether the sense is partitive (*in a part of a feast, or of a new moon, or of Sabbaths*) or expressing apposition (*in the matter of a feast, or of a new moon, or of Sabbaths*).

Verse 17 contains a genitive noun located within a verbless statement that is hard to understand: τὸ δὲ σῶμα τοῦ Χριστοῦ (literally, *Moreover, the body of Christ*). Debate turns on the meaning of the word translated as *substance* (σῶμα) which more typically means *body* (physical or corporate entity). But here, *body* may be contrasted with the word *shadow* (σκιά) as is attested in a few instances in ancient literature (see "σκιά" BDAG 931.c) and supported by BDAG (984.4). Translations that agree with this meaning still disagree with the sense, however. The NLT has "Christ himself is that reality" which takes the genitive "of Christ" as an appositional genitive. Other translations retain the possessive sense: "the substance belongs to Christ" (ESV). I wonder whether τὸ σῶμα refers to the corporate *body* of believers. If the genitive is possessive, then Paul is simply saying *Moreover, the body belongs to Christ*, meaning that Christ has jurisdiction over rules and regulations in the body that belongs to Him as its political head.

Verse 18 contains two interesting genitives. *The worship of angels* is an excellent example of an objective genitive in which the genitive noun is like the object to the verbal idea in the head noun, thus translated *the worshipping of angels*. The second genitive translated literally is *by his mind of flesh* or *by the mind of his flesh*. The genitive may be attributive in which the noun in the genitive case ascribes an attribute to the main noun, namely one of *fleshliness*. Or, the sense may be possessive—*by the mind belonging to the flesh*, i.e., *the mind that the flesh controls*. Paul may be describing a situation in which religious visions are actually the product of fanciful thinking arising out of one's own person or flesh. (How often does this happen today?) As we will ponder below, "the Flesh" is a force for persons to have mastery over; the question is how this mastery is achieved.

In contrast to this is the genitive idea of 2:19: *a growth which is from God*. This would appear to be a relatively rare genitival use—the genitive of producer (see Wallace 104-6)—in which the genitive noun produces the noun it governs. The point is that there are two sources of the spiritual life: One can (try to) live independently by living out of the Flesh or one may participate in the dynamically growing body, which God grows (cf. Gal 3:16-24; Eph 4:15-16). A fuller explanation on how one comes to participate in this God-growing body is provided in Col 2:20-22, which entails two more genitives that describe dying to *the elementary principles of the world* and not submitting to *the teachings of humans*. Both genitives may be attributive Genitives (*worldly principles* and *human teachings*) or possessive genitives (*principles belonging to the World* and *the teachings belonging to the(se) humans* [notice the article with τῶν ἀνθρώπων]).

Verse 23 explains the nature of such teachings. The beginning of 2:23 is translated: *which are indeed having a word of wisdom*, which may be an attributive genitive (*wise* word). Such wisdom, however, only leads to *severe treatment of the body*, which is another clear instance of an objective genitive. Taken as such, we understand the genitive noun as the object of the verbal idea of *severe treatment*, and translate this as *severely treating the body*. Paul argues that such severe treatment has no value for curbing *the indulgence of the flesh*. This final genitive noun could be an attributive genitive (*fleshly* indulgence) as the NASB95 translates it. However, notice that the noun *flesh* has an article while the lead noun does not; this imbalance is unusual and breaks a general rule called Apollonius' Canon (see §24.6 and Wallace 239-40). This suggests to me that we should preserve the identity of *the flesh* as an active entity and understand the construction as an objective genitive, translating it as *indulging the flesh*. Thus, it would appear here that *the flesh* is presented as a powerful force that must be denied, which corresponds to Paul's ethical understanding in anthropological and theological perspective. In Rom 8:3-13 and Gal 3:3; 5:16-24 Paul contrasts *the flesh* with the power of God in the Holy Spirit. In each context, Paul calls believers to die with Christ to the flesh in order to live in Christ to God (Col 2:20; 3:3; Gal 2:19-21; Rom 6:7-8; 7:6).

This picture is from the south side of the Altar of Peace (*Ara Pacis*) at Rome.[2] It was made by Augustus. This exposure of the frieze shows the imperial family walking in procession. Notice how the women will have their hair covered. In the Greek world in the east, Aristotle had earlier described the existence of various city officials (called magistrates) to help retain gender and social distinctions in public and primarily with respect to religious activities. Their provenance extended as far south as Alexandria, as far west as Syracuse, and as far north as Thasos in the Northern Aegean sea.[3] One such group oversaw the conduct of women—called γυναικονόμοι ("the controllers of women"). These made sure women dressed properly without too much ornamentation, mourned properly at funerals, were proper distinguished in religious ceremony, spent money properly, etc. Their roles varies slightly from city to city. Riet van Bremen summarizes the role of these magistrates:

> Aristotle, in the *Politics*, does indeed describe the *gynaikonomos*, together with the *paidonomos* and 'other magistracies exercising similar supervisory functions'…; he also lists the *gynaikonomia* with the *paidonomia*, *nomophylakia* and *gymnasiarchia* under the heading of magistracies that 'are concerned with *eukosmia* (good order, decorum) and specific to cities that have a certain amount of leisure and wealth' (*Pol.* 1300a4; 1322b39; 1323a4)…. In our period, these magistracies had developed from being specific only to certain types of cities to being virtually ubiquitous and characteristic of cities' concern with acculturating the young and with guarding the public decorum and moral integrity of those groups that were deemed to be in need of supervision precisely because they were essential to the integrity of the citizen body as a whole.[4]

---

[2] The photo (here slightly edited) was taken by MM. It is in the public domain and used under CC BY-SA 3.0.

[3] Daniel Ogden, *Greek Bastardy in the Classical and Hellenistic Periods* (Oxford: Clarendon Press, 1996), 366. Ogden's is the most extensive treament of γυναικονόμοι.

[4] Riet van Bremen, "Family Structures," in *A Companion to the Hellenistic World*, ed. Andrew Erskine, Blackwell Companions to the Ancient World: Ancient History (Oxford: Blackwell, 2003), 313–30 at 323-24.

CHAPTER 12

How important is it to determine the referent to a pronoun? Very. The CASE IN POINT *demonstrates* this (pun intended).

This chapter introduces **Third Declension Nouns** and **Adjectives**. The Third Declension is comprised of Masculine, Neuter, and Feminine nouns. Next, a group of adjectives are presented that deal with **number** and **amount**. Such adjectives are significant because they often contribute **quantitative emphasis** to what is being communicated. Next, the **Demonstrative Pronouns** are introduced, which use the First and Second Declension endings. Additionally, demonstrative pronouns provide contour to discourse by pointing out words spatially (near and far), by pointing forward to a target statement, or by sometimes being placed in a forward position indicating **demonstrative emphasis**. Finally, students are shown how to **Navigate Major NT Lexicons**.

VOCABULARY 12 THIRD DECLENSION NOUNS, ADJECTIVES, DEMONSTRATIVES

Third Declension Nouns:

ὁ αἰών, αἰῶνος [122]	age, era; life span; eternity
ὁ ἀνήρ, ἀνδρός [216]	man; husband
ὁ ἄρχων, ἄρχοντος [37]	ruler
ὁ πατήρ, πατρός [413]	father
ὁ πούς, ποδός [93]	foot
τὸ ὕδωρ, ὕδατος [76]	water; rain
τὸ φῶς, φωτός [72]	light; torch
τὸ πῦρ, πυρός [71]	fire
ὁ Σίμων, Σίμονος [75]	Simon

Demonstrative Pronouns:

ἐκεῖνος, -η, -ο [243]	that (one); those (*pl.*)
οὗτος, αὕτη, τοῦτο [1387]	this (one); these (*pl.*)

Adjectives and Pronouns of Number or Amount:

ἅπας, -ασα, -αν [34]	(quite) all, every; whole
εἷς, μία, ἕν (gen.= ἑνός, μίας, ἑνός) [344]	one, single
μέγας, μεγάλη, μέγα [243]	great, large
ὅλος, -η, -ον [108]	whole, entire
οὐδείς, οὐδεμία, οὐδέν [227]	no; no one; nothing
πᾶς, πᾶσα, πᾶν [1243]	every, all; each
πολύς, πολλή, πολύ [415]	much, many

Partially Declinable Adjectives of Number:

δυό (δυσί=dat.pl.) [135]	two
τρεῖς (M/F), τρία (N) [68]	three
τέσσαρες (M/F), τέσσαρα (N) [41]	four
ἑπτά [88]	seven
δώδεκα [75]	twelve

After learning vocabulary to this point, you will know 66.3% of the words in the GNT. If you are able, listen to audio recordings of VOCABULARY 12 and complete the CROSSWORD PUZZLE in the WORKBOOK EXERCISES.

NOTES ON VOCABULARY 12:

Most of the words above have English cognates: <u>aeon</u>, <u>android</u> (man-like robot), <u>arch</u>-bishop, <u>pater</u>-nal, <u>pod</u>-iatry, <u>pyro</u>-maniac, <u>hydrau</u>-lics, <u>photo</u>-graphy, <u>heno</u>-theism (worship one God; ἕν means *one*), <u>mega</u>-phone, <u>hol</u>-istic, <u>pan</u>-theism, <u>poly</u>-theism. (The ὖ ψιλόν vowel comes into English as a "*y*.") These English derivatives should greatly reduce your memorization work. Additionally, some words are cognates with the others: οὐδείς, οὐδεμία, οὐδέν *no; no one; nothing* may be classified among the Negative Pronouns (ἀντωνυμίαι ἀρνητικαί) along with μηδείς (in ch. 22) and is formed from οὐ (*no*) and εἷς, μία, ἕν *one*. ἅπας and πᾶς are cognates and have similar meanings, with the former being less frequent and, with the additional morpheme, more marked.

Although most of the meanings above are simple, a few words deserve a comment or two. First, ἀνήρ can mean a *man* or *male* in general or a *husband*. This noun is to be distinguished from ἄνθρωπος *person*, which nevertheless is too often translated as "man." The determination that ἀνήρ may mean *husband* is significant for interpreting those passages in the NT on male-female relations, since these passages discuss women's roles within the context of husband-wife relationships (1 Cor 14:34-35; 1 Tim 2:11-15; cf. Eph 5:22; Col 3:18; 1 Pet 3:1-6).

The word αἰών is often found in an idiomatic expression that should perhaps be memorized separately due to its frequency and special meaning: εἰς τοὺς αἰῶνας (τῶν αἰώνων) literally, *into the ages (of the ages),* often translated *forever.*

The first set of adjectives given above are fully declinable: They have masculine, feminine, and neuter formations. However, their forms are a bit odd and will be discussed further below. It should be said now that two adjectives—πᾶς, πᾶσα, πᾶν and εἷς, μία, ἕν—are peculiar in that the masculine and neuter forms have Third Declension endings, whereas the feminine has the First Declension endings (see §12.2.B. below). Also, ἅπας *quite all, every; whole* is "strengthened for πᾶς" (LSJ, 181). The final set of adjectives of number are partially declinable in that they usually show no case, but occasionally gender. Some English cognates will help in their memorization: "the dynamic <u>duo</u>," <u>tri</u>-cycle, <u>tessaract</u> (four-dimensional cube), <u>hepta</u>-gon.

Finally, the demonstrative pronoun οὗτος, αὕτη, τοῦτο *this, these* is marked *+proximity*, whereas ἐκεῖνος, -η, -ο *that, those* is marked *+remoteness*.

12.1 NOUNS OF THE THIRD DECLENSION (Τρίτη Κλίσις)

A. **General Information:** The Third Declension contains all three genders. Despite this, however, the endings are similar in formation with some variations. This group of nouns can be broken down into two smaller subdivisions: stems ending in consonants (consonant stems) and vowels (vowel stems). Vowel stems are a bit more difficult and are presented in CHAPTER 16. Consonant stems are relatively easy.

B. **Endings:** The endings for the Third Declension are as follow:

	Masc./Fem. Stems	Neuter Stems	Masc./Fem. Stems	Neuter Stems
sg. nom.	-ς	- or -ς	ἀνήρ	φῶς
gen.	-ος →	-ος	ἀνδρός	φωτός
dat.	-ι →	-ι	ἀνδρί	φωτί
acc.	-α or ν	- or -ς	ἄνδρα	φῶς

	Masc./Fem. Stems	Neuter Stems	Masc./Fem. Stems	Neuter Stems
pl. nom.	-ες	-α	ἄνδρες	φῶτα
gen.	-ων →	-ων	ἀνδρῶν	φώτων
dat.	-σι(ν) →	-σι(ν)	ἀνδράσι	φωσί(ν)
acc.	-ας	-α	ἄνδρας	φῶτα
Stems→			ἀνδρ-	φωτ-

<u>Notice</u>: (1) The endings joined by arrows are the same; the neuter and masculine endings in genitive and dative cases are the same both singular and in the plural. (2) The neuter Third Declension nominative singular sometimes takes a σίγμα. (3) Always, the neuter nominative and accusative endings will be the same for singular and plural respectively. (4) In the plural, the neuter endings will always end in ἄλφα.

C. **Some Keys to the Third Declension:**

1. <u>Learn both the Nominative and Genitive Singular Forms</u>. Third Declension nouns and adjectives have hidden stems. These stems become manifest in the genitive singular. There are occasional exceptions: the actual stem of πατήρ is πατερ- not πατρ-; thus, the singular is πατήρ, πατρός, πατρί, πατέρα; the plural is πατέρες, πατέρων, πατράσι(ν), πατέρας.

2. <u>Stems Ending in Liquid Consonants (λ, μ, ν, ρ) will reject σίγμα</u>. This can be seen in virtually all the masculine nouns in this lesson. Thus, the nominative case ending -ς, *which is normally added*, is rejected (e.g. ἀνήρ).

3. <u>Stems Ending in Mute Consonants will act accordingly</u>. When a σίγμα is added to a mute consonant, combinations or changes will result. The most remarkable is with the Dentals,

where the σίγμα for the nominative singular and the dative plural ending replaces the mutes. Study the full paradigm below.

Labial	π	β	φ	+ σ	→ ψ
Dental*	τ	δ	ϑ or ζ	+ σ	→ σ
Palatal	κ	γ	χ	+ σ	→ ξ

4. <u>The Article</u>. Most importantly, let the article help you parse these Third Declension nouns. Many times, but not always, of course, Third Declension nouns will be accompanied by the article, or there will be other contextual considerations that will assist your parsing of them.

D. **Full Paradigms of Third Declension Nouns from This Chapter:**

	Art.	**Masculine Stems**				Art.	**Neuter Stems**	
sg.								
nom.	ὁ	ἀνήρ	αἰών	ἄρχων	πούς	τὸ	φῶς	ὕδωρ
gen.	τοῦ	ἀνδρός	αἰῶνος	ἄρχοντος	ποδός	τοῦ	φωτός	ὕδατος
dat.	τῷ	ἀνδρί	αἰῶνι	ἄρχοντι	ποδί	τῷ	φωτί	ὕδατι
acc.	τὸν	ἄνδρα	αἰῶνα	ἄρχοντα	πόδα	τὸ	φῶς	ὕδωρ
pl.								
nom.	οἱ	ἄνδρες	αἰῶνες	ἄρχοντες	πόδες	τὰ	φῶτα	ὕδατα
gen.	τῶν	ἀνδρῶν	αἰώνων	ἀρχόντων	ποδῶν	τῶν	φώτων	ὑδάτων
dat.	τοῖς	ἀνδράσιν	αἰῶσιν	ἄρχουσιν	ποσίν	τοῖς	φωσίν	ὕδασιν
acc.	τοὺς	ἄνδρας	αἰῶνας	ἄρχοντας	πόδας	τὰ	φῶτα	ὕδατα

E. **Vocative Endings of the Third Declension:**

1. <u>Plural</u>. The vocative case endings in the plural are the same as the nominative endings.

2. <u>Singular</u>. In the singular, however, the vocative form is different. Below are given all the forms of the Vocative Case (First, Second, and Third Declension).

Feminine sg.			Masculine sg.			Neuter sg.	
1st decl.	2nd decl.	3rd decl.	1st decl.	2nd decl.	3rd decl.	2nd decl.	3rd decl.
-α or -η	-ος	none (the pure stem)	-α or -η	-ε	none (the pure stem)	-ον	-ν or none

Note: In the singular, for 3rd declension nouns with the final syllable with ἦτα, the final vowel will change to ἒ ψιλόν when forming the vocative Thus, πατήρ "father," μήτηρ "mother," θυγάτηρ "daughter," and ἀνήρ "husband" become in the vocative singular πάτερ, μῆτερ, θύγατερ, and ἄνερ (notice, too, the change of accents). For vowel stem 3rd Declension (covered in §16.1 VOWEL STEM NOUNS OF THE THIRD DECLENSION), the pure stem is seen after removing the final σίγμα; thus, βασιλεύς becomes βασιλεῦ to form the vocative (notice the change in accent).

12.2 ADJECTIVES (Ἐπίθετα) OF NUMBER AND AMOUNT

A. **Some General Characteristics:** There are many adjectives that indicate number or amount. These adjectives share some several common features:

1. Commonly used as Substantives. This occurs with or without the article.

> πάντες εἶδον = *(they) all* saw
> (οἱ) πολλοὶ εἶδον = (the) *many* saw

2. As Anarthrous Modifier of a Substantive. As an adjectival modifier, the adjective of number may not often have the article before it, yet still agrees with the noun they modify in gender, case, and number. However, εἷς, μέγας, πᾶς, and πόλυς occasionally will have an article. For example, consider these phrases:

> πᾶσα ἡ Ἰουδαία = *all Judea*
> ὅλην τὴν ἡμέραν = *the whole day*
>
> BUT
>
> τοῦ μεγάλου βασιλέως = *of the great king*
> οἱ πάντες ἄνδρες = *all the men*

B. **Endings:** These adjectives display all the noun declension endings, sometimes within the same word. For example, the adjective πᾶς, πᾶσα, πᾶν shows Third Declension endings in the masculine and neuter, but First Declension endings for the feminine. This is a 3-1-3 pattern: masc. (3rd), fem. (1st), neut. (3rd). Also, the adjectives πολύς, πολλή, πολύ *much, many* and μέγας, μεγάλη, μέγα *great, large* show a different stem (πολλ- and μεγαλ-) much like the Third Declension, yet all their endings are from the First and Second Declensions. Here is a summary of their endings.

1. First and Second Declension. ὅλος, -η, -ον *whole, entire*

2. 3-1-3 Pattern: Masculine (3rd)—Feminine (1st)—Neuter (3rd).

> πᾶς, πᾶσα, πᾶν *every, all*
> εἷς, μία, ἕν *one*
> οὐδείς, οὐδεμία, οὐδέν *no one*

	πᾶς, πᾶσα, πᾶν *every, all*			εἷς, μία, ἕν *one*		
Gender:	**Masculine**	**Feminine**	**Neuter**	**Masculine**	**Feminine**	**Neuter**
Declension:	3rd	1st	3rd	3rd	1st	3rd
sg. nom.	πᾶς	πᾶσα	πᾶν	εἷς	μία	ἕν
gen.	παντός	πάσης	παντός	ἑνός	μιᾶς	ἑνός
dat.	παντί	πάσῃ	παντί	ἑνί	μιᾷ	ἑνί
acc.	πάντα	πᾶσαν	πᾶν	ἕνα	μίαν	ἕν
pl. nom.	πάντες	πᾶσαι	πάντα	The same endings are also used for οὐδείς, οὐδεμία, οὐδέν and μηδείς, μηδεμία, μηδέν. There are no plural forms, since *one* cannot be plural!		
gen.	πάντων	πασῶν	πάντων			
dat.	πᾶσι(ν)	πάσαις	πᾶσι(ν)			
acc.	πάντας	πάσας	πάντα			

3. <u>Slightly Irregular in Masculine and Neuter Nominative and Accusative Endings.</u>

πολύς, πολλή, πολύ *much, many*
μέγας, μεγάλη, μέγα *great, large*

	μέγας, μεγάλη, μέγα *great*			πολύς, πολλή, πολύ *much, many*		
	Masculine	**Feminine**	**Neuter**	**Masculine**	**Feminine**	**Neuter**
sg. nom.	μέγας*	μεγάλη	μέγα*	πολύς*	πολλή	πολύ*
gen.	μεγάλου	μεγάλης	μεγάλου	πολλοῦ	πολλῆς	πολλοῦ
dat.	μεγάλῳ	μεγάλῃ	μεγάλῳ	πολλῷ	πολλῇ	πολλῷ
acc.	μέγαν*	μεγάλην	μέγα*	πολύν*	πολλήν	πολύ*
pl. nom.	μεγάλοι	μεγάλαι	μεγάλα	πολλοί	πολλαί	πολλά
gen.	μεγάλων	μεγάλων	μεγάλων	πολλῶν	πολλῶν	πολλῶν
dat.	μεγάλοις	μεγάλαις	μεγάλοις	πολλοῖς	πολλοῖς	πολλοῖς
acc.	μεγάλους	μεγάλας	μεγάλα	πολλούς	πολλάς	πολλά

12.3 THE GREEK ALPHABET AND NUMERIC VALUES

The Greeks had no separate numbers; so they represented numbers by their alphabet, including archaic letters that dropped out of language use. Abbreviated numbers using the alphabet are often times represented with lines on top of the letters; in the stele below, letters as numbers are isolated by dashes on either side.

You should recognize all the letters below but the numbers 6 (F a *digamma*, ϛ a later form called *stigma*), 90 (Ϙ a *kōppa*), and 900 (ϡ a *sampi*). If the number appears written out in the GNT, it is included in the table below.

GREEK ALPHABET FOR NUMBERS AND WRITTEN OUT								
1	A	εἷς, μία, ἕν	10	I	δέκα	100	P	
2	B	δύο	20	K		200	Σ	διακόσιοι, -αι, -α
3	Γ	τρεῖς, τρία	30	Λ	τριάκοντα	300	T	
4	Δ	τέσσαρες	40	M	τεσσαράκοντα	400	Υ	
5	E	πέντε	50	N	πεντήκοντα	500	Φ	
6	F, ϛ	ἕξ	60	Ξ	ἑξήκοντα	600	X	
7	Z	ἑπτά	70	O		700	Ψ	
8	H	ὀκτώ	80	Π		800	Ω	
9	Θ		90	Ϙ		900	ϡ	

Additional numbers occurring in the GNT are written out as follows:

11 = ἕνδεκα, 12 = δώδεκα, 14 = δεκατέσσαρες, 24 = εἰκοσιτέσσαρες
1000 = ἡ χιλιάς, -άδος, 1000s = χίλιοι, -αι, -α
4000 = τετρακισχίλιοι, 5000 = πεντακισχίλιοι, 6000 = ἑξακόσιοι

Ancient Mediterranean graffiti has been found that has converted a person's name into numbers. In the GNT, "the number of a person" (ἀριθμὸς ἀνθρώπου) is said to add up to 666 (ἑξακόσιοι ἑξήκοντα ἕξ), which is written out in the text with a line over the letter: χ̅ξ̅ϛ̅. One fairly early textual variant, however, reads 616 (ἑξακόσιοι δέκα ἕξ) which is abbreviated in the manuscript as χ̅ιϛ̅. Bruce M. Metzger comments: "Perhaps the change was intentional, seeing that the Greek form *Neron Caesar* written in Hebrew characters (נרון קסר) is equivalent to 666, whereas the Latin form *Nero Caesar* (נרו קסר) is equivalent to 616."[1] The ancient practice of rendering a person's name into numeric value is called gematria.[2] You can convert arabic numbers into the Greek system at **The Greek Number Converter** website.[3]

Below, a funerary stele honors two dead sons and their tutor, or παιδαγωγός (see 1 Cor 4:15; Gal 3:24, 25), who died in an earthquake.[4] The funerary stele from Nicomedia (modern İzmit) in Bithynia, white marble, c. 120 BC. The inscription reads:

---

[1] Bruce M. Metzger, *A Textual Commentary on the Greek New Testament*, 2nd ed. (New York: United Bible Societies, 1994), 676.

[2] For a discussion in relation to Revelation, see G. K. Beale, *The Book of Revelation: A Commentary on the Greek Text*, New International Greek Testament Commentary (Grand Rapids: Eerdmans, 1999), 718-19.

[3] http://www.russellcottrell.com/greek/utilities/GreekNumberConverter.htm.

[4] This photograph is in the public domain. The artifact is found the Louvre Museum, Department of Greek Antiquities, Denon, ground floor, room 2, accession number Ma 4498 (MND 1770).

Funerary Stele (c.120 BC)

In the translation below, I have deliberately left their ages blank. Are you able to calculate how many "years" old each son was, and their tutor?[5]

Θράσων Διογένους τήνδε ἀνέστησεν στυλλεῖδαν <u>υἱῶν Β'</u> Δεξιφάνους <u>ἐτῶν Ε'</u> Ξράσοωνος <u>ἐτῶν Δ'</u> Ἑρμῇ θρέψαντος αὐτῶν <u>ἐτῶν ΚΕ'</u> ἐν τῇ συμπτώσει τοῦ σεισμοῦ οὕτως αὐτὰ περιειλήφει.

"Thrason, son of Diogenes, erected this funerary stele for his <u>two sons</u>, Dexiphanes, age ___, and Thrason, age ___, and for Hermes, age ___, who brought them up. In the earthquake collapse, so did he hold them in his arms."

---

[5] Dexiphanes was age 4, Thrason was age 5, and Hermes was age 25.

12.4 QUANTITATIVE EMPHASIS

A. **Numbers Signify Quantity and Significance:** Any specification of quantity is exegetically significant. Numeric modification will restrict or limit the referent. One must ask, Why? Does this clarify identity? Does the numeric value add vividness to the description or clarity? In any case, the numeric specificity contributes to larger discursive meaning. *We must understand that numbers in the Mediterranean world were as much about significance as quantity.* This contrasts often with Western cultures (although there is certainly variation among them), where numbers are primarily about quantity for mathematic and scientific calculation. For example, consider this: Why was Jesus tempted in the desert for 40 days? Was there something significant about 40? Yes. This signified something of Israel's history of wandering in the wilderness for 40 years. In this context, when tempted by the Devil, it is not surprising that Jesus three times quotes Scripture from Deuteronomy 6-8, a passage that concerned the people of Israel's wilderness wandering. The difference, however, between Jesus and Israel is critical: Where Israel gave way to temptation, Jesus did not. So, pay attention to numbers, but not simply for their quantities, but additionally for their significance.

B. **Quantitative Emphasis of Scale and Scope:** Certain adjectives of quantity do not *specify* numeric quantity, but only relative quantity of **scope** on a **scale**. Consider the difference between these descriptors: *all, many, much, some, few, little, one, none.* One should discern a scale. What difference does it make that one or another of these modifiers is used to describe unspecified or relative quantity? The adjectives ἅπας, *(quite) all, every; whole* and πᾶς *all, entire,* for example, **stress inclusive scope**. So does ὅλος *whole, entire.* Additionally, the initial ἄλφα on ἅπας shows morphological marking to increase emphasis and is a strengthened form of πᾶς. The modification of sentence elements that stress inclusive scope is contextually significant. The same can be said for πολύς *much, many* which signifies scope on a slightly lesser scale than πᾶς. These adjectives emphasize complete/entire or broad participation, or what I call **quantitative emphasis**. Such emphasis also attends cognate forms of these words.[6] For a corresponding discussion on qualitative emphasis, see §26.4 QUALITATIVE EMPHASIS.

C. **Examples of Quantitative Emphasis:**

1. **Mark 12:44.** πάντες γὰρ ἐκ τοῦ <u>περισσεύοντος</u> αὐτοῖς ἔβαλον, αὕτη δὲ ἐκ τῆς <u>ὑστερήσεως</u> αὐτῆς <u>πάντα,</u> <u>ὅσα</u> εἶχεν ἔβαλεν, <u>ὅλον</u> τὸν βίον αὐτῆς.

   For <u>all</u> of them cast in from their <u>abundance</u>, but this woman from her <u>poverty</u> cast in <u>all</u>, how <u>much</u> she was having, her <u>whole</u> means of living!

---

[6] On πᾶς as a compound, see R. S. W. Hawtrey, "Παν Compounds in Plato," *The Classical Quarterly* 33.1 (1983): 56–65.

Apart from the initial πάντες that creates a contrast between the *one poor widow* of 12:43, there are descriptors *abundance* and *poverty* that refer to quantity. The last sentence, however, is highly marked for quantitative emphasis, deploying πάντα and ὅσα, both indicating inclusive scope, as well as ὅλον with inclusive scope, which also has appositional emphasis. Jesus is the speaker here, and he points out the tragic contrast between the wealthy and this poor widow, who should rather be the recipient of assistance from the temple authorities, rather than to feel obligated to throw in her whole livelihood.

2. **Eph 4:4-5**. Consider also Eph 4:4-5 which is arranged with *one Lord* in the center of the affirmations of "one" and builds to a climax with quantitative emphasis using πᾶς with regard to God the Father:

⁴ Ἓν σῶμα   *(There is) One Body*

    καὶ ἓν πνεῦμα,   *and One Spirit*

        καθὼς καὶ ἐκλήθητε ἐν μιᾷ ἐλπίδι τῆς κλήσεως ὑμῶν·

        just as also you were called in One Hope of your calling.

      ⁵ εἷς κύριος,   *One Lord*

    μία πίστις,   *One Faith*

  ἓν βάπτισμα,   *One Baptism*

⁶ εἷς θεὸς καὶ πατὴρ πάντων, *One God and Father of all things/people*

    ὁ ἐπὶ πάντων   *The one (who is) over all*

      καὶ   *and*

    διὰ πάντων   *through all*

      καὶ   *and*

  ἐν πᾶσιν.   *in all.*

The climax of *all* with respect to God the Father is notable. Such functioned to affirm the supremacy of the One God amidst alternative claims within the pagan world where, for example, Jupiter-Zeus was thought to govern all things; see, e.g., Aelius Aristides's speech in praise "For Zeus" (c. AD 160) which culminates with a similar emphasis. For another fruitful passage that also has a good display of quantitative emphasis, see John 6:5-13.

3. **Mark 5:25-27**. An excellent example of quantitative emphasis is found in Mark 5:25-27, which is also remarkable in its use of seven participles to describe the woman's medical and financial condition before coming to Jesus![7] The main sentence is the last clause in

---

[7] I am particularly indebted to Benson Goh for bringing these passages to my attention within his final paper on quantitative emphasis (at my behest) in my advanced Greek course J-Term 2014.

bold. Notice how the first five participle clauses introduced with conjunctions show some sort of quantity contributing to a larger rhetorical effect.

²⁵ Καὶ γυνὴ οὖσα ἐν ῥύσει αἵματος <u>δώδεκα ἔτη</u>	²⁵ And a woman being in a flow of blood <u>12 years</u>
²⁶ καὶ <u>πολλὰ</u> παθοῦσα ὑπὸ <u>πολλῶν</u> ἰατρῶν	²⁶ and suffering <u>many things</u> by <u>many</u> doctors,
καὶ δαπανήσασα <u>τὰ</u> παρ' αὐτῆς <u>πάντα</u>	and spending <u>everything</u> on it [the flow],
καὶ <u>μηδὲν</u> ὠφεληθεῖσα	and benefiting <u>nothing</u>,
ἀλλὰ <u>μᾶλλον</u> εἰς τὸ <u>χεῖρον</u> ἐλθοῦσα,	but <u>more/rather</u> (be)coming <u>worse</u>,
²⁷ ἀκούσασα περὶ τοῦ Ἰησοῦ,	²⁷ hearing about Jesus,
ἐλθοῦσα ἐν τῷ ὄχλῳ ὄπισθεν	coming in the crowd from behind
ἥψατο τοῦ ἱματίου αὐτοῦ·	**she touched his garment.**

What is communicated here? One notices first specificity (*12 years*), but eventually the woman's suffering *many things* through *many doctors* (broad scope), and then expenditure of *everything* (inclusive scope) with the result of *nothing* but a *worse* condition.

12.5 DEMONSTRATIVE PRONOUNS (Δεικτικαὶ Ἀντωνυμίαι)

A. **General Information:**

1. <u>NT Greek has three Proper Demonstrative Pronouns.</u>

   a. οὗτος, αὕτη, τοῦτο *this, these* (1387x) refers to things near and marked +*proximity*.

   b. ἐκεῖνος, -η, -ο *that, those* (243x) refers to things far away and marked +*remoteness*.

   c. ὅδε, ἥδε, τόδε (10x) *this* prepares for what follows (+*anticipatory*). This is relatively rare in the GNT. For an example of one in broader cultural setting, see the funerary stele image above, which contains the statement τήνδε ἀνέστησεν στυλλεῖδαν *he erected this funerary stele*. The statement was physically placed above and pointing down at the stele, to which this demonstrative pronoun thus points, anticipating it.

2. <u>Pointers and Modifiers.</u> Demonstrative Pronouns point to entities and can even modify them directly. They draw attention by pointing out certain persons or things. They function very much like the article. The article, in fact, was a demonstrative earlier in the Greek language; the remnants of the article are seen on the rare demonstrative ὅδε, ἥδε, τόδε *this* that points to or anticipates often the postcedent that follows. Because of their already inherently pointing nature, *these proper demonstratives will never take an article even if modifying a substantive that has an article*. For more discussion of Demonstrative Pronouns, see Wallace 325-35.

3. <u>Correlative Demonstratives.</u> There are additionally four correlative demonstrative forms that combine demonstrative and correlative senses. These are not given in the vocabulary here, but are included for some degree of completeness. But "Correlative" signifies that two

words work in conjunction with each other to balance ideas, typically of quality or quantity. These pronouns are rather rare, but enjoyable to see because they convey either quantitative or qualitative emphasis.

a. τοιόσδε, -άδε, -όνδε (1x) *such as this, of this kind* (quality) occurs once as τοιᾶσδε in 2 Pet. 1:17.

b. τηλικοῦτος, αὐτη, οὖτο (4x) *so great, so large* (quantity) is a "strengthened form of τηλίκος 'so great'" (BDAG).

c. τοιοῦτος, -αύτη, -οῦτον (57x in Ch.26) *of such a kind, such as this* (quality) and works sometimes with its correlative οἷος, α, ον (14x) *of what sort, such.*

d. τοσοῦτος, -αύτη, -οῦτον (20x) *so many* (quantity) and can sometimes be found with its correlative ὅσος, α, ον (111x in Ch.26) *how many, as much as*

B. **Endings:** Both ἐκεῖνος, -η, -ο and οὗτος, αὕτη, τοῦτο use the First and Second Declension adjective endings. The full declension of οὗτος, αὕτη, τοῦτο is included below only because of the addition of a ταῦ in the gen., dat., and accusative forms:

		Masculine	Feminine	Neuter
sg.	nom.	οὗτος	αὕτη	τοῦτο
	gen.	τούτου	ταύτης	τούτου
	dat.	τούτῳ	ταύτῃ	τούτῳ
	acc.	τοῦτον	ταύτην	τοῦτο
pl.	nom.	οὗτοι	αὗται	ταῦτα
	gen.	τούτων	τούτων	τούτων
	dat.	τούτοις	ταύταις	τούτοις
	acc.	τούτους	ταύτας	ταῦτα

Notice that the masculine and feminine nominative forms have *rough breathing marks*. This rough breathing mark helps to distinguish two otherwise identical forms: αὕτη is the demonstrative pronoun (*this woman*) whereas αὐτή is the 3rd person personal pronoun (*she*).

C. **Semantics and Pragmatics of the Demonstrative Pronoun:** Levinsohn argues,

> The core meaning of the demonstratives in Greek is NOT thematic or athematic. The core meaning of *ekeinos* is 'distal' (not at the deictic centre) and the core meaning of *houtos* is 'proximal' (close to the deictic centre). Nevertheless, in certain contexts, a pragmatic effect of using *ekeinos* is to identify the referent as athematic.

Conversely, a pragmatic effect of using *houtos* in certain contexts is to identify the referent as thematic. (emphasis original)[8]

Runge likewise maintains, "The primary function of the demonstrative is to assign a near/far distinction to a discourse entity. This is what has traditionally been called the *regular* or *deictic* usage. As has been noted, οὗτος is used for the near entity, ἐκεῖνος for the far entity, whether that is a literal or a figurative distinction" (368). Within this basic understanding, we can describe usage in terms of grammatical function as adjectival, substantival, pronominal, but also in terms of discourse pragmatics as marking thematic or athematic participants, as forward-pointing device, and additionally as marking an element by fronted position:

1. Functional Uses.

    a. **Adjectival.** Modifies a noun or substantive. Here it must agree in gender, case, and number. Here are several examples:

    (common) ἐν ἐκείναις ταῖς ἡμέραις in *those* days

    John 21:7 λέγει οὖν ὁ μαθητὴς ἐκεῖνος… Therefore, *that* disciple said…

    John 21:23 ἐξῆλθεν οὖν οὗτος ὁ λόγος… Therefore, *this* word went out…

    b. **Substantival.** The demonstrative pronoun can stand alone and act like a noun:

    ἐκεῖνοι = *those men*
    αὗται = *these women*

    Notice how, as like with adjectives, that a generic noun (men, women, things, etc.) may need to be supplied in the English translation based upon context and the gender of the pronoun.

    c. **Pronominal.** Especially in the gospels, the demonstratives appear to function like 3rd person personal pronouns. Their referents will be very close in the context. In this usage, the demonstratives are often translated *he, she, it, they*, **and yet their +proximate and +distal marking should not be neglected** (see further below). For example, consider two examples from John:

    John 14:21 ὁ ἔχων τὰς ἐντολάς μου καὶ τηρῶν αὐτὰς ἐκεῖνος ἐστιν ὁ ἀγαπῶν με.
        The one having my commands and keeping them, he is the one loving me.

---

[8] Stephen H. Levinsohn, *Self-Instruction Materials on Narrative Discourse Analysis* (Dallas: SIL International, 2012), Ch.9 Appendix 1: Demonstratives in Koiné Greek, 142.

John 1:8 οὐκ ἦν <u>ἐκεῖνος</u> τὸ φῶς. <u>*He*</u> *(John the Baptist) was not the light.*

2. <u>Discourse Pragmatic Uses</u>.

  a. ***Marking Thematic and Athematic <u>Participants</u>***.

  i. <u>*ἐκεῖνος*</u>. Levinsohn states, "**animate** participants in a narrative text who are designated with *ekeinos* are usually **athematic and not salient**."[9] In John 1:8, John the Baptist is athematic in relation to Jesus.

  John 1:8 οὐκ ἦν <u>ἐκεῖνος</u> τὸ φῶς. <u>*That One*</u> *(John the Baptist) was not the light.*

  ii. <u>*οὗτος*</u>. "Because the core meaning of *houtos* is 'proximal' (close to the deictic centre), **animate** participants in a narrative text who are designated with *houtos* are usually **thematic and salient**."[10]

  Matt 5:19 *Therefore, the one whoever annuls one of the least of <u>these</u>* [τούτων] *commandments and teaches people in this manner, he will be called least in the kingdom of the heavens. However, the one whoever does and teaches [them], <u>this one</u>* [οὗτος] *will be called great in the kingdom of the heavens.*

  The Sermon of the Mount will have been about Jesus' words and teaching (i.e. his commandments), and so <u>*these*</u> *(τούτων) commandments* and <u>*this one*</u> *[οὗτος]* who does and teaches them are +proximate to the theme line.

  iii. <u>*An Exception?*</u> The Sower Parable in Mark 4:10-20 provides an interesting case of recognizing theme line versus non-theme line based upon the use of the distal and proximate demonstrative pronouns. After Jesus tells the parable of the Sower with four different seed locations, he explains the meaning of the parable and these seed locations to the disciplines "alone" (4:10). Oddly, he explains the first three locations (along the road, in the rocky places, and among the thorns) using the + proximate οὗτοι *these ones* (4:15, 16, 18), yet for the good soil, the + distal ἐκεῖνοί *those ones* (4:20) is used. But why? Wouldn't the thematic material (surely, the seeds on the good soil) use the proximate pronoun οὗτοι? Well, what is thematic and athematic here? Jesus frames his whole explanation of the parable with the disciples alone by reference to Isa 6:9-10 in Mark 4:11-12, which speaks of a time of judgment upon the people who hear but don't understand, see but don't perceive,

---

[9] Levinsohn, *Self-Instruction Materials on Narrative Discourse Analysis*, 142 (emphasis original).
[10] Ibid., 143 (emphasis original).

etc. So, in fact, the theme line is one of judgment and Jesus' need to speak in parables, and so the use of οὗτοι appropriately marks thematic and salient participants.

b. Marking *Continuous vs. Discontinuous <u>Events</u>*.

i. <u>*ἐκεῖνος may mark Distal Time and Discontinuity in Theme Line*</u>. Levinsohn states,

- o "Use of *ekeinos* may imply the **same distal** time (past or future in relation to the time of speaking or writing) as that of the events just described. This is particularly clear when an earlier reference to time has just been made."[11]
- o "Use of *ekeinos* may imply a **loose chronological relation** between episodes when there is a **discontinuity** in the theme-line." And "The pragmatic effect of using the distal demonstrative is to imply a **discontinuity in the theme line** between the episodes so linked."[12]

ii. <u>*οὗτος may mark Theme Line Event and Continuity with the Theme Line*</u>. Levinsohn once again summarizes,

- o "The referent of the proximal demonstrative may be the **theme-line event** or events that were mentioned immediately before" (2012, p. 144, emphasis original).
- o "When the proximal demonstrative *houtos* is used in a **temporal expression** to refer to a past time, the pragmatic effect is typically to imply **continuity in the theme-line**, even when the chronological relation between the episodes is vague" (2012, p. 143, emphasis original).

Consider the example of John 14:19–26 (NASB95, with slight modifications with Greek and underlining added):

John 14:19–26

[19] "After a little while the world will no longer see Me, but you *will* see Me; because I live, you will live also. [20] "In <u>that</u> day [ἐν ἐκείνῃ τῇ ἡμέρᾳ] you will know that I am in My Father, and you in Me, and I in you. [21] "He who has My commandments and keeps them, <u>that one</u> [ἐκεῖνός] is the one who loves Me; and he who loves Me will be loved by My Father, and I will love him and will disclose Myself to him." [22] Judas (not Iscariot) said to Him, "Lord, what then has happened that You are going to disclose Yourself to us and not to the world?" [23] Jesus answered and said to him, "If anyone loves Me, he will keep My word; and My Father will love him, and We will come to him and make Our abode

---

[11] Ibid., 142 (emphasis original).
[12] Ibid., 143 (emphasis original).

with him. [24] "He who does not love Me does not keep My words; and the word which you hear is not Mine, but the Father's who sent Me. [25] "These things [Ταῦτα] I have spoken to you while abiding with you. [26] "But the Helper, the Holy Spirit, whom the Father will send in My name, That One [ἐκεῖνος] will teach you all things, and bring to your remembrance all that I said to you.

The use of ἐκεῖνος in the expression *in that day* of 14:20 is marked +distal event in relation to the mainline events that consist of Jesus' farewell discourse in which he is speaking "these things [Ταῦτα]" of 14:25, which is marked +proximate. Within this distal situation, however, two prominent participants (the one keeping Jesus' commands and the Holy Spirit) are nevertheless marked +distal with ἐκεῖνος *that one*, because they are within a distal Jesus provides an explanation of the future "that day."

c. **Forward Pointing Reference**. One pragmatic use of the demonstrative pronoun is as a forward pointing reference to a target, increasing the anticipation of the target reference. The demonstrative pronoun effectively introduces and sets off the actual content target to which it points (Runge, §3.3.2). Occasionally, this target is explicitly indicated with ὅτι translated *that (is)* or *namely*.

Luke 10:20 πλὴν ἐν τούτῳ μὴ χαίρετε ὅτι τὰ πνεύματα ὑμῖν ὑποτάσσεται, χαίρετε δὲ ὅτι τὰ ὀνόματα ὑμῶν ἐγγέγραπται ἐν τοῖς οὐρανοῖς.

> *However, in this do not rejoice, NAMELY THAT the spirits obey you, but rejoice THAT your names have been written in the heavens.*

It must be stated that the target of the demonstrative pronoun is emphasized. In the example above, the emphasis is one of contrast.

d. **Demonstrative Emphasis by Fronted Position**. The location of the demonstrative pronoun may place additional force on the demonstrative's modification. Porter argues of near and far demonstratives that the unmarked position is following their head term (85% in Paul and 78% in Luke). Thus, "In a construction where the demonstrative adjective precedes the headterm of its group, the demonstrative functions at the level of the group, foregrounding the near or remote semantic features indicated by the form."[13] Thus, *demonstrative adjectives placed before their substantives are especially emphasized.* Consider these examples:

---

[13] Stanley E. Porter, "Prominence: An Overview," in *The Linguist as Pedagogue: Trends in the Teaching and Linguistic Analysis of the Greek New Testament*, ed. Stanley E. Porter and Matthew Brook O'Donnell, New Testament Monographs 11 (Sheffield: Sheffield Phoenix, 2009), 45–74 at 68.

In **John 14:19-26** (given above), the expression *In that day* [ἐν ἐκείνῃ τῇ ἡμέρᾳ] has a fronted ἐκείνη, even though this is marked +distal event in relation to the theme line of Jesus delivering a farewell discourse. The importance of this distal set of events is seen further in emphatic constructions involving thematically prominent words (love, obey, commandments), participants (Father, Jesus, one keeping Jesus' word, and Holy Spirit), subject pronouns, and even left dislocations (see §21.3) involving two important participants, the one keeping Jesus' commandments (14:21) and the Holy Spirit (14:26).

In **2 Cor 1:12-15**, the Apostle Paul first explains his sincerity and integrity towards the Corinthians and how he and they will mutually boast in each other in the day of the Lord. He continues with this statement:

2 Cor 1:15 Καὶ <u>ταύτῃ</u> τῇ πεποιθήσει ἐβουλόμην πρότερον πρὸς ὑμᾶς ἐλθεῖν, ἵνα δευτέραν χάριν σχῆτε,
> *And with* <u>*THIS*</u> *confidence I was intending formerly to come to you, in order that you would have a second favor…*

Here in 1:15 we see that Paul generalized what he had just described in 1:12-14 and brings it forward in order to frame what he "was intending" (βούλομαι) to do—this verb and cognate repeats 4x in 1:15-17—namely, to visit the Corinthians twice, which was a point of contention with them when Paul failed to do so.

Consider also this example in the final section of the Sermon on the Mount

Matt 7:22-23 <u>*Many*</u> *will say to me in* <u>*THAT*</u> *day* [ἐν ἐκείνῃ τῇ ἡμέρᾳ], "<u>*Lord, Lord, in your name*</u> *did we not prophesy, and* <u>*in your name*</u> *cast out demons, and* <u>*in your name*</u> *perform many miracles?*" [23] *And then I will say to them* [*that*], *"I never knew you; depart from me, you who are doing lawlessness."*

Matt 7:22-23 <u>πολλοὶ</u> ἐροῦσίν μοι ἐν ἐκείνῃ τῇ ἡμέρᾳ· <u>κύριε κύριε</u>, οὐ <u>τῷ σῷ ὀνόματι</u> ἐπροφητεύσαμεν, καὶ <u>τῷ σῷ ὀνόματι</u> δαιμόνια ἐξεβάλομεν, καὶ <u>τῷ σῷ ὀνόματι</u> δυνάμεις <u>πολλὰς</u> ἐποιήσαμεν; [23] καὶ τότε ὁμολογήσω αὐτοῖς <u>ὅτι</u> οὐδέποτε ἔγνων ὑμᾶς· ἀποχωρεῖτε ἀπ᾽ ἐμοῦ οἱ ἐργαζόμενοι τὴν ἀνομίαν.

What a startling day *THAT* will be. The forward positioning marks that event, making it more prominent to audiences. Additionally, there are several other ways that this passage shows emphasis. The emphasized elements are underlined. Are you able to identify and describe them? See Answers below.

<u>πολλοὶ</u> = *quantitative emphasis* (broad scope)
<u>κύριε κύριε</u> = *vocative emphasis* and *repeated element*

τῷ σῷ ὀνόματι = *repeated element* and *dative of means*; there is also a rare possessive
   adjective σός, σή, σόν *your*
πολλὰς = *quantitative emphasis* (broad scope)
ὅτι = *recitative* ὅτι

Additionally, the question that is asked of the Lord expects a positive reply in the Greek
text. See §14.2 QUESTIONS IN GREEK.

12.6 NAVIGATING MAJOR LEXICONS

One of the basic tools for students learning and studying a language is a dictionary, or, what is
more technically called, a lexicon. In §3.1 GREEK WORDS AND LEXICAL MEANINGS, students
were given a basic description of types of lexicons. In §6.7 A FIRST LOOK AT MAJOR LEXICONS:
BDAG, L&N, AND LSJ we looked at the basic lexical entries for the verb κτίζω, in which we,
while we have confidence in these resources, we still need to exercise caution, and consult several
lexicons for comparison. In §14.7 LEXICAL INFORMATION ON THE CASE OF VERBAL OBJECTS, we
discuss specifically a verbal entry, noting how direct objects and related matters are given and
abbreviated. Here I would like to show you what the various entries will look like, preserving the
formatting as much as possible, in order to begin to orient you to basic features and differences
between the lexicons. I have chosen the noun πολιτεία, typically glossed *citizenship*, to begin
explaining what kind of information is contained in the major lexicons for NT study. It should also be said that the order of the definitions tends to be given from the most common/basic sense to
the less common and/or particular or idiomatic. There are many considerations that attend such
decisions!

A. **BDAG:** Bauer, Walter and F. W. Danker, W. F. Arndt, and F. W. Gingrich. *Greek-English
   Lexicon of the New Testament and Other Early Christian Literature.* 3rd ed. Revised. Chicago: The University of Chicago Press, 2000.

> **πολιτεία, ας, ἡ** (πολίτης; Hdt.+; ins, pap; 2, 3, 4 Macc; TestAbr A 20 p. 104, 7 [Stone p. 56]; ApcMos
> prol.; Philo, Joseph., Just., Tat.)
>   ❶ **the right to be a member of a sociopolitical entity,** *citizenship* (Hdt. 9, 34; X., Hell. 1, 1, 26; 1, 2,
> 10; 4, 4, 6; Polyb. 6, 2, 12; Diod S 14, 8, 3; 14, 17, 3; Cyr. Ins. 57; 59; Gnomon [=BGU V 1] 47; 3 Macc
> 3:21, 23; Jos., Ant. 12, 119) lit., of Roman citizenship (Dio Chrys. 24 [41], 2 Ῥωμαίων π.; Ael. Aristid. 30,
> 10 K.=10 p. 117 D.; IG IV2/1, 84, 33 [40/42 A.D.]; Jos., Bell. 1, 194 and Vi 423 π. Ῥωμαίων.—
> WRamsay, The Social Basis of Roman Power in Asia Minor '41) πολιτείαν ἐκτησάμην **Ac 22:28**.—In a
> transf. sense, this transl. is poss. (EHaupt, PEwald et al.) for **Eph 2:12**, but not very probable (s. 2 below).
>   ❷ **a sociopolitical unit or body of citizens,** *state, people, body politic* (Thu. 1, 127, 3; Pla., Rep. 10,
> 619c; Diod S 5, 45, 3; Appian, Bell. Civ. 2, 19 §68; Just., A II, 10, 6) ἀπηλλοτριωμένοι τ. πολιτείας τοῦ
> Ἰσραήλ *alienated from the people of Israel* **Eph 2:12** (so HvSoden, MDibelius, NRSV et al.; s. 1 above).

❸ **behavior in accordance with standards expected of a respectable citizen,** *way of life, conduct* (Athen. 1, 19a; Herm. Wr. in Stob. p. 486, 24 Sc. ἡ τῶν ἀνθρώπων ἄγριος πολιτεία; Ps.-Liban., Charact. Ep. p. 34, 2; 47, 8; 10; Biogr. p. 261; TestAbr A 20 p. 104, 7 [Stone p. 56]; ApcMos prol.; Just., A I, 4, 2 al.; Tat.) Dg 5:4; ἀγαθὴ πολ. MPol 13:2; ἡ ἀπ᾽ ἀρχῆς ἀνεπίληπτος πολ. 17:1; ἡ πανάρετος καὶ σεβάσμιος πολ. 1 Cl 2:8. οἱ πολιτευόμενοι τὴν ἀμεταμέλητον πολιτείαν τοῦ θεοῦ *those who follow God's way of life, that brings no regrets* 54:4 (πολιτεύεσθαι πολιτείαν in Nicol. Dam.: 90 Fgm. 126 Jac. and in the Synagogue ins fr. Stobi [c. 100 A.D.] lines 6f: ZNW 32, '33, 93f).—DELG s.v. πόλις. M-M. TW. Spicq.

<u>Comments</u>: Looking at this entry, one can easily be overwhelmed with information! The use of abbreviations is taken to a new level, but the introduction explains this reduces the size of the lexicon as well as the cost to users (!). Let me explain this entry briefly.

After the lexical form (**πολιτεία, ας, ἡ**), which indicates this is a feminine noun, one sees in parentheses the noun from which **πολιτεία** was derived πολίτης. This is followed by a summary of where the word is found, starting chronologically: πολίτης; Hdt.+; ins, pap; 2, 3, 4 Macc; TestAbr A 20 p. 104, 7 [Stone p. 56]; ApcMos prol.; Philo, Joseph., Just., Tat. Often it may be Homer, Hesiod, Aristotle, etc. One can become familiar with these authors' names and dates by reference to the abbreviations information in the front of the lexicon. (It should be said that in electronic versions, like Logos Bible Software, these abbreviations are immediately explained by hovering over the "hyperlinked" abbreviated information.) In the case of **πολιτεία**, "Hdt.+" refers to Herodotus, a fifth century BC Greek historian, and the plus (+) indicates the word is found in subsequent authors. The abbreviations "ins, pap" indicate the word is found is inscriptions and papyri dated broadly. This is a publically recognized word. Then one sees a listing of Jewish Intertestamental literature where the word is found (2, 3, 4 Maccabees; Testament of Abraham; Apocalypse of Moses prologue), then two Jewish authors (Philo and Josephus), before then finally two church fathers (Justin and Tatian). For verb entries, one additionally finds a summary of forms (tenses, moods, etc.) in relation to ancient authors.

Next we see a listing of definitions that are numbered with block numbers. BDAG provides first "extended definitions" in **bold** that may be followed by "formal equivalents" in ***bold italics***. The reason for starting with extended definitions is for users to be given a broader understanding of the sense of the meaning before being given shorter glosses. In parentheses are given references where the term is found in Classical and Jewish Literature, sometimes with portions of texts given. Outside of the parentheses, one will then find Greek text with *italicized* English followed by the NT verse reference in bold for easy identification. The *italicized* English portions are "suggested translation equivalents" for those NT passages. Notice that there is debate about which definition Eph 2:12 should be placed within, and a few supporters for each are indicated. Also notice that the third definition contains no NT references; however, BDAG is a lexicon also for "Other Early Christian Literature"; in this case, the third entry features Dg (*The Letter of Diognetus*), MPol (*Martyrdom of Polycarp*), and 1 Cl (*1 Clement*).

Finally, users of the entry are directed here and there and at the end to important secondary studies (articles, books, dictionary entries, and other lexical books). So, under the first definition, users are directed to William Ramsay, *The Social Basis of Roman Power in Asia Minor* (Aberdeen University Press: 1941). In the second definition, users are told that Eph 2:12 is translated as *the people of Israel* by support by "HvSoden, MDibelius, NRSV et al." meaning the interpreters Hermann Von Soden and Martin Dibelius and the NRSV translation and some others. At the end of lexical entries after the emdash, one can see if other important wordbooks contain entries; here "—DELG s.v. πόλις. M-M. TW. Spicq." In the list of abbreviations, one can identify these books. The first, DELG, is a massive reference work in French.

B. L&N: Louw, Johannes and Eugene Nida. *Greek-English Lexicon of the New Testament Based on Semantic Domains*. 2 Vols. 2nd ed. New York: United Bible Societies, 1988.

Comments: Before providing the lexical information from L&N, it is important to know that the authors (world-class linguists) have arranged Greek words according into ninety-three "Semantic Domains" (e.g. 1 Geographical Objects and Features; 2 Natural Substances, etc.) with many subdomains underneath these: e.g. A Universe, Creation (1.1-4); B Regions Above the Earth (1.5-16), etc. For **πολιτεία** the Index in Volume 2 contains this basic information (p. 202):

> **πολιτεία, ας** *f*
> a citizenship: 11.70
> b state: 11.67

This tells us that there are two senses for πολιτεία, but both occur in the same domain 11 for "Groups and Classes of Persons and Members of Such Groups and Classes." Then users can see a more detailed explanation in Volume 1 by looking up the L&N numbers. These entries are given below. In the first entry, an extended discussion is provided for what sense the noun may carry in Eph 2:12.

> **11.67 πολιτεία**[b], **ας** *f*: a group of people constituting a socio-political unit—'state, people.' ἀπηλλοτριωμένοι τῆς πολιτείας τοῦ Ἰσραήλ 'you were excluded from the people of Israel' Eph 2:12.
>
> It is possible that in Eph 2:12 the use of πολιτεία suggests not merely a socio-political but also a socio-religious grouping. Such a conclusion would, in a sense, be true of any and all designations of a Jewish constituency, since religion and ethnic identification were so inextricably bound together.

> **11.70 πολιτεία**[a], **ας** *f*: the right to be a citizen of a particular socio-political entity (see 11.67 and 11.68)—'citizenship.' ἐγὼ πολλοῦ κεφαλαίου τὴν πολιτείαν ταύτην ἐκτησάμην 'I acquired this citizenship with a large sum of money' Ac 22:28. In some languages Ac 22:28 may be rendered as 'I obtained the right to be counted as a citizen' or 'I became a person who belongs to that nation.'

C. LSJ: Liddell, H. G., R. Scott and H. S. Jones. *A Greek-English Lexicon*. 9th ed., revised. Oxford: Clarendon, 1996.

> **πολῖτεία**, Ion. **-ηΐη**, ἡ, *condition and rights of a citizen, citizenship*, Hdt.9.34, Th.6.104, etc.; π. δοῦναί τινι X.HG1.2.10: pl., *grants of citizenship*, Arist.Ath.54.3.

2. *the daily life of a citizen*, And.2.10, D.19.184; ἐν εἰρήνῃ καὶ π. Id.20.122; *life, living*, ἡ ἐν Βοιωτίᾳ π. Plb.1843.6; so perh.Ep.Eph.2.12.

3. concrete, *body of citizens*, Arist.Ath.4.3, IG9(2)517.17 (Larissa, iii B.C.).

4. = Lat. *civitas* in geographical sense, SIG888.118 (Scaptopara, iii A.D.), Mitteis Chr.78.6 (iv A.D.), etc.
II. *government, administration*, Ar.Eq.219, X.Mem.3.9.15, etc.; ἄγειν τὴν π. Th.1.127; θρασύτατα καὶ ἀσελγέστατα τῇ π. κεχρῆσθαι Hyp.Eux.29; *course of policy*, τῇ π. καὶ τοῖς ψηφίσμασι D.18.87, cf. 9.3 (pl.), 18.263; ἡ Κλεοφῶντος π. Aeschin.3.150; ἡ πρὸς Ῥωμαίους ὁμιλία καὶ π. Str.16.2.46: pl., *acts of policy*, J.Vit.65.

2. *tenure of public office*, πᾶσαν π. ἐπιφανῶς ἐκτελέσαι IG4.716.6 (Hermione); ἐν τοῖς τῆς π. χρόνοις IPE12.32 B 76 (Olbia, iii B.C.).
III. *civil polity, constitution of a state*, Antipho 3.21, Th.2.37, etc.; τὴν ἐλευθερίαν .., μᾶλλον δὲ καὶ τὰς π. D.18.65; *form of government*, Pl.R.562a, etc.; ὁμολογοῦνται τρεῖς εἶναι π., τυραννὶς καὶ ὀλιγαρχία καὶ δημοκρατία Aeschin.1.4, cf. Arist.Pol.1293a37, etc.; αἱ τέτταρες π. Pl.R.544b; ἥτις ἂν π. συμφέρῃ Lys.25.8; π. ἐστὶ τάξις ταῖς πόλεσιν ἡ περὶ τὰς ἀρχάς Arist.Pol.1289a15, cf. 1274b26 (pl.), 1289b27 (pl.); ὅπου μὴ νόμοι ἄρχουσιν οὐκ ἔστι π. ib. 1292a32; τὴν ἀρίστην πολιτεύεσθαι π. ib. 1288b32, cf. X.Ath.1.1, etc.

2. esp. *republican government, free common-wealth*, Arist.EN1160a34, Pol.1293b22; ὅταν δὲ τὸ πλῆθος πρὸς τὸ κοινὸν πολιτεύηται συμφέρον, καλεῖται π. ib. 1279a39; ἄπιστον ταῖς π. ἡ τυραννίς D.1.5; οὐ γὰρ ἀσφαλεῖς ταῖς π. αἱ πρὸς τοὺς τυράννους .. ὁμιλίαι Id.6.21; τοὺς τὰς π. μεθιστάντας εἰς ὀλιγαρχίαν Id.15.20; ταῖς μὲν π. πολεμοῦσι τὰς δὲ μοναρχίας συγκαθιστᾶσι Isoc.4.125; ἔστι δήμου ἡ π. βίος Plu.2.826c.

Comments: Just a few comments are offered here. One will once again find lots of abbreviations, so consult the "Abbreviations" provided in the frontal material. (It should be said again that electronic versions, such as are found in Logos Bible Software, often, but not always, supply what these abbreviations mean.) The LSJ entry will begin with alternative forms as found in the Greek dialects (here Ion. means Ionic). Then the main English glosses are provided in italics. Notice that sub-glosses are provided beginning with "2." and other major gloss categories with II. and III. etc. What can be confusing is that one does not see **I.** or **1.** *These numbers are assumed.* What this means is that the first English gloss (above *condition and rights of a citizen, citizenship*) is really understood as definition "**I. 1.** …" Another nice feature is that, if there is a clear Latin word equivalent, it will often be included, as in **I. 4.** "= Lat. *civitas* in geographical sense."

D. **LSJ (Int)**: Liddell, H. G. *A Lexicon: Abridged from Liddell and Scott's Greek-English Lexicon*. Oxford: Clarendon, 1963. [Int = Intermediate]

πολιτεία, Ion. -ηΐη, ἡ, (πολιτεύω) *the condition and rights of a citizen, citizenship*, Lat. *civitas*, Hdt., Thuc., etc.; πολιτείαν δοῦναί τινι Xen.

2. *the life of a citizen, civic life*, Dem.

3. as a concrete, *the body of citizens*, Arist.

II. *the life and business of a statesman, government, administration*, Ar., Thuc., etc.:—in a collective sense, *the measures of a government*, Dem.

III. *civil polity, the condition or constitution of a state*, Thuc., etc.:—*a form of government*, Plat., etc.

2. *a republic, commonwealth*, Xen., etc.

Comments: One can see the value of the Intermediate LSJ (or "Middle Liddell"), since it contains the same essential information easily displayed without detailed references. However, just after the lexical form one finds in parentheses πολιτεύω, which is the form from which πολιτεία was derived. This differs from BDAG's indication of πολίτης. Why? Well, BDAG provides the *ultimate source* of related forms, whereas Middle Liddell provides the actual word from which πολιτεία is *directly derived*, namely, the verb πολιτεύω. If one looks up πολιτεύω in Middle Liddell, then one sees that πολιτεύω is derived from πολίτης.

Complete WORKBOOK EXERCISES 12 and consult the ANSWER KEY & GUIDE as needed.

CASE IN POINT 12: DEMONSTRATIVE ANTECEDENTS

We have learned that when studying pronouns, we should seek to identify the referent: If it comes before or precedes the pronoun, it is called an antecedent; if after, it is a postcedent. The first place to look for the referent is in an antecedent position. However, there are instances when the referent comes <u>after</u> the pronoun as a postcedent. The determination of the referent has tremendous exegetical consequences. Consider these examples of demonstrative pronouns <u>underlined</u> in the NASB95 and Greek texts.

1 Thess 4:3 <u>Τοῦτο</u> γάρ ἐστιν θέλημα τοῦ θεοῦ, ὁ ἁγιασμὸς ὑμῶν, ἀπέχεσθαι ὑμᾶς ἀπὸ τῆς πορνείας,

> For <u>this</u> is the will of God, your sanctification; *that is*, that you abstain from sexual immorality;

Notice how the demonstrative pronoun (here functioning adjectivally) comes before and anticipates its postcedent referent. It points the reader to the topic of "the will of God," which is further explained by the grammatical construction of apposition by "your sanctification" and then is further elaborated in the sentences that follow.

Here is another example from **John 20:30-31** (NASB95):

> [30] Therefore many other signs Jesus also performed in the presence of the disciples, which are not written in this book; [31] but <u>these</u> have been written so that you may believe that Jesus is the Christ, the Son of God; and that believing you may have life in His name.
> [30] Πολλὰ μὲν οὖν καὶ ἄλλα σημεῖα ἐποίησεν ὁ Ἰησοῦς ἐνώπιον τῶν μαθητῶν [αὐτοῦ], ἃ οὐκ ἔστιν γεγραμμένα ἐν τῷ βιβλίῳ τούτῳ· [31] <u>ταῦτα</u> δὲ γέγραπται ἵνα πιστεύ[σ]ητε ὅτι Ἰησοῦς ἐστιν ὁ χριστὸς ὁ υἱὸς τοῦ θεοῦ, καὶ ἵνα πιστεύοντες ζωὴν ἔχητε ἐν τῷ ὀνόματι αὐτοῦ.

Interpreters consider that these verses are a purpose statement for John's Gospel. What, however, is the referent to <u>these</u> in John 20:31? It is commonly held that <u>these</u> is backward looking, referring to all the signs in the preceding narrative based upon the previous statement in 20:30. However, notice how 20:30 brings our attention to *"many other signs also...which are not written in this book."* The adverbial additive καί stresses the adjective ἄλλα *other*. Also, notice the contrast in 20:31. It suggests to the reader a contrast not between *signs* (in the book) and *other signs*, but between *other signs not written* in book vs. *other signs written* in the book. What other signs written in this book would these be? Well, in the next chapter (John 21) there are additionally recorded miraculous things that Jesus performed in the presence of his disciples. What I would suggest is that *these* in 20:31 has a postcedent referent other signs that are written in John 21. This interpretation would also help scholars ponder over the proper relationship of John 21 to the rest of the gospel, since for many interpreters, the last chapter of John seems ancillary; some interpreters even speculate that John 21 was not original to John's Gospel. More evidence can be provided to establish my proposal. For example, the conjunctions μὲν οὖν ... δέ signal a resumption of the narrative and thus point forward to what follows. However, please understand the point of this Case in Point: Consider carefully what the referent to a pronoun is, whether it is antecedent, postcedent, or even implied.

Another good debatable example is determining the referent to *these commandments* in Matt 5:19. If you are able, look up this verse in context. Do *these commandments* have antecedent in the Law and Prophets of 5:17-18 or postcedent in Jesus' commands throughout the Sermon of the Mount in Matt 5:19–7:27 (or possibly even throughout Matthew's Gospel)? We must consider what importance the οὖν *therefore* has in 5:19, which was untranslated in the NIV84, but rectified in the NIV 2011. If Jesus is so concerned about obeying all *these commandments* of the Law (assuming that the Law is the antecedent), then why would Jesus conclude the Sermon on the Mount explaining that the wise person hears and does *these words of mine* (**μου** τοὺς λόγους τούτους) in 7:24? (Notice the forward placed **μου** for genitival emphasis.) It just may be that *these commandments* in 5:19 have their postcedent in Jesus' teaching as commands for God's renewed covenant people as found in the Sermon on the Mount.

To the right is a Roman relief dating to the 4th century AD (now lost) showing scrolls with title tabs.[14] In a private villa in Pompei, one private collection consisting largely of works of Philodemus (an Epicurean philosopher in Rom c. 75-40 BC). It contained a room 3 meters square with shelved walls up to eye level holding scrolls, 1,800 hundred in all, with immediate access to  an adjacent colonnade for comfortable reading. Such private library collections were often copied for building up public library holdings.[15] In addition, authors would contribute their own works.

---

[14] Image is slighty edited from Theodor Birt, *Die Buchrolle in Der Kunst: Archäologische-Antiquarische Untersuchungen Zum Antiken Buchwesen* (Leipzig: B. G. Teubner, 1907), 247.

[15] Lionel Casson, *Libraries in the Ancient World* (New Haven: Yale University Press, 2001), 74 and 102.

CHAPTER 13

13.0 VOCABULARY

13.1 PERFECT (Παρακείμενος) AND PLUPERFECT (Ὑπερσυντέλικος) TENSES: TENSE MARKERS AND VERBAL ASPECT

13.2 PERFECT AND PLUPERFECT TENSES: FORMATION AND TRANSLATION

13.3 REDUPLICATION: SPECIAL RULES AND EXAMPLES

13.4 PLUPERFECT OF οἶδα IS ᾔδειν

13.5 DISCOURSE PRAGMATIC OPTIONS TO REPRESENT PAST TIME IN THE INDICATIVE MOODS

13.6 MORE NOUNS OF THE THIRD DECLENSION (Τρίτη Κλίσις)

    CHECK POINT 13.6 PARSE THESE THIRD DECLENSION NOUNS

CASE IN POINT 13: PERFECTED LOVE IN 1 JOHN

Love is primary in the fruit of the Spirit, the core virtue of the Christian life. In 1 John, the Perfect Tense was chosen to help communicate what is important about love. Take a look.

    This lesson introduces the **Fourth** and **Fifth Principal Parts**. The Fourth Principal Part covers the **Perfect** and **Pluperfect Tenses**, **Active Voice** only. The Fifth Principal Part includes the **Perfect** and **Pluperfect Tenses**, **Middle/Passive Voice** only. **Reduplication** is the prefix used to form both the Perfect and Pluperfect Tenses. The Pluperfect of οἶδα (ᾔδειν) is discussed. Then, the Verbal Aspect of both the Perfect and Pluperfect Tenses is explained within the context of the available options to indicate past time in the Indicative Mood. Lastly, in the Vocabulary are given more Third Declension nouns.

VOCABULARY 13   MORE THIRD DECLENSION NOUNS

Feminine Third Declension Nouns:

ἡ γυνή, γυναικός [216]	woman; wife
ἡ ἐλπίς, ἐλπίδος [53]	hope
ἡ ματήρ, μήτρος [83]	mother
ἡ νύξ, νυκτός [61]	night
ἡ σάρξ, σαρκός [147]	flesh
ἡ χάρις, χάριτος [155]	grace; favor; thankfulness
ἡ χεῖρ, χειρός [176]	hand

Neuter Third Declension Nouns:

τὸ αἷμα, -ατος [97]	blood; bloodshed
τὸ θέλημα, -ατος [62]	will, desire
τὸ ὄνομα, -ατος [229]	name
τὸ πνεῦμα, -ατος [379]	spirit; breath; (Holy) Spirit
τὸ ῥῆμα, -ατος [67]	word, saying; thing
τὸ σπέρμα, -ατος [43]	seed; offspring
τὸ στόμα, -ατος [78]	mouth, opening
τὸ σῶμα, -ατος [142]	body

After learning vocabulary to this point, you will know 67.8% of the words in the GNT. If you are able, listen to audio recordings of VOCABULARY 13 and complete the CROSSWORD PUZZLE in the WORKBOOK EXERCISES.

NOTES ON VOCABULARY 13:

Many of the words above have English cognates: <u>gyne</u>-cology, <u>mater</u>-nal, <u>nycta</u>-lopia (night blindness) or <u>noct</u>-urnal, <u>sarco</u>-phagus (stone coffin for dead flesh), Eu-<u>charist</u>, <u>chiro</u>-practic (manipulation of spinal column <u>by hand</u>), <u>hema</u>-tic or an-<u>emia</u>, <u>onomato</u>-poeia (formation of names in imitation of natural sounds) or pseudo-<u>nym</u> (false name), <u>pneuma</u>-tic, sperm, <u>stoma</u>-ch (the mouth empties into stomach), <u>soma</u>-tic.

The image shows the famous hands of the bronze statue *Boxer at Rest* (4th century BC) located at Museo Delle Terme, Rome. The hands are wrapped with a "sharp thong" (ἱμὰς ὀξύς), which was not to soften the blow to the boxer's hand, but to increase the impact against one's opponent.[1] No wonder the boxer's face is scared and gashed with a broken nose.

The type of neuter nouns presented in this vocabulary is very regular in formation. They form a class of nouns called –μα nouns. Because of their regularity, the entire word's stem is not repeated when providing genitive ending; instead, one often finds a dash demarcating when the stem ends and then the genitive ending -ατος. As for the word ῥῆμα *word, saying; thing*, remember that conventionally the letter ῥῶ has a rough breathing mark when it begins a word. Finally, students may be interested to know that nouns formed with –μα endings are typically "result" words; the word formed signified the result or effect of some action or activity, although sometimes we may not quite understand the derivation (e.g. αἷμα *blood*). Smyth (§841) provides these examples: "γράμ-μα *thing written* (γράφ-ω *write*), νόη-μα *thought* (νοέω *think*), ποίη-μα *poem* (ποιέ-ω *make*), δέρ-μα *hide* (δέρ-ω *flay*), τμῆ-μα *section* (τέμ-νω *cut*, τεμ-, τμη-,…)." Robertson (151, 153) provides many others and explains that many new –μα words were formed in the Koine era.

One interesting resultative –μα noun is χάραγμα, *stamp, imprinted mark* from χαράσσω *I engrave*. The word χάραγμα is found seven times in Revelation in the expressions "the mark of the beast" etc. (13:16, 17; 14:9, 11; 16:2; 19:20; 20:4). A hundred years ago, Adolf Deissmann brought to light recent discoveries from papyri documents that included a red imperial χάραγμα *mark*. Many examples were found stamped on official documents of sales. He summarizes the significance of the word, which

(1) Is connected with the Roman Emperor,

(2) Contains his name (possibly also his effigy) and the year of his reign,

---

[1] Walter Woodburn Hyde, *Olympic Victor Monuments and Greek Athletic Art* (Washington, DC: Carnegie Institution of Washington, 1921), 237-38. The image is modified from the original photo by Marie-Lan Nguyen (2009).

(3) Was necessary upon documents relating to buying, selling, etc., and

(4) Was technically known as χάραγμα.[2]

The image above is one such χάραγμα with a 5.5 cm diameter. It dates to the 35th year of Caesar Augustus' reign (AD 5-6) and has the text **L ΛΕ ΚΑΙΣΑΡΟΣ** (35 *Caesar)* around a **ΓΡ** (which probably signified the abbreviated word γραφεῖον meaning *tax).* Deissmann concludes, "The χάραγμα of the Apocalypse is not, of course, wholly identical with its contemporary prototype. The seer acted with a free hand; he has it that the mark is impressed on forehead or hand, and he gives the number a new meaning."[3]

13.1 PERFECT (*παρακείμενος*) AND PLUPERFECT (*ὑπερσυντέλικος*) TENSES: TENSE MARKERS AND VERBAL ASPECT

A. **Tense Markers:** We have already learned that tense in the Greek verb can be signaled in five ways: (1) affixing a **prefix** to the front of a verb stem; (2) **changing** the verb stem; (3) supplying a **tense indicator**; (4) supplying a **coupling vowel**; and (5) adding types of **endings**.

Prefix + Stem Change + Tense Indicator + Coupling Vowel + Endings

   (1)   (2)   (3)   (4)   (5)

The Perfect and Pluperfect Tenses have a prefix called **reduplication** (marked for resultative-stative verbal aspect), and may show a stem change or none at all. The Perfect Active has a κάππα tense indicator with α/ε coupling vowel and the Secondary Tense Endings. The Perfect Middle/Passive is truly odd: it is formed with <u>no</u> tense indicator, <u>no</u> coupling vowel, and the Primary Middle/Passive Endings.

B. **Verbal Aspect:** The Perfect and Pluperfect Tenses have **resultative-stative verbal aspect**, in which the action reflects "a given (often complex) state of affairs."[4] In the Indicative Mood, the Perfect Tense indicates a resultant state, arising from some prior past event(s), that continues into the present time. With the Pluperfect Tense, which is often marked for past time through augmentation, this resultative-stative aspect is placed into a past timeframe: Something happened that created a resultant state for a time, but this resultant state is no longer effective at present. See below §13.5; cf. Wallace 572-86.

---

[2] Quoted from Adolf Deissmann, *Bible Studies: Contributions, Chiefly from Papyri and Inscriptions, to the History of the Language, the Literature, and the Religion of Hellenistic Judaism and Primitive Christianity,* trans. A. Grieve, 2nd ed. (Edinburgh: T&T Clark, 1903), 242. The corresponding image on page 243 has been colored red, flipped, and re-oriented for easier reading here.

[3] Deissmann, *Bible Studies,* 247.

[4] Porter 21–22; cf. Porter, *Verbal Aspect,* 258–59 and Porter, Reed, and O'Donnell, *Fundamentals,* 319.

13.2 PERFECT AND PLUPERFECT TENSES: FORMATION AND TRANSLATION

A. **The Addition of the Reduplication to the Front of the Verb Stem:** Regular reduplication is simply the doubling of the initial consonant from the verb stem with an ἒ ψιλόν placed in between. The reduplication for πιστεύω is πε-πιστευ. To form the Pluperfect Tenses, typically an additional ἒ ψιλόν (ἐ-) is affixed to the front of the reduplication. For example, πιστεύω would become ἐπεπιστευ.... This ἒ ψιλόν (ἐ-) is optional for the pluperfect. The endings distinguish a pluperfect from a perfect form.

B. **The Perfect and Pluperfect Active Endings:** Both the Perfect and Pluperfect Active Endings use a κάππα as a tense indicator. This κάππα is then joined with a coupling vowel(s)—α/ε for the Perfect and ει for the Pluperfect—and the universal secondary endings.

	PERFECT ACTIVE		PLUPERFECT ACTIVE	
	sg.	pl.	sg.	pl.
1	-κα	-κα-μεν	-κει-ν	-κει-μεν
2	-κα-ς	-κα-τε	-κει-ς	-κει-τε
3	-κε-(ν)	-κα-σιν*	-κει-	-κει-σαν*

*The 3rd plural forms are somewhat unique. Sometimes one sees -καν for the Perfect 3rd pl.

1. <u>Adding These Κάππα Endings to the Stem</u>: When the verb stem ends in a vowel, these κάππα endings are added directly onto the reduplicated stem:

Lexical Form	**Fourth Principal Part**	Notes
λύω	λέλυκα	Pluperfect → ἐ-λέλυκειν
ἀναβαίνω	ἀναβέβηκα	stem change → -βη
γινώσκω	ἔγνωκα	<u>Notice</u> the irregular reduplication.

2. <u>Verb Stems Ending in a Consonant</u>: When a κάππα is added to a consonant, either the κάππα totally replaces it, or the κάππα is rejected by the consonant and is not added.

a. **Often κάππα completely replaces ζῆτα (ζ):**

Lexical Form	**Fourth Principal Part**	Notes:
ἐγγίζω	ἤγγικα	
ἑτοιμάζω	ἡτοίμακα	
καθίζω	κεκάθικα	
σῴζω	σέσωκα	The ὦ μέγα losses its ἰῶτα.
κράζω	κέκραγα	Γάμμα is found instead of κάππα.

b. Κάππα in the following verbs is completely rejected: These verb formations are often called *Second Perfects* because they lack a κάππα (and some have stem changes).

Lexical Form	Fourth Principal Part	Lexical Form	Fourth Principal Part
ἀνοίγω	ἀνέῳγα	πάσχω	πέπονθα
γράφω	γέγραφα	πείθω	πέποιθα
ἔρχομαι	ἐλήλυθα	προσφέρω	προσενήνοχα
λαμβάνω	εἴληφα		

C. Translating the Perfect and Pluperfect Active Voice: Capturing the sense of the Perfect Tense in English is very difficult. It is preferable to use the English linking verbs *have* or *has* for the Perfect Tense and *had* for the Pluperfect.

PERFECT ACTIVE

sg.	1	πεπίστευκα	*I have trusted.*
	2	πεπίστευκας	*You have trusted.*
	3	πεπίστευκε(ν)	*He/She/It has trusted.*
pl.	1	πεπιστεύκαμεν	*We have trusted.*
	2	πεπιστεύκατε	*You have trusted.*
	3	πεπιστεύκασι(ν)	*They have trusted.*

PLUPERFECT ACTIVE*

sg.	1	ἐπεπίστευκειν	*I had trusted.*
	2	ἐπεπίστευκεις	*You had trusted.*
	3	ἐπεπίστευκει	*He/She/It had trusted.*
pl.	1	ἐπεπιστεύκειμεν	*We had trusted.*
	2	ἐπεπιστεύκειτε	*You had trusted.*
	3	ἐπεπιστεύκεισαν	*They had trusted.*

*Note: The augment ἐ- may or may not be present along with the reduplication.

D. Perfect and Pluperfect Middle/Passive Endings: There is no tense indicator or coupling vowel. The Perfect Middle/Passive uses the Primary Middle/Passive Endings with no coupling vowels added. The Pluperfect Middle/Passive uses the Secondary Middle/Passive endings:

	PERFECT MIDDLE/PASSIVE		PLUPERFECT MIDDLE/PASSIVE	
	sg.	pl.	sg.	pl.
1	-μαι	-μεθα	-μην	-μεθα
2	-σαι*	-σθε	-σο*	-σθε
3	-ται	-νται	-το	-ντο

<u>Notice</u>: (1) All these endings begin with a consonant. This will cause some trouble when adding them to a verb stem that ends in a consonant. See Below. (2) The 2nd singular forms with (*) are the original forms of Primary and Secondary Middle/Passive Endings.

1. <u>Adding These Endings to the Stem</u>. When the verb stem ends in a vowel, these endings are added directly onto the reduplicated stem.

Lexical Form	**Fifth Principal Part**	**Notes**
λύω	λέλυμαι	-Pluperfect is ἐ-λελύ-μην
βάλλω	βέβλημαι	-stem change → βλη
γινώσκω	ἔγνωμαι	-irregular reduplication

2. <u>Verb Stems Ending in a Consonant</u>. When these endings are added to a stem ending in a consonant they (1) turn dentals and ζῆτα into σίγμα, or (2) in the case of palatals, they change that consonant:

a. *Endings change ζῆτα (ζ) and dentals (δ, τ, ϑ) into σίγμα.*

Lexical Form	**Fifth Principal Part**	**Notes:**
βαπτίζω	βεβάπτισμαι	
δοξάζω	δεδόξασμαι	
εὐαγγελίζω	εὐηγγέλισμαι	
σῴζω	σέσω(σ)μαι	Sometimes the σίγμα is missing.
ἑτοιμάζω	ἡτοίμασμαι	
πείϑω	πέπεισμαι	

b. *Consonant changes occur in these verbs.* These changes are for easier pronunciation (i.e. euphony):

Lexical Form	**Fifth Principal Part**
γράφω	γέγραμμαι
διώκω	δεδίωγμαι
δέχομαι	δέδεγμαι

E. **Translating the Perfect and Pluperfect Middle/Passive Voices:** As was mentioned above, capturing the sense of the Perfect Tense in English may be difficult. Generally, the English linking verbs *have* or *has* for the Perfect Tense and *had* for the Pluperfect help convey resultant effect. The Middle and Passive forms are identical. *However, always try to translate the forms below first as if they were passive.* If a passive sense does not work, then follow the guidelines for translating the middle voice in §3.4.E.

PERFECT MIDDLE/PASSIVE

sg.	1	πεπίστευμαι	*I have been trusted.*
	2	πεπίστευσαι	*You have been trusted.*
	3	πεπίστευται	*He/She/It has been trusted.*
pl.	1	πεπιστεύμεθα	*We have been trusted.*
	2	πεπίστευσθε	*You have been trusted.*
	3	πεπίστευνται	*They have been trusted.*

PLUPERFECT MIDDLE/PASSIVE

sg.	1	ἐπεπιστεύμην	*I had been trusted.*
	2	ἐπεπίστευσο	*You had been trusted.*
	3	ἐπεπίστευτο	*He/She/It had been trusted.*
pl.	1	ἐπεπιστεύμεθα	*We had been trusted.*
	2	ἐπεπίστευσθε	*You had been trusted.*
	3	ἐπεπίστευντο	*They had been trusted.*

F. **Common and Special Uses of the Perfect Tense:** Here are some of the major uses of the Perfect tense. See Wallace 573-82 for a description of these and others.

1. Intensive or Resultative Perfect. Emphasizes the present resultant state

2. Extensive Perfect. Emphasizes the completed action of the verbal idea from which the resultant effect comes

3. Aoristic or Dramatic Perfect. A rare usage to stress some past event dramatically

G. **Examples of Perfect Tense Verbs:** Consider the significance of each verse (especially in context). The verses are translated literally with the perfect tense verb underlined.

Rom 3:21a *But now apart from the law, righteousness from God has been revealed, …*

Rom 5:5 *And hope does not put us to shame, because the love of God has been poured into our hearts by the Holy Spirit, whom was given to us.*

Rom 13:8b *For the one who loves the other person has fulfilled the law.*

1 Cor 15:20 *But even Christ has been raised from the dead, the firstfruits of the ones having fallen asleep.*

2 Cor 12:9a *And he [the Lord] has spoken to me, "My grace is sufficient for you, for my power is completed in weakness."*

13.3 REDUPLICATION: SPECIAL RULES AND EXAMPLES

A. **Reduplication:** Both the Perfect and Pluperfect Tenses add a prefix called reduplication to the front of the verb stem. The Pluperfect Tense, however, in order to put the Perfect into the past time, **often** has added an augment before the reduplication. This phenomenon of augmentation added to the reduplication of the Pluperfect is not emphasized below, but rather simple reduplication is. This is because the Perfect Tense occurs much more frequently than does the Pluperfect Tense. By far, "simple reduplication" is the most common. *Learn simple reduplication first before attempting to memorize the special cases or exceptions described below in 2.– 4.*

1. Simple Reduplication. Basically, reduplication is when the initial verb stem consonant is (1) doubled, (2) and an ἒ ψιλόν (ε) is squeezed between the doubled and initial consonant:

Initial Stem:	πιστευ-	
Step 1	π πιστευ-	
Step 2	πεπιστευ-	πε is the reduplication

Stem	Reduplicated Stem	Note:
βαπτιζ-	βεβαπτισ-	
γραφ-	γεγραφ-	
δοξαζ-	δεδοξασ-	
σωζ-	σεσωσ-	The ὦ μέγα losses its ἰῶτα.
καθιζ-	κεκαθισ-	

2. Reduplicating Verb Stems that Begin with a Vowel. For verb stems that begin with a vowel, there is no consonant to double. Nonetheless, an ἒ ψιλόν (ε) is added to the front. The result is that the reduplication looks like an augment (ε), although it is not. Basically, the same rules apply for reduplication under this circumstance as with augmentation. These rules are summarized below:

a. *If the verb stem begins with ι, υ, η, or ω, then no visible reduplication is seen.*

b. *Otherwise, see below:*

Vowel	Reduplicated	Examples	
α	η	εὐ-αγγελίζω	→ εὐηγγελισ-
ε	η	ἑτοιμάζω	→ ἡτοιμασ-
ο	ω	ὁρίζω	→ ὡρισ- (this verb form occurs 3x)
		ὁράω	→ ἑωρα- (you will see this odd form most often)

c. *Monophthongs and Diphthongs are also affected by reduplication.* Along with the initial vowel lengthening, if an ἰῶτα is present, it becomes an ἰῶτα *subscript*.

Mono-/Diphthong	Reduplicated	Examples		Reduplicated Stem
αι →	η	αἰτέω	→	ᾐτη-
αυ →	ηυ	αὐξάνω	→	ηὔξαν-

Notice that frequently with ευ and οι, no change occurs with reduplication.

d. *Compound verbs are reduplicated at their stem.* (Note example in b. above.)

3. Reduplicating Σίγμα Consonant Clusters. Verbs stems beginning with ζ, ξ, ψ, or σ followed by any consonant (e.g. στ-, σπ-) reject doubling and simply take an ἑ ψιλόν.

Σίγμα Consonant Cluster	**Reduplicated**
σταυρόω	→ ἐσταυρ-
σπείρω	→ ἐσπαρ- This verb also has a stem change.

4. Reduplicating Aspirated Mutes. There are three aspirated mutes: φ, θ, χ. These three are pronounced with a push of air as one speaks. When these consonants are reduplicated, they are doubled using the corresponding non-aspirated mute. For example,

φ →	π	φανερόω	→	πεφανερο-
θ →	τ	θεραπεύω	→	τεθεραπευ-
χ →	κ	χαίρω	→	κεχαιρ-

Only three verbs in the vocabularies begin with an aspirated mute and have Perfect forms in the NT. These are: θεραπεύω, φανερόω, and τίθημι (a special verb).

13.4 PLUPERFECT OF οἶδα IS ᾔδειν

Already you are familiar with the fact that οἶδα is really Perfect Tense in form, but translated as a Present Tense verb. To make οἶδα past time, the Greeks used the Pluperfect Tense forms. There are 86 Pluperfect Tense forms in the GNT. The Pluperfect of οἶδα in the Indicative Mood accounts for 33 of these:

		TRANSLATION	FREQUENCY IN GNT
sg. 1	ᾔδειν	*I knew.*	5x
2	ᾔδεις	*You knew.*	3x
3	ᾔδει	*He/She/It knew.*	14x
pl. 1	(ᾔδειμεν)	*We knew.*	-
2	ᾔδειτε	*You knew.*	3x
3	ᾔδεισαν	*They knew.*	8x

13.5 Discourse Pragmatic Options to Represent Past Time in the Indicative Mood

A. **Greek Indicative Past Tenses:** As you have learned, Greek has four "past time" verb formations for the Indicative Mood: the Imperfect, Aorist, Perfect, and Pluperfect. This contrasts with only one present time formation (the Present Tense) and one future time formation (the Future Tense, excluding the rather rare Future Perfect). Obviously, an author had many options for how to represent past time events in narrative, especially if one throws in the Historic Present, which, remember, is used to highlight significant action or speech (see §6.6 Historic Present (HP) and Discourse Pragmatics). It may be helpful to recall Verbal Aspect in Relation to Verb Tenses:

Verbal Aspect	Greek Tenses
1. *Imperfective*. Action as viewed internally as in progress or incomplete	**Present, Imperfect**
2. *Perfective*. Action as viewed as a whole externally or as complete (but not necessarily completed)	**Aorist**
3. *Resultative-Stative*. Action reflects "a given (often complex) state of affairs"	**Perfect, Pluperfect**
4. *Future*. Action reflects expectation or intention of occurrence in the future	**Future**

B. **Discourse Pragmatic Functions in Narrative Materials:** One must distinguish between semantics (i.e., meaning in the Greek forms) and pragmatic function (i.e., use the forms for discursive effect).

1. Aorist Tense. As will be presented in the respective chapters, the unique semantics of the Aorist Indicative is suitable to mark the mainline information of the narrative—the Aorist Indicative moves the narrative forward. All the other tenses are unmarked for mainline information; instead, they are marked for some kind of prominence in the narrative.

2. Historic Present (HP) is Forward Pointing. The HP has the pragmatic effect to highlight the unfolding **subsequent** events, actions, or speech. The *imperfective aspect of "incompleteness"* opens up the narrative to look forward to subsequent speech or action. In this respect, the Historic Present is to be differentiated from the Imperfect Tense, which rather instead preserves an imperfective verbal aspect in relation to the verbal action itself. Also, the location of the HP may be at the start of a new unit, but also need not be. See again §6.6 Historic Present (HP) and Discourse Pragmatics.

3. <u>Imperfect Tense</u>. The Imperfect Tense represents the verbal action as *imperfective*, i.e. as internal and in progress without view of beginning and ending. As such, the presence of the Imperfect Tense alerts audiences to envision such *ongoing past action* in relation to the verbal action itself. This distinguishes the Imperfect Tense from the HP, which rather points forward to the unfolding narrative. In terms of pragmatic effect, since the Imperfect Tense verbs is marked +*internal incomplete representation*, it may add vividness, highlight significant events in the narrative, and/or serve to introduce a new scene.

4. <u>Perfect and Pluperfect Tenses</u>. Since the Perfect Tense has *resultative-stative aspect*, its use emphasizes resultant effect or state of actions. To put this resultant effect or state into remote, distant, past time, then an augment may be added to form the Pluperfect Tense. Because of their rarity and the complex resultative aspect, the Perfect and Pluperfect Tenses are the most prominent of the tenses. By their use, authors indicate important actions/states.

5. <u>Semantic and Pragmatic Function of Past Indicative Tenses</u>. These discourse pragmatic functions in the Indicative Mood may be summarized as follows:

	AUGMENT	ASPECTUAL SEMANTIC SIGNIFICANCE			PRAGMATIC FUNCTION		
	Remoteness (There-ness)	Perfective	Imperfective	Resultative-Stative	Main-line	Fore-ground	Front-ground
Aorist	+	+			+		
Historic Present			+			+ +subsequent focus	
Imperfect	+		+			+ +vividness	
Perfect				+			+
Pluperfect	+			+			+

To summarize, the **augment** (+remoteness) is added to verbs in the Indicative Mood when forming the Aorist Tense, Imperfect Tense, and Pluperfect Tense; the augment marks remoteness and thus often past time. In narratives, the perfective aspect (i.e., *complete[d] action*) of the **Aorist Tense** indicates mainline material or the storyline that is <u>not marked for prominence</u> (Porter calls this <u>background</u>). The **Imperfect Tense** in narrative shows imperfective aspect (i.e., *in progress* or *incomplete*) and makes vivid and <u>foregrounded</u> the verbal event itself. The **Pluperfect Tense** represents stative aspectual actions that are <u>frontgrounded</u>, but have remoteness, i.e. have already occurred in the past and have already had stative results that are already concluded. Also with stative aspect, the **Perfect Tense** represents actions that are <u>frontgrounded</u> but are not-marked for remoteness. In other words, the resultant stative effects still persist and/or these results are prominently presented. Finally, the **Historic Present** with imperfective aspect (i.e., *in progress* or *incomplete*) highlights the narrative's immediately unfolding subsequent speech or actions. Thus, each tense makes a distinctive contribution to narrative discourse that corresponds both to the semantics related to the tense form (e.g. "remoteness" signaled by augmentation) and to the pragmatics of verbal aspect in contextual use.

C. **Discourse Pragmatic Functions in Non-Narrative Materials:** The description above pertains primarily to narrative materials, but in many respects one may extend the principles to non-narrative discourse (such as Paul's letters) with the main exception being the HP, which would not occur. Also, the mainline material in Paul would be the present tense (i.e., Paul's current circumstances, and need to write church assemblies) although one should expect him to switch between past, present, and future time frames, depending on the needs of his presentation. For example, consider how Paul in 2 Cor 1:8-14 in a matter of seven verses utilized the Present (6x), Aorist (4x), Future (3x), and Perfect (2x) Tenses in the Indicative Mood (I have not identified non-Indicative moods.):

2 Cor 1:8–14 [8] For we are not wanting [Present] you to be unaware, brethren, of our affliction that occurred in Asia Minor, that excessively we were burdened [Aorist] beyond our strength, so that we despaired even of living; [9] but we ourselves have had [Perfect] the sentence of death within ourselves in order that we would not trust in ourselves, but in God who raises the dead, [10] who delivered [Aorist] us from so great a death, and will deliver [Future], in whom have set our hope [Perfect] that also he will deliver [Future] us still, [11] while you also are joining us through your prayers, in order that the favor for us by many persons would be thanked on our behalf. [12] For our boast is [Present] this, the testimony of our conscience, that in sincerity and purity, not in fleshly wisdom but in the grace of God, we conducted [Aorist] ourselves in the world, and especially toward you. [13] For we are not writing [Present] anything to you other than what you are reading [Present] and are understanding [Present], and I am hoping [Present] that you will understand [Future] until the end, [14] just as also you knew [Aorist] us in part, that we are [Present] your boast, just as you *are* ours, in the day of our Lord, Jesus Christ.

Despite the predominance of the Indicative Present Tense by frequency, Paul was concerned here primarily to convey the gravity of what **had happened** to him in Asia Minor in the past (a death sentence). This time frame switches to the Future due to Paul's expectation of God's further future deliverance (1:10) coupled with the Corinthians' prayer (1:11). This leads to Paul's further present testimony about his past conduct (1:12). Paul then reflects on the clarity of his current writing (1:13), which involves self-reflectively an extensive "metacomment" about the reception of the current epistle, ending with a future tense expectation (see §10.8 META-COMMENTS AND PRAGMATICS). Paul concludes (1:14) by comparing what he hopes the Corinthians will understand about him in their future understanding after reading the letter with their past partial knowledge of him about the future: They will boast about each other in the day of the Lord. So, we observe Paul utilizing each tense strategically in view of past, present, and future realities.

13.6 MORE NOUNS OF THE THIRD DECLENSION (Τρίτη Κλίσις)

In the last chapter, we looked at Third declension nouns. Review once more, if you need to, §12.1 NOUNS OF THE THIRD DECLENSION.

A. **Feminine:** All Third Declension nouns share common endings with only slight variation. Feminine Third Declension nouns are no exception. **Notice**, however, the following:

1. The accusative singular of χάρις can be either χάριν or χαρίτα.

2. The dative plural for σάρξ, νύξ, and γυνή is -ξι(ν). This is the result of the stem (σαρκ-, νυκτ-, and γυναικ-) combining with the -σι(ν) to become -ξι(ν). Thus,

$$\sigma\alpha\rho\kappa + \sigma\iota(\nu) \rightarrow \textbf{σαρξίν} \qquad \nu\upsilon\kappa\tau + \sigma\iota(\nu) \rightarrow \textbf{νυξίν} \qquad \gamma\upsilon\nu\alpha\iota\kappa + \sigma\iota(\nu) \rightarrow \textbf{γυναιξίν}$$

B. **Neuter:** The Neuter Third Declension nouns share the same endings with the other genders. Every noun that ends in -μα is a Third Declension Neuter noun.

CHECK POINT 13.6 PARSE THESE THIRD DECLENSION NOUNS	
Gender (M, F, N), Case (N, G, D, A), and Number (S,P)	
1. τῇ μητρὶ	9. πατρί
2. χάριτος	10. ἀνδρὲς
3. αἰῶνας	11. τοὺς πόδας
4. πνεύματα	12. σάρκα
5. θελήματος	13. ἐλπίδος
6. τὸ αἷμα	14. φῶς
7. πυρί	15. ὑδάτων
8. ἀνδράσιν	16. νυκτός
ANSWERS	
1. τῇ μητρὶ F D S	9. πατρί M D S
2. χάριτος F G S	10. ἀνδρὲς M N P
3. αἰῶνας M A P	11. τοὺς πόδας M A P
4. πνεύματα N N/A P	12. σάρκα F A S
5. θελήματος N G S	13. ἐλπίδος F G S
6. τὸ αἷμα N A S	14. φῶς N N/A S
7. πυρί N D S	15. ὑδάτων N G P
8. ἀνδράσιν M D P	16. νυκτός F G S

Complete WORKBOOK EXERCISES 13 and consult the ANSWER KEY & GUIDE as needed.

CASE IN POINT 13: PERFECTED LOVE IN 1 JOHN

In the First Epistle of John, the verb τελειόω (*I perfect; I complete*) is found four times. In each occurrence, it is found in the Perfect Tense (1 John 2:5; 4:12, 17, 18). A brief study of the first two occurrences will help to illustrate the significance of the Perfect Tense. The verses are given below with the relevant forms highlighted.

1 John 2:5 *but whoever keeps* [present tense] *His word, (then) truly in this person the love of God <u>has been perfected</u>. By this we know that we are in Him:*

1 John 2:5 ὃς δ' ἂν τηρῇ αὐτοῦ τὸν λόγον, ἀληθῶς ἐν τούτῳ ἡ ἀγάπη τοῦ θεοῦ <u>τετελείωται</u>, ἐν τούτῳ γινώσκομεν ὅτι ἐν αὐτῷ ἐσμεν.

The subject of the verb *perfected* is "the love of God." Immediately, we need to consider whether this is a subjective genitive (*God's love for us*) or objective genitive (*Our love for God*). As we consider more the logic of the verse, we see that there is an implied "if...then" structure: "If someone keeps His word, then the love of God is perfected in that person." This structure indicates that a precondition for the love of God being perfected is our keeping His word. If it is our "keeping" that is necessary, then we should understand the love of God as objective, *our love of God*. We might be able to restate the idea this way: *If we keep His word, our love for God is perfected*. This reading goes well with the second part of the verse that indicates how ("by this") we may know that "we are in Him." Such assurance comes as we are keeping His word.

Now, what is the significance of the Perfect Tense here? Well, it suggests that something has happened (a complex action) with continuing results. What happened? It must be something related to keeping God's word; this keeping/obeying is in the Present Tense, which reflects imperfective aspect, and hence progressive, habitual, or ongoing action. This progressive keeping of God's Word has continued results for the present in terms of having love for God. This interpretation may shed light on how and why people might lose their sense of assurance of being in God, and thus why they experience a loss of love for God: If persons are not keeping His word, they are not loving God. John's statements are clear, to the point, and refreshing, causing us to reflect more deeply about how people show love for God.

The next occurrence of τελειόω is in 1 John 4:12, which is thematically related to 2:5:

1 John 4:12 *No one has ever seen God; if we are loving one another, then God keeps abiding in us and His love <u>is perfected</u> in/among us.*

1 John 4:12 θεὸν οὐδεὶς πώποτε τεθέαται. ἐὰν ἀγαπῶμεν ἀλλήλους, ὁ θεὸς ἐν ἡμῖν μένει καὶ ἡ ἀγάπη αὐτοῦ ἐν ἡμῖν <u>τετελειωμένη</u> ἐστίν.

John's "cause and effect" logic is present once again: "If we love one another, then...." There are two stated consequences: (1) *God abides in us*; (2) and *His love is perfected in us*. The Perfect Tense form used here involves a special participle construction (see §19.5 PERIPHRASTIC USE OF THE PARTICIPLE) that stresses the attribute of *having been perfected* in relation to God's love. In other words, the verbal construction directs one to consider the "perfectedness" of God's love in us or among us as an active attribute of believers. The question that arises is, How does this occur? Notice that the condition for this to occur is our love of one another. God's love is perfected if we love one another.

We should meditate on these verses. One theological and anthropological implication is that human beings have the faculty and prerogative of loving one another. But more than this, humans have a divine sanctioning to do so *in participation with God's love*. In other words, it was in God's plan to involve humans in the fulfillment of His love for us. We become participants in God's love for us through loving one another. Another implication might very well be that our failure to love one another would result in a failure of the realization or actualization of God's love in our lives in relation to one another. This may partially explain why there is such heartache and hurt in the world since God has entrusted us as humans, who are made in His image, with so much, even participating in the spread of God's love. So, Jesus as a human being provides us with the example of sacrificial love, in order to demonstrate God's love and encourage us to love one another, strangers, and our enemies (1 John 4:9-11; cf. Matt 5:43-48).

To the right is an image of a bronze rabbit that was an *ex-voto* offering (an offering to fulfill a vow) to the god Apollo at Priene.[5] Such offerings reflected an understanding of humans fulfilling one's vows as a dire responsibility to the gods. This hare was hung by its front paws as sacrificed and dead. Beginning with its head and repeating again partially on the underside (the lower image) the inscription reads as follows:

Τῷ Ἀπόλλωνι τῷ Πριηλῆι μ' ἀνέθηκεν Ἡφαιστίων.

"To Apollo the Prieleus, Hephaistion dedicated me."

This dates to the sixth century BC and shows right to left writing and superscripted ἰῶτα.

---

[5] Image slightly modified from Victor Duruy, *History of Greece, and of the Greek People: From the Earliest Times to the Roman Conquest*, trans. M. M. Ripley, Vol. 2, Sect. 1 (London: Kegan Paul, Trench, Trübner & Co., 1898), 261.

CHAPTER 14

One topic of interest for believers is the gifting by the Holy Spirit. Do all believers have all the gifts? Or, is there one gift available to all? Importantly, Paul's use of questions in 12:29 helps to resolve these questions.

    This chapter introduces the **Interrogative** and **Indefinite Pronouns**. Although the meaning and uses of these pronouns are different, they look exactly alike, except for their accents (or lack thereof). Then **Questions** in Greek are covered along with **Interrogative Adverbs**. These adverbs may be used within **indirect questions**. The common uses of the **Dative Case** are discussed. Lastly, the Vocabulary contains more adjectives of the First and Second Declensions and **non-declinable adjectives of number**.

VOCABULARY 14   MORE ADJECTIVES; INDEFINITE PRONOUNS AND INTERROGATIVE PRONOUNS, ADVERBS, AND CONJUNCTIONS

Adjectives:

ἀγαπητός, -ή, -όν [61]	beloved, dearly loved
αἰώνιος, -ον [69]	eternal, ever-lasting
δεξιός, -ά, -όν [54]	right (vs. left)
ἔσχατος, -η, -ον [52]	last; end
κακός, -ή, -όν [50]	bad; evil
λοιπός, -ή, -όν [55]	rest; remaining
μέσος, -η, -ον [58]	middle (of) (+ *gen.*)
μόνος, -η, -ον [113]	only; alone (*adv.*)
πρεσβύτερος, -α, -ον [66]	elderly, old; Elder
τυφλός, -ή, -όν [50]	blind

Interrogative and Indefinite Pronouns:

τίς, τί [551]	Who? What? Why?
τις, τι [534]	someone, something

Interrogative Adverbs and Conjunction:

μή [1038] or μήτι [18]	no; (*expects a negative answer*)
οὐ or οὐχί [54]	no; (*expects a positive answer*)
ἤ [346]	or, whether (a conjunction)
ποῦ [48]	where (?)
πότε [19]	when (?)
πῶς [105]	how (?); in what way (?)

After learning vocabulary to this point, you will know 70.5% of the words in the GNT. If you are able, listen to audio recordings of VOCABULARY 14 and complete the CROSSWORD PUZZLE in the EXERCISES.

NOTES ON VOCABULARY 14:

Many of the adjectives have English cognates: agape love, aeon (related to αἰών *age*), dex-tral (right-handedness), eschat-ology, caco-phony (bad sound), Meso-lithic, mono-theism (*only one God*), presbyter, typhl-osis (blindness).

Also, note that the adjective αἰώνιος, -ον belongs to a group of adjectives that only have "dual termination" (cf. Smyth §312), which means that there are no independent feminine forms. Instead, the masculine form is considered also feminine and thus is used to modify feminine nouns. A rather common example is seen in the phrase ἡ αἰώνιος ζωή (*the) eternal life*. Such dual termination adjectives are normally compounded words; for example, ἀ-χειρο-ποίητος, -ον (*not-hand-made*) and αἰώνιον from the noun αἰών *age*, which may have been derived from ἀεί *ever* and ὤν *being* (see Thayer, 18).

14.1 Interrogative and Indefinite Pronouns

A. **Formation and Translation:** As already mentioned, these two pronouns look exactly alike except for their accent marks. Both use the Third Declension endings, *but notice the following*: *The interrogative pronoun is always accented on the first ἰῶτα; and if the indefinite pronoun is accented, it will always be on the second syllable.*

Interrogative Pronoun	Masc./ Fem.	Neut.	Masc./Fem	Neut.
sg. nom.	τίς	τί	Who?	What? Why?
gen.	τίνος	τίνος	Whose?	What's?
dat.	τίνι	τίνι	To whom?	To what?
acc.	τίνα	τί	Whom?	What? Which?
pl. nom.	τίνες	τίνα	Who?	What things?
gen.	τίνων	τίνων	Whose?	Of what things?
dat.	τίσι(ν)	τίσι(ν)	To whom?	To what things?
acc.	τίνας	τίνα	Whom?	Which things?

Indefinite Pronoun	Masc./Fem	Neut.	Masc./Fem.	Neuter
sg. nom.	τις	τι	someone	something
gen.	τινός	τινός	of someone	of something
dat.	τινί	τινί	to someone	to something
acc.	τινά	τι	someone	something
pl. nom.	τινές	τινά	some people	some things
gen.	τινῶν	τινῶν	of some people	of some things
dat.	τισί(ν)	τισί(ν)	to some people	to some things
acc.	τινάς	τινά	some people	some things

Notice: (1) The masculine and feminine forms of the Interrogative and Indefinite pronouns are identical. (2) The Interrogative Pronoun is always accented on the first syllable on the ἰῶτα. (3) The Indefinite Pronoun, <u>if</u> accented, is always accented on the second syllable.

B. **Interrogative and Indefinite Pronouns used as Adjectives:** These two pronouns can be used independently as pronouns or with a noun as adjectives. (For Interrogative and Indefinite Pronouns, see Wallace 345-46 and 347 respectively.) As pronouns, these words must agree with their antecedents in gender and number. Of course, if functioning as adjectives, they must agree in gender, case, and number. Here are several examples. Can you determine which are pronominal and which are adjectival uses?

Matt 12:48b <u>Τίς</u> ἐστιν ἡ μήτηρ μου, καὶ <u>τίνες</u> εἰσιν οἱ ἀδελφοί μου;
<u>Who</u> is my mother and <u>who</u> are my brothers?

Luke 9:57b ἐν τῇ ὁδῷ εἶπεν <u>τις</u> πρὸς αὐτόν, Ἀκολουθήσω σοι...
<u>Someone</u> on the road said to him, 'I will follow you...'

Luke 10:30a ὁ Ἰησοῦς εἶπεν, <u>Ἄνθρωπός τις</u> κατέβαινεν ἀπὸ Ἰερουσαλὴμ εἰς Ἰεριχὼ...
Jesus said, '<u>A certain person</u> was going down from Jerusalem to Jericho...'

14.2 QUESTIONS IN GREEK

A. **Punctuation:** Questions have been indicated in the UBS and NA Greek NT texts by a semi colon (;). The student needs to observe carefully the punctuation at the end of a sentence. However, one must remember that adding punctuation marks is a later convention; so there are places where the presence or absence of a question mark is in question in the Greek text. Consider 1 Cor 7:23.

1 Cor 7:23 τιμῆς ἠγοράσθητε· μὴ γίνεσθε δοῦλοι ἀνθρώπων.
You were bought with a price; don't be slaves of people!
Or,
You were bought with a price; you aren't becoming slaves of people, are you? (No!)

Although I could find no translation of the verse above with a rhetorical question expecting a negative response, the forms and grammar would allow it. However, the context probably does not, since Paul is not treating slavery *per se*, but more generally the station or circumstance a believer finds himself or herself when they are converted to the Lord.

B. **No Interrogative Words are Needed to Begin a Question:** Questions in Greek, as in English, need no interrogative word to introduce them. For example, *Are you coming?* English usually inverts the sentence order in a question by putting the helping verb first (*Have you understood?*). However, Greek does not necessarily do this:

Σὺ εἶ ὁ διδάσκολος τοῦ Ἰσραὴλ;
Are you the teacher of Israel?

C. **Questions Introduced with an Interrogative Adverb:** If present, interrogative words normally introduce Greek questions (both direct and indirect); as such, they are forward pointing. Interrogative words or phrases include the following (but there are many others):

PRONOUN	TRANSLATION	GRAMMATICAL FUNCTION
τίς, τί	Who? What?	–ascertains facts
ποῦ	Where?	–seek to identify a *location*
πῶς	How? In what way?	–considers *manner*
τί	Why?	–asks for a *reason* or *purpose*
διὰ τί	Why?	–asks for a *reason* or *purpose*

Notice that the neuter singular form τί may be used to ascertain a fact (*What?*) or a reason (*Why?*). Context must determine its meaning. Here are some examples:

John 9:26b Τί ἐποίησεν σοι; = *What did he do to you?*
John 9:12b Ποῦ ἐστιν ἐκεῖνος; = *Where is that man (he)?*
Luke 1:34b Πῶς ἔσται τοῦτο...; = *How will this be?*
John 8:46b διὰ τί ὑμεῖς οὐ πιστεύετε μοι; = *Why do you not believe me?*

D. **Direct or Indirect Questions:** Like other types of verbal expressions, questions may be direct or indirect. Here is an example of an indirect question: Matt 26:70 οὐκ οἶδα τί λέγεις. *I do not know what you are saying.* The direct question would simply have been Τί λέγεις; *What are you saying?*

E. **Questions Expecting a "Yes" or "No" Answer:** Greeks, when asking a question, could indicate whether they expected a *yes* or *no* answer. Such is done by using the negative adverbs οὐ(κ) or οὐχί or μή or μήτι, which point forward and anticipate answers.

1. Questions Expecting a Positive Answer. A question expecting *yes* answer is introduced by οὐ(κ) or οὐχί, usually located at the beginning of the sentence:

John 11:9b Οὐχὶ δώδεκα ὧραί εἰσιν τῆς ἡμέρας;
Are there not twelve hours during the day? (Yes!)

Luke 4:22c <u>Οὐχὶ</u> υἱός ἐστιν Ἰωσὴφ οὗτος;
Is this <u>not</u> the son of Joseph? (Yes!)

Translating such questions is somewhat tricky. Imitate how the above examples have been worded and understand the argumentative significance of the question.

2. <u>Questions Expecting a Negative Answer</u>. A question expecting a *no* answer is introduced by μή or μήτι. Again these words will begin the question:

John 18:35 ἀπεκρίθη ὁ Πιλᾶτος, <u>Μήτι</u> ἐγὼ Ἰουδαῖός εἰμι;
Pilate answered, 'I am <u>not</u> a Jew, <u>am I</u>?' (No!)

Matt 12:23b οἱ ὄχλοι ἔλεγον, <u>Μήτι</u> οὗτός ἐστιν ὁ υἱὸς Δαυίδ;
The crowd was saying, 'This man is <u>not</u> the son of David, <u>is he</u>?' (No!)

Admittedly, questions that expect a negative reply are harder to translate into English. Simply try your best, and if any doubt exists, put in parentheses *no*.

3. <u>The Rule of MNOP</u>: It is easy to forget whether οὐκ/οὐχί or μή expects a positive answer or vice versa. However, we all know the alphabet: MNOP.

<u>μ</u>ή	→	<u>n</u>egative answer	<u>ο</u>ὐκ	→	<u>p</u>ositive answer
M		**N**	**O**		**P**

CHECK POINT 14.1-2 QUESTIONS IN GREEK

Given these verses from Luke 6:39-42 with literal translation and minimal punctuation, <u>first</u>, determine which sentences are questions; <u>second</u>, consider whether the question may be expecting a negative or positive answer; and, <u>third</u>, provide a suitable translation for each question asked.

39 Εἶπεν δὲ καὶ παραβολὴν αὐτοῖς·
Additionally he also spoke a parable to them

μήτι δύναται τυφλὸς τυφλὸν ὁδηγεῖν;
A blind person is not able to lead a blind person

οὐχὶ ἀμφότεροι εἰς βόθυνον ἐμπεσοῦνται;
Both will not fall into a pit

40 οὐκ ἔστιν μαθητὴς ὑπὲρ τὸν διδάσκαλον·
A disciple is not above the teacher

κατηρτισμένος δὲ πᾶς ἔσται ὡς ὁ διδάσκαλος αὐτοῦ.
But everyone will be prepared like his teacher

41 Τί δὲ βλέπεις τὸ κάρφος τὸ ἐν τῷ ὀφθαλμῷ τοῦ ἀδελφοῦ σου, τὴν δὲ δοκὸν τὴν ἐν τῷ ἰδίῳ ὀφθαλμῷ οὐ κατανοεῖς;
Moreover what/why you see the speck (that is) in your brother's eye but the wood beam (that is) in your own eye you do not notice

42 πῶς δύνασαι λέγειν τῷ ἀδελφῷ σου· ἀδελφέ, ἄφες ἐκβάλω τὸ κάρφος τὸ ἐν τῷ ὀφθαλμῷ σου, αὐτὸς τὴν ἐν τῷ ὀφθαλμῷ σου δοκὸν οὐ βλέπων;
How you are able to speak to your brother, "Brother, permit (that) I extract the speck (that is) in your eye" yourself not seeing the wood beam in your eye

ὑποκριτά, ἔκβαλε πρῶτον τὴν δοκὸν ἐκ τοῦ ὀφθαλμοῦ σου, καὶ τότε διαβλέψεις τὸ κάρφος τὸ ἐν τῷ ὀφθαλμῷ τοῦ ἀδελφοῦ σου ἐκβαλεῖν.
Hypocrites, extract first the wood beam from your eye and then you will see in order to extract the speck (that is) in your brother's eye

SUGGESTED ANSWERS WITH FULL PUNCTUATION

There may be other ways to render questions expecting negative or positive answers.

39 Εἶπεν δὲ καὶ παραβολὴν αὐτοῖς·
Additionally, he also spoke a parable to them:

μήτι δύναται τυφλὸς τυφλὸν ὁδηγεῖν;
A blind person is not able to lead a blind person, is he? (No!)

οὐχὶ ἀμφότεροι εἰς βόθυνον ἐμπεσοῦνται;
Will not both fall into a pit? (Yes!)
Or, *Surely, won't both fall into a pit? (Yes!)*

40 οὐκ ἔστιν μαθητὴς ὑπὲρ τὸν διδάσκαλον·
A disciple is not above the teacher;

κατηρτισμένος δὲ πᾶς ἔσται ὡς ὁ διδάσκαλος αὐτοῦ.
But everyone will be prepared like his teacher.

41 Τί δὲ βλέπεις τὸ κάρφος τὸ ἐν τῷ ὀφθαλμῷ τοῦ ἀδελφοῦ σου, τὴν δὲ δοκὸν τὴν ἐν τῷ ἰδίῳ ὀφθαλμῷ οὐ κατανοεῖς;

Moreover, why do you see the speck (that is) in your brother's eye, but the wood beam (that is) in your own eye you do not notice?

42 πῶς δύνασαι λέγειν τῷ ἀδελφῷ σου· ἀδελφέ, ἄφες ἐκβάλω τὸ κάρφος τὸ ἐν τῷ ὀφθαλμῷ σου, αὐτὸς τὴν ἐν τῷ ὀφθαλμῷ σου δοκὸν οὐ βλέπων;

How are you able to speak to your brother, "Brother, permit (that) I extract the speck (that is) in your eye" yourself not seeing the wood beam in your eye?

ὑποκριτά, ἔκβαλε πρῶτον τὴν δοκὸν ἐκ τοῦ ὀφθαλμοῦ σου, καὶ τότε διαβλέψεις τὸ κάρφος τὸ ἐν τῷ ὀφθαλμῷ τοῦ ἀδελφοῦ σου ἐκβαλεῖν.

Hypocrites, extract first the wood beam from your eye and then you will see in order to extract the speck (that is) in your brother's eye.

14.3 INTERROGATIVE EMPHASIS

Questions are naturally more prominent because they invite participation from the audience or bring focus to specific sentence elements. Questions often serve to point forward in the discourse. Moreover, additional interrogative emphasis attends to marked constructions when questions are asked that expect a negative (with μή or μήτι) or positive (οὐ or οὐχί) answer, and when intensive affixes are added (such as the -τι on μήτι) or when non-routine interrogative phrases are used to initiate questions that take more space and become more explicit (e.g., διὰ τί rather than τί). Also, questions may be formed with different pronominal reference, mode (null, what? when? How many? What sort of quality? Why?), time frame, and rhetorical force and location.

A. **Natural Prominence:** Questions have natural prominence because they call upon audiences to engage the topic either by formulating responses in their minds or because the question is rhe-torical and making a point, driving the argument forward. In addition to this natural promi-nence, additional emphasis is afforded sentence elements in the following ways.

B. **Rhetorical Questions are More Emphatic:** When questions are asked that expect either a yes or no question with οὐ(κ) or οὐχί and μή or μήτι, they are especially emphatic. See 14.E.2 above. Additionally, if questions are asked and then answers are immediately given, then the point of the question is even more emphasized. Additional emphasis attends to such questions in the follow ways.

1. *The Forms οὐχί and μήτι are more Marked.* Whenever these forms are used, they add mor-phological emphasis in the extra syllables -χί and -τι to make the make the question more marked and emphatic.

a. Οὐχί. The affix –χί on οὐ expects "a somewhat more emphatic affirmative response" than simply οὐ (L&N 69.12; cf. 1:17 on μήτι).

b. Μήτι. The affix –τι with μήτι adds emphasis and makes the μήτι more prominent: "This marker is somewhat more emphatic than the simple μή" (BDAG, 649; cf. LN 69.16).

c. See the examples given above in 14.E.2.

2. *Forward positioning of Sentence Elements before the Verb.* Levinsohn (51) argues, "When a *rhetorical question* begins with a negative, placing a constituent [i.e. sentence element] immediately after the negative and before the verb again gives it more prominence." Thus, consider Matt 13:55.

Matt 13:55 οὐχ <u>οὗτός</u> ἐστιν ὁ τοῦ τέκτονος υἱός;
   Isn't <u>this guy</u> the son of the builder?

The stress is on *this guy* (Jesus), because of the shock of his wisdom and miraculous power (Matt 13:54). Consider also John 7:51.

John 7:51 μὴ <u>ὁ νόμος ἡμῶν</u> κρίνει τὸν ἄνθρωπον ἐὰν μὴ ἀκούσῃ πρῶτον παρ' αὐτοῦ;
   <u>Our law</u> doesn't judge the person unless it hears first from him, does it?

Stress is on *our law* and the unlawful action of judging before hearing.

3. *Immediately Answered Questions are Very Prominent.* Why? Because they slow down the discourse in providing the answer. Let's look at some examples. Levinsohn discusses the first example.[1] Notice the linking of questions building to the final question being answered itself by Paul, which forms an inclusion with the beginning of the unit in 11:17 with the exact same statement: οὐκ ἐπαινῶ, *I do not praise (you).*

1 Cor 11:22a μὴ γὰρ οἰκίας οὐκ ἔχετε εἰς τὸ ἐσθίειν καὶ πίνειν;
   For its not that you don't have houses to eat and drink, is it? (No!) [the Corinthians do, in fact, have houses in which to eat and drink]

1 Cor 11:22b ἢ τῆς ἐκκλησίας τοῦ θεοῦ καταφρονεῖτε, καὶ καταισχύνετε τοὺς μὴ ἔχοντας;
   Or, do you despise the assembly of God, and shame those not having (means to provide food)?

---

[1] Stephen H. Levinsohn, *Self-Instruction Materials on Non-Narrative Discourse Analysis* (Dallas: SIL International, 2011), 88. He refers readers to John Beekman, "Analyzing and Translating the Questions of the New Testament," *Notes on Translation* 44 (1972): 3-21.

1 Cor 11:22c τί εἴπω ὑμῖν;
What should I say to you?

1 Cor 11:22d ἐπαινέσω ὑμᾶς; ἐν τούτῳ οὐκ ἐπαινῶ.
Should I praise you? In this I do not praise (you).

These later two questions involve "deliberative questions" (hence, the use of *should*) that involve the Subjunctive Mood; these will be treated in CHAPTER 22. This is true also in the next two examples from Romans 6.

Rom 6:1-2a Τί οὖν ἐροῦμεν; ἐπιμένωμεν τῇ ἁμαρτίᾳ, ἵνα ἡ χάρις πλεονάσῃ; <u>μὴ γένοιτο</u>.
What therefore shall we say? Should we remain in sin, in order that grace would abound? <u>No way!</u>

Rom 6:15 Τί οὖν; ἁμαρτήσωμεν, ὅτι οὐκ ἐσμὲν ὑπὸ νόμον ἀλλὰ ὑπὸ χάριν; μὴ γένοιτο.
What therefore? Should we sin, because we are not under law but under grace? <u>No way!</u>

It is absolutely critical to understand Paul's emphatic rhetorical questions within his progressive argument. Paul's responses entail the rare optative mood, *No way!* These questions string Paul's argument together preparing for his description of one living unsuccessfully under the law (7:7-25) and the solution to live by the law of the Spirit (Romans 8). In fact, let me say here that 7:5 and 7:6 outline each major section, respectively (check out the verb tenses!). So, in the end, paying attention to the rhetorical forcefulness of questions will help you interpret a passage.

C. **Non-Routine Interrogative Phrases:** Questions can be asked with the translation of *Why?* in English but with a different underlying construction. For example, τί is often translated *Why?* but so are the prepositional phrases διὰ τί, εἰς τί, and others. These prepositional phrases require more cognitive processing effort; thus, the addition of the preposition διά or εἰς makes the question *asking for rationale* more marked and emphatic. Διὰ τί is better translated *On account of what reason...?* or *For what reason...?* to indicate a more explicit and emphatic interrogative introduction. Consider these examples:

Matt 14:31 εὐθέως δὲ ὁ Ἰησοῦς ἐκτείνας τὴν χεῖρα ἐπελάβετο αὐτοῦ καὶ **λέγει** αὐτῷ· **ὀλιγόπιστε**, <u>εἰς τί</u> ἐδίστασας;
*And immediately Jesus, stretching out the hand, grabbed him and **says** to him, "**You of little faith**, <u>for what reason/why</u> did you doubt?"*

Here Jesus was speaking to Peter who had been sinking into the water and had just yelled out *Save me!* The question begun with <u>εἰς τί</u> is more marked and fittingly emphasizes Jesus's pointed question to Peter. Notice how two other emphatic features (**placed in bold and highlighted**) contribute to the impact. First, the Historical Present **λέγει** highlights what follows, and the vocative **ὀλιγόπιστε** admonishes Peter for not having more faith.

Matt 15:2 <u>διὰ τί</u> οἱ μαθηταί σου παραβαίνουσιν τὴν παράδοσιν τῶν πρεσβυτέρων; οὐ γὰρ νίπτονται τὰς χεῖρας [αὐτῶν] ὅταν ἄρτον ἐσθίωσιν.
For what reason do your disciples transgress the tradition of the elders? For they do not wash their hands, whenever they eat bread.

In context, the Pharisees and Scribes have just arrived from Jerusalem (Historic Present) and this is the question asked of Jesus. Also, the following sentence introduced with γάρ provides the supporting rationale that uses a Present General Condition—a marked conditional sentence (see §26.2 TYPES OF GREEK CONDITIONS) with unusual clause ordering that fronts the proposition *they do not wash their hands* rather than the supposition (*whenever....*). Finally, Jesus *answered back* (using ἀποκρίνομαι—see §18.5 TAKING CONTROL OR "ANSWERING BACK" IN CONVERSATION) in 15:3 with his own emphatic question (διὰ τί) with supporting emphatic features including additive καί, emphatic subject pronoun ὑμεῖς, and turning the subjects *transgress* and *tradition* back upon the religious leaders:

15:3 <u>διὰ τί</u> καὶ ὑμεῖς παραβαίνετε τὴν ἐντολὴν τοῦ θεοῦ διὰ τὴν παράδοσιν ὑμῶν;
On account of what reason also do you transgress the commandment of God on account of your tradition?

D. **Interrogative Modes and Referential Complexity:** Since questions are naturally prominent in that audiences are "asked" to engage in participatory thought related to communicative goals, they are a window into understanding an author's communicative intentions. It is possible to study questions according to points of pronominal reference (*third, second, first*), with first person plural "we" calling audiences to be most engaged with the speaker. There are also different modes to questions (*null, what, when, where, how,* and *why*), with the higher modes of *how* and *why* requiring more processing effort. We may also speak of time frames, in which past is least prominent generally, and present and future more prominent. Finally, we should consider the rhetorical force and location of a question: Those questions that are more directive and volitionally forceful, guiding audiences to a negative or positive answer (denial or assent), are more prominent. Those questions that lead the audience to negative conclusions, in denial of potentially held views, are more prominent. Those questions that occur within argumentative or disputative contexts (like a diatribe exchange) for thematic development are more prominent than those which do not. The following list describes these areas of investigation. The items lower down in each category are generally more prominent. In general, more prominence attends to those questions that have the more prominent elements within each of the categories.

1. PERSON REFERENT
3rd Person
2nd Person
1st Person
2. INTRODUCTION AND MODE
null; not introduced
τίς, τί *What?*; ποῦ *Where?*; πότε *When?* (definition; location; time)
πῶς *How?* (means or manner)
τί *Why?* (purpose)
διὰ τί *For what reason?* (marked purpose)
πόσος *How many?* (quantity) See Vocabulary in CH.26.
ποῖος *What sort of?* (quality) See Vocabulary in CH.26.
3. TIME FRAME
Past
Present
Deliberative Present (*What should we do?* See §22.2).
Future (may present vivid consequences)
4. RHETORICAL FORCE AND LOCATION
Expect positive response (οὐ or οὐχί).
Expect negative response (with μή or μήτι).
Diatribe and supplied with explicit positive answer.
Diatribe and supplied with explicit negative answer (e.g. μὴ γένοιτο).
Other grammatical features (word choice)
Questions with other questions or that are climactic

When all is said and done, Greek questions show much variation and nuance; hence, paying attention to the construction within context will often pay good interpretive dividends.

E. **Example Analysis from Romans:** A fruitful exercise would be to track the use of questions in Romans 1-8 to evaluate the markedness of questions. However, one extremely prominent set of questions occurs at a critical juncture at 6:1-3, where Paul through four successive questions leads the audience to an important conclusion (οὖν) in 6:4 that *we also thus* [οὕτως καὶ ἡμεῖς] *walk in newness of life* (not remaining in sin).

TEXT	CATEGORICAL DESCRIPTION
6:1 Τί οὖν ἐροῦμεν; *Therefore, what shall we say?*	1. <u>Person Referent</u>: 1st Plural 2. <u>Introduction and Mode</u>: Simple Τί (what?) 3. <u>Time Frame</u>: Future, which moves the discussion forward 4. <u>Rhetorical Force and Location</u>: Within Diatribe and showing progression with new development (οὖν).
ἐπιμένωμεν τῇ ἁμαρτίᾳ, ἵνα ἡ χάρις πλεονάσῃ; ² μὴ γένοιτο. *Should we remain in sin, in order that grace abounds? ²No way!*	1. <u>Person Referent</u>: 1st Plural 2. <u>Introduction and Mode</u>: Null 3. <u>Time Frame</u>: Deliberative Present 4. <u>Rhetorical Force and Location</u>: Diatribe continues with a question with an explicit purpose statement (ἵνα) and explicit emphatic answer provided (μὴ γένοιτο.)
οἵτινες ἀπεθάνομεν τῇ ἁμαρτίᾳ, πῶς ἔτι ζήσομεν ἐν αὐτῇ; *We who have died to sin, how still will we live in it?*	1. <u>Person Referent</u>: 1st Plural 2. <u>Introduction and Mode</u>: πῶς ἔτι expresses manner and time 3. <u>Time Frame</u>: Future tense about past time realities 4. <u>Rhetorical Force and Location</u>: The third question within a diatribal exchange. The forward placement of the οἵτινες relative clause, implicates a negative answer.
³ ἢ ἀγνοεῖτε ὅτι, ὅσοι ἐβαπτίσθημεν εἰς Χριστὸν Ἰησοῦν, εἰς τὸν θάνατον αὐτοῦ ἐβαπτίσθημεν; *³ or, are you ignorant that, however many of us were baptized into Christ Jesus, were baptized into his death?*	1. <u>Person Referent</u>: 2nd person question about 1st person content. 2. <u>Introduction and Mode</u>: Null. But the conjunction ἢ *or* suggests an alternative that builds upon the previous diatribal question *how still will we live in sin?* 3. <u>Time Frame</u>: Present time frame about past time realities. 4. <u>Rhetorical Force and Location</u>: The suggestion of ignorance is rather prominent; this question is rather making a statement. This final question of the series leads the audience to Paul's conclusions in 6:4 (οὖν).

14.4 INDIRECT STATEMENTS OF MANNER AND LOCATION

A. **Manner:** The adverb πῶς can be used both to introduce a question of manner and to introduce an indirect statement of manner. When introducing an indirect question or statement, πῶς is like ὅτι *that*. Indirect statements, remember, are usually found after verbs of communication, like *saying, teaching, showing*, etc.

Acts 9:27b καὶ διηγήσατο αὐτοῖς <u>πῶς</u> ἐν τῷ ὁδῷ εἶδεν τὸν κύριον.
And he described to them <u>how</u> in the road he saw the Lord.

B. **Location:** In like fashion, the adverb ποῦ can be used both to introduce a question and to introduce an indirect statement of location.

John 14:5b οὐκ οἴδαμεν <u>ποῦ</u> ὑπάγεις· *We do not know <u>where</u> you depart;*

14.5 COMMON USES OF THE DATIVE CASE

A. **Introduction:** In §11.6 we learned that there are several other common uses of the genitive case. Here we briefly cover the most common uses of the dative case. Remember that in constituent marking, the special uses of the noun cases are indicated by using curly braces {…}. For the general discussion of the Dative Case, see Wallace 137-40.

B. **Most Common Specific Uses:**

1. <u>Indirect Object</u>. This use is the most common and has already been covered (Wallace 140-42). <u>How to translate</u>: *to, for*.

2. <u>Dative of Means or Instrument</u>. This is very common (Wallace 162-63). Personality is not in view. However, the means involves an agent who uses it (whether the agent is stated or implied). <u>How to translate</u>: *by means of* or *with*. It has been covered in CHAPTER 6.3.

3. <u>Dative of Advantage (Interest)</u>. This use is common (Wallace 142-44). The noun in the dative case indicates the person(s) interested in the action of the main verb. <u>How to translate</u>: *to, for, in the interest of, for the benefit of*.

   1 Cor 6:13a τὰ βρώματα <u>τῇ κοιλίᾳ</u>   *food is for the stomach*

   2 Cor 5:13 εἴτε γὰρ ἐξέστημεν, <u>θεῷ</u>· εἴτε σωφρονοῦμεν, <u>ὑμῖν</u>.
   For if we are crazy, <u>it is for God</u>. If we are in our right mind, <u>it is for you</u>.

4. <u>Dative of Disadvantage (Interest)</u>. This use is common (Wallace 142-44). It is the converse of the dative of advantage. <u>How to translate</u>: *for, against, to the detriment of, to the disadvantage of*.

   Matt 23:31 μαρτυρεῖτε <u>ἑαυτοῖς</u>   *You testify <u>against yourselves</u>...*

   1 Cor 11:29a ὁ γὰρ ἐσθίων καὶ πίνων <u>κρίμα ἑαυτῷ</u> ἐσθίει καὶ πίνει
   For the one eating and drinking eats and drinks <u>judgment upon himself</u>

5. <u>Dative of Reference or Respect</u>. This use is common (Wallace 144-46). The dative case word specifies and qualifies the action of the verb with reference or respect to itself. <u>How to translate</u>: *with reference to, concerning, about, in regard to*.

   Rom 6:2b οἵτινες ἀπεθάνομεν <u>τῇ ἁμαρτίᾳ</u>, πῶς ἔτι ζήσομεν ἐν αὐτῇ;
   Those of us who died <u>with reference to sin</u>, how can we still live in it?

   Luke 18:31b πάντα τὰ γεγραμμένα διὰ τῶν προφητῶν <u>τῷ υἱῷ τοῦ ἀνθρώπου</u>.
   all the things written through the prophets <u>concerning the Son of Man</u>.

6. <u>Dative of Sphere/Location</u>. This use is common (Wallace 153-55). The dative case word indicates the sphere within which the word to which it is related exists. <u>How to translate</u>: *in, in the sphere of, in the realm of*.

Acts 16:5 Αἱ...ἐκκλησίαι ἐστερεοῦντο <u>τῇ πίστει</u>
The churches were growing <u>in the realm of faith</u>.

Luke 3:16 ἐγὼ μὲν <u>ὕδατι</u> βαπτίζω ὑμᾶς   *Indeed, I baptize you <u>in water</u>.*

7. <u>Dative of Direct Object</u>. This use is common (Wallace 171-73). Some verbs take the dative as their direct object. These verbs often involve some *personal relationship*. The verb πιστεύω can take the dative case (see CHAPTER 7.4).

Matt 4:9b ταῦτά σοι πάντα δώσω, ἐὰν πεσὼν προσκυνήσῃς <u>μοι</u>.
I will give all these things to you, if falling you worship <u>me</u>.

8. <u>Dative of Association or Accompaniment</u>. This use is relatively common (Wallace 159-61). The dative case noun describes an association with some other persons in the sentence, often the subject. This use is common with σύν. <u>How to translate</u>: *in association with*.

John 6:22 οὐ συνεισῆλθεν <u>τοῖς μαθηταῖς</u> αὐτοῦ ὁ Ἰησοῦς εἰς τὸ πλοῖον
Jesus did not enter into the boat <u>with his disciples</u>.

Eph 2:5b συνεζωοποίησεν <u>τῷ Χριστῷ</u>   *He made us alive <u>with Christ</u>*

9. <u>Dative of Manner</u>. This use is relatively common (Wallace 161-62). The dative case noun explains *how* the action of the verb occurs in terms of its *quality*. This distinguishes it from the dative of means that focuses on its *method*. <u>How to translate</u>: *with, in*.

Rev 5:12 λέγοντες <u>φωνῇ μεγάλῃ</u>· ἄξιόν ἐστιν τὸ ἀρνίον...
Saying <u>with a loud voice</u>, 'Worthy is the Lamb...'

Acts 11:23 καὶ παρεκάλει πάντας <u>τῇ προθέσει τῆς καρδίας</u> προσμένειν τῷ κυρίῳ
And <u>with steadfastness of heart</u> he was encouraging them all to remain with the Lord.

10. <u>Dative of Cause</u>. This use is fairly common (Wallace 167-68). The dative of cause indicates *why* the action takes place in terms of its basis or cause. The dative of means indicates *how* the action occurs in terms of method. <u>How to translate</u>: *because of, on the basis of*.

Luke 15:17b ἐγὼ δὲ <u>λιμῷ</u> ὧδε ἀπόλλυμαι;
But am I perishing here <u>because of famine</u>?

Rom 11:30 νῦν δὲ ἠλεήθητε <u>τῇ τούτων ἀπειθείᾳ</u>
But now you were shown mercy <u>because of their disobedience</u>.

11. <u>Dative of Time</u>. This use is common enough (Wallace 155-57). The dative of time expresses a *point* in time; not to be confused with *kind* of time (genitive of time) or *extent* of time (accusative of time). <u>How to translate</u>: *on, at (precisely) that moment*.

Matt 17:23 καὶ <u>τῇ τρίτῃ ἡμέρᾳ</u> ἐγερθήσεται.
And he will be raised <u>on the third day</u>.

12. <u>Dative of Possession</u>. Not terribly common, the dative can be used to denote possession with an animate entity (i.e. a person); this usage is marked + (personal) proximity.[2] This differentiates it from the genitive, which is unmarked for such proximity. Often, one can perceive personal involvement/attachment.[3] <u>How to translate</u>: *belong(ing) to, of*.

Acts 17:2 κατὰ δὲ τὸ εἰωθὸς <u>τῷ Παύλῳ</u>   *But according to the custom <u>of Paul</u>*

Rom 7:3 ἐὰν γένηται <u>ἀνδρὶ ἑτέρῳ</u>,   *if she belongs <u>to another husband</u>,*

Mark 1:24 τί <u>ἡμῖν</u> καὶ <u>σοί</u>, Ἰησοῦ Ναζαρηνέ;
What is ours and yours [in common], Jesus the Nazarene
Or, *What belongs to us and to you, Jesus the Nazarene?*

In the context, the unclean spirit is adressing Jesus. This dative usage could alternatively be a dative of respect. Once again, we see that we should not force grammatical labels onto constructions, nor lean too heavily on them to support our idiosyncratic views.

---

[2] See Silvia Luraghi, *On the Meaning of Prepositions and Cases: The Expression of Semantic Roles in Ancient Greek*, Studies in Language Companion Series 67 (Amsterdam: Benjamins, 2003), 51, 65.

[3] This view is to be distinguished from discussions in NT Greek grammars. For example, Wallace (149) citing BDF §189 summarizes, "The dative substantive possesses the noun to which it is related. In other words, the dative of possession is that to which the subject of an equative verb belongs. This occurs with equative verbs such as εἰμί, γίνομαι, and ὑπάρχω. It possesses the subject of such verbs. The usage is not especially common." BDF §189 indicates, " (1) The classical distinction, whereby the genitive is used when the acquisition is recent or the emphasis is on the possessor (e.g. R[om] 14:8) and the dative when the object possessed is to be stressed, is customarily preserved. (2) Exceptions appear only occasionally: R[om] 7:3 ἐὰν γένηται ἀνδρὶ ἑτέρῳ,…" However, the supposed exception of Rom 7:3 reveals the dative of possession is marking +personal proximity. The construction of the dative with εἰμί in view here, in my view, may be understood as other uses, like dative of (dis)advantage (e.g. Matt 16:22; Rom 14:8).

14.6 Verbs that take Genitive, Accusative, or Dative Objects

A. **Introduction:** The use of different cases for the objects of verbs can be perplexing for students of Greek. In John 10:27-28 one sees the diversity. These two verses contain six independent clauses. Below, constituent marking has been provided for <u>direct objects</u>, <u>indirect objects</u>, and (prepositional phrases).

Comments on Objects

John 10:27 τὰ πρόβατα τὰ ἐμὰ <u>τῆς φωνῆς</u> μου ἀκούουσιν,
my sheep hear my <u>voice</u>

<u>genitive direct object</u> with the verb ἀκούω.

κἀγὼ γινώσκω <u>αὐτὰ</u>
and I know <u>them</u>

<u>accusative direct object</u> with the verb γινώσκω.

καὶ ἀκολουθοῦσίν <u>μοι</u>,
and they follow <u>me</u>

<u>dative direct object</u> with the verb ἀκολουθέω

10:28a κἀγὼ δίδωμι <u>αὐτοῖς</u> <u>ζωὴν αἰώνιον</u>
and I give <u>to them</u> <u>eternal life</u>

"Standard" <u>direct</u> and <u>indirect</u> objects with the verb δίδωμι.

καὶ οὐ μὴ ἀπόλωνται (εἰς τὸν αἰῶνα)
and they will never ever perish (into the age)

No objects with the verb ἀπόλλυμι in the middle voice.

καὶ οὐχ ἁρπάσει τις <u>αὐτὰ</u> (ἐκ τῆς χειρός μου)
and someone will not seize <u>them</u> (from my hand)

"Standard" <u>direct object</u> with the verb ἁρπάζω.

B. **General Patterns:** It may be helpful for students here to provide a summary of rules that help explain what types of verbs take the genitive or the dative for their direct objects.

1. <u>Middle Voice</u>. It is important to know that for some of these verbs, it is not until they are formed in the middle voice that they take the genitive. Thus, λείπω *I leave* (active voice) is the lexical form, yet the first entry in BDAG shows middle and passive forms with the second sub-definition (b) provided as ***be/do without, lack, be in need or want (of)***, which will take a genitive object. Also, ἀπέχω *I receive in* full (active voice) is the lexical form, but in the fifth entry BDAG provides the gloss "***keep away, abstain, refrain from***" with the middle voice that occurs with a "genitive of thing" as the object.

2. <u>Persons and Things</u>. Another general rule is that if a verb shows two objects, the person may be indicated by the accusative or the genitive, but the object typically only by the genitive. One needs, however, to carefully study the lexical entries for verbs. §14.7 Lexical Information on the Case of Verbal Objects.

C. Verbs that have Genitive Objects:[4]

1. Verbs with a partitive sense *to partake of* (μεταλαμβάνω, μετέχω), *to taste* (γεύομαι), *to touch* (ἅπτομαι), *to seize* (ἐπιλαμβάνομαι), *to hold* (κρατέω), etc.

2. Verbs meaning *to be full* or *to fill* (πίμπλημι, πληρόω, γέμω, γεμίζω), etc.

3. Verbs denoting perception, such as *to hear* (ἀκούω), which is also followed by the accusative case

4. Verbs denoting emotion or volition, etc. such as *to desire* (ἐπιθυμέω), *to care for/take care of* (ἐπιμελέομαι), *to attain* (τυγχάνω), *to bear with* (ἀνέχομαι), etc.

5. Verbs denoting separation or abstention from or hindering, want or need, such as *to deprive of* (ἀποστερέω), *to beseech, make request of* (δέομαι), *to cease from* (παύομαι), *to have need of* (χρῄζω), *to need/be lacking of* (ὑστερέω, λείπομαι), *to abstain from* (ἀπέχομαι)

6. Verbs meaning *to rule* (ἄρχω, κυριεύω, etc.) or *to excel* (διαφέρω)

7. Verbs meaning *to remember* (μιμνήσκομαι; μνημονεύω) or *to forget* (ἐπιλανθάνομαι)

8. Many verbs compounded with κατά are followed by a simple Genitive case. These include καταγελάω (*I laugh at*), κατακαυχάομαι (*I boast myself against*), and καταφρονέομαι (*I despise*)

D. Verbs that take Dative Objects:

1. Certain verbs meaning *to worship* (προσκυνέω)

2. Verbs meaning *to serve* (δουλεύω, διακονέω, ὑπηρετέω)

3. Verbs meaning *to obey* (πείθομαι, ὑπακούω) or *to disobey* (ἀπειθέω)

4. Verbs meaning *to believe* (πιστεύω)

5. Verbs meaning *to rebuke* (ἐπιτιμάω, ἐμβριμάω)

6. Verbs meaning *to command* (ἐπιτάσσεω, παραγγέλλω)

7. Compounded verbs with certain prepositions such as ἐν, σύν, ἐπί, παρά, and πρός

14.7 LEXICAL INFORMATION ON THE CASE OF VERBAL COMPLEMENTS

A. **Introduction:** Beyond the handful of verbs learned in beginning grammars that may take genitive or dative direct objects, there are a good number. Additionally, verbs may take multiple objects. How does one identify which case or cases are allowable for the direct object? How

---

[4] This summarizes and reformates H. P. V. Nunn, *A Short Syntax of New Testament Greek* (Cambridge: Cambridge University Press, 1920), 45-46.

do you find them? Well, the standard lexicons will typically provide that information. In the Master Vocabulary List at the back of this textbook one will find words occurring 20 times or more, with basic entries for the verbs indicating the case of the objects. But really there is much more to it than this. One needs a proper introduction to the robust (and complicated!) entries in our standard Lexicon BDAG. Further below is given the entry for the verb ἐρωτάω *I ask, request*, in order to explain basic format, abbreviations, and conventions to explain object complements and adjuncts. The discussion below presupposes familiarity with §6.7 A FRIST LOOK AT MAJOR LEXICONS: BDAG, L&N, AND LSJ and §12.6 NAVIGATING MAJOR LEXICONS. But first, students need an introduction to complements and adjuncts.

B. Verbal Complements, Adjuncts, Absolute Usage, and Valency:

1. Verbal Complements. Verbs may necessarily take objects, or such objects may be assumed. If such is the case, we are dealing with **complements**. *Verbal complements are generally required or assumed when a particular verb is used.* For example, consider the verb *to hit*. This verb normally takes an object to complete its meaning, or it is assumed. If I were to say the following sentence alone, *John hits*, you would wonder *what John hits*. In context, one could determine by implication *what* John hits—*the baseball* or *his brother* or *the cat*. However, the point is that the verb *to hit* normally takes an object or assumes one from context. Such complements become a part of the **semantic field** of the verb.

2. Adjuncts. Relatedly, in actual usage in this or that context, verbs may take additional modifiers, which are called **adjuncts**. *Adjuncts are not strictly required or assumed for the semantics of the verb.* Adjuncts may include prepositional phrases, adverbs, nouns, etc. For example, *John hits in the batting cage*. Or, *John hits hard*. The two modifiers (the first, a prepositional phrase of location; the second, an adverb of manner) are not normally expected for the verb *to hit*; one does not assume them in the semantics. They are verbal adjuncts.

3. Absolute Usage. Verbs sometimes are used without complements or absolutely, which is indicated by the abbreviation Abs. Working with our example with the verb *to hit*, if given the sentence, *Johnny is hitting*, it would make sense alone and without assuming an object. Why? It relates to a specific social sports situation of a baseball game where *is hitting* means *is at bat*. Literally, Johnny is not then and there *hitting the ball;* he is only attempting to hit it.

4. Verbal Valency. It is sometimes difficult to determine how many complements a verb has or to adjudicate between what are obligatory complements, optional complements, and adjuncts; such is the concern of verbal **valency** studies. So, **verbal valency** concerns a verb's semantic relation to required, assumed, or optional object complements and unnecessary, but possible, adjuncts.

C. Verbal Complements and Adjuncts in BDAG:

1. Orientation. Fortunately, our standard GNT lexicon will provide a verb's definition with a description of possible cases of the objects; there may be multiple objects for a verb. This information is often buried within a verb's entry. Additionally, adjuncts may be included here and there. Unfortunately, this vast information needs re-evaluation according to recent valency research. However, the information on objects is still very helpful; but it takes some practice to navigate this dimension of BDAG.

2. Lexical Entry for ἐρωτάω. So, let's get started by looking at the relatively simple verb entry ἐρωτάω in BDAG (395). Information on absolute usage or complements is highlighted.

ἐρωτάω fut. ἐρωτήσω; 1 aor. ἠρώτησα; 2 aor. ἠρόμην, fr. ἔρομαι, s. Schwyzer I 746, 7 (Just., D. 3, 5; Ath. 35, 1). Pass.: 1 aor. 3 sg. ἠρωτήθη 2 Km 20:18, inf. ἐρωτηθῆναι (TestAbr B 4 p. 108, 22 [Stone p. 64]), ptc. ἐρωτηθείς (TestSol 11, 1 C); pf. ptc. ἠρωτημένος 2 Km 20:18.

❶ to put a query to someone, *ask, ask a question* (Hom.+) abs. (Da 2:10; 1 Macc 10:72) **Lk 22:68.** τινά *someone* (Lucian, D. Deor. 7, 1; Gen 24:47; 40:7; Ex 13:14 al.; En 22:6; TestSol 7:4 al.; TestJob 47:5; Just., D. 3, 5) **J 1:25; 8:7; 9:21; 16:19, 30** al. τινά τι *someone about someth.* (X., Mem. 3, 7, 2, Cyr. 3, 3, 48; Job 21:29; TestSol 3:6 D; Jos., Ant. 6, 48; Just., D. 68, 4) ὑμᾶς λόγον ἕνα *ask you one question* **Mt 21:24**=Lk 20:3 (cp. Pla., Leg. 10, 895e; Jer 45:14; ApcSed 8:5 al.; TestJob 36:5); αὐτὸν τὰς παραβολάς *ask him about the parables* **Mk 4:10.** Certainly **J 16:23** belongs here too. τινὰ περί τινος *someone about someth.* (2 Esdr 11:2; Is 45:11; Just., D. 94, 4) **Mt 19:17; Lk 9:45; J 18:19.** W. τινά and direct question (X., An. 1, 6, 7; TestSol 15:2 al.; TestAbr A 10 p. 87, 30 [Stone p. 22]; GrBar 9:5 al.; Just., D. 99, 3) **Mk 8:5; Lk 19:31; J 1:19, 21; 5:12; 16:5;** the direct quest. introduced by λέγων or λέγοντες (En 23:3; TestSol 7:3 al.; TestJob 44:4; ParJer 2:4) **Mt 16:13; J 9:2, 19.** W. τινά and indir. quest. foll. (X., Cyr. 8, 5, 19; Just., A I, 17, 2, D. 64, 3) **9:15.** Cp. **Lk 23:6** P⁷⁵ (s. ed. note and s.v. ἐπερωτάω 1a; ἐρωτ. εἰ also Thu. 1, 5, 2).

❷ to ask for someth., *ask, request* (Babrius 42, 3; 97, 3; Apollon. Dysc., Synt. 3, 167 Uhlig ἐρωτῶ σε νῦν ἐν ἴσῳ τῷ παρακαλῶ σε, λιτανεύω, ἱκνοῦμαι; SIG 705, 56 [112 b.c.]; 741, 5 [after 88 b.c.]; POxy 744, 6; 13 [1 b.c.]; 292, 7 [c. 25 a.d.]; 110; 111; 113; 269; 745; 746 al.; Jer 44:17; Jos., Ant. 7, 164; TestSim 4:1.—Dssm., B 30; 31; 45, NB 23f [BS 195f; 290f]) τὶ *for someth.* **Lk 14:32** (s. εἰρήνη 1 a). περί τινος *for someth.* Hv 3, 1, 6b (w. ἵνα foll.). τὶ περί τινος *for someth. concerning a thing* 3, 1, 6a. W. acc. of pers.: τινά *someone* **J 14:16** (Field, Notes 101f). τ. κύριον Hv 2, 2, 1 (Jos., Ant. 5, 42 ἐ. τ. θεόν; SibOr 2, 309). Foll. by λέγων, which introduces the request in direct discourse **Mt 15:23; Lk 7:4** v.l.; **J 4:31; 12:21.** W. impv. foll. (BGU 423, 11 ἐρωτῶ σε οὖν, γράψον μοι ἐπιστόλιον; POxy 745, 7; 746, 5) **Lk 14:18f; Phil 4:3.** τινὰ περί τινος *beseech someone on someone's behalf* (JosAs 15:7 περὶ τῶν μετανοούντων ἐρωτᾷ αὐτόν [about the topic Μετάνοια]) **Lk 4:38; J 16:26; 17:9, 20;** *concerning someth.* **1J 5:16,** sim. ὑπέρ τινος **2 Th 2:1** (on the interchange of περί and ὑπέρ s. B-D-F §229, 1; 231; Rob. 629; 632). τινὰ κατὰ τοῦ κυρίου *beseech someone by the Lord* Hv 3, 2, 3 (B-D-F §225). W. ἵνα foll. (POxy 744, 13 [1 b.c.]) **Mk 7:26; Lk 7:36; 16:27; J 4:47; 17:15; 19:31, 38; 2J 5.** W. ὅπως foll. (SIG 741, 5 [after 88 b.c.]; PTebt 409, 4; 6; En 13:4) **Lk 7:3; 11:37; Ac 23:20.** W. inf. foll. (Chariton 8, 7, 3; PTebt 410, 11; PRyl 229, 8 [38 a.d.]; POxy 292, 7 [c. 25 a.d.]; Jos., Ant. 6, 328) **Lk 5:3; 8:37; J 4:40; Ac 3:3; 10:48; 16:39; 18:20; 1 Th 5:12.** Foll. by εἰς and subst. inf. **2 Th 2:1.**—ἐ. and παρακαλέω together (POxy 744, 6; 294, 28 [22 a.d.]. S. the quot. fr. Apollon. Dysc., above) **1 Th 4:1.**—*Urge* w. inf., impv. et al. B 4:6; 21:2, 4, 7.—B. 1264; 1271. DELG s.v. ἐρέω. M-M. TW.

3. <u>Abbreviations</u>. To understand the information, one needs to understand the abbreviations (see frontal material in BDAG). Here are some that are found above.

> abs. = absolute
> indir. quest. = indirect question
> *someth.* = something
> acc. = accusative
> pers. = person
> foll. = following
> sim. =similarly
> W. = with
> subst. = substantive(ly)
> inf. = infinitive
> impv. =imperative

4. <u>Conventional Use of Τις, Τι</u>. Also, you will encounter the indefinite pronoun as a convention to indicate the case of the object/complement. The masculine/feminine forms (τις, τινος, τινι, τινα) are used to represent the case of an object in reference to a *person*; the neuter forms (τι, τινος, τινι, τι) are used to represent the case of the object in reference to a *thing*. Also, some knowledge of Latin is required, since the Latin ablative form *rei* from *re* ("thing") and other Latin abbreviations may be used in Lexicons; again, see the list of Abbreviations in the frontal material.

5. <u>Reading the Entry</u>. In BDAG, after an initial description of verbal forms (the first paragraph), one encounters boxed numbers: **❶**, **❷**, **❸**, **❹**, and **❺**. As needed, beneath these are sub-definitions/uses indicated by circled letters ⓐ, ⓑ, ⓒ, etc. Beneath these may be further sub-uses indicated by lowercase Greek letters (α., β., γ., etc.). For the first definition provided, here is an explanation of verb usage in reference to object and adjunct.

> **❶ to put a query to someone, *ask, ask a question***
>   abs. = absolute use of the verb (i.e. no complements)
>   τινά *someone* = accusative object of person
>   τινά τι *someone about someth.* = double accusative objects: one for person, one for thing
>   τινά περί τινος *someone about someth.* = accusative object of person with περί and the genitive
>   indicating thing.
>   W. τινά and direct question = accusative object of person followed by a direct question
>   the direct quest. introduced by λέγων or λέγοντες = the participles introduce direct question
>   W. τινά and indir. quest. foll. = accusative object of person followed by indirect question
> **❷ to ask for someth., *ask, request***
>   τι *for someth.* = accusative object of thing
>   περί τινος *for someth.* = object thing indicted by περί with the genitive
>   τι περί τινος *for someth. concerning a thing* = accusative object of thing with περί with the genitive indicated another thing
>   W. acc. of pers.: τινά *someone* = accusative object of person

Foll. by λέγων, which introduces the request in direct discourse = the participle λέγων introduce
    direct question/discourse

W. impv. foll. = the request is provided in the command form that follows

τινὰ περί τινος *beseech someone on someone's behalf*

W. ἵνα foll. = the request is provided in the ἵνα content clause that follows

W. ὅπως foll. = the request is provided in the ὅπως content clause that follows

W. inf. foll. = the request is provided in the infinitive clause that follows

Foll. by εἰς and subst. inf. = the request is provided the clause that follows formed with εἰς and the
    substantive infinitive that follows

Urge w. inf., impv. et al. = having the meaning *Urge*, the content may be indicated by an infinitive,
    imperative/command, etc.

D. **Greek Verbal Valency:** Believe it or not, ἐρωτάω is not as complex as many other verbs. Similar research as has begun on the Hebrew verb and needs to be done for the Greek Verb.[5]

Complete WORKBOOK EXERCISES 14 and consult the ANSWER KEY & GUIDE as needed.

CASE IN POINT 14: GOD'S GIFTS AND 1 COR 12:29

One perennial question for believers concerns the spiritual gifts and speaking in tongues. Are the gifts still in existence today? Which gifts should believers expect to have? I remember as a student at the University of Illinois being encouraged to pray in tongues "because every Christian has the ability to do so." Like many young Christians, I was confused; I read and reread 1 Corinthians 12-14 looking for answers. What I needed was a little knowledge of how questions may be constructed in Greek.

In 1 Cor 12-14, the apostle Paul was engaged in a struggle to promote a proper understanding of the origin and use of spiritual gifts. The chapters have a basic thought flow: Ch. 12 "The Theology and Communal Context for Gifts," Ch. 13 "The Motivation of Love for the Use of Gifts," and Ch. 14 "The Intelligibility and Practice of the Gifts of Prophecy and Tongues." At the end of Ch. 12 where Paul establishing a theology of spiritual gifts, he asks a series of seven questions:

1 Cor 12:29 μὴ πάντες ἀπόστολοι;
      μὴ πάντες προφῆται;
      μὴ πάντες διδάσκαλοι;
      μὴ πάντες δυνάμεις;
   ³⁰ μὴ πάντες χαρίσματα ἔχουσιν ἰαμάτων;

---

[5] See, e.g., John A. Cook, "Valency: The Intersection of Syntax and Semantics," *Ancient Hebrew Grammar*, December 5, 2012, n.p. Online: http://ancienthebrewgrammar.wordpress.com/2012/12/05/biblical-hebrew-valency/ [cited 17 June 2014] and the work of his doctoral student, James Wilson, "Verbal Valency in Biblical Hebrew: An Analysis of the Valency of עבר" (Masters Thesis, Wilmore, KY: Asbury Theological Seminary, May 2014).

μὴ πάντες γλώσσαις λαλοῦσιν;
μὴ πάντες διερμηνεύουσιν;

How are we to understand and translate these questions? What do you notice about them? First, they are verbless; so, we must imply and supply a verb of *being*. Second, each question begins with a μή πάντες, which would produce tremendous aural impact through the repetition of the words and sounds. Third, each question has quantitative emphasis with πάντες, which marks inclusive scope: What Paul affirms, he affirms for all believers. Fourth, the questions begin with μή. What significance does this have? Remember the MNOP rule (M̲ή expects a N̲egative answer; O̲ὐ expects a P̲ositive answer). These questions expect a negative answer. Thus, we would correctly understand and translate these questions as follows: *Are all apostles?* <u>*No.*</u> *Are all prophets?* <u>*No.*</u> *Are all teachers?* <u>*No.*</u> *Do all work miracles?* <u>*No.*</u> *Do all have gifts of healing?* <u>*No.*</u> *Do all speak with languages?* <u>*No.*</u> *Do all interpret?* <u>*No.*</u> Again, all these questions expect a negative response. What are the implications? One is that speaking in tongues is not a gift that all believers have.

Paul's rhetorical questions are very clear in the Greek. These questions are one strategy to teach the Corinthians the relative value of tongue speaking as only one gift among many that not all people in the one body of Christ have. His strategy was necessary in order to prevent misunderstanding and divisions between Corinthian believers based upon the possession of one gift as opposed to other spiritual gifts. Rather than being divisive, Paul argues that God's spiritual gifts are to help believers build up one another as the body of Christ (12:12-27); they are to be intelligible, understandable and mutually edifying (see 14:5, 6, 9, 13, 19). Far from dismissing the giftedness of believers, Paul urges for the proper manifestation of the gifts motivated by God's love.

Honor was a common motivator for individuals, especially in the Roman colony of Corinth that was founded by Julius Caesar and was devoted to the Imperial family. The Apostle Paul's application of the metaphor of the "body" to the church assembly drew upon ancient political thought, in which the body politic was often represented in various iconography as a person. To the right is the personification of *Roma* (the Roman People). Cowering beside Roma is a captured barbarian. This statuary is from Aphrodisias in Asia Minor (photo, slightly edited, courtesy of Rosemary Canavan).

CHAPTER 15

How important are lists in your life? Where do you encounter them? When someone provides you with a list, how important is it typically? Lists are prominent within human discourse if not simply because they orient our attention to an arrangement of items. The exact nature of the arrangement, however, varies; it may be completely haphazard or it may be quite intentional and profound. My experience identifying and interpreting lists in Scripture, especially the NT, has helped me see the value of careful observation of lists. Paul's second letter to the Corinthians is a masterpiece, and contains several lists–the one at 6:1-10 will likely not fail to impress you. But what was Paul trying to communicate to the Corinthians?

This lesson covers the **Sixth Principal Part** used to form the **Passive Forms** of the **Aorist Tense** and the **Future Tense**. Both formations use a ϑῆτα (-ϑ-) tense indicator combined with an ῆτα (η) thematic vowel along with endings you already know. Also, in addition to more First Declension Nouns and Adverbs, the Vocabulary contains two important types of words. The first are **Interjections** that serve as forward pointing **Attention-Getting Devices**. The second are **Particles** and **Conjunctions** that are connecting words. The lack of connecting conjunctions between sentences is called **Asyndeton**. More typical, however, is that each sentence is "connected" to the next with conjunctions, which is called **Polysyndeton**. The arranging sentences or sentence elements together in lists with or without particles and conjunctions creates **Correlative Emphasis**.

VOCABULARY 15   MORE FIRST DECLENSION NOUNS; PARTICLES AND CONJUNCTIONS, INTERJECTIONS, AND ADVERBS

More First Declension Nouns:

ἡ ἀγαπή [116]	love, adoration
ἡ ἁμαρτία [172]	sin, failure; guilt
ἡ Γαλαλία [61]	Galilee
ἡ γενεά [43]	generation; age; kind
ἡ γῆ [250]	land; earth

Particles and Conjunctions:

μέν [178]	indeed, certainly
μέν … δέ	on the one hand … on the other hand
οὐδέ [143]	nor; not even; neither
οὐδέ … οὐδέ	neither … nor (+new development)
οὔτε [87]	nor; not even; neither

ἡ δόξα [165]	glory, splendor; reputation	οὔτε ... οὔτε	neither ... nor (+sameness)
ἡ ἐξουσία [102]	authority; power	τέ [213]	and; both (*enclitic and postpositive*)
ἡ θάλασσα [91]	lake, sea	τε καί	both ... and
ἡ καρδία [156]	heart	Interjections:	
ἡ κεφαλή [75]	head; superior	ἀμήν [128]	Amen! Certainly!
ἡ οἰκία [93]	house, building; family	ἰδού [200]	Behold! Look! (*draws attention*)
ἡ φυλακή [47]	prison; guard; watch	οὐαί [46]	Woe! Alas!
ἡ φωνή [139]	voice; sound	Adverbs:	
ἡ ψυχή [102]	soul; life; mind	ἐκεῖ [95]	there (as in a place)
ἡ ὥρα [106]	hour	οὕτως [207]	thus, in this manner

After learning vocabulary to this point, you will know 72.4% of the words in the GNT. If you are able, listen to audio recordings of Vocabulary 15 and complete the Crossword Puzzle in the Workbook Exercises.

NOTES ON VOCABULARY 15:

Many of these nouns have English cognates: agape love, <u>hamarto</u>-logy (study of sin), <u>genea</u>-logy, <u>geo</u>-logy, <u>doxo</u>-logy (a word of glory or praise), thalassic (pertaining to smaller seas versus oceans), cardiac, en-<u>cephal</u>-itis (inflammation of the head/brain), par-<u>ochial</u> (pertaining to a parish, i.e. a minister's home), <u>phono</u>-logy, <u>psycho</u>-logy, hour.

One pair of nouns is particularly interesting, because of their use together to indicate the extent of one's rule "of land and sea." Below is an pedestal inscription from Pergamum in honor of Augustus, hailing Augustus as "overseer of every land and sea."[1]

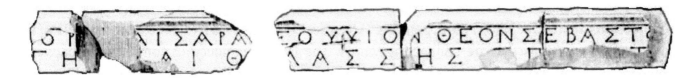

Αὐτοκράτορα Καίσαρα θεοῦ υἱὸν θεὸν Σεβαστὸν
πάσης γῆς καὶ θαλάσσης ἐπόπτην

"The Emperor, Caesar, son of a god, the god Augustus,
the overseer of every land and sea"

In this vocabulary, more conjunctions and particles are introduced. Particles are indeclinable words that contribute semantic nuance to Greek discourse; conjunctions are a subset of parti-

---

[1] Image is based upon G. Adolf Deissmann, *Light from the Ancient East the New Testament Illustrated by Recently Discovered Texts of the Graeco-Roman World*, trans. L. R. M. Strachan (London: Hodder & Stoughton, 1910), 350, fig. 53. The inscription reference is *IvP* II 381 and the physical pedestal is at the Berlin Museum. The image has been enhanced.

cles, and provide semantic meaning by relating sections, sentences, clauses, phrases, or words within a Greek discourse. It is critical to understand the discourse function and constraint of each conjunction (see 4.8 SOME COORDINATING CONJUNCTIONS). The conjunction μέν *indeed, certainly,* when working alone, is marked +affirmative emphasis (derived from μήν "used w. other particles for emphasis" BDAG). However, μέν often correlates with other conjunctions and particles and is marked for +continuity, +correlation, and +forward pointing (Runge 57 Table 3). Μέν occurs with δέ (+new development) to mark transition to the new development within the discourse: μέν ... δέ *on the one hand ... on the other hand,* which may involve concession (*although ... but*), contrast, or simply separation of thoughts or items in a series (BDAG 630.1). But these relationships are not inherent in the pairing of μέν ... δέ but rather must be ascertained by the context. The connectives are correlated as a marked set, but the semantics will vary according to the context.

The particle τέ is an *enclitic,* which means that it throws off its accent to the word before it whenever possible. It is also a postpositive (i.e. coming second in its clause). Τέ is marked for +addition and +sameness (not of identity, but function). Levinsohn argues, "Τέ solitarium ... adds distinct propositions that are characterized by *sameness,* in the sense that they refer to different aspects of the same event, the same occasion, or the same pragmatic unit" (106–7; emphasis original). However, τέ may work together with καί in the correlative expression ... τε καί ... *both ... and* that marks an addition to the sentence and sameness between the items connected by ... τε καί.... In such cases there is correlative emphasis. However, the translation *both* will not work if there are more than two items being formed in a list, which looks like τε καί ... καί ... καί ... etc.

The two pairings οὐδέ ... οὐδέ and οὔτε ... οὔτε may be translated the same *neither... nor* in a sequence of two or more items (forming correlative emphasis), but the pairings are different. Οὐδέ ... οὐδέ correlates items that are marked for new development and thus different, whereas οὔτε ... οὔτε correlates items that are marked for sameness, not of identity, but in function within the context. See the extended example below in 15.6.C. from 1 Thess 2:3-6 which illustrates this difference.

The interjections should be relatively easy to memorize. Just sound them out. Ἀμήν *Amen! Certainly!* translates well into English. In Greek, it is the transliteration of the Hebrew אָמֵן. Interestingly, ἀμήν is represented numerically in papyri as the number 99 (α=1 + μ=40 + η=8 + ν=50; BDAG 53). Οὐαί sounds a lot like *Woe!* And the interjection ἰδού *behold!* is related to εἶδον *I saw,* which is formed from the primitive root ϝιδ that contains a δίγαμμα (or ϝαῦ) from which the English word *video* is derived.

Finally, the adverb ἐκεῖ *there* signals +distant location (in distinction from ὧδε *here* +near location) and οὕτως *thus, in this way* signals +manner, which is often significant for interpretation. Also, οὕτως can function with other adverbs or conjunctions (esp. καθώς *just as* in CH.16) to form connective correlative emphasis. See the example below in 15.6.C. from 1 Thess 2:3-6.

15.1 SIXTH PRINCIPAL PART

A. **Tenses of the Sixth Principal Part:** You have learned all the Principal Parts except the Sixth Principal Part until now. This Principal Part is used to form the passive forms of the Aorist and Future Tenses. Remember that you have already learned the Aorist and Future Middles. Both the Aorist Passive and the Future Passive are easily recognized by their characteristic -ϑη- and respective endings.

B. **General Information:** The Aorist and Future Passives always share the same verb stem. Therefore, they are grouped together in the Sixth Principal Part. The form of the verb given in the sixth column for the Sixth Principal Part is always the Aorist Passive Indicative of that verb. This Aorist Passive Indicative *is always augmented*. Thus, to form the Future Passive, one must *first remove the augment* and then replace the Aorist Passive endings with the Future Passive endings. See below.

15.2 AORIST PASSIVE: FORMATION, ASPECT, AND TRANSLATION

A. **Formation and Endings of the Aorist Passive:** Many verbs will show a slight to major stem change from their lexical form. Check the comprehensive list given in APPENDICES §§25-27 PRINCIPAL PARTS OF VERBS. Compare the First and Sixth Principal Parts to see if any change takes place. You may want to highlight those verbs in which the stem changes radically.

     1. <u>Same Augmentation Rules</u>. The Aorist Passive Indicative is augmented just as the Imperfect and Aorist Active/Middle Indicative Tenses (see §8.3 AUGMENTATION).

     2. <u>Tense Suffix and Coupling Vowel</u>. The tense suffix for the Aorist Passive is ϑῆτα. The coupling vowel is ῆτα. Together the tense suffix and coupling vowel form the Aorist Passive morpheme -ϑη-.

     3. <u>Secondary Active Endings added to ϑη-</u>. To this ϑη- are added the secondary active endings:

		SECONDARY ENDINGS			AORIST PASSIVE ENDINGS	
		-ν	-μεν		-ϑην	-ϑημεν
ϑη-	+	-ς	-τε	→	-ϑης	-ϑητε
		-	-σαν*		-ϑη	-ϑησαν

     ****Notice** that the 3rd person plural ending is -σαν instead of -ν, which has the effect of differentiating the 3rd plural from the 1st singular ending (-ϑην).

B. **Aorist Verbal Aspect:** The Aorist Passive has the same *perfective* verbal aspect as the Aorist Active, in which the action is viewed as a whole externally or as complete, possibly even completed (cf. Wallace 554-65). See §10.1.B.2.

C. **Translation of the Aorist Passive:**

			English Simple Past
sg.	1	ἐπιστεύθην	*I was entrusted.*
	2	ἐπιστεύθης	*You were entrusted.*
	3	ἐπιστεύθη	*He, She, or It was entrusted.*
pl.	1	ἐπιστεύθημεν	*We were entrusted.*
	2	ἐπιστεύθητε	*You were entrusted.*
	3	ἐπιστεύθησαν	*They were entrusted.*

Notice the important distinction in translation between the Imperfect Passive and Aorist Passive. The helping verb *being* is reserved only for the Imperfect Passive. Why? Because the addition of *being* reflects more the imperfective verbal aspect of the Imperfect Tense, i.e. the action of the verb is internal and as in progress.

15.3 FUTURE PASSIVE: FORMATION, ASPECT, AND TRANSLATION

A. **Formation and Endings of the Future Passive:** As with the Aorist Passive formation, many verbs will show a slight to major stem change from their lexical form. Check the comprehensive list given in APPENDICES §§25-27 PRINCIPAL PARTS OF VERBS. Compare the First and Sixth Principal Parts to see if any change in verb stem takes place. You may want to highlight those verbs that have radical stem changes.

1. Un-Augment the Aorist Passive. Remember that in the standard listing of the principal parts of a verb, the sixth column shows the Aorist Passive Indicative forms that are augmented. Thus, this Aorist Passive Indicative form must be unaugmented to form the Future Passive.

2. Tense Indicator and Future Tense Suffix -θησ-. The tense indicator for the Future Passive is θη- + σ→ θησ-. This σίγμα is similar to the σίγμα added to form the Future Active and Middle.

3. Primary Middle/Passive Endings added to θησ-.

		Primary Endings			**Future Passive Endings**	
		–ομαι	–όμεθα		<u>–θήσομαι</u>	<u>–θησόμεθα</u>
θησ-	+	–η	–εσθε	→	<u>–θήση</u>	<u>–θήσεσθε</u>
		–εται	–ονται		<u>–θήσεται</u>	<u>–θήσονται</u>

B. **Future Tense Verbal Aspect:** The Future Passive has the same verbal aspect as the Future, which entails action that is intended and expected to occur. Stated again, the future tense reflects expectation or intention of occurrence in the future (cf. Wallace 566-71). See again §10.1.B.1.

C. **Translation of the Future Passive:**

			English Simple Future
sg.	1	πιστευθήσομαι	*I will be entrusted.*
	2	πιστευθήση	*You will be entrusted.*
	3	πιστευθήσεται	*He, She, or It will be entrusted.*
pl.	1	πιστευθησόμεθα	*We will be entrusted.*
	2	πιστευθήσεσθε	*You will be entrusted.*
	3	πιστευθήσονται	*They will be entrusted.*

CHECK POINT 15.1-3

Parse these verb Aorist and Future Passive forms (provide lexical form) and translate.

1. ἐδοξάσθη		
2. σωθήσονται		
3. ἐγνώσθησαν		
4. ἐπέμφθην		
5. ἐπείσθησαν		
6. ἀνοιχθήσεται		
7. συνήχθητε		
8. ἀπεκρίθη		
9. δοξασθήσεται		
10. ἐκηρύχθημεν		

ANSWERS

1. ἐδοξάσθη	API 3S δοξάζω	*s/he was glorified*
2. σωθήσονται	FPI 3P σῴζω	*they will be delivered*
3. ἐγνώσθησαν	API 3P γινώσκω	*they were known*
4. ἐπέμφθην	API 1S πέμπω	*I was sent*
5. ἐπείσθησαν	API 3P πείθω	*They were persuaded*
6. ἀνοιχθήσεται	FPI 3S ἀνοίγω	*it will be opened*
7. συνήχθητε	API 2P συνάγω	*you were gathered together*
8. ἀπεκρίθη	API 3S ἀποκρίνομαι	*s/he answered back* (middle formed)
9. δοξασθήσεται	FPI 3S δοξάζω	*s/he will be glorified*
10. ἐκηρύχθημεν	API 1P κηρύσσω	*we were preached*

15.4 INTERJECTIONS AS ATTENTION-GETTING DEVICES

A. **Introduction:** Interjections, along with vocatives, are attention-getting devices. An attention-getting interjection draws "special attention to the events or statements" it introduces.[2] Runge (§5.4.2) describes interjections as "attention-getters" when discussing forward-pointing devices; such words point forward to mark what follows as especially important.

2 Cor 6:2 λέγει γάρ· καιρῷ δεκτῷ ἐπήκουσά σου καὶ ἐν ἡμέρᾳ σωτηρίας ἐβοήθησά σοι. ἰδοὺ νῦν καιρὸς εὐπρόσδεκτος, ἰδοὺ νῦν ἡμέρα σωτηρίας.

> *For he says, "At the right time I heard you and in the day of salvation I helped you. Behold, now is the acceptable time; behold, now is the day of salvation!*

The Apostle Paul has been building up the discourse to this moment, where he pleads for the Corinthians to be reconciled to God (5:20). After quoting Isa 49:8, Paul applies the quotation immediately to the Corinthians. The repeated interjection ἰδοὺ and temporal adverb form a correlative emphasis (see §15.6 below). The double occurrence of ἰδοὺ as an attention getting device marks Paul's statement as extremely important. Paul's exhortation is building to the exhortative material in 6:14–7:1.

B. **Ἀμήν Meaning *Amen*! May be Backward Referencing:** The affirmative interjection ἀμήν *Amen! Certainly!* adds importance to what is said, but may be backward referencing to the previous speech or actions rather than forward pointing.[3] Why? Because such an understanding comports with its liturgical backward referencing in Hebrew Scripture to affirm what has been said (BDAG 53.1a). This is quite a different way of understanding ἀμήν than is commonly translated. Typically, when Jesus uses ἀμήν, it is with verbs of saying, which are regularly translated "Truly I say to you…", thus pointing forward "beginning a solemn declaration but used only by Jesus" (BDAG 53.1b.). What is problematic here is that such a solemn declaration is "used only by Jesus"—and no one else in this manner. However, given the typical use of ἀμήν in Hebrew idiom to conclude important statements and prayers, it seems quite possible that ἀμήν *Amen*! affirms previous action or speech and connects such recent action or speech with subsequent speech statements (often with metacomments pointing forward). For example, the use of ἀμήν often accentuates a response to an event or speech. In Matt 8:10b, Jesus responds to the Centurion's expression of faith in 8:8-10a with the marked statement:

Matt 8:8-10a The Centurion expresses faith.
Matt 8:10b ἀμὴν λέγω ὑμῖν, παρ' οὐδενὶ τοσαύτην πίστιν ἐν τῷ Ἰσραὴλ εὗρον.

> *Amen! I say to you from no one have I found such kind of faith in Israel!*

---

[2] Robert E. Smith, "Recognizing Prominence Features in the Greek New Testament," *Selected Technical Articles Related to Translation* 14 (1985): 16–25 at 19.

[3] This suggestion was first made to me by Michael Halcomb. This view and translation of ἀμήν as *Amen!* is implemented in our book, *Mark: GlossaHouse Illustrated Greek-English New Testament*, Accessible Greek Resources and Online Studies (Wilmore, KY: GlossaHouse, 2014).

Here it seems ἀμήν affirms the Centurion's faith and then is followed immediately (as often it is) with a metacomment (λέγω ὑμῖν *I say to you*) that is forward pointing to an important statement. The demonstrative modifier τοσαύτην *such kind of* also stresses the quality of the *faith* held by the Centurion. Thus, it is worth considering how the use of ἀμήν affirms what has been said or done and conjoins such with forward pointing statements of "saying."

C. **Constituent Marking and Diagramming Interjections:** Since interjections modify the whole sentence and do so within the environment of the surrounding verses, they function similarly to initial conjunctions, which are boxed in the Constituent Marking Method, and thus so should ⌐interjections¬ be boxed. In the Reed-Kellogg diagramming method, interjections are placed on a suspended line unattached to the rest of the diagram like this:

Matt 8:10b

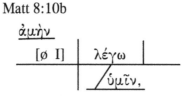

15.5 ASYNDETON (Ἀσύνδετον) AND POLYSYNDETON (Πολυσύνδετον)

A. **Asyndeton Defined:** Greek typically connects sentences with conjunctions. But, *asyndeton is the abutting of two or more independent sentences <u>without</u> an intervening or connecting conjunction*. The inter-sentential relationship is unmarked. Runge (20) discusses this phenomenon: "Asyndeton means that the writer did not feel compelled to specify a relation. If they had wanted to constrain a specific relation, there are plenty of conjunctions to make the intended relation explicit. The choice to use asyndeton represents the choice not to specify a relation.... In Koiné Greek, asyndeton is the default means of connecting clauses in the Epistles and in speeches reported within narrative. It is also used in the narrative of the Gospel of John."

B. **Discourse Pragmatic Impact of Asyndeton:** In terms of information processing effort, the audience is required <u>either</u> to closely connect the ideas as "of equal importance and parallel to each other" (Levinsohn 120) with structural emphasis or emotive effect <u>or</u> to disconnect them for sectional division, which will also show a change of topic. The brief summary of Wallace captures these uses: "Asyndeton is a vivid stylistic feature that occurs often for emphasis, solemnity, or rhetorical value (staccato effect), or when there is an abrupt change in topic" (658).

1. <u>Asyndeton for Close Connection and Rhetorical-Structural Emphasis.</u> Moulton and Turner (MHT III.340) discuss asyndeton from a Greek language historical perspective, "Except occasionally for effect, this is contrary to the genius of Greek, but Paul and Hebrews are full of it (e.g. 1 Co 7:27 Heb 11:32ff)." It is notable that the two examples cited here involve questions, summaries, and lists for rhetorical effect. Robertson (1178) indicates that conjunctions "may be consciously avoided for rhetorical effect... Cf. also 1 Cor 13:4-7 where the verbs follow one another in solemn emphasis with no connective save one δέ."

2. <u>Asyndeton for Amplification and Emotive Effect</u>. Abutted sentences may make parallel statements that build upon and amplify one another for effect. Grammarians have noted how asyndeton may create a certain atmosphere or reflect "emotion"; Robertson (443) describes the creation of a "mood"; BDF (§462) affirms that asyndeton lends an unconscious "solemnity and weight to the words"; Levinsohn, quoting Kathleen Callow's study on δέ, affirms that such emotion may signify "a further motivation for asyndeton" (121).[4]

3. <u>Asyndeton for Disconnection to Signal Discourse Boundaries</u>. In addition to this principle of "effect," Moulton and Turner (MHT III.341) conclude their brief discussion by describing a change in topic: "Asyndeton makes the beginning of new long sections conspicuous, e.g. Ro 9:1 10:1 13:1 1 Pt 5:1 2 Pt 3:1." So also BDF §463. It is notable, too, that the textual manuscript tradition attempts to rectify asyndeton (MHT III.340; BDF §462).

4. <u>Within the Pauline Epistles</u>. While discussing style, Moulton and Turner (IV.85) summarize the use of asyndeton: "Paul's asyndeton is effective in all his letters, whether emphasizing a new section (Eph 1:3 3:1 5:6.22.25.32 6:1.5.10 Rom 9:1 10:1 11:1 etc.), leading successively to a climax (Eph 4:5.6.12.13 6:12 1 Cor 4:8 2 Cor 7:2 1 Thes 5:14 Phil 3:5), marking contrast (Eph 2:8 1 Cor 15:42f), or otherwise making for stylistic liveliness (Eph 1:10 3:8 4:4.28.29.31 6:11 Rom 1:29ff 2:19 1 Cor 3:2 13:4–8 14:26 al.)." Compare this also to the evaluation of BDF 241: "There are, however, many and, in part, brilliant examples of rhetorical asyndeton in the Epistles, particularly Paul's."

C. **Carefully Consider Asyndeton:** Asyndeton is typically significant varying in degree on the particular NT author.

1. <u>Section Break</u>. Isolated instances of asyndeton may signal section breaks especially if there is a sudden shift of topic and other transitional indicators (e.g., vocatives, "Brothers").

2. <u>Different Connection</u>. If no break, then asyndeton may reflect a relationship between propositions that is beyond or different from what may be conveyed by the available connectors. Such relationships may entail providing **evaluation**, moving from **general to specific**, or **summarization** (Levinsohn, 119-20). One kind of evaluation in Paul occurs within diatribe amidst questions and their answers; asyndeton may here reflect a different speaker offering answers to questions posed (e.g., Rom 3:2, 4, 9b, 27, 29; 6:1-2, 15-16; 1 Cor 6:12a, 13a, 18b [perhaps]).

3. <u>Intense Emotion</u>. Additionally, the motivation for asyndeton may be emotional, signaling intense feeling and focus on a particular topic, especially in the midst of rhetorical questions.

4. <u>In Verbal Lists</u>. Finally, asyndeton may occur in lists where a sequence of verbal actions is described, which may produce "a vivid and impassioned effect" (BDF §460).

D. **Polysyndeton in Lists:** The use of conjunctions to connect items in lists of items *when otherwise unnecessary* is called polysyndeton. "Asyndeton and polysyndeton often, though by no means always, lend rhetorical emphasis: polysyndeton produces the impression of extensiveness and abundance by means of an exhausting summary; asyndeton, by breaking up the series and introducing the items staccato fashion, produces a vivid and impassioned effect" (BDF §460). Polysyndeton within lists entails correlative emphasis. See immediately below.

---

[4] Kathleen Callow, "Patterns of Thematic Development in 1 Corinthians 5:1-13," in *Linguistics and New Testament Interpretation: Essays on Discourse Analysis*, ed. David Alan Black (Nashville: Broadman, 1992), 194–206 at 192.

15.6 CORRELATIVE EMPHASIS: LISTS AND COORDINATED CONNECTIVES

A. **Definition:** *Correlative emphasis occurs when two or more words, phrases, or clauses are placed together in parallel or complementary fashion in order to stress their interrelationship to each other and to the broader discursive context.* In addition to parallel or complementary structures, the correlation may be (more) explicitly marked through the use of two or more conjunctions, particles, and adverbs. Just what interpretive effect attends the correlated elements must be determined by investigating the communicative context and the constraints conveyed by presence of any correlating conjunctions, particles, and adverbs (see D. below).

B. **Lists involve Correlative Emphasis:**

1. <u>Lists Defined</u>. Most basically, *lists involve three or more items presented together to provide greater understanding about what is deemed important.* By this definition, *two items do not constitute a list* (but this should not lessen their interpretive importance as "a doublet"). Lists implicitly involve the semantic relationship of reoccurrence of three or more items, the importance of which is typically guaranteed by the space and prominence given to them in the discourse. Although biblical writers used lists for a variety of purposes, and each purpose must be determined in context, the use of lists can be related to what cognitive scientists and linguists describe as "information structure." Lists function to organize and prioritize items, which additionally often facilitates easier recollection. The items in lists are correlated intentionally, and thus lists are marked +correlation of ideas. The interpretation must be made in context.

2. <u>Attributes of Lists</u>. The proper interpretation of biblical lists will always contribute to the proper interpretation of the entire passage, and for understanding the overarching concerns of the biblical authors. Scripture contains many lists, whether of persons or agencies (genealogical, biographical, etc.), places (geographical), events (chronological, grouped, etc.), processes (steps, stages, etc.), attributes (qualities, etc.), or concepts (moral, theological, etc.). Within biblical materials, lists function to make reference to what has been already discussed (backward referencing), or to what will be discussed (forward referencing), or possibly both (transitional or medial). Lists may build to a climax, and may show particularization (from general to particular), generalization (a movement from particular to general), or a more specific form of each called summarization (headings as outline for the particulars). Other relationships are possible. The emphasizing of items in a list may be achieved by correlating each with a conjunction like καί. For example, the list of 1 Pet 4:3 does not contain correlative emphasis, since "the insertion of καί each time would make the separate items too important" (BDF §460.2). Also, "the use of a particle repeatedly in longer enumerations produces polysyndeton … [which] often, though by no means always, lend[s] rhetorical emphasis" (BDF §460.3).

C. **Interpreting Lists:** When interpreting lists, consider the following areas:

1. Material Content.

    a. *persons* or *agencies* (genealogical, biographical, etc.)
    b. *places* (geographical, etc.)
    c. *events* (chronological, grouped, etc.)
    d. *processes* (steps, stages, etc.)
    e. *attributes* (qualities, etc.)
    f. *concepts* (moral, theological, etc.)
    g. *other?*

2. Scope.

    a. *exhaustive (inclusive)*—all possible items are included in the list
    b. *massive (majority)*—many, but not all.
    c. *open* (*indefinite*)—unrestricted and open; any or some.
    d. *limited (exclusive)*—selected items are included in the list
        i. *representative*—items are a sampling of general representation
        ii. *exemplary*—the most critical or important items are included.
        iii. *Other* limitation?

3. Referencing.

    a. *backward*—primarily related to what precedes
    b. *forward*—primarily related to what follows
    c. *dual*—both backward and forward referencing
        i. *transitional*—bridging what comes before to the new coming after
        ii. *medial*—occupying middle position in the development of the argument.

4. Formal Structure. Often more than one characteristic applies simultaneously:

    a. *collective*—the group of items coheres together evenly
    b. *grouped*—items within a list are paired or grouped together among other groupings
    c. *progressive*—items build upon one another in a development
    d. *prioritized*—one or more item is preeminent to the others (initial, center, final)
    e. *inner-outer movement*—related to above, the list describes intra-personal and moves to inter-personal realities, or vice versa.
    f. *alternating*—items are presented back & forth between 2 poles or vantage points
    g. *chiastic*—items are arranged around a central notion in ABC-CBA fashion
    h. *bracketed*—the list begins and ends with the same/similar item.

5. <u>Semantic (Structural) Relations</u>—Implicitly, lists involve reoccurrence, but may also involve one or more of the following semantic relations:[5]

    a. *climactic*—items culminates with a high point (determined from literary context)

    b. *particularizing*— items provide details of a general notion

    c. *generalizing*— items move from specific to more general concepts

    c. *contrastive*—items are contrasted with one another

    d. *comparative*—items are compared with one another

    e. *causative*—items lead consequently to something

    f. *purposive means*—items are intended as a means to something

    g. *manner*—items describe the "manner" of something (like behavior or action)

    h. *resultative*—items come from or result from something

D. **Coordinated Correlative Connectives:** *Connective correlative emphasis occurs when two or more adverbs, conjunctions, correlative pronouns, or particles are used in coordinated proximity to mark two or more clauses, phrases, or words.* Where simple coordination, subordination, or asyndeton might have been used (e.g., in lists), the deployment of stylized pairings and/or sequences of adverbs, conjunctions, and particles signals correlative semantic relationships between the elements involved.

CORRELATIVE COMBINATIONS	BASIC SEMANTIC CONSTRAINTS
εἴτε ... εἴτε (*whether... or whether*)	alternative of similar kind
ἐάν ... ἄρα or εἰ ... ἄρα (*if ... then*)	condition; cause to effect
ἤ ... ἤ (*either ... or*)	alternative
καθὼς ... οὕτως (*just as ... thus*)	correspondence (comparison and basis)
καί ... καί (*both ... and*)	association
μέν ... δέ (*on the one hand ... on the other hand*)	contrast
μήτε ... μήτε (*neither ... nor*)	exclusion of similar alternatives
οἷος ... τοιοῦτος (*of what sort ... such*)	quality
ὅπου ... ἐκεῖ (*where ... there*)	locative
ὅταν ... τότε (*when[ever] ... then*)	temporal
ὅτε ... τότε (*when ... then*)	temporal
οὐκ ... ἀλλά or δέ (*not ... but*)	point/counterpoint set
οὔτε ... οὔτε (*neither ... nor*)	exclusion of similar alternatives
ποτέ ... νῦν (*once ... now*)	past/present temporal contrast
τε ... καί (*both ... and*)	association of similar items
τε ... τε (*as ... so*)	association of similar items

---

[5] Cf. Robert A. Traina, who related some structural relationships to the interpretation of what he called "series of facts." He indicated, "Comparison, contrast, enumeration, or progression from the general to the specific may be involved in this type of relation" (Robert A. Traina, *Methodical Bible Study: A New Approach to Hermeneutics* [Wilmore, KY: Robert A. Traina, Asbury Theological Seminary, 1952; repr., Grand Rapids: Zondervan, 2002], 42 n.26).

As one can see, the type of semantic relationship (contrast, correspondence, alternative, association, etc.) depends on the adverbs, conjunctions, and particles utilized. However, the pragmatic effect of co-relating items places them into a "common folder of understanding." *When such constructions occur, an important point is being made; so pay careful attention.* Note: students will not have learned all of the grammar and constructions attending these connectives and adverbs; some conjunctions like ὅταν take the subjunctive mood covered in ch.22.

E. **Extended Examples:**

2 Cor 12:12 τὰ μὲν σημεῖα τοῦ ἀποστόλου κατειργάσθη ἐν ὑμῖν ἐν πάσῃ ὑπομονῇ,
σημείοις <u>τε</u> <u>καὶ</u> τέρασιν <u>καὶ</u> δυνάμεσιν.
Indeed, the signs of the apostle were accomplished among you in all endurance, with <u>indeed</u> signs <u>and</u> wonders <u>and</u> miracles.

The conjunction μέν *indeed* is working alone here and is marked +affirmative emphasis. This sets off Paul's statements on miraculous signs as important in his developing argument. Just how important is discerned in the list that follows beginning σημείοις τε. Here τε is difficult to translate (I used *indeed*). To use *both … and* would not work, since there are three items in the list, and *both* implies only two elements. Remember that τε is marked +addition and +sameness (not of identity, but function). The items in the list are of a same kind (i.e. *miraculous activities*); the addition relates to the already stated direct object (τὰ … σημεῖα *the signs*) at the beginning of the sentence. Thus, the connective correlative emphasis marks the importance of the list: It is an elaboration that contributes to Paul's point that he also performed apostolic miracles among the Corinthians (although for rhetorical effect, Paul states this indirectly using the passive voice!). Finally, notice, too, that both the final placement in the sentence and the special use of the dative case (dative of means) add additional marking and emphasis.

Consider this next lengthy example that contains multiple instances of connective correlative emphasis.

1 Thess 2:3 ἡ γὰρ παράκλησις ἡμῶν <u>οὐκ</u> ἐκ πλάνης <u>οὐδὲ</u> ἐξ ἀκαθαρσίας <u>οὐδὲ</u> ἐν δόλῳ,
For our exhortation was <u>not</u> out of deception, <u>nor</u> out of impurity, <u>nor</u> by cunning,

The correlative emphasis connects the three prepositional phrases that emphasize Paul's denial of any bad basis for the exhortation. The choice to use οὐδὲ signifies +new development indicating the complementary nature of the prepositional phrases rather than the sameness that would be communicated by οὔτε (see below).

1 Thess 2:4 <u>ἀλλὰ</u> <u>καθὼς</u> δεδοκιμάσμεθα ὑπὸ τοῦ θεοῦ πιστευθῆναι τὸ εὐαγγέλιον,
<u>οὕτως</u> λαλοῦμεν, <u>οὐχ ὡς</u> ἀνθρώποις ἀρέσκοντες <u>ἀλλὰ</u> θεῷ τῷ δοκιμάζοντι τὰς καρδίας ἡμῶν.

But, just as we have been approved by God to be entrusted with the gospel, thus also we speak, not as pleasing people but God who approves of our hearts.

There are three instances of connective correlative emphasis. The first is a continuation from 2:3 where the οὐκ ... οὐδὲ ... οὐδὲ *not ... nor ... nor* are correlated with the ἀλλὰ *but* to form a point-counterpoint set (see discussion on Ἀλλά in §4.8 SOME COORDINATING CONJUNCTIONS). The counterpoint initiated with ἀλλά presents positively how Paul's exhortation was made, *having God's approval*. Within this counterpoint, the second emphasis consists of the καθὼς ... οὕτως *just as ... thus* pairing that stresses the relationship of correspondence (καθὼς +comparison and +basis) and manner (οὕτως +manner). What is communicated is that God's approval and entrusting of the gospel to Paul is the basis for and has the likeness of how Paul speaks the gospel. The third instance involves another point-counterpoint set, οὐχ ὡς ... ἀλλὰ, that stresses the manner of contrast between whom Paul is trying to please: humans or God. It is God and not humans that Paul seeks to please.

1 Thess 2:5-6 Οὔτε γάρ ποτε ἐν λόγῳ κολακείας ἐγενήθημεν, καθὼς οἴδατε, οὔτε ἐν προφάσει πλεονεξίας, θεὸς μάρτυς, [6] οὔτε ζητοῦντες ἐξ ἀνθρώπων δόξαν οὔτε ἀφ᾽ ὑμῶν οὔτε ἀπ᾽ ἄλλων

*For not once ever did we come with flattering speech, **just as you know**, nor with a pretense of greed, **God is witness**, [6] nor seeking glory from people, neither from you nor from others.*

Two instances of connective correlative emphasis occur. The first involves the first three instances of οὔτε and the second involves the last two instances of οὔτε. In both sets, the τε component marks +addition and +sameness. In the second or last set, the addition entails two prepositional phrases with ἀπό supplementing and specifying who among the prepositional phrase ἐξ ἀνθρώπων may be the source of glory (δόξαν). The element of sameness concerns the elements of *you* and *others* in that both are possible sources of glory. In the first set, the additive dimension connects back to the negative denial in 2:4 that Paul *was not seeking to please people*. The sameness concerns the fact that the list of activities in 2:5-6 all pertain to the ways in which Paul denied that he was seeking to please people: flattering speech, pretense of greed, and seeking glory from people. What might seem odd to us is that these activities share a common sameness of pleasing people. But this is how the discourse is marked. Additional emphasis has been indicated by bold. What kind of statements are these? Metacomments (see §10.8 METACOMMENTS AND PRAGMATICS) that point forward to the denials that Paul makes. Why does Paul make such emphatic statements of denial? Well, to answer that properly would require us to investigate the broader book context and the rhetorical situation of the discourse.

Complete WORKBOOK EXERCISES 15 and consult the ANSWER KEY & GUIDE as needed.

CASE IN POINT 15: 2 COR 6:1-10 AND PAUL'S IMPASSIONED APPEAL

By this point in learning Greek, you should be able to recognize many types of marked constructions and to ponder their interpretive significance. In this chapter, we have looked at interjections as attention getting devices that anticipate what is said next. We have also considered correlative emphasis through the strategic use of lists and conjoining connective words like conjunctions, particles, and adverbs.

Well, Paul's appeal to the Corinthians in 2 Cor 6:1-10 is a remarkable example of lists and connectives to form correlative emphasis. Plus, by paying attention to other kinds of emphasis (like quantitative), we can begin to discern just where Paul is next heading in the subsequent discourse, namely, to address the financial giving of the Corinthians. So, let's look at the Greek text in conjunction with my fairly literal translation. This translation and some of the discussion comes slightly edited from my *2 Corinthians: A Handbook on the Greek Text*, Baylor Handbook on the Greek New Testament (Waco, TX: Baylor University Press, 2015). I will place the Greek and English in parallel columns, as well as arranging the sentences to highlight semantic relationships (see §16.4 SEMANTIC DIAGRAMMING: INTRODUCTION AND PROCEDURES).

2 CORINTHIANS 6:1–10 WITH TYPES OF EMPHASIS UNDERLINED AND IN BRACKETS	

¹ Συνεργοῦντες
 δὲ
   καὶ
  παρακαλοῦμεν
        μὴ εἰς κενὸν τὴν
        χάριν τοῦ θεοῦ
        δέξασθαι ὑμᾶς·
² λέγει
γάρ·
    καιρῷ δεκτῷ ἐπήκουσά σου
     καὶ
   ἐν ἡμέρᾳ σωτηρίας ἐβοήθησά σοι.
ἰδοὺ
   νῦν καιρὸς εὐπρόσδεκτος,
ἰδοὺ
   νῦν ἡμέρα σωτηρίας.
 	
³ Μηδεμίαν ἐν μηδενὶ διδόντες
προσκοπήν, ἵνα μὴ μωμηθῇ ἡ διακονία,
	¹Now
	   since we are working together,
	   also [**additive**]
	  we urge
	       that you not receive
	       the grace of God in vain.
	²For
	   He says,
	      [From Isaiah 49:8]
	   "At the right time I listened to you
	      and
	  on the day of salvation I helped you."
	<u>Look,</u> [**attention getting** and **asyndeton**]
	  <u>now</u> is the truly right moment!
	<u>Look,</u> [**attention getting** and **asyndeton**]
	  <u>now</u> is the day of salvation!
	  [νῦν... νῦν **correlative**]
	³In <u>no way</u> are we providing <u>any</u> opportunity that the ministry be criticized. [**asyndeton** and **negative**]

4 ἀλλ'
  ἐν παντὶ
συνιστάντες ἑαυτοὺς ὡς θεοῦ διάκονοι,
 	
  ἐν ὑπομονῇ πολλῇ,
  ἐν θλίψεσιν,
  ἐν ἀνάγκαις,
  ἐν στενοχωρίαις,
5 ἐν πληγαῖς,
  ἐν φυλακαῖς,
  ἐν ἀκαταστασίαις,
  ἐν κόποις,
  ἐν ἀγρυπνίαις,
  ἐν νηστείαις,
6 ἐν ἁγνότητι,
  ἐν γνώσει,
  ἐν μακροθυμίᾳ,
  ἐν χρηστότητι,
  ἐν πνεύματι ἁγίῳ,
  ἐν ἀγάπῃ ἀνυποκρίτῳ,
7 ἐν λόγῳ ἀληθείας,
  ἐν δυνάμει θεοῦ·
  διὰ τῶν ὅπλων τῆς δικαιοσύνης
        τῶν δεξιῶν καὶ ἀριστερῶν,
8 διὰ δόξης
    καὶ ἀτιμίας,
  διὰ δυσφημίας
    καὶ εὐφημίας·
  ὡς πλάνοι
    καὶ ἀληθεῖς,
9 ὡς ἀγνοούμενοι
    καὶ ἐπιγινωσκόμενοι,
  ὡς ἀποθνῄσκοντες
    καὶ ἰδοὺ ζῶμεν,
 	
  ὡς παιδευόμενοι
    καὶ μὴ θανατούμενοι,
10 ὡς λυπούμενοι
    ἀεὶ δὲ χαίροντες,
	4Rather, [μή ... ἀλλ' **correlative**]
	  in <u>every way</u> [**quantitative**]
	we are commending ourselves as servants
	        of God [**genitival**]
	  in <u>much</u> endurance, [**quantitative**]
	  in afflictions,
	  in tough spots,
	  in difficulties,
	5 in beatings,
	  in prisons,
	  in riots,
	  in toils,
	  in sleepless nights,
	  in fasts,
	6 in purity,
	  in knowledge,
	  in patience,
	  in kindness,
	  in the Holy Spirit,
	  in unhyprocritical love,
	7 in truthful word,
	  in the power of God,
	  through weapons of righteousness
	        in the right and left hand,
	8 through honor
	    and disrepute,
	  through slander
	    and praise,
	  <u>as</u> (being) deceivers
	    <u>and</u> truthful, [series of **correlative**]
	9 <u>as</u> (ones) unrecognized
	    <u>and</u> completely known,
	  <u>as</u> (ones) dying
	    <u>and</u>, <u>look</u>, we are living(!),
	    [**attention getting**]
	  <u>as</u> (ones) punished
	    <u>and</u> not put to death,
	10 <u>as</u> (ones) grieving
	    <u>but</u> <u>always</u> rejoicing,
	    [**quantitative**]

<u>ὡς</u> πτωχοὶ
    πολλοὺς δὲ πλουτίζοντες,
<u>ὡς</u> μηδὲν ἔχοντες
    καὶ <u>πάντα</u> κατέχοντες.
	<u>as</u> poor
	    <u>but</u> enriching <u>many</u>, [**quantitative**]
	<u>as</u> (ones) having <u>nothing</u>
	    <u>and</u> possessing <u>all things</u>.
	                        [**quantitative**]

In 6:1 additive emphasis with καί highlights the already lexically repeated and thus emphatic word group "encouragement" of Paul that the Corinthians "not receive the grace of God in vain." The γάρ in 6:2 initiates support for Paul's encouragement as originating from God's reported speech in Isaiah 49:8. This quotation is reworked and repeated with the **emphatic attention-getter** ἰδού and the temporal adverb νῦν, drawing even more attention to the statements as **correlative**: "Look, now is the acceptable time! Look, now is the day of salvation!" Both statements involve **asyndeton**, indicating a moment of high emotional appeal. The word σωτηρία is naturally and contextually prominent, since it entails all of God's saving activity in the gospel of Christ as related by Paul in the discourse to this point. Paul will be admonishing the Corinthians in 6:14-7:1 to leave their idolatrous relationships.

But more is taking place in 6:1-10. Striking indeed is Paul's conjoining the participial clause "giving…." in 6:3 (μηδεμίαν ἐν μηδενὶ διδόντες προσκοπήν) to 6:2 with asyndeton. Other emphatic features include the repeated and abutted negative words from μηδεῖς *no one* (Μηδεμίαν ἐν μηδενὶ) with μή (covered in Chapter 22) that powerfully convey **negative emphasis** (see §22.6 NEGATIVE EMPHASIS). Together these words develop an extensive **point/counterpoint set** with ἀλλ' in 6:4 (Μηδεμίαν ἐν μηδενὶ … μή… ἀλλ') entailing **correlative emphasis**. The focus of these emphatics indicators relate to the integrity of Paul's ministry. Why does this affect Paul's appeal for the Corinthians to accept God's salvation? Further insight comes from what follows.

The list that follows in 6:4-10 entails extensive **correlative emphasis** by correlating certain items together in contrast or mutual paradoxical existence. The list begins in 6:4 with ἐν παντὶ *in every way* providing **quantitative emphasis**. Then, the list builds momentum first by shifting from the preposition ἐν to διά and then by having more complex items in the lists in which the prepositions have compound objects starting at 6:7b: διὰ δόξης καὶ ἀτιμίας *through honor and disrepute*. Finally, the list builds to a climax at 6:8b with several marked constructions:

1. more explicit **correlative emphasis** of conjunction pairs (ὡς … καί 5 times; ὡς … δέ 2 times),
2. the emphatic **attention getter** ἰδού in 6:9, and
3. several instances of **quantitative emphasis** in 6:10: ἀεί *always*; μηδὲν *nothing*; πολλοὺς *many*; πάντα *all things*.

The content of the final climactic build up concerns matters of rich/poor, ownership of wealth, and making others rich. These concluding notions are cohesive with latter portions of 2 Corinthians, specifically chs. 8-9, where Paul will appeal to the Corinthians to complete their giving to the collection effort, by which others will be enriched out of Christ's poverty in making others rich. This collection was an international relief fund that shows the unity of the Gentile churches with the Jewish churches. Particularly at issue for Paul were suspicions of his handling of money and sending others in his place to receive the money (7:2; 8:20-24; 11:8; 12:14-18). All in all, 6:1-10 shows diverse types of emphasis including the remarkable **patterned emphasis** in the list of 6:4-10. Attending to these emphatic features of the Greek text allows one to understand how Paul underscores the integrity and purposes of his ministry despite adverse affliction (cf. 1:3-7).

Below is a reconstruction of Ancient Olympia (Ἀρχαία Ὀλυμπία) in Greece, with the temple of Zeus prominently in the center. Here was hosted the quadrennial athletic Olympic games from the 8th century BC to the 4th century AD.[6] The square structure is the *Leonidaion* (Λεωνίδαιον) where athletes resided during the games. It is possible that the Apostle Paul viewed similar games at Corinth when he traveled through there. His descriptions and lists of sufferings contain elements that recall athletic or military contests; in 2 Cor 4:9 Paul is "knocked down" (καταβάλλω) but "not destroyed." See especially Paul's explicit reference to games, racing, boxing, and training in 1 Cor 9:24-27 and elsewhere (Phil 1:30; 1 Tim 1:18; 6:12; 2 Tim 2:5; 4:7-8).

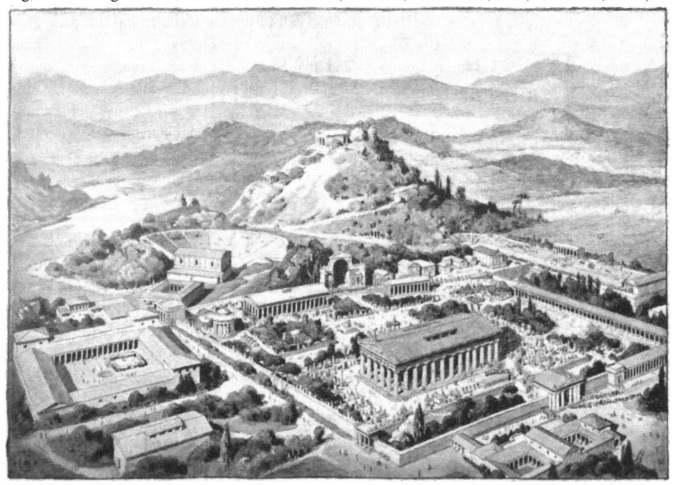

---

[6] Image has been edited from William Carey Morey, *Outlines of Greek History: With a Survey of Ancient Oriental Nations* (New York: American Book, 1903), 152.

CHAPTER 16

The main sentence may be thought to be the most important point of the sentence. However, subordinate clauses may be the most important because they provide important clarifying and elaborative information. Such is the case with John 13:31-35.

This chapter introduces you to a method of **Semantic Diagramming** and **Analysis**. This method is extremely productive in any language (including especially Greek and English) and can work alongside of that which was introduced in §4.7 CONSTITUENT MARKING FOR NAVIGATING A GREEK SENTENCE. Also, this chapter features the last of the Third Declension nouns. These are **Vowel Stem Third Declension nouns.** Then, we look at some subordinating conjunctions.

VOCABULARY 16   LAST OF THE THIRD DECLENSION

Feminine:

ἡ ἀνάστασις, -εως [42]	resurrection
ἡ δύναμις, -εως [119]	power; miracle
ἡ θλῖψις, -εως [45]	affliction; persecution
ἡ κρίσις, -εως [47]	judging, judgment
ἡ πίστις, -εως [242]	faith; faithfulness
ἡ πόλις, -εως [163]	city

Neuter:

τὸ ἔθνος, ἔθνους [160]	nation; Gentile
τὸ ἔτος, ἔτους [49]	year
τὸ μέρος, μέρους [42]	part, portion
τὸ ὄρος, ὄρους [63]	mountain, hill
τὸ τέλος, τέλους [40]	end, result, purpose

Masculine:

ὁ ἀρχιερεύς, -έως [122]	high priest, chief priest
ὁ βασιλεύς, -έως [115]	king
ὁ γραμματεύς, -έως [63]	scribe, law expert
ὁ Μωϋσῆς, -έως [80]	Moses

Irregular Name:

ὁ Ἰούδας, -α [49]	Judas

Subordinating Conjunctions:

ὅπου [81]	where
ὅτε [102]	when
ὡς [504]	as, corresponding to; while
καθώς [182]	just as, corresponding to

After learning vocabulary to this point, you will know 74% of the words in the GNT. If you are able, listen to audio recordings of VOCABULARY 16 and complete the CROSSWORD PUZZLE in the WORKBOOK EXERCISES.

NOTES ON VOCABULARY 16:

Many of the nouns have English cognates: <u>dynam</u>-ite, <u>criti</u>-cal, <u>poli</u>-tical, ethnic, <u>etes</u>-ian (periodical; yearly), poly-<u>mer</u> (many parts), <u>oro</u>-graphy (study of mountains) or <u>oro</u>-geny (mountain formation), telic (denoting the end or goal of something), basilic (royal), <u>grammati</u>-cal. These 3rd Declension noun endings are covered below.

The forms for the Masculine and Feminine include the genitive endings (demarcated with a dash) that are added to the noun stem. So, for ἡ κρίσις, -εως the genitive form is τῆς κρίσεως. For the Neuter nouns, the full genitive form is given (without its genitive article). For a complete listing of endings, see below. The proper name for Judas is included with this vocabulary; it has its nominative form as ὁ Ἰούδας and its genitive form as τοῦ Ἰούδα.

Finally, the conjunctions ὡς and καθώς are marked +correspondence, which entails +comparison and +basis/support; for ὡς additionally +correspondence may ential +estimation or approximation. The additional καθ- (from the preposition κατά) gives καθώς more markedness due to morphological emphasis. Both ὡς and καθώς occur with οὕτως *thus* to provide connective correlative emphasis: καθώς ... οὕτως (*just as... thus...*); this combination entails the notions of +correspondence (καθώς/ὡς) and +manner (οὕτως).

Below is the silver tetradrachm coin of Antiochus IV Epiphanes ("god manifest") dating 167-165 BC. This king sacked the Jerusalem temple in 167, beginning a three year period where the temple was rededicated to Zeus. Antiochus is identified as pagan king who brings "the desolating sacrilege" of Daniel 9:27; 11:31; 12:11 (cf. Mark 13:14). On the obverse is the head of Antiochus IV facing right; on the reverse we have ΒΑΣΙΛΕΩΣ ΑΝΤΙΟΧΟΥ ΘΕΟΥ ΕΠΙΦΑΝΟΥΣ ΝΙΚΗΦΟΡΟΥ "Of King Antiochus, god manifest, victorious" with Zeus seated left holding the god Nike (Νίκη, *victory*) with crowning wreath. These epithets will later be taken up by the Roman emperors. The apostle Paul describes the believers' hope in awaiting the day of "the appearance of our Savior Christ Jesus" (τῆς ἐπιφανείας τοῦ σωτῆρος ἡμῶν Χριστοῦ Ἰησοῦ, 2 Tim 1:10) in which there awaits him "the crown of righteousness" (ὁ τῆς δικαιοσύνης στέφανος, 2 Tim 4:8).

Source M. Ernest Babelon, *Catalogue des Monnaies Grecques: Les Rois de Syrie, d'Arménie, et de Commagène* (Paris: Rollin & Feuardent, 1890), Plate XII no.11. The coin is located at Paris, Cabinet des Médailles.

16.1 VOWEL STEM NOUNS OF THE THIRD DECLENSION (Τρίτη Κλίσις)

A. **Two Basic Types of Third Declension:** Already you have encountered the first type of this declension, the **consonant stems** in CH. 12. A second class is called **vowel stems**. Three sets of endings that correspond to each gender (although Masculine and Feminine differ only at one point) are illustrated below.

B. **Same Third Declension Endings Changed Slightly:** Vowel Stem Nouns basically take the same Third Declension endings. However, because the stem ends in a vowel, the normal Third Declension endings are slightly altered. For comparison sake, the standard Third Declension endings are listed below left and the slightly changed (*) vowel stem endings are on the right:

	THIRD DECLENSION CONSONANT STEM ENDINGS				VOWEL STEM ENDINGS		
	Masc./Fem. Stems		**Neuter Stems**		**Masculine Stem**	**Feminine Stem**	**Neuter Stem**
sg. nom.	-ς		- or -ς		-ς	-ς	- or -ς
gen.	-ος	→	-ος		-ως*	-ως*	-ους*
dat.	-ι	→	-ι		-ι	-ι	-ι
acc.	-α		- or -ς		-α	-ν*	- or -ς
pl. nom.	-ες		-α		-ις*	-ις*	-η*
gen.	-ων	→	-ων		-ων	-ων	-ων
dat.	-σι(ν)	→	-σι(ν)		-σι(ν)	-σι(ν)	-σι(ν)
acc.	-ας		-α		-ις*	-ις*	-η*

Note: (1) The Masculine and Feminine endings are virtually the same in the vowel stem endings except for the accusative singular. (2) The genitive singular of all genders changes from -ος to -ως or -ους. (3) The nominative/accusative plural of all genders is identical in each respective gender. (4) The changes seen are the result of a vowel, normally an ἒ ψιλόν (-ε) at the end of the noun stem.

C. **Forms of Vowel Stem Third Declension Nouns:**

	art.	Masculine	art.	Feminine	art.	Neuter
sg. nom.	ὁ	βασιλεύς	ἡ	πίστις	τὸ	ἔθνος
gen.	τοῦ	βασιλέως	τῆς	πίστεως	τοῦ	ἔθνους
dat.	τῷ	βασιλεῖ	τῇ	πίστει	τῷ	ἔθνει
acc.	τὸν	βασιλέα	τὴν	πίστιν	τὸ	ἔθνος

pl. nom.	οἱ βασιλεῖς	αἱ πίστεις	τὰ ἔθνη
gen.	τῶν βασιλέων	τῶν πίστεων	τῶν ἐθνῶν
dat.	τοῖς βασιλεῦσι(ν)	ταῖς πίστεσι(ν)	τοῖς ἔθνεσι(ν)
acc.	τοὺς βασιλεῖς	τὰς πίστεις	τὰ ἔθνη

Base Stems: βασιλεύ/έ- **Note** that this base stem is the vocative form: βασιλεῦ (note change in accent).	πίστι/ε-	ἔθνε-

16.2 SOME SUBORDINATING CONJUNCTIONS

A. **Definition of *Subordinating and Coordinating*:** Remember that conjunctions connecting two independent sentences or equal sentence components are called **coordinating conjunctions**. However, other conjunctions are called **subordinating conjunctions**, because they introduce a subordinate clause that is governed by the main sentence. In fact, the conjunction "because" (that I just used) is a subordinating conjunction introducing a subordinate clause.

B. **Particular:** Below are subordinating conjunctions with uses described and examples given:

1. Ὡς has three main uses.

    a. *Comparison.* Ὡς can be used in comparisons and means *like, as, just as.*

      Luke 6:40b κατηρτισμένος δὲ πᾶς ἔσται <u>ὡς</u> ὁ διδάσκαλος αὐτοῦ.
          Now every person trained will be <u>like</u> his teacher.

      Eph 5:23a ἀνήρ ἐστιν κεφαλὴ τῆς γυναικὸς <u>ὡς</u> καὶ ὁ Χριστὸς κεφαλὴ τῆς ἐκκλησίας.
          A husband is the head of the wife <u>as</u> even Christ is the head of the church.

    b. *Time.* Ὡς can indicate a time *while, when, since* something happened.

      John 7:10a <u>ὡς</u> δὲ ἀνέβησαν οἱ ἀδελφοὶ αὐτοῦ εἰς τὴν ἑορτήν, τότε καὶ αὐτὸς ἀνέβη.
          <u>When</u> his brothers went up to the feast, then he himself also went up.

      John 12:36a <u>ὡς</u> τὸ φῶς ἔχετε, πιστεύετε εἰς τὸ φῶς.
          <u>Since</u> you have the light, believe in the light.

c. *Estimation*: Ὡς can indicate an estimation (with numbers, etc.) *about*

John 6:10 b ἀνέπεσαν οὖν οἱ ἄνδρες τὸν ἀριθμὸν ὡς πεντακισχίλιοι.
Thus, the men reclined, the number (being) about five thousand.

John 1:39b ὥρα ἦν ὡς δεκάτη.
The hour was about the tenth.

d. *Various other Uses in context that include* **Purpose**, **Substantiation**, **Indirect Address**, *and the formation of* **Noun Clauses**, *in additional to others. Thus,* ὡς *can be found in contexts such that its uses approximate that of* ὅτι. *Consult BDAG or Louw-Nida for a list and description.*

2. Καθώς has the same meanings as ὡς, but is not used for estimation.

Mark 16:7 ἐκεῖ αὐτὸν ὄψεσθε, καθὼς εἶπεν ὑμῖν.
You will see him there, just as he told you.

Luke 17:26 καὶ καθὼς ἐγένετο ἐν ταῖς ἡμέραις Νῶε, οὕτως ἔσται καὶ ἐν ταῖς ἡμέραις τοῦ υἱοῦ τοῦ ἀνθρώπου·
Even just as it was in the days of Noah, thus it will be in the days of the Son of Man.

3. Ὅτε describes a time *when*.

Luke 22:14 Καὶ ὅτε ἐγένετο ἡ ὥρα, ἀνέπεσεν καὶ οἱ ἀπόστολοι σὺν αὐτῷ.
And when the hour came, the apostles also reclined with him.

Rev 12:13a Καὶ ὅτε εἶδεν ὁ δράκων ὅτι ἐβλήθη εἰς τὴν γῆν, ἐδίωξεν τὴν γυναῖκα.
And when the dragon saw that it was cast into the earth, it persecuted the woman.

4. Ὅπου describes a location *where*.

John 1:28 ταῦτα ἐγένετο πέραν τοῦ Ἰορδάνου, ὅπου ἦν ὁ Ἰωάννης.
These things happened near the Jordan, where John was.

Matt 26:57b ...ὅπου οἱ γραμματεῖς καὶ οἱ πρεσβύτεροι συνήχθησαν.
...where the scribes and the elders were gathered.

16.3 SINGULAR VERBS WITH NEUTER PLURAL SUBJECTS

The Greek Language at times confounds our English common sense. Here is one example: A neuter plural subject may be used with a 3rd singular verb (Wallace 399-400).

Luke 11:26b γίνεται <u>τὰ ἔσχατα</u>. . . .χείρονα τῶν πρώτων.
  The <u>last things</u> become...worse than the first things.

John 1:3a <u>πάντα</u> δι' αὐτοῦ ἐγένετο.
  <u>All things</u> were made through him.

This phenomenon seldom occurs when neuter plural nouns refer to human beings:

Matt 25:32a συναχθήσονται ἔμπροσθεν αὐτοῦ <u>πάντα τὰ ἔθνη</u>,
  <u>All the nations</u> were gathered before him,

16.4 SEMANTIC DIAGRAMMING: INTRODUCTION AND PROCEDURES

A. **More Diagramming?!** Thus far you have been shown how to do Constituent Marking that helps navigate a Greek Sentence (§4.7) as well as the Reed-Kellogg Sentence Diagramming Method. From this point on, I heartily recommend using the Semantic Diagramming Method, which corresponds to approaches used elsewhere.[1] Some interpreters describe such an approach (or something very similar) as "block diagramming." I allow students to adjust, modify, enhance semantic diagramming to suite their needs as long as certain essential parameters are preserved. The reason for this flexibility is that students learn differently! Some love to add color-coding; others not. Some are more visual and love to add arrows and lines, etc., while other students do not like this. Some perform this work by hand, others using computer, or creating an Excel Spreadsheet. So, enjoy!

B. **Definition of Semantic Diagramming and Analysis:**

1. <u>Semantic Diagramming</u>. The word *semantic* concerns the notion of *meaning*; hence, this method has as its goal the clarification of the meaning of the sentence components in relation to each other within the context of surrounding sentences. *Semantic Diagramming involves aligning and layering each constituent or element of the Greek sentence in order to show the basic inner relations of these constituents or elements.* **Semantic Diagramming attempts to answer these two essential questions:**

---

[1] The approach here is very similar to that found in George H. Guthrie and J. Scott Duvall, *Biblical Greek Exegesis* (Grand Rapids: Zondervan, 1998). Compare also the "Structural Analysis" of Gordon D. Fee, *New Testament Exegesis: A Handbook for Students and Pastors*, 3rd ed. (Louisville: Westminster John Knox, 2002 [1st ed. 1983]).

a. What are the main constituents or elements in the clause, such as conjunctions, subject, verb, compliments, modifiers?

b. And, what modifies each element in the clause?

A basic premise of semantic diagramming is to preserve the original Greek sentence order as much as possible, which differs drastically from the Reed-Kellogg Sentence Diagramming Method. Semantic Diagramming is the first step in a more comprehensive process of observation and analysis.

2. <u>Semantic Analysis</u>. Semantic diagramming should be followed by detailed semantic analysis (see §16.5 below). *Semantic Analysis entails the observation and analysis of the semantic relationships within and between sentences and their elements using grammatical and linguistic categories of meaning, many of which incidentally are familiar to the average person (active, passive, comparison, contrast, cause-effect, climax, purpose, etc.).* **Semantic analysis attempts to answer these two questions:**

a. How do sentence elements modify each other?

b. And how do clauses and their elements relate to the surrounding clauses and their elements?

During Semantic Analysis, you can make any or all observations possible, identify key words for word study, and ask questions needing more research for interpretation. Based upon the combined Semantic Diagramming and Analysis, often times an expository sermon or teaching outline will become readily apparent.

C. Foundational Concepts to Perform Semantic Diagramming:

1. <u>Slot Zones, Aligning, and Layering Greek Sentence Elements</u>. One of the first conceptual landmarks of Semantic Diagramming is the concept of Zones as Slots within which to place and align the appropriate sentence elements. The basic zones from left to right are: verse reference numbers, initial coordinating conjunction, subject, main verb, and verbal complements (including predicate nominatives). These elements may or may not be expressed. If they are not expressed, the elements may be represented as null (ø). For example, the subject is often implied in the verbal ending; the verb may itself be implied from the context (see §9.4 ELLIPSIS: SUPPLYING AN IMPLIED WORD). These slots are arranged as vertical zones, preserving word order by layering elements horizontally (with a hard return in a word processor). So, students will be expected to align and layer the sentence elements into perceivable *zones* and *relative positions* while preserving sentence word order.

2. <u>Basic Sentence Components and Zones Slots</u>. You begin with aligning into zones or slots the basic sentence parts, which include initial coordinating conjunction, subject, main verb, object compliments.

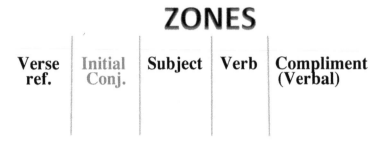

ZONES

Verse ref.	Initial Conj.	Subject	Verb	Compliment (Verbal)

Two further points can be made here. First, it may be advantageous to layer sentence elements in order to provide room to note observations, questions, and other interpretive comments to the right within brackets [...].

ZONES Layered with Comments

Verse ref.	Initial Conj.	Subject	Verb	Compliment
John 3:16	For [*substantiation of 3:17*]			
		God [*divine subject*]		
			loved [*simple past; affective sense?*]	
				the world

Second, the content of speech, thought, or feeling in direct or indirect statements is placed in the verbal complement zone. Consider the equivalence of these two sentences, which are placed in zones as follows (no verse reference is needed).

And	Jesus	said	something
And	Jesus	said,	"We [NOTE: Relative Zones] are going ---to Jerusalem"

The second sentence entails direct discourse ("We are going to Jerusalem"), which is placed within the verbal complement zones. It is equivalent in slot function to "something" from the first sentence. Notice, too, that "---to Jerusalem" (indicating destination) is a modifier (see immediately below) and so is layered under the verb "are going" and indented three spaces (---). This direct discourse shows relative zones for each clause. In these examples, you first have the main clause ("And Jesus said *something*") and then the subordinate clause of direct discourse ("We are going to Jerusalem"). See further examples below.

3. <u>Modifiers</u>. Then you continue by layering/placing any modifiers (such as indirect object, adverbs, adjectives, prepositional phrases, and subordinate clauses) into relative positions under or above the sentence elements they modify. The modifiers are indented three spaces from the start of the element, which may be indicated by three dashes (---) and helps to set them apart. Students may improvise here, adding lines, arrows, or other markings to help set off and demarcate modifiers. Decisions must be made about what modifies what–does a preposition modify the verb or a noun? If you are ever uncertain, leave a question mark in the Semantic Diagram and a note. Here is a hypothetical diagram.

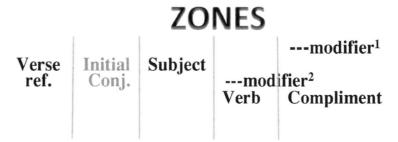

Notice that the diagram became more complex. In this depiction there are two modifiers, one adjectival and the other adverbial. The first one from top down is placed on top of the verbal Compliment. Why? Because it occurred first in the sentence. The hypothetical sentence would have read like this: Verse reference, (discontinuous) modifier[1], initial conjunction, subject, modifier[2], verb, object compliment. One can always see the sentence word order from top to bottom and left to right. The second modifier is adverbial, since it is aligned on top of the verb. Notice that it extends into the next zone. This intrusion is incidental, and depends on how wide one makes the zones. For some students, this extension into another zone is intolerable; so they will widen their zones in order to try to keep modifiers within the boundaries of their zone. This is fine (good luck!). There is flexibility here. The point, however, is to understand what are the main sentence elements (initial conjunction, subject, verb, object complement) and what are modifiers, and what each modifier modifies. Below is depicted the zones with modifiers that receive comments.

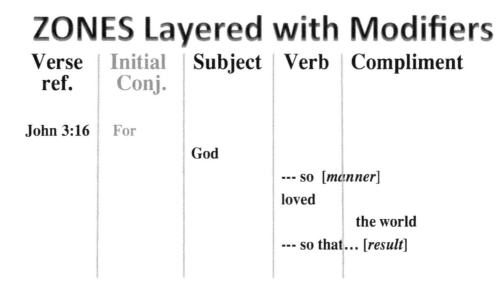

4. Types of Modifiers.

   a. *General Classifications.* It may be helpful to reflect on what types of modifiers Greek regularly deploys. These can be broadly categorized as adjectival (nouns and substantives), adverbial (verbs and adverbs), and sentential (sentences and discourse).

ADJECTIVAL Modifiers of Nouns and Substantives	ADVERBIAL Modifiers of Verbs and Adverbs	SENTENTIAL Modifiers of Sentences & Discourse

o article
o attributive adjective and equivalent
o any type of pronoun, but especially these types:
  ▪ genitive
  ▪ possessive
  ▪ demonstrative
  ▪ relative (begins clause)
o genitive noun
o prepositional phrase
o appositional phrase
o vocatives
	o adverbs
	o indirect object
	o prepositional phrase
	o adverbial uses of the noun cases–genitive, accusative, dative (e.g. dative of means)
	o subordinate clauses, including these types:
	  ▪ conjunctive
	  ▪ adverbial participle (including genitive absolute)
	  ▪ infinitive constructions
		o conjunctions
		o interjections
		o vocatives

   b. *Specific Discussions.*

      i. **Substantives.** It should be reminded that many types of modifiers may function as substantives (if so marked by the article), and thus like subjects and compliments. So, an adjective may function as a substantive, and be the subject of the clause.

      ii. **Articles.** Technically the article is a modifier, and could be diagrammed as such (layered and indented). I tend to keep the article with its substantive for simplicity's sake. But, you may want to align articles as modifiers under what they qualify, but this makes the semantic diagram more complex.

      iii. **Sentence Level Modifiers.** Sentential level modifiers are sometimes difficult to diagram. Some **interjections** (like ἰδού) may function to introduce the whole sentence, and may be well-placed in the initial conjunction zone. Also, **vocatives** give prominence to what follows in the clause. In such cases, I recommend treating the voca-tive like an initial conjunction. However, sometimes vocatives will have an explicit referential relationship to a sentence element (like the subject or an implied subject) while also supplying critical information about the (perception of) identity of the persons so specified. In such cases, the vocative is probably better diagrammed as an appositional modifier. For example, consider the proximity of the vocative to its logical referent in 2 Cor 6:11. In such a case, I recommend treating the vocative as modifying the substantive appositionally (=) and diagrammed like this:

2 Cor 6:11 Τὸ στόμα ἡμῶν ἀνέῳγεν πρὸς ὑμᾶς, <u>Κορίνθιοι</u>, ἡ καρδία ἡμῶν πεπλάτυνται·

Our mouth has been opened to you, <u>Corinthians</u>; our heart has been expanded.

2 Cor 6:11 Τὸ στόμα
     ---ἡμῶν
         ἀνέῳγεν
         ---πρὸς ὑμᾶς,
               =--<u>Κορίνθιοι</u>,
    ἡ καρδία
      ---ἡμῶν
        πεπλάτυνται·

5. <u>Subordinate Clauses and "Relative" Zone Slots</u>. Because of the complexity added by the presence of subordinate clauses, they receive special treatment here. Indeed, the same zone slots apply in the formation of subordinate clauses–but the slot zones begin at the point of modification of which the subordinate clause initiates. For adverbial modifiers that begin with conjunctions, the zone slots begin with the conjunction and are relative to the location of the subordinating conjunction. Relative zoning, however, is more complex for relative pronouns that modify a noun, since the relative pronoun will be aligned under this noun three spaces over; then from this position, the subordinate clause will build around it with its own "relative" zones. This can get tricky.

CHECK POINT 16.4

In English in the space given below, make a layered Semantic Diagram of John 3:16 and 3:17. Watch for subordinate clauses. Check your work with the Suggested Answer provided further below.

3:16 For God loved the world in this way, that He gave His unique Son, in order that the one who believes in Him would not perish, but would have eternal life.

Ref.	Conj.	Subj.	Verb	Complement Zone
3:16				

3:17 For God did not send the Son into the world in order to judge the world, but in order that the world would be saved through Him.

Ref.	Conj.	Subj.	Verb	Complement Zone
3:17				

SUGGESTED ANSWER

Subordinate clauses are shown in grey highlighting; in 3:16 there are three layers of grey shading which reflect three layers of subordinate clauses. Remember that within subordinate clauses, the zones are relative beginning where the clause begins to be diagrammed. Implied elements are placed within brackets […], italicized, and diagrammed. To the right, observations are placed within brackets. John 3:17 has more extensive comments.

Ref.	Conj.	Subj.	Verb	Complement Zone
3:17	For			
		God	loved	
				the world,
			---in this way	

Subordinate Clause I   --- that [*conjunction of result; relative zones begin*]

         He

          gave

              --- His

              --- unique

            Son,

Subordinate Clause II   --- in order that [*conjunction of purpose*]

            the one [*qualified by believing*]

Subordinate Clause III   --- who believes in Him

Subordinate Clause II (Continued)   would

              --- not [*DENIAL*]

            perish,

     --- but [*in order that*]   [*CONTRAST*]

         [*the one*] would have ---eternal

         [*AFFIRMATION*] life.

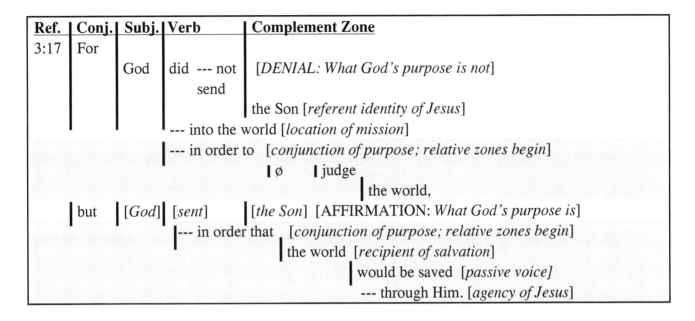

6. Examples from Matt 18:23 and Rom 3:21-23. Now I'll demonstrate these principles in Greek with Matt 18:23 and then the more complex Rom 3:21-23. Each clause will be semantically diagrammed with relative zones, alignment marks (three dashes), comments, and notes. A vertical stroke (|) will separate individual sentence zones and also the relative zones inside subordinate clauses. **Warning**: This diagramming may look more difficult than it actually is; so hang in there! Here are the Greek and English translations of Matt 18:23 and Rom 3:21-23:

Matt 18:23 Διὰ τοῦτο ὡμοιώθη ἡ βασιλεία τῶν οὐρανῶν ἀνθρώπῳ βασιλεῖ,
On account of this, the kingdom of the heavens is likened to a person, a king,

ὃς ἠθέλησεν συνᾶραι λόγον μετὰ τῶν δούλων αὐτοῦ.
who wanted to settle a matter with his servants.

Reference | Conj. Zone | Subj. Zone | Verb Zone | Complement Zone

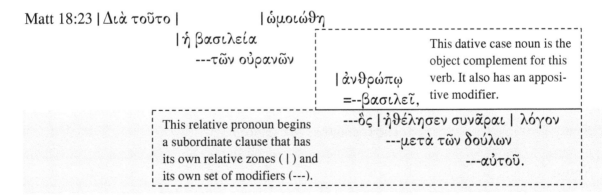

The sentence begins with the prepositional phrase Διὰ τοῦτο that functions like a conjunction, and is thus placed within the conjunction zone. Also, the relative pronoun clause includes a verb

that takes an infinitive to complete its verbal contribution (covered in CH.23). Please read the text boxes explaining some other important matters. The next step involves aligning modifiers three spaces from the beginning of the word they modify. Romans 3:21-23 is an enlarged example and contains participles (covered in CHS.17-19).

Rom 3:21 Νυνὶ δὲ χωρὶς νόμου δικαιοσύνη θεοῦ πεφανέρωται μαρτυρουμένη ὑπὸ τοῦ νόμου καὶ τῶν προφητῶν, ²² δικαιοσύνη δὲ θεοῦ διὰ πίστεως Ἰησοῦ Χριστοῦ εἰς πάντας τοὺς πιστεύοντας. οὐ γάρ ἐστιν διαστολή, ²³ πάντες γὰρ ἥμαρτον καὶ ὑστεροῦνται τῆς δόξης τοῦ θεοῦ

Rom 3:21 *But now apart from the Law God's righteousness/justice has been manifested, although being testified by the Law and the Prophets,* ²² *moreover God's justice through the faithfulness of Jesus Christ for all those that believe; for there is no distinction;* ²³ *for all sinned and are falling short of the glory of God,*

```
Reference | Conj. | Subj. Zone  | Verb Zone        | Complement Zone
          | Zone |
Rom 3:21                          --- Νυνὶ
          | δὲ                    --- χωρὶς νόμου
                   |δικαιοσύνη
                     --- θεοῦ     |πεφανέρωται
                                   --- μαρτυρουμένη  [an adverbial participle; see ch.17]
                                       --- ὑπὸ τοῦ νόμου
                                                καὶ
                                                τῶν προφητῶν,
22                 |δικαιοσύνη
          | δὲ --- θεοῦ           | ø [=has been manifested]
                                   --- διὰ πίστεως
                                       --- Ἰησοῦ
                                           =-- Χριστοῦ
                                   --- εἰς --- πάντας
                                             τοὺς πιστεύοντας.
                                   --- οὐ
          |γάρ |[there]           |ἐστιν            |διαστολή,
23                 |πάντες
          |γὰρ                    |ἥμαρτον
                                     καὶ
                                   |ὑστεροῦνται  |τῆς δόξης
                                                  — τοῦ θεοῦ
```

Notes:

o When the coordinating conjunction καί is not clause initial, but connects two sentence elements, the καί is indented and placed between what it is coordinating, as, for example, with the καί within the prepositional phrase in 3:21 (ὑπὸ τοῦ νόμου καὶ τῶν προφητῶν) and connecting the verbs 3:23 (ἥμαρτον καὶ ὑστεροῦνται).

o In 3:22 the verb is elliptical (null ø), and may be reconstructed within brackets in English ([= *has been manifested*]).

o In 3:22, the adjective πάντας modifies τοὺς πιστεύοντας *those that believe.*

o In 3:23, the verb ὑστεροῦνται takes the genitive for its object complement.

7. Video Examples. Here are some video links to watch my creation of Semantic Diagrams (SD) with some Semantic Analysis (SA) in English and Greek biblical texts. You will notice development and flexibility of performing SD and SA.

SD English of Eph 2:17-18 http://screencast.com/t/807eNGAtPh4

SD Greek of Eph 2:17-18 http://screencast.com/t/K9caI94KcmM1

SD Greek and English Part 1 of Eph 2:19-22 http://screencast.com/t/pzcAnfb7U

SD Greek and English Part 2 of Eph 2:19-22 http://screencast.com/t/0F6HReZgOBIA

SD Greek and English Part 3 of Eph 2:19-22 http://screencast.com/t/sNiwtqyONuF0

16.5 SEMANTIC ANALYSIS: MAJOR LINGUISTIC CATEGORIES OF MEANING

A. **Analysis of Sentence Elements and Their Modification:** Detailed Semantic Analysis attempts to analyze modifying relations within and between clauses and ponder what meaning they have. The scale of observation is at the phrase and clause level, but also may include patterns, structures, and themes of the surrounding verses. Such analysis may involve *identifying significant words* for a detailed word study (for directions how, see Ch.27). You may also ponder the *significance of various aspects of Greek grammar.* You may also consider raising *interpretive questions.* Before I work through an example from Rom 5:10-11 showing Semantic Diagramming and Analysis, we must discuss linguistic categories that will aid our analysis of the Greek grammar and the logic of any particular passage.

B. **Categories of Relationships:** In the field of linguistics significant advances have been made cataloguing and categorizing types of foundational and of modifying relationships. Below I will present some of these as they have been summarized in several books treating biblical interpretation. You will notice some overlap in categories as well as differences in nomenclature.

1. Major Structural Relationships (MSRs).[2] Robert A. Traina in *Methodical Bible Study* has described universal patterns of relating ideas in order to convey meaning in communication.[3] These structural relations operate between phrases and clauses, sentences and paragraphs, and paragraphs and whole books. Below are descriptions as have been further de-

---

[2] For a discussion of the history of structural relationships within the Inductive Bible study movement, see Fredrick J. Long, "Major Structural Relationships: A Survey of Origins, Development, Classifications, and Assessment," *The Journal of Inductive Biblical Studies* 1 (2014): 22-58.

[3] Robert A. Traina, *Methodical Bible Study* (New York: Biblical Seminary in New York, 1952; repr. Grand Rapids: Zondervan, 2001).

veloped by one of Traina's students David R. Bauer at Asbury Theological Seminary. Together, Bauer and Traina have written a comprehensive update that discusses inductive biblical studies and how to make observations, which include the following:[4]

a. **Introduction**—the giving of necessary background information which prepares the reader for the material which follows; e.g. Luke 1:1-4

b. **Interrogation or Problem/Solution**—The movement from a problem to its solution or a question and its answer; e.g. 1 Cor 7:1

c. **Comparison**—the process of showing how two or more items/ideas/people are alike; key words: *like, as*

d. **Contrast**—the process of showing how two or more items/ideas/people are different; key words: *but, however*

e. **Climax**—the movement from lower to higher intensity within a passage/book with focus on the highest or greatest point being realized; e.g. the Gospels and the crucifixion.

f. **Pivot *or* Cruciality**—a movement of events or ideas to an crucial point on which the subject matter moves in another unexpected direction

g. **Particularization**—the movement from general idea(s) to particular ideas. Usually one may detect a general statement which is then particularized. See Rev 1:1.

h. **Generalization**—the movement from particular ideas to a general statement or broad topic. See Heb 13:22. It is the converse to particularization.

i. **Recurrence**—the repetition of the same terms, phrases, clauses, or themes; repetition of word family; e.g. "joy/rejoice" in Philippians.

j. **Summarization**—the conclusion to some discussion by way of reiterating specific elements or themes; e.g. Matt 28:18-20 (Make disciples of all nations, baptizing, commanding)

k. **Causation**—the move from cause to effect, from action to the result(s) produced from that action; e.g. Rom 12:1; Key words: *Therefore, Thus, Consequently.*

l. **Substantiation**—the move from effect to cause or basis, from the result produced to the source/action; from the conclusion to the basis or rationale of an argument; e.g. Rom 1:16. It is the converse to causation. Key terms: *For, because, since.*

m. **Instrumentality**—a description of the means by which an end or goal is achieved; or, the specification of an end or goal; e.g. Matt 5:17; Key terms: *in order that, so that.*

2. Four Supporting Major Structural Relationships. These patterns help convey MSRs.

a. **Inclusion**—beginning and ending a unit with the same words or ideas; this "brackets" the section and may help to convey key topics of the passage or an entire book; e.g. Mark's Gospel and heavens "torn apart"—Mark 1:10; 15:38.

---

[4] David R. Bauer and Robert A. Traina, *Inductive Bible Study: A Comprehensive Guide to the Practice of Hermeneutics* (Grand Rapids: Baker Academic, 2011).

b. **Chiasm**—discussing topics A...B...C and then continuing to discuss the same topics but by inverting their order C...B...A; so you have ABC-CBA; e.g. Mark 2:27 "The <u>Sabbath</u> was made for <u>humans</u>, not <u>humans</u> for the <u>Sabbath</u>"

c. **Alternation**—going "back and forth" between material: ABABABAB; this is a good way to compare or contrast two ideas; e.g. 1 Cor 14:1-5.

d. **Intercalation**—the insertion of seemingly unrelated material (B) in the midst of a larger narrative or argument (A); thus, A-B-A; e.g. the cleansing of the temple in Mark 11:15-18 surrounded by Jesus' cursing of the fig tree surrounding it in Mark 11:12-14 and Mark 11:19-21.

3. <u>Types of Clause Relationships</u>. Remember that clauses are groups of words that contain a verb. These lists of subordinate and coordinating clause relations have been adapted from Grant Osborn.[5]

a. <u>Subordinate Clauses</u>	b. <u>Coordinating Clauses</u>
Temporal (time connection)	**Contrast**
Cause	**Progression**
Concessive (*although*…)	**Series** or **List**
Conditional (*if*…)	**Comparison**
Result	**General to Particular**
Relative (*who, in which*…)	**Particular to General**
Purpose	**Expansion** or **Elaboration**
Manner	**Question-Answer**
Instrumental or **Means**	**Problem-Solution**
Ground or **Substantiation**	
Location	
Attendant Circumstance (i.e., happening concurrently)	

4. <u>Phrase and Miscellaneous Modifying Relationships</u>. Remember that phrases are smaller grouping of words that have no verb. This list is slightly adapted from David A. Black.[6]

a. **Location**; <u>key word(s):</u> *in, out, at, into*, etc.

b. **Temporal**; <u>key word(s):</u> *at, before, during*, etc.

c. **Direction**; <u>key word(s):</u> *towards, away*, etc.

d. **Purpose**; <u>key words:</u> *for*

e. **Beneficiary**; <u>key word(s):</u> *on behalf of, for, to*

f. **Reference**; <u>key word(s):</u> *concerning, with reference to*

g. **Instrumental** or **Means**; <u>key word(s):</u> *by, through, in, with*

h. **Agency**; <u>key word(s):</u> *through, by*

---

[5] Grant Osborn, *The Hermeneutical Spiral* (Downers Grove, IL: InterVarsity Press, 1997), 31-35.

[6] David A. Black, *Linguistics for Students of New Testament Greek*, 2nd ed. (Grand Rapids: Baker, 1995), 111-12.

i. **Cause**; key word(s): *because of, on account of*

j. **Origin** or **Source**; key word(s): *from, out of*

k. **Manner**; describes *how*

l. **Association**; key word: *with*

m. **Substitution**; key word: *in place of, instead of*

n. **Comparison**; key words: *in accordance with, according to*

5. Argument vs. Adjunct Roles. One may be more precise while considering semantic function of sentence elements *by distinguishing between elements that are* **required** *and elements that are* **auxiliary**. The choice of the main verb, around which sentences are constructed, will require or imply certain sentence elements to be present to have proper sense. In the sci-ence of linguistics, such required elements are called "arguments." *Arguments* are to be distinguished from "adjuncts," which instead are not strictly needed for the sentence to make sense; in other words, adjuncts are completely optional. The distinction between ar-guments and adjuncts delimits what semantic roles are possibly in play in any given sen-tence. Sentence elements that are arguments (i.e. integral and necessary for the verb used) will typically have one of these roles. Paul R. Kroeger provides this "Inventory of Seman-tic Roles":[7]

AGENT: causer or initiator of events

EXPERIENCER: animate entity which perceives a stimulus or registers a particular mental or emotional process or state

RECIPIENT: animate entity which receives or acquires something

BENEFICIARY: entity (usually animate) for whose benefit an action is performed

INSTRUMENT: inanimate entity used by an agent to perform some action

THEME: entity which undergoes a change of location or possession, or whose location is being specified

PATIENT: entity which is acted upon, affected, or created; or of which a state or change of state is predicated

STIMULUS: object of perception, cognition, or emotion; entity which is seen, heard, known, remembered, loved, hated, etc.

LOCATION: spatial reference point of the event (the source, goal, and path roles are often considered to be sub-types of location)

SOURCE: the origin or beginning point of a motion

GOAL: the destination or end-point of a motion

PATH: the trajectory or pathway of a motion

ACCOMPANIMENT (or COMITATIVE): entity which accompanies or is associated with the performance of an action

---

[7] As summarized by Paul R. Kroeger, *Analyzing Grammar: An Introduction*, Cambridge Textbooks in Linguistics (Cambridge: Cambridge University Press, 2005), 54-55.

Additionally, adjunct roles include time, location, manner, purpose, etc.

For example, consider the simplified sentences below adapted from Galatians 2 (yet reflecting accurately the Greek) as told by the Apostle Paul. The verbs are in bold. The arguments are followed by brackets with their functions indicated in ALL CAPS. The underlined constituents are "optional" adjuncts; consider how their inclusion reveal important aspects of Paul's argumentation.

2:11a   *Peter* [AGENT] ***came*** *to Antioch* [LOCATION] .

2:11b   *I* [AGENT] ***opposed*** *Peter* [RECIPIENT] <u>*to his face*</u>.

2:12b   *He* [AGENT] ***used to eat*** *with the Gentiles* [ACCOMPANIMENT].

2:12c   *James* [AGENT] ***came***.

2:12d   *Peter* [AGENT] ***withdrew*** *and* ***separated*** <u>*himself,*</u> <u>*fearing those of the Circumcision*</u> <u>*group*</u>.

2:13a   *The rest* [AGENT] <u>*of the Jews*</u> ***joined*** *him* [ACCOMPANIMENT] <u>*in hypocrisy.*</u>

2:13b   *Even Barnabas* [AGENT] ***was carried away*** *by their hypocrisy* [INSTRUMENT].

2:14a   *I* [AGENT] ***saw*** *that they* [AGENT] ***were*** *not* ***progressing*** *toward the truth of the Gospel* [GOAL].

2:14b   *I* [AGENT] ***spoke*** *to Cephas* [RECIPIENT] <u>*in the presence of all*</u>....

A consideration of the adjuncts would indicate that Paul was augmenting his own courage (confronting Peter <u>to his face</u> and <u>in the presence of all</u>), while at the same time showing Peter's separating <u>himself,</u> because of <u>fearing those of the Circumcision group</u> which further affected <u>the Jews</u> present who were led astray <u>in hypocrisy</u>.

C. **Using Paper or Computer to Make Observations:** Semantic diagramming should be accompanied with semantic analysis. If you have done the diagramming in a word processor, I recommend printing it out and then writing out your analysis on it. Alternatively, one can embed interpretive questions and observations within a word processor, but it can be time-consuming to draw arrows, use color, etc.; but I have observed some magnificent computer-created analyses. Types of observations to make during this analysis include:

1. particular modifying expressions and the meaning they have;
2. larger structural observations spanning several verses;
3. significant words or themes for further word study;
4. significant points of Greek grammar to be studied and pondered;
5. interpretive questions that should be answered to better understand the passage; or
6. other observations that may contribute to one's understanding of the passage;
7. conclude by summarizing the most significant observations and questions.

D. Example of Detailed Semantic Analysis of Gal 2:19:

1. Text and Translation.

2:19 ἐγὼ γὰρ διὰ νόμου νόμῳ ἀπέθανον, ἵνα θεῷ ζήσω. Χριστῷ συνεσταύρωμαι·

2:19 *For I died through the law to the law, in order that I would live for God. I have been crucified with Christ.*

2. Semantic Diagram.

Ref.	Conj.	Subj.	Verb	Complement
2:19		ἐγὼ		
	γὰρ			
			---διὰ νόμου	
			---νόμῳ	
			ἀπέθανον,	
			⊢--- ἵνα [NOTE: begins relative zones with a subordinating conj.]	
			---θεῷ	
			∣ø ∣ζήσω.	
	ø			
				Χριστῷ
		ø	συνεσταύρωμαι·	

3. Semantic Diagram with *Analysis*.

Ref.	Conj.	Subj.	Verb	Complement
2:19		ἐγὼ	[emphatic pronoun usage, stressing Paul as agent and example]	
	γὰρ		[support for claim in 2:18b that Paul's repentance proves him a sinner]	
			---διὰ νόμου [intermediate agency; How? Paul admits the law is right about universal sin? see Rom 3:1-19]	
			---νόμῳ [dative of reference; νόμου νόμῳ abutted; aural impact]	
			ἀπέθανον, [Aorist tense; perfective aspect complete(d) action]	
			⊢--- ἵνα [purpose subordinate clause (see ch.22)—"dying to the law" is the MEANS for Paul's END, "living to God"]	
			---θεῷ [dative of reference or advantage?]	
			∣ ø ∣ζήσω. [Aorist subjunctive mood verb; see ch.22]	
	ø		[Asyndeton! Why? Emotional highpoint?]	
				Χριστῷ [Object of compound verb with συν-]
		ø	συνεσταύρωμαι· [Perfect tense; resultative! Paul co-identifies with Christ in crucifixion; how???]	

4. <u>Summary Conclusion and Key Questions</u>:
    a. Emphatic use of ἐγώ draws attention to Paul as agent and likely example.
    b. The abutting of forms of νόμος would suggest a focal point, and "law" as an intermediate means to bring about Paul's death (past complete[d] action).
    c. Living for God is the Purpose of Paul's death via the law. How accomplished?
    d. Asyndeton and perfect tense emphasizes Paul's co-crucifixion with Christ.

CHECK POINT 16.5

Given the Greek and English translation of Gal 2:20, provide a semantic diagram with analysis of the Greek text. Conclude with summary conclusion with key questions. Check your work with the Suggested Answer provided below.

2:20 ζῶ δὲ οὐκέτι ἐγώ, ζῇ δὲ ἐν ἐμοὶ Χριστός· ὃ δὲ νῦν ζῶ ἐν σαρκί, ἐν πίστει ζῶ τῇ τοῦ υἱοῦ τοῦ θεοῦ τοῦ ἀγαπήσαντός με καὶ παραδόντος ἑαυτὸν ὑπὲρ ἐμοῦ. [ζῶ (1st sg.) and ζῇ (3rd sg.) from ζάω]

2:20 *Moreover, I myself no longer live; but Christ lives in me. Additionally, that which now I live in the flesh, I live in faithfulness to the Son of God, the one loving me and giving himself on behalf of me.*

Ref.	Conj.	Subj.	Verb	Complement

Summary Conclusion and Key Questions:

SUGGESTED ANSWER

Subordinate clauses (that have relative zones) are placed in gray highlight.

2:20 ζῶ δὲ οὐκέτι ἐγώ, ζῇ δὲ ἐν ἐμοὶ Χριστός· ὃ δὲ νῦν ζῶ ἐν σαρκί, ἐν πίστει ζῶ τῇ τοῦ υἱοῦ τοῦ θεοῦ τοῦ ἀγαπήσαντός με καὶ παραδόντος ἑαυτὸν ὑπὲρ ἐμοῦ. [ζῶ (1st sg.) and ζῇ (3rd sg.) from ζάω]

2:20 *Moreover, I myself no longer live; but Christ lives in me. Additionally, that which now I live in the flesh, I live in faithfulness to the Son of God, the one loving me and giving himself on behalf of me.*

Ref.	Conj.	Subj.	Verb	Complement
2:20			ζῶ	[recurring verb/word; how and why used?]
	δέ	[new development from previous statement]		
			---οὐκέτι	[temporal denial vs. relative past]
		ἐγώ,	[emphatic pronoun use stressing Paul as agent and example]	
			ζῇ	[repeated verb]
	δέ	[contrastive clause with δέ where two elements are contrasted]		
			---ἐν ἐμοὶ	[sphere; mystical union?]
		Χριστός·		
	δέ		ὃ	[object of main & relative clause]
			---νῦν	[contemporaneous vs. past]
			ζῶ	[repeated verb]
			---ἐν σαρκί,	[dative of sphere?]
			---ἐν πίστει	[manner and/or sphere? "faithfulness"?]
			ζῶ	[repeated verb]
			---τῇ	[discontinuous modifier of πίστει]
			---τοῦ υἱοῦ	[objective genitive]
			---τοῦ θεοῦ	["son of God"; imperial title?]
			=--τοῦ ἀγαπήσαντός	[in apposition to son; *cause*]
			μ ε	
			καὶ	
			παραδόντος	[apposition and sacrificial theme]
			ἑαυτὸν	[*effect*]
			---ὑπὲρ ἐμοῦ.	[beneficiary]

Summary Conclusion and Key Questions:

1. Repetition of the verb ζάω "I live"–why? Why is this important in context?
2. How are the prepositional phrases "in flesh" and "in faith(fullness)" related or contrasted? Why are they seemingly contrasted?
3. Implicit contrast between Paul's past and the current "now";

> 4. The identity of the Christ as "Son of God" is stressed by the discontinuous modification as the object of Paul's "faith(fulness)"; also, Son of God is given explicit elaboration through appositional description of what Christ has done (loved and given himself for Paul) which has sacrificial overtones (cf. Eph 5:1-2); is there any implicit contrast to the imperial title of the current Caesar as "son of the deified one" (Latin: *divi filius*)??
> 5. Repetition of Paul as referent; emphatic pronoun (ἐγώ) with the verb ζῶ, the prepositional phrase ἐν ἐμοί, the verb form ζῶ again, and finally Paul signified through the pronouns as the beneficiary (ὑπὲρ ἐμοῦ) of Christ's sacrificial love (με). Why this focus on Paul? How would this help identify Paul as an example or model to follow?

Complete WORKBOOK EXERCISES 16 and consult the ANSWER KEY & GUIDE as needed.

CASE IN POINT 16: THE LOVE COMMAND IN JOHN 13:31-35

The surrounding context of Jesus' command to love in John 13 affords us an opportunity to observe how the subordinate conjunctions presented in this chapter function and may aide our interpretation of a passage. Below are the relevant verses in the NASB95 with these subordinate conjunctions placed in bold. In the Greek text, subordinate clauses are placed in brackets. Preposed sentence elements are underlined.

John 13:31 Therefore **when** he [Judas] had gone out, Jesus said, "<u>Now</u> is the Son of Man glorified, and <u>God</u> is glorified in Him; ³² if <u>God</u> is glorified in Him, <u>God</u> will also glorify Him in Himself, and will glorify Him <u>immediately</u>. ³³ "Little children, I am <u>with you a little while</u> longer. You will seek Me; and **as** I said to the Jews, now I also say <u>to you</u>, '**Where** <u>I</u> am going, <u>you</u> cannot come.' ³⁴ "<u>A new commandment</u> I give to you, that you love one another, **even as** I have loved you, that <u>you</u> also love one another. ³⁵ "<u>By this</u> all men will know that you are <u>My</u> disciples, if you have <u>love</u> for one another."

John 13:31 [Ὅτε οὖν ἐξῆλθεν], λέγει Ἰησοῦς· <u>νῦν ἐδοξάσθη ὁ υἱὸς τοῦ ἀνθρώπου καὶ ὁ</u> <u>θεὸς ἐδοξάσθη ἐν αὐτῷ.</u> ³² [εἰ ὁ θεὸς ἐδοξάσθη ἐν αὐτῷ,] καὶ <u>ὁ θεὸς δοξάσει</u> αὐτὸν ἐν αὐτῷ, καὶ <u>εὐθὺς</u> δοξάσει αὐτόν. ³³ τεκνία, <u>ἔτι μικρὸν μεθ' ὑμῶν εἰμι·</u> ζητήσετέ με, καὶ [¹**καθὼς** εἶπον τοῖς Ἰουδαίοις [²ὅτι [³**ὅπου** <u>ἐγὼ</u> ὑπάγω ³] <u>ὑμεῖς</u> οὐ δύνασθε ἐλθεῖν ²] ¹], καὶ <u>ὑμῖν</u> λέγω ἄρτι. ³⁴ Ἐντολὴν καινὴν δίδωμι ὑμῖν, [¹ ἵνα ἀγαπᾶτε ἀλλήλους, [² **καθὼς** ἠγάπησα ὑμᾶς [³ ἵνα καὶ <u>ὑμεῖς</u> ἀγαπᾶτε ἀλλήλους ³] ²] ¹]. ³⁵ <u>ἐν τούτῳ</u> γνώσονται πάντες ὅτι <u>ἐμοὶ μαθηταί</u> ἐστε, ἐὰν <u>ἀγάπην</u> ἔχητε ἐν ἀλλήλοις.

Notice first the presence of οὖν *therefore*, which marks +continuity and +development from the preceding context: Jesus had predicted Judas' betrayal and Judas has just departed. The ὅτε in

13:31 functions to connect these two events temporally: *When Judas went out* provides a framework for Jesus' statement, *Now the Son of Man is glorified*. How are these two events linked together? Well, Judas' departing to betray Jesus would eventually result in Jesus' death and exaltation, which Jesus considers his glorification. This glorification will place Jesus with God and fulfill his purpose to save those who would believe in Him in the world (see 3:14-17 and ch. 17).

Jesus' glorification necessarily involves his own departure; thus, Jesus in 13:33 turns to prepare his disciples for this departure. He compares his statements to the Jewish leaders in 8:21-22 (when he said "as [καθώς] I said..., Where [ὅπου] I am going, you are not able to come") to what he now speaks the disciples. The comparison with the conjunction καθώς suggests that Jesus is fully aware of what is happening—He remains in control of his fate and knows His destiny (see 13:1-3).

However, Jesus' statement involving his *movement* (ὑπάγω "I depart") to another *location* (note ὅπου); this understandably is very troubling to the disciples. As the discourse unfolds, Jesus qualifies his statement, because he discloses that the disciples will in fact have *a place prepared for them* where Jesus will also be (14:2-3). This matter of Jesus' coming from God in heaven and returning there to the Father is a very important theme in John's Gospel (3:13, 31; 6:33, 38, 41, 50-51, 58; 7:33; 8:14; 8:21; 13:1-3, 36; 14:4-5, 28; 16:5, 10, 17, 28*; 17:24; 18:36).

Finally, Jesus moves quickly to the heart of the matter when he issues the love command in 13:34. This command to love one another is given a particular shape by using καθώς, which is marked +correspondence. This correspondence clause indicates simultaneously the basis of our loving others as well as the example of what that love looks like: We are to love *because* and *just as* Jesus loved us. Furthermore, see that Jesus loved us in order that we would love one another. So, Jesus' love is central to the ethical conduct of believers; this is the hallmark of Jesus' disciples (John 13:35; cf. Matt 5:44-48). The Apostle Paul twice describes Jesus' "loving" and sacrificial "giving himself" as an example for us all to follow (Gal 2:20; Eph 5:1-2).

There are many other significant or marked and emphatic features in these verses. I have listed them here for your further consideration. Most of these we have already encountered thus far:

1. Historic Present λέγει in 13:31.
2. Preposed constituents are underlined.
3. The strategic use of the adverbs νῦν, ἔτι, and ἄρτι.
4. Repetition of δοξάζω verb (5x in 13:31-32)
5. Additive καί in 13:32, 33, 34.
6. Thematic Address: the vocative τεκνία in 13:33.
7. The special use of the Accusative μικρόν for extension of time.
8. Emphatic Subject Pronouns: ἐγὼ in 13:33 and ὑμεῖς in 13:33, and 34.
9. Quantitative emphasis with πάντες in 13:35.
10. Forward Pointing Demonstrative prepositional phrase ἐν τούτῳ in 13:35.
11. Possessive Pronoun ἐμοί (see §19.3 POSSESSIVE PRONOUNS) in 13:35.
12. Final Emphasis (in terms of placement) by locating the supposition (the "if" clause) last in 13:35, which is the most important command of Jesus.

CHAPTER 17

One of my favorite passages to illustrate the value of studying Greek, and participles in particular, is Eph 5:18-21. In context, Paul exhorts his audience to walk wisely, to understand the Lord's will, and to be filled with the Spirit. This last command relates to perennial questions that I have heard, "What does it mean to be filled with the Spirit? How do I know that I am filled with the Spirit?" People need to know. Sadly, our English translations often obscure what Paul communicates here. See the CASE IN POINT at the end of this chapter.

Participles are often described as verbal adjectives. I call them "party-ciples" because they are so fun, interesting, and dynamic. They always attract a crowd. This lesson provides the endings of the **Present Active, Aorist Active, Aorist Passive,** and **Perfect Active Participles,** since they use very similar endings. Lastly, the semantic and pragmatic functions of participles are introduced and discussed along with some translation strategies.

VOCABULARY 17   MORE FIRST DECLENSION NOUNS

First Declension Nouns:

ἡ ἀρχή [55]	beginning; rule, power	ἡ τιμή [41]	honor
ἡ γλῶσσα [50]	language; tongue	ἡ χαρά [59]	joy, delight, gladness
ἡ γραφή [49]	scripture; writing	ἡ χρεία [49]	need
ἡ ἐπαγγελία [52]	promise		
ἡ σοφία [51]	wisdom	Verb often found as a Participle:	
ἡ συναγωγή [56]	gathering; synagogue	ὑπάρχω [60]	I exist
ἡ σωτηρία [46]	salvation		

Negative Adverb for Non-Indicative Moods:

μή [(1038)]   no, not

After learning vocabulary to this point, you will know 74.5% of the words in the GNT. If you are able, listen to audio recordings of VOCABULARY 17 and complete the CROSSWORD PUZZLE in the WORKBOOK EXERCISES.

NOTES ON VOCABULARY 17:

In this vocabulary, several nouns have English cognates: <u>arche</u>-ology, <u>gloss</u>-ary (list of difficult or foreign [language] words) or <u>glos-so</u>-lalia (speaking in tongues/languages), <u>graph</u>-ics, <u>soph</u>-omore (wise fool), synagogue, <u>soteri</u>-ology (doctrine of salvation).

These important nouns have many cognates. For example, σωτήρ *savior, deliverer, preserver* (found 24 times in the GNT) was a common title for military/political rulers, as seen in this silver drachm coin of Menander I Soter (Μένανδρος Α΄ ὁ Σωτήρ) of the Indo-Greek kingdom.[1] He reigned 165-130 BC. In the far east, this Greek king interacted with Buddhist monks and adopted Buddhism. After dying, he was succeeded by his wife Agathokleia. The Obverse (top) reads ΒΑΣΙΛΕΩΣ ΣΩΤΗΡΟΣ ΜΕΝΑΝΔΡΟΥ "of the King Savior Menander." The reverse below has the same but written in Kharosthi script of Sanskrit language; it shows Athena Alkidemos holding a shield and throwing a thunderbolt.

The verb ὑπάρχω *I exist* is often found as a participle; for example, as a substantive participle like τὰ ὑπάρχοντα *the belongings*. Occasionally, the meaning of ὑπάρχω *I exist* or *I am* requires a predicate nominative such as are used with εἰμί and γίνομαι.

Finally, although the negative adverb μή is typically used with non-Indicative moods (e.g. participles, subjunctive mood verbs), occasionally οὐ is used.

17.1 INTRODUCTION TO THE PARTICIPLE (ἡ Μετοχή)

A. **Verbal Adjectives:** Participles are often treated as a Mood alongside the Indicative, Subjunctive, Imperative, Optative and Infinitives (verbal nouns), but technically participles are simply **verbal adjectives**; they are derived from verb stems and use adjective endings. Participles are a dynamic hybrid of form and function.

1. <u>Basic Features of Form</u>. Like verbs, participles have tense, voice, and mood. Like adjectives, participles have gender, case, and number. Thus participles have six parsing characteristics: **tense, voice, mood,** and **gender, case,** and **number**.

2. <u>Basic Features of Function</u>. Broadly speaking, Participles function **adjectivally** and **adverbially**. Participles function **adjectivally**, being found in *the attributive and predicative positions* and being formed into *substantives* (i.e. nouns). For a review of adjectival functions, see §7.3 ADJECTIVAL FUNCTIONS AND CONSTRUCTIONS. Participles are like verbs and

---

[1] Photo by PGHCOM in the public domain is slightly modified. The coin is found at the British Museum.

function **adverbially** by sometimes *taking subjects, object complements, indirect objects,* and *modifiers,* and in *supplementing the verb in complementary and periphrastic constructions*, and in *forming circumstantial clauses*. Importantly, too, participles serve **pragmatic functions** that are discernible depending on the verb chosen and relative location before or after the main or "nuclear verb."

3. <u>Categories of Participial Usage</u>: The following chart summarizes the major participle functions and may be considered a Road Map for this textbook.

CATEGORY	PARTICULAR FUNCTIONS	WHERE TREATED
Adjectival	◆Attributive (modifying noun) ◆Substantive (alone acting as noun) ◆Predicative (predicate position)	§17.3 ADJECTIVAL PARTICIPLES
Circumstantial	◆Segue, Procedure, or Frame (pre-nuclear) ◆Explication of particulars (post-nuclear) ◆Adverbial logical-semantic relations (pre- or post-nuclear, contextually dependent)	§17.4 CIRCUMSTANTIAL PARTICIPLES
Supplementary	◆Periphrastic ◆Complementary	§19.5 PERIPHRASTIC USE OF THE PARTICIPLE §19.6 COMPLEMENTARY USE OF THE PARTICIPLE
Pragmatic	◆Switch Reference Marker (genitive absolute construction)	§20.4 THE GENITIVE CIRCUMSTANTIAL PARTICIPLE (AKA GENITIVE ABSOLUTE)

B. **Frequency of Moods and of Participle Tenses:** Participles are the second most frequently occurring mood in the GNT with 6,667 occurrences. Compare this frequency with approximately 15,773 Indicative Mood verbs, 2294 Infinitives, 1,887 Subjunctives, and 1,685 Imperatives. (Numbers vary a bit depending of the database searched.) As far as the tenses, In the GNT (NA[28]), participles are found primarily in three tenses: Present (3,689 times), Aorist (2,285 times), and Perfect (673 times). Future Tense participles occur only 12 times.

C. **Verbal Aspect is Retained; "Time Frame" is Relative:**

1. <u>No Absolute Time</u>. Participles are unmarked for time; they **show no absolute time**, but are dependent on the time frame of the main clause in context. Citing several authorities, Porter indicates, *"the temporal reference of a participle is established relative to its use in context"* (Porter, 187, emphasis original).

2. <u>Pre- or Post-Nuclear Verb Positions</u>. As will be discussed more below, the position of a participle vis-à-vis the main verb (the nuclear verb) provides one important piece of evidence

(among others) of the significance of and of the relative time of the participle. In general, a participle occurring before the verb is understood "before" it or preceding it, and this may help indicate action occurring **time prior** to the main verb. Conversely, a post-nuclear participle may indicate **time contemporaneous** or **time subsequent** to the main verb (Porter, 188). These generalizations of position are consonant with information processing in the discourse flow.

3. <u>Aspectual Significance Retained</u>. Another piece of evidence is the selective use of one participle tense (say, Perfect) over another (say, Aorist); such a choice has **aspectual significance**. So, one must pay attention to which Greek tense to help determine the significance of and the relative time of the participle.

    a. *Present Tense*. Present Tense participles convey an imperfective aspect (action in progress or incomplete); thus Present Tense participles often convey **action contemporaneous** with the main verb.

    b. *Aorist Tense*. Aorist Tense participles convey a perfective aspect (seen as a whole, complete or completed); thus Aorist Tense participles often describe **action prior** to the main verb.

    c. *Perfect Tense*. Perfect Tense participles convey a stative/resultative aspect (complex action often with resultant effects), which may indicate **action prior to and contemporaneous** with the main verb. However, this resultative aspect may be difficult to render in English without encumbering one's translation.

    d. *Future Tense*. Future Tense participles are rare in the GNT and express expectation, specifically **purpose**.

D. <u>No</u> **Augmentation outside the Indicative Mood, but Reduplication Persists:** Participles are generally treated as a mood. Thus, Aorist Participles will never have an augment. However, the reduplication of the Perfect Tense is **always** found outside the Indicative Mood.

E. **Negation with Mή:** Normally, μή (or forms derived from μή) is used to negate participles; however, οὐ is occasionally found (less than 20 times).

17.2 PARTICIPLE FORMATION

A. **The Basics:** In English, the present participle is simply formed by adding *–ing* to the end of a verb; e.g., *going, walking, teaching.* However, Greek participles are much more complex, because participles have six characteristics: **tense, voice, mood, gender, case,** and **number.** Yet, patterns exist that will help you learn the forms.

1. <u>The active participle endings (with the Aorist Passive) are already familiar to you</u>. The masculine and neuter endings use the Third Declension endings from ἄρχων:

	Masculine		Neuter	
	sg.	pl.	sg.	pl.
nom.	-ων	-οντες	-ον	-οντα
gen.	-οντος	-οντων	-οντος	-οντων
dat.	-οντι	-ουσι(ν)	-οντι	-ουσι(ν)
acc.	-οντα	-οντας	-ον	-οντα

Notice that the neuter forms are identical to the masculine forms except for the nominative and accusative.

The Feminine endings are formed from the First Declension noun endings that are added to a coupling syllable:

Feminine		sg.	pl.
	nom.	-α	-αι
Coupling +	gen.	-ης	-ῶν
Syllable	dat.	-ῃ	-αις
	acc.	-αν	-ας

Both the Masculine/Neuter and the Feminine Participle endings are added to a <u>tense suffix and coupling vowel</u> forming a <u>coupling syllable</u>; the tense suffixes should already be familiar to you, having already learned similar forms for each tense of the Indicative Mood. Thus, this coupling syllable varies according to the tense of the participle. A list of **the genitive singular forms** below allows one to see the coupling syllable (<u>underlined</u>) that is used to form the active participles endings (and the Aorist Passive participle endings).

Genitive Sg. Forms (in order to show coupling syllable)

	MASCULINE	FEMININE	NEUTER
Present:	πιστεύ-<u>οντ</u>-ος	πιστευ-<u>ούσ</u>-ης	πιστεύ-<u>οντ</u>-ος
Aorist:	πιστεύ-<u>σαντ</u>-ος	πιστευ-<u>σάσ</u>-ης	πιστεύ-<u>σαντ</u>-ος
Perfect:	πεπιστευ-<u>κότ</u>-ος	πεπιστευ-<u>κυί</u>-ας	πεπιστευ-<u>κότ</u>-ος
Aorist Passive:	πιστευ-<u>θέντ</u>-ος	πιστευ-<u>θείσ</u>-ης	πιστευ-<u>θέντ</u>-ος

B. **Present Active Participle:** Remember that participles have six characteristics: tense, voice, mood, gender, case, and number. Below is given all three genders of the Present Active Participle for πιστεύω.

sg.	MASCULINE	FEMININE	NEUTER
nom.	πιστεύ-ων*	πιστεύ-ουσ-α	πίστευ-ον*
gen.	πιστεύ-οντ-ος	πιστευ-ούσ-ης	πιστεύ-οντ-ος
dat.	πιστεύ-οντ-ι	πιστευ-ούσ-ῃ	πιστεύ-οντ-ι
acc.	πιστεύ-οντ-α	πιστευ-ουσ-αν	πίστευ-ον*

pl. nom.	πιστεύ-οντ-ες	πιστεύ-ουσ-αι	πιστεύ-οντ-α
gen.	πιστευ-όντ-ων	πιστευ-ουσ-ῶν	πιστευ-όντ-ων
dat.	πιστεύ-ου-σι(ν)*	πιστεύ-ούσ-αις	πιστεύ-ου-σι(ν)*
acc.	πιστεύ-οντ-ας	πιστεύ-ούσ-ας	πιστεύ-οντ-α

Notice: (1) The coupling syllable for the Masculine and Neuter Active Present Tense participle is -οντ-; the exceptions are noted by an asterisk (*). To this syllable are added the Third Declension endings. (2) The coupling syllable for the feminine active Present Tense participle is -ουσ-. The First Declension endings are added to this syllable.

C. **1st Aorist Active Participle:** The Aorist Active Participle uses the exact same endings as above with a different coupling syllables: -σαντ- for the Masculine/Neuter and -σασ- for the Feminine. Each has the familiar –σα of the 1st Aorist Tense forms.

sg.	**MASCULINE**	**FEMININE**	**NEUTER**
nom.	πιστεύ-σας*	πιστεύ-σασ-α	πίστευ-σαν*
gen.	πιστεύ-σαντ-ος	πιστευ-σάσ-ης	πιστεύ-σαντ-ος
dat.	πιστεύ-σαντ-ι	πιστευ-σάσ-ῃ	πιστεύ-σαντ-ι
acc.	πιστεύ-σαντ-α	πιστεύ-σασ-αν	πίστευ-σαν*
pl. nom.	πιστεύ-σαντ-ες	πιστεύ-σασ-αι	πιστεύ-σαντ-α
gen.	πιστευ-σάντ-ων	πιστευ-σάσ-ων	πιστευ-σάντ-ων
dat.	πιστεύ-σα-σι(ν)*	πιστευ-σάσ-αις	πιστεύ-σα-σι(ν)*
acc.	πιστεύ-σαντ-ας	πιστευ-σάσ-ας	πιστεύ-σαντ-α

Notice: The Masculine and Neuter forms with an asterisk (*) break the pattern.

D. **Aorist Passive Participle:** The Aorist Passive Participle uses the exact same endings. However, the masculine and neuter tense suffix is -θέντ- (except for the forms with an asterisk) and the feminine coupling syllable is -θείσ-. These coupling syllables are related to the -θη- of the Aorist Passive Indicative formation.

sg.	**MASCULINE**	**FEMININE**	**NEUTER**
nom.	πιστευ-θείς*	πιστευ-θεῖσ-α	πιστευ-θέν*
gen.	πιστευ-θέντ-ος	πιστευ-θείσ-ης	πιστευ-θέντ-ος
dat.	πιστευ-θέντ-ι	πιστευ-θείσ-ῃ	πιστευ-θέντ-ι
acc.	πιστευ-θέντ-α	πιστευ-θεῖσ-αν	πιστευ-θέν*
pl. nom.	πιστευ-θέντ-ες	πιστευ-θεῖσ-αι	πιστευ-θέντ-α
gen.	πιστευ-θέντ-ων	πιστευ-θεισ-ῶν	πιστευ-θέντ-ων
dat.	πιστευ-θεῖ-σι(ν)*	πιστευ-θείσ-αις	πιστευ-θεῖ-σι(ν)*
acc.	πιστευ-θέντ-ας	πιστευ-θείσ-ας	πιστευ-θέντ-α

E. **Perfect Active Participle:** The Perfect Active Masculine and Neuter Participle has **reduplication** and uses the Perfect Tense indicator κάππα to form -κότ-, that notably **lacks the νῦ** compared to the Present Active Participle coupling syllable (-οντ-). The Feminine forms have -κυί- as a coupling syllable. Distinctive about the Perfect participles is the **retention of the accent** on either the ultima (last syllable) or penult (second to last). Normally, the recessive nature of verb accents would move the accent on the antepenult, if possible (i.e. on the third syllable from the end) (see "I. Verb Accent Rules" in §24 SYNOPSIS OF GREEK ACCENT RULES).

sg.	MASCULINE	FEMININE	NEUTER
nom.	πεπιστευ-κώς*	πεπιστευ-κυῖ-α	πεπιστευ-κός*
gen.	πεπιστευ-κότ-ος	πεπιστευ-κυί-ας	πεπιστευ-κότ-ος
dat.	πεπιστευ-κότ-ι	πεπιστευ-κυί-ᾳ	πεπιστευ-κότ-ι
acc.	πεπιστευ-κότ-α	πεπιστευ-κυῖ-αν	πεπιστευ-κός*
pl.			
nom.	πεπιστευ-κότ-ες	πεπιστευ-κυῖ-αι	πεπιστευ-κότ-α
gen.	πεπιστευ-κότ-ων	πεπιστευ-κυι-ῶν	πεπιστευ-κότ-ων
dat.	πεπιστευ-κό-σι(ν)*	πεπιστευ-κυί-αις	πεπιστευ-κό-σι(ν)*
acc.	πεπιστευ-κότ-ας	πεπιστευ-κυί-ας	πεπιστευ-κότ-α

F. **2nd Aorist Participles:** 2nd Aorist verbs, since they don't take –σα in their Indicative endings, *use the same coupling syllable and endings of the Present Participle.* Of course, the 2nd Aorist stem is changed and remains **unaugmented**. Thus, one needs to review the 2nd Aorist unaugmented changed stem forms given in §11.3, especially learning the very common participle forms made with ειπ- and ιδ-. Here are the 2nd Aorist active participle endings for ἔρχομαι:

sg.	MASCULINE	FEMININE	NEUTER
nom.	ἐλθ-ών	ἐλθ-οῦσ-α	ἐλθ-όν
gen.	ἐλθ-όντ-ος	ἐλθ-ούσ-ης	ἐλθ-όντ-ος
dat.	ἐλθ-όντ-ι	ἐλθ-ούσ-ῃ	ἐλθ-όντ-ι
acc.	ἐλθ-όντα	ἐλθ-οῦσ-αν	ἐλθ-όν
pl.			
nom.	ἐλθ-όντ-ες	ἐλθ-οῦσ-αι	ἐλθ-όντ-α
gen.	ἐλθ-όντ-ων	ἐλθ-ουσ-ῶν	ἐλθ-όντ-ων
dat.	ἐλθ-οῦ-σι(ν)	ἐλθ-ούσ-αις	ἐλθ-οῦ-σι(ν)
acc.	ἐλθ-όντ-ας	ἐλθ-ούσ-ας	ἐλθ-όντ-α

G. **Present Participle of Εἰμί:** Once you have learned the Present Active Participle endings, *you already know the participle forms for εἰμί.* Εἰμί only has the Present Tense Participles.

sg.	**MASCULINE**	**FEMININE**	**NEUTER**
nom.	ὤν	οὖσ-α	ὄν
gen.	ὄντος	οὔσ-ης	ὄντος
dat.	ὄντι	οὔσ-η	ὄντι
acc.	ὄντα	οὖσ-αν	ὄν

pl.			
nom.	ὄντες	οὖσ-αι	ὄντα
gen.	ὄντων	οὐσ-ῶν	ὄντων
dat.	οὖσι(ν)	οὔσ-αις	οὖσι(ν)
acc.	ὄντας	οὔσ-ας	ὄντα

17.3 ADJECTIVAL PARTICIPLES

A. **Introduction:** Already it has been noted that participles are verbal adjectives. *When used as adjectives, participles will **often** have an article.* This article must agree in gender, case, and number with its participle. Thus, when reading the GNT, whenever you come upon a participle that has an article in agreement with it, the participle must be functioning adjectivally. HOW-EVER, the converse is not necessarily true: that if you find a participle that has <u>no</u> article, it is <u>not</u> adjectival. In fact, anarthrous participles may be adjectival, modifying anarthrous substantives. BUT, your initial assessment that anarthrous participles are adverbial *would often be right* (see §17.4 below). Adjectival participles function the same ways as adjectives.

B. **Attributive Use:** Participles, like adjectives, can *modify nouns or substantives.* They give the reader more information about a particular noun (see also Wallace 617-19). Remember that while modifying a noun, participles may take a direct object and other modifiers.

τὴν σωτηρίαν τὴν <u>κηρυχθεῖσαν</u>
the salvation <u>preached</u>
Or, *the salvation <u>that was preached</u>*   [rendered as a relative clause in English]

τὴν <u>κηρυχθεῖσαν</u> σωτηρίαν
the <u>preached</u> salvation   [rendered in literal order; makes some English sense]

ὁ <u>διδάσκων</u> ἀπόστολος
The <u>teaching</u> apostle   [rendered in literal word order, but not good English!]

ὁ ἀπόστολος ὁ <u>διδάσκων</u> τὴν ἐκκλησίαν
The apostle <u>that is teaching</u> the church   [rendered as a relative clause with "that"]

ὁ ἀπόστολος ὁ <u>διδάσκων</u> <u>τοὺς ἄλλους</u> (περὶ τῆς βασιλείας)...
The apostle <u>that is teaching</u> <u>the others</u> (about the kingdom)...

Notice: (1) Participles occur in any case depending on how they are used in the sentence, whether as subject, genitive modifier, indirect object, direct objects, vocatives, etc. (2) Adjectival participles may often be translated by using an English relative pronoun *that* as in the examples above [note that I preserve *who* or *which* for relative pronoun clauses]. (3) In the last example, the participle has an object complement (double-underlined) as well as an adverbial prepositional phrase (…).

C. **Substantive Use:** The participle may function as a substantive or noun. In this usage, the participle stands alone and simply acts like a noun. See Wallace 619-21. A generic noun such as *one, man, woman, thing* is normally helpful to supply for English sense. Consider the following examples:

ὁ διδάσκων τοὺς ἄλλους περὶ τῆς βασιλείας...
*The **one** that is teaching the others about the kingdom...*

τὰ ὑπάρχοντα τῶν μαθητῶν
*the existing **things** of the disciples* (i.e. *the belongings of the disciples*)

Notice again that substantive participles can occur in any case and may have objects and modifiers.

D. **Predicate Use:** Rather rare. See Wallace 618-19 for brief description and some other examples. In the example below, the copula [is] is implied.

Heb 4:12 Ζῶν γὰρ ὁ λόγος τοῦ θεοῦ καὶ ἐνεργὴς... (Ζῶν is from ζάω *I live*)
For the Word of God [is] *living and active...*

E. **The Pragmatic Use of Adjectival Participles:**

1. More Robust Description. When functioning as adjectives, the choice to use a participle results in a more robust and dynamic description as opposed to an adjective or other modifier. Why? Because participles are *verbal* adjectives reflecting verbal aspect and may additionally take necessary objects (called arguments) and optional modifiers (called adjuncts); thus, participles add more complexity in their modification. At the same time, however, participles may be added to restrict the referent, i.e. a restrictive use, to delimit or disambiguate a referent. However, my sense is that a "purely" restrictive use of the attributive participle is not common; the information added is usually descriptive.

2. 1st Attributive Position is Often (not always) Unremarkable and Unmarked. The use of the participle in 1st Attributive Position sandwiched between an article and substantive is not especially marked apart from the modification conveyed by the participle itself, which of-

ten does not contain modifiers, but in fact may. Consider this example that has two 1st Attributive Position participles, the first one with modifiers and the second without.

Luke 3:7 Ἔλεγεν οὖν τοῖς <u>ἐκπορευομένοις</u> ὄχλοις βαπτισθῆναι ὑπ᾽ αὐτοῦ· γεννή-
ματα ἐχιδνῶν, τίς ὑπέδειξεν ὑμῖν φυγεῖν ἀπὸ τῆς <u>μελλούσης</u> ὀργῆς;
Therefore, he was saying to the <u>outcoming</u> crowds to be baptized by him,
"Brood of vipers! Who showed you to flee from the <u>coming</u> wrath!"

Both attributive participles may simply be restrictive (i.e. differentiating one crowd from others or one wrath from another), yet they each contribute to the narrative in quite important ways. The first attributive participle, ἐκπορευομένοις *outcoming*, has a purpose clause (*to be baptized*) attending it, describing not just that the crowds came out to see John, but more than this, that they agreed with his message to the point of being baptized. In Luke's Gospel, the narrator draws attention to persons' response to John as paradigmatic, whether or not they are baptized by him, thus agreeing with him (7:29-30). The second participle μελλούσης *coming* has no modifiers, yet it is attached to the noun ὀργῆς *wrath*, which occurs only again elsewhere in Luke referring to the tragic fall of Jerusalem soon to happen (21:23) that John the Baptist here was foreseeing and foretelling.

Importantly, *it would be wrong to suppose that the 1st Attributive Position is chosen because the participle has no modifiers*. In Eph 2:11, the 1st attributive participle has the modifier in the prepositional phrase with ὑπό. Likewise, the attributive participle in Jas 1:5 has an indirect object and adverbial modifier.

Eph 2:11b ... ποτὲ ὑμεῖς τὰ ἔθνη ἐν σαρκί, οἱ <u>λεγόμενοι</u> ἀκροβυστία ὑπὸ τῆς
<u>λεγομένης</u> περιτομῆς ἐν σαρκὶ χειροποιήτου,
... once you were the gentiles in flesh, the ones <u>being called</u> "uncircumcision"
by the <u>called</u> "circumcision" handmade in the flesh,...

Jas 1:5b ... αἰτείτω παρὰ τοῦ <u>διδόντος</u> θεοῦ <u>πᾶσιν ἁπλῶς</u>...
... let one ask from the <u>giving</u> God <u>to all</u> generously...
Or, *... let one ask from the God <u>giving</u> <u>to all</u> generously...*

Cf. other examples of 1st Attribtuive Position participles with adjunct modifiers at Luke 3:7; 23:48; 1 Pet 5:1; 2 Peter 3:2. What this means is that there is intentionality behind placing participles in the 2nd Attributive Position.

3. <u>2nd Attributive Position Often Creates Elaborative Emphasis</u>. When participles function attributively, and especially in the 2nd Attributive Position, their modification is more marked. For translation into English, it becomes difficult to distinguish whether the participle should be translated with a relative pronoun clause or not, which may be either restrictive or non-restrictive in sense.

Luke 6:8b εἶπεν δὲ τῷ ἀνδρὶ <u>τῷ</u> ξηρὰν <u>ἔχοντι</u> τὴν χεῖρα...

> *Moreover, he said to the man <u>having</u> the withered hand...*
>
> Or, *Moreover, he said to the man <u>who was having</u> the withered hand...*

In such cases, since the participle conveys additional extra information, it could have been written with a relative pronoun clause:

> * εἶπεν δὲ τῷ ἀνδρὶ, ὃς ξηρὰν <u>εἶχεν</u> τὴν χεῖρα, ...
>
> *Moreover, he said to the man, <u>who was having</u> the withered hand,...*

Using the relative pronoun clause reduces similar sounds found in <u>τῷ</u> ἀνδρὶ <u>τῷ</u> ... <u>ἔχοντι</u> and appears to set off the information more than would an adjectival participial modifier. In both cases, the writer has deemed such information important—notice that *withered hand* involves a more marked, discontinuous construction (ξηρὰν ... τὴν χεῖρα) that draws attention to the "witheredness" of the hand since it is preposed before the participle ἔχοντι.

To illustrate the difference between the 1st and 2nd Attributive Position, consider this instance of a participle in the 1st Attributive Position:

John 6:57a ἀπέστειλέν με ὁ <u>ζῶν</u> πατήρ...

> *The <u>living</u> Father sent me....*

The attributive participle ζῶν (from ζάω *I live*) is in the 1st Position. The acclamation of God as "living" reflects the Jewish affirmation of the One True God in distinction to pagan gods and handmade idols, which are not alive or ***living***.[2] But this acclamation of God as *living* could be even more stressed by placing the participle in the 2nd Attributive Position, as such in fact occurs in the two following statements:

Matt 16:16b σὺ εἶ ὁ χριστὸς ὁ υἱὸς τοῦ θεοῦ τοῦ <u>ζῶντος</u>.

> *You are the Christ, the Son of the <u>living</u> God.*

Matt 26:63b καὶ ὁ ἀρχιερεὺς εἶπεν αὐτῷ· ἐξορκίζω σε κατὰ τοῦ θεοῦ τοῦ <u>ζῶντος</u> ἵνα ἡμῖν εἴπῃς εἰ σὺ εἶ ὁ χριστὸς ὁ υἱὸς τοῦ θεοῦ.

> *And the high priest said to him: "I adjure you according to the <u>living</u> God that you tell to us if you yourself are the Messiah, the Son of God."*

---

[2] See, e.g., the apocryphal account of the prophet Daniel in "Bel and the Dragon" (LXX), discussed by Mark Goodwin, *Paul, Apostle of the Living God: Kerygma and Conversion in 2 Corinthians* (Harrisburg, PA: Trinity Press International, 2001). A reading guide for "Bel and the Dragon" is found in the EXERCISE READING for CH.27.

Both statements are in emotionally charged contexts. In the first, Peter is emphatically proclaiming who Jesus is at a climactic point of God's revelation. In the second example, the high priest adjures Jesus in an oath before *the living God* to state clearly whether he is the Messiah or not. For examples of 2nd Attributive participles where the 2nd Attributive Position does not appear motivated due to adjuncts or other modification, but rather for elaborative emphasis, see Matt 10:6; 15:24; Mark 10:30; 16:6; Luke 13:4; John 4:11; 5:35; 6:27, 51; 11:42; Acts 11:22; 24:25; 28:2; 1 Cor 15:37; 2 Cor 1:1, 8; 8:1; and Heb 2:5.

17.4 CIRCUMSTANTIAL PARTICIPLES

A. **Definitions and Semantics:** Robertson rightly says: "the circumstantial participle is an additional statement and does not form an essential part of the verbal notion of the principal verb. The circumstantial participle may be removed and the sentence will not bleed" (1124). Sometimes called "adverbial"—which is a term better reserved to describe the contextually implied logical-semantic relations of a circumstantial participle (see F. below)—the circumstantial use of the participle involves an anarthrous participle modifying the action of a nuclear verb in forming a subordinate clause. *The nature of the modification is constrained by the relative location of the participle to the nuclear verb, as pre-nuclear verb or post-nuclear verb, and the verbal aspect of the participle.* Again, let me repeat, although it is common to describe various adverbial logical-semantic relationships that participles may convey (see F. below), it is critical to understand the following point (BDF 215):

> The logical relation of the circumstantial participle to the rest of the sentence is not expressed by the participle itself (apart from the future participle), but is to be deduced from the context; it can be made clear, however, by the addition of certain particles. Other more extended but more precise constructions are available for the same purpose: prepositional phrases, conditional, causal, temporal clauses, etc., and finally the grammatical co-ordination of two or more verbs.

So, **the circumstantial participle is unmarked regarding logical-semantic relations**; any such sense of the participle must *instead* be deduced from the context.

B. **Rules for Identification of Circumstantial Participle:**

1. <u>Anarthrous.</u> *When used circumstantially, the participle will **never** have an article with it.* Thus, a participle that does not have an article should *initially* be considered as adverbial-circumstantial. Occasionally, however, the biblical context demands that a participle lacking the article is, in fact, acting adjectivally, since it will be discovered to be modifying a

substantive as an adjective would. 74% of participles are anarthrous.[3]

2. <u>Always Nominative Case? No, but very often.</u> In addition to the anarthrous rule above, another rule has been recently proposed: "Adverbial participles will always be nominative, except in genitive absolute constructions or when they modify an infinitive."[4] [Note: these exceptions are covered in subsequent chapters–Genitive Absolutes are covered in §20.4 THE GENITIVE CIRCUMSTANTIAL PARTICIPLE (AKA GENITIVE ABSOLUTE) and infinitives in CHAPTER 23]. However, it is my view that this rule does not quite hold, even though a vast majority of adverbial participles will in fact be nominative (94.4%).[5] For example, consider this counter example involving the dative case.

Matt 8:23 Καὶ <u>ἐμβάντι</u> αὐτῷ εἰς τὸ πλοῖον ἠκολούθησαν αὐτῷ οἱ μαθηταὶ αὐτοῦ.

LITERAL: *And to/with him <u>entering</u> into the boat his disciples followed him.*
Adverbial: *And <u>after</u> he <u>entered</u> into the boat, his disciples followed him.*

In this example, the anarthrous dative case participle is not only pre-verbal, it is sentence initial. It looks like a circumstantial participle and should be understood as one, since the pronominal subject (αὐτῷ) is found again in identical form as the direct object of the main verb (which takes a dative as its object). This adverbial participle frames the disciples' following of Jesus; the three-fold pronominal reference to Jesus keeps the focus clearly on Jesus. This example is not an isolated exception.[6]

3. <u>Additional Contextual Factors.</u> Phyllis M. Healey & Alan Healey have noted other factors that may help students recognize circumstantial participle constructions:[7]

a. they represent whole clauses;
b. they are often lineally separated from the substantive/noun they agree with;

---

[3] Ben Straub, "The Case of Greek Participles: Distinguishing between Adjectival and Adverbial Uses" (Paper, 2010), 1; accessed on Oct 2, 2014 and available online at https://www.academia.edu/3488970/The_Case_of_Greek_Participles_Distinguishing_between_Adjectival_and_Adverbial_Uses.

[4] Martin M. Culy, "The Clue is in the Case: Distinguishing Adjectival and Adverbial Participles," *Perspectives in Religious Studies* 30 (2003): 441–53 at 441.

[5] This number comes from figures from Table 2 in James L. Boyer, "The Classification of Participles: A Statistical Study," *Grace Theological Journal* 5, no. 2 (1984): 163–79. Boyer counted 2881 adverbial participles (not counting genitive absolutes) of which 2719 are found in the nominative case compared to 13 genitive, 29 dative, and 120 accusative case adverbial participles.

[6] See also the review of Culy's work with analysis of the participle in the GNT by Grant G. Edwards, "The Validity of Oblique Adverbial Participles in the Greek of the New Testament" (Th.M., Dallas Theological Seminary, 2007). Accessed Oct 2, 2014 and available online http://place.asburyseminary.edu/trendissertations/5855.

[7] Phyllis M. Healey and Alan Healey, *Greek Circumstantial Participles: Tracking Participants with Participles in the Greek New Testament*, Occasional Papers in Translation and Textlinguistics Vol. 4, No. 3 (Dallas: Summer Institute of Linguistics, 1990), 179-80. This list is slightly altered from Culy's summary ("Clue is in the Case," 441-42 n.3).

    c. they are typically initial in sentences within narratives but late in the sentence in non-narrative materials;

    d. they frequently introduce the setting for what follows;

    e. they sometimes provide "back reference" to connect segments of text; and

    f. they have a semantic relationship to another whole clause or larger unit rather than a single substantive.

Sometimes it is difficult to determine whether we observe a circumstantial or adjectival use. Given Healey & Healey's additional criteria, what would you conclude in this case?

John 11:33a Ἰησοῦς ... εἶδεν <u>αὐτὴν κλαίουσαν</u>.
        Jesus ... saw her <u>(as she was?) weeping</u>.

Since the participle is singular and not representing a whole clause structure (a.), is not separated from its substantive (b.), is sentence final within a narrative (c.), and is connected to a singular substantive (f.), it is best to understand <u>κλαίουσαν</u> as an attributive (adjectival) participle.

C. **Who performs the action of the adverbial-circumstantial participle?** Actually, any person in the sentence can perform a subordinate action using a circumstantial participle: the subject, direct object, indirect object, object of a preposition, genitive modifier, etc. However, 94.4% of the time it is the subject of the main verb who is performing the subordinate action (as in the first example); but rarely the direct object (as in the second example).

Matt 9:36a <u>Ἰδὼν</u> δὲ τοὺς ὄχλους ἐσπλαγχνίσθη περὶ αὐτῶν
        And <u>after seeing</u> the crowds, he had compassion for them.

Matt 9:27a Καὶ παράγοντι ἐκεῖθεν τῷ Ἰησοῦ ἠκολούθησαν [αὐτῷ] δύο τυφλοὶ
        And, <u>as</u> Jesus <u>went along</u> from there, two blind men followed [him]

<u>Notice</u> that the circumstantial participle agrees with its "subject" noun in all respects: gender, case, and number.

D. **Pre-Nuclear Placement:** Circumstantial participles that are pre-nuclear, i.e. placed somewhere before the main verb, are used to subordinate or "background" actions respective to the main verb. Such material may be viewed as having secondary importance (Levinsohn 183-86). However, *pre-nuclear participles often have quite significant interpretive value*. In pre-nuclear locations, circumstantial participles may: 1) mark a transitional segue showing *continuity* with the previous narrative, 2) provide procedurally necessary action prior to the main verb, and 3) frame the action of the main clause with important description that is otherwise unnecessary. In each usage, the inclusion of the circumstantial participle was deemed important.

1. <u>Sentence Initial as a Transitional Segue Marking Continuity</u>. Circumstantial participles that are sentence initial and thus pre-nuclear (i.e. before the main verb) may have the pragmatic function of making a transition while yet maintaining continuity with the situation. Their use contrasts with the use of a temporal conjunction that forms an adverbial clause of time. Levinsohn (188) describes this pragmatic function as follows:[8]

Sentence Initial	signals:
adverbial clause of time	+discontinuity of time
participle	–discontinuity

Below is an example to illustrate the difference.

Mark 1:14-20 *And after John was delivered up* [Μετὰ δὲ τὸ παραδοθῆναι], *Jesus came into Galilee preaching the gospel of God,* [15] *and saying this: "The time has been fulfilled and the kingdom of God has come near; repent and believe in the gospel."* [16] *And <u>while passing along</u>* [Καὶ παράγων] *beside the Sea of Galilee, he saw Simon and Andrew, the brother of Simon, casting a net in the sea, for they were fishermen.* [17] *And Jesus said to them, "Come behind me, and I will make you become fishers of people."* [18] *And immediately <u>after leaving</u>* [καὶ εὐθὺς ἀφέντες] *the nets, they followed him.* [19] *And <u>after going on</u> a little farther* [Καὶ προβὰς ὀλίγον], *he saw Jacob the son of Zebedee and John his brother, and them in the boat readying the nets.* [20] *And straightaway he called them. And <u>after leaving</u>* [καὶ ἀφέντες] *their father Zebedee in the boat with the hired workers, they departed behind him.*[9]

Mark 1:14-20 begins with an adverbial temporal clause (a special infinitive clause not yet covered in this textbook) that works along with the δέ that is marked +discontinuity in the narrative—a scene change occurs with a new development. However, in 1:16, 18, 19, and 20 one observes sentence initial participles with καί, that are marked –discontinuity; in other words, there is **no** discontinuity signalled even though there may be a change of settting (1:16).

Another example is seen in Matt 2:11, which has three pre-nuclear circumstantial participles, with the first providing a segue with continuity from the preceding verses where the Magi are present with King Herod, who then follow the star. The second two

---

[8] Levinsohn explains: "In practice, this means that continuity of situation and other relevant factors between the contiguous nuclear clauses is implied. Thus, while a prenuclear participial clause may present some modification in circumstances, if it begins with the participle the overall continuity of situation and other factors between the foreground events described in the nuclear clauses is preserved" (187). Levionsohn directs students to further examples in Levinsohn, *Textual Connections in Acts* (Atlanta: Scholars Press, 1987), 71-79.

[9] The English translation is from T. Michael W. Halcomb and Fredrick J. Long, *Mark: GlossaHouse Illustrated Greek-English New Testament*, Accessible Greek Resources and Online Studies (Wilmore, KY: GlossaHouse, 2014).

circumstantial, pre-nuclear participles provide procedural actions (*falling down* and *opening…*) in relation to the main verbs (*making obeisance* and *offering gifts*).

Matt 2:11 καὶ <u>ἐλθόντες</u> εἰς τὴν οἰκίαν εἶδον τὸ παιδίον μετὰ Μαρίας τῆς μητρὸς αὐτοῦ, καὶ <u>πεσόντες</u> προσεκύνησαν αὐτῷ καὶ <u>ἀνοίξαντες</u> τοὺς θησαυροὺς αὐτῶν προσήνεγκαν αὐτῷ δῶρα, χρυσὸν καὶ λίβανον καὶ σμύρναν.

And <u>coming</u> into the house [SEGUE], they saw the child with Mary, his mother, and <u>falling down</u> [PROCEDURAL] they made obeisance to him, and <u>opening</u> their treasure chests [PROCEDURAL], they offered gifts to him, gold and frankincense, and myrrh.

2. <u>Procedural Action Prior to the Main Verb</u>. Pre-nuclear participles may sometimes provide subordinate action that is *procedurally necessary or descriptive*. Occasionally, the circumstantial participle may seem completely unnecessary, yet may be following Mediterranean narrative descriptive and/or social conventions. The participle's inclusion has descriptive value that may be worth considering further in context. If the description moves beyond *mere procedure*, then it may provide an important "framework" (see 3.) within which to understand the main action.

Matt 2:8 *And <u>sending</u> [πέμψας] the Magi into Bethlehem, he said: "<u>Going</u> [Πορευθέντες], inquire accurately about the child. And whenever you find out, report it to me, in order that I also, <u>going</u> [ἐλθών], would bow down to him."*

The first pre-nuclear participle πέμψας *sending* provides a descriptive framework (see 3. below) within which to understand Herod's speech to the Magi; there is no segue here, since the Magi are already on stage and Herod has just summoned them. Within the speech of 2:8, however, one observes two procedural pre-nuclear participles. The first is the aorist passive participle Πορευθέντες *going* that describes the necessary prior action required before accurate inquiry can be accomplished. (Compare the same participle form in the Great Commission in Matt 28:19.) The second is ἐλθών *going*, which seems like an unnecessary detail to add. One must consider, however, what the contextual significance of adding such "seemingly unnecessary" description might be. Altogether, each of the pre-nuclear participles contributes to a repetition of movement (*sending* and *going*) to Bethlehem. This stresses the importance of what has occurred there. Additionally, as the narrative continues, readers will learn that Herod's intention of *going* there is in fact not in order to "bow down" (as he said!), but rather to murder the child.

3. <u>Contextual Framing for the Main Verb and Subsequent Event(s)</u>. Beyond providing a segue or a procedural description, *pre-nuclear participles may very well describe a very important context or framework within which the audience is to understand and interpret the*

main verb. Consider these three examples, the first two are simple, but the third provides a much more extreme example of circumstantial participles providing a graphic, important framework within which to understand the healing that occurs (the main clause).

John 9:25b ἓν οἶδα ὅτι τυφλὸς <u>ὢν</u> ἄρτι βλέπω.
One thing I know, that, <u>being</u> blind, now I see!

When questioned by the religious authorities, the once-blind man explains how he can now see. Although *being blind* is secondary to the miraculous subsequent main statement, *now I see!*, the fact of being blind is an important framework within which to understand the miracle. Additionally, one detects a logical-semantic relation of concession (*although I was blind...*; see F. below), which however is not inherently marked in the participle form itself, but is deduced by the context of contrast (blind vs. see) in time (ἄρτι = *now*).

Acts 1:24 καὶ <u>προσευξάμενοι</u> εἶπαν· σὺ κύριε καρδιογνῶστα πάντων, ἀνάδειξον ὃν ἐξελέξω ἐκ τούτων τῶν δύο ἕνα...

> and <u>praying</u> they said, "You, Lord, heart-knower of all people, show which one you have chosen from these two men..."

The action of *praying* may be considered a redundant usage (see E.2. below), but, in either case, the participle stresses the devout mindset (a framework) out of which these early believers asked the Lord to show who should replace Judas. The participle *praying* importantly frames the speech act. Indeed, in Luke's Gospel Jesus is shown praying more often than in the other gospels.[10] One concludes, then, that Luke intends for his audience to see continuity between Jesus and his faithful disciples.

In this next example, I have isolated and layered the circumstantial participle clauses for ease of observation (alternatively, one may understand the first five as attributive):

Mark 5:25 Καὶ <u>γυνὴ</u> <u>οὖσα</u> ἐν ῥύσει αἵματος δώδεκα ἔτη [Present Tense]
    26 καὶ πολλὰ <u>παθοῦσα</u> ὑπὸ πολλῶν ἰατρῶν [Aorist Tense]
    καὶ <u>δαπανήσασα</u> τὰ παρ' αὐτῆς πάντα [Aorist Tense]
    καὶ μηδὲν <u>ὠφεληθεῖσα</u> [Aorist Tense]
    ἀλλὰ μᾶλλον εἰς τὸ χεῖρον <u>ἐλθοῦσα</u>, [Aorist Tense]
    27 <u>ἀκούσασα</u> περὶ τοῦ Ἰησοῦ, [Aorist Tense]
    <u>ἐλθοῦσα</u> ἐν τῷ ὄχλῳ ὄπισθεν [Aorist Tense]
    ἥψατο τοῦ ἱματίου αὐτοῦ·

---

[10] "Praying" (προσεύχομαι) occurs in the Gospels and Acts as follows (bolded references indicate Jesus' praying): Matt 5:44; 6:5-7, 9; 14:23; 19:13; 24:20; 26:36, 39, 41-42, 44; Mark 1:35; 6:46; 11:24-25; 12:40; 13:18; 14:32, 35, 38-37; Luke 1:10; 3:21; 5:16; 6:12, 28; 9:18, 28-29; 11:1-2; 18:1, 10-11; 20:47; 22:40-41, 44, 46; Acts 1:24; 6:6; 8:15; 9:11, 40; 10:9, 30; 11:5; 12:12; 13:3; 14:23; 16:25; 20:36; 21:5; 22:17; 28:8.

Mark 5:25 *And a woman, <u>being</u> with a flow of blood for twelve years,*
26 and <u>having suffered</u> many things by many physicians
and <u>having spent</u> everything belonging to her,
and <u>having benefitted</u> nothing
but rather to a greater degree <u>having come</u> worse,
27 <u>hearing</u> about Jesus,
<u>coming</u> in the crowd from behind,
she touched his clothing.

This list of circumstantial participles creates emphasis along with the repeated modifiers specifying amount and quantity (see §12.4 QUANTITATIVE EMPHASIS). All of this provides critical context for her action to touch Jesus' clothing; these participle clauses frame her critical action of risking to touch Jesus and make him unclean due to her *being with a flow of blood*, the only circumstantial participle that is in the Present Tense and thus contemporaneous with the main verb *touched*.

CHECK POINT 17.4

Below is given Acts 20:36 containing two pre-nuclear circumstantial participles (underlined) and the literal translation. First, explain the pre-nuclear use of the participles. Second, from the list of adverbial logical-semantic relations, consider which are most fitting, if any, for these two participles.

Acts 20:36 Καὶ ταῦτα <u>εἰπὼν</u> <u>θεὶς</u> τὰ γόνατα αὐτοῦ σὺν πᾶσιν αὐτοῖς προσηύξατο.
And <u>having said</u> these things, <u>setting</u> on his knees, he prayed with all of them.

εἰπὼν =

θεὶς =

SUGGESTED ANSWERS

εἰπὼν = The prenulcear participle εἰπὼν is in a sentence initial participial clause, so it provides a *segue with continuity* from the previous speaking event in Acts 20 to the subsequent praying event. The speaking and praying events are marked with continuity. The most likely adverbial logical-semantic relation would be temporal, *after.*

θεὶς = The pre-nuclear participle θεὶς may indicate procedural information, namely that the praying proper was preceded by setting down on their knees. However, it is possible that *setting on his knees* provides a contextual framework for the main action of praying. Why? Importantly, kneeling before praying is indicated elsewhere in Luke's writings (e.g. Luke 22:41; Acts 9:40; 21:5; cf. Eph 3:14; Phil 2:10); so, Luke's description may be more than procedural and greater contextual significance may attend to Luke's recording Paul's kneeling before praying. The most likely adverbial logical-semantic relation would be temporal, *after*.

E. **Post-Nuclear Placement:** There are two main uses of post-nuclear circumstantial participles: 1) to explicate and qualify particulars of the main verbal action (Runge 262-63); or 2) by redundant statements, to point forward and emphasize subsequent speech.

1. Explication and/or Qualification of Particulars. The circumstantial participle's placement after the nuclear verb explicates some particular dimensions of the main verb and/or emphasizes subsequent activity arising out of the main verb. Consider these examples.

Acts 19:9 ἀφώρισεν τοὺς μαθητάς, καθ᾽ ἡμέραν <u>διαλεγόμενος</u> ἐν τῇ σχολῇ Τυράννου,
he separated the disciples, each day <u>dialoging/instructing</u> [them] in the school of Tyrannus.

John 6:6 τοῦτο δὲ ἔλεγεν <u>πειράζων</u> αὐτόν,
and this he said <u>testing</u> him.

Luke 19:20a ὁ ἕτερος ἦλθεν <u>λέγων</u>...
The other one came, <u>saying</u>...

In Acts 19:9, the participle διαλεγόμενος explicates what was entailed in separating the disciples (from the adversity)—namely, dialoging with them (or instructing them) daily in the school of Tyrannus. It is likely that διαλεγόμενος here indicates the intention or purpose behind separating them. In John 6:6, the participle πειράζων explicates and even qualifies the nature of Jesus' speech, also highlighted by the imperfect tense (ἔλεγεν). Finally, in Luke 19:20a the participle λέγων explicates what happened when the servant came, as invited, to give account of his stewardship in context. So, the speech is a particular aspect of his coming (ἦλθεν; the main verb).

2. Redundant Forward Pointing and Emphasizing Device. In this very common sense, the participle appears to convey the same action as the main verb. This usage is particularly common with verbs of saying. Although in English translations the participle is not often translated, nevertheless the participle serves an important function to emphasize the speech that follows as particularly important in the discourse. In other words, the participle pauses before the giving of speech. Thus, it is advisable somehow to translate the forward pointing emphasis that is thus contained. Cf. Wallace 649-50 and Runge ch.7.

Matt 8:29 ἔκραξαν <u>λέγοντες</u>, τί ἡμῖν καὶ σοί, υἱὲ τοῦ θεοῦ; ἦλθες ὧδε πρὸ καιροῦ βασανίσαι ἡμᾶς;

> They cried out, <u>saying</u>, "What do our (things) and yours (have in common), Son of God? You came here ahead of time to punish us?"

Luke 12:17 καὶ διελογίζετο ἐν ἑαυτῷ <u>λέγων</u>· τί ποιήσω, ὅτι οὐκ ἔχω ποῦ συνάξω τοὺς καρπούς μου;

> And he was thinking within himself, <u>saying</u>: "What should I do, because I don't have [a place] where I will gather my products?"

It may seem odd that in Matt 8:29 that the demons should be given emphasized speech; yet, they perceive that Jesus is *the Son of God*. In Luke 12:17, the wealthy man reasons *in himself* how to handle his excess wealth. The emphasized reported speech represents exactly the wrong thing to do, because in 12:20 the man's soul will be asked of him *at this very night* (ταύτῃ τῇ νυκτὶ); we should notice the demonstrative emphasis (*this* is fronted).

F. **Adverbial:** Grammarians have described various adverbial logical-semantic relations used to identify and translate circumstantial participles. What do adverbs do? Adverbs answer **how**, **why**, **when**, and **where**. Thus, in this understanding, adverbial participles modify the action of the verb by providing more information in one of these ways. However, to consider participles inherently "adverbial" in this sense is misleading; as explained above, "circumstantial" is a better label for this participle usage. Why? Because **the circumstantial participle is unmarked for any particular adverbial function**. However, the common adverbial senses are given below as described by grammarians (e.g. Wallace 621-53). This catalogue is provided to assist students in understanding the translational "options" that ultimately, however, must be decided upon by contextual considerations.

1. *Temporal.* Here the participle answers when an action took place, either prior to the main verb (Aorist participle *after*) or simultaneous to it (Present participle *while*). See Wallace 623-27.

   Acts 1:9 Καὶ ταῦτα <u>εἰπὼν</u> <u>βλεπόντων</u> αὐτῶν ἐπήρθη καὶ νεφέλη ὑπέλαβεν αὐτὸν ἀπὸ τῶν ὀφθαλμῶν αὐτῶν.

   > And <u>after He had said</u> these things, <u>while they were looking on</u>, He was lifted up and a cloud received Him out of their sight.

   Note in this example that the Present Tense participle and pronoun βλεπόντων αὐτῶν is a special type of circumstantial participle called a genitive absolute that is covered in §20.4 THE GENITIVE CIRCUMSTANTIAL PARTICIPLE (AKA GENITIVE ABSOLUTE).

2. *Substantiation or Causal.* Here the participle is translated *because* and indicates the cause or grounds for the action of the main verb. See Wallace 631-32.

> **Matt 1:19** Ἰωσὴφ δὲ ὁ ἀνὴρ αὐτῆς, δίκαιος <u>ὢν</u> καὶ μὴ <u>θέλων</u> αὐτὴν δειγματίσαι, ἐβουλήθη λάθρα ἀπολῦσαι αὐτήν.
>
> *And Joseph her husband, because he <u>was</u> a righteous man and <u>was</u> not <u>wanting</u> to disgrace her, planned to send her away secretly.*

3. *Purpose (Instrumental).* Here the participle is translated *in order that* and indicates the intention or purpose behind some action. See Wallace 635-37.

> **Mark 10:2** Καὶ προσελθόντες Φαρισαῖοι ἐπηρώτων αὐτὸν εἰ ἔξεστιν ἀνδρὶ γυναῖκα ἀπολῦσαι, <u>πειράζοντες</u> αὐτόν.
>
> *Some Pharisees came up to Jesus, <u>in order to test</u> Him, and began to question Him whether it was lawful for a man to divorce a wife.*

4. *Concession.* Here the participle is used to concede some point or to offer a concession and is translated *although*. See Wallace 634-35.

> **Matt 7:11a** εἰ οὖν ὑμεῖς πονηροὶ <u>ὄντες</u> οἴδατε δόματα ἀγαθὰ διδόναι τοῖς τέκνοις ὑμῶν
>
> *If you then know how to give good gifts to your children, <u>although</u> you <u>are</u> evil*

5. *Conditional.* Here the participle forms the protasis or supposition of a conditional idea and is translated *if*. See Wallace 632-33.

> **1 Cor 11:29** ὁ γὰρ ἐσθίων καὶ πίνων κρίμα ἑαυτῷ ἐσθίει καὶ πίνει μὴ <u>διακρίνων</u> τὸ σῶμα
>
> *For the one eating and drinking eats and drinks judgement upon him- or herself, <u>if</u> not <u>discerning</u> the body.*

6. *Result.* Here the participle describes the result or outcome and is translated *so that*, or *resulting in*. See Wallace, 637-39.

> **Luke 4:15** καὶ αὐτὸς ἐδίδασκεν ἐν ταῖς συναγωγαῖς αὐτῶν <u>δοξαζόμενος</u> ὑπὸ πάντων.
> *And he himself was teaching in their synagogues <u>resulting in being glorified</u> by all.*

7. *Means*. Here the participle describes the intention or purpose of the action of the main verb and is translated *by means of*. See Wallace, 628-30.

> **Mark 15:30** σῶσον σεαυτὸν <u>καταβὰς</u> ἀπὸ τοῦ σταυροῦ.
> *Save yourself, <u>by coming down</u> from the cross!*

8. *Manner*. Here the participle indicates *how* in terms of the manner of the completion of some action (Wallace, 627-28).

> **Acts 2:13** ἕτεροι δὲ <u>διαχλευάζοντες</u> ἔλεγον ὅτι γλεύκους μεμεστωμένοι εἰσίν.
> *Additionally, others <u>mockingly</u> were saying this: "They are full of sweet wine!"*

9. *Relative Time and Adverbial Sense*. Below is a representation of a chart by Wallace that attempts to describe the various adverbial uses of the Participles by Tense in relation to the Main Verb (Wallace 626, Chart 82 - *The Tenses of Adverbial Participles*).

RELATIVE TIME	ANTECEDENT to main verb	CONTEMPORANEOUS with main verb	SUBSEQUENT to main verb
Tense of Participle	1. <u>Aorist</u> or <u>Perfect</u>	2. <u>Present</u>; (sometimes <u>Aorist</u>)	3. <u>Future</u>; (sometimes <u>Present</u>)
Possible Adverbial Senses	CAUSE CONDITION CONCESSION	RESULT MEANS MANNER	PURPOSE

How to interpret this chart: Start with the middle Row entitled on the left as "Tense of Participle" to see what participle tense(s) occupies what vertical column. The first tenses are the Aorist Tense and Perfect Tense participles, which tend to have "Antecedent" relative time in relation to the main verb (i.e., such participles describe events/actions that occur before the main verb). Following the chart downward into the Adverbial sense row, most commonly the Aorist or Perfect adverbial participle will flow into causal, conditional, or concessive senses; but also possibly means and manner. The second tense is the Present Tense, which typically describes the relative time of contemporaneous action in relation to the main verb (sometimes also the Aorist Tense seems to mean this); below this, the Present Tense participle column opens into the Adverbial Sense Row flooding all lower chambers: the Present Tense participle may take any adverbial participle function. The Future participle (very rare in the GNT) may mean purpose, or possibly result. For that matter, too, the Aorist participle may mean result or purpose.

Complete WORKBOOK EXERCISES 17 and consult the ANSWER KEY & GUIDE as needed.

Here is the NIV84 translation (cf. NLT) of Eph 5:18-21:

Eph 5:18 Do not get drunk on wine, which leads to debauchery. Instead, be filled with the Spirit. [19] Speak to one another with psalms, hymns and spiritual songs. Sing and make music in your heart to the Lord, [20] always giving thanks to God the Father for everything, in the name of our Lord Jesus Christ. [21] Submit to one another out of reverence for Christ.

Notice how 5:19-21 contains a series of commands: *Speak to one another...Sing and make music...Submit to one another*. What relationship do these commands have with the preceding context? Is there any relationship with *being filled with the Spirit*? Yes there is.

Actually, 5:19-21 contains five circumstantial participle clauses qualifying the imperative verb form "Be filled" in 5:18. A semantic diagram and analysis of these verses shows this.

Greek	English (slightly modified from NASB95)

[18] καὶ ---μὴ
   μεθύσκεσθε
   ---οἴνῳ, [means]
    ---ἐν ᾧ [sphere?]
    ἐστιν ἀσωτία,
ἀλλὰ [contrast of correction]
   πληροῦσθε
   ---ἐν πνεύματι, [means, sphere?]
[19] [1]--- λαλοῦντες
    --- ἑαυτοῖς [indirect object]
    ---[ἐν] ψαλμοῖς [manner]
     καὶ
     ὕμνοις
     καὶ
     ᾠδαῖς πνευματικαῖς,
  [2]--- ᾄδοντες
     καὶ
  [3]--- ψάλλοντες
    ---τῇ καρδίᾳ ὑμῶν [sphere?]
    ---τῷ κυρίῳ, [recipient]
[20] [4]--- εὐχαριστοῦντες
    --- πάντοτε [temporal]
    --- ὑπὲρ πάντων [reference?]
	[18] And
	   do not get drunk
	   ---with wine,
	    ---in which
	    there is dissipation,
	but
	  be filled
	  ---with the Spirit,
	[19] [1]--- speaking
	    --- to one another
	    --- in psalms
	     and
	     hymns
	     and
	     spiritual songs,
	  [2]--- singing
	     and
	  [3]--- making melody
	    --- with your heart
	    --- to the Lord;
	[20] [4]--- giving thanks
	    --- always
	    --- for all things

--- ἐν ὀνόματι [cause/basis?]	--- in the name
--- τοῦ κυρίου	--- of --- our
--- ἡμῶν	Lord
=-- Ἰησοῦ Χριστοῦ	=-- Jesus Christ
--- τῷ θεῷ [recipient]	--- to God,
=-- καὶ πατρί.	=-- even the Father;
[21] [5]--- ὑποτασσόμενοι	[21] [5]--- submitting
--- ἀλλήλοις [indirect object]	--- to one another
--- ἐν φόβῳ [manner]	--- in the fear
--- Χριστοῦ,	--- of Christ.

These Present Tense circumstantial participles are post-nuclear, specifying ongoing details and particulars pertaining to "being filled with the Spirit." As such, they describe what it looks like to be filled with the Spirit. Adverbially, they may be understood logically-semantically as participles of *result*. You may be surprised at what is present and what is lacking from Paul's description.

Certainly, a careful study of what each participle means would be prudent. Let me share some thoughts and reflections. *Speaking to each other* is the first particular. The pronoun is reflexive (*yourselves*), and not simply reciprocal (*one another*). The implication is that this speaking involves *oneself* as well as others. (See CHAPTER 19 for a discussion of these pronouns.) Here, the list of what is spoken is noteworthy: *psalms and hymns and spiritual odes* (with correlative emphasis). One wonders whether these psalms are scriptural Hebrew Psalms. Also, are these hymns and spiritual odes related to the early Christian gospel summaries and creeds that are forming and present in Paul's and Peter's writings, as suspected lies behind Eph 5:14; Phil 2:5-11, 1 Tim 3:16, Titus 2:11-14; 3:4-7, and 1 Pet 3:21-22? If so, I suspect that such *speaking* is a form of Christian theological instruction to learn about Christ and to encourage each other mutually to respond accordingly. Thus, one particular result of being filled with the Spirit is the interest in learning about Christ, especially how to live as His disciples (see Eph 4:17-24 and CASE IN POINT 24).

Another evidence of being filled with the Spirit is *singing* that has its origin or location *from the heart* and is directed *to the Lord*, who is the recipient, an Audience of One. This suggests a certain degree of joy and celebration and worship. Related to this, but stated distinctly (we should ask why?), is *giving thanks*. This thanksgiving is done *always* while acknowledging that Jesus is Lord of all, and trusting in His providence. Such thanksgiving is explicitly to be directed to our God and Father; we are eternally grateful for what God, the Father, has accomplished for us in Christ.

Finally, *submitting to one another* is further evidence of being filled in the Spirit. I suspect that this submission involves respecting the vocation and position to which God has called each person, valuing and caring for persons in their diverse giftedness and roles (Eph 4:11-13; Rom 12:3-8; 1 Cor 12:18-30). In the immediate context of Ephesians, Paul develops this notion of mutual respect with regard to various fundamental social relationships: husband and wife, child and parent, and servant and master. Each person in these relationships has a respective role, and each person should voluntarily submit to the other respectively as Paul describes in Eph 5:22–6:9.

So, Paul provides basic benchmarks of what the Spirit-filled life looks like through a series of post-nuclear, circumstantial participles. Since we are commanded to *be filled*, Paul implies that we have a real role in submitting to God to allow this filling by the Holy Spirit to happen. In context, to be filled with the Holy Spirit is contrasted with *being drunk with wine*, which was a major form of entertainment in the Mediterranean cultures of that time. To venture into one application for today, we must not waste time with desiring other things that take control of us (like alcohol, watching television, playing video games, gambling, pornography, workaholism, etc.) and begin and continue to be filled with the Spirit through our submission to God and knowing and doing his will.

Below is a scene of the drunken god Dionysos followed by his parading throng (θίασος) arriving at a man's home (1st century AD).[11] Many details are worth noting, such as the Dionysian temple in the background, the satyr attending to the feet of Dionysos, and the instruments of the satyrs, including Silenus playing his flute. At some point, this marble relief was modified by chiseling off two (immodest?) women, one reclining on the couch and the other (a drunken nymph) supported by the last satyr on the right. Such a parading scene was commonly depicted in various media. Dionysian cults enjoyed involvement at all levels of society: domestic (home), civic, provincial, and imperial. Contests and re-enactment performances included dancers and choral singers called "hymnodoi" (ὑμνῳδοί). In the first century AD, one well-known group was "the dancing cowherds of Pergamum."[12]

---

[11] This edited-enhanced image located in the British Museum is from Ernest Arthur Gardner, *A Handbook of Greek Sculpture* (London: Macmillan, 1911), 439.

[12] On this and related subjects, see Philip A. Harland, *Associations, Synagogues, and Congregations: Claiming a Place in Ancient Mediterranean Society* (Minneapolis: Fortress, 2003).

CHAPTER 18

Although participles are not the main verb, they often provide important information by way of elaboration. In Matt 8:14, Jesus saw Peter's mother-in-law sick in bed with a fever. How do the three participles function in this simple verse to convey a sense of urgency that prepares for Jesus' immediate response and the subsequent results?

This chapter covers the rest of the participle voices: **Present** and **Perfect Middle/Passive** and **Aorist Middle**. These voices of the participle use the First and Second Declension endings, already well known by you. The functions of these participles are the same as in the previous chapter. Since the middle/passive participle endings are not that difficult to learn, the student should re-read CHAPTER 17, which contains a lot of important information about "Party-ciples." Lastly, the Vocabulary contains more Second Declension nouns.

VOCABULARY 18   MORE SECOND DECLENSION NOUNS

Neuter Nouns:

τὸ θηρίον [46]	wild beast
τὸ ἱερόν [72]	temple; holy place
τὸ ἱμάτιον [60]	garment
τὸ μνημεῖον [40]	tomb
τὸ παιδίον [52]	little child; young servant
τὸ πλοῖον [67]	boat
τὸ πρόσωπον [76]	face, appearance; presence
τὸ σάββατον [68]	Sabbath; rest
τὸ σημεῖον [77]	sign, mark; miracle

Masculine Nouns:

ὁ θρόνος [62]	throne, chair, seat
ὁ καρπός [66]	fruit, produce; profit
ὁ λίθος [59]	stone
ὁ ναός [45]	temple (edifice); sanctuary
ὁ φόβος [47]	fear, respect
ὁ χρόνος [53]	time, occasion

After learning vocabulary to this point, you will know 75.1% of the words in the GNT. Congratulations! You may be able to recognize 3 out of 4 words. If you are able, listen to audio recordings of VOCABULARY 18 and complete the CROSSWORD PUZZLE in the EXERCISES.

NOTES ON VOCABULARY 18:

Many of these words have English cognates: <u>mnemon</u>-ics (memory tactics), <u>ped</u>-agogy (instruction of children), <u>prosopo</u>-poeia (personification; literally *to make face*), Sabbath, <u>Semeio</u>-logy (science of sign language), throne, <u>litho</u>-graphy (writing on stone to make impressions), claustro-<u>phobic</u> (fear of tight places), <u>chrono</u>-logical. Of cultural significance, ὁ ναός *the*

sanctuary more properly refers to the inside of a temple, as opposed to the τὸ ἱερόν that refered more generally to the temple structure, courtyards, and precincts (holy grounds around the site). The physical temple structures were a standard feature of Mediterranean cities; the expediture of resources for them was enormous, and so the most visible locations were preserved for them (see a restored city plan for Olympia at the end of this chapter).

The image below depicts the layout for the temple of Zeus at Olympia, where one sees the innermost ναός and the πρόναος is the *front hall* of the temple. The στυλοβάτης is the base that supports the row of columns. The ὀπισθόδομος is the *back chamber*, formed from the words δόμος *house* and ὀπίσθιος, α, ον, *hinder, back part*. The Greeks decorated the columns with colors and elaborate patterns (on the right), which included 1. the fret; 2. the egg and dart; 3. the bead and fillet; and 4. the honeysuckle.[1]

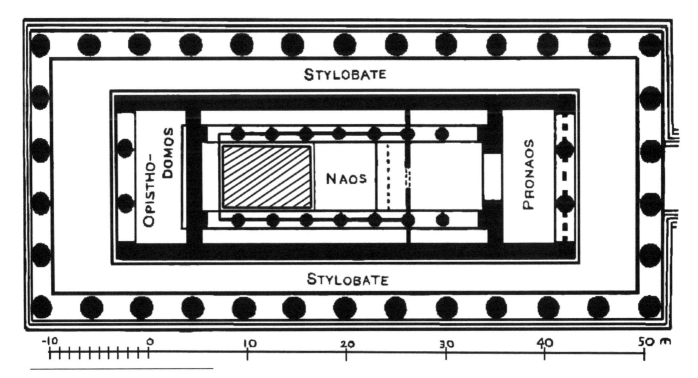

---

[1] William Carey Morey, *Outlines of Greek History: With a Survey of Ancient Oriental Nations* (New York: American Book, 1903), 157.

[2] Cf. Mark 3:3 where an Aorist Tense participle is used of the same verb root, but uncompounded τὴν χεῖρα ... <u>ξηρὰν</u>

18.1 FORMATION OF THE MIDDLE/PASSIVE AND MIDDLE PARTICIPLES

A. **Present and Perfect Middle/Passive and Aorist Middle:** The middle/passive and middle participle endings are easy to learn. All genders use either the First or Second Declension endings. These First and Second Declension endings are added to the coupling syllable –ομεν- for the Present Middle/Passive, –σαμεν- for the Aorist Middle, and –μέν- for the Perfect Middle/Passive. Here are the endings of the Present Middle/Passive Participle.

	MASCULINE	FEMININE	NEUTER
sg. nom.	–όμεν-ος	–ομέν-η	–όμεν-ον
gen.	–ομέν-ου	–ομέν-ης	–ομέν-ου
dat.	–ομέν-ῳ	–ομέν-ῃ	–ομέν-ῳ
acc.	–όμεν-ον	–ομέν-ην	–όμεν-ον
pl. nom.	–όμεν-οι	–όμεν-αι	–όμεν-α
gen.	–ομέν-ων	–ομέν-ων	–ομέν-ων
dat.	–ομέν-οις	–ομέν-αις	–ομέν-οις
acc.	–ομέν-ους	–ομέν-ας	–όμεν-α

B. **Present Middle/Passive Participle:** These endings are added directly to the verb stem.

	MASCULINE	FEMININE	NEUTER
sg. nom.	πιστευ-όμενος	πιστευ-ομένη	πιστευ-όμενον
gen.	πιστευ-ομένου	πιστευ-ομένης	πιστευ-ομένου
dat.	πιστευ-ομένῳ	πιστευ-ομένῃ	πιστευ-ομένῳ
acc.	πιστευ-όμενον	πιστευ-ομένην	πιστευ-όμενον
pl. nom.	πιστευ-όμενοι	πιστευ-όμεναι	πιστευ-όμενα
gen.	πιστευ-ομένων	πιστευ-ομένων	πιστευ-ομένων
dat.	πιστευ-ομένοις	πιστευ-ομέναις	πιστευ-ομένοις
acc.	πιστευ-ομένους	πιστευ-ομένας	πιστευ-όμενα

C. **Aorist Middle Participle:** The Aorist middle participle uses the exact same endings, except that the tense suffix σίγμα and coupling vowel ἄλφα replace the ὂ μικρόν.

	MASCULINE	FEMININE	NEUTER
sg. nom.	πιστευ-σάμενος	πιστευ-σαμένη	πιστευ-σάμενον
gen.	πιστευ-σαμένου	πιστευ-σαμένης	πιστευ-σαμένου
dat.	πιστευ-σαμένῳ	πιστευ-σαμένῃ	πιστευ-σαμένῳ
acc.	πιστευ-σάμενον	πιστευ-σαμένην	πιστευ-σάμενον
pl. nom.	πιστευ-σάμενοι	πιστευ-σάμεναι	πιστευ-σάμενα
gen.	πιστευ-σαμένων	πιστευ-σαμένων	πιστευ-σαμένων
dat.	πιστευ-σαμένοις	πιστευ-σαμέναις	πιστευ-σαμένοις
acc.	πιστευ-σαμένους	πιστευ-σαμένας	πιστευ-σάμενα

D. **Perfect Middle/Passive Participle:** To form these endings, first, retain the reduplication and then add the same endings (minus the ὃ μικρόν) to form the Perfect middle/passive participle. The omission of the ὃ μικρόν is very similar to Perfect Tense in the Indicative Mood.

		MASCULINE	FEMININE	NEUTER
<u>sg.</u>	nom.	πεπιστευ-μένος	πεπιστευ-μένη	πεπιστευ-μένον
	gen.	πεπιστευ-μένου	πεπιστευ-μένης	πεπιστευ-μένου
	dat.	πεπιστευ-μένῳ	πεπιστευ-μένῃ	πεπιστευ-μένῳ
	acc.	πεπιστευ-μένον	πεπιστευ-μένην	πεπιστευ-μένον
<u>pl.</u>	nom.	πεπιστευ-μένοι	πεπιστευ-μέναι	πεπιστευ-μένα
	gen.	πεπιστευ-μένων	πεπιστευ-μένων	πεπιστευ-μένων
	dat.	πεπιστευ-μένοις	πεπιστευ-μέναις	πεπιστευ-μένοις
	acc.	πεπιστευ-μένους	πεπιστευ-μένας	πεπιστευ-μένα

18.2 A SUMMARY OF PARTICIPLE FORMS

Below is a **Master Chart for Identifying and Parsing Participles**. Consider this chart a Master Chart for identifying participle forms (including even the rare Future Participle).

TENSE FORM		MASCULINE/NEUTER Coupling Syllable + Type of Declension Ending	FEMININE Coupling Syllable + Type of Declension Ending	NOTES AND OTHER FEATURES
Present	A	-οντ- + 3rd Decl. (ἄρχων)	-ουσ- + 1st Decl.	▪ masc. sg. –ων
	M/P	-ομεν- + 2nd Declension	-ομεν- + 1st Decl.	
Future	A	-σοντ- + 3rd Decl. (ἄρχων)	-σουσ- + 1st Decl.	▪ 12 times; masc. sg. –σων
	M	-σομεν- + 2nd Declension	-σομεν- + 1st Decl.	
	P	-θησομεν- + 2nd Decl.	-θησομεν- + 1st Decl.	
Aorist	A	-σαντ- + 3rd Decl. (ἄρχων)	-σασ- + 1st Decl.	▪ <u>no</u> augment; masc. sg. –σας
	M	-σαμεν- + 2nd Declension	-σαμεν- + 1st Decl.	▪ <u>no</u> augment
	P	-θέντ- + 3rd Decl. (ἄρχων)	-θεισ- + 1st Decl.	▪ <u>no</u> augment; masc. sg. –θείς
2nd Aorist		-οντ- + 3rd Decl. (ἄρχων)	-ουσ- + 1st Decl.	▪ <u>no</u> augment; stem change
Perfect	A	-κότ- + 3rd Decl. (ἄρχων)	-κυί- + 1st Decl.	▪ masc. sg. –κώς; removes the νῦ from –οντ-
	M/P	-μέν- + 2nd Declension	-μέν- + 1st Decl.	▪ M/P voice removes ὃ μικρόν from –ομεν- ▪ <u>All</u> perfects participles have retained accents and normal reduplication

18.3 A GUIDE TO TRANSLATING ADJECTIVAL AND CIRCUMSTANTIAL PARTICIPLES

A. Initial Steps:

1. First, consider between these broad usages:

   a. Adjectival Participles are **often articular** and will either modify a noun or substantive or will act alone as. Go to B. below.

   b. Circumstantial Participles are **always anarthrous** and often in the nominative case (but not always!). Go to C. below.

   c. Other Specialized Participle uses are covered in §19.5-6.

2. Second, consider the significance of the verbal aspect of the participle tense:

   a. Present is imperfective aspect with the action as repeated or ongoing; time simultaneous.

   b. Aorist is perfective aspect with the action viewed as a whole as complete(d); time prior.

   c. Perfect is stative aspect with complex action and resultant state, whether in the past or present.

B. Adjectival Participles in Translation:

1. Present Tense and Time Contemporaneous. The verbal imperfective aspect of a Present Tense adjectival participle may indicate time contemporaneous in relation to the main verb. With a Present Tense adjectival participle, catching this time contemporaneous notion in English depends on the tense of the main verb. Thus, if the main verb is present time, the Present Tense adjectival participle may best rendered ***the one (that is) ____ing*** or in the plural ***the ones (that are)____ing***. If the main verb is given in past time, then translate the adjectival participle in this way: ***the one (that was) ____ing*** or ***the ones (that were) ____ing***. Study these examples, the first with a substantive participle and the second with an attributive participle.
   Example 1: ὁ <u>ἀκούων</u> τὸν λόγον μου ἔχει ζωήν.

   The one <u>that is hearing</u> my word has life. [using a relative pronoun *that*]
   or
   The <u>one hearing</u> my word has life.

Example 2: οἱ μαθηταὶ οἱ βλέποντες αὐτὸν ἀπῆλθον.

> *The disciples that were seeing him departed* [using a relative pronoun *that*]
>
> or
>
> *The disciples seeing him departed.*

2. Aorist Tense and "Time Prior". The verbal perfective aspect with an Aorist Tense adjectival participle may often indicate "time prior" action in relation to the main verb. The English translation depends on the time frame of the main verb. Thus, if the main verb represents present time, the Aorist Tense adjectival participle may be rendered ***the one(s) having*** _____, where the blank (___) is the English past passive participle form (like *seen*, *heard*, *taught*, *sent*, etc.). This translation also works if the main verb is given in past time. However, alternatively, you can create an English relative pronoun clause using *that* as follows: If the main verb is in past time frame, then the Aorist participle may translated as what may be called the "past-past" time frame (or as an English pluperfect verb): ***the one that had taught*** or ***had walked***. If the main verb is present or future in time frame, then translate as ***the one that taught*** or ***walked***. Study these examples, the first with a substantive participle and the second with attributive participle.

Example 1: ὁ ἀκούσας τὸν λόγον μου ἔχει ζωήν.

> *The one that heard my word has life.*   [using the relative pronoun *that*]
>
> or
>
> *The one hearing my word has life.* [no verbal aspect is evident]

Example 2: οἱ μαθηταὶ οἱ βλέψαντες αὐτὸν ἀπῆλθον.

> *The disciples that saw him departed.* [using a relative pronoun *that*]
>
> or
>
> *The disciples having seen him departed.* [no verbal aspect is evident]

3. Perfect Tense and Resultant Effects. Perfect tense participles represent a special difficulty, because of the stress on the resultant effects and how to represent such in translation. Study these examples. For example, consider these examples with an attributive participle or substantive participles:

John 11:44a ἐξῆλθεν ὁ τεθνηκὼς

> *the one that had been in a state of death came out.* [using *that*]

Titus 3:8b οἱ πεπιστευκότες θεῷ

> *The ones that have believed God...* [using a relative pronoun *that*]

2 Cor 12:21 πολλοὺς τῶν <u>προημαρτηκότων</u>

> *many of the ones <u>having sinned (with continued results)</u>*
>
> or
>
> *many of the ones <u>that have sinned (with continued results)</u>*
>
> [using a relative pronoun *that*]

Mark 3:1 <u>ἐξηραμμένην</u>... τὴν χεῖρα[2]

> *the <u>completely withered up</u> hand*

4. Summary Chart of Adjectival Participle Translation (here in Substantive Use). Note that all middle/passive forms below are translated as passives. Also, the Aorist middle is not included below since it often occurs in middle-formed verbs and therefore carries an active meaning.

A GUIDE TO ADJECTIVAL PARTICIPLE TRANSLATION				
PARTICIPLE			**TIME FRAME OF MAIN VERB**	**PARTICIPLE TRANSLATION**
Tense	Voice	Form (masc. pl.)		
Present	A	οἱ πιστεύοντες	Present	*The ones that are believing*
	M/P	οἱ πιστευόμενοι		*The ones that are being entrusted*
	A	οἱ πιστεύοντες	Past	*The ones that were believing*
	M/P	οἱ πιστευόμενοι		*The ones that were being entrusted*
Aorist	A	οἱ πιστεύσαντες	Present	*The ones that believed*
	P	οἱ πιστευθέντες		*The ones that were entrusted*
	A	οἱ πιστεύσαντες	Past	*The ones that had believed*
	P	οἱ πιστευθέντες		*The ones that had been entrusted*
Perfect	A	οἱ πεπιστευκότες	Present	*The ones that have believed*
	M/P	οἱ πεπιστευμένοι		*The ones that have been entrusted*
	A	οἱ πεπιστευκότες	Past	*The ones that had believed*
	M/P	οἱ πεπιστευμένοι		*The ones that had been entrusted*

---

[2] Cf. Mark 3:3 where an Aorist Tense participle is used of the same verb root, but uncompounded τὴν χεῖρα ... <u>ξηράν</u> that is translated *the <u>withered</u> hand*.

C. **Circumstantial Participles:** First, determine the participle's location as either pre-nuclear (see 1. and 2. below) or post-nuclear verb (see 3. below); then consider tense aspect for translation. (The same considerations also apply to Genitive Absolutes that are covered in §20.4 THE GENITIVE CIRCUMSTANTIAL PARTICIPLE (AKA GENITIVE ABSOLUTE).)

   1. <u>Pre-nuclear Placement</u>. Circumstantial participles located before the main verb (i.e. pre-nuclear participles) often provide a relative sequencing of events.

      a. *Present Tense participles* are translated as contemporaneous (e.g. "while going along"). A Greek writer generally used a Present participle if he/she wanted that action to be understood as happening at the same time as the main verb. This kind of action is well suited to the Present Tense because it often indicates progressive, on-going action. With a Present Tense circumstantial participle, begin your translation with **While (was/is) ____ing**. My preference is for the first translation in the examples below, because the translation reflects the generic nature of the participle.

      <u>διδάσκων</u> ὁ Παῦλος εἶδε τὸν ἀρχιερέα.
      <u>While teaching</u>, Paul saw the high priest.
      or *<u>While he was teaching</u>, Paul saw the high priest.*

      b. *Aorist Tense participles* are translated as antecedent or time prior (e.g. *after going…*). In keeping with the perfective aspect of the Aorist Tense, a Greek writer generally used Aorist participles *if that action occurred prior to the main verb*. To capture the time-prior notion of the Aorist circumstantial participle, if active in voice, simply translate using **after having _____**. If passive in voice, then translate **after having been _____**. What is supplied in the blanks is actually called the "past passive participle" form of the English verb (e.g., *seen, heard, taught, sent*). Consider these two examples:

      <u>διδαχθεὶς</u> ὑπὸ Βαρναβᾶ ὁ Παῦλος εἶδε τοὺς ἀποστόλους.
      <u>After having been taught</u> by Barnabas, Paul saw the apostles.

      <u>διδάξας</u> Βαρναβᾶν ὁ Παῦλος εἶδε τοὺς ἀποστόλους.
      <u>After having taught</u> Barnabas, Paul saw the apostles.

      c. *Perfect Tense Participles* are translated as antecedent or time prior with resultant effects (e.g. *after having gone …*).

      Mark 5:33 ἡ δὲ γυνὴ…<u>εἰδυῖα</u> ὅ γέγονεν αὐτῇ ἦλθεν καὶ προσέπεσεν αὐτῷ καὶ εἶπεν αὐτῷ….
         Moreover, the woman … <u>after having seen</u> what had happened to her, came and fell before him and said to him.…

d. One consistent exception is the aorist middle-formed participle ἀποκριθείς, for which see §18.5 Taking Control or "Answering Back" in Conversation.

A Guide to Pre-Nuclear Temporal Adverbial Participle Translation

Present Tense Participle: *While...*
Aorist Tense Participle: *After...*
Perfect Tense Participle: *After...* (*rare as circumstantial*)

PARTICIPLE			TIME FRAME OF MAIN VERB	PARTICIPLE TRANSLATION (translated into 3rd person *they*)
Tense	Voice	Form (masc. pl.)		
Present	A	πιστεύοντες	Present	*While (they are) believing*
	M/P	πιστευόμενοι		*While (they are) being entrusted*
	A	πιστεύοντες	Past	*While (they were) believing*
	M/P	πιστευόμενοι		*While (they were) being entrusted*
Aorist	A	πιστεύσαντες	Present	*After having believed*
	P	πιστευθέντες		*After having been entrusted*
	A	πιστεύσαντες	Past	*After having believed*
	P	πιστευθέντες		*After having been entrusted*

However, if a temporal sense does not make sense, then translate the circumstantial participle with *–ing*. If context would justify a more specific semantic relation, then consider possible adverbial logical-semantic relations (see 3. immediately below).

2. <u>Post-Nuclear Placement</u>. Circumstantial participles that come after the verb (i.e. post-nuclear participles), since they tend to further describe the activity of the nuclear verb, may need simply to be translated as English participles ("seeing, walking"). Where the semantic relation from the semantics of the verb and context is so clear that to render it so generically strains English sense, then supply a conjunction in italics to indicate one of these semantic senses. Remember that such a decision should be justified from contextual considerations. There are **a variety of adverbial logical-semantic relations** (see §17.4.F.):

a. **Temporal** (*while, after*)   f. **Conditional** (*if*)
b. **Substantiation** (*because*)   g. **Result** (*so that, with the result that*)
c. **Purpose** (*in order that*)   h. **Means** (*by means of*)
d. **Concession** (*although*)   i. **Manner** (relates *how* something is done).

1 Cor 9:26b οὕτως πυκτεύω <u>ὡς</u> οὐκ ἀέρα δέρων·
    I am boxing in a manner <u>as</u> not <u>beating</u> the air.

In 1 Cor 9:26b the participle communicates *manner* and there are an explicit adverb and conjunction that establish that meaning (οὕτως ... ὡς, forming a correlative emphasis).

2 Cor 11:7a Ἢ ἁμαρτίαν ἐποίησα ἐμαυτὸν ταπεινῶν ἵνα ὑμεῖς ὑψωθῆτε,
   Or, I committed a sin, <u>because</u> I <u>humbled</u> myself in order that you yourselves would be exalted, ... ?

In 2 Cor 11:7a the participle is likely causal *because*, indicating the cause of Paul's sinning; importantly, he is being ironic here.

John 9:19a καὶ ἠρώτησαν αὐτοὺς <u>λέγοντες</u>· οὗτός ἐστιν ὁ υἱὸς ὑμῶν, ὃν ὑμεῖς λέγετε ὅτι τυφλὸς ἐγεννήθη;
   And they asked them, <u>saying</u>: "This is your son, whom you yourselves say that he was born blind?"

In John 9:19a, the parents of the blind man who had been healed are being asked a question. Here the participle λέγοντες *saying* is redundant; there is no special semantic sense. Instead, we are observing a discourse pragmatic use of the participle to emphasis the speech that follows (a question in a heated conversation). This use of the participle was covered in §17.4.E.2.

D. Cautions about Translating Circumstantial Participles:

1. <u>Beware of Over-Interpreting Participles</u>. As indicated in the discussion above, especially given the many possible adverbial "labels" of meanings, **participles are dynamic and therefore liable to over-interpretation**. The above list of possible adverbial meanings should not be understood as a smorgasbord of equal possibilities for every occurrence of a circumstantial participle. Instead, an informed understanding of the unmarked nature of participles, their relative position, tense aspectual significance, and contextual information should constrain interpreters of the import of the participles, if not to one basic sense and use, then to a constrained set of good possibilities. Robertson (1124) rightly says:

> But it is distinctly misleading to treat this [circumstantial] participle as adverbial. In fact, there is a constant tendency to read into this circumstantial participle more than is there. In itself, it must be distinctly noted, the participle does not express time, manner, cause, purpose, condition or concession. These ideas are not in the participle, but are merely suggested by the context, if at all, or occasionally by a particle like ἅμα, εὐθύς, καίπερ, ποτέ, νῦν, ὡς. There is no necessity for one to use the circumstantial participle. If he wishes a more precise note of time, cause, condition, purpose, etc., the various subordinate clauses (and the infinitive) are at his command, besides the co-ordinate clauses.

2. <u>Beware of Overly-Restrictive Translations.</u> Nor is it helpful to think that only one possible adverbial meaning should be pressed as a meaning in a particular case, unless contextual indicators would so delimit it to such. Remember that participles are unmarked for adverbial logical-semantic relations; had an author wanted to mark semantic relationships, other subordinate clause constructions could have been chosen. Smyth correctly states: "The force of these circumstantial participles does not lie in the participle itself, but is derived from the context. Unless attended by some modifying adverb, the context often does not decide whether the participle has a temporal, a causal, a conditional, a concessive force, etc.; and some participles may be referred to more than one of the above classes" (§2069). So, participles represent one efficient way to communicate, with the logical-semantic sense(s) either made explicit in the context so as to be readily implied, or with the deliberate openness for more than one sense to be implied. It is possible that a circumstantial participle may be translated into English (or any language) by more than one adverbial sense in any given sentence; thus translation becomes highly interpretive and may be too restrictive (since usually only one sense can be supplied in translation) beyond what is actually constrained semantically by the participle itself.

3. <u>Other Categories of Participle Usage: Attendant Circumstance and Imperatival.</u> When reading other grammars, you will probably encounter these other participle uses, and some comment is offered here to explain their omission in this grammar.

   a. *Attendant Circumstance.* According to this usage, the participle is thought to describe a different independent action, but one that is related (often in prior sequence) to the main verb. For translation, then, it has been advised (but I disagree) that one translate the participle as a regular verb and adding an *and* to form a compound sentence (see Wallace 640-45). For example, "he answered and said...." However, such a translation often obscures which verb has the main verb status in the sentence, which is always contextually significant since an author's choice to use the participle *subordinates* it to the nuclear verb. Consider Matt 2:13b and in particular the direct discourse of 2:13a that contains a purported participle of attendant circumstance:

   Matt 2:13a Ἀναχωρησάντων δὲ αὐτῶν ἰδοὺ ἄγγελος κυρίου φαίνεται κατ᾽ ὄναρ τῷ Ἰωσὴφ λέγων·
   So, when they departed, behold an angel of the Lord appears in a dream to Joseph, saying:

   Matt 2:13a <u>ἐγερθεὶς</u> παράλαβε τὸ παιδίον καὶ τὴν μητέρα αὐτοῦ καὶ φεῦγε
   "<u>Rising up</u>, take the child and his mother and flee ...!
   "<u>Get up!</u> Take the Child and His mother and flee...! (NASB95)

The angel is speaking to Joseph. Where is the stress? On *getting up* or on *taking the child and his mother* (*and fleeing*)? It is on the later based upon the Greek syntax. Additionally, the use of the participle ἐγερθεὶς recalls Joseph's prior action of *awaking* after the dream in 1:24 with ἐγερθεὶς, and immediately *doing* what was asked him. So, the use of ἐγερθεὶς **again** in 2:13 serves to frame Joseph's obedient action by recalling Joseph's earlier obedient action. Also, the participle participates in the urgency of the situation, since it is attached to an imperative entailing *taking the child and his mother* and *fleeing*. Finally, it is notable that the multiple emphatic indicators in 2:13a (attention getting ἰδοὺ, historic present with φαίνεται, and λέγων introducing the speech act) all set off the speech as important. Again, what is the focal point of the speech act? *Getting up* or *taking the child and fleeing*?

b. *Imperatival.* A questionable category of the participle is the imperatival use (see Wallace 650-51). Here it is thought that the participle may be used by itself in the place of a command form in the context where a command form would be expected. Robertson (1133-34) rightly says, "In general it may be said that no participle should be explained in this way that can properly be connected with a finite verb." However, good examples are lacking that would justify the creation of such a category of usage. Better ways to understand possible instances of such kind of participle are that it frames (pre-nuclear) or explicates (post-nuclear) a nearby main verb or is involved with implied forms of εἰμί for rhetorical effect (brevity or softening the force) in context.[3]

CHECK POINT 18.3

Luke 7:10 contains three participles (underlined), which are given a very basic translation using –*ing*. First, parse the participles. Second, identify the use of the participles as adjectival-attributive, adjectival-substantive, adjectival-predicative, or circumstantial. Third, briefly discuss what implications attend to sentence placement (pre-nuclear or post-nuclear) and/or verbal aspect for each participle. Fourth, if circumstantial, discuss possible adverbial logical-semantic relations that are fitting for translation. Fifth, provide a more robust translation with explanation. Vocabulary help for two verbs is provided in brackets.

Luke 7:10 Καὶ ὑποστρέψαντες εἰς τὸν οἶκον οἱ πεμφθέντες εὗρον τὸν δοῦλον ὑγιαίνοντα. [ὑποστρέφω = *I return*; ὑγιαίνω = *I am healthy, sound*]

Luke 7:10 *And returning into the house, the ones being sent found the servant being healthy.*

---

[3] In the case of independent participle ἔχοντες in 1 Pet 2:12, there is simply a breakdown of grammar agreement with the accusative plural in the previous and rather distant accusative referents παροίκους καὶ παρεπιδήμους working with the infinitive of indirect command in 2:11; however, the post-nuclear sense of ἔχοντες is readily apparent: explicating the goal of abstaining from lusts, having (instead) good behavior among the Gentiles (τὴν ἀναστροφὴν ὑμῶν ἐν τοῖς ἔθνεσιν ἔχοντες καλήν).

ὑποστρέψαντες

1. Parsing:
2. Identify Use:
3. Position and/or Aspect:
4. Adverbial-logical-semantic relation:
5. More Robust Translation:

πεμφθέντες

1. Parsing:
2. Identify Use:
3. Position and/or Aspect:
4. Adverbial-logical-semantic relation:
5. More Robust Translation:

ὑγιαίνοντα

1. Parsing:
2. Identify Use:
3. Position and/or Aspect:
4. Adverbial-logical-semantic relation:
5. More Robust Translation:

SUGGESTED ANSWERS

ὑποστρέψαντες

1. AAPMNP = Aorist Active Participle Masculine Nominative Plural
2. Circumstantial
3. Pre-nuclear, segueing with continuity; the Aorist's perfective aspect views action as a whole as complete(d)
4. Temporal
5. *"After they returned…"*

πεμφθέντες

1. APPMNP = Aorist Passive ParticipleMasculine Nominative Plural
2. adjectival-substantive participle
3. position does not apply; Aorist perfective aspect refers to complete(d) action
4. not applicable
5. *"the ones that had been sent…"*

ὑγιαίνοντα

1. PAP MAS = Present Active Participle Masculine Accusative Singular
2. adjectival-attributive, although possibly circumstantial
3. If adjectival-attributive, position does not apply; however, if circumstantial, then the participle describes further particulars of "how" they found the servant. The Present Tense imperfective aspect stresses continuous condition.
4. if circumstantial, an adverbial logical-semantic relation is difficult to assign.
5. same; cf. "in good health" (NASB95); "completely healed" (NLT); "well" (NIV; ESV).

18.4 MARKING AND DIAGRAMMING PARTICIPLES

A. **Marking and Diagramming Adjectival Participles:** One should not treat attributive or substantive participles as subordinate clauses. Instead, treat such participles as you would any adjective or substantive/noun. Even though we may use a relative pronoun clause (which are subordinate clauses) to render such participles in English (e.g. "the one, who is believing, sees Jesus…"), we ought to avoid creating or describing Greek grammatical phenomenon based on English translation considerations.

1. <u>Constituent Marking</u>. The adjectival participle will be marked according to its function. (To review Constituent Marking, see §4.6.) If modifying a noun, then mark the adjectival participle along with that noun; if acting as a substantive, then mark it according to its sentence function. What may get tricky is when the participle has its own elements (direct object, modifiers). Mark these attending elements with the participle, because they are within the participle's sphere of influence. If needed, draw arrows back to the participle to show what these elements are modifying. Also, you may find it helpful to demarcate the direct object of a participle by using a double upright line (…‖…). For example, consider both Luke 6:28a and 6:28b marked:

Luke 6:28a εὐλογεῖτε <u>τοὺς καταρωμένους</u> ‖ <u>ὑμᾶς</u>,
    Bless <u>the ones cursing</u> ‖ <u>you</u>

Luke 6:28b <u>προσεύχεσθε</u> (περὶ <u>τῶν ἐπηρεαζόντων</u> ‖ <u>ὑμᾶς</u>.)
    <u>Pray</u> (concerning <u>the ones abusing</u> ‖ <u>you</u>.)

Notice how the participle and elements are treated together; double underlined as the direct object or placed in parentheses within a prepositional phrase. In these two examples, the initial verb forms are commands that are formed with the Imperative Mood (see CHAPTER 25).

2. <u>Semantic Diagramming</u>. Once again, the adjectival participle will be treated according to its function, placed in zone slots and layered, and then aligned above or below what it is modifying. Consider this wonderfully robust example from Mark 5:15 that contains five participles. The first participle is substantive, acting as the object of the main verb. The second adjectival participle is modifying the first as a predicate adjective with an implied form of εἰμί [*was*]. The third and fourth are circumstantial participles modifying the second participle. And the final adjectival participle is in apposition to the first.

Mark 5:15 *And they come to Jesus, and they behold [that] the <u>demon-possessed person</u> [was] <u>sitting</u>, <u>having been dressed</u> and <u>thinking clearly</u>—<u>the one who had had the legion</u>—and they feared.*

Mark 5:15 καὶ ἔρχονται πρὸς τὸν Ἰησοῦν καὶ θεωροῦσιν τὸν <u>δαιμονιζόμενον</u> <u>καθήμενον</u> <u>ἱματισμένον</u> καὶ <u>σωφρονοῦντα</u>, τὸν <u>ἐσχηκότα</u> τὸν λεγιῶνα, καὶ ἐφοβήθησαν.

ZONES

Ref.	Conj.	Subj.	Verb	Complement Zone
5:15	καὶ			
		ø	ἔρχονται ---πρὸς τὸν Ἰησοῦν	
	καὶ			
		ø	θεωροῦσιν	τὸν <u>δαιμονιζόμενον</u> [was] <u>καθήμενον</u> ---<u>ἱματισμένον</u> καὶ ---<u>σωφρονοῦντα</u>, =--τὸν <u>ἐσχηκότα</u> ‖ τὸν λεγιῶνα,
	καὶ	ø	ἐφοβήθησαν.	

3. <u>Reed-Kellogg Sentence Diagramming</u>. Adjectival Participles are placed on a pedestal on the location in the sentence grammar they occupy. In the diagram below, the adjectival participle would be a substantive (noun-like) and functioning as the direct object in the sentence. For actual examples, see B.2. below.

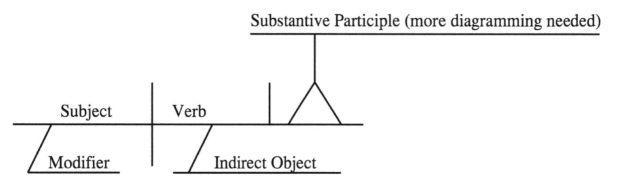

B. **Constituent Marking and Diagramming Circumstantial Participles:** In contrast to adjectival participles, one should treat circumstantial participles as subordinate clauses. So, treat such participles as you would any subordinate clause understanding that the clause begins with the adverbial participle typically (although subjects, adverbs, and other elements may actually precede the participle itself at times).

1. Constituent Marking and Semantic Diagramming. Since adverbial participles form subordinate clauses, they are placed inside brackets. For example, consider John 19:25b, which has been marked up first and then semantically diagrammed:

John 19:25b ἓν οἶδα ὅτι τυφλὸς <u>ὢν</u> ἄρτι βλέπω.

One thing I know, that, <u>being</u> blind, now I see!

Marked: <u>ἓν</u> οἶδ|α [¹ὅτι [²τυφλὸς <u>ὢν</u>²] ⌜ἄρτι⌝ βλέπ|ω.¹]

Semantic Diagram and Analysis:

Ref.	Conj.	Subj.	Verb	Complement Zone
19:25b	ø			ἓν [*quantitive emphasis, limited focus*]
		ø [*I*]	οἶδα	[*metacomment, emphasizing what is known*]
				ὅτι [*particularizing* ἓν*; important knowledge*]
				τυφλὸς [*predicate nominative of* <u>ὢν</u>]
RELATIVE ZONES				--- <u>ὢν</u> [*significance of aspect? Concessive?*]
				--- ἄρτι [*temporal adverb*]
				ø [*I*]
				βλέπω. [*contrast with* τυφλὸς]

2. Reed-Kellogg Diagramming. Circumstantial participles are diagrammed just like any subordinate clause (see §9.5). Study these examples, each with a circumstantial and adjectival participle.

Luke 19:32 ἀπελθόντες δὲ οἱ ἀπεσταλμένοι εὗρον καθὼς εἶπεν αὐτοῖς.

And <u>after departing</u>, <u>the ones (who were) sent</u> found it just as He had said to them.

Luke 19:32

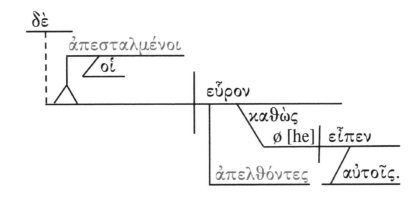

Mark 14:40a καὶ πάλιν <u>ἐλθὼν</u> εὖρεν αὐτοὺς <u>καθεύδοντας</u>,
And <u>after coming</u> again, He found them <u>sleeping</u>,

Mark 14:40a

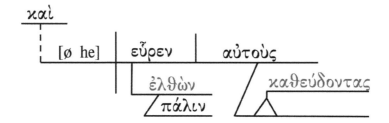

Gal 4:8 Ἀλλὰ τότε μὲν οὐκ <u>εἰδότες</u> θεὸν ἐδουλεύσατε <u>τοῖς</u> φύσει μὴ <u>οὖσιν</u> θεοῖς·
However at that time, when you did not know God, you were slaves <u>to the ones</u> <u>who</u> by nature <u>are</u> no gods.

Gal 4:8

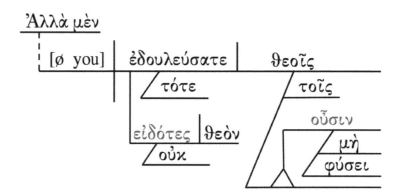

18.5 TAKING CONTROL OR "ANSWERING BACK" IN CONVERSATION: Ἀποκρίνομαι

A. **Introduction:** The verb ἀποκρίνομαι is typically glossed as *I answer*. Bruce M. Metzger, when discussing the impact of compounded prepositions, mused, "Thus, the force of ἀπό in ἀποκρίνομαι and in ἀποθνῄσκω is no longer obvious. Perhaps originally the former verb meant 'I answer back' and the latter 'I die off'."[4] Metzger was close to recovering an important aspect of this verb's usage. Indeed, the gloss *I answer* does not do justice to how the verb commonly functions in dialogue.

---

[4] Bruce Metzger, *Lexical Aids for Students of New Testament Greek*, new ed. (Princeton, NJ: Bruce M. Metzger, 1978), 79.

B. **Pragmatic Use:** The verb ἀποκρίνομαι shows dialogue participants *taking back control of the conversation or controlling the conversation by making an important statement* (Levinsohn 231-35). Ἀποκρίνομαι is commonly found as an aorist passive circumstantial participle ἀποκριθείς, but may occur as a main verb, which may make the "taking control" more pronounced as an independent action. In current English idiom, a better gloss that typically reflects this pragmatic use is *I answer back.*[5] Such a translation helps capture a person's or group's attempt to control a conversation or to manage a situation that is confronting them.

1. <u>In Response to Events</u>. This may involve an event, as when Peter, being confronted with Jesus' transfiguration and talking with Elijah and Moses, "responds/answers back" to Jesus (Oh, Peter!) by suggesting they build three tents (Mark 9:5).

> **Mark 9:5b** καὶ ἀποκριθεὶς ὁ Πέτρος λέγει τῷ Ἰησοῦ, ...
> *And responding [to the transfiguration event] Peter says to Jesus, ...*

2. <u>In Response to Speech</u>. More often, however, the verb ἀποκρίνομαι reflects the agonistic environment of challenge-riposte or statement and response back. Consider how Jesus "answers back" to the statement made to him in Mark 3:32-33:

> **Mark 3:32** καὶ ἐκάθητο περὶ αὐτὸν ὄχλος, καὶ λέγουσιν αὐτῷ· ἰδοὺ ἡ μήτηρ σου καὶ οἱ ἀδελφοί σου [καὶ αἱ ἀδελφαί σου] ἔξω ζητοῦσίν σε. 33 καὶ <u>ἀποκριθεὶς</u> αὐτοῖς λέγει· τίς ἐστιν ἡ μήτηρ μου καὶ οἱ ἀδελφοί [μου];
>
> [32] *And a crowd was sitting around him and they say to him, "Behold, your mother and your brothers are outside seeking you."* [33] *And <u>answering back</u> to them, he says, "Who is my mother or my brothers?"* (GEV)

C. **Importance for Exegesis:** Noticing when ἀποκρίνομαι is used will enhance one's understanding of the dynamics of discourse exchange or the (problematic) response to some event. While teaching through Luke's Gospel, paying attention to this verb has afforded my students and me many opportunities to observe important dynamics that affect interpretation. In the extended example below from Luke 13 (NASB95) and the brief commentary that follows, consider how the verb ἀποκρίνομαι marks significant moments in the conversation that involve making important assertions or taking control. The final instance in these occurrences uses ἀποκρίνομαι in the Indicative Mood, which makes that controlling statement more pronounced than a (dependent) circumstantial participle would have. I think you will enjoy paying attention to the strategic use of ἀποκρίνομαι to mark *answering back* as controlling a conversational exchange.

---

[5] This translation of ἀποκρίνομαι works well and is thoroughly implemented in the GlossaHouse English Translation (GEV) used in T. Michael W. Halcomb and Fredrick J. Long. *Mark GlossaHouse Illustrated Greek-English New Testament*, Accessible Greek Resources and Online Studies (Wilmore, KY: GlossaHouse, 2014).

Luke 13:1–3   Now on the same occasion there were some present who reported to Him about the Galileans whose blood Pilate had mixed with their sacrifices. [2] And Jesus said to them [καὶ ἀποκριθεὶς εἶπεν αὐτοῖς], "Do you suppose that these Galileans were *greater* sinners than all *other* Galileans because they suffered this *fate?* [3] "I tell you, no, but unless you repent, you will all likewise perish.

Notice that in 13:2, the fairly literal translation of the NASB95 misses translating ἀποκριθείς altogether, which otherwise would help mark Jesus' control of the conversation.

Luke 13:6–9 [6] And He *began* telling this parable: "A man had a fig tree which had been planted in his vineyard; and he came looking for fruit on it and did not find any. [7] "And he said to the vineyard-keeper, 'Behold, for three years I have come looking for fruit on this fig tree without finding any. Cut it down! Why does it even use up the ground?' [8] "And he <u>answered</u> and said to him [ὁ δὲ <u>ἀποκριθεὶς</u> λέγει αὐτῷ·], 'Let it alone, sir, for this year too, until I dig around it and put in fertilizer; [9] and if it bears fruit next year, *fine;* but if not, cut it down.' "

In 13:8, the circumstantial participle <u>ἀποκριθείς</u> marks the retort of the vineyard-keeper to the owner. A better way to translate would be *And he, answering back, said to him…*

Luke 13:11–16 [11] And there was a woman who for eighteen years had had a sickness caused by a spirit; and she was bent double, and could not straighten up at all. [12] When Jesus saw her, He called her over and said to her, "Woman, you are freed from your sickness." [13] And He laid His hands on her; and immediately she was made erect again and *began* glorifying God. [14] But [<u>ἀποκριθεὶς</u> δὲ] the synagogue official, indignant because Jesus had healed on the Sabbath, *began* saying to the crowd <u>in response</u>, "There are six days in which work should be done; so come during them and get healed, and not on the Sabbath day." [15] But the Lord <u>answered</u> him and said [<u>ἀπεκρίθη</u> δὲ αὐτῷ ὁ κύριος καὶ εἶπεν], "You hypocrites, does not each of you on the Sabbath untie his ox or his donkey from the stall and lead him away to water *him?* [16] "And this woman, a daughter of Abraham as she is, whom Satan has bound for eighteen long years, should she not have been released from this bond on the Sabbath day?"

In this final exchange we observe heightened intensity and "escalation." Notice the how the synagogue official offers a retort to Jesus' action of healing. In this case, the circumstantial participle ἀποκριθείς at the start of the sentence frames the subsequent description as "answering back" in an argumentative environment. Jesus retorts back strongly, so strongly that ἀποκρίνομαι in found in the Indicative Mood.

Complete WORKBOOK EXERCISES 18 and consult the ANSWER KEY & GUIDE as needed.

CASE IN POINT 18: A LOOK AT SOME PARTICIPLES IN MATTHEW 8:14

You have now learned all the forms of the participles. Participles are very common, and a careful look at them will usually be exegetically rewarding. Here is one passage that is given greater vividness after one considers the meaning of the participles (underlined). These are not always well represented in the English translations; some are included for comparison.

Matt 8:14 Καὶ <u>ἐλθὼν</u> ὁ Ἰησοῦς εἰς τὴν οἰκίαν Πέτρου εἶδεν τὴν πενθερὰν αὐτοῦ <u>βεβλη-μένην</u> καὶ <u>πυρέσσουσαν</u>· [πυρέσσω= *I am feverish*]

Matt 8:14 *And <u>after</u> Jesus <u>came</u> into Peter's home, He saw his mother-in-law <u>having been cast (in bed)</u> and <u>having a fever</u>.*

Matt 8:14 <u>When</u> Jesus <u>came</u> into Peter's home, He saw his mother-in-law <u>lying sick in bed</u> with a fever. (NASB95)

Matt 8:14 <u>When</u> Jesus <u>arrived</u> at Peter's house, Peter's mother-in-law <u>was sick in bed</u> with a high fever. (NLT)

Matt 8:14 And <u>when</u> Jesus <u>entered</u> Peter's house, he saw his mother-in-law <u>lying sick</u> with a fever. (ESV)

This verse begins with a circumstantial participle that has an adverbial temporal sense. Since it is Aorist in tense, a translation indicating its "time priorness" is preferable. The temporal conjunction *after* would help accomplish this. So, Matt 8:14 presents the reader with a sequence of events: *After Jesus came…, He saw….*

Now, let's look at the next two participles. Can you parse them? The first, βεβλημένην, is RM/PP FAS (Perfect, middle/passive, participle, feminine, accusative, singular). The second, πυρέσσουσαν, is PAP FAS; so, it has the same gender, case, and number, but it is present active in tense and voice. Are these participles functioning as circumstantial or adjectival? Well, since they have no definite article, we initially assume circumstantial. This would seem to be confirmed, since the noun they are modifying has a definite article, so if they were adjectival, we would expect them to have a definite article. They are modifying τὴν πενθερὰν *mother-in-law*.

As circumstantial and post-nuclear, we observe that the participles explain more about what Jesus saw. With the first participle βεβλημένην and translated as passive *having been cast*, we meet with an idiomatic expression; it indicates that she was laid onto a bed. The perfect tense vividly portrays a person being "cast-placed" onto a bed. The passive voice indicates that she was moved into the location by another person (or others). The other participle πυρέσσουσαν is present in tense and vividly portrays Peter's mother-in-law *continuously* burning with fever. Taken together, the Greek text depicts a woman cast onto a bed and burning up with fever. This is a very troubling situation. A closer investigation of both participles adds vividness to the situation. When preaching, such vividness could help us elaborate upon the pressing need of the situation. In fact, Jesus acts immediately:

Matt 8:15 καὶ ἥψατο τῆς χειρὸς αὐτῆς, καὶ ἀφῆκεν αὐτὴν ὁ πυρετός, καὶ ἠγέρθη καὶ διηκόνει αὐτῷ.

And he held her hand, and the fever departed her, and she arose and began serving him.

And there are immediate results and consequences, as stressed by four successive main verbs conjoined with καί.

Below is a bas-relief of a sacrificial scene at an Asklepieion (Ἀσκληπιεῖον), a temple dedicated to the god Asklepeios.[6] Such healing temples were located in various cities and sites around the Mediterranean world, with magnificent examples at Epidaurus and Pergamum. People would travel to an Asklepieion and spend the night there, report their dreams to the priests. Testimonials of healings were then posted outside. This relief is located inside a church building at Merbaka near Argos in the Peloponnese. It is ex-voto scene where supplicants offer sacrifices to fulfill a vow, here a ram sacrifice. The large gods Asclepius and his daughter Hygeia recline eating, with the snake below Asklepeios, his calling card. Sometimes the snake is depicted as receiving food. A servant boy dips a cup into the vase (κρατήρ) full of drink. The family of supplicants has hands slightly raised as a sign of adoration or prayer (προσευχή), a word commonly used in the GNT.

_____

[6] The image and description has been edited from Victor Duruy, *History of Greece, and of the Greek People, from the Earliest Times to the Roman Conquest*, trans. M. M. Ripley, vol. I, sect. II (Boston: Estes and Lauriat, 1890), 417.

CHAPTER 19

19.0 VOCABULARY
19.1 REFLEXIVE PRONOUNS (Ἀντανακλαστικὴ Ἀντωνυμία)
19.2 RECIPROCAL PRONOUNS (ἡ Ἀμοιβαία Ἀντωνυμία)
19.3 POSSESSIVE PRONOUNS (Κτητικαὶ Ἀντωνυμίαι)
19.4 INDEFINITE RELATIVE PRONOUNS (Ἀντωνυμίαι Ἀόριστοι καὶ Ἀναφορικαί)
    CHECK POINT 19.1-4 PRONOUNS
19.5 PERIPHRASTIC USE OF THE PARTICIPLE
19.6 COMPLEMENTARY USE OF THE PARTICIPLE
CASE IN POINT 19: SPECIAL USES OF PARTICIPLES IN MATT 9:35-36

Participles are dynamic; they often help to elaborate events in narrative discourse or advance arguments in non-narrative discourse, such as in the Apostle Paul's epistles. As such, participles carry much weight in their usage. Another look at participles will help to consolidate your learning. In particular, Matt 9:35-36 is worth looking at more closely, since Jesus' ministry is programmatically described using participles. Furthermore, Jesus sees the crowds and has compassion on them. Why? How might Jesus' ministry practices and concerns be exemplary, indeed, programmatic for our ministry practices and concerns today?

In this chapter, two further uses of the participle are covered: **Periphrastic** and **Supplementary**. Before this, however, you will encounter four more types of pronouns: **Reflexive**, **Reciprocal**, **Possessive**, and **Indefinite Relative**.

VOCABULARY 19   SPECIAL PRONOUNS

Reflexive Pronoun:

ἐμαυτοῦ [37]	of myself
σεαυτοῦ [43]	of yourself
ἑαυτοῦ [321]	of himself, herself, itself

Indefinite Relative Pronoun:

ὅστις, ἥτις, ὅτι [144]	who(soever), what(soever)

Reciprocal Pronoun:

ἀλλήλων [100]	one another

Possessive Pronouns:

ἐμός, ἐμή, ἐμόν [68]	my, mine
σός, σή, σόν [24]	your, yours (sg.)
ἡμέτερος, -α, -ον [7]	our, ours
ὑμέτερος, -α, -ον [11]	your (pl.)

After learning this vocabulary, you will know 75.7% of the words in the GNT. If you are able, listen to the audio of VOCABULARY 19 and complete the CROSSWORD PUZZLE in the EXERCISES.

NOTES ON VOCABULARY 19:
These pronouns use the First and Second Declension endings. The indefinite relative pronoun *also* uses the 3rd Declension endings. So, no new endings need to be learned. For all the Greek pronouns in one chart, see APPENDIX §10.

19.1 REFLEXIVE PRONOUNS (Ἀντανακλαστικὴ Ἀντωνυμία)

A. **Introduction and Semantics:** These pronouns reflect back upon the subject of their clause. As such, and when they are so used, they bring even more attention to the subject, i.e. they are emphatic in significance. Wallace (350) states: "the reflexive pronoun is used to *highlight the participation of the subject* in the verbal action, as direct object, indirect object, intensifier, etc." Such attention must be studied carefully for contextual significance. Functionally, too, "The reflexive pronoun itself is really possessive when in the genitive case" (Robertson 289).

B. **Formation:** The forms of the Greek reflexive pronoun are similar to the 3rd person personal pronoun (αὐτός, -ή, -όν). However, there are two differences. First, the reflexive pronouns have **no** nominative forms. Second, to the front of αὐτοῦ, -ῆς, -οῦ are added a **person prefix**:

ἐμ = 1st person *myself*
σε = 2nd person *yourself*
ἑ = 3rd person singular *himself, herself, itself* with singular endings
ἑ = 1st, 2nd, 3rd plural *ourselves, yourselves, themselves* with plural endings

All <u>plural</u> reflexives (regardless of person) use simply an ἑ ψιλόν prefix. **Thus, first, second, and third persons have the same form in the plural.** Context must determine how to translate these identical forms. Here are the forms:

	FIRST PERSON *myself*		**SECOND PERSON** *yourself*		**THIRD PERSON** *himself, herself, itself*		
sg.	Masc.	Fem.	Masc.	Fem.	Masc.	Fem.	Neut.
gen.	ἐμ-αυτοῦ	ἐμ-αυτῆς	σε-αυτοῦ	σε-αυτῆς	ἑ-αυτοῦ	ἑ-αυτῆς	ἑ-αυτοῦ
dat.	ἐμ-αυτῷ	ἐμ-αυτῇ	σε-αυτῷ	σε-αυτῇ	ἑ-αυτῷ	ἑ-αυτῇ	ἑ-αυτῷ
acc.	ἐμ-αυτόν	ἐμ-αυτήν	σε-αυτόν	σε-αυτήν	ἑ-αυτόν	ἑ-αυτήν	ἑ-αυτό

Plural forms are same for 1st, 2nd, and 3rd Persons.

	ourselves, yourselves, themselves		
pl.	Masc.	Fem.	Neut.
gen.	ἑ-αυτῶν	ἑ-αυτῶν	ἑ-αυτῶν
dat.	ἑ-αυτοῖς	ἑ-αυταῖς	ἑ-αυτοῖς
acc.	ἑ-αυτ-ούς	ἑ-αυτάς	ἑ-αυτά

C. **Examples and Discussion:** Consider these examples with the reflexive pronoun:

John 7:35a εἶπον οὖν οἱ Ἰουδαῖοι πρὸς <u>ἑαυτούς</u>,
Therefore, the Jewish Officials said to <u>themselves</u>,

John 7:28b ἀπ᾽ ἐμαυτοῦ οὐκ ἐλήλυθα.
I have not come from myself.

Luke 2:3 καὶ ἐπορεύοντο πάντες ἀπογράφεσθαι, ἕκαστος εἰς τὴν ἑαυτοῦ πόλιν.
And all of them were travelling to register, each into his own city.

In each example, the reflexive pronoun refers back to the subject, emphasizing their participation (or in John 7:28b, the denial of such). In John 7:35a, the prepositional phrase with reflexive pronoun communicates conversation amongst themselves. In John 7:28b, the reflexive pronoun is used in Jesus' denial of originating *from himself* (ἀπ᾽ ἐμαυτοῦ). Finally, the reflexive pronoun in Luke 2:3 is sandwiched in 1st attributive position between the article and its substantive. Such occurs 36 times in the GNT; personal possession is emphasized in such usage.

19.2 RECIPROCAL PRONOUNS (ἡ Ἀμοιβαία Ἀντωνυμία)

A. **Introduction and Semantics:** The reciprocal pronoun is always plural and carries the notion of a group of people acting in relation to themselves, i.e., upon *one another*.[1] For example, *We were caring for one another*. **Integral to this pronoun is it being marked + communal reciprocity.** It has been said that behind every use of the reciprocal pronoun is an important point about Christian community to be made in preaching.

B. **Formation:** This pronoun is always masculine plural in form and has no nominative form.

gen.	ἀλλήλων	*of one another*
dat.	ἀλλήλοις	*to/for one another*
acc.	ἀλλήλους	*one another*

C. **Example:**

John 4:33 ἔλεγον οὖν οἱ μαθηταὶ πρὸς ἀλλήλους,...
Therefore, the disciples were speaking to one another, ...

19.3 POSSESSIVE PRONOUNS (Κτητικαὶ Ἀντωνυμίαι)

A. **Introduction and Semantics:** The possessive pronoun ἐμός, -ή, -όν may very well be treated as an adjective (Wallace 348 n.90). It indicates possession (*my, mine*), but can also be used as an agent or object, as in the statement *do this in remembrance of me* (εἰς τὴν ἐμὴν ἀνάμνησιν) (BDAG 323). In this latter example, the *of me* is similar in sense to an objective genitive, receiving here the action of *remembering*. So, semantically what does ἐμός, -ή, -όν inherently communicate? It would appear that the possessive pronoun is marked + proximity

---

[1] However, it is interesting that Luke 23:12 reports that two individuals, Herod and Pilate, (not groups) became friends *with one another* (μετ᾽ ἀλλήλων), unless the social circles surrounding each political leader is implied.

of personal relationship, which may often indicate possession, but may not always be restricted to this. Regardless, Robertson states correctly: "When these possessive forms occur in the N. T. there is emphasis" (684). See D. further below.

B. **Formation:** The possessive pronoun ἐμός, -ή, -όν *my, mine* has masculine, feminine, and neuter endings (like an adjective), in order to agree in gender, number, and case with the noun it is modifying. The endings are from the First and Second Declension:

ἐμός, -ή, -όν[68]	*my, mine*
ἡμέτερος, -α, -ον[7]	*our, ours*
σός, σή, σόν[24]	*your, yours* (sg.)
ὑμέτερος, -α, -ον[11]	*your* (pl.)

C. **Examples:** Here are examples with the first in the 1st attributive position and the second in the 2nd attributive position.

1st attributive position:	εἰς τὸ <u>ἐμὸν</u> ὄνομα	ἡ <u>ἐμὴ</u> διδαχὴ
	or	or
2nd attributive position:	εἰς τὸ ὄνομα τὸ <u>ἐμὸν</u>	ἡ διδαχὴ ἡ <u>ἐμὴ</u>
	into <u>my</u> name	*<u>my</u> teaching*

D. **Further Discussion of Emphasis and Regional Influence:** Because of significant disagreement about the emphatic nature of the possessive pronoun, it would be helpful to describe what is said, weigh the evidence, and consider the question in some detail. Such a review should help remind students of the history of interpretation, the disagreements therein, and the historical and regional (geographic) dimension of the study of language.

1. <u>Ambivalence on Emphatic Nature in Lexicons and Philologists.</u>

   a. <u>BDAG</u>. In this standard NT lexicon, there is ambivalence whether this possessive pronoun should be considered emphatic. The pronoun is described initially as an adjective as follows: "in attributive [position], often without special emphasis, frequently used"; yet, in the immediately following subentry, it reads: "for the possessive genitive, where μου could be used in nearly all cases...; with emphasis ....τῇ ἐμῇ χειρί *w. my own hand* ... **1 Cor 16:21**" (BDAG 323.a.α.). So, it is acknowledged that the possessive pronoun can have emphasis. How is such determined? Is this inherent to the pronoun itself or by its use in context?

   b. <u>LSJ</u>. In this classical lexicon, it is acknowledged that the genitive form of the personal pronoun αὐτός may strengthen this possessive notion (LSJ-Int 253.1). By implication, by itself ἐμός, -ή, -όν is not strengthened.

c. <u>Moulton and Milligan (MM)</u>. In their summary of scholarly studies of usage of ἐμός, Moulton and Milligan indicate that in Ptolemaic papyri (i.e. from Egypt in the era of Ptolemy dynasties, 3rd century BC and onward) there is a tendency for ἐμός to be replaced by ἐμαυτοῦ.[2]

d. <u>Deissmann</u>. In his discussion of a latter instance where ἐμός was used (dated AD 192) in the statement at the end of the brief letter providing details on who should receive wheat, concludes with this statement: καὶ ἤδη ποτὲ δὸς τῇ ἐμῇ παιδίσκῃ τὰς τοῦ ϝγ ε. *And now at length give to my maid the 3 ¾ artabae of wheat.* Deissmann adds a footnote to ἐμῇ: "ἐμός unemphatic as, for example, in Rom 10:1."[3] However, this brief letter concludes a list, and is set off oddly with the adverbs ἤδη ποτὲ (as Deissmann also notes is found in Rom 1:10!) meaning *now at last*; there is here an implied contrast with those first receiving wheat and *now at last* the owner himself receiving wheat given to his maid. So, the use of ἐμός may emphasize a slight degree of contrast (if only we understood more of the social context!) that the genitive personal pronoun μου would not have.

e. <u>Rom 10:1 Unemphatic or Emphatic?</u> Moulton and Milligan cite (seemingly approvingly) Deissmann's view that Rom 10:1 is unemphatic. I flatly diasgree. Let's look at Paul's heartfelt sentiment about the ultimate salvation of his kinsfolk (cf. Rom 9:1-5!).

Rom 10:1 Ἀδελφοί, ἡ μὲν εὐδοκία τῆς ἐμῆς καρδίας καὶ ἡ δέησις πρὸς τὸν θεὸν ὑπὲρ αὐτῶν εἰς σωτηρίαν.
Brethren, indeed the desire of <u>my</u> heart and petition to God for them [is] for salvation.

Ref.	**Conj.**	**Subj.**	**Verb.**
Rom 10:1 Ἀδελφοί			[vocative emphasis]
		ἡ	
	μὲν		[+affirmative emphasis]
		εὐδοκία	
		---τῆς ἐμῆς καρδίας	[emphatic possession]
		καὶ	
		ἡ δέησις	[is] [implied verb sets off PPs]
		---πρὸς τὸν θεὸν	
		---ὑπὲρ αὐτῶν	
		---εἰς σωτηρίαν. [goal of prayer]	

---

[2] James Hope Moulton and George Milligan, *The Vocabulary of the Greek Testament* (London: Hodder and Stoughton, 1930), 206.

[3] G. Adolf Deissmann, *Light from the Ancient East: The New Testament Illustrated by Recently Discovered Texts of the Graeco-Roman World*, trans. L. R. M. Strachan, 2nd ed. (London: Hodder & Stoughton, 1910), 186.

Several emphatic features work together to indicate that this is no trite statement, but rather is an earnest statement that reflects Paul's proximate heart-level concern that is conjoined with his investment in petitionary prayer. First, the vocative Ἀδελφοί sets off what follows. Second, the μέν signals +affirmative emphasis and advances beyond the conclusion of ch. 9, which stressed Israel's stumbling (9:31-33), to Paul's heart's desire and prayer for their salvation. Third, the lack of a main verb places more weight on the prepositional phrases, which culminate in the naturally prominent notion of salvation (εἰς σωτηρίαν). So, the presence of the possessive pronoun acting adjectivally in the phrase τῆς ἐμῆς καρδίας contributes in communicating Paul's proximity of concern in his own heart for petition for his kinsfolk, which participates in the larger sense of urgent concern that Paul expresses at transitional moments in Romans 9-11 as is marked by his self-referentiality in the discourse (e.g. 9:1-3; 10:2; 11:1, 13-14).

2. <u>A Regional Idiom?</u> Moulton and Milligan also report the following possibility: "The use of ἐμός is very characteristic of the Johannine writings... and Thumb (*ThLZ*, 1903, p. 421) regards this as a sign of their connexion with Asia Minor, in view of the fact that ἐμός survives in modern Pontic—Cappadocian Greek, as against μου elsewhere...".[4] Robertson (288-89) cautions about making too much of this:

> The large amount of dialogue in the Gospel of John perhaps explains the frequency of the pronoun there. The possessive ἐμός is naturally in the mouth of Jesus (or of John his reporter) more than σός, for Jesus is speaking so much about himself. The possessive is more formal and more emphatic in the solemn words of Jesus in this Gospel. This is probably the explanation coupled with the fact that John was doubtless in Asia also when he wrote the Gospel and was open to whatever influence in that direction was there.

3. <u>Emphatic</u>. In agreement with Robertson, the use of the possessive pronoun should be considered emphatic for these reasons:

o the pronoun is relatively rare, and so its use is more noticeable, even if influenced by broader regional practices;
o the 1st sg. forms are accented and have a prefixed morpheme ἐ- that make this form look much like or even identical to the emphatic personal pronoun forms that have ἐ- prefixed (ἐμού, ἐμοί, ἐμέ);
o the 2nd sg. forms are accented like the emphatic forms of the 2nd personal pronoun (σύ, σού, σοί, σέ).
o the pronoun contains longer formations for the 1st and 2nd person plural: ἡμέτερος, -α, -ον and ὑμέτερος, -α, -ον as opposed to the genitive equivalents ἡμῶν and ὑμῶν.
o the pronoun often occurs in the 2nd attributive position, which repeats the article in the construction, marking even more the possessive pronoun.

---

[4] Moulton and Milligan, *Vocabulary*, 207.

In the end, a simpler and more typical way to indicate pronominal possession would be to use genitive forms of the personal pronoun: μου/ἡμῶν, σου/ὑμῶν, and αὐτοῦ/αὐτῶν or the genitive form of the reflexive pronoun

E. **Scales of Pronominal Possesive Modification and Emphasis:** By now we have learned that possession using pronouns and like words (such as ἴδιος *one's own*; see Robertson 289) may be accomplished in a variety of ways: personal pronouns and their relative position before or after the substantive possessed; the reflexive pronoun in the gentive case; the possessive pronouns in 1st or 2nd attributive position or alone as a substantive; and ἴδιος *one's own*. Are these equal in semantic import? Choice implies meaning; not all ways are equal. One should notice which construction is used and consider whether a scale of emphasis exists on the type of possessive marked by one construction as opposed to another. Let me list all these indicators of possession (assumed as occuring in the genitive case where needed):

1. The personal pronouns (ἐγώ, σύ, and αὐτός) in the genitive can mean many things, one of which is possession; these are thus unmarked for any special attention drawn to the possession and could be considered the default construction. However, the emphatic forms of ἐγώ and σύ would reflect elevated attention to these pronouns, and if used possessively as determined by context, then would indicate intensification of possessive import. Likewise, genitive forms of αὐτός may be added to genitives indicating possession, thus increasing the possessive emphasis. See example further below with Luke 2:35.
2. Ἴδιος is marked + unique possession (as opposed to belonging to others of a similar kind).
3. The reflexive pronoun ἐμαυτοῦ, σεαυτοῦ, etc. is marked + subject involvement in the possession somehow in relation to the verbal action.
4. The possessive pronoun ἐμός is marked + proximity of personal relationship.

Apart from considering where to place reflexive pronouns (with possessive meaning) and instances of ἴδιος *one's own*, which admittedly might be quite strong in asserting possession, I would propose the following two-dimensional scale (which is inherently flawed!) from least marked (or default) to most marked as far as emphasizing pronominal possession.

SCALE OF PROMINENCE IN PRONOMINAL POSSESSION			
1. Least marked	Default	τὴν ψυχήν <u>σου</u>	Personal Pronoun
2.	Emphatic Form	τὴν ψυχὴν <u>σοῦ</u>	
3	Sandwiched Genitive	τήν <u>σου</u> ψυχὴν	
4.	Fronted Genitive	<u>σου</u> τὴν ψυχήν	
5.	Fronted Emphatic Form	<u>σοῦ</u> τὴν ψυχήν	
6.	1st Attributive Position	τὴν <u>σὴν</u> ψυχήν	Possessive Pronoun
7. Most marked	2nd Attributive Position	τὴν ψυχήν τὴν <u>σήν</u>	

However, it seems likely that the middle options are nearly equivalent (e.g. the fronted forms of 4. and 5. may be more marked than 6.). A three dimensional model would be more suitable, but more research would be necessary. However, if this scale is more or less correct, it would indicate that Greek speakers had an array of options not simply to communicate pronominal possession, but to stress that possessive relationship *simply by using the pronouns themselves*. Indeed, other factors must be accounted for to discern the presence and degree of emphasis: relative location (before or after the noun possessed), sentence location (fronted vs. final position), additional emphatic words (additive adverbial καί, intensive αὐτός, etc.), and other types of collaborative emphasis (abutment, structural, lexical repetition, aspectual, etc.). For example, consider how the fronted placement, the presence of additive-adverbial καί before the genitive pronoun form, and the intensive use of αὐτός all occur together to strengthen the already emphatic pronoun form σοῦ (accented) in the possessive statement of Luke 2:35 when Simeon prophesies to Mary about her child Jesus.[5]

Luke 2:35 καὶ σοῦ [δὲ] αὐτῆς τὴν ψυχὴν διελεύσεται ῥομφαία ...
moreover also your very own soul a sword will pierce....

19.4 INDEFINITE RELATIVE PRONOUNS (Ἀντωνυμίαι Ἀόριστοι καὶ Ἀναφορικαί)

A. **Introduction and Semantics:** Although this pronoun is a combination of the Relative and Indefinite Pronouns in form, its function is essentially like the relative pronoun. As such, it begins a relative clause, which, remember, may be classified as restrictive (i.e. disambiguating reference) or non-restrictive/explanatory (see §9.3.E. RELATIVE PRONOUNS). The explanatory nature of the indefinite relative pronouns is suitable for use to indicate a causal sense such that they can be translated with *because* or *since*. Maximilian Zerwick explains that ὅστις, when having a determinate antecedent, "may easily have a causal sense ('in as much as') or consecutive one ('such as')."[6] This sense and usage arises from the contribution of the indefinite pronoun τις (*someone*), which generalizes the indefinite relative pronoun to mean *whosoever*. See examples below (cf. Wallace 343-45).

B. **Formation:** This pronoun combines the forms of the Relative and Indefinite Pronouns. In this way, the indefinite-relative pronoun shows all the forms of the three declensions (1st, 2nd, 3rd)! Remarkable! However, it occurs most frequently in the nominative case.

---

[5] "The accented forms are used in the oblique cases of the sing. when emphasis is to be laid on the pron. or when a contrast is intended σοῦ" (BDAG 950.b.α.).

[6] Maximilian Zerwick, *Biblical Greek: Illustrated by Examples*, trans. Joseph Smith, 4th ed., Scripta Pontificii Instituti Biblici 114 (Rome: Editrice Pontificio Istitutio Biblico, 1963), §163.

who(soever); what(soever)

	Masc.	**Fem.**	**Neut.**
sg. nom.	ὅστις	ἥτις	ὅτι*
gen.	οὗτινος	ἧστινος	οὗτινος
dat.	ᾧτινι	ᾗτινι	ᾧτινι
acc.	ὅντινα	ἥντινα	ὅτι*

sg. nom. ...	*This form does not occur in the GNT; so don't confuse this with the conjunction ὅτι.*

pl. nom.	οἵτινες	αἵτινες	ἅτινα
gen.	ὧντινων	ὧντινων	ὧντινων
dat.	οἷστισι	αἷστισιν	οἷστισιν
acc.	οὕστινας	ἅστινας	ἅτινα

C. Examples and Discussion:

Matt 7:15 Προσέχετε ἀπὸ τῶν ψευδοπροφητῶν, <u>οἵτινες</u> ἔρχονται πρὸς ὑμᾶς ἐν ἐνδύμασιν προβάτων, ἔσωθεν δέ εἰσιν λύκοι ἅρπαγες.

Watch out for the false prophets, <u>who</u> come to you in sheep's clothing, but inside they are ravenous wolves.

Notice how in Matt 7:15, the indefinite relative clause (beginning with <u>who</u>) could well be translated at its start *since they...*

Matt 19:12 εἰσὶν γὰρ εὐνοῦχοι <u>οἵτινες</u> ἐκ κοιλίας μητρὸς ἐγεννήθησαν οὕτως,

For they are eunuchs <u>who</u> are born thus from the womb of (their) mother,

Matt 27:55 Ἦσαν δὲ ἐκεῖ γυναῖκες πολλαὶ... <u>αἵτινες</u> ἠκολούθησαν τῷ Ἰησοῦ ἀπὸ τῆς Γαλιλαιας

There were many women there...<u>who</u> followed Jesus from Galilee

In these last two examples, one can see how the explanatory function of the indefinite relative pronouns has a supportive meaning (replace <u>who</u> with <u>since they...</u>). We should remember that the conjunction ὅτι *that, because* originated from this neuter singular pronoun form. In terms of pragmatics, the choice of an indefinite relative pronoun as opposed to a coordinating conjunction like γάρ, subordinating conjunctions like ὅτι, διότι, ἐπεί, ἐπειδή, and ἐπειδήπερ, or other special construction using prepositions (e.g., διά) to indicate support is likely motivated by the open scope of the pronoun (i.e., *anyone, someone*) and its nominal focus and thus efficiency, since it simply elaborates upon some referent.

CHECK POINT 19.1-4 PRONOUNS

Explain the exegetical significance of the underlined pronouns in the verses below. Notice that other pronouns are found.

John 5:30 Οὐ δύναμαι ἐγὼ ποιεῖν ἀπ' <u>ἐμαυτοῦ</u> οὐδέν· καθὼς ἀκούω κρίνω, καὶ ἡ κρίσις ἡ <u>ἐμὴ</u> δικαία ἐστίν, ὅτι οὐ ζητῶ τὸ θέλημα τὸ <u>ἐμὸν</u> ἀλλὰ τὸ θέλημα τοῦ πέμψαντός με.

I am not able to do anything from <u>myself</u>; just as I hear, I judge, and <u>my</u> judgment is righteous, because I am not seeking <u>my</u> will, but the will of the One who sent me.

<u>ἐμαυτοῦ</u> =

<u>ἐμὴ</u> =

<u>ἐμὸν</u> =

John 15:12 Αὕτη ἐστὶν ἡ ἐντολὴ ἡ <u>ἐμή</u>, ἵνα ἀγαπᾶτε <u>ἀλλήλους</u> καθὼς ἠγάπησα ὑμᾶς.

This is <u>my</u> commandment, that you love <u>one another</u> just as I loved you.

<u>ἐμή</u> =

<u>ἀλλήλους</u> =

Matt 18:4-5 <u>ὅστις</u> οὖν ταπεινώσει <u>ἑαυτὸν</u> ὡς τὸ παιδίον τοῦτο, οὗτός ἐστιν ὁ μείζων ἐν τῇ βασιλείᾳ τῶν οὐρανῶν. **5** καὶ <u>ὃς</u> ἐὰν δέξηται ἓν παιδίον <u>τοιοῦτο</u> ἐπὶ τῷ ὀνόματί μου, <u>ἐμὲ</u> δέχεται.

*Therefore, <u>who(soever)</u> will humble <u>himself</u> [or <u>herself</u>] as this little child, this person is rather great in the kingdom of the heavens. **5** And <u>the one who</u> receives one little child <u>such as this</u> in my name, receives <u>me</u>.*

ὅστις =

ἑαυτὸν =

BONUS: Discuss the following pronouns in 18:5:

ὃς =

ἐμὲ =

EXTRA CREDIT (see CH.26):

τοιοῦτο =

Eph 4:32 γίνεσθε [δὲ] εἰς <u>ἀλλήλους</u> χρηστοί, εὔσπλαγχνοι, χαριζόμενοι <u>ἑαυτοῖς</u>, καθὼς καὶ ὁ θεὸς ἐν Χριστῷ ἐχαρίσατο ὑμῖν.

Moreover, be kind to <u>one another</u>, compassionate, forgiving <u>yourselves</u>, just as also God in Christ forgave you.

<u>ἀλλήλους</u> =

<u>ἑαυτοῖς</u> =

SUGGESTED ANSWERS

John 5:30 Οὐ δύναμαι ἐγὼ ποιεῖν ἀπ᾿ <u>ἐμαυτοῦ</u> οὐδέν· καθὼς ἀκούω κρίνω, καὶ ἡ κρίσις ἡ <u>ἐμὴ</u> δικαία ἐστίν, ὅτι οὐ ζητῶ τὸ θέλημα τὸ <u>ἐμὸν</u> ἀλλὰ τὸ θέλημα τοῦ πέμψαντός με.

I am not able to do anything from <u>myself</u>; just as I hear, I judge, and <u>my</u> judgment is right-eous, because I am not seeking <u>my</u> will, but the will of the One who sent me.

<u>ἐμαυτοῦ</u> = Reflexive, relates back to the already emphatically expressed subject ἐγὼ (Jesus as referent). Helps stress Jesus' point that he did not act alone or independent to the Father.

<u>ἐμὴ</u> = Possessive pronoun with emphasis on Jesus. Again, this pronoun contributes to Jesus' point of having judgment, but a judgment dependent on the One who sent him.

ἐμὸν = Possessive pronoun with emphasis; the phrase structurally is parallel and found in a point-counter point set with οὐ ... ἀλλά. What is contrasted is whose will Jesus follows (not his own, but the One who sent him).

John 15:12 Αὕτη ἐστὶν ἡ ἐντολὴ ἡ ἐμή, ἵνα ἀγαπᾶτε ἀλλήλους καθὼς ἠγάπησα ὑμᾶς.

This is my commandment, that you love one another just as I loved you.

ἐμή = Possessive pronoun with emphasis on Jesus as the owner/source of the this central command to love one another.

ἀλλήλους = The reciprocal pronoun stresses the mutuality of the love. It is shared within community relationships.

Matt 18:4-5 ὅστις οὖν ταπεινώσει ἑαυτὸν ὡς τὸ παιδίον τοῦτο, οὗτός ἐστιν ὁ μείζων ἐν τῇ βασιλείᾳ τῶν οὐρανῶν. 5 καὶ ὃς ἐὰν δέξηται ἓν παιδίον τοιοῦτο ἐπὶ τῷ ὀνόματί μου, ἐμὲ δέχεται.

Therefore, who(soever) will humble himself [or herself] as this little child, this person is rather great in the kingdom of the heavens. 5 And the one who receives one little child such as this in my name, receives me.

ὅστις = The indefinite relative pronoun produces a relative pronoun clause that has supportive or causal function, here almost functioning as a supposition (the "if" part) of a conditional sentence. It is often open in scope.

ἑαυτὸν = The reflexive pronoun stresses self-response of humbling; this is something that a person does in relation to self; it is not forced by another.

BONUS: Discuss the following pronouns in 18:5:

ὃς = The relative pronoun creates a subordinate clause, and here with ἐάν actually forms a conditional sentence.

ἐμὲ = This is an emphatic form of the personal pronoun με. It stresses Jesus as co-identified with the little child. God aligns with the poor, the humble, and the lowly.

EXTRA CREDIT (see CH.26):

τοιοῦτο = This is a demonstrative pronoun of quality, that entails qualitative emphasis; it stresses the quality of the little child as the recipient of hospitality and loving care.

Eph 4:32 γίνεσθε [δὲ] εἰς ἀλλήλους χρηστοί, εὔσπλαγχνοι, χαριζόμενοι ἑαυτοῖς, καθὼς καὶ ὁ θεὸς ἐν Χριστῷ ἐχαρίσατο ὑμῖν.

Moreover, be kind to one another, compassionate, forgiving yourselves, just as also God in Christ forgave you.

ἀλλήλους = The reciprocal pronoun stresses the mutuality of the kindness. It is shared within community relationships.

ἑαυτοῖς = The reflexive pronoun indicates that forgiveness of self is critical, and perhaps even prior, to the kindness and compassion shown to one another.

19.5 PERIPHRASTIC USE OF THE PARTICIPLE

A. **Supplementary Participles:** Periphrastic and Complementary Participles are generally classified as supplementary participles, because in each construction the participles are added as supplements to a finite verb. "The attributive and circumstantial participles are commonly not necessary to the *construction*; but the removal of a supplementary participle may make the construction incomplete" (Smyth 455).

B. **Periphrastic Participles in Construction:**

1. <u>Verb of Being Plus Participle</u>. The periphrastic construction involves a verb of being, usually εἰμί, but also γίνομαι, or more rarely ὑπάρχομαι or ἔχω, in any tense and a Present or Perfect Tense participle. Very rarely is the Aorist participle used. Wallace (648, Table 11-*The Forms of the Periphrastic Participle*) helpfully charts the tense equivalence of the various periphrastic constructions in the NT. The Imperfect Tense equivalent is the most frequently occurring construction.

Finite Verb (of εἰμί)	+	*Participle*	=	*Finite Tense Equivalent*
Present	+	Present	=	Present
Imperfect	+	Present	=	Imperfect
Future	+	Present	=	Future
Present	+	Perfect	=	Perfect
Imperfect	+	Perfect	=	Pluperfect

2. <u>Anarthrous Participle</u>. The periphrastic participle **<u>never</u>** occurs with the article.

3. <u>Nominative and Agreeing with the Verb in Number</u>. The participle must be in the nominative case (unless in a somewhat rare accusative infinitive construction). The periphrastic participle must agree in number with the verb and subject.

4. <u>With Other Verbal Moods</u>. In addition to the Indicative Mood, the periphrastic construction occurs with the other moods—the Imperative, Subjunctive, and Infinitive, and another Participle. Each mood will offer distinctive dimensions to the semantics of the construction—which is usually important for exegesis. These other moods will be briefly treated in §25.4 PERIPHRASTIC PARTICIPLES WITH NON-INDICATIVE MOODS. For example, here is a periphrastic construction used with the participle ὄντες *being* (masc.nom.pl.).

> **Eph 4:18a** ἐσκοτωμένοι τῇ διανοίᾳ <u>ὄντες</u>...
>> *since they <u>are</u> (having been) darkened in (their) understanding...*

5. <u>Close but Not Near Proximity</u>. Usually, the participle occurs in close proximity, but may be separated by many intervening modifiers or objects.[7] Here are a few examples:

Matt 19:22 ἦν γὰρ ἔχων κτήματα πολλά
For <u>he was having [had]</u> many possessions

Matt 10:22 καὶ ἔσεσθε μισούμενοι ὑπὸ πάντων διὰ τὸ ὄνομά μου.
And <u>you will be hated</u> by many because of my name.

Acts 8:13a ὁ δὲ Σίμων καὶ αὐτὸς ἐπίστευσεν καὶ βαπτισθεὶς ἦν.
Simon even himself believed and <u>was baptized</u>.

Luke 18:34b καὶ ἦν τὸ ῥῆμα τοῦτο κεκρυμμένον ἀπ᾽ αὐτῶν.
This word <u>was hidden</u> from them.

C. Periphrastic Emphasis:

1. <u>An Alternative Expression with More Cognitive Processing Effort</u>. The periphrastic participle is a round about way of saying something (literally, because *peri* means *around* and *phrastic* means *saying*). Often a regular verb could convey virtually the same idea. For example,

προσεύχομαι *I am praying.*
εἰμί προσευχόμενος *I am praying.*

Thus, the periphrastic participle constructions involve more space and audience processing effort, and thus emphasize the verbal action and modifiers as an attribute to the subject.

2. <u>Descriptive Emphasis</u>. J. Gonda explains the pragmatics of periphrastic participles as "semi-nominal sentences" that in classical authors, "were largely preferred in descriptions, statements, elucidations, explications, characterizations, exclamations, indications of time or circumstances, transitional formulas etc."[8] Such sentences describe "a state of affairs"; and "Being more graphic in character and distracting the attention of the audience from an individual point of time at which something narrated happens, the semi-nominal expression [including periphrastic constructions] is apt, on the one hand, to create the impression of

---

[7] *Pace* the view of Porter (44-45) that, "In determining whether a given instance of εἰμί and a participle is periphrastic, it is useful to keep in mind that no elements may intervene between the auxiliary verb and the participle except for those which complete or directly modify the participle (not the verb εἰμί)" (44). This unnecessarily delimits the pragmatics of the periphrastic construction, which may entail flexibility of word order to convey special emphasis and relationship to other sentence elements, which is why the construction is used. See C.2. below.

[8] J. Gonda, "A Remark on 'Periphrastic' Constructions in Greek," *Mnemosyne* 12 (1959): 97–112 at 99.

being more forceful.... and on the other hand, to bring out the object or adjuncts amplifying the predicate."[9] Also, concerning periphrastic constructions, Porter correctly concludes, "grammarians who wish to stress that the periphrastic is more emphatic or significant, or that it draws attention to the participle and its modifiers, are probably correct" (46). And, Porter, Reed, and O'Donnell surmise, "most grammarians think that the periphrastic was in some way more emphatic, probably drawing attention to the participle and its modifiers."[10] So, to answer the question, "Why would an author use a periphrastic construction?"—the construction often emphasizes *some verbal characteristic or attribute of the subject as is thus communicated via the participle (verbal aspect, gender, number) and its complements and adjuncts*.

3. <u>Brief Examples</u>. Consider the aspectual and descriptive significance conveyed in these examples above and below. The Present Tense usually emphasizes ongoing action. The Perfect Tense emphasizes a resultant state.

Luke 4:44 Καὶ ἦν <u>κηρύσσων</u> εἰς τὰς συναγωγὰς τῆς Ἰουδαίας.
He was <u>preaching</u> in the synagogues of the Jews.

Luke 4:31 καὶ ἦν <u>διδάσκων</u> αὐτοὺς ἐν τοῖς σάββασιν.
He was <u>teaching</u> them on the Sabbath(s).

Eph 2:8a τῇ γὰρ χάριτί ἐστε <u>σεσῳσμένοι</u> διὰ πίστεως.
For by grace you are <u>(having been) saved</u> through faith.

Heb 4:2a καὶ γὰρ ἐσμεν <u>εὐηγγελισμένοι</u> καθάπερ κἀκεῖνοι.
For even we are <u>(having been) evangelized</u> just as even they (are).

D. **Pragmatics in Luke:** It is helpful here to provide the abstract summary of Carl E. Johnson from his dissertation, "A Discourse Analysis of the Periphrastic Imperfect in the Greek New Testament Writings of Luke" (The University of Texas at Arlington, 2010). Johnson's fine abstract summary (only slightly modified in 1. and 2. below) may serve as a basis for further reflection and research on the periphrastic participle.

1. <u>Important Background or Linking (Segue) of Location or Action</u>. The Periphrastic imperfect highlights background for introductory or linking purposes by presenting particularly salient information concerning location and/or action. This suggests the following four categories:

---

[9] Gonda, "Periphrastic," 100.
[10] Stanley E. Porter, Jeffrey T. Reed, and Matthew Brook O'Donnell, *Fundamentals of New Testament Greek* (Grand Rapids: Eerdmans, 2010), 349.

a. INTRODUCTORY LOCATIVE which highlights action whose placement in a specific location or time is important to the subsequent narrative. Both location and action are important.

b. LINKING LOCATIVE which highlights action in a specific physical location or time which links the passage to a previous or subsequent narrative which involves the same participants in the same or similar action. Both location and action are important.

c. INTRODUCTORY ACTION which highlights the involvement of the subject(s) in an action which is important to the subsequent narrative.

d. LINKING ACTION which highlights involvement of the subject(s) in an action which links the passage to a previous or subsequent narrative involving the same participant(s) in the same or similar action.

2. <u>Highlighted Agent Action</u>. Therefore, a Lukan periphrastic imperfect unites an imperfect form of εἰμί (*be*) with a nominative present participle that agrees in number with the subject of the copula in order to express a highlighted, ongoing state or action which may occur in a spatial or temporal sphere. Said action is usually agentive.

19.6 COMPLEMENTARY USE OF THE PARTICIPLE

A. **Introduction:** A final use of the participle that is not terribly common in the GNT is called the complementary participle. Here the participle participates integrally with the main or nuclear verb to form a whole verbal idea. The complementary participle may be classified as a type of supplementary participle. What distinguishes this use from the periphrastic participle (also a sub-class of supplementary participles) is that certain nuclear verbs semantically may need to use the participle to complete their meaning, whereas the nuclear verb in the periphrastic construction (εἰμί or γίνομαι) does not need the participle; instead, the periphrastic construction is simply one option for conveying verbal action. Sometimes the line between circumstantial and complementary may be blurred.[11] For example, consider these few examples:

Matt 11:1a Καὶ ἐγένετο ὅτε <u>ἐτέλεσεν</u> ὁ Ἰησοῦς <u>διατάσσων</u> τοῖς δώδεκα μαθηταῖς αὐτοῦ,
And it happened, when Jesus <u>finished</u> <u>instructing</u> his twelve disciples, ...

Eph 1:18a οὐ <u>παύομαι</u> <u>εὐχαριστῶν</u> ὑπὲρ ὑμῶν...
I do not <u>cease</u> <u>giving thanks</u> for you...

---

[11] This summary draws upon Robertson (1119-24) and K. L. McKay, *A New Syntax of the Verb in New Testament Greek: An Aspectual Approach*, Studies in Biblical Greek 5 (New York: Peter Lang, 1994), 65; both are too generous in applying the category (Robertson, 1121-24; McKay, 105-6).

2 Pet 2:10b τολμηταὶ αὐθάδεις, δόξας οὐ <u>τρέμουσιν</u> <u>βλασφημοῦντες</u>, ...
Daring, self-willed, they <u>do</u> not <u>tremble</u> <u>blaspheming</u> glories, ...

Acts 16:34b καὶ <u>ἠγαλλιάσατο</u> πανοικεὶ <u>πεπιστευκὼς</u> τῷ θεῷ.
And he <u>rejoiced</u> with the entire household <u>trusting</u> in God.

In the first two examples, the participle is clearly complementary. The latter two examples, however, may be understood more simply as circumstantial: 2 Pet 2:10b would be temporal (*while blaspheming*) or concessive (*even though blaspheming*); Acts 16:34b could be causal-substantiation (*because he trusted in God*). Below are given some verbs that may be used with a participle, but are not always used with one. Their frequency in the GNT is included in the superscripts.

B. **Verbs of Continuing or Ending:** (Frequency is indicated by the superscript numbers.)

1. παύομαι[15] *I cease* (middle)
2. διατελέω[1] *I continue, remain* (intransitive); (Acts 27:33)
3. τελέω[28] *I finish*
4. ἐπιμένω[16] *I remain*; (16 occurrences)
5. διαλείπω[1] *I stop*; (Luke 7:45)
6. ἐγκακέω[6] *I grow weary*; (see esp. Gal 6:9 and 2 Thess 3:13)

C. **Other Verbs:**

1. λανθάνω[6] *I escape notice*
2. προφθάνω[1] *I anticipate*; (Matt 17:25)

D. **Others Types of Supplementary Participles?**

1. <u>Verbs of Emotion</u>. Grammarians have often extended the category of supplementary participle to include verbs of emotion, as in the examples of 2 Pet 2:10b and Acts 16:34b above (e.g. Smyth §2048).

2. <u>Participles in Indirect Statements</u>. K. L. McKay has described one use of supplementary participles to form indirect statements: "When statements ... are indirectly quoted in dependence on most verbs of knowing and perceiving, the verbs in their principal clauses are sometimes expressed as supplementary participles, with case usage the same as in the infinitive construction...."[12] These are two examples among several others that McKay cites:

---

[12] K. L. McKay, *New Syntax*, §12.5 (p. 105). He treats these instances involving participles as indirect statements: Matt 1:18; Luke 8:46; Acts 7:12; 8:23; 9:12; 17:16; 24:10; 2 Cor 8:22; 12:2; Heb 13:23.

Acts 9:12a καὶ εἶδεν ἄνδρα... εἰσελθόντα καὶ ἐπιθέντα αὐτῷ [τὰς] χεῖρας

and I saw a man <u>coming</u> and <u>setting</u> hands upon him

2 Cor 12:2 οἶδα ἄνθρωπον ἐν Χριστῷ ... <u>ἁρπαγέντα</u>...ἕως τρίτου οὐρανοῦ.

I know a person in Christ ...<u>caught up</u> ... until the third heaven.

It may be better to understand some of these examples as simply attributive uses or as entailing ellipsis with an implied form of the infinitive εἶναι (see the discussion under D. in §23.4 INFINITIVES OF INDIRECT DISCOURSE, CONTENT, AND EPEXEGETICAL STATEMENTS).

Complete WORKBOOK EXERCISES 19 and consult the ANSWER KEY & GUIDE as needed.

CASE IN POINT 19: SPECIAL USES OF PARTICIPLES IN MATTHEW 9:35-36

Another look at participles will help to consolidate your learning. Below is given the Greek text and the NASB95, with participles underlined and one bracketed item added (an underlying participle in the Greek). As you can see, there are several participles underlined in the verses below. All of them happen to be anarthrous–but are they all circumstantial participles? What type of participles do we have? What tense aspect? Are they located before the main verb (i.e. prenuclear) or after the main verb (i.e. post-nuclear)?

Matt 9:35 Καὶ περιῆγεν ὁ Ἰησοῦς τὰς πόλεις πάσας καὶ τὰς κώμας διδάσκων ἐν ταῖς συναγωγαῖς αὐτῶν καὶ κηρύσσων τὸ εὐαγγέλιον τῆς βασιλείας καὶ θεραπεύων πᾶσαν νόσον καὶ πᾶσαν μαλακίαν

Matt 9:35 *Jesus was going [Imperfect Tense] through all the cities and villages, <u>teaching</u> in their synagogues and <u>proclaiming</u> the gospel of the kingdom, and <u>healing</u> every kind of disease and every kind of sickness.*

Matt 9:36 <u>ἰδὼν</u> δὲ τοὺς ὄχλους ἐσπλαγχνίσθη περὶ αὐτῶν, ὅτι ἦσαν <u>ἐσκυλμένοι</u> καὶ <u>ἐρριμμένοι</u> ὡσεὶ πρόβατα μὴ <u>ἔχοντα</u> ποιμένα.

Matt 9:36 *<u>Seeing</u> the people, He felt compassion for them, because they were <u>distressed</u> and <u>dispirited</u> like sheep [<u>having</u>] without a shepherd.*

Matthew 9:36 begins with an aorist tense circumstantial participle. It might be translated temporally with *after*. Or, might the participle be causal, translated ***Because*** *he saw the crowds, he felt compassion*? Delimiting one adverbial semantic sense would here be over-interpreting; hence the NASB95 helpfully does not "lock in" the semantics. In the context, Jesus is in the midst of teaching among the people; he is concerned for the harvest of needy souls (9:37-38). There is something about "seeing the need" by being physically present that moves us to a more acute form of compassion.

The explicit reason for Jesus' compassion is stated within a ὅτι clause: *because they were distressed and dispirited...* This description of the people is accomplished by two perfect tense periphrastic participles. Let's consider the significance.

First, the perfect tense suggests that something had happened to them with continuing results. The nature of the verbs, which involve emotional states, places emphasis on their final resultant state. The picture is not pretty. The condition of the crowds is further amplified by the use of the periphrastic construction. Remember that the periphrastic construction *ascribes a verbal attribute upon the subjects*; in this case, the crowds are in a final condition of being distressed and dispirited. Furthermore, they are the recipients of this condition (passive voice); this situation seems beyond their control.

This description is supported by a comparison. Here another participle is used to describe the crowds. They are *like sheep without a shepherd*. The present tense participle emphasizes the continual nature of this condition. It is an awful picture—sheep continually without a caretaker, bewildered, confused, lost. Jesus is so moved by this state of affairs that he responds with an appeal to his disciples to pray for God to send out harvesters (9:38) and then sends them out (10:1).

In the final analysis, we see a sequence of events unfolding within the Matthean narrative: Jesus goes to where the people are (9:35); he sees their needs (9:36a), and has compassion (9:36b); and he responds by calling his disciples to prayer (9:37-38) and finally sends out his disciples (10:1-5). Where are we in our journeying with Jesus?

Below is a depiction of Alexander the Great's conquest on the north side of his sarcophagus in Constantinople (modern day Istanbul).[13] Tutored by Aristotle, Alexander led his troops even into modern day India and would have continued, but his soldiers requested to stop because they were tired of fighting and wanted to reap the benefits of their efforts and live in leisure.

---

[13] Ernest Arthur Gardner, *A Handbook of Greek Sculpture* (London: Macmillan, 1911), 429 fig. 106.

CHAPTER 20

We may take for granted how often and in what ways the writers of the NT describe God. The biblical texts are saturated not only with references to God, but descriptions of God's identity, will, and involvements in the world. One such passage is 1 Cor 12:4-6; a look at the context and special pronoun usage will help reveal the mystery of the Godhead as revealed in the Lord Jesus, the Messiah.

This lesson introduces verbs whose stem ends in a single vowel (either ε, α, or ο) called **Contract Verbs**. Certain verb endings will combine with these contract vowels to form a **contraction,** resulting in a slight change in the verb ending. Two further **Adjectival Uses of the 3rd Person Personal Pronoun** (αὐτός, -ή, -ό) are introduced: **the Intensive** and **the Identical**. Finally, we look at the last special use of the participle—the **Genitive Circumstantial Participle**, otherwise known as the **Genitive Absolute**.

VOCABULARY 20   CONTRACT VERBS

__ἐ ψιλόν Contract Verbs:__

αἰτέω [70]	I ask, demand
ἀκολουθέω [89]	I follow, obey (+ dative)
δοκέω [62]	I think; I suppose; I seem
ζητέω [117]	I seek, search; I inquire
θεωρέω [58]	I behold, see, view (as a spectator)
καλέω [148]	I call; I name; I invite
λαλέω [297]	I speak
μαρτυρέω [76]	I testify, witness
παρακαλέω [109]	I exhort; I encourage; I advise
περιπατέω [95]	I walk; I live, behave
ποιέω [568]	I do; I make

προσκυνέω [60]	I worship; I bow down
τηρέω [71]	I keep, guard; I obey
φοβέω [95]	I fear, am afraid; I respect

__ἄλφα Contract Verbs:__

ἀγαπάω [143]	I love, adore, value
γεννάω [97]	I bear, give birth; I parent
ἐπερωτάω [156]	I ask, inquire
ἐρωτάω [63]	I ask, inquire
ζάω [140]	I live

__ὂ μικρόν Contract Verbs:__

πληρόω [86]	I fill; I fulfill
φανερόω [49]	I make manifest; I reveal

After learning this vocabulary, you will know 77.6% of the words in the GNT. If you are able, listen to audio recordings of VOCABULARY 20 and do the CROSSWORD PUZZLE in the WORKBOOK.

NOTES ON VOCABULARY 20:

Several of these verbs have related noun forms that have already been learned: ἀγαπάω (ἀγάπη *love*), ζάω (ζωή *life*), καλέω (ἐκ-κλησία *church*, literally *those called out*) and φοβέω (φόβος *fear*). Other verbs also have English cognates or related derived forms: γεννάω is related to *genesis* (the origin of something); δοκέω is the root for *docet-ism* (the Christian heresy that Jesus only *seemed* to be really human); θεωρέω *theorize* (to see something); λαλέω *glosso-lalia* (tongue-speaking); μαρτυρέω *martyr* (one who testifies to the truth, even to the point of death); περιπατέω *peripatetic* (walking around); ποιέω *poem* (a literary making); φανερόω (from φαίνω *I shine; I appear*) *epi-phany* or *theo-phany* (i.e., God appearing, revealing).

Also, you need to understand that the lexical forms given above are not actually found in Greek literature. Instead, for example, you would find ἀγαπῶ, αἰτῶ, πληρῶ. In lexicons, it has become customary to list these verbs so that we can see the *contract vowel* that becomes "hidden" in the first person singular forms (ἀγαπάω, αἰτέω, πληρόω).

20.1 CONTRACT VERBS IN GENERAL

A. **Regular Verb Stems:** Contract verbs have the most stable verb stems. There are no 2nd Aorist contract verbs. Thus, they are relatively easy to parse, except that in the Present and Imperfect Tense (i.e. the first Principal Part), the contract vowels at the end of the verb stem combine ("contract") with the vowels of the endings.

B. **Contract Vowels:** Only in the First Principal Part (Present and Imperfect Tenses) does a problem exist. The contract vowels (ε, α, or ο) will contract or blend with the endings. This contraction usually changes the look of the coupling vowel (see below). However, outside of the First Principal Part, the contract vowels lengthen before the endings like this: ε → η, α → η, and ο → ω. Here are the Principal Parts of three contract verbs to illustrate this last point:

FIRST	SECOND	THIRD	FOURTH	FIFTH	SIXTH
λαλέω*	λαλήσω	ἐλάλησα	λελάληκα	λελάλημαι	ἐλαλήθην
ἀγαπάω*	ἀγαπήσω	ἠγάπησα	ἠγάπηκα	ἠγάπημαι	ἠγαπήθην
πληρόω*	πληρώσω	ἐπλήρωσα	πεπλήρωκα	πεπλήρωμαι	ἐπληρώθην

Notice how the lengthened contract vowel really will assist your parsing outside the First Principal Part. In effect, the endings are put out "on display" by the lengthened contract vowel. The asterisk (*) indicates a hypothetical form.

20.2 CONTRACT VERBS: CONTRACTION CHART, RULES, AND FORMATION

A. **Contraction Chart and Basic Rules:** When adding endings for the Present and Imperfect Tenses in the First Principal Part, contractions occur. These contractions are predictable and follow fixed patterns. Here is a chart and basic rules to help you.

Contract Vowel +	Initial Vowel or Monophthong of Ending						
	ε	ει	η	ῃ	ο	ου	ω
-ε	ει	ει	η	ῃ	ου	ου	ω
-α	α	ᾳ	α	ᾳ	ω	ω	ω
-ο	ου	οι	ω	οι	ου	ου	ω

1. All contractions result in a monophthong or long vowel.
2. An ἒ ψιλόν contract verb *scarcely* changes Present Indicative endings.
3. Often a circumflex accent is found over the contraction.
4. An ἰῶτα within endings always remains there in one form or another.
5. An ἄλφα contract vowel always wins out, except when added to an "o" vowel in which case it is always contracted to ὦ μέγα.
6. An ὂ μικρόν contract vowel always results in an "o" vowel in the ending.
7. Focus on ἒ ψιλόν and ἄλφα contracts since these are the most common.

B. **Ἒ ψιλόν Contract:** *Ἒ ψιλόν contract verbs are the most common in the GNT.* With contract verbs, small changes occur in the endings of the First Principal Part. This is so because the personal endings have no tense suffix or consonant on the front of them that would "buffer" the coupling vowel from the contract vowel. Thus, the contract vowel and the coupling vowel come into direct contact and a contraction results. Here are the contractions from ἒ ψιλόν (-έω) contract verbs:

PRESENT ACTIVE		Example:	IMPERFECT ACTIVE		Example:
sg.		δοκέω *I seem*	sg.		δοκέω *I seem*
έ + ω	→ ῶ	δοκῶ	ε + ον	→ ουν	ἐδόκουν
έ + εις	→ εῖς	δοκεῖς	ε + ες	→ εις	ἐδόκεις
έ + ει	→ εῖ	δοκεῖ	ε + ε	→ ει	ἐδόκει
pl.			pl.		
έ + ομεν	→ οῦμεν	δοκοῦμεν	έ + ομεν	→ οῦμεν	ἐδοκοῦμεν
έ + ετε	→ εῖτε	δοκεῖτε	έ + ετε	→ εῖτε	ἐδοκεῖτε
έ + ουσιν	→ οῦσιν	δοκοῦσιν	ε + ον	→ ουν	ἐδόκουν

Notice the following:
1. In the Present singular, the endings do not change (except for the accent). In the plural, only the 1st and 2nd person changes.
2. The accent location often changes, and if so, involves a circumflex.
3. In the Imperfect, <u>all</u> the endings are changed slightly.
4. Also, many of the Imperfect endings look exactly like the Present endings. *How will you distinguish between the two tenses?* (Augmentation!)
5. The middle/passive endings for both tenses are not presented above because the same, predictable contractions occur.

C. Ἄλφα **Contract:** Ἄλφα contract verbs are the 2nd most common in frequency in the Greek NT. Here are the contractions from ἄλφα (-άω) contract verbs:

PRESENT ACTIVE			Example:	IMPERFECT ACTIVE			Example:
sg.			ἀγαπάω *I love*	sg.			ἀγαπάω *I love*
ά + ω	→	ῶ	ἀγαπῶ	α + ον	→ ων		ἠγάπων
ά + εις	→	ᾷς	ἀγαπᾷς	α + ες	→ ας		ἠγάπας
ά + ει	→	ᾷ	ἀγαπᾷ	α + ε	→ α		ἠγάπα
pl.				pl.			
ά + ομεν	→	ῶμεν	ἀγαπῶμεν	ά + ομεν	→ ῶμεν		ἠγαπῶμεν
ά + ετε	→	ᾶτε	ἀγαπᾶτε	ά + ετε	→ ᾶτε		ἠγαπᾶτε
ά + ουσιν	→	ῶσιν	ἀγαπῶσιν	α + ον	→ ων		ἠγάπων

Notice the following:
1. All but one ending has changed.
2. An ἄλφα that contracts with an ἒ ψιλόν ending always wins out.
3. An ἄλφα that contracts with an "*o*" class vowel always yields ὦ μέγα.
4. Every ἰῶτα remains after contraction as an ἰῶτα subscript.

D. Ὂ μικρόν **Contract:** This is the least common of the contract verbs. Here are the contractions from ὂ μικρόν (-όω) contract verbs:

PRESENT ACTIVE			Example:	IMPERFECT ACTIVE			Example:
sg.			πληρόω *I fulfill*	sg.			πληρόω *I fulfill*
ό + ω	→	ῶ	πληρῶ	ο + ον	→ ουν		ἐπλήρουν
ό + εις	→	οῖς	πληροῖς	ο + ες	→ ους		ἐπλήρους
ό + ει	→	οῖ	πληροῖ	ο + ε	→ ου		ἐπλήρου
pl.				pl.			
ό + ομεν	→	οῦμεν	πληροῦμεν	ό + ομεν	→ οῦμεν		ἐπληροῦμεν
ό + ετε	→	οῦτε	πληροῦτε	ό + ετε	→ οῦτε		ἐπληροῦτε
ό + ουσιν	→	οῦσιν	πληροῦσιν	ο + ον	→ ουν		ἐπλήρουν

Notice the following:
1. All but two endings are changed.
2. An ὂ μικρόν vowel will win out over an ἒ ψιλόν ending.
3. Every ἰῶτα remains in one form or another.

E. **A Complete Paradigm Chart of Contract Verbs is provided in** APPENDIX §21.

20.3 INTENSIVE AND IDENTICAL USES OF Αὐτός (Σύντονος Ἀντωνυμία)

A. **Introduction:** Up to this point, you have thoroughly learned how to recognize αὐτός, -ή, -ό as a personal pronoun. When used as a pronoun, αὐτός, -ή, -ό never had an article, and always was by itself. However, when found with an article and/or with a noun, αὐτός, -ή, -ό takes on special adjective meanings; that is to say, it functions like an adjective. There are two adjectival meanings that αὐτός, -ή, -ό has when in these situations: *same* and *-self*.

B. **Identical Use and Emphasis:** Αὐτός, -ή, -ό takes on the adjectival meaning *same* whenever it has an article.

    1. <u>Attributively</u>. Agrees in gender, number, and case with a substantive/noun and αὐτός, -ή, -ό is always with an article.

        1 Cor 12:5b ὁ <u>αὐτὸς</u> κύριος *The <u>same</u> Lord*

        1 Cor 12:9 ἐκ τοῦ <u>αὐτοῦ</u> στόματος *from the <u>same</u> mouth*

        Jas 3:10 ἐν τῷ <u>αὐτῷ</u> πνεύματι *in the <u>same</u> Spirit*

    2. <u>Substantively</u> = Stands alone and αὐτός, -ή, -ό is always with an article. In English translation, a generic noun needs to be supplied (e.g. *one, person, thing, man, woman*).

        Heb 1:12b σὺ δὲ ὁ αὐτὸς εἶ *You are <u>the same one</u>*

        Matt 5:46b <u>τὸ αὐτὸ</u> ποιοῦσιν *They do <u>the same thing</u>*

        Note again that whenever αὐτός, -ή, -ό has this meaning *same*, it is typically found **with** the article. Also, so used, it can be found in any case (nom., gen., dat., acc.).

C. **Intensive Use and Emphasis:** As already treated in §9.2 PERSONAL PRONOUNS, whenever αὐτός, -ή, -ό is found in the nominative case with the verb, it emphasizes the subject; we can call this subjective intensive emphasis. In a similar way, when anarthrous αὐτός, -ή, -ό accompanies a noun agreeing with it in gender, case, and number, αὐτός may carry the adjectival meaning pertaining to *–self*; for example, *myself, yourself, herself, itself, themselves*. See examples below and Wallace 321-23.

    1. <u>Subject Intensive</u>. In this use, αὐτός, -ή, -ό adds more emphasis on the subject of the verb. This subject may be 1st person, 2nd person, or 3rd person. It is found in the nominative case, but never with an article.

Matt 1:21b αὐτὸς σώσει *he himself will save*

Acts 28:28b αὐτοὶ ἀκούσονται *they themselves will hear*

1 Thess 2:1a Αὐτοὶ γὰρ οἴδατε *You yourselves know*

Note that αὐτός, -ή, -ό as a subject intensive can be used with 2nd person (*yourself, yourselves*) or 1st person (*myself, ourselves*). However, the frequency of this use with 1st and 2nd persons is approximately 50 times in the GNT.

Rom 7:25b ἄρα οὖν αὐτὸς ἐγὼ ... δουλεύω ... *Therefore then, I myself serve...*

Notice that αὐτός is used in Rom 7:25b to intensify the subject *I* that is already made emphatic by the presence of ἐγώ. Rom 7:25b is the most emphatic way to emphasis the subject and one must consider carefully what is the Apostle Paul's point. Is he making an autobiographical remark about himself (*I, Paul, was in this state or am in this state*)? Or, is he emphasizing the desperate state of any person who attempts to rely on the Law to overcome sin, dramatically indicated by the 1st person? (I think the latter.) Other examples of doubly emphatic subjects occur at Acts 10:26b, Rom 15:14, and 2 Cor 10:1; 12:13.

2. <u>Noun Intensive</u> = Agreeing with a noun, αὐτός, -ή, -ό <u>never</u> has an article itself. Sometimes the word *very* catches the sense of intensification.

Heb 9:24a εἰσῆλθεν Χριστός εἰς αὐτὸν τὸν οὐρανόν.
Christ entered into heaven itself.

Acts 16:18 καὶ ἐξῆλθεν αὐτῇ τῇ ὥρᾳ.
It went out at that very hour.

John 14:11b διὰ τὰ ἔργα αὐτὰ πιστεύετε.
You believe on account of the deeds themselves.

D. **Discourse and Pragmatic Considerations:** Robertson (685) indicates at the start of his discussion of these uses: "The intensive use is more emphatic." Concerning the nominative use of αὐτός, he further muses: "it is not always clear whether we have the emphatic 'he' or the intensive 'self' with αὐτός in the nominative." True enough for English translation. The pragmatic effect of either use (if they are truly of a different nature) is simply to draw attention to the agent or object. Both uses are untypical uses of αὐτός, and are thus marked and emphatic. The type of emphasis—such as contrastive, focal, thematic, recurrence—must be determined in context.

20.4 The Genitive Circumstantial Participle (AKA the Genitive Absolute)

A. **Introduction:** One distinct and notable use of the circumstantial-adverbial participle can be called the Genitive Circumstantial Participle (GCP), traditionally labeled the Genitive Absolute (GA). The GCP has been so-called "absolute," because the participle and its subject are placed into the genitive case but remain grammatically unconnected and thus separated from the rest of the sentence. In other words, there is no agreement in the genitive case linking the GA to another sentence element. Additionally, the subject of the GA is typically different than that of the main clause. For example, in Matt 21:10a *he* (= Jesus) is the subject of the GA subordinate clause; but the subject of the main clause is *the entire city*:

Matt 21:10a Καὶ <u>εἰσελθόντος</u> αὐτοῦ εἰς Ἱεροσόλυμα ἐσείσθη πᾶσα ἡ πόλις...
     And, <u>after</u> he <u>entered</u> into Jerusalem, the entire city was stirred up...

However, this grammatical "absoluteness" or separation must be properly understood; in fact, the genitive subject of the GA may find a referent in the main clause (like an object of the main verb; Smyth §2073.c), and in exceptional cases even the subject (!), in violation of the definition; in fact, this is for emphasis.

B. **Genitive Absolutes in Construction:**

1. <u>Genitive Case</u>. Why the Greeks put this construction into the genitive case is due to a development of **the genitive case as a modifying or delimiting case**. Thus, the genitive absolute will always be in the genitive case. Both the participle and its subject will agree in gender and number (besides already agreeing in case).

2. <u>Location in the Sentence</u>. A genitive absolute **normally precedes the main verb**. Also, this subordinate clause may have modifiers (adverbs, prepositional phrases, etc.) and a direct object. Thus, one must determine when the genitive absolute construction begins and ends.

3. <u>Sometimes a Missing Genitive Subject</u>. It is not uncommon that the genitive case subject is missing. In these cases, context should determine who is acting. Usually the student will have no trouble supplying the generic *he* or *they* as the subject of the genitive absolute.

4. <u>Circumstantial Participle</u>. The CGP creates a circumstantial clause. Thus, **the participle in the GA will never have an article**. The same rules concerning circumstantial participles apply here in all regards. Reread §17.4 Circumstantial Participles.

    a. *Aorist Participle.*

       Matt 5:1b καὶ <u>καθίσαντος</u> αὐτοῦ προσῆλθαν αὐτῷ οἱ μαθηταὶ αὐτοῦ.
        And <u>after he sat down</u>, his disciples came to him.

b. *Present Participle.*

Acts 1:9a καὶ ταῦτα εἰπὼν <u>βλεπόντων αὐτῶν</u> ἐπήρθη,
And after saying these things, <u>while they were looking</u>, he was taken up,

c. *No Genitive Noun.*

Matt 17:14 Καὶ <u>ἐλθόντων πρὸς τὸν ὄχλον</u> προσῆλθεν αὐτῷ ἄνθρωπος...
And <u>after [they were] coming to the crowd</u>, a person came to him...

5. <u>Basic Functions</u>. As will be discussed in D. below, there are two major reasons for using the GA or GCP: 1) to show switch-reference, i.e. a change of subject is taking place within the sentence; and/or 2) to provide a segue or an important framework (context, time, or place) for the action/events of the main verb.

C. **Definitions, Frequency of Occurrences, and Broader Koine Usage:** The definition for the GA construction will delimit obviously how many of these constructions are accounted for in the GNT. One issue is whether the subject of the GA can be the same as the subject of the main clause, and what this might indicate. Let me summarize three important contributions in understanding the GCP or GA.

1. <u>Phyllis M. Healey & Alan Healey</u>.[1] In an important study, Healey & Healey correlate the GA with switch-reference devices found in languages. In their accounting, the NT contains 313 occurrences. But for over 40% of these instances, the GA is not so "absolute" (i.e. separate, isolated), since the subject of the GA is in fact grammatically connected to some other element (in any case) of the main clause: "130 of the 313 instances (42 percent) of this construction in the New Testament do in fact have and expressed co-referent in the same UBS [critical text] sentence" (186).

2. <u>Levinsohn</u>. Within his discussion of "Adverbial Participial Clauses," Levinsohn summarizes: "The GA is used 336 times in the Greek New Testament. Only six do not manifest a change of surface subject between the GA and the nuclear clause, and five of them involve changes in the role of the subject between experiencer and agent."[2] So, in the GNT, there are six instances where the genitive subject of the GA is the same as the subject of the main clause. At this point, the statement concerning classical Greek by Smyth (§2073, 460) may help explain the import of this rare circumstance: "Exceptionally, the subject of the genitive absolute is the same as that of the main clause. The effect of this irregular construction is to emphasize the idea contained in the genitive absolute."

---

[1] Phyllis M. Healey and Alan Healey, *Greek Circumstantial Participles: Tracking Participants with Participles in the Greek New Testament* (Occasional Papers in Translation and Textlinguistics Vol. 4, No. 3; Dallas: Summer Institute of Linguistics, 1990).

[2] Stephen H. Levinsohn, "Adverbial Participial Clauses in Koiné Greek: Grounding and Information Structure" (presented at the The International Conference on Discourse and Grammar (DG2008) Illocutionary force, information Structure and Subordination between Discourse and Grammar, Universeit Ghent, Belgium, May 2008).

3. <u>Lois K. Fuller</u>. In her recent study of the GA construction, Fuller investigates 313 instances of the construction in the GNT (of which 26% are grammatically connected to some element in the nuclear sentence), as well as extra-biblical instances. *She contests the notion that the GA is a switch-reference device.* Fuller concludes: "They are adverbial constructions, and their main uses in narrative are (1) to signal important prior background information that provides necessary context for the action, and (2) to provide cohesion. Another relatively common use, usually in exposition, is (3) to give accompanying confirming circumstance."[3] Additionally, Fuller provides very helpful summaries of frequency data and discussions of extrabiblical usage in the papyri. Most notably, Fuller analyzes extra-biblical data showing the use of the GA *when the subject is the same as that of the nuclear main verb*. For her, this evidence argues against the switch-reference usage.

D. **Semantic and Pragmatic Functions:**

1. <u>Semantic: Important Remote Framework for the Main Clause</u>. The Genitive Absolute can be said to be marked +important remote framework/background information. Fuller describes a fascinating example from Acts 27:7-32, which contains twelve GCPs (!): "All occur before the indicative verb of the sentence; most start the sentence and appear to be causal. The common pattern is that the GC [Genitive Circumstantial Participle] gives remote background and the nominative participles give close background."[4] Fuller's study demonstrates that most GCPs precede the main verb and provide important information that frames what follows; in other words, they are pre-nuclear participles and function as such. Like other pre-nuclear participles, they can provide a segue from the previous material to subsequent material; or they can describe an important framework for the actions/events of the main verb.

However, this latter function of providing a framework is true even in the numerous extra-biblical examples in which the genitive subject of the GCP is the same as the subject of the main clause. *When such happens, the information in the GA clause is emphasized (as Smyth indicates) as it is providing an important framework to understand the main verb*. Alternatively, Levinsohn proposes that the role of the subject changes between the GA construction and the main clause, e.g., from AGENT to EXPERIENCER.

Bringing this all together, one can begin to discern a hierarchy of possible subordinate clause constructions that could precede and postcede the main verb, depending on what type of subordinate clause is constructed: 1) conjunctions (marking the most distal; segue), 2) GAs (marked distal and important), or 3) circumstantial participles (the most proximate). These constructions can be displayed in chart form in relation to the main verb.

---

[3] Lois K. Fuller, "The 'Genitive Absolute' in New Testament/Hellenistic Greek: A Proposal for Clearer Understanding," *Journal of Greco-Roman Christianity and Judaism* 3 (2006): 142–67 at 167.

[4] Fuller, "Genitive Absolute," 155.

Positioning: **PRE-NUCLEAR** Contribution: **Segue or Framework**				Positioning: **POST-NUCLEAR** Contribution: **Explication of Particulars or Reasons**	
(←Distal or Proximate→)					
←	← and →	→	**MAIN VERB**	← and →	←
Conjunctive Adverbial Clause	GA or Genitive Circumstantial Clause	Nominative Circumstantial Participle Clause		Post-Nuclear Participle (GCP etc.)	Conjunctive Adverbial Clauses
Segue & more Distal; change of context, time, or place	*Segue or Important Distal Background or Framework: context, time, or place*	*Important & Proximate; introduction of agency*		*Explicate Specifics and/or Reasons*	*Marked Reasons, Means, etc.*

To illustrate the "framework function" of the pre-nuclear GA that is grammatically more remote than a grammatically-linked circumstantial participle, consider this example.

Matt 21:23a Καὶ <u>ἐλθόντος</u> αὐτοῦ εἰς τὸ ἱερὸν προσῆλθον αὐτῷ <u>διδάσκοντι</u> οἱ ἀρχιερεῖς καὶ οἱ πρεσβύτεροι τοῦ λαοῦ ...
And <u>after</u> he <u>came</u> into the temple, the chief priests and elders of the people came to him, <u>while or because [he was] teaching</u>, ...

The essential background framework (+distal but important) is provided by the pre-nuclear GA in the aorist tense *after he came* (ἐλθόντος αὐτοῦ) *into the temple*. The main verbal action (*the chief priests and elders of the people came*) comes next, but this action is given elaboration by the circumstantial participle (marked +proximate) *while or because [he=Jesus was] teaching* (διδάσκοντι). So, Jesus' agency of entering the temple is important, but subordinted to the main verbal action involving the high priesnts and elders. Their action of coming to Jesus attends the circumstance of Jesus teaching, which may be temporal (*while* or *as*) or causal (*because*).

Another good example occurs in Mark 16:20 where we find the following:[5]

| **[Mark 16:20]** | ἐκεῖνοι δὲ <u>ἐξελθόντες</u> ἐκήρυξαν πανταχοῦ, τοῦ κυρίου <u>συνεργοῦντος</u> καὶ τὸν λόγον <u>βεβαιοῦντος</u> διὰ τῶν ἐπ-ακολουθούντων σημείων. | *But these ones, <u>having gone out</u>, preached everywhere, with the Lord <u>working along</u> and <u>confirming</u> the word through the accompanying signs.* |

---

[5] Although this is from the longer secondary ending to Mark's Gospel, it still reflects Koine Greek.

In this example, ἐκεῖνοι δὲ marks a return to the disciples (after 16:19 being about the ascended Lord) and the pre-nuclear verb nominative circumstantial participle provides an important proximate framework to understand the main verb clause. Yet, the content of the post-nuclear GA could also provide an important framework (the Lord's *co-working and confirming the word*), although it is post-nuclear placement disrupts the more typical placement of GA as pre-nuclear. How are we to understand this? Fuller creates a new category of usage, the "confirmatory circumstance"; yet, this does not seem necessary, since the GA still describes an important framework or background for the disciples' preaching. In fact, the final placement of the GA may point forward to the continued confirmatory work of the risen Lord as the Word is preached.

2. <u>Pragmatic Switch-Reference</u>. A further extension of the background framework function of the GCP is that the GA may be used to mark switch-reference within the same sentence. Despite the criticism of Fuller, the conclusion of Healey & Healey (followed by Levinsohn) is still sound:

> Many living languages around the world have a grammatical device, currently being called a switch-reference device, for showing in one clause that there is a change of subject in the next following clause or in the higher ranking clause to which it is subordinate. This is one of the ways that participants who are moving on and off the center of the stage in narrative can be identified and kept track of without frequent recourse to cumbersome noun phrases. Switch reference is very commonly marked on a dependent verb. The genitive circumstantial participle is just such a switch-reference device in New Testament Greek.

Levinsohn agrees with their conclusions:

> Now, a construction that indicates switch reference provides a natural way of highlighting the introduction to an existing scene of participants who perform significant actions that change the direction of the story, etc. This is because, when the GA has the *same* subject as the *previous* clause, the scene is set for a *different* participant to be the subject of the nuclear clause. The employment of the GA with the same subject as the previous clause thus gives natural prominence to the event described in the following nuclear clause.[6]

The exceptions in which the subject of the GA is the same as the main verb can be explained either as exceptional and thus **emphatic** (Smyth) or due to a fundamental **change in the role of the subject** (Levinsohn). A striking example may be found in Matt 1:18-19 (with 1:19 summarized); the formal narrative begins here after Matthew's genealogy:

Matt 1:18a Τοῦ δὲ Ἰησοῦ Χριστοῦ ἡ γένεσις οὕτως ἦν.
> *Now the origin of Jesus Messiah was in this manner:*

---

[6] Stephen H. Levinsohn, *Self-Instruction Materials on Non-Narrative Discourse Analysis* (Dallas: SIL International, 2011), 182.

Matt 1:18b μνηστευθείσης τῆς μητρὸς αὐτοῦ Μαρίας τῷ Ἰωσήφ,
After his mother Mary was betrothed to Joseph,

Matt 1:18c πρὶν ἢ συνελθεῖν αὐτοὺς
before even they were joined intimately,

Matt 1:18d εὑρέθη ἐν γαστρὶ ἔχουσα ἐκ πνεύματος ἁγίου.
she was found pregnant from the Holy Spirit.

Matt 1:19 Joseph wanted to release Mary.

Mary is the subject of the GA in 1:18b, but there is no switch reference, since Mary remains the subject of the main verb. However, it is clear that Mary's role switches from AGENT-PARTICIPANT (she is *engaged to Joseph*) to EXPERIENCER (she is *found pregnant*).[7] Also, the information in the GA is being emphasized (Mary's betrothal); and such emphasis relates to the narrative development as seen in 1:19, namely that Joseph was going to release Mary from their planned marriage. In this regard, Fuller's excellent analysis shows how the five GA constructions in Matt 1-2 provide cohesion by interlinking important events.[8]

CHECK POINT 20.4

Just before Paul speaks to his Jewish kinsfolk, the Roman commander grants him permission in Acts 21:40. This verse contains four participles (underlined and parsed), which are presented below using a very basic translation with *–ing*. First, identify the use of the participles as either genitive circumstantial or nominative circumstantial. Second, briefly discuss what implications attend to sentence placement (pre-nuclear or post-nuclear) Third, consider the significance of verbal aspect for each participle. Fourth, discuss possible adverbial logical-semantic relations that are fitting for translation. Fifth, provide a more robust translation with explanation.

Acts 21:40 ἐπιτρέψαντος [AAP-MGS] δὲ αὐτοῦ ὁ Παῦλος ἑστὼς [RAP-MNS] ἐπὶ τῶν ἀναβαθμῶν κατέσεισεν τῇ χειρὶ τῷ λαῷ. πολλῆς δὲ σιγῆς γενομένης [AAP-FGS] προσεφώνησεν τῇ Ἑβραΐδι διαλέκτῳ λέγων [PAP-MNS] ·

Acts 21:40 *So, he [the commander] giving permission, Paul, having stood upon the stairs, motioned with hand to the people. Then, a great silence occuring, he [Paul] spoke out in the Hebrew dialect, saying:*

---

[7] As I study the other examples that Fuller ("Genitive Absolute") provides of GA constructions used when the same subject occurs with the main verb, I also notice the same possibility that there is a change in the role of the GA subject versus the same subject of the main clause (e.g., see the lengthy example from the papyrus on p. 157).

[8] Fuller, "Genitive Absolute," 162-63.

ἐπιτρέψαντος

    1. GCP or NCP:

    2. Sentence Placement:

    3. Tense Aspect:

    4. Adverbial Logical-semantic Relation:

    5. Improved Translation:

ἑστὼς

    1. GCP or NCP:

    2. Sentence Placement:

    3. Tense Aspect:

    4. Adverbial Logical-semantic Relation:

    5. Improved Translation:

γενομένης

    1. GCP or NCP:

    2. Sentence Placement:

    3. Tense Aspect:

    4. Adverbial Logical-Semantic relation:

    5. Improved Translation:

λέγων

    1. GCP or NCP:

    2. Sentence Placement:

    3. Tense Aspect:

    4. Adverbial Logical-semantic Relation:

    5. Improved Translation:

SUGGESTED ANSWERS

ἐπιτρέψαντος

    1. GCP or NCP: *GCP*

    2. Sentence Placement: *Pre-nuclear. Important Distal Background.*

    3. Tense Aspect: *Aorist Tense, perfective (action complete[d])*

    4. Adverbial Logical-semantic Relation: *Temporal (time antecedent or prior), although possibly causal: "So, because he [the commander] gave permission, ..."*

    5. Improved Translation: *"So, after he [the commander] gave permission, ..."*

ἑστώς

1. <u>GCP or NCP</u>: *NCP*
2. <u>Sentence Placement</u>: *Pre-nuclear. Important Proximate Framework/Setting.*
3. <u>Tense Aspect</u>: *Perfect Tense, stative-resultative aspect. Paul as "addressor" of the people "standing" is made prominent*
4. <u>Adverbial Logical-semantic Relation</u>: *logically antecedent action*
5. <u>Improved Translation</u>: *Paul, <u>(after) having stood</u> upon the stairs,*

γενομένης

1. <u>GCP or NCP</u>: *GCP*
2. <u>Sentence Placement</u>: *Pre-nuclear. Important Distal Background. Notice the quantitative emphasis in the use of* πολλῆς *great to modify* σιγῆς.
3. <u>Tense Aspect</u>: *Aorist Tense, perfective (action complete[d])*
4. <u>Adverbial Logical-semantic Relation</u>: *Temporal (time antecedent or prior)*
5. <u>Improved Translation</u>: *"Then, <u>after</u> a great silence <u>occured</u>,.."*

λέγων

1. <u>GCP or NCP</u>: *NCP*
2. <u>Sentence Placement</u>: *Post-nuclear*
3. <u>Tense Aspect</u>: *Present Tense, imperfective*
4. <u>Adverbial Logical-semantic Relation</u>: *none; redundant use (see Ch.17.4.E.2) that stresses what follows as important*
5. <u>Improved Translation</u>: *difficult to convey other than to translate the participle and informing readers to its importance: "saying, …"*

Complete WORKBOOK EXERCISES 20 and consult the ANSWER KEY & GUIDE as needed.

CASE IN POINT 20: THE UNIFIED GODHEAD IN 1 COR 12:4-6

The Greco-Roman world of the Apostle Paul was full of deities and religious experiences. The first Gentile believers had various religious commitments and had taken part in various religious practices, some of which probably continued. In fact, Paul had to warn them to stop attending feasts at pagan temples (1 Cor 10). Some of these cultic and religious practices have been described in ancient documents. Certain deities were renowned for certain types of manifestations and miraculous happenings. However, many religious practices remain a mystery, especially the mystery cults, because those people initiated into the worship of this or that god or goddess were strictly prohibited from disclosing their experiences on penalty of injury or death from the deity.

In 1 Cor 12:1-2, we observe that Paul has "framed" his entire discussion "concerning spiritual things" (Περὶ δὲ τῶν πνευματικῶν) found in 1 Cor 12-14 by explicit reference to the Corinthians' pagan background:

1 Cor 12:2 Οἴδατε ὅτι ὅτε ἔθνη ἦτε πρὸς τὰ εἴδωλα τὰ ἄφωνα ὡς ἂν ἤγεσθε ἀπαγόμενοι

> *You know that when pagans, you were being led astray to mute idols, however you were being led.*

This verse contains many types of "marked" constructions that bring prominence to important notions. First, Paul slows down the discourse using a "metacomment" construction, "You know that…." to highlight "the introduction of important propositions."[9] Second is the preposed notion of "pagans" (ἔθνη) before the verb to bring it into focus, i.e. stressing the previous identity of the Corinthians. Third is the periphrastic participle construction (ἔθνη ἦτε…ἀπαγόμενοι) that ascribes emphatically the verbal attribute of "being led astray" to the subject "(you as) pagans." Fourth, there is attributive emphasis on "mute" since it is in the 2nd attributive position, repeating the article (πρὸς τὰ εἴδωλα τὰ ἄφωνα). What is implied here is that pagan religion focused on "speaking" on behalf of the gods in various utterances and manifestations or discerning what the gods were communicating through portends and studying the entrails of sacrificed animals. Fifth is the adverbial clause of manner with the imperfect tense (ὡς ἂν ἤγεσθε), which indicates both "manner" and repeated action within a past time frame. Finally, Paul has poignantly repeated and abutted the verbal root ἀγαγ* "lead" and "lead astray" (ἤγεσθε ἀπαγόμενοι) and in so doing explicitly evokes the Corinthians' not so distant pagan past. Thus, the Greek word order and special constructions of this verse are highly marked, emphasized, and prominent, thus supporting the critical role that 12:2 plays as a "frame" for what follows.[10]

Paul's appeal to the Corinthians' pagan past is the framework to understand how Paul speaks of God in 1 Cor 12:4-6.

1 Cor 12:4-6 Διαιρέσεις δὲ χαρισμάτων εἰσίν, τὸ δὲ αὐτὸ πνεῦμα· ⁵ καὶ διαιρέσεις διακονιῶν εἰσιν, καὶ ὁ αὐτὸς κύριος· ⁶ καὶ διαιρέσεις ἐνεργημάτων εἰσίν, ὁ δὲ αὐτὸς θεὸς ὁ ἐνεργῶν τὰ πάντα ἐν πᾶσιν.

> *Now there are varieties of gifts, but the same Spirit. ⁵ And there are varieties of ministries, and the same Lord. ⁶ And there are varieties of effects, but the same God [is] the one working all things in all persons.*

In this present chapter we learned about a particular grammatical construction involving the personal pronoun αὐτός. One of its uses is as an adjective taking on the meaning *same*. Can you identify the construction above? How often is it used and with what nouns?

Paul mentions the persons of the Trinity: the *same* Spirit and the *same* Lord (i.e. Jesus—see 12:3) and subsumes their activity under *the same God who works **all** things in **all***. It would seem that Paul wanted the Corinthians to understand that despite the different gifts, ministries, and effects, there is but ***same one* Spirit** and ***same one* Lord** and the ***same one*** God working them all in all. Rather than the plethora of pagan deities in tension and conflict with one another, under

---

⁹ Runge ch.5, quoting here from p.124.

¹⁰ This summarizes Fredrick J. Long, "Paul's Prophesying Isa 28:11 in Context: The Signs of Unbelievers and Believers in 1 Corinthians 14," in *Kingdom Rhetoric: New Testament Explorations in Honor of Ben Witherington III*, ed. T. Michael W. Halcomb (Eugene, OR: Wipf & Stock, 2013), 133–69.

the Lord Jesus one finds a Godhead unified even in the display of diversity of gifts and services.

However, these foundational thoughts are just the start of Paul's larger argument. He wants the Corinthians to accept and respect the diversity of giftedness (ch.12), while acting out of love for the other (ch.13) and in harmony for edification within this diversity (ch.14). Paul's repeated adjectival identical use of the personal pronoun αὐτός in 12:4-6 conveyed the foundational theological truth that behind the worship and body life of Christ's church assembly, there is a unified Godhead, who gives diverse gifts.

On the next page is a representation of a chiseled marble relief (approx. 3x5 feet) dated to the 2nd or 1st century BC.[11] It is known as the Apotheosis (ἀποθέωσις, *deification*) of Homer. The figures of the bottom row are identified in the relief by name, many of which you have learned or can sound out. At the bottom left, Homer (Ὅμηρος) is seated, being crowned by a woman identified as Οἰκουμένη, "the inhabited world." Next to her is a male personification, Χρόνος. Under Homer are two upright scrolls named: Ἰλιάς and Ὀδύσσεια. Then is given Homer's name, and then approaching the altar to make pagan sacrifice are the personified genres of ancient Mediterranean literature: Μῦθος, Ἱστορία, Ποίησις, Τραγῳδία, and Κωμῳδία· (Sound them out.) Behind them are a little child representing Φύσις ("nature"), and then Ἀρετή ("moral excellence, virtue"), Μνήμη ("remembrance"), Πίστις, and Σοφία. The next rows contain various gods identifiable by physical attribute. At top sits enthroned Zeus holding thunderbolt and attended at right by his representation, the eagle. To Zeus' left is Mnemosyne, the mother of the nine Muses, who follow wrapping around in this order: Τερψιχόρα/Terpsichore *Dance*, Εὐτέρπη/Euterpe *Well-Pleasing Music*, Μελπομένη/Melpomene *Singing in Tragedy and Lyric Poetry*, Θάλεια/Thalia *Festivity of Comedy*, Κλείω/Clio *Renown in History*. On the next row standing beneath Terpsichore is likely a poet standing, in whose honor this relief was made, having won a competition. Then the Muses continue with Ἐρατώ/Erato *the Muse for Lyric and Love Poetry*, then Apollo playing his harp in a cave; then Πολύμνια/Polyhymnia *Much praised in Song* (literally, *many hymned*), Οὐρανία/Urania *Heavenly One of Astronomy*, and Καλλιόπη/Calliope *Beautiful Voice*, chief of the Muses and for Epic Poetry. The purported author of the work singed it below Zeus: "Archelaos, son of Apollonius, from Priene, made [this]" (Ἀρχέλαος Ἀπολλωνίου ἐποίησε Πριηνεύς).

This monument attests to four realities in the Ancient Mediterranean world. First, the pervasive and continued influence of Homer in education, the arts, and society in general. Homer remained central in ancient education. Second, the performing arts were almost everywhere celebrated with contests of various kinds occurring frequently. We have only a fraction of the hundreds and hundreds of poems produced by ancient poets. Among the most popular that we have extant include those by Sophocles, Euripides, and Aeschylus from the 5th and 4th centuries BC. Third, a pervasive belief in gods existed, who were known by various manifestations/gifts. Fourth, one might hope that upon death to attain something more than Hades by becoming (like) a god.

---

[11] Image edited and enhanced from Victor Duruy, *History of Greece, and of the Greek People: From the Earliest Times to the Roman Conquest*, trans. M. M. Ripley, vol. Vol. 2, Sect. 1 (London: Kegan Paul, Trench, Trübner & Co., 1898), 13. This inscription may be found under IG XIV.1295 at the Packham Humanities Institute.

The Apotheosis of Homer

CHAPTER 21

How important is one's identity and social status in relation to Jesus? How about one's ethnicity or religious status? At the end of this chapter, we will look at *the* Samaritan woman, who remains nameless to us. However, looking carefully at the use of the article (*the*) and its absence will help us probe the meaning and significance of the episode.

This chapter covers a group of verbs that have stems ending in λ, μ, ν, or ρ. Such verbs are called **Liquid Verbs**. We look at common uses of the **Nominative Case** (beyond indicating Subject). Lastly, two intermediate features of discourse are investigated: **Left (Dis)Located Topics and Frames** and the **Pragmatic Use of the Article with Names of People**.

VOCABULARY 21   LIQUID VERBS

Liquid Verbs:		ἐγείρω [143]	I raise up; I rise
αἴρω [101]	I raise, lift up; I take away	κρίνω [115]	I judge, decide; I condemn
ἀπαγγέλλω [45]	I report, declare	μένω [118]	I remain, continue
ἀποκτείνω [74]	I kill, slay	σπείρω [52]	I sow seed; I scatter
ἀποστέλλω [131]	I send (off)	χαίρω [74]	I rejoice, am glad; I welcome

---

After learning vocabulary to this point, you will know 78.2% of the words in the GNT. If you are able, listen to audio recordings of VOCABULARY 21 and complete the CROSSWORD PUZZLE in the WORKBOOK EXERCISES.

NOTES ON VOCABULARY 21:

Several of these verbs have related noun forms that have already been learned: ἀπαγγέλλω (an ἄγγελος is a messenger who *declares* God's message); ἀποστέλλω (ἀπόστολος *one who is sent*); κρίνω (κρίσις *judging, judgment*); and χαίρω (χαρά *joy*). Also, the verb σπείρω is used in *dia-spora*—the term that describes the Jewish *dispersion* (*sowing*) throughout the Greco-Roman empire after the Babylonian Exile.

21.1 LIQUID VERBS

A. **Definition: Liquid verbs** are those verbs that have a stem ending in λ, μ, ν, or ρ. One student of mine commented that they are not **NoRMaL**. Liquid verbs reject the σίγμα of the Future and Aorist endings, leaving behind the remainder of the ending.

B. **Liquids in the Aorist Tense:** As indicated above, the Aorist endings will be lacking a σίγμα, but will show the ἄλφα or ἒ ψιλόν coupling vowel and the rest of the ending. Also, the verb form will have the augment (in the Indicative Mood). For example,

PRESENT			AORIST	
ἀποκτείνω	I kill	→	ἀπέκτειν-α	I killed
ἀποστέλλομεν	We send	→	ἀπεστείλ-αμεν	We sent
ἐγείρει	He raises up	→	ἤγειρ-ε	He raised up

Notice: A slight stem change may also occur, as in ἀποστέλλω above.

The Aorist Participle (as well as the other moods yet to be covered) also drop the σίγμα from the endings:

PRESENT INDICATIVE	AORIST PARTICIPLES		
	M	F	N
ἀποκτείνω	ἀπόκτειν-ας,	-ασα,	-αν
ἀποστέλλω	ἀπόστειλ-ας,	-ασα,	-αν
ἐγείρω	ἔγειρ-ας,	-ασα,	-αν

C. **Liquids in the Future:** In the Future Tense, liquid verbs also drop the σίγμα from their endings. However, to avoid confusion with the Present Tense endings (which, remember, are identical except for the σίγμα), *the future verb stem becomes an ἒ ψιλόν contract stem.* Thus, the contraction that takes place will distinguish the Future Tense from the Present Tense in liquid verbs.

PRESENT			FUTURE	
ἀποκτείνω	I kill	→	ἀποκτενῶ	I will kill
ἀποστέλλομεν	We send	→	ἀποστελοῦμεν	We will send
ἐγείρει	He raises up	→	ἐγερεῖ	He will raise up

Notice: There is the characteristic accent shift using the circumflex accent. Also, there is often a slight stem change. Each of the above verbs shows this.

D. **Liquid Comparison:** Here is the Present, Future, and 1st Aorist Indicative of ἐγείρω:

		PRESENT ACTIVE	FUTURE ACTIVE	FUTURE MIDDLE	AORIST ACTIVE	AORIST MIDDLE
sg.	1	ἐγείρω	ἐγερῶ	ἐγεροῦμαι	ἤγειρα	ἠγειράμην
	2	ἐγείρεις	ἐγερεῖς	ἐγερῇ	ἤγειρας	ἠγείρω
	3	ἐγείρει	ἐγερεῖ	ἐγερεῖται	ἤγειρε(ν)	ἠγείρατο
pl.	1	ἐγείρομεν	ἐγεροῦμεν	ἐγερούμεθα	ἠγείραμεν	ἠγειράμεθα
	2	ἐγείρετε	ἐγερεῖτε	ἐγερεῖσθε	ἠγείρατε	ἠγείρασθε
	3	ἐγείρουσιν	ἐγεροῦσιν	ἐγεροῦνται	ἤγειραν	ἠγείραντο

E. **2nd Aorist Verbs are not Liquid in Third Principal Part:** There are a few verbs which one might think are liquid. But remember that 2nd Aorists take the Imperfect endings and have no σίγμα. Hence, the σίγμα is not dropped!

PRESENT	FUTURE	2ND AORIST	
ἀναβαίνω καταβαίνω	ἀναβήσομαι	ἀνάβην	
βάλλω ἐκβάλλω	βαλῶ*	ἔβαλον	*liquid in the Future
πίνω	πίομαι	ἔπιον	
λέγω	ἐρῶ*	εἶπον	*liquid in the Future

However, a few verbs such as εὑρίσκω, λέγω, and ὁράω sometimes show (alongside their regular 2nd Aorist forms) Aorist forms that resemble liquids: Εὗρα, εἶπα, εἶδα. (These last two are not liquids, since they end in *pi* (π) and *delta* (δ).)

F. **Principal Parts of the Liquid Verbs:** Notice irregular forms and patterns. A dash (-) signifies that no such tense form occurs in the Greek NT.

FIRST	SECOND	THIRD	FOURTH	FIFTH	SIXTH
αἴρω	ἀρῶ	ἦρα	ἦρκα	ἦρμαι	ἤρθην
ἀπαγγέλλω	–	–	–	–	–
ἀποκτείνω	ἀποκτενῶ	ἀπέκτεινα	–	–	ἀπεκτάνθην
ἀποστέλλω	ἀποστελῶ	ἀπέστειλα	ἀπέσταλκα	ἀπέσταλμαι	ἀπεστάλην
ἐγείρω	ἐγερῶ	ἤγειρα	–	ἐγήγερμαι	ἠγέρθην
κρίνω	κρινῶ	ἔκρινα	κέκρικα	κέκριμαι	ἐκρίθην
μένω	μενῶ	ἔμεινα	μεμένηκα	–	–
σπείρω	–	ἔσπειρα	–	ἔσπαρμαι	ἐσπάρην
χαίρω	χαιρήσομαι	–	–	–	ἐχάρην

21.2 SPECIAL USES OF THE NOMINATIVE CASE (Πτῶσις Ὀρθή, Εὐθεῖα, Ὀνομαστική)

A. **Introduction:** We learned in §4.2.C.2 that the nominative case is the case for *naming* or *designation*; most commonly, the nominative case specifies the subject of a verb. Beyond this, however, students must understand that the nominative case will "render the topic of the sentence prominent whether or not it is the grammatical subject" (Wallace 61 n.90). Within this basic understanding, additional special uses of the nominative are described below.

B. **Special Uses of the Nominative:**

1. <u>Nominatives in Predicates that Refer Back to the Subject</u>. In general, substantives or adjectival modifiers that are predicated of the subject (i.e. part of the verbal statement) will be in the nominative case. Often, grammarians will sub-categorize such uses as follows:

    a. ***Predicate Nominatives and Adjectives***. You have already learned in §5.3 that the nominative case is used with verbs of *being* like εἰμί, γίνομαι, and ὑπάρχω to indicate predicate nominatives or predicate adjectives.

    b. ***Nominative of Appellation***. With verbs of naming, calling, and the like, one commonly observes a nominative referring to the subject that is thus named or called.

    Matt 5:9 αὐτοὶ <u>υἱοὶ</u> θεοῦ κληθήσονται.
    They will be called <u>sons</u> of God.

    Matt 21:13b [Isa 56:7 LXX] ὁ οἶκός μου <u>οἶκος</u> προσευχῆς κληθήσεται,
    My house will be called <u>a house </u>of prayer,

    Notice that the verb of calling or naming is in the passive voice; the verb predicates a name upon the subject. Importantly, we need to understand that had these verbs been active in voice, then they would have normally taken two accusatives as follows:[1]

    Matt 22:43b Δαυὶδ ... καλεῖ <u>αὐτὸν</u> <u>κύριον</u>...
    David ... calls <u>him</u> <u>Lord</u>....

    So, this observation leads us to the next sub-category of use.

---

[1] The statement in John 13:13 ὑμεῖς φωνεῖτέ με· ὁ διδάσκαλος, καί· ὁ κύριος, *You yourselves call me "The Teacher," and "The Lord,"* involves nominatives of direct quotation, as indicated by the NA27 punctuation setting them off as commas (Robertson, *A Short Grammar of the Greek New Testament: For Students Familiar with the Elements of Greek* [New York: Hodder & Stoughton, 1908], 90).

c. ***Passive-Middle Verbs that Would Otherwise Take Double Accusatives or an Accusative and an Infinitive.*** When such verbs are found in the passive voice, they retain one object as a nominative referring back to the subject of the passive voice verb.

James 4:4b ὃς ἐὰν οὖν βουληθῇ φίλος εἶναι τοῦ κόσμου, <u>ἐχθρὸς</u> τοῦ θεοῦ καθίσταται.
Therefore, whoever wants to be a friend of the world is established as <u>an enemy</u> of God.

In this first example, there are two special nomintive uses. For an explanation of the first (φίλος *friend*), see d. below. The second nominative is explained in that the verb καθίστημι *I establish* can take a double accusative (LSJ 835.A.II.4):[2] *God established <u>a friend</u> of the world (as) <u>an enemy</u>.* But, if the sentence was recreated using the passive voice, in which one object becomes the subject, then the second object is retained as a nominative, since it refers back to the subject, as follows: *A friend of the world was estabished (as) <u>an enemy</u>.*

Titus 2:11 Ἐπεφάνη γὰρ ἡ χάρις τοῦ θεοῦ <u>σωτήριος</u> πᾶσιν ἀνθρώποις..
For God's Grace was manifested (as) <u>salvific</u> for all humans.

This second example likely implies an infinitive, since this verb is attested as taking the accusative and infinitive meaning *to make it manifest that...* (LSJ 669.I.2.). If placed in the passive voice construction, the verb would be *it was manifested that....* Thus, in Titus 2:11, the translation supplying the implied infinitive would be: *God's grace was manifested (to be) salvific....* Finally, consider this example, which involves a passive voice construction. Can you reconstruct what the active voice construction was?[3]

1 Pet 2:5a καὶ αὐτοὶ ὡς λίθοι ζῶντες οἰκοδομεῖσθε <u>οἶκος πνευματικὸς</u>...
And you yourselves, as living stones, are being built (into) <u>a spiritual house</u>...

d. **Nominative referents in Infinitive Clauses.** Infinitives and their subjects will be treated in §23.1.F. However, for the sake of complete coverage here, substantives that refer back to the subject will retain the nominative case, even though students might expect an accusative according to the general rule that "infinitives take accusative subjects." See the first nominative in James 4:4b above; and then consider this example.

---

[2] *Pace* Robertson who identifies this as a predicate nominative (*Word Pictures in the New Testament* [Nashville: Broadman, 1933], s.v.)

[3] Put actively, the sentence would read: *God built <u>you</u> (as) <u>a spiritual house</u>.*

1 Cor 14:37 Εἴ τις δοκεῖ <u>προφήτης</u> εἶναι ἢ <u>πνευματικός</u>....

If someone thinks that he is <u>a prophet</u> or <u>spiritual</u>...

2. <u>Pendent Nominative</u>. The word *pendent* means *suspended* or *hanging*. Here the nominative phrase or clause (a substantive or participle) is hanging on to the main clause, only loosely connected logically to some referent in the main clause. Pendent nominatives will often form **left (dis)locations**, which because of their importance in the discourse, will receive extensive treatment below in §21.3 LEFT (DIS)LOCATED TOPICS & FRAMES WITH A TRACE. On the pendent nominative, Wallace summarizes: "The pendent nominative carries one of two semantic forces: *emotion* or *emphasis*. The second usage, which is far more common, could be labeled *nominative of reference*" (52, emphasis original).

John 17:2b ἵνα <u>πᾶν</u> ὃ δέδωκας αὐτῷ δώσῃ <u>αὐτοῖς</u> ζωὴν αἰώνιον.

that <u>everyone</u>, whom you have to him (the Son), he would give <u>to them</u> eternal life.

Here the πᾶν *everyone* is a nominative hanging, but referentially and logically connected to the αὐτοῖς *to them* of the main clause.

Rev 3:12a Ὁ νικῶν ποιήσω <u>αὐτὸν</u> στῦλον ἐν τῷ ναῷ τοῦ θεοῦ μου.

<u>The one conquering</u>, I will give <u>him</u> a pillar in the temple of my God.

Other specific uses of nominative case approach the semantic and pragmatic contribution of suspended nominatives. These include proverbial nominatives (nominative clauses with a participle that preserve a proverb), "parenthetic nominatives," which are sentences strikingly placed in the midst of others (Wallace 53-54), and "nominatives of exclamation" (Wallace, 59-60).

Matt 24:15 ὁ ἀναγινώσκων νοείτω *Let the reader understand!*

Rom 7:24 ταλαίπωρος ἐγὼ ἄνθρωπος *O wretched person I (am)!*

3. <u>Nominative Absolute (Possibly with Implied Verbs)</u>. In epistolary openings or other formulaic statements, nominatives are found. Such statements probably involve implied verbs.

1 Thess 1:1 <u>Παῦλος</u> καὶ <u>Σιλουανὸς</u> καὶ <u>Τιμόθεος</u> τῇ ἐκκλησίᾳ Θεσσαλονικέων ἐν θεῷ πατρὶ καὶ κυρίῳ Ἰησοῦ Χριστῷ, <u>χάρις</u> ὑμῖν καὶ <u>εἰρήνη</u>.

<u>Paul</u> and <u>Silvanus</u> and <u>Timothy</u> [writing] to the church of the Thessalonians in God the Father and the Lord Jesus Christ. <u>Grace</u> [be] to you and <u>Peace</u>!

4. <u>As Vocatives or Articular Nominatives in Apposition with Vocatives</u>. Anarthrous nominatives can function as vocatives, with or without ὦ *O!* Wallace reports that nearly 600 occur in the GNT (57 n.72). On the significance of vocatives, see §5.5 VOCATIVES OF DIRECT ADDRESS.

Luke 9:41b ὦ <u>γενεὰ ἄπιστος</u> καὶ <u>διεστραμμένη</u>, ἕως πότε ἔσομαι πρὸς ὑμᾶς καὶ ἀνέξομαι ὑμῶν;

> *Oh <u>foolish generation</u> and <u>crooked</u>, for how long will I be with you and put up with you?*

With the article, however, Zerwick helpfully summarizes a rule: "the nominative with the article is always used in appositions added to a vocative."[4] There are about 60 instances in the GNT.[5] The key is the article: Since the article does not have a vocative form, the nominative suffices.

Rev 15:3b Μεγάλα τὰ ἔργα σου, Κύριε <u>ὁ Θεὸς ὁ παντοκράτωρ</u>...
> *Great are your works, Lord, <u>The God Almighty</u>...*

Rom 8:15b κράζομεν· αββα <u>ὁ πατήρ</u>. *We Cry out: Abba <u>(the) Father</u>.*

5. <u>Various Uses in the Book of Revelation</u>. The Book of Revelation has several striking examples of nominatives, which basically function to keep the focus on the major Agent. So, consider these examples.

Rev 1:4 ἀπὸ <u>ὁ ὢν</u> καὶ <u>ὁ ἦν</u> καὶ <u>ὁ ἐρχόμενος</u>
> *from <u>the One being</u> and <u>the One (who) was</u> and <u>the coming One</u>.*

<u>Notice</u>: One would expect a genitive case noun with the preposition ἀπό, but the nominative likely emphasizes the referent.

Rev 1:5 ἀπὸ Ἰησοῦ Χριστοῦ, <u>ὁ μάρτυς ὁ πιστός</u>
> *from Jesus Christ, <u>the faithful witness</u>*

<u>Notice</u>: One would expect the appositional noun to be in the genitive case; it may be that ὁ μάρτυς ὁ πιστός may be an exclamation.

---

[4] Maximilian Zerwick, *Biblical Greek: Illustrated by Examples*, trans. Joseph Smith, 4th ed., Scripta Pontificii Instituti Biblici 114 (Rome: Editrice Pontificio Istitutio Biblico, 1963), 11.

[5] James Hope Moulton, *A Grammar of New Testament Greek: Volume 1, Prolegomena*, 3rd ed. (Edinburgh: T&T Clark, 1967), 70.

21.3 LEFT (DIS)LOCATED TOPICS & FRAMES WITH A TRACE

A. **Introduction:** A not uncommon occurrence in Greek is the extreme fronting (to the left) of some sentence constituent (word, phrase, or clause) to the sentence initial slot. Such positioning may be considered "left (dis)located." Then, in the main clause, a "trace element" will refer back to the left (dis)located constituent. Consider this example:

2 Cor 12:17 μή <u>τινα</u> ὧν ἀπέσταλκα πρὸς ὑμᾶς, δι' αὐτοῦ ἐπλεονέκτησα ὑμᾶς;

> *Not with any one of those whom I have sent to you—through him I didn't exploit you, did I?!*[6]

The direct object <u>τινα</u> *someone* is placed in far left position to draw attention to it; then, a pronominal trace δι' αὐτοῦ *through him* refers back to it. This particular example also shows grammatical discontinuity between the initially left located constituent (accusative) and its trace (genitive), making this an even more striking example of the phenomenon. Paul created this dislocation within a rhetorical question expecting a negative response amidst a highly emotionally charged letter. The left (dis)location helped emphasize the point that he did **not** exploit the Corinthians.

1. <u>Far Left Placement with a Trace.</u> What sets left (dis)locations apart from other similar constructions is that in the main clause they will have some resumptive element or "trace" that refers back to the left (dis)location anaphorically. For example, consider the placement of the topic ***the movie*** and its trace <u>*it*</u> in example (1):

(1) *The movie*, I knew <u>it</u> would end that way!

Although we don't have the whole conversation before us, we can image one. The statement "the movie" would probably mark a return to a known topic (hence, only the article and no specific movie title is needed). The left (dis)located topic (LDT) draws extra attention to the constituent as a topic of important focus.

Consider these next two examples. In Matt 10:22b and Rev 3:12a, the **left-(dis)location topics** (LDTs) are nominative substantives that have a resumptive <u>pronoun</u> or "<u>trace</u>" that anaphorically refers back to them. In Matt 10:22b, the trace is the nominative demonstrative pronoun <u>οὗτος</u> *this one*. In Rev 3:12a, the LDT is nominative but the trace is accusative; in this case there is no grammatical relationship, but only a referential one: the anaphoric pronoun αὐτόν *him*.

---

[6] Translation is from Fredrick J. Long, *2 Corinthians: A Handbook on the Greek Text*, Baylor Handbook on the Greek New Testament (Waco, TX: Baylor University Press, 2015), 234.

Matt 10:22b ὁ δὲ **ὑπομείνας εἰς τέλος** οὗτος σωθήσεται.
*Moreover, **the one enduring to the end**, this one will be saved.*

Rev 3:12a Ὁ **νικῶν** ποιήσω αὐτὸν στῦλον ἐν τῷ ναῷ τοῦ θεοῦ μου...
***The one overcoming**, I will make him a pillar in the temple of my God...*

2. <u>Nomenclature</u>. What I am calling left (dis)locations are commonly simply called left dislocations (LD): "In grammatical description, a type of sentence in which one of the constituents appears in initial position and its canonical position is filled by a pronoun or a full lexical noun phrase with the same reference, e.g. *John, I like him/the old chap.*"[7] Left dislocations are found across languages and have received extensive treatment in linguistic research.[8] Studies differentiate clitic left dislocation (CL LD) from hanging topic left dislocation (HT LD); however, their component parts and properties are similar.[9] I am assuming similar characteristics for the GNT.

In my discussion of left (dis)location, I prefer placing the "dis" in parentheses, because in Greek, the left (dis)location may be quite proper grammatically and syntactically; so there is no true "dislocation." Of the four categories of (dis)locations that I describe below, only two may be considered to violate normal sentence constructions, i.e. what are *anacoluthon* and *prolepsis*.

3. <u>Important Topics and Frameworks</u>. Remember that fronted sentence elements typically indicate important topics or frameworks. I distinguish **nominal** left (dis)located topics (LDTs) from **adverbial** left (dis)located frames (LDFs). By topic I mean a (simpler) nominal phrase that entails a substantive or noun phrase, whereas by frame, I mean a more complex conjunctive adverbial subordinate clause that begins with a subordinating conjunction. Interestingly, relative pronoun clauses, which combine nominal and subordinate clause features, may function like an LDT or LDF, or both simultaneously. My research of the GNT indicates that *LDTs usually, if not always, mark both +immediate alternative discontinuity and +larger discourse continuity; whereas LDFs simply seem to introduce important complex adverbial frameworks marked +discontinuity.*

---

[7] David Crystal, *Dictionary of Linguistics and Phonetics*, 6th ed. (Malden, MA: Blackwell, 2008), 273, the original all-small caps were removed.

[8] E.g., Knud Lambrecht, "Dislocation," pages 2:1050-78 in Martin Haspelmath, Ekkehard König, Wulf Oesterreicher, and Wolfgang Raible, eds., *Language Typology and Language Universals: An International Handbook*, 2 vols., Handbücher zur Sprach- und Kommunikationswissenschaft 20 (Berlin: de Gruyter, 2001); idem., *Information Structure and Sentence Form: Topic, Focus, and the Mental Representations of Discourse Referents* (Cambridge University Press, 1996). See especially the fascinating dissertation, worthy of mentioning simply for its application to exegesis more generally, by Mathias Irmer, "Bridging Inferences in Discourse Interpretation" (Ph.D. diss., Universität Leipzig, 2009), ch.8 "Bridging by Clitic Left Dislocation."

[9] So, Luis López, *A Derivational Syntax for Information Structure*, Oxford Studies in Theoretical Linguistics 23 (Oxford: Oxford University Press, 2009). Lopez first distinguishes CLLD and HTLD and then concludes, "However, from a Universal Grammar perspective, one has to view these constructions as built from similar sets of ingredients and therefore as having similar properties" (7).

B. **More Research on Left (dis)Locations Needed:** In 2000, Levinsohn indicated, "Research is needed to determine the effect of using left-dislocation rather than simple preposing to establish a point of departure" (26 n.33). Since then, Runge provides the most extensive discussion of left dislocation for the GNT, although his examples and discussion focus primarily on frameworks, or what I have called LDFs. My research into nominal LDTs will supplement and refine Runge's discussion. His nuanced and complex view is summarized in this paragraph (290):

> Generally speaking, left-dislocations serve to streamline the introduction of an entity into the discourse. They have the effect of either announcing or shifting the topic of the clause that follows. This attracts more attention to the topic than it would have otherwise received with one of the more conventional methods. Where the topic needs to be activated from scratch, left-dislocations serve a necessary function, activating the entity into the discourse.

C. **Pragmatic Functions of LDFs and LDTs:** In general, from Runge's research and examples, we can summarize the first three functions below for left dislocations with some modification (esp. the dimension of particularization in #3); the fourth restates Knud Lambrecht's understanding (quoted, but not elaborated upon by Runge). The fifth and sixth represent my own extension of Lambrecht's understanding in concert with more recent work on left dislocations which indicates that they mark local discontinuity of alternatives (real or implied) but at the same time they also mark discourse continuity. For the GNT, this discontinuity appears especially true of LDTs, but less often with LDFs, unless the LDF is marked by a conjunction (ἀλλά or δέ) or constrained by contextual sense.

1. <u>To Generally Mark a Topic or Framework as Especially Important</u>. As stated by Runge, a fundamental purpose involves "thematically highlighting the introduction of an entity because of its significance to the discourse…. Fundamentally, use of the construction adds prominence to the entity" (291).

2. <u>Re-introduction of Topics back into the discourse with Particularization (LDTs)</u>. The left location re-activates an already established topic within the hearer's mental representation (drawing upon Knud Lambrecht[10]). Additionally, linguistic studies have noted that an LDT will have "a somewhat complex relationship with its antecedent–the relationship can be part/whole, set, subset, etc."[11] In Inductive Bible Study categories, this relationship is called "particularization."

---

[10] Lambrecht, *Information Structure*, 174. See also Irmer, "Bridging Inferences," 227.
[11] Lopez, *Derivational Syntax*, 6; Irmer, "Bridging Inferences," 222-24.

3. <u>To Streamline the first time Introduction of a Complex Framework (LDFs)</u>. As stated by Runge, the purpose involves "streamlining the introduction of a complex entity into one clause instead of two" (291); important here is the trace to mark the transition, "making it easier for the reader/hearer to properly process the discourse."[12]

4. <u>To Mark Topical Shifts</u>. Additionally, as indicated in Lambrecht's description, "left-dislocation constructions are reserved for topic announcing or topic shifting contexts."[13] Implicitly, such shifts would entail contrast and discontinuity (see 5. below).

5. <u>LDTs are marked +immediate alternative discontinuity and +discourse continuity</u>. LDTs are marked +contrastive/discontinuity by introducing an actual or implied set of alternatives.[14] At the same time, LDTs are marked +discourse continuity. How are both possible? The reintroduction of a topic by means of LD, which creates an immediate contrast, is for the purpose of advancing larger unit cohesion or discourse themes.[15] Consider once again the biblical examples already given above:

Matt 10:22b ὁ δὲ <u>**ὑπομείνας εἰς τέλος**</u> <u>οὗτος</u> σωθήσεται.
*Moreover, **the one enduring to the end**, this one will be saved.*

Rev 3:12a Ὁ <u>**νικῶν**</u> ποιήσω <u>αὐτὸν</u> στῦλον ἐν τῷ ναῷ τοῦ θεοῦ μου...
The one overcoming, *I will make <u>him</u> a pillar in the temple of my God...*

For Matt 10:22b where Jesus describes believers as missionaries, Jesus first discussed how family members would betray family member (10:21), then how disciples as *you* (pl.) will be hated (10:22a) and eventually be persecuted (10:23), just as Jesus had been (10:25). So, 10:22b interupts hatred and persecution (*you* pl.) by specifying an individual (*the one* 3rd sg.) who will endure and be saved (+discontinuity). Additionally, a broader book theme in Matthew is salvation (+continuity). The same is true of Rev 3:12a. The preceding verse concludes with the call to persevere (*hold fast*) "in order that no one would take your crown" (3:11). So, 3:12a is discontinuous with the last thought of 3:11; additionally, 3:12a

---

[12] See also Irmer, "Bridging Inferences," 221.

[13] Runge, 290, citing Lambrecht, *Information Structure*, 204; see also Irmer, "Bridging Inferences," 226-27.

[14] Irmer concludes, "speakers fundamentally use Left Dislocations in order to change the discourse topic and to mark discourse discontinuity" and regarding contrastiveness in CLLD constructions, "it can be seen that no matter whether contrast is seen as an inherent property or as arising from independent grounds, a set of alternatives seems to be involved" ("Bridging Inferences," 229 and 231, respectively).

[15] Summarizing one aspect of the dissertation of Raquel Hidaldo Downing, Irmer's description of how both are possible makes excellent sense: "On the one hand, in a strategy of topic shift [+immediate discontinuity], a global aspect of coherence is emphasized [+discourse continuity], in the sense that referents which stand in some relation to former subjects of a conversation are (re-)introduced. On the other hand, strategies of topic continuity create links between adjacent discourse segments and are thus a means to express local discourse coherence [again +discourse continuity]" (229, my comments in brackets added).

pertains to the larger discursive theme of conquering (νικάω) through faithful witness, even to the point of death.[16] Consider also 1 Cor 15:36.

1 Cor 15:36 ἄφρων, **σὺ** ὃ σπείρεις, οὐ ζωοποιεῖται ἐὰν μὴ ἀποθάνῃ·
*Fool! **You**, that which you sow does not come to life, (if) unless it dies.*

Here Paul is correcting the view that the dead are not raised bodily (15:35), so this has +immediate discontinuity. Yet, Paul advances the broader theme of resurrection in the unit of 1 Cor 15, while also rebuking/correcting the Corinthians, which is a discourse wide theme across 1 Corinthians; so 15:36 shows +discourse continuity.

6. <u>LDFs Introduce Important Complex Adverbial Frameworks with +Discontinuity</u>. The use of subordinating conjunctions and their clauses are placed far left in the sentence, and then will have an adverbial trace.

Matt 6:21 **ὅπου** γάρ ἐστιν ὁ θησαυρός σου, ἐκεῖ ἔσται καὶ ἡ καρδία σου.
*For **where** your treasure is, there will be also your heart.*

The locative conjunction **ὅπου** *where* introduces the LDF and has the adverbial trace ἐκεῖ *there*. There is some discontinuity and specificity with the preceding verse, since in 6:20 Jesus has spoken in 2nd plural (whereas 6:21 is 2nd singular).

D. **Classification of Left (Dis)Location Constructions:** Grammarians and linguists have observed these "odd" constructions, which are the first four constructions described here: *prolepsis*, suspended phrases (*pendens* constructions), *anacoluthon*, and fronted relative pronoun clauses. These grammatical categories still have grammatical, descriptive value. These first four constructions are nominal, i.e. they are LDTs. Additionally, I include a discussion of two possible types of left (dis)locations, which are better deemed "left locations," since grammatically fronted adverbial clauses are not so unusual in placement. In the fifth construction, I treat adverbial subordinate clauses, which may be considered LDFs. Finally, I treat a sixth construction, the relative conditional clause (a subtype of adverbial clauses), which may combine features of LDTs and LDFs.

1. <u>LDT: Syntactical *Prolepsis* (πρόληψις)</u>. The term *prolepsis* in grammar refers to anticipating a sentence element before its subordinate clause begins. Robertson (423) provides this excellent summary with examples:

> PROLEPSIS is not uncommon where either the substantive is placed out of its right place before the conjunction in a subordinate clause like τὴν ἀγάπην ἵνα γνῶτε (2

---

[16] Rev 2:7, 11, 17, 26; 3:5, 12, 21²; 5:5; 6:2²; 11:7; 12:11; 13:7; 15:2; 17:14; 21:7.

Cor. 2:4) and βιωτικὰ κριτήρια ἐὰν ἔχητε (1 Cor. 6:4), or the subject of the subordinate clause even becomes the object of the previous verb like ἰδεῖν τὸν Ἰησοῦν τίς ἐστιν (Lu. 19:3).

Other examples of *prolepsis* identified by Robertson include Mark 8:24; Luke 10:26; Acts 3:12; 13:32; Rom 9:19, 20; 14:4, 10; 1 Cor 15:36. To these could be added others like Matt 6:6 and Luke 11:19b. Let's look closely at 2 Cor 2:4.

2 Cor 2:4 ἔγραψα ὑμῖν διὰ πολλῶν δακρύων, οὐχ ἵνα λυπηθῆτε ἀλλὰ **τὴν ἀγάπην** [¹ ἵνα γνῶτε [²ἣν ἔχω περισσοτέρως εἰς ὑμᾶς²] ¹].

> *I wrote to you with many tears, not in order that you would be grieved, but **the love** [¹in order that you would know X, [²which I abundantly have towards you²] ¹].*

The direct object τὴν ἀγάπην *the love* is pulled out of the boundaries of its subordinate clause [¹...¹] and fronted. The trace is implied (X), and elaborated in the relative pronoun clause [²...²]. The proleptic left (dis)located ***The love*** here is marked +immediate discontinuity in regard to the negated purpose of grieving the Corinthians (notice the point-counterpoint set οὐχ ... ἀλλὰ), but also +discourse continuity across 2 Corinthians, since Paul's love for the Corinthians is a major theme.[17]

Consider also the σὺ in Luke 4:7, which involves grammatical prolepsis by placing an emphasized sentence element in forward position even outside the limits of its subordinate claques boundary.[18]

Luke 4:7 **σὺ** οὖν [¹ἐὰν προσκυνήσῃς ἐνώπιον ἐμοῦ²], ἔσται σοῦ πᾶσα.

> ***You**, therefore, if you bow before me, all will be yours.*

Here the **σὺ** ***you*** has its trace in the verbal form. In context, the **σὺ** ***you*** returns back to the devil's addressing of Jesus found in 4:6a that had been interrupted by the more generalized statements about the devil's authority to give authority and glory "to whomever" he wants in 4:6b. Immediately following this, 4:7 is marked +immediate discontinuity and +particularity (Jesus vs. whomever), but also +discourse continuity, since it relates to the discourse unit of Jesus' temptation.

---

[17] See my discussion of τὴν ἀγάπην in *2 Corinthians*, 46.

[18] The σύ is not removed from its clause for the sake of ἐὰν not occuring before οὖν, since ἐὰν οὖν occurs sentential initial frequently enough (in the GNT, Matt 5:23; 6:22b; 24:26; Luke 6:62; 8:36; Rom 2:26; 1 Cor 14:11, 23; 2 Tim 2:21; Rev 3:3b).

2. <u>LDT: Suspended phrases (*pendens*) with grammatical agreement with the trace</u>. To be differentiated from *anacoluthon* below (because the LDT has grammatical agreement with the trace), these LDTs provide an alternative topical focus from the immediate context (+discontinuity).

Luke 8:21b <u>**μήτηρ**</u> μου καὶ <u>**ἀδελφοί**</u> μου <u>οὗτοί</u> εἰσιν οἱ τὸν λόγον τοῦ θεοῦ ἀκούοντες καὶ ποιοῦντες.

> *My **mother** and my **brothers**, these are the ones hearing and doing the Word of God.*

Both LDTs are nominative and together agree with the trace in case and number. Jesus was speaking here "answering back" (ἀποκριθεὶς) to someone pointing out that his mothers and brothers were present; the LDT is thus +discontinuity, since he redefines and specifies (+particularization) kinship to be one's obedience to the Word of God, which he is preaching in Luke (+discourse continuity).

Another example that contains repeated LDTs is Jesus' explanation of the soils parable in Luke 8, where after the first soil type is explained in 8:12 (no LDT construction), the subsequent specific descriptions of distinct soils (thus, +immediate discontinuity and +particularization) each entail LDTs (8:13, 14, 15). However, taken together, the LDTs show +discourse continuity through their explaining the same parable.

3. <u>LDT: *Anacoluthon* (ἀνακόλουθον)</u>. Unlike suspended phrases that agree in case with its trace, *anacolouthon* "refers to a syntactic break in the expected grammatical sequence within a sentence, as when a sentence begins with one construction and remains unfinished,..."[19] *Anacoluthon* involves a jarring ungrammatically connected constituent, which, however, has a trace in the main clause that is referentially connected.

Acts 7:40 εἰπόντες τῷ Ἀαρών· ποίησον ἡμῖν θεοὺς οἳ προπορεύσονται ἡμῶν· <u>**ὁ**</u> γὰρ <u>**Μωϋσῆς οὗτος**</u>, ὃς ἐξήγαγεν ἡμᾶς ἐκ γῆς Αἰγύπτου, οὐκ οἴδαμεν τί ἐγένετο <u>αὐτῷ</u>.

> *saying to Aaron: "Make for us gods which will go before us. For **this Moses**, who led us out of Egypt, we do not know what has happened <u>to him</u>!"*

Moses as leader (and "his" God, whom the Israelites ignore!) is placed in contrast to Aaron, to whom the Israelites turned for an alternative idolatrous leadership.

---

[19] Crystal, *Dictionary of Linguistics and Phonetics*, 24.

4. <u>LDT: Fronted Relative Pronoun Clauses with Pronominal Traces</u>. Fulfilling the same constraints, relative pronoun clauses that are left (dis)located introduce entities that are marked +immediate discontinuity and +discourse continuity. Such relative pronoun clauses are LDTs. More typically, relative pronoun clauses (immediately) follow what they modify; so, when they are moved to the far left, they divert from the normal expectation, even though they have properly grammatical relationship to their referent. For instance, in John 1:12a, the LDT is a quantitative relative pronoun clause (i.e. ὅσος is marked +quantity; see vocabulary in CH.26) that has its referent in the pronoun **αὐτοῖς** *them* that follows subsequently.[20]

John 1:11-12a εἰς τὰ ἴδια ἦλθεν, καὶ οἱ ἴδιοι αὐτὸν οὐ παρέλαβον. **12** **ὅσοι** δὲ **ἔλαβον αὐτόν**, ἔδωκεν <u>αὐτοῖς</u> ἐξουσίαν τέκνα θεοῦ γενέσθαι, ...

[11] *He came to his own and his own did not receive him.* [12a] *But **as many as receiving him**, to them he gave authority to become children of God, ...*

The relative pronoun ὅσος has been placed far left in the sentence to provide focal contrast (+immediate discontinuity) with those who did not receive the Word (1:11b). However, the whole Gospel of John concerns Jesus' work to reveal the Father and allow people to become God's children (see 17:1-8); thus, this construction is marked +discourse continuity. Students may also be interested to know that 1:11-12 forms the center of a chiastic arrangement (ABCDEFG-GFEDCBA) in 1:1-18.

5. <u>LDF: Adverbial Clauses with Adverbial Trace</u>. In his discussion of left dislocations, Runge includes fronted adverbial subordinate clauses (e.g. ὅταν, ὅπου, and καθως) that have corresponding adverbial traces in the main clause (e.g. respectively, τότε, ἐκεῖ, and οὕτως). However, subordinate clauses regularly are found fronted in left location in order to provide a framework for what follows. This is true especially of ὅταν, which is a temporal-conditional subordinate clause, where such conditional clauses are typically clause initial.[21] So, these adverbial clauses may not be true left dislocations. What is intriguing, however, is the presence of an adverbial trace, which may rightly signal a left (dis)location construc-

---

[20] Oddly, Wallace (52) includes John 1:12 to illustrate a pendent nominative. It is not.

[21] There are 123 instances of ὅταν in the GNT, which is not clause initial in 29 instances, and of these, six are in Gospel parallel passages: Matt 5:11 (//Luke 6:22); 9:15(//Mark 2:20//Luke 5:35); 15:2; 26:29 (//Mark 14:25); Mark 8:38 (//Luke 9:26); 9:9; 13:4 (//Luke 21:7); Luke 6:26; 11:36; 13:28; 23:42; John 13:19; Acts 23:35; Rom 11:27; 1 Cor 15:24; 16:5, 12; 2 Cor 10:6; 13:9; Jas 1:2; 1 John 5:2; Rev 9:5; 18:9. Of these that occur sentence final, a number involve climactic eschatological descriptions; in others, one senses some thematic emphasis (a final punch line statement). On the other hand, Rev 9:5 seems only to be further descriptive in a none emphatic way.

tion, which then may function like other LDTs or LDFs as I have here described them.[22] Additionally, one can often discern discontinuity, although it may not be very strong.

In this first example, the adverbial clause is sentence initial and has a trace. In the context, there is no strong discontiuity, although a change in setting exists (20:29).

Matt 21:1 Καὶ **ὅτε** ἤγγισαν εἰς Ἱεροσόλυμα καὶ ἦλθον εἰς Βηθφαγὴ εἰς τὸ ὄρος τῶν ἐλαιῶν, **τότε** Ἰησοῦς ἀπέστειλεν δύο μαθητὰς

> And, **when** they drew near into Jerusalem and came into Bethphage into the Mountain of Olives, **then** Jesus sent two disciples.

Colossians 3:4 involves a LDF with ὅταν occurring in the middle of a discourse thought.

Col 3:3 ἀπεθάνετε γὰρ καὶ ἡ ζωὴ ὑμῶν κέκρυπται σὺν τῷ Χριστῷ ἐν τῷ θεῷ·
> For you died and your life has been hiddne with Christ in God.

Col 3:4 **ὅταν ὁ Χριστὸς φανερωθῇ, ἡ ζωὴ ὑμῶν**, **τότε** καὶ ὑμεῖς σὺν αὐτῷ φανερωθήσεσθε ἐν δόξῃ.
> **Whenever Christ is manifested**, **our Life**, **then** also you yourselves with him will be manifested in glory.

In Col 3:3, Paul has affirmed that presently life in *Christ is hidden*, but in 3:4 he describes the future when *Christ will be manifest* (+immediate discontinuity). Additionally, 3:4 continues the larger discourse theme of believers' attachment to Christ. Notable are the three emphatic constructions in καὶ ὑμεῖς σὺν αὐτῷ *also you yourselves with Him*.[23] Thus, 3:4 shows +discourse continuity.

6. <u>LDT & LDF: Conditional Relative Clauses.</u> Although conditional sentences are given full treatment in Ch.26, a brief comment is necessary here. Relative pronouns can combine with conditional particles ἄν or ἐάν (*if*) to form the "if" part (called the supposition) of a condition, which is a subordinate relative clause. The relative pronoun forms the supposition or protasis of a relative conditional clause ("*whoever…*"). However, since the supposition in Greek constructions normally are placed first, and this is especially true of ὅς ἐάν or ὅς ἄν,[24] there may not be, in fact, any dislocation, but simply a typical fronted left location.

---

[22] Alternatively, the adverbial trace may simply underscore the semantic temporal or locative marking indicated by the subordinate clause (temporal and locative). I consider and treat such pairings as indicating correlative emphasis (see §15.6 Correlative Emphasis: Lists and Coordinated Connectives); in these instances with ὅταν … τότε (temporal) and ὅπου … ἐκεῖ (locative), the pairings more intimately connect the subordinate clause events with the main clause events.

[23] Additive καὶ, redundant pronoun subject ὑμεῖς, and this latter's abutment with σὺν αὐτῷ.

[24] Of fifty-eight occurrences of ὅς ἐάν or ὅς ἄν (with our without intervening conjunction), in all but three instances after a cleft construction (Matt 11:6//Luke 7:23; Acts 2:21) are these clause initial.

Runge provides Matt 18:6 as the first example of a left dislocation in his treatment (293). Significant discontinuity exits, since in 18:5 Jesus has just compared welcoming the little one in his name with welcoming himself.

Matt 18:6 Ὃς δ' ἂν σκανδαλίσῃ ἕνα τῶν μικρῶν τούτων τῶν πιστευόντων εἰς ἐμέ, συμφέρει αὐτῷ ἵνα κρεμασθῇ μύλος ὀνικὸς περὶ τὸν τράχηλον αὐτοῦ καὶ καταποντισθῇ ἐν τῷ πελάγει τῆς θαλάσσης.

But **whoever** *trips up one of these small ones believing in me, it is better* *for him* *that a heavy millstone be hung around his neck and that he be drowned in the depth of the sea.*

E. **Prominence Factors Related to Information Processing:** It is important to understand that *left (dis)location constructions are always prominent* (Runge 291). Several factors contribute to prominence on the basis of information flow, context, and cognitive processing.

- Sentence Initial Position
- Immediate Contrastive Context (discontinuity)
- The Complexity of Description (when present)
- Redundancy of the Trace referring back to the Left (Dis)location
- Broader Discursive Coherence of Theme (continuity)

The following chart may help conceptualize the relative and scalar prominence effect of these factors in relation to the six constructions described above.

Scale of Prominence	LD CONSTRUCTION	RESUMPTIVE TRACE
	singular proleptic word	implied verbal subject or object
	simple suspended nominative	nominative demonstrative pronoun
	relative pronoun clause	pronominal trace; agreement optional
	adverbial clause	adverbial trace
	conditional relative clause	pronominal trace; agreement optional
Most	jarring *anacoluthon*	pronoun of different case

In evaluating these types of constructions, other contextual factors must be considered, such as the presence of intensive particles, contrastive conjunctions (like ἀλλά), and other emphatic features.

CHECK POINT 21.3

Given these sentences from John 15:4-6, in the space given in the right:

1. Identify any left (dis)location constructions by underlining them and their traces.
2. Identify the classification of the left (dis)location (see C. above). Be sure to identify whether the construction is an LDT or an LDF.
3. Briefly describe the semantic and pragmatic functions of the LDFs and LDTs (see B. above).
4. Consider the level of prominence based upon the type of LD construction, the factors present, and other contextual reasons.

John 15:4a μείνατε ἐν ἐμοί, κἀγὼ ἐν ὑμῖν. *Remain in me, and I [will remain] in you.*	
John 15:4b καθὼς τὸ κλῆμα οὐ δύναται καρπὸν φέρειν ἀφ᾽ ἑαυτοῦ ἐὰν μὴ μένῃ ἐν τῇ ἀμπέλῳ, οὕτως οὐδὲ ὑμεῖς ἐὰν μὴ ἐν ἐμοὶ μένητε. *Just as the branch is not able to bear fruit by itself, if it does not remain in the vine, thus neither you [are able to] if you do not remain in me.*	
John 15:5a ἐγώ εἰμι ἡ ἄμπελος, ὑμεῖς τὰ κλήματα. *I am the vine, you [are] the branches.*	
John 15:5b ὁ μένων ἐν ἐμοὶ κἀγὼ ἐν αὐτῷ οὗτος φέρει καρπὸν πολύν, ὅτι χωρὶς ἐμοῦ οὐ δύνασθε ποιεῖν οὐδέν. *The one remaining in me and I in him, this one bears much fruit, because without me you are not able to do anything.*	
John 15:6 ἐὰν μή τις μένῃ ἐν ἐμοί, ἐβλήθη ἔξω ὡς τὸ κλῆμα καὶ ἐξηράνθη καὶ συνάγουσιν αὐτὰ καὶ εἰς τὸ πῦρ βάλλουσιν καὶ καίεται. *If someone does not remain in me, he was cast outside like the branch and dried up and they gather them and cast into the fire and he is burned.*	

SUGGESTED ANSWERS

There are only two left (dis)location constructions in John 15:4-6; they are discussed in turn.

1. **John 15:4b** <u>καθὼς</u> τὸ κλῆμα οὐ δύναται καρπὸν φέρειν ἀφ᾽ ἑαυτοῦ ἐὰν μὴ μένῃ ἐν τῇ ἀμπέλῳ, <u>οὕτως</u> οὐδὲ ὑμεῖς ἐὰν μὴ ἐν ἐμοὶ μένητε.
   Just as the branch is not able to bear fruit by itself, if it does not remain in the vine, thus neither you [are able to] if you do not remain in me.

2. This is an LDF: Adverbial Clause with Adverbial Trace.

3. The semantic and pragmatic functions are as follows. The conjunction καθώς *just as* intro-duces a complex comparison, which also entails a conditional idea (the *if* clause) that is resumed by the adverbial trace οὕτως *thus*. The LDF construction in 15:4b about the branch <u>not</u> remaining connected to the vine is discontinuous with remaining in Christ in 15:4a; yet, there is continuity with the larger discourse to remain attached to Christ. Additionally, one may detect some movement of particularity by discussing a single branch that stands in particular relation to the whole main vine.

4. This particular construction is located in the middle of the scale; however, there are additional modifications, includding two conditional "if" clauses that keep repeat the critical theme of remaining. Also, the use of οὐδὲ *neither* further drives home the comparison of "a branch need a vine", so also "you need Jesus" to bear fruit.

1. **John 15:5b** ὁ μένων ἐν ἐμοὶ κἀγὼ ἐν αὐτῷ <u>οὗτος</u> φέρει καρπὸν πολύν, ὅτι χωρὶς ἐμοῦ οὐ δύνασθε ποιεῖν οὐδέν.
   The one remaining in me and I in him, this one bears much fruit, because without me you are not able to do anything.

2. This is an LDT: Suspended phrase with grammatical agreement with the trace.

3. The semantic and pragmatic functions are as follows. The LDT is discontinuous with the previous LDF in 15:4b (that denies branch's ability to bear fruti apart from attachment ot the vine) by describing how one can bear fruit. In this way, it continues the theme of remaining in Christ (+discourse continuity). It also describes a singular person inn 3rd singular (+particularity) in distinction to the previous clause in 15:5a that has 2nd plural referents.

4. This simple suspended nominative with demonstrative trace is not as prominent as other types of LD constructions; however, there is some additional complexity by adding *and I* [*remaining*] *in him*. Also, the verb *remain* is an important and repeated discourse theme. So, these additional factors would increase the LDTs prominence.

21.4 Discourse Pragmatic Use of the Article or its Absence

A. **Introduction:** This material presumes that you have read §4.5 The Article (Τὸ ἄρθρον) and Lack of an Article (Ἄναρθρος). So, reread this now if needed. The discussion below will treat Proper Names of Participants, Proper Names of Places, and General Nouns before providing some Examples and concluding with a comment about textual variants involving the article.

B. **Proper Names of Participants:** A complicating factor to a more traditional understanding of the Greek article has been to recognize that the presence or absence of articles functions pragmatically to signal discourse activation, status, and emphasis of Participants. *Activation* concerns whether a participant (person) has been brought on stage in a scene (i.e. within a limited range of verses) or the entire discourse. *Status* concerns whether participants remain on the stage in the scene or discourse or move off when another takes the stage. *Emphasis* concerns prominence afforded to participants that are already activated. The basic discourse principles explained below summarize the discussion of Levinsohn (ch.9) and Jenny Read-Heimerdinger.[25]

1. <u>Initial Introduction/Activation of Participant is through Anarthrous Identification.</u> A participant or unique entity is typically introduced or "activated" into a scene within a narrative without the article (anarthrous). Importantly, direct speech represents a new scene, so participants will generally need to be activated within them (i.e. be anarthrous) from the perspective of the audience of the speech.

2. <u>Continued Activation through Arthrous Identification.</u> In that scene, as long as that participant or unique entity remains activated, he/she will normally be articular.

3. <u>Global VIP Status is Assumed through Continuous Arthrous Identification.</u> Some participants may be granted "global VIP" (Very Important Participant) status in the narrative—i.e., they are assumed known or important throughout, like God—and need no activation in the discourse or reactivation; so, such participants will normally be found with the article.

4. <u>Local VIP Status is Maintained through Arthrous Identification.</u> Even if a participant disappears for a time from the narrative, once returning, the participant enters articular. One's observation of this phenomenon helps identify a participant with Local VIP status. For ex-

---

[25] Read-Heimerdinger gave a presentation entitled "The Discourse Use of Articles with Personal Names in Acts" at the Discourse Studies Workshop sponsored Logos Bible Software and co-organized by her and Steven Runge before the annual meeting of the Society of Biblical Literature Nov 22, 2013 in Baltimore. Her presentation was a summary of her more detailed study in her book, *The Bezan Text of Acts: A Contribution of Discourse Analysis to Textual Criticism*, JSNTSS 236 (London: Sheffield Academic, 2002), 116-44.

ample, in Acts 13-28 Paul goes on and off stage throughout, yet is frequently arthrous on his return. This is because (apparently) he is being viewed as a Local VIP for this portion of Acts, although he is not a global VIP in the same sense as God is.[26]

5. <u>Unless the participant is a Global or Local VIP, his/her Removal from a Scene Requires Re-Activation later via Anarthrous Identification</u>. (= principle #1) A participant can be deactivated by removal from the scene by being "upstaged" by another participant being activated. Then, re-activation of a previously activated participant without global or local VIP status is through anarthrous identification.

6. <u>Emphasis is given to an activated participant through Anarthrous Identification</u>. Participants that have been activated through anarthrous referent may continue to be highlighted or emphasized as a "local VIP" through anarthrous reference (see Levinsohn 156-58). The type of emphasis must be determined from context: it may include contrast with another participant or highlighting some important action or speech of the participant.

7. <u>Exceptions to these principles include the following</u>:
   a. "Set phrases" may be anarthrous, such as "in the name of Jesus (Christ)" (ἐν τῷ ὀνόματι Ἰησοῦ Χριστοῦ), where we might otherwise expect to find Jesus articular in Acts, since he is the global VIP.
   b. Indeclinable names may be (unexpectedly) articular, since the article may be provided to indicate the noun's case (Wallace 240). So, in Matt 1:18 the first occurrence of Joseph is articular (τῷ Ἰωσήφ); in Acts 7:8 at the first mention of Isaac, we find τὸν Ἰσαάκ (examples from Levinsohn 151). In this latter case, the accusative article indicates that Isaac is not the subject, but the direct object of the verb. Alternatively, one may account for these articles on the basis of the knowledge of the audience in Matthew (Joseph is a known person or knowable from the genealogical context) and the Jewish audience who was listening to Stephen's speech in Acts 7.[27]

C. **Cities and Regions:** Jenny Read-Heimerdinger maintains, "names of cities … are usually (but not always) anarthrous at first mention whereas names of regions/provinces/countries are arthrous."[28] For example, the region of Samaria is always articular (John 4:4, 5, 7; Acts 1:8; 8:1, 5, 9, 14; 9:31; 15:3), except one instance in Luke 17:11 (διὰ μέσον Σαμαρείας καὶ Γαλιλαίας).

D. **General Nouns:** The introduction of a place, space, or situation will also assume the items/persons commonly understood as present therein; therefore, when explicitly mentioned, such items/persons will be articular, even though it is their first mention. For example, an entity (like *a home*) may imply the existence of other entities, like *the atrium* in the home or *the*

---

[26] This example was provided by Read-Heimerdinger while reading through and critiquing this material.

[27] Read-Heimerdinger has indicated this latter explanation to me.

[28] In an email correspondence.

master of the home, etc. So, once a *home* is introduced in the discourse, then afterwards the first reference will be made to *the* atrium (articular) or *the* master (articular), since these are assumed as known in the previous reference to the home.

E. **Examples:**

1. In general, Levinsohn reveals interesting observations in the Gospels and Acts (151-55).
    o In Matthew and Mark, once Jesus has been activated by anarthrous reference in Mark 1:9 and Matt 1:16 (shown above), he then shows a global VIP status and is never again reactivated, *EXCEPT* after his resurrection (Matt 28:9 is anarthrous, but thereafter arthrous in 28:10, 16, 18).
    o In Luke 1-3 Jesus is always anarthrous, but after activation at the start of his ministry in 4:1 (anarthrous), Jesus achieves global VIP status (arthrous in 4:4, 8, 12, 14, etc.) until his resurrection, after which he is reactivated by being anarthrous (24:15).
    o In Matthew 14, Herod the tetrarch is activated by anarthrous reference in 14:1, and thereafter remains on stage with articular reference (14:3, 6a, 6b).
    o In Mark 15, Pilate is activated by anarthrous reference in 15:1, and thereafter remains on stage with articular reference (15:2, 4, 5, 9, 12, 14, 15, etc.).
    o In Luke 9, Peter is reactivated with anarthrous reference (9:28) and thereafter remains on stage with articular reference (9:32, 33; and 12:41 and 18:28).

2. In Acts 9:2 Saul asks for *letters* (anarthrous) from the high priest *for Damascus* (εἰς Δαμασκὸν, anarthrous) to be carried along *to the synagogues* (πρὸς τὰς συναγωγάς, arthrous); then in 9:3 Paul traveled and approached near to *the Damascus* (τῇ Δαμασκῷ). The explanation according to the principles above is as follows: *Letters* are anarthrous because they are not specific letters previously mentioned; they are simply letters. Since *Damascus* is a city, so its first reference is anarthrous (more common), but the second is arthrous, probably anaphoric. *The synagogues* are arthrous because they have a distinct referential identity, being known to exist in the setting of the city of Damascus, which has already been introduced.

3. In 1 Tim 2:15, Paul's articular reference to "the childbearing" (τῆς τεκνογονίας) has presented interpreters with problems. With the article, Paul was indicating specificity of an entity that is known or knowable in the discourse context; but what? Although some have suggested *this childbearing* refers to Christ's incarnational birth through Mary, it is simpler to understand that Paul has been discussing a husband in relation to a wife in 2:11-15, and so *the childbearing* referred to would naturally occur from the marriage relationship.[29]

F. **Textual Critical Matters Regarding the Article:** Read-Heimerdinger has rightly urged me to let students know the following:

---

[29] See my article, "A Wife in Relation to a Husband: Greek Discourse Pragmatic and Cultural Evidence for Interpreting 1 Tim 2:11-15," *The Journal of Inductive Biblical Studies* 2.2 (2015): 6–43 available online at http://place.asburyseminary.edu/jibs/vol2/iss2/3/.

Some mention is needed of the large amount of variant readings regarding the presence of the article in the Gospels and Acts – esp. with proper names. The editors of the NA edition … made their choice of [best] readings without the knowledge of the 'principles' you present here, but instead adopted the reading that was most in line with the author's 'style' – which your principles show is not relevant or applicable in the case of the article.[29]

Also, Levinsohn (ch. 9) shows awareness of variant readings as are sometimes and sometimes not given in the critical editions of the GNT when discussing the use or absence of the article.

CHECK POINT 21.4 ARTICLE USAGE

Below articles (*the*) or lack of articles (Ø) are indicated by being placed within parentheses. First, identify the type of noun: Proper Name or General Noun. Second, explain the absence and presence of the article referring to any principle from above.

A. 1 Cor 10:4b [4] ἔπινον γὰρ ἐκ πνευματικῆς ἀκολουθούσης <u>πέτρας</u>, ἡ <u>πέτρα</u> δὲ ἦν ὁ <u>Χριστός</u>. [4] For they were drinking from (Ø) spiritual <u>rock</u> that was following, and (*the*) <u>rock</u> was (*the*) <u>Christ</u>

1. (Ø) *spiritual rock*
2. (*the*) *rock*
3. (*the*) *Christ*

B. John 1:43-48 Note that Galilee, Philip, Bethsaida, Nathanael, Bethsaida, Nazareth, Israelite, the Prophets (pl.), and Joseph are here first introduced. The other nouns have already occurred at least once in the narrative.

[43] On the next day, he goes out into (*the*) <u>Galilee</u> and finds (Ø) <u>Philip</u>. And (*the*) <u>Jesus</u> says to him, "Follow me!"

[44] Now (*the*) <u>Philip</u> was from (Ø) <u>Bethsaida</u>, from (*the*) city of (Ø) <u>Andrew</u> and (Ø) <u>Peter</u>.

[45] (Ø) <u>Philip</u> finds (*the*) <u>Nathanael</u> and says to him, "The one, whom (Ø) <u>Moses</u> wrote about in (*the*) <u>Law</u> and (*the*) <u>Prophets</u> [wrote about], we have found, (Ø) <u>Jesus</u>, (Ø) son of (*the*) <u>Joseph</u>, (*the*) one from (Ø) <u>Nazareth</u>.

[46] And (Ø) <u>Nathanael</u> said to him, "From (Ø) <u>Nazareth</u> is anything good able to come?!" [(*The*)] <u>Philip</u> says to him, "Come and see!"

[47] (*The*) <u>Jesus</u> saw (*the*) <u>Nathanael</u> coming to Him, and said of him, "Behold, (Ø) <u>Israelite</u> indeed, in whom there is no deceit!"

[48] (Ø) <u>Nathanael</u> said to Him, "How do You know me?" (Ø) <u>Jesus</u> answered back and said to him, "Before (Ø) <u>Philip</u> called you, when you were under the fig tree, I saw you."

---

[29] Read-Heimerdinger offered this while reading through and critiquing this material (slightly edited for clarity).

1:43

   1. (*the*) Galilee

   2. (Ø) Philip

   3. (*the*) Jesus

1:44

   4. (*the*) Philip

   5. (Ø) Bethsaida

   6. (*the*) city

   7. (Ø) Andrew and (Ø) Peter

1:45

   8. (Ø) Philip

   9. (*the*) Nathanael

   10. (Ø) Moses

   11. (*the*) Law

   12. (*the*) Prophets

   13. (Ø) Jesus

   14. (Ø) son

   15. (*the*) Joseph

   16. (*the*) one

   17. (Ø) Nazareth

1:46

   18. (Ø) Nathanael

   19. (Ø) Nazareth

   20. [(*The*)] Philip

1:47

   21. (*The*) Jesus

   22. (*the*) Nathanael

   23. (Ø) Israelite

1:48

   24. (Ø) Nathanael

   25. (Ø) Jesus

   26. (Ø) Philip

SUGGESTED ANSWERS

A. 1 Cor 10:4b

1. (Ø) *spiritual rock* = **A general noun is introduced.** An indefinite translation ("a") is justified.

2. (*the*) *rock* = **The general noun is repeated.** Once the rock has been introduced, the article marks an anaphoric referent; i.e. it identifies a previous referent (a rock) and identifies it (*the* rock).

3. (*the*) *Christ* = **Proper noun.** Christ has been present through 1 Corinthians (see 1:1-3); he is already on stage in the discourse and is well known. It is also significant that in 1 Corinthians Χριστός rarely has the article; the exception is when Χριστός functions as a modifier of articular nouns, as is similar here. Given this predicate nominative construction (see §5.3), the article functions to co-identify *the Christ* with *the Rock*, as Paul interpreted this OT event.

B. John 1:43-48

1:43

1. (*the*) Galilee = **Proper noun.** Regions are generally introduced as arthrous.
2. (Ø) Philip = **Proper noun.** Introduced for the first time (**PRINCIPLE 1**)
3. (*the*) Jesus = **Proper noun.** The article signifies that Jesus is already on stage (**PRINCIPLE 2**). Moreover, Jesus may have global VIP status (**PRINCIPLE 3**).

1:44

4. (*the*) Philip = **Proper noun.** The article signifies that Philip is already on stage (**PRINCIPLE 2**).
5. (Ø) Bethsaida = **Proper noun.** Cities are generally introduced as anarthrous.
6. (*the*) city = **General noun** that now has a specific referent (anaphoric use).
7. (Ø) Andrew and (Ø) Peter = **Proper nouns.** Since these participants have already been introduced, their anarthrous status highlights their relation to the city of Bethsaida (**PRINCIPLE 6**). Alternatively, this may be an Exception to the Rules involving "a set phrase" (**PRINCIPLE 7**).

1:45

8. (Ø) Philip = **Proper noun.** The lack of article highlights Philip's purposeful action of finding Nathanael (**PRINCIPLE 6**).
9. (*the*) Nathanael = **Proper noun.** Introduced for the first time (**PRINCIPLE 1**).
10. (Ø) Moses = **Proper noun.** Already introduced and well-known; the lack of article may highlight Moses performing the important role of writing about Jesus (**PRINCIPLE 6**).
11. (*the*) Law = **General noun** with a specifically known referent.
12. (*the*) Prophets = **General noun** with a specifically known referent.
13. (Ø) Jesus = **Proper noun.** Within this speech act, the lack of article indicates that Jesus is being introduced to Nathanael (**PRINCIPLE 1**).

14. (Ø) son = **General noun.** The lack of article may continue the introduction of Jesus as a son within the speech act to Nathanael (**PRINCIPLE 1**). Additionally, the indefiniteness may indicate that Jesus is only one son among other sons of Joseph.

15. (*the*) Joseph = **Proper noun.** Assumed as already known in the speech act; in other words, Philip and Nathanael already know this Joseph.

16. (*the*) *one* = **No noun,** simply the article, which specifies the identity of Jesus.

17. (Ø) Nazareth = **Proper noun.** Cities are generally introduced as anarthrous.

1:46

18. (Ø) Nathanael = **Proper Noun.** The lack of article highlights Nathanael's purposeful action of speaking (**PRINCIPLE 6**).

19. (Ø) Nazareth = **Proper noun.** Cities are generally introduced as anarthrous.

20. [(*The*)] Philip = **Proper noun.** There is a textual variant here regarding the article. At issue it would seem is how important is Philip's speech. Since he is already on stage, the article's presence would simply indicate as much (**PRINCIPLE 2**). If there is no article here, then the lack of article would highlight Philip's purposeful action of directing Nathanael to go and see Jesus (**PRINCIPLE 6**).

1:47

21. (*The*) Jesus = **Proper noun.** The article signifies that Jesus is already on stage (**PRINCIPLE 2**). Moreover, Jesus may have global VIP status (**PRINCIPLE 3**).

22. (*the*) Nathanael = **Proper noun.** The article signifies that Nathanael is already on stage (**PRINCIPLE 2**).

23. (Ø) Israelite= **Proper noun.** Within this speech discourse (Jesus speaking to Nathanael), this is the first instance of *Israelite*, so it is introduced (**PRINCIPLE 1**). Alternatively, the indefiniteness of this noun may stress its essence or quality, which may be indicated by the adverb ἀληθῶς *truly*. An indefinite translation ("an") is justified.

1:48

24. (Ø) Nathanael = **Proper Noun.** The lack of article highlights Nathanael's purposeful action of speaking (**PRINCIPLE 6**).

25. (Ø) Jesus = **Proper Noun.** The lack of article highlights Jesus' purposeful action of speaking (**PRINCIPLE 6**).

26. (Ø) Philip = **Proper Noun.** Within the reported speech, the lack of article introduces or activates Philip as participant (**PRINCIPLE 1**). This is true even though in John's Gospel, Philip (Ø) has already been introduced in 1:43. But to Nathanael, whom Jesus addresses here, this has not been the case. Alternatively, the lack of article may highlight Philip's important action of calling Nathanael (**PRINCIPLE 6**).

Complete WORKBOOK EXERCISES 21 and consult the ANSWER KEY & GUIDE as needed.

CASE IN POINT 21: THE *SAMARITAN* WOMAN IN JOHN 4:9

John 4:9a λέγει οὖν αὐτῷ <u>ἡ γυνὴ ἡ Σαμαρῖτις</u>·
   4:9b πῶς σὺ <u>Ἰουδαῖος</u> ὢν παρ' ἐμοῦ πεῖν αἰτεῖς γυναικὸς <u>Σαμαρίτιδος</u> οὔσης;
   4:9c οὐ γὰρ συγχρῶνται <u>Ἰουδαῖοι Σαμαρίταις</u>.

John 4:9a *Therefore the Samaritan woman said to Him,*
   4:9b *"How is it that You, being a Jew, ask me for a drink since I am a Samaritan woman?"*
   4:9c *(For Jews have no dealings with Samaritans.)* (NASB95)
OR, **4:9c** *For Jews have no dealings with Samaritans."*

A closer look at the Greek text reveals a special emphasis on the woman at the well. The woman (ἡ γυνὴ) has an article, and this article is anaphoric, referring back to *a woman from Samaria* (γυνὴ ἐκ τῆς Σαμαρείας) who came to get water in 4:7. But in 4:9 this *woman* is (again) described as *the Samaritan* using the 2nd attributive construction (ἡ γυνὴ ἡ Σαμαρῖτις). This particular attributive construction is the most emphatic attributive construction (see §7.3.C.2), since it repeats the article, drawing more attention to the adjective modifier *Samaritan*. Why? As the conversation continues, we understand exactly why: The Samaritan woman herself raises the issue of ethnicity, pointing out Jesus' *Jewishness* in contrast to her *Samaritan-ness* (notice the repetition of words denoting ethnicity). The 2nd attributive position stresses the woman's ethnicity as a Samaritan.

   Now, 4:9c is commonly understood and translated as the narrator's comment; this sentence is missing in a couple of important manuscripts (ℵ* D), although it is present in our earliest ones. So, the NASB95 (and every translation I consulted) places 4:9c inside parentheses. However, it is possible that the statement is the Samaritan woman's own statement supporting the basis of her question: "You, a Jew, shouldn't be asking me, a Samaritan, to get something to drink. *For Judeans/Jews don't associate with Samaritans.*" In either case, this explanation contains a gnomic use of the present tense verb, which relates a general truth/reality. This becomes an important piece of evidence as we continue interpreting 4:9c.

   Notable in 4:9c is the lack of article for both *Jews* and *Samaritans*. What might this suggest? Let's list important considerations. First, these nouns have unique referential identity. Second, the lack of article may occur with nouns with unique referential identity under two conditions: When they are introduced into the narrative or brought on stage) or are emphasized for some reason (like performing some significant action or speech). Third, the lack of article may indicate indefiniteness (*a Samaritan*), but this does not apply with plural nouns. Fourth, the lack of article may stress the quality or essence signified by the noun; here, those who are *in essence* Samaritans or Judeans). Of these options in 4:9, the best for Ἰουδαῖοι and Σαμαρίταις are qualitative meaning, stressing the *ethnicity* of those involved. Which option is best?

At this point a feature of John's Greek style provides important evidence. In John's Gospel the word Ἰουδαῖος occurs 71 times, and it is with an article 67 times. One time it has no article with a clearly indefinite sense when it is the object of the preposition (3:25) and once it is a predicate adjective where its quality is emphasized (18:35). The other two occurrences where it has no article are in 4:9, our verse. From this evidence in addition to the context, we should understand these two substantives Ἰουδαῖοι and Σαμαρίταις as qualitative in meaning. The final force of the close of 4:9 is then this: *A person having an intrinsic alignment with Judaism does not have anything to do with anyone being Samaritan.*

The Samaritan woman was indeed shocked that Jesus, a Jew, was engaging her in any kind of conversation. What was her response to such interaction? Joyful witness about Him (4:28-30, 39-42). Jesus, as one ushering in the Kingdom of God, in his social interactions exemplifies the obliteration of national or ethnic barriers that are often erected within human communities. As Paul has said in Gal 3:28, "There is neither Jew nor Greek, there is neither slave nor free man, there is neither male nor female; for all of you are one in Christ Jesus." As Jesus' disciples, we are called to love, value, relate to, and do good to others likewise (Gal 6:9-10).

Collecting water was normally a social event. Below is a vase painting (6th century BC) of women collecting water for a nuptial bath at the well in Athens called Callirrhoe (Καλλιρρόη *beautiful flow*), named after one of the mythological daughters of Oceanus.[30] This bath was customary. Later the fountain was called the "Nine Springs" (Ἐννεάκρουνος), when the Greek King Peisistratus diverted its flow into nine streams (560s BC). The bride Σιμυλίς (her name is written top down) bows before the fountain ΚΑΛΙΡΕ ΚΡΕΝΕ (abbrev. of Καλλιρρόη κρηνη, *well*). The five other maidens are named. At top is a statement for the bridegroom: Ἱπποκράτες κάλος.

---

[30] Victor Duruy, *History of Greece, and of the Greek People: From the Earliest Times to the Roman Conquest*, trans. M. M. Ripley, Vol. 1, Sect. 2 (Boston: Estes and Lauriat, 1890), 557.

CHAPTER 22

What might the use of the Subjunctive Mood in John 20:31 tell us about the purpose of John's Gospel? After learning about the Subjunctive mood in this chapter, students will be able to consider this question as is presented in CASE IN POINT 22: SUBJUNCTIVE TENSES IN JOHN 20:31. In addition to the forms and uses of **Subjunctive Mood**, this chapter discusses **adverb formation and function**. At this point, students will learn one special use of "negative" adverbs and adjectives: **Negative Emphasis**. But first, in the Vocabulary are given more adjectives, adverbs, and some important words for the Subjunctive Mood.

VOCABULARY 22   ADJECTIVES, CONJUNCTIONS, AND ADVERBS

First and Second Declension Adjectives:

ἁμαρτωλός, -όν* [47]	sinful; sinner (*noun*)	
ἄξιος, -α, -ον [41]	worthy	
δεύτερος, -α, -ον [43]	second	
ἔρημος, -ον* [48]	desolate; desert (*noun*)	
ὅμοιος, -α, -ον [45]	like, liken to (+ *dat.*)	
καινός, -ή, -όν [42]	new	
μικρός, -ά, -όν [46]	small, little	
ὀλίγος, -η, -ον [40]	little; few	
τρίτος, -η, -ον [56]	third	

Third Declension Adjectives:

ἀληθής, -ές* [26]	true, truthful
ἀσθενής, -ές* [26]	weak; sick

Conjunctions for the Subjunctive Mood:

ἄχρι(ς) [49]	as far as (+ *gen.*); until (*conj.*)
ἐάν [330]	if, (when)ever
ἵνα [663]	in order that; that
ὅπως [53]	in order that; how

Negative words for Non-Indicatives:

μηδείς, μηδεμία, μηδέν [91]	no; no one; nothing
μηδέ [56]	and not; not even; neither...nor
μήποτε [25]	never; lest ever; whether perhaps

Adverbs:

ἔξω [62]	outside
εὐθύς, εὐθεώς [59]	immediately, at once; directly
ὧδε [61]	here; thus

After learning vocabulary to this point, you will know 79.6% of the words in the GNT. If you are able, listen to audio recordings of VOCABULARY 22 and complete the CROSSWORD PUZZLE in the WORKBOOK EXERCISES.

NOTES ON VOCABULARY 22:

Several adjectives above are marked with an asterisk (*). Notice that they have only two endings: The first is both masculine and feminine and the second neuter. These are called *dual termination* adjectives. Dual termination adjectives occur often when the adjective form is made from two or more word components.[1] Consider the following as examples:

- ἁμαρτωλός,-όν *sinful* is possibly created with the prefix ἀ- which is called an ἄλφα *privative* (i.e. a negating ἄλφα), found as either ἀ- or ἀν- (before a vowel) and root μέρος *share* ("ἁμαρτάνω" Thayer, 30).[2] Ἁμαρτωλός,-όν *sinful* is often used as a substantive adjective to mean *sinner*.

- ἀληθής,-ές, *true*, too, is formed with ἄλφα *privative* (ἀ-) and the Greek root λαθ* basically meaning *unknown, hidden*; so also is the noun ἀλήθεια *truth* in Chapter 4. Both words have as a cognate word, the verb λανθάνω *I escape notice, am unknown* which has the 2nd Aorist stem λαθ- that reveals its Greek root.

- Likewise, ἀσθενής,-ές *weak* is formed with an ἄλφα *privative* added onto a stem σθέν- that means *strength, might* (cf. τὸ σθένος *strength*; σθένω *I have strength*).

Δεύτερος,-α,-ον *second* can sometimes be found in a neuter singular form δεύτερον or as a prepositional phrase ἐκ δευτέρου to carry the adverbial meaning *a second time*.

The adjective ἔρημος,-ον is commonly used as a feminine noun, ἡ ἔρημος *desert* with "masculine looking" endings, and so may be considered dual termination.[3] Remember that Greek often treats geographical locations as feminine. This adjective is used frequently with the prepositions εἰς and ἐν to mean *into/in the desert*.

Ὅμοιος,-α,-ον introduces a comparison of some type. It will agree with the noun it is modifying. However, the noun to which the comparison is made *will be put into the dative case*. This is called a **dative of comparison.**

Καινός,-ή,-όν *new* may be used in contrast to παλαιός,-ά,-όν *old*.

Μικρός,-ά,-όν *small* is sometimes found in the neuter singular form, μικρόν, with an adverbial meaning of *in a little bit* or *for a little while longer*.

Ἄξιος,-η,-ον and τρίτος,-η,-ον can both be used as adverbs and will thus be found in the neuter singular forms and in prepositional phrases. Of course, these and all adjectives can be used as substantives (nouns).

Ἄχρι(ς) is "A function word used to indicate an interval between two points" (BDAG, 160). It may also be considered an improper preposition, because it can function as a conjunction

---

[1] But this is not always demonstrable, as is the case with ἔρημος, -ον *desolate*, which, however, in Homeric and Attic Greek had a commonly used feminine form ἐρήμη (LSJ).

[2] More likely to me, ἁμαρτωλός would derive from ἄλφα privative the adjective ἄρτιος *complete, perfect for function* with the –ολος ending denoting chief characteristic.

[3] However, ἔρημος is not a compounded word and historically showed feminine endings in Homeric and Attic Greek (LSJ).

often working with a relative pronoun (e.g. ἄχρι οὗ... or ἄχρι ἧς...) meaning, "until..." taking the subjunctive mood (e.g., Luke 21:20; 21:24).

Ἐάν will take the subjunctive mood and begins a conditional, subordinate clause. CHAPTER 26 treats the wide variety of conditional sentences.

Ἵνα is a very common subordinating conjunction, found 663 times in the GNT. It will begin its clause, so, when you are performing Constituent Marking, be sure to bracket this subordinating conjunction [ἵνα...]. Ἵνα functions "to alert the reader to expect a thought, desire or intention of the speaker."[4] Under this semantic constraint, ἵνα carries several uses based upon contextual indicators. The verb within the ἵνα clause is normally in the Subjunctive Mood; but occasionally the Future Indicative is found. Ἵνα can often be translated *(in order) that*. As simply *that*, ἵνα functions as content clause of prayers, requests, commands or as a noun clause. In usage, ἵνα is somewhat analogous to ὅτι *that* (see §8.5.B.4), but ἵνα can express the logical content of (intentional) **purpose**, and is then translated as *in order that*. Ὅπως is less frequent than ἵνα, but often indicates purpose.

Μηδείς *no one* and μηδέ *and not, neither* are negative words that are used with all non-Indicative Moods. Μηδείς is classified among the Negative Pronouns (ἀντωνυμίαι ἀρνητικαί) with οὐδείς, οὐδεμία, οὐδέν from CH.12. Μηδέ may be used by itself or in correlative emphasis as μηδέ ... μηδέ to mean *neither ... nor*. Finally, μήποτε *never; lest ever; whether perhaps* is an adverb/conjunction indicating negative purpose or expressing uncertainty in direct or indirect questions. Context must determine how to translate this versatile conjunction/adverb.

The adverb ἔξω *outside* is a cognate of the preposition ἐκ *from, out of*. The adverbs εὐθύς and εὐθέως *immediately* are found primarily in the Gospels and Acts, often as a transitional word, not necessarily indicating immediate temporal sequence, but narrative sequence. Ὧδε is a locative adverb indicating the location *here*.

Finally, VOCABULARY 22 contains two Third Declension adjectives. Their stem ends in a vowel and a contraction results (→) when endings are added. Here are their endings:

		MASCULINE/FEMININE		NEUTER	
sg.	N	ἀληθής		ἀληθές	
	G	ἀληθέ + ος	→ ἀληθοῦς	ἀληθοῦς	
	D	ἀληθέ + ι	→ ἀληθεῖ	ἀληθεῖ	
	A	ἀληθέ + α	→ ἀληθῆ	ἀληθές	
pl.	N	ἀληθέ + ες	→ ἀληθεῖς	ἀληθέ + α → ἀληθῆ	
	G	ἀληθέ + ων	→ ἀληθῶν	ἀληθῶν	
	D	ἀληθέ + σι(ν)	→ ἀληθέσι(ν)	ἀληθέσι(ν)	
	A	ἀληθέ + ες	→ ἀληθεῖς	ἀληθέ + α → ἀληθῆ	

---

[4] Margaret G. Sim, *Marking Thought and Talk in New Testament Greek: New Light from Linguistics on the Particles* Ἵνα *and* Ὅτι (Eugene, OR: Pickwick, 2010), 4.

22.1 THE SUBJUNCTIVE MOOD (ἡ ὑποτακτικὴ ἔγκλισις): FORMATION

The basic purpose and uses of Subjunctive Mood are described under §22.2-4 below. The abbreviation for subjunctive mood verbs when parsing them is "S." So, first, let's learn the endings.

A. **No Augmentation:** As with all moods outside the Indicative Mood, the Aorist Tense has no augmentation in the Subjunctive Mood.

B. **Endings:** The Subjunctive endings are formed using the *primary endings* with a *lengthened coupling vowel*, either an ἦτα (η) or an ὦ μέγα (ω).

<table>
<tr><td colspan="3" align="center">**ACTIVE**
SUBJUNCTIVE</td><td colspan="3" align="center">**MIDDLE/PASSIVE**
SUBJUNCTIVE</td></tr>
<tr><td></td><td>sg.</td><td>pl.</td><td></td><td>sg.</td><td>pl.</td></tr>
<tr><td>1</td><td>-ω</td><td>-ωμεν</td><td>1</td><td>-ωμαι</td><td>-ωμεθα</td></tr>
<tr><td>2</td><td>-ης</td><td>-ητε</td><td>2</td><td>-η*</td><td>-ησθε</td></tr>
<tr><td>3</td><td>-η*</td><td>-ωσι(ν)</td><td>3</td><td>-ηται</td><td>-ωνται</td></tr>
</table>

Notice that the ὂ μικρόν (o-) coupling vowels lengthen to ὦ μέγα (ω-) and the ἒ ψιλόν (ε- or ει-) coupling vowels lengthen to ἦτα (η- or η-). Also **notice** that the 3rd singular active form -η looks like the 2nd singular middle/passive form -η*. Context must determine the parsing and translation.

C. **Tenses and Tense Indicator:** Only two tenses use these subjunctive endings: **Present** and **Aorist**. *Both tenses use the exact same endings*, but are differentiated by tense indicators placed on the front of the endings. Below, the Active endings are separated from the Middle and Middle/Passive endings.

TENSE/VOICE	TENSE IN-DICATOR	EXAMPLES WITH πιστεύω
PRESENT A	→ none	πιστεύ-ω, -ης, -η, -ωμεν, -ητε, -ωσι(ν)
AORIST A	→ -σ-	πιστεύ-σω, -σης, -ση, -σωμεν, -σητε, -σωσι(ν)
AORIST P	→ -θ-	πιστευ-θῶ, -θῇς, -θῇ, -θῶμεν, -θῆτε, -θῶσι(ν)
PRESENT M/P	→ none	πιστεύ-ωμαι, -η, -ηται, -ώμεθα, -ησθε, -ωνται
AORIST M	→ -σ-	πιστεύ-σωμαι, -ση, -σηται, -σώμεθα, -σησθε, -σωνται

Notice that the Aorist Passive uses the Active endings (!); fortunately, the θῆτα tense indicator (-θ-) helps identify the Aorist Passive forms, since the θῆτα is used to form the Indicative Mood, Participle endings, and, in fact, all the Aorist Passive endings.

Here are the full endings for each tense:

	PRESENT A	PRESENT M/P	1ST AORIST A	1ST AORIST M	AORIST P
sg. 1	πιστεύ-ω	πιστεύ-ωμαι	πιστεύ-σω	πιστεύ-σωμαι	πιστευ-θῶ
2	πιστεύ-ῃς	πιστεύ-ῃ	πιστεύ-σῃς	πιστεύ-σῃ	πιστευ-θῇς
3	πιστεύ-ῃ	πιστεύ-ηται	πιστεύ-σῃ	πιστεύ-σηται	πιστευ-θῇ
pl. 1	πιστεύ-ωμεν	πιστεύ-ωμεθα	πιστεύ-σωμεν	πιστευ-σώμεθα	πιστευ-θῶμεν
2	πιστεύ-ητε	πιστεύ-ησθε	πιστεύ-σητε	πιστεύ-σησθε	πιοστευ-θῆτε
3	πιστεύ-ωσι(ν)	πιστεύ-ωνται	πιστεύ-σωσι(ν)	πιστεύ-σωνται	πιστευ-θῶσι(ν)

D. 2nd Aorist Verbs: These verbs will use the Subjunctive endings with no Aorist tense indicator (thus, no σίγμα); so how will they be recognizable as in the Aorist tense? Look for their stem change. Thus, ἔρχομαι will appear as follows:

AORIST A

	sg.	pl.
1	ἔλθω	ἔλθωμεν
2	ἔλθῃς	ἔλθητε
3	ἔλθῃ	ἔλθωσι(ν)

E. Present Subjunctive Forms of εἰμί:

	sg.	pl.
1	ὦ	ὦμεν
2	ᾖς	ἦτε
3	ᾖ	ὦσι(ν)

Notice that these forms are the same as the Active Subjunctive endings, except that they all have smooth breathing marks and a circumflex accent. Εἰμί has **no** Aorist Subjunctive forms.

22.2 OVERVIEW OF THE SUBJUNCTIVE MOOD

A. **General Information:** Why did the Greek language develop the Subjunctive Mood? It is a mood of future possibility, volition, and deliberation.[5] Its names from antiquity reflect the diversity of the Mood's usage: ἡ ὑποτακτικὴ ἔγκλισις (*the subordinate mood*); ἡ διστακτική (from διστακτικός, ή, όν *expressive of doubt*, LSJ) and ἡ συμβουλευτική (from συμβουλευτικός, ή, όν, *of* or *for advising, hortatory*, LSJ). If Greek writers wanted to express purpose, intention, potentiality, or possibility, they could use the Subjunctive Mood; the modal reality is marked +potentiality. This is in distinction to the Future Tense in the Indicative Mood that presents the future more *concretely* or *vividly*.

---

[5] These categories correspond to Robertson's description of the Subjunctive broadly under futuristic, volitive, and deliberative (928-35).

B. **Negation:** Μή and cognate forms (like μηδείς and μηδέ) are used to negate Subjunctive verbs. Emphatic negation is indicated by οὐ μή together (see F.4. below).

C. **Time and Verbal Aspect:** It is extremely important to understand that *the Subjunctive Mood carries no inherent time significance*. There is no augmentation. Thus, the Aorist Subjunctive *does not* refer to past time. In actual translation, the only difference between the Present and Aorist Subjunctive is the verbal aspect that each tense entails. A Present Subjunctive represents imperfective aspect (internal view and as in progress) whereas the Aorist Subjunctive represents perfective aspect (external and as complete, but not necessarily completed) (cf. Wallace 461-80).

D. **Future Tense Substitutions:** Occasionally, the future tense will be found in the place of the subjunctive mood verb. In such cases, the verbal description is marked +concreteness or vividness, which is due to the import of the Indicative Mood. For example, notice how the Future Tense makes Peter's emphatic negation statement (normally with the Subjunctive Mood) more concrete or vivid:

> **Mark 14:31** ὁ δὲ ἐκπερισσῶς ἐλάλει· ἐὰν δέῃ με συναποθανεῖν σοι, οὐ μή σε ἀπαρνήσομαι.
>
> *Moreover, he emphatically kept saying: "If it should be necessary that I die with you, I <u>will</u> never ever <u>deny</u> you!"*

Notice how the presence of the adverb ἐκπερισσῶς *emphatically* and the (iterative) imperfect verb ἐλάλει *he kept saying* also support the intensity of Peter's vivid denial.

E. **Translating the Subjunctive Mood:** Unfortunately, there is no single way to translate all Subjunctive mood verbs into English—it truly depends on the construction in which one finds them. Often students will be taught or will opt for "may" or "might"; you should avoid this. So, we need to think through the semantics involved in each construction before we can translate them into English or any other language. The discussion of the Subjunctive Mood is divided into DEPENDENT USES (§22.3) and INDEPENDENT USES (§22.4).

22.3 DEPENDENT USES OF THE SUBJUNCTIVE MOOD

Dependent Subjunctive clauses will begin with subordinating conjunctions like ἵνα (common), ἐάν (common), ὅπως (much less common), μήποτε (infrequent), etc. The presentation below is based on semantic uses rather than on individual conjunctions. However, at the end of this discussion the various uses of ἵνα are summarized.

A. **Positive Purpose (*in order that*):** The primary subordinating conjunction used to express purpose is ἵνα, although others are found much less frequently, like ὅπως. Purpose involves the intentionality of action of an agent (God, humans, etc.) towards some intended goal. It should be added that occasionally the notion of purpose is difficult to perceive in the context, and so ἵνα may be understood to convey result (*so that*), which normally lacks the notion of intentionality.

1 John 5:13 Ταῦτα ἔγραψα ὑμῖν <u>ἵνα</u> εἰδῆτε ὅτι ζωὴν ἔχετε αἰώνιον,
> *I write these things to you in order that you would know that you have eternal life,*

Acts 8:15 ...οἵτινες...προσηύξαντο περὶ αὐτῶν <u>ὅπως</u> λάβωσιν πνεῦμα ἅγιον.
> *... which ones...prayed about them in order that they would receive the Holy Spirit.*

Certain other conjunction-functioning words may carry the sense of purpose in context. For instance, consider the improper preposition μέχρι that can act like a conjunction with the subjunctive. Μέχρι has a relatively low frequency, only occuring 18 times in the GNT.

Eph 4:13 <u>μέχρι</u> καταντήσωμεν οἱ πάντες
                    εἰς τὴν ἑνότητα τῆς πίστεως
                              καὶ τῆς ἐπιγνώσεως τοῦ υἱοῦ τοῦ θεοῦ,
                    εἰς ἄνδρα τέλειον,
                    εἰς μέτρον ἡλικίας τοῦ πληρώματος τοῦ Χριστοῦ,
> *until we all would attain*
> > *to the unity of the Faith*
> > > *and of the knowledge of the Son of God,*
> > *to the perfect Man,*
> > *to the measure of the stature of the fulfillment of the Christ.*

Paul's statement reaches a climactic moment in the discourse. The improper preposition μέχρι carries the semantic constraint +temporal extension up to a point; however, in a small handful of instances, it is used as a conjunction with the Subjunctive Mood to describe extension of time leading to a goal or purpose (Mark 13:30; Gal 4:19), as here in Eph 4:13 where the goal of unity centers around Jesus as the Son of God, perfect Man, and Christ (Messiah).

B. **Negative Purpose (*lest, in order that not*):** Negative purpose clauses are typically formed with ἵνα μὴ (*in order that not*), and much less often with μήποτε (*lest ever*).

Luke 9:43b-45 (NASB95)

> [43b] But while everyone was marveling at all that He was doing, He said to His disciples, [44] "Let these words sink into your ears; for the Son of Man is going to be delivered into the hands of men." [45] But they did not understand this statement, and [καὶ] it was concealed from them <u>so that</u> they would not perceive it [ἵνα μὴ αἴσθωνται αὐτό]; and they were afraid to ask Him about this statement.

Although the NASB95 translates the ἵνα μή in 9:45 as *so that*, leaving it ambiguous whether the construction indicates *result* or *purpose*, Luke's use of the passive voice in "was concealed" indicates divine agency (a divine passive), and hence, intentionality. God did not prevent them from understanding; God simply did not assist their understanding. Luke first says "But they did not understand" (9:45a), and then adds (καί), but not substantiates (using γάρ), that "it was concealed from them." What Luke expresses here is that God does not assist the disciples past their own lack of understanding of the matter (9:45a); God kept the significance of Christ's death from them *in order that they would not understand it* (purpose). Why? This is a significant question. Perhaps for the disciples to have such an understanding would have caused so much fear that they would reject Jesus then and there; instead, God intended that they stay longer with Jesus. Had they fully understood his need to die, they may have abandoned Jesus prematurely before he could teach them further about his Mission and the New Covenant. As it turned out, the disciples fled Jesus when he was arrested.

C. **Content Clause or Indirect Discourse (*that*):** The content of some verbal idea may be expressed either positively with ἵνα or negatively with μή or cognates. Such content may be deemed as *indirect discourse* or a *verbal complement*. It is important to understand that ἵνα (or negative statements μή) may be used with the Subjunctive Mood to indicate content.

1. *Ἵνα indicating Positive Content of Verbal Idea.* Ἵνα with the Subjunctive Mood sometimes is best rendered by *that* indicating the content of some verbal notion. "Many ἵνα clauses in the NT follow verbs of praying, asking, commanding or instructing. These verbs, however, are not always followed by this construction"; the semantic constraint indicated by ἵνα is + "desirable outcome" or "a desirable state of affairs, from the perspective of the subject."[6] The idea of *purpose* may be close at hand. In this regard, ἵνα is analogous with the content marking use of ὅτι (§8.5.B.4), except that ὅτι remains unmarked for *desirable outcome*.

   Luke 4:3 εἶπεν δὲ αὐτῷ ὁ διάβολος· εἰ υἱὸς εἶ τοῦ θεοῦ, εἰπὲ τῷ λίθῳ τούτῳ <u>ἵνα</u> γένηται ἄρτος.
   And the devil said to him: "If you are the Son of God, speak to this stone <u>that</u> it become bread."

   1 Cor 4:2 ζητεῖται ἐν τοῖς οἰκονόμοις, <u>ἵνα</u> πιστός τις εὑρεθῇ.
   It is sought among stewards <u>that</u> some be found faithful.

2. *Μή and cognates indicating Undesirable Outcome.* After verbs of warning or watching (out), you may find μή (or cognates such as μήποτε) and the subjunctive (or equivalent) to express the negative content of the warning.

---

[6] Sim, *Marking Thought*, 17-18.

Luke 21:8b βλέπετε <u>μὴ</u> πλανηθῆτε· Watch <u>that</u> you <u>not</u> be deceived!

Heb 3:12a Βλέπετε, ἀδελφοί, <u>μήποτε</u> ἔσται ἔν τινι ὑμῶν καρδία πονηρὰ ἀπιστίας...
Watch, brothers, <u>lest ever</u> an evil heart will be in any one of you...

D. **Epexegetical Use with Nouns, Adjectives, Demonstratives:** The ἵνα clause may specify the content of a noun or pronoun clause.[7] This is very similar to content clauses (immediately above C.), which however pertain to verbs. Sometimes a demonstrative pronoun like οὗτος *this* may help prepare for the epexegetical use of ἵνα. Occasionally, the idea of *purpose* or *desirable outcome* is close at hand (see Wallace 475-76). In John 2:25a the *need* that Jesus had no need of is indicated by the ἵνα clause. In 2 John 1:6a-b, the demonstrative pronouns help to set up the use of ἵνα that defines the terms *love* and *command*.

John 2:25a οὐ χρείαν εἶχεν <u>ἵνα</u> τις μαρτυρήσῃ περὶ τοῦ ἀνθρώπου.
He was having no need <u>that</u> someone testify concerning humans.

2 John 1:6a καὶ αὕτη ἐστὶν ἡ ἀγάπη, <u>ἵνα</u> περιπατῶμεν κατὰ τὰς ἐντολὰς αὐτοῦ·
And this is love, <u>that</u> we walk according to his commands.

2 John 1:6b αὕτη ἡ ἐντολή ἐστιν, καθὼς ἠκούσατε ἀπ᾽ ἀρχῆς, <u>ἵνα</u> ἐν αὐτῇ περιπατῆτε.
This is his command, just as you heard from the beginning, <u>that</u> we walk in it [love].

E. **Indeterminate and Contingent/Conditional Clauses with ἐάν, ὅς ἄν, ὅταν, etc.:** The Subjunctive is used with some form of ἄν to indicate potential circumstance and contingency, sometimes translatable in English as *ever*, as in the following examples: *if (ever), who(ever), when(ever), where (ever), how(ever),* etc. Moreover, the combination of εἰ (*if*) with ἄν (*ever*) results in the Greek form ἐάν, signaling a conditional clause. These various types of indeterminate clauses of manner (*however*), location (*wherever*), time (*whenever*), or relative person (*whoever*) introduce subordinate clauses that may function within a conditional sentence. CHAPTER 26.2 will explain these various types of conditional sentences.

Matt 5:46a ἐὰν γὰρ ἀγαπήσητε τοὺς ἀγαπῶντας ὑμᾶς, τίνα μισθὸν ἔχετε;
For <u>if</u> you love those loving you, what reward do you have?

F. **Summary Uses of Ἵνα:** The presence of ἵνα almost always signals the presence of a subjunctive Mood verb (the only exception being possibly the rare Future tense verb). Below are the many uses of ἵνα.

---

[7] Sim argues, "Many of the uses of ἵνα in the NT are described as 'noun clauses'. These are frequently epexegetic in that they explicate a noun, adjective or demonstrative in the main clause" (*Marking Thought*, 18).

1. <u>Purpose</u>: *in order that*

2. <u>Result</u> (rare): *so that*

3. <u>Negative Purpose</u>: *in order that not, lest*

4. <u>Content Clause or Indirect Discourse</u>: *that*

5. <u>Epexegetical Use with Nouns, Adjectives, Demonstratives</u>: *that*.

Notice that the conjunction ἵνα does not simply indicate purpose. But, how are we to account for the variety of uses? Margaret G. Sim's important study on the matter deserves our attention. Sim's research in to Classical and Koine usage led her to understand that ἵνα's main "function is to alert the reader to expect a thought, desire or intention of the speaker."[8] Her conclusion about ἵνα is as follows:

> its function is that of a procedural marker alerting the reader to expect an indication of the speaker or subject's thought, often his desire or intention. It is the responsibility of the reader to draw from the text the most relevant logical relation between the clause introduced by ἵνα and the rest of the sentence. This claim is based on the assumption that a communicator presents information which is relevant to his hearers or readers, and that by using a clause introduced by this particle and in the subjunctive mood, he is inviting the recipients of his communication to draw inferences which would not have been as easily recovered if he had used other grammatical constructions. The use of ἵνα enables the reader or hearer to access the communicative intention of the implied author in a more perspicacious manner than if she was presented with an infinitival construction.[9]

22.4 INDEPENDENT USES OF THE SUBJUNCTIVE MOOD

Verbs in the Subjunctive Mood may be used independently. Such clauses are not subordinate. Thus, they need no conjunction to introduce them. Below are the main independent uses of the Subjunctive Mood.

A. **Hortatory Subjunctive:** This usage occurs exclusively with a 1st person plural subjunctive verb. *The Hortatory Subjunctive is a polite injunction or command.* As such, the speaker includes himself in the urging to do this or that. See Wallace 464-65. The translation is something like *Let us do this or that… .*

John 11:16b <u>Ἄγωμεν</u> καὶ ἡμεῖς ἵνα ἀποθάνωμεν μετ' αὐτοῦ.
   <u>Let us also go</u> in order that we ourselves would die with him.

---

[8] Sim, *Marking Thought*, 4.
[9] Sim, *Marking Thought*, 20. This statement concludes her introductory survey of her monograph.

B. **Prohibition with Μή:** The Aorist Subjunctive with the negative particle μή is used for a negative command, which is called **prohibition**. See Wallace 469. The translation would be something like *Don't do this or that ... !*

Heb 3:8a μὴ σκληρύνητε τὰς καρδίας ὑμῶν. . . . *Don't harden your hearts ... !*

The pragmatics of choosing the Aorist Subjunctive with μή to form prohibition as opposed to using the Imperative Mood will be treated in CH. 25.

C. **Deliberative Question:** A question that is raised in deliberation (with various options potentially being considered) may be put in the Subjunctive Mood and is called a deliberative question. These questions are usually direct questions and will therefore end with a semi-colon punctuation mark (;). See Wallace 465-68. The translation is something like this: *Should we do such and such...?* or *What should we do?*

John 6:5b Πόθεν ἀγοράσωμεν ἄρτους ἵνα φάγωσιν οὗτοι;
	From where should we buy bread in order that these ones eat?

In the following example, consider carefully what is lost by an English translation that uses the simple future to translate the deliberative questions.

Matt 6:31 μὴ οὖν μεριμνήσητε λέγοντες· τί φάγωμεν; ἤ· τί πίωμεν; ἤ· τί περιβαλώμεθα;

NASB95 *Do not worry then, saying, 'What will we eat?' or 'What will we drink?' or 'What will we wear for clothing?'*
BETTER *Therefore, do not worry, saying: 'What should we eat?' or 'What should we drink?' or 'What should we wear for clothing?'*

The issue is not *in having nothing*, i.e. someone having no clothing and so saying "What will I wear [since I have nothing]?" Instead, the context is one where people eagerly seek to beautify themselves in appearance and distinguish themselves by what they eat. Jesus immediately says in 6:32: "For the Gentiles eagerly seek all these things...." Instead, Jesus urges his followers not to seek after such things as important pursuits, but rather to pursue God's Kingdom.

D. **Emphatic Negation:** To make a very emphatic denial of possibility, the Greeks would use both negative particles οὐ μή (in this same order) with the Subjunctive Mood (or, sometimes with the Future Tense). The translation is something like: *Such and such will never ever happen.* This is called **emphatic negation**.

Matt 24:25 ὁ οὐρανὸς καὶ ἡ γῆ παρελεύσεται, οἱ δὲ λόγοι μου οὐ μὴ παρέλθωσιν.
	Heaven and earth will pass away, but my words will never ever pass away.

See Wallace 468-69 and Smyth §2754a.[10] Students will be surprised at how common this construction is and in what well-known verses, since the English translations often do not help readers catch the urgency or tone of the emphatic negation. See, e.g., Luke 6:37; 9:27; 10:19; 12:59; 18:7, 17; 21:18; 22:16, 18, 67, 68; John 4:14, 48. For example, are you able to discern the emphatic negation in Luke 10:19 (NLT)? (Hint: See the end.) Notice also the word order.

Luke 10:19 Look, I have given you authority over all the power of the enemy, and you can
walk among snakes and scorpions and crush them. Nothing will injure you. (NLT)

Luke 10:19 ἰδοὺ δέδωκα ὑμῖν τὴν ἐξουσίαν τοῦ πατεῖν ἐπάνω ὄφεων καὶ σκορπίων, καὶ
ἐπὶ πᾶσαν τὴν δύναμιν τοῦ ἐχθροῦ, καὶ οὐδὲν ὑμᾶς οὐ μὴ ἀδικήσῃ.

E. **Imperatival Ἵνα?** Very rarely one finds a ἵνα unconnected to a main clause in the context of exhortation. See Mark 5:23; 2 Cor 8:7; Eph 5:33; Gal 2:9.[11] Grammarians have struggled to explain this, and this grammatical label, Imperatival Ἵνα, has been used. However, it is probably better to understand an implied verb from the context.

2 Cor 8:7 Ἀλλ' ὥσπερ ἐν παντὶ περισσεύετε, πίστει καὶ λόγῳ καὶ γνώσει καὶ πάσῃ
σπουδῇ καὶ τῇ ἐξ ἡμῶν ἐν ὑμῖν ἀγάπῃ, <u>ἵνα</u> καὶ ἐν ταύτῃ τῇ χάριτι
περισσεύητε.
*But just as in every way you are overflowing, in faith and in word and in knowledge
and in all eagerness and in love from us among you, (I urge) <u>that</u> you also overflow
in this grace.*[12]

Here the context of *urging* is clearly present, so the verbal notion *I urge* is implied and may be included within parentheses.

F. **Final Word on Translation:** Proper translation of a Subjunctive Mood verb entirely depends on the construction it is in. Be sure to use the helping verbs to translate as described above and as demonstrated in the examples. I would clarify here that "would be" is best for purpose statements. Why? Because purpose statements are statements of intention; the helping verbs "may be" or "might be" convey statements of possibility, not of intention. Authors include statements of purpose to express not primarily what "might be" (the possibility of existence) but what **agents intend "would be."** Whether the event *may* or *might* happen is another question; it is a step removed away from the intention of the agent who acts and plans that the event *would* happen.

---

[10] Smyth summarizes as follows: "οὐ μή marks strong personal interest on the part of the speaker. In its original use it may have belonged to colloquial speech and as such we find it in comedy; but in tragedy it is often used in stately language. οὐ μή is rare in the orators."

[11] See the summary of Sim: "He [Cadoux 1941, 166] claimed that it then became common to omit the main verb 'so that the ἵνα-clause virtually became as much a main sentence as if the plain imperative had been used' and gave evidence both from the papyri and Epictetus. For the NT he gave 'at least four unmistakable cases' from Mark 5:23, 2 Corinthians 8:7, Ephesians 5:33 and Galatians 2:9" (*Marking Thought*, 11).

[12] Translation from Long, *2 Corinthians: A Handbook on the Greek Text* (Waco: Baylor University Press, 2015), 150.

CHECK POINT 22.1-4 SUBJUNCTIVE MOOD VERBS

Given these verses in Greek and an English translation (NASB95),

1. **First**, identify whether each Subjunctive verb is Independent or Dependent and which conjunction or adverb helps signal this;
2. **Second**, indicate what particular use of the Subjunctive Mood is present;
3. **Third**, briefly discuss possible ways to improve the translation in view of the construction and verbal aspect. Present Tense subjunctives are indicated; all others are Aorist Tense.

Rom 6:1 Τί οὖν ἐροῦμεν; ἐπιμένωμεν τῇ ἁμαρτίᾳ, ἵνα ἡ χάρις πλεονάσῃ;
Rom 6:1 What shall we say then? Are we to continue in sin so that grace may increase?

ἐπιμένωμεν (Present Tense) =

πλεονάσῃ =

Rom 14:13a Μηκέτι οὖν ἀλλήλους κρίνωμεν·
Rom 14:13a Therefore let us not judge one another anymore,

κρίνωμεν (take as Present Tense) =

Luke 22:67-68 εἰ σὺ εἶ ὁ χριστός, εἰπὸν ἡμῖν. εἶπεν δὲ αὐτοῖς· ἐὰν ὑμῖν εἴπω, οὐ μὴ πιστεύσητε· [68] ἐὰν δὲ ἐρωτήσω, οὐ μὴ ἀποκριθῆτε.
Luke 22:67-68 If You are the Christ, tell us." But He said to them, "If I tell you, you will not believe; [68] and if I ask a question, you will not answer.

εἴπω =

πιστεύσητε =

ἐρωτήσω =

ἀποκριθῆτε =

Matt 7:6 Μὴ δῶτε τὸ ἅγιον τοῖς κυσὶν μηδὲ βάλητε τοὺς μαργαρίτας ὑμῶν ἔμπροσθεν τῶν χοίρων, μήποτε καταπατήσουσιν αὐτοὺς ἐν τοῖς ποσὶν αὐτῶν καὶ στραφέντες ῥήξωσιν ὑμᾶς.
Matt 7:6 "Do not give what is holy to dogs, and do not throw your pearls before swine, or they will trample them under their feet, and turn and tear you to pieces."

δῶτε =

βάλητε =

ῥήξωσιν =

Bonus = Explain καταπατήσουσιν.

Luke 16:27-30 εἶπεν δέ· ἐρωτῶ σε οὖν, πάτερ, ἵνα <u>πέμψῃς</u> αὐτὸν εἰς τὸν οἶκον τοῦ πατρός μου, ²⁸ ἔχω γὰρ πέντε ἀδελφούς, ὅπως <u>διαμαρτύρηται</u> αὐτοῖς, ἵνα μὴ καὶ αὐτοὶ <u>ἔλθωσιν</u> εἰς τὸν τόπον τοῦτον τῆς βασάνου. ²⁹ λέγει δὲ Ἀβραάμ· ἔχουσιν Μωϋσέα καὶ τοὺς προφήτας· ἀκουσάτωσαν αὐτῶν. ³⁰ ὁ δὲ εἶπεν· οὐχί, πάτερ Ἀβραάμ, ἀλλ᾽ ἐάν τις ἀπὸ νεκρῶν <u>πορευθῇ</u> πρὸς αὐτοὺς μετανοήσουσιν.

Luke 16:27-30 "And he said, 'Then I beg you, father, that you <u>send</u> him to my father's house— ²⁸ for I have five brothers—in order that he may <u>warn</u> them, so that they will not also <u>come</u> to this place of torment.' ²⁹ "But Abraham *said, 'They have Moses and the Prophets; let them hear them.' ³⁰ "But he said, 'No, father Abraham, but if someone <u>goes</u> to them from the dead, they will repent!'

πέμψῃς =

διαμαρτύρηται (Present Tense) =

ἔλθωσιν =

πορευθῇ =

SUGGESTED ANSWERS

Rom 6:1 Τί οὖν ἐροῦμεν; <u>ἐπιμένωμεν</u> τῇ ἁμαρτίᾳ, ἵνα ἡ χάρις <u>πλεονάσῃ</u>;
Rom 6:1 What shall we say then? <u>Are we to continue</u> in sin so that grace <u>may increase</u>?

ἐπιμένωμεν (Present Tense) = **1.** Independent; **2.** deliberative question that ends with a question mark (;); **3.** The NASB95 does well to capture imperfective aspect with a translation suggesting ongoing action.

πλεονάσῃ = **1.** Depedent; **2.** Positive Purpose with ἵνα; **3.** An improvement in translation would be to use the stronger auxiliary verb "would" (rather than "may") to better express purpose; also a conjunction like *"in order that"* would indicate clearly purpose instead of result.

Rom 14:13a Μηκέτι οὖν ἀλλήλους <u>κρίνωμεν·</u>
Rom 14:13a Therefore <u>let</u> us not <u>judge</u> one another anymore,

---

* **A star** (*) is used to mark verbs that are historical presents in the Greek which have been translated with an English past tense in order to conform to modern usage. The translators recognized that in some contexts the present tense seems more unexpected and unjustified to the English reader than a past tense would have been. But Greek authors frequently used the present tense for the sake of heightened vividness, thereby transporting their readers in imagination to the actual scene at the time of occurence [sic]. However, the translators felt that it would be wise to change these historical presents to English past tenses.

κρίνωμεν (take as Present Tense) = **1.** Independent; **2.** Hortatory Subjunctive; **3.** The form may be either Aorist or Present Subjunctive. If Present (as it is parsed in databases), then a translation may help stress the imperfective aspect: "Let us no longer keep/continue judging one another."

Luke 22:67-68 εἰ σὺ εἶ ὁ χριστός, εἰπὸν ἡμῖν. εἶπεν δὲ αὐτοῖς· ἐὰν ὑμῖν <u>εἴπω</u>, οὐ μὴ <u>πιστεύσητε</u>· ⁶⁸ ἐὰν δὲ <u>ἐρωτήσω</u>, οὐ μὴ <u>ἀποκριθῆτε</u>.

Luke 22:67-68 If You are the Christ, tell us." But He said to them, "If <u>I tell</u> you, <u>you will</u> not <u>believe</u>; ⁶⁸ and if <u>I ask</u> a question, <u>you will</u> not <u>answer</u>.

εἴπω = **1.** Dependent; **2.** Conditional Subjunctive with ἐάν; **3.** no improvements.

πιστεύσητε = **1.** Independent; **2.** Emphatic Negation with οὐ μή; **3.** Somehow the emphatic negation should be translated; consider adding "never" and an exclamation point: "you will never (ever) believe!"

ἐρωτήσω = **1.** Dependent; **2.** Conditional Subjunctive with ἐάν; **3.** no improvements.

ἀποκριθῆτε = **1.** Independent; **2.** Emphatic Negation with οὐ μή; **3.** Somehow the emphatic negation should be translated; consider adding "never (ever)" and an exclamation point: "you will never (ever) answer!"

Matt 7:6 Μὴ <u>δῶτε</u> τὸ ἅγιον τοῖς κυσὶν μηδὲ <u>βάλητε</u> τοὺς μαργαρίτας ὑμῶν ἔμπροσθεν τῶν χοίρων, μήποτε <u>καταπατήσουσιν</u> αὐτοὺς ἐν τοῖς ποσὶν αὐτῶν καὶ στραφέντες <u>ῥήξωσιν</u> ὑμᾶς.

Matt 7:6 "<u>Do</u> not <u>give</u> what is holy to dogs, and <u>do</u> not <u>throw</u> your pearls before swine, or <u>they will trample</u> them under their feet, and turn and <u>tear</u> you to pieces."

δῶτε = **1.** Independent; **2.** Prohibition with Aorist Subjunctive and Μή; **3.** no improvements.

βάλητε = **1.** Independent; **2.** Prohibition with Aorist Subjunctive and μηδέ; **3.** no improvements.

ῥήξωσιν = **1.** Dependent; **2.** Negative purpose with μήποτε; **3.** One improvement would be to translate μήποτε more clearly as expressing negative purpose "lest perchance" or "in order that ... not...."

Bonus = Explain καταπατήσουσιν. Future Indicative is used in place of Subjunctive Mood. Why? This may add some level of "concreteness" in depicting the negative consequences of giving to dogs and swine what is precious.

Luke 16:27-30 εἶπεν δέ· ἐρωτῶ σε οὖν, πάτερ, ἵνα <u>πέμψῃς</u> αὐτὸν εἰς τὸν οἶκον τοῦ πατρός μου, ²⁸ ἔχω γὰρ πέντε ἀδελφούς, ὅπως <u>διαμαρτύρηται</u> αὐτοῖς, ἵνα μὴ καὶ αὐτοὶ <u>ἔλθωσιν</u> εἰς τὸν τόπον τοῦτον τῆς βασάνου. ²⁹ λέγει δὲ Ἀβραάμ· ἔχουσιν Μωϋσέα καὶ τοὺς προφήτας· ἀκουσάτωσαν αὐτῶν. ³⁰ ὁ δὲ εἶπεν· οὐχί, πάτερ Ἀβραάμ, ἀλλ᾽ ἐάν τις ἀπὸ νεκρῶν <u>πορευθῇ</u> πρὸς αὐτοὺς μετανοήσουσιν.

> **Luke 16:27-30** "And he said, 'Then I beg you, father, that <u>you send</u> him to my father's
> house— ²⁸   for I have five brothers—in order that <u>he may warn</u> them, so that
> they <u>will</u> not also <u>come</u> to this place of torment.' ²⁹ "But Abraham *said, 'They
> have Moses and the Prophets; let them hear them.' ³⁰ "But he said, 'No, father
> Abraham, but if someone <u>goes</u> to them from the dead, they will repent!'
>
> πέμψης = **1.** Dependent; **2.** Content of ἐρωτῶ with ἵνα; **3.** no improvements.
> διαμαρτύρηται (Present Tense) = **1.** Dependent; **2.** Positive Purpose with ὅπως; **3.** One
>   improvement would be to use the auxilliary verb "would" (rather than "may"); ad-
>   ditionally, the translation should draw more attention to the imperfective aspect and
>   the foregrounding of this important action, "in order that he would be warning
>   them" or in order that he would keep warning them."
> ἔλθωσιν = **1.** Dependent; **2.** Negative Purpose with ἵνα μὴ; **3.** An auxiliary verb "would" ra-
>   ther than "will" may better express purpose; also a conjunction like *"in order that"*
>   (rather than "so that") would indicate clearly purpose instead of misunderstanding
>   this as result.
> πορευθῇ = **1.** Dependent; **2.** Conditional Subjunctive with ἐὰν; **3.** no improvements.

22.5 ADVERBS (Ἐπιρρήματα): MORE ON FORMATION AND FUNCTION

A. Formation:

1. Many adverbs may be formed from adjectives; e.g., the neuter accusative singular form may function as an adverb. For example, if not working as or with a substantive, μικρόν means *in a little while*. See §7.1 ADVERBS: A FIRST LOOK.

2. Additionally, some adverbs may be formed by adding an -ως to the stem of the adjective. The adverbial ending -ως indicates *manner*.

δίκαιος	*righteous*	→	δικαίως	*righteously*
καλός	*good*	→	καλῶς	*well*
κακός	*bad*	→	κακῶς	*in an evil way; badly*

3. Moreover, Greek adverbs show a great variety of endings that convey certain meanings. Actually, many of these endings are old case endings (this is true also for prepositions). Just look at the variety of endings in the adverbs from VOCABULARY 7, VOCABULARY 15, and VOCABULARY 22.

4. Finally, here is a list of adverbial endings with their basic sense or meaning:

ADVERBIAL ENDINGS AND EXAMPLES				
Ending & Meaning	**EXAMPLES**			
-ως *manner*	ἀδίκως	*unjustly*	κακῶς	*wickedly, badly*
	ἀληθῶς	*truly*	ὄντως	*really, certainly*
	δικαίως	*justly*	οὕτως	*in this manner, thus*
	εὐθέως	*immediately*	πώς	*somehow*
	ἡδέως	*gladly*	πῶς	*how?*
	καλῶς	*well, beautifully*	ταχέως	*quickly*
-τε *time*	ὅτε	*when*	πότε	*when?*
	οὐδέποτε	*never*	πώποτε	*ever*
	πάντοτε	*always*	τότε	*then*
-ι *time*	ἀεί	*always*	οὐκέτι	*no longer*
	ἄρτι	*now, just*	πάλαι	*long ago*
	ἔτι	*yet, still*	πέρυσι	*last year*
	νυνί	*now*	πρωΐ	*early*
-ι *place where*	ἐκεῖ	*there, to that place*		
-ου *place where*	πανταχοῦ	*everywhere*	ὅπου	*where*
	ποῦ	*where?*	οὗ	*where (gen. form of ὅς that became an adv. of place)*
-θεν *place where from*	ἄνωθεν	*from above, again*	ἔσωθεν	*from within*
	ἐκεῖθεν	*from there*	μάκροθεν	*from afar*
	ἔμπροσθεν	*in front*	ὅθεν	*from where*
	ἐντεῦθεν	*from here*	ὄπισθεν	*from behind*
	ἔξωθεν	*from the outside*	πόθεν	*whence?*
-δε *direction to where*	ἐνθάδε	*here*	ὧδε	*here*
-ις *denoting number*	δίς	*two times; twice*	πεντάκις	*five times*
	ἑβδομη-κοντάκις	*seventy times*	πολλάκις	*many times; often*
	ἑπτάκις	*seven times*	ποσάκις	*how often (?)*
	ὁσάκις	*as often as*	τρίς	*three times; thrice*

B. Adverb Functions:

1. <u>Adverbial</u>. Adverbs are words that generally *modify verbs, adjectives,* or *other adverbs*. In English, certain adverbs may quickly be recognized when they end in *–ly: slowly, quietly,* etc. In Greek, the adverb is typically found right beside the word that it is modifying.

John 13:13 ὑμεῖς φωνεῖτέ με Ὁ διδάσκαλος καὶ Ὁ κύριος, καὶ <u>καλῶς</u> λέγετε, εἰμὶ γάρ. *You call me 'Teacher and Lord,' and you speak <u>well</u>, for I am.*

1 Cor 15:34 ἐκνήψατε <u>δικαίως</u> καὶ μὴ ἁμαρτάνετε, ἀγνωσίαν γὰρ θεοῦ τινες ἔχουσιν
Be <u>righteously</u> sober minded and don't continue sinning! For some have ignorance about God.

Matt 26:39a καὶ προελθὼν <u>μικρὸν</u> ἔπεσεν ἐπὶ πρόσωπον αὐτοῦ προσευχόμενος
and going forward <u>a little bit</u>, he fell on his face praying

2. <u>Adjective-Like</u>. Beyond their more typical adverbial function, adverbs may function on occasion like adjectives, either in the substantive position or, much more rarely, in the attributive position. Adverbs will also be formed in the comparative and superlative degrees; see §25.5 COMPARATIVE AND SUPERLATIVE ADJECTIVES AND ADVERBS.

   Acts 13:42 εἰς τὸ <u>μεταξὺ</u> σάββατον *at the next sabbath*
   ἀπὸ τοῦ <u>νῦν</u> *from now on*   εἰς τὸ <u>πέραν</u> *to the across,* i.e. *to the other side*

3. <u>Conjunction-Like</u>. Adverbs may work together with conjunctions to form correlative emphasis (e.g., οὐκ ... ἀλλά *not ... but*). See §15.6.D. Additionally, adverbs may function like conjunctions as οὕτως in 1 Cor 2:11b, although their adverbial sense should not be ignored. So, e.g., οὕτως in Rom 11:26 is not primarily "therefore" but "thus" indicating manner.

22.6 NEGATIVE EMPHASIS

A. **Introduction:** Since Greek has a variety of words to indicate negation or denial, it is important to understand the difference. We have already seen how in questions that a negative or a positive answer is explicitly indicate by the presence of μή or οὐ (and their cognate forms), respectively (§14.3 INTERROGATIVE EMPHASIS). Remember the rule of MNOP. Moreover, unlike proper English, Greek may add double or triple negatives to underscore the denial of what is stated. Such emphasis may be seen in English, although only in breaking the norms of the language, as in this example: "I hain't nohow seen nobody nowhere." This emphatic denial is signaled by repetition of negative words.

B. **Distinguishing Οὐ and Μή:** It is helpful, first, to understand the difference between οὐ and μή. Robertson helpfully summarizes:

> In general the New Testament uses the negative οὐ and μή in accordance with the idiom of the earlier Greek. The distinction is well observed between the outright negation by οὐ and the subtle and subjective μή.... Οὐ is direct, positive, categorical, definite; μή is doubtful, indirect, indefinite, hypothetical. Μή is a negative with a "string tied to it." If a girl should say οὐ to a proposal of marriage (especially οὐχί), there would be little hope. But μή would leave room for another trial. The bluntness of οὐ in its strengthened form οὐχί is well shown in Luke 1:60. On the other hand μήτι in Jo. 4:29 (μήτι οὗτός ἐστιν ὁ Χριστός;) but dimly conceals the woman's real conviction about Jesus.[13]

---

[13] Robertson, *A Short Grammar of the Greek New Testament, for Students Familiar with the Elements of Greek* (New York: Hodder & Stoughton, 1908), 199.

Second, one immediately application of the difference is seen with which negative adverb is used to negate the participle. For instance, Robertson maintained, "The negative of the participle in the New Testament is μή, unless a very emphatic negative is desired, when οὐ is used…. In general οὐ is only found with the participle when a distinct and strong negative is desired. So in Lu. 6:42 οὐ βλέπων. In 1 Pet. 1:8 we have οὐκ ἰδόντες and μή ὁρῶντες and the distinction can be seen."[14]

C. **Negative Words:** Students have already learned that there are several words that indicate quantity (§12.4 QUANTITATIVE EMPHASIS). Likewise, *there are a variety of words to indicate negation*. Along with the adverb οὐ *no, not*, there is the negative pronoun οὐδείς *no one; nothing*. Additionally, there are other words built with οὐ signifying negation, some included in the chapter vocabularies and others with lower frequency not included: οὐκέτι[47] *no longer*, οὔπω[26] *not yet*, and οὔτε[87] *nor, not even, neither* (CH.15), etc. Moreover, there is also a negative adverb μή *no* (CH.14) that also has words derived from it: μηδέ[56] *and not; neither* (CH.22), μηκέτι[22] *no longer*, μήποτε[25] *never*, μήτε[34] *and not, neither*, etc. The following chart shows the variety of Greek negative words built from οὐ and μή. Those in brackets do not occur in the GNT.

GREEK NEGATING WORDS		
οὐ Cognates	μή Cognates	Meaning
οὐ, οὐκ, οὐχ	μή	*no, not*
οὐχί	μήτι	*no, not* (+intensity)
οὐδέ	μηδέ	*additionally no, not* (+new development)
οὔτε	μήτε	*and not* (+addition and +sameness)
οὐδείς	μηδείς	*no one, nothing*
οὐκέτι	μηκέτι	*no longer*
οὔπω	μήπω	*not yet*
[οὔπως]	μήπως	*nohow, not at all*
οὐδέπω	μηδέπω	*not yet* (+new development)
[οὔποτε]	μήποτε	*not ever; never, in order that not, lest*
οὐδαμῶς	μηδαμῶς	*by no means*
οὐδέποτε	μηδέποτε	*never* (+new development)
οὐκοῦν		*therefore yes* (used to ask affirmative question in John 18:37)

In general, the more morphological elements attached, the more emphatic the negative word becomes. For example, BDAG indicates of οὐδαμῶς, only found in Matt 2:6: "marker of emphatic negation, *by no means*."

---

[14] Robertson, *Short Grammar*, 198.

D. Two or More Negative Words in the Same Clause Add Emphasis: Importantly, in Greek multiple negative words do not cancel each other out when occurring within the same clause, but they rather strengthen the negative denial being made. Consider these examples, where some attempt is made to communicate the extra force of the emphasized negation:

Luke 4:2b οὐκ ἔφαγεν οὐδέν... *Jesus did not eat a single thing...*

Rom 13:8a μηδενὶ μηδὲν ὀφείλετε εἰ μὴ τὸ ἀλλήλους ἀγαπᾶν·
Owe not one thing to any single person, except to love one another!

Mark 12:34 καὶ οὐδεὶς οὐκέτι ἐτόλμα αὐτὸν ἐπερωτῆσαι.
And no one any longer dared to question him.

Mark 14:25b οὐκέτι οὐ μὴ πίω ἐκ τοῦ γενήματος τῆς ἀμπέλου...
I will never ever any longer drink from the fruit of the vine...

Acts 4:12a καὶ οὐκ ἔστιν ἐν ἄλλῳ οὐδενὶ ἡ σωτηρία
and salvation is not in any single other.

Rodney J. Decker compiles a list of double or triple negatives in Mark's Gospel when commenting on **μηδενὶ μηδὲν** in Mark 1:44:

μηδενὶ μηδὲν. The double negative conveys emphatic negation in Greek (it does not result in a positive statement as in English). The following compound (double or triple) negatives occur in Mark: οὐ μή (9:1, 41; 10:15; 13:2 [2x], 30, 31; 14:31); οὐ οὐδείς (3:27; 5:37; 6:5; 12:14; 14:60, 61; 15:4); οὐδὲ οὐκέτι οὐδείς (5:3, a triple negative!); οὐδεὶς οὔπω (11:2); οὐδεὶς οὐκέτι (12:34); οὐδενὶ οὐδὲν (16:8); οὐκέτι οὐδὲν (7:12; 9:8; 15:5); οὐκέτι οὐ μή (14:25, a triple negative!); μὴ μηδὲ (3:20; 6:11); μηδενὶ μηδὲν (1:44); μηκέτι μηδὲ (2:2); and μηκέτι μηδείς (11:14).[15]

Robertson (1165) summarizes the impact of compound negatives nicely, "These compound negatives merely strengthen the previous negative. This emphatic repetition of the compound negative was once good vernacular in both English and German, but it gave way in literary circles before the influence of the Latin. It was always good Greek." After considering examples from Luke 10:19, Heb 13:5, and Rev 18:14, Robertson comments "There is no denying the power of this accumulation of negatives. Cf. the English hymn, 'I'll never, no never, no never forsake.' This view is also expressed in BDF §431, along with some exceptions. See E. below.

---

[15] Rodney J. Decker, *Mark 1-8: A Handbook on the Greek Text*, Baylor Handbook on the Greek New Testament (Waco, TX: Baylor University Press, 2014), 41.

E. **Simple Single Negative in the Second Clause Retains Force:** Robertson explains this according to whether the second negative is a single (i.e. simple) negative word, i.e. the simple forms of οὐ and μή. He explains:

> But when the second negative is a single negative, it retains its force. So οὐ παρὰ τοῦτο οὐκ ἔστι ἐκ τοῦ σώματος (1 Cor. 12:15); οὐκ ἔχομεν ἐξουσίαν μὴ ἐργασίαν (1 Cor. 9:6); μὴ οὐκ ἤκουσαν (Rom. 10:18); ὁ μὴ πιστεύων ἤδη κέκριται ὅτι μὴ πεπίστευκεν (Jo. 3:18). Cf. οὐδὲν γάρ ἐστιν κεκαλυμμένον ὃ οὐκ ἀποκαλυφθήσεται (Matt. 10:26), and οὐ μὴ ἀφεθῇ ὧδε ... ὃς οὐ καταλυθήσεται (Matt. 24:2). See 1 Cor. 6:9 (οὐ ... οὐ). Cf. also μή ποτε οὐ μή (or μή ποτε οὐ, mg.) in Matt. 25:9. In Matt. 13:29 οὔ, μή ποτε ... ἐκριζώσητε each negative has its full force. Cf. μή, μή ποτε (Mk. 14:2). Cf. Mk. 12:24 for οὐ μή in question and μή with participle.[16]

A closer look at these "exceptions" reveals that the second (simple) negative adverb functions (1) either in its own clause explicitly (Matt 10:26; 24:2; John 3:18 1 Cor 6:9; 9:6) or implicitly (1 Cor 12:15), (2) after an initial negative reply to a question (Matt 25:9, *No way, there won't ever be sufficient [oil]...*), or (3) after the initial negative adverb that negates the whole clause in a rhetorical question (Rom 10:18, *It's not that they haven't heard, is it? [No!]*).

F. **Conclusion:** Pay attention to the type of negative adverb used, whether οὐ and μή, and whether it is appropriately used (see B.). Also consider the particular type of negative adverb, whether it carries a special adverbial meaning or negative emphasis (see the chart in C.). Finally, consider whether two or more negative words are included in the sentence and consider the discursive significance in location and the type of emphasis conveyed (see D.). However, understand that there may be some exceptional circumstances that need to be understood, such as when a second negative legitimately retains its negative force when it occurs in its own distinct clause or in a rhetorical question (see E.).

CHECK POINT 22.5-6 ADVERBS

Given these verses provided in Greek with English translation (NASB95) and definition gloss for words not yet learned, 1. **First**, comment on the significance of the adverb or negative word present (what is the meaning of the type of adverb, i.e. consider its morphology), and 2. **Second**, comment on the English translation and whether it may be improved.

Luke 1:3 ἔδοξεν κἀμοὶ παρηκολουθηκότι ἄνωθεν πᾶσιν ἀκριβῶς καθεξῆς σοι γράψαι, κράτιστε Θεόφιλε,
  It seemed fitting for me as well, having investigated everything carefully from the beginning, to write it out for you in consecutive order, most excellent Theophilus;

---

[16] Robertson, *Short Grammar*, 203.

κἀμοί (καὶ ἐμοί) =

ἄνωθεν ("from above/the beginning") =

ἀκριβῶς ("accurately, carefully") =

καθεξῆς ("in sequence/order") =

Luke 11:40 ἄφρονες, οὐχ ὁ ποιήσας τὸ ἔξωθεν καὶ τὸ ἔσωθεν ἐποίησεν;
You foolish ones, did not He who made the outside make the inside also?

οὐχ =

ἔξωθεν ("from outside") =

καὶ =

ἔσωθεν ("from inside") =

Luke 23:53b καὶ ἔθηκεν αὐτὸν ἐν μνήματι λαξευτῷ οὗ οὐκ ἦν οὐδεὶς οὔπω κείμενος.
and laid Him in a tomb cut into the rock, where no one had ever lain.

οὗ ("where") =

οὐκ =

οὐδεὶς =

οὔπω ("not yet") =

SUGGESTED ANSWERS

Luke 1:3 ἔδοξεν κἀμοὶ παρηκολουθηκότι ἄνωθεν πᾶσιν ἀκριβῶς καθεξῆς σοι γράψαι,
κράτιστε Θεόφιλε,
*it seemed fitting for me as well, having investigated everything carefully from the
beginning, to write it out for you in consecutive order, most excellent Theophilus;*

κἀμοί (καὶ ἐμοί) = **1.** the additive καὶ "also" indicates that Luke includes himself to others
who have *also* taken up the task to write a gospel. **2.** Translation is good.

ἄνωθεν ("from above/the beginning") = **1.** means place from where, here indicating the beginning of Jesus' life. **2.** Translation is good.

ἀκριβῶς ("accurately, carefully") = **1.** adverb of manner. **2.** Translation is good.

καθεξῆς ("in sequence/order") = **1.** No specialized meaning for the adverb (which, incidentally, is formed from the genitive ending -ης), although καθεξῆς is probably

> strengthened by the preposition κατά prefixed to the adverb ἐξῆς *in the next place*. **2.** Translation is good.
>
> General Comments: In translation, we must decide what each adverbs is modifying. For example, καθεξῆς ("in sequence/order") is fronted before its verb "to write," although it is translated after this clause begins; by its position, Luke is stressing καθεξῆς. Also, an important question concerns ἀκριβῶς ("accurately, carefully"): Is it modifying Luke's investigating, or his writing it out his gospel?

> **Luke 11:40** ἄφρονες, οὐχ ὁ ποιήσας τὸ ἔξωθεν καὶ τὸ ἔσωθεν ἐποίησεν;
>
> *You foolish ones, did not He who made the outside make the inside also?*
>
> οὐχ = **1.** This negative adverb expects a positive answer in the question. **2.** Translation is adequate, since this positive expectation is conveyed.
>
> ἔξωθεν ("from outside") = **1.** adverb of place from where. The adverb functions substantivally: *the outside*. **2.** In translation and sense, the "from-where-ness" indicated by the adverb suffix –θεν is not indicated. One wonders whether these adverb forms were chosen to emphasis outwardness vs. inwardness by using such morphologically "extra" marked forms. Or, does the issue in the argumentative context actually concern "from where" one might become ritually unclean (contamination from the outside of a cup) in contrast "from where" one acts wickedly, i.e. the sinful inward heart. One must study this more in context.
>
> καί = **1.** additive καί indicates that the same person (God) made the outside and also the inside, so that humans should be concerned to clean both the inside and the outside. **2.** Translation is good.
>
> ἔσωθεν ("from inside") = **1.** adverb of place from where. The adverb functions substantivally: *the outside*. **2.** On translation, see discussion for ἔξωθεν.

> **Luke 23:53b** καὶ ἔθηκεν αὐτὸν ἐν μνήματι λαξευτῷ οὗ οὐκ ἦν οὐδεὶς οὔπω κείμενος.
>
> *and laid Him in a tomb cut into the rock, where no one had ever lain.*
>
> οὗ = **1.** adverb indicating place where; this begins a relative clause. **2.** Translation is good.
>
> οὐκ = **1.** participates with three other negative words. **2.** This is not easily translated.
>
> οὐδεὶς = **1.** participates with three other negative words. **2.** "No one" is translated fine.
>
> οὔπω = **1.** participates with three other negative words; means "not yet." **2.** The translation "ever" seems to stress the negative statement being made, but "not yet" would also work. It is difficult to represent in English the three negatives. Literally, this clause might be rendered in poor English, *where there was not no one not yet laid down.* I might suggest this translation *where not a single person was ever yet laid down.*
>
> General Comments: We must ask, why does Luke make such a strong denial? Does this help underscore the uniqueness of Jesus's death and his subsequent resurrection? Or, is Luke helping us understand the irony of Jesus dying such an ignoble death (crucifixion), yet being given such an honorable burial? The one was justified, the other not.

Complete WORKBOOK EXERCISES 22 and consult the ANSWER KEY & GUIDE as needed.

CASE IN POINT 22: SUBJUNCTIVE TENSES IN JOHN 20:31

John 20:30 Πολλὰ μὲν οὖν καὶ ἄλλα σημεῖα ἐποίησεν ὁ Ἰησοῦς ἐνώπιον τῶν μαθητῶν [αὐτοῦ], ἃ οὐκ ἔστιν γεγραμμένα ἐν τῷ βιβλίῳ τούτῳ· ³¹ ταῦτα δὲ γέγραπται ἵνα πιστεύ[σ]ητε ὅτι Ἰησοῦς ἐστιν ὁ Χριστὸς ὁ υἱὸς τοῦ θεοῦ, καὶ ἵνα πιστεύοντες ζωὴν ἔχητε ἐν τῷ ὀνόματι αὐτοῦ.
³⁰ Therefore indeed, Jesus also performed many other signs before his disciples, which are not written in this book. ³¹ However, these (signs) have been written in order that you would [come to] believe that Jesus is the Christ, the Son of God, and in order that, while believing, you would (continue to) have life in His name.

Central themes and a final statement of purpose for John's Gospel are indicated clearly in 20:30-31: Jesus' relationship with his disciples, Jesus' miraculous signs, Jesus's identity as the Christ, Jesus' relationship with God the Father as God's Son, and the goals of discipleship which include *believing* and *life*. Indeed, in 20:31 the purpose of the entire Gospel is indicated by two purpose clauses, each introduced by ἵνα *in order that*.

The first purpose is that the hearers of the gospel *would [come to] believe*. This verb, πιστεύ[σ]ητε, is in the subjunctive mood. The only dispute is whether or not it is aorist or present tense. The brackets indicate the existence of textual variation concerning the presence of the σίγμα. What is the difference in form? A σίγμα would indicate an aorist subjunctive; no σίγμα would indicate a present subjunctive. However, the aorist subjunctive reading is considered the more likely in the UBS and NA texts, although some doubt remains and so the σίγμα is placed within brackets. What is the difference in meaning? Πιστεύω in the present tense with imperfective aspect indicates *a continuation of believing*; it often signifies *believers*, i.e., *those who continue to believe*. Πιστεύω in the aorist tense with perfective aspect presents the action as a whole or complete; it often signifies converts who newly *enter into believing*. So, the variant readings of πιστεύ[σ]ητε in 20:31 reflect scribal attempts to understand the purpose of the John's Gospel: Is this purpose to encourage the hearers *to become new converts* (aorist subjunctive)? Or, is the purpose to help those who already believing *to continue to believe* (present subjunctive)?

I tend to believe the gospel of John functions both ways. One reason for this lies in the fact that there is an expressed second purpose for writing: *in order that you would (continue to) have life while believing*. Notice that ἔχητε is a present subjunctive with imperfective aspect. As such, it marks *a continued possession of life*. The word *life*, ζωὴν, is anarthrous, making it likely qualitative in meaning, since readers have already encountered the term (see CASE IN POINT 4: WHAT IS *(THE) ETERNAL LIFE?*). Also, the present tense participle πιστεύοντες probably refers to believers, those who *continue to believe*. Overall, then, we observe in 20:31 the two-fold purpose of John's gospel that represents a progression. First, the signs of the Gospel are written in order that the reader may come to faith (i.e., be converted; πιστεύω in the aorist tense with perfective aspect); and, second, and equally as important, the signs are written down in order that believers would continuously have life, the kind of life that is described in John's Gospel (see especially 17:3 and CASE IN POINT 4).

It is apparent, then, that Christians rightly direct people seeking to have faith in Christ to read John's Gospel. John's is a great gospel to help people come to faith. At the same time, the Gospel of John is directs believers to have *eternal life* now. Those who are already believers learn about *the kind of life* that is given through Jesus.

Below is a picture of the recto side of document P. Oxy. 847.[17] It contains John 2:11-22, here 2:11 at top beginning with ΑΥΤΟΥ· ΚΑΙ. The second line reads: ΤΟΝ ΟΙ ΜΑΘΗΤΑΙ ΑΥΤΟΥ· before beginning 2:12. This important manuscript is catalogued as Uncial number 0162. It dates to the 4th century. It is currently housed in the New York Metropolitan Museum of Art.

[17] Image is from Bernard Pyne Grenfell and Arthur Surridge Hunt, *The Oxyrhynchus Papyri*, vol. 6 (London: Egypt Exploration Fund, 1908), Plate VI.

CHAPTER 23

This chapter is dedicated to describe the **Greek Infinitive Formation and Uses** as well as the **Common Uses of the Accusative Case**. In the case in Point, 1 Thess 4:9-12 will illustrate several uses of the Infinitive.

VOCABULARY 23   VERBS THAT CAN TAKE AN INFINITIVE

Verbs regularly taking infinitives:		Irregular verb:	
ἄρχομαι [86]	I begin to; I am	κάθημαι [91]	I sit, am sitting
δεῖ [101]	it is necessary to	**Conjunction:**	
δύναμαι [209]	I am able to	ὥστε [83]	so that, that; therefore
θέλω [208]	I will, wish, want to	**Preposition:**	
μέλλω [109]	I am going to, am about to	πρό [47]	gen. before; in front of

After learning this vocabulary, you will know 80.2% of the words in the GNT. If able, listen to audio recordings of VOCABULARY 23 and complete the CROSSWORD PUZZLE in the WORKBOOK.

NOTES ON VOCABULARY 23:

Several of these verbs have words that have already been learned: δύναμαι (δύναμις *power, ability*); θέλω (θέλημα *will*); and κάθημαι (καθίζω *I sit*). The preposition πρό is found in numerous English words: prologue (the introduction before the main discourse) and prophet (one who speaks before hand or in front of people).

The verb ἄρχομαι is the middle voice form of the verb ἄρχω *I rule* (ἄρχων *ruler*). In the middle voice, this verb has the sense of *beginning to* do something and normally has an infinitive to complete its meaning.

Ὥστε used with an infinitive carries the logical relation of **result** (the unplanned outcome of some action as opposed to **purpose**, the intended outcome). However, when ὥστε is used with the Imperative and Indicative Moods, it often brings some argument to a summarizing conclusion and means *therefore*.

23.1 THE INFINITIVE (ἡ Ἀπαρέμφατος Ἔγκλισις)

A. **Definition:** Infinitives in English are those "verbals" (words derived from verbs) that place the preposition *to* before the verb: *to walk*, *to eat*, *to learn*, *to feel*, etc. Infinitives in Greek are sometimes translated this same way. In Greek, Infinitives are often described as **verbal nouns**, although they are more dynamic than nouns. They are **neuter in gender**, and in certain constructions will have a neuter article. See Wallace 587-611. The abbreviation for infinitives when parsing them is "N."

B. **Negation of the Infinitive:** Μή and cognates are used to negate infinitives.

C. **No Augmentation:** Infinitives are unmarked for remoteness (of time), but show verbal aspect.

D. **Infinitive Formation and Principal Parts:**

1. <u>Tenses and Voice</u>. Infinitives occur mainly in two tenses: Present and Aorist. However, Perfect and even Future Tense Infinitives also occur, but with less frequency. The Infinitive endings and approximate frequencies (based upon Tense & Voice) are presented below.

TENSE & VOICE Freq.	ENDING	TENSE & VOICE Freq.	ENDING
Present A [761]	-ειν	Perfect A [116]	-κεναι
Present M/P [239]	-εσθαι	Perfect M/P [11]	-σθαι
Aorist A [958]	-σαι	Future A [0]	-σειν
Aorist M [112]	-σασθαι	Future M [5]	-σεσθαι[1]
Aorist P [171]	-θῆναι	Future P [0]	-θήσεσθαι

<u>There are several important things to notice about these endings:</u>
   a. All the Infinitive endings show the typical tense indicators: Aorist Active (-σα), Perfect Active (-κ), Perfect Middle/Passive (no coupling vowel), Future Active (-σ), and, Aorist/Future Passive (-θη).
   b. The first column of endings above is the most important to learn: The Present and Aorist Infinitives (since these are the most common).
   c. Middle-Formed verbs, as would be expected, use the Middle/Passive, or Middle or Passive Infinitive Endings.
   d. Finally, in reality the actual frequency of each specific Aorist Tense form may be less, since the 2nd Aorist verbs will use the Present Infinitive Endings. For example, I was able to count only 35 Aorist Middle endings (–σασθαι).

---

[1] Four of these are the future infinitive form ἔσεσθαι from εἰμί.

2. <u>Infinitives and Principal Parts</u>. The Infinitive Endings above are placed upon the appropriate verb Principal Part:

PRINCIPAL PART	TENSE VOICE	ENDINGS	REGULAR VERB πιστεύω	2ND AORIST VERB λέγω/εἶπον
1ST	PRESENT A	-ειν	πιστεύειν	λέγειν
	PRESENT M/P	-εσθαι	πιστεύεσθαι	λέγεσθαι
2ND	FUTURE A	-σειν	πιστεύσειν	ἐρεῖν
	FUTURE M	-σεσθαι	πιστεύσεσθαι	ἐρεῖσθαι
3RD	AORIST A	-σαι	πιστεύσαι	εἰπεῖν*
	AORIST M	-σασθαι	πιστεύσασθαι	εἰπέσθαι*
4TH	PERFECT A	-κεναι	πεπιστευκέναι	εἰρηκέναι
5TH	PERFECT M/P	-σθαι	πεπιστεῦσθαι	εἰρῆσθαι
6TH	AORIST P	-θηναι	πιστευθῆναι	ἐρρεθῆναι

<u>Notice the following</u>:
a. There are *no augments* in the Aorist Infinitives.
b. Reduplication persists in Perfect infinitives, as in other non-Indicative Moods.
c. 2nd Aorist Verbs (such as λέγω above) use the Present Infinitive endings (*).

3. <u>Εἰμί</u>. The Present Infinitive of εἰμί is εἶναι. The Future Infinitive is ἔσεσθαι.

4. <u>Formation of Ἄλφα Contract and Ὁ μικρόν Contract Verbs</u>. Ἄλφα and ὁ μικρόν Contract Verbs have unusual looking contracted Present Active Infinitive Endings.

PRESENT ACTIVE INFINITIVE
ἀγαπάω → ἀγαπᾶν
σταυρόω → σταυροῦν

These forms are difficult to derive from –ειν. However, the reason for them is that the Present Active Infinitive Ending –ειν is itself a contraction:

ε + εν → –εεν → –ειν

So, the ἄλφα or ὁ μικρόν contract vowel combines with each ἒ ψιλόν individually. Thus, the ἰῶτα does not stay (as it typically does in contractions). Here is the progression of contraction for the contraction:

	Ἄλφα CONTRACTION	**Ὁ μικρόν CONTRACTION**
Step 1:	–ά + ε + εν → –ά + εν	–ό + ε + εν → –οῦ + εν
Step 2:	–ά + εν → –ᾶν	–οῦ + εν → –οῦν

E. **Verbal Aspect in Infinitives:** Like participles, the aspectual significance of the verbal tense is retained. The choice to use a Present, Perfect, or Aorist Tense infinitive conveys **aspectual significance**.

1. <u>Present Tense</u>. Present Tense infinitives convey an imperfective aspect (action in progress or incomplete); thus Present Tense infinitives convey **ongoing** or **attempted action.**

2. <u>Aorist Tense</u>. Aorist Tense infinitives convey a perfective aspect (seen as a whole, complete or completed); thus Aorist Tense infinitives convey the **action viewed as a whole**.

3. <u>Perfect Tense</u>. Perfect Tense infinitives convey a stative/resultative aspect (complex action often with resultant effects).

4. <u>Future Tense</u>. Future Tense infinitives are very rare in the GNT and express expectation.

F. **Subjects of Infinitives:**

1. <u>Accusative Subject</u>. When Infinitives are used to form subordinate clauses, an accusative case substantive will normally be the subject, if a subject needs to be expressed.

> **Acts 20:1** Μετὰ δὲ τὸ παύσασθαι <u>τὸν θόρυβον</u>, ...
> *Now after <u>the uproar</u> stopped, ...*

2. <u>Implied Unexpressed Subject</u>. However, the subject of the infinitive may not be expressed and thus must be inferred from the context.

> **Matt 2:13c** μέλλει γὰρ Ἡρῴδης ζητεῖν τὸ παιδίον <u>τοῦ ἀπολέσαι αὐτό</u>.
> *For Herod is about to seek the child <u>in order to destroy him</u>.*

Here, the subject of the infinitive <u>*to destroy*</u> is unexpressed, but the agent behind the action is clearly Herod. But this example also raises a question–how does one know whether an accusative substantive with an infinitive is a subject or object?

3. <u>Differentiating Subject and Object</u>. This grammatical phenomenon may create a situation where an infinitive subordinate clause may have two accusative case nouns, one the subject of the infinitive and the other the direct object. However, the subject will occur before the direct object:

> **Matt 6:8** οἶδεν γὰρ ὁ πατὴρ ὑμῶν ὧν χρείαν ἔχετε πρὸ τοῦ <u>ὑμᾶς</u> αἰτῆσαι <u>αὐτόν</u>.
> *For your Father knows which need you have before <u>you</u> ask <u>him</u>.*

In this next example, interpreters differ in their determination of which accusative case word is the subject and which is the object, supplying contextual evidence. The first translation, however, is preferred. Why? The position of the accusatives.

Phil 1:7b διὰ τὸ ἔχειν <u>με</u> ἐν τῇ καρδίᾳ <u>ὑμᾶς</u>
    because <u>I</u> have <u>you</u> in the heart
OR, *because <u>you</u> have <u>me</u> in the heart*

4. <u>Nominative Subjects and Predicates</u>. The only exception to having an accusative case subject is when the subject of the infinitive clause is expressed as the same as the subject of the main clause, in which case the nominative case is used:

Rom 9:3a ηὐχόμην γὰρ ἀνάθεμα εἶναι <u>αὐτὸς ἐγὼ</u> ἀπὸ τοῦ Χριστοῦ...
    For I could wish that <u>I myself</u> would be accursed from Christ...

1 Cor 14:37 Εἴ τις δοκεῖ <u>προφήτης</u> εἶναι ἢ <u>πνευματικός</u>....
    If someone thinks that he is <u>a prophet</u> or <u>spiritual</u>...

Luke 15:19a οὐκέτι εἰμὶ ἄξιος κληθῆναι <u>υἱός</u> σου
    I am no longer worthy to be called your <u>son</u>.

23.2 COMPLEMENTARY INFINITIVES

A. **Completing the Meaning of Verbs:** As in English, Greek infinitives may be used to complete the meaning of certain verbs, like those found in this chapter's vocabulary. Additional verbs could be added, like βούλομαι *I want, intend* (see §23.5.D.1.b below). See Wallace 598-99. When seeing one of these verbs, one should regularly look for an infinitive, which, however, may or may not always immediately follow the main verb. Here are several examples:

John 21:23b θέλω <u>μένειν</u>... *I want <u>to remain</u>...*

John 18:32b ἤμελλεν <u>ἀποθνήσκειν</u>. *He was about <u>to die</u>.*

John 7:35b μέλλει <u>πορεύεσθαι</u> καὶ <u>διδάσκειν</u> *He is about <u>to come</u> and <u>to teach</u>*

Luke 12:12b δεῖ <u>εἰπεῖν</u> *it is necessary <u>to say</u>*

John 15:5b οὐ δύνασθε <u>ποιεῖν</u> οὐδέν *you are not able <u>to do</u> a single thing*

John 12:39a οὐκ ἀδύναντο <u>πιστεύειν</u> *they were not able <u>to believe</u>*

Luke 4:21a ἤρξατο δὲ <u>λέγειν</u> πρὸς αὐτούς... *And he began <u>to say</u> to them...*

B. **Some Nouns or Adjectives will on occasion take an infinitive.** For example, ἐξουσία *authority*, ἱκανός,-ά,-όν *able, sufficient*, καλός,-ά,-όν *good*, ἄξιος,-α,-ον *worthy*. Wallace (607) will categorize these as epexegetical infinitives that explain or clarify the head word.

> **Luke 3:16b** οὐκ εἰμὶ ἱκανὸς <u>λῦσαι</u> τὸν ἱμάντα τῶν ὑποδημάτων αὐτοῦ.
> *I am not sufficient <u>to untie</u> the strap of his shoes.*

> **1 Cor 9:4** μὴ οὐκ ἔχομεν ἐξουσίαν <u>φαγεῖν</u> καὶ <u>πεῖν</u>;
> *It's not that we don't have authority <u>to eat</u> and <u>to drink</u>, is it?*

23.3 SUBSTANTIVAL INFINITIVES

This use is not common. Here the Greek Infinitive acts like a neuter noun and may often simply be translated as *to do, to act, to be* or as a gerund, *the doing, the acting* etc. It usually functions as a subject or direct object. See Wallace 600-603. For example,

> **Phil 1:21** ἐμοὶ γὰρ <u>τὸ ζῆν</u> Χριστὸς καὶ <u>τὸ ἀποθανεῖν</u> κέρδος.
> *For for me <u>to live</u> is Christ and <u>to die</u> is gain.*

Notice the emphatic personal pronoun form ἐμοί.

> **Rom 13:8a** Μηδενὶ μηδὲν ὀφείλετε εἰ μὴ <u>τὸ ἀλλήλους ἀγαπᾶν</u>·
> *Owe nothing to anyone, except <u>to continue loving</u> one another.*

Notice the negative emphasis with Μηδενὶ μηδὲν and the exceptive clause with εἰ μή.

> **Phil 2:13** θεὸς γάρ ἐστιν ὁ ἐνεργῶν ἐν ὑμῖν καὶ <u>τὸ θέλειν</u> καὶ <u>τὸ ἐνεργεῖν</u> ὑπὲρ τῆς εὐδοκίας.
> *For God is the One that is enabling among you both <u>the willing</u> and <u>the enabling</u> for what is well pleasing.*

23.4 INFINITIVES OF INDIRECT DISCOURSE, CONTENT, AND EPEXEGETICAL STATEMENTS

A. **Indirect Discourse:** The infinitive can function to indicate indirect discourse with verbs of *saying*. See Wallace 603-605. Here are some examples.

> **John 4:40** ὡς οὖν ἦλθον πρὸς αὐτὸν οἱ Σαμαρῖται, <u>ἠρώτων</u> αὐτὸν <u>μεῖναι</u> παρ' αὐτοῖς· καὶ ἔμεινεν ἐκεῖ δύο ἡμέρας.
> *So when the Samaritans came to Jesus, <u>they were asking</u> Him <u>to stay</u> with them; and He stayed there two days.*

Rom 12:1 Παρακαλῶ οὖν ὑμᾶς, ἀδελφοί, διὰ τῶν οἰκτιρμῶν τοῦ θεοῦ <u>παραστῆσαι</u> τὰ σώματα ὑμῶν θυσίαν ζῶσαν ἁγίαν εὐάρεστον τῷ θεῷ, τὴν λογικὴν λατρείαν ὑμῶν·

Therefore <u>I urge</u> you, brethren, by the mercies of God <u>to present</u> your bodies a living, holy sacrifice, acceptable to God, which is your reasonable service of worship.

B. **Content Clauses:** The infinitive can be used to provide the actual content of knowing, aspirational or emotive verbs or words. This use is very similar to indirect discourse, except that it does not involve verbs of *saying*.

Matt 3:9 καὶ μὴ <u>δόξητε λέγειν</u> ἐν ἑαυτοῖς· πατέρα ἔχομεν τὸν Ἀβραάμ.

and do not <u>suppose that you can say</u> to yourselves, 'We have Abraham for our father.'

Phil 2:19a Ἐλπίζω δὲ ἐν κυρίῳ Ἰησοῦ Τιμόθεον ταχέως <u>πέμψαι</u> ὑμῖν...

Moreover, <u>I am hoping</u> in the Lord Jesus quickly <u>to send</u> Timothy to you...

C. **Epexegetical Statements:** Sometimes demonstrative pronouns (*this*, or *that*) will function as forward pointing devices, "serving up" the delivered content. Wallace calls this usage appositional (606-7); a major clue to identification is supplying in English, *namely*, or *that is*.

Jas 1:27 θρησκεία καθαρὰ καὶ ἀμίαντος παρὰ τῷ θεῷ καὶ πατρὶ <u>αὕτη</u> ἐστίν, <u>ἐπισκέπτεσθαι</u> ὀρφανοὺς καὶ χήρας ἐν τῇ θλίψει αὐτῶν, ἄσπιλον ἑαυτὸν <u>τηρεῖν</u> ἀπὸ τοῦ κόσμου.

Pure and undefiled religion before the God and Father is <u>this</u>, [namely],
<u>to visit</u> orphans and widows in their distress,
<u>to keep</u> oneself spotless from the world.

D. **Implied Infinitive of Εἰμί (Εἶναι) with Accusative Subjects and Accusative Participles:** Grammarians will often describe a use of the accusative case participle and accusative case subject (hence, a double accusative situation) as if this was indirect discourse or a content clause; hence, this would be yet another function of the participle.[2] (This view was briefly presented in §19.6.D.2.) For example consider the content clause of the verb ἰδὼν *seeing* in Mark 11:13a:

Mark 11:13a καὶ ἰδὼν <u>συκῆν</u> ἀπὸ μακρόθεν <u>ἔχουσαν</u> φύλλα ἦλθεν...

and, seeing <u>a fig tree</u> from far away <u>having</u> leaves, he went...

---

[2] For example, K. L. McKay, *A New Syntax of the Verb in New Testament Greek: An Aspectual Approach*, Studies in Biblical Greek 5 (New York: Peter Lang, 1994), §12.5 (p. 105). He treats these instances involving participles as indirect statements: Matt 1:18; Luke 8:46; Acts 7:12; 8:23; 9:12; 17:16; 24:10; 2 Cor 8:22; 12:2; Heb 13:23.

What is seen (i.e., the content) is *a fig tree* (συκῆν) *having* (ἔχουσαν) leaves. This sense could have been expressed with ὅτι and the indicative mood (imperfect tense) or with an infinitive.

> ἰδὼν ὅτι συκῆ ... εἶχεν...
> ἰδὼν συκῆν ... ἔχειν ...

However, it may be that such double accusative constructions with an accusative participle imply an infinitive εἶναι *to be*.

Mark 11:13a καὶ ἰδὼν συκῆν ἀπὸ μακρόθεν [εἶναι] ἔχουσαν φύλλα ἦλθεν...
> *and, seeing a fig tree from far away [to be] having leaves, he went...*

One evidence for an implied εἶναι is that the accusative participle is often the second of two accusatives; the first is a substantive that is then followed by the participle functioning like periphrastic participle with implied εἶναι. (See §25.4 PERIPHRASTIC PARTICIPLES WITH NON-INDICATIVE MOODS). Consider the following examples, which could be translated with a "that" to help convey the content or indirect discourse and implied periphrastic construction.

2 Cor 8:22b τὸν ἀδελφὸν ἡμῶν ὃν ἐδοκιμάσαμεν ἐν πολλοῖς πολλάκις σπουδαῖον ὄντα
> *...our brother whom we approved often in many ways [to be] being eager.*
> Or, *...our brother whom we approved often in many ways that [he was] being eager.*

Acts 7:12 ἀκούσας δὲ Ἰακὼβ ὄντα σιτία εἰς Αἴγυπτον ἐξαπέστειλεν τοὺς πατέρας ἡμῶν πρῶτον.
> *But Jacob, having heard grain [to be] being in Egypt, sent out first our fathers.*
> Or, *But Jacob, having heard that [there was] grain being in Egypt, sent out first our fathers.*

Luke 8:46b ἐγὼ γὰρ ἔγνων δύναμιν ἐξεληλυθυῖαν ἀπ' ἐμοῦ.
> *for I myself knew power [to be] having gone out from me.*
> Or, *for I myself knew that power [was/had] gone out from me.*

John 17:13b ...ἵνα ἔχωσιν τὴν χαρὰν τὴν ἐμὴν πεπληρωμένην ἐν ἑαυτοῖς.
> *...in order that they would have my joy [to be] fulfilled among themselves.*
> Or, *...in order that they would have that my joy [is] fulfilled among themselves.*

Acts 9:12a καὶ εἶδεν ἄνδρα ... εἰσελθόντα καὶ ἐπιθέντα αὐτῷ [τὰς] χεῖρας
> *and I saw a man ... [to be] coming and setting hands upon him*
> Or, *and I saw that a man ... [was] coming and setting hands upon him*

2 Cor 12:2 οἶδα ἄνθρωπον ἐν Χριστῷ ... ἁρπαγέντα...ἕως τρίτου οὐρανοῦ.
> *I know a person in Christ ... [to be] caught up ... up to the third heaven.*
> Or, *I know that a person in Christ ... [was] caught up ... up to the third heaven.*

These content constructions would then entail periphrastic participles with the form of εἰμί as infinitive being implied. Alternatively, some of these participles may be understood as attributive modifiers.

F. **Imperatival Infinitives (rare):** There is a use of the Infinitive in which it functions like a command form. Moulton helpfully summarizes, "The infinitive for imperative was familiar in Greek, especially in laws and in maxims."[3] There may only be three examples in the NT (Wallace 608).

> **Rom 12:15** χαίρειν μετὰ χαιρόντων, κλαίειν μετὰ κλαιόντων.
> _Rejoice_ with the ones that are rejoicing, _weep_ with the ones that are weeping.

See also Phil 3:16 and 2 Thess 3:14; it is important to note that each of these contexts has commands preceding these infinitives; so the context helps to identify the sense.

23.5 ADVERBIAL INFINITIVES

A. **To Form Adverbial Subordinate Clauses:** This use of the Greek infinitive will be most unfamiliar to English speakers. The Greek infinitive is used in several types of subordinate clauses, such as substantiation, causation, purpose, time, and result. See Wallace 590-98. These subordinate constructions are formed in three ways treated below: B. Articular and Anarthrous Infinitives, C. Preposition Constructions, and D. Conjunction Construction with ὥστε.

B. **Articular and Anarthrous Infinitives:** The infinitive alone, anarthrous or articular, can be found in contexts where the adverbial senses of purpose and (much less commonly) result are present. Inherently, however, the infinitive is unmarked for purpose or result. Articular infinitives within a context of **purpose** occur 33 times and with a sense of **result** only 2-5 times. If present, the article will be genitive neuter singular (τοῦ). The anarthrous infinitive is found in contexts of specific or general **purpose** (253 times) and of **result** (12 times).[4] See Wallace 590-94.

1. Purpose. _in order that_

    a. _articular infinitive_ (33 times)

> **Matt 11:1b** μετέβη ἐκεῖθεν <u>τοῦ διδάσκειν καὶ κηρύσσειν</u> ἐν ταῖς πόλεσιν αὐτῶν.
> _He went from there (in order) to teach and preach in their cities._

> **Acts 18:10a** διότι ἐγώ εἰμι μετὰ σοῦ καὶ οὐδεὶς ἐπιθήσεταί σοι <u>τοῦ κακῶσαί</u> σε,
> _For I am with you and no one will touch you in order to harm you,_

---

[3] James Hope Moulton, _A Grammar of New Testament Greek: Prolegomena_ (Edinburgh: T&T Clark, 1967), 179.

[4] Clyde W. Votaw, "The Use of the Infinitive in Biblical Greek" (Ph.D. diss., The University of Chicago, 1896), 10-13, 4-849. The number of specific or general purpose infinitives combines Votaw's "Distinct and Specific" with "Modified and General" categories.

b. *anarthrous infinitive* (253 times).

> **Mark 4:9b** ὃς ἔχει ὦτα <u>ἀκούειν</u> ἀκουέτω.
> *(The one) who has ears (in order) <u>to hear</u>, let him hear.*

> **John 1:33a** ὁ πέμψας με <u>βαπτίζειν</u> ἐν ὕδατι
> *the one that sent me <u>(in order) to baptize</u> with water*

> **Acts 18:27b** βουλομένου δὲ αὐτοῦ <u>διελθεῖν</u> εἰς τὴν Ἀχαΐαν...
> *Moreover, as he was wanting (in order) <u>to pass through</u> into Achaia...*

Notice with Acts 18:27b, the sense of purpose derives from the intentionality of the verb (here βουλομένου in the genitive absolute construction) and the inifnitive may be understood as complementary.

2. <u>Result</u>. *so that* or *with the result that*

a. *articular infinitive* (2-5 times; see also Acts 10:47; cf. Matt 21:32; Acts 7:19; 18:10).

> **Rom 7:3b** ἐὰν δὲ ἀποθάνῃ ὁ ἀνήρ, ἐλευθέρα ἐστὶν ἀπὸ τοῦ νόμου, <u>τοῦ μὴ εἶναι</u> αὐτὴν μοιχαλίδα γενομένην ἀνδρὶ ἑτέρῳ.
>
> *But if the husband dies, she is free from the law, <u>with the result that</u> she is <u>not</u> an adulteress, if marrying another man.*

b. *anarthrous infinitive* (12 times).

> **Rev 5:5b** ἰδοὺ ἐνίκησεν ὁ λέων ὁ ἐκ τῆς φυλῆς Ἰούδα, ἡ ῥίζα Δαυίδ, <u>ἀνοῖξαι</u> τὸ βιβλίον καὶ τὰς ἑπτὰ σφραγῖδας αὐτοῦ.
>
> *Behold the Lion from the tribe of Judah, the Root of David, has conquered, <u>with the result that</u> he may open the book and its seven seals.*

C. **Preposition Constructions:** Certain prepositions may be used with infinitives to begin various adverbial clauses (approx. 200 times).[5] These are εἰς[72], ἐν[55], διά[32], μετά[15], πρός[12], πρό[9], ἀντί[1], ἕνεκεν[1], ἐκ[1], and ἕως[1]. The specific grammatical construction has these four components, usually in this order:

preposition	+	article	+ infinitive	+ accusative case subject
1st		2nd	3rd or 4th	3rd or 4th

---

[5] The frequencies are from Votaw, "The Use of the Infinitive," 20.

For example, consider this clause:

διὰ τὸ αὐτὸν πιστεύειν   Notice that the accusative case is used for the subject of the
because he believes   infinitive. Also, prepositions will carry slightly different
                                         meanings than what you may be used to by now.

The first two components (preposition and article) are always in this order. The infinitive and accusative case subject can alternate positions. Modifiers, such as μή (*not*), come after the article. This construction is hardest to translate, because the infinitive must be translated like a regular verb (*he believes*) and not like an infinitive (*to believe*). Below are the main uses.

1. <u>Purpose</u>. εἰς (common; 72 times) and πρός (rare; 12 times) are both used to mean *in order that*. See Wallace 590-92. In a few instances, εἰς may indicate result (e.g. Rom 1:20).

   2 Thess 2:10b <u>εἰς τὸ σωθῆναι αὐτούς.</u> <u>*in order that*</u> *they would be saved.*

   Luke 18:1 ἔλεγεν παραβολὴν αὐτοῖς <u>πρὸς τὸ δεῖν πάντοτε προσεύχεσθαι</u> αὐτούς
   He was speaking a parable to them <u>(in order) that it was necessary always</u> for them to pray. . . . [this is like indirect discourse]

2. <u>Substantiation</u>. The preposition διά means *because* (somewhat common; 32 times). See Wallace 596-97.

   Luke 2:4c <u>διὰ τὸ εἶναι αὐτὸν</u> ἐξ οἴκου καὶ πατριᾶς Δαυίδ,
   <u>*because he was*</u> *from the house and family of David,*

3. <u>Temporal</u>. A temporal meaning is conveyed by the following prepositions. See Wallace 594-96.

   a. ἐν *while* (most common; 55 times)

   Luke 9:29 καὶ ἐγένετο <u>ἐν τῷ προσεύχεσθαι αὐτόν.</u> . . . .
   And it happened <u>while he was praying</u>. . . .

   b. μετά *after* (less common; 15 times)

   Matt 26:32 <u>μετὰ δὲ τὸ ἐγερθῆναί με</u> προάξω ὑμᾶς εἰς τὴν Γαλιλαίαν.
   And <u>after I am raised</u>, I will go before you into Galilee.

   c. πρό *before* (somewhat rare; 9 times)

Gal 3:23b <u>Πρὸ τοῦ δὲ ἐλθεῖν τὴν πίστιν</u> ὑπὸ νόμον ἐφρουρούμεθα
And <u>before faith came</u>, we were being kept under the law

D. Conjunction Construction: With ὥστε, the infinitive and accusative case subject is mainly used to express **result,** but also rarely **purpose** and **description**.

1. <u>Result</u>.

1 Pet 1:21b <u>ὥστε</u> τὴν πίστιν ὑμῶν καὶ ἐλπίδα εἶναι εἰς θεόν.
<u>so that</u> our faith and hope are in God.

2. <u>Purpose</u>.

Luke 4:29 καὶ ἀναστάντες ἐξέβαλον αὐτὸν ἔξω τῆς πόλεως καὶ ἤγαγον αὐτὸν ἕως ὀφρύος τοῦ ὄρους ἐφ᾽ οὗ ἡ πόλις ᾠκοδόμητο αὐτῶν <u>ὥστε κατακρημνίσαι αὐτόν·</u>
And standing, they cast him outside the city and led him as far as the edge of the mountain upon which their city had been built <u>in order to</u> <u>cast</u> him <u>down</u>.

It is interesting that certain manuscripts/scribes (namely, A C Ψ) have changed the ὥστε construction into a εἰς τό... purpose construction. Another example often provided is Matt 10:1.

Matt 10:1 Καὶ προσκαλεσάμενος τοὺς δώδεκα μαθητὰς αὐτοῦ ἔδωκεν αὐτοῖς ἐξουσίαν πνευμάτων ἀκαθάρτων <u>ὥστε ἐκβάλλειν</u> αὐτὰ καὶ <u>θεραπεύειν</u> πᾶσαν νόσον καὶ πᾶσαν μαλακίαν.

And after calling his twelve disciples, he gave to them authority over unclean spirits, <u>in order to</u> <u>cast</u> them out and <u>to heal</u> every disease and every weakness.

In this latter example, it is conceivable that Matthew provides a "narrative accounting," which would be more resultative-consequential rather than a "motivational description" of Jesus' intentions, which would be more purposive.

3. <u>Description</u>. Takamitsu Muroaka has argued that ὥστε may carry a descriptive sense, which corresponds with its derivation from ὡς to indicate comparison or manner.[6] Only a few examples are found in the GNT. Often this occurs with correlative pronouns or adverbs. John 3:16 is considered an example of this with the adverb of manner οὕτως:

---

[6] Takamitsu Muraoka, "Purpose or Result: Ὥστε in Biblical Greek," *Novum Testamentum* 15.3 (1973): 205–19. He is supported by Trent Rogers, "The Functions of Ὥστε in the New Testament," *Annali Di Storia Dell'esegesi* 30.2 (2013): 317–31 at 320.

John 3:16 <u>οὕτως</u> γὰρ ἠγάπησεν ὁ θεὸς τὸν κόσμον, <u>ὥστε</u> τὸν υἱὸν τὸν μονογενῆ ἔδωκεν, ἵνα πᾶς ὁ πιστεύων εἰς αὐτὸν μὴ ἀπόληται ἀλλ᾽ ἔχῃ ζωὴν αἰώνιον.

For God loved the world <u>in this way</u>: <u>that</u> he gave his unique son, in order that everyone that believes in him would not perish, but would have eternal life.

4. Ὥστε with Indicative or Imperative Verbs to Indicate a Summative Conclusion. It is important to point out that ὥστε may also be used with the Indicative and Imperative Moods to draw an argument to a conclusion, and in this sense to carry a inferential conclusion. Stephen Levinsohn recently has studied logical connectors used in the NT and has concluded that ὥστε marks +conclusion: "When *hoste* introduces an independent clause or sentence, it constrains it to be interpreted as the conclusion of a section or sub-section (+Conclusion)."[7] Thus, from a discourse perspective, ὥστε concludes a larger argument; it focalizes content by way of generalizing or summarizing the preceding argument as a conclusion. Just how far backwards the conclusion reaches must be determined in context.[8]

Mark 2:28 <u>ὥστε</u> κύριός ἐστιν ὁ υἱὸς τοῦ ἀνθρώπου καὶ τοῦ σαββάτου.

<u>Therefore</u> the son of man is Lord even of the Sabbath.

CHECK POINT 23.1-5 INFINITIVES

Given the infinitives in the following verses with a woodenly literal translation, **first**, parse them, **second**, identify the particular use (complementary, substantival, indirect discourse/content, epexegetical, or adverbial) with an semantic relationship, and then, **third**, retranslate the infinitive portion trying also to represent the verbal aspect of the infinitive.

Luke 12:5b φοβήθητε τὸν μετὰ τὸ <u>ἀποκτεῖναι</u> ἔχοντα ἐξουσίαν <u>ἐμβαλεῖν</u> εἰς τὴν γέενναν.

Fear the One, after <u>to kill</u>, having authority <u>to cast</u> into Gehenna.

ἀποκτεῖναι =

ἐμβαλεῖν =

Luke 20:20 Καὶ παρατηρήσαντες ἀπέστειλαν ἐγκαθέτους ὑποκρινομένους ἑαυτοὺς δικαίους <u>εἶναι</u>, ἵνα ἐπιλάβωνται αὐτοῦ λόγου, ὥστε <u>παραδοῦναι</u> αὐτὸν τῇ ἀρχῇ καὶ τῇ ἐξουσίᾳ τοῦ ἡγεμόνος.

And watching [him] closely, they sent spies pretending themselves <u>to be</u> righteous, in

---

[7] Stephen H. Levinsohn "'Therefore' or 'Wherefore': What's the Difference?" (presented at the SBL Greek Language and Linguistics Section, San Francisco, CA, 2011), as stated in the abstract.

[8] For my study of this use of ὥστε in 1 Corinthians, see my "Paul's Prophesying Isa 28:11 in Context: The Signs of Unbelievers and Believers in 1 Corinthians 14," in *Kingdom Rhetoric: New Testament Explorations in Honor of Ben Witherington III*, ed. T. Michael W. Halcomb (Eugene, OR: Wipf & Stock, 2013), 133–69 at 153-57.

> *order that the would catch his speech, so that to hand over him to the rule and authority of the governor.*

εἶναι =

παραδοῦναι =

---

1 Cor 14:39 Ὥστε, ἀδελφοί [μου], ζηλοῦτε τὸ προφητεύειν, καὶ τὸ λαλεῖν μὴ κωλύετε γλώσσαις·

> *So then, my brothers, seek to prophesy, and to speak do not hinder with tongues.*

προφητεύειν =

λαλεῖν =

Acts 14:1 Ἐγένετο δὲ ἐν Ἰκονίῳ … εἰσελθεῖν αὐτοὺς εἰς τὴν συναγωγὴν τῶν Ἰουδαίων καὶ λαλῆσαι οὕτως ὥστε πιστεῦσαι Ἰουδαίων τε καὶ Ἑλλήνων πολὺ πλῆθος.

> *And it happened in Iconia … to enter them into the synagogue of the Jews and to speak in a manner so that to believe a great multitude both of Jews and Greeks.*

εἰσελθεῖν =

λαλῆσαι =

πιστεῦσαι =

SUGGESTED ANSWERS

Luke 12:5b φοβήθητε τὸν μετὰ τὸ ἀποκτεῖναι ἔχοντα ἐξουσίαν ἐμβαλεῖν εἰς τὴν γέενναν.

> *Fear the One, after to kill, having authority to cast into Gehenna.*

ἀποκτεῖναι = **1.** AAN; **2.** adverbial preposition construction with μετά, temporal; **3.** better translation: "after killing"

ἐμβαλεῖν = **1.** AAN; **2.** epexegetical with ἐξουσίαν; **3.** better translation: the same.

Luke 20:20 Καὶ παρατηρήσαντες ἀπέστειλαν ἐγκαθέτους ὑποκρινομένους ἑαυτοὺς δικαίους εἶναι, ἵνα ἐπιλάβωνται αὐτοῦ λόγου, ὥστε παραδοῦναι αὐτὸν τῇ ἀρχῇ καὶ τῇ ἐξουσίᾳ τοῦ ἡγεμόνος.

> *And watching [him] closely, they sent spies pretending themselves to be righteous, in order that the would catch his speech, so that to hand over him to the rule and authority of the governor.*

εἶναι = **1.** PAN; **2.** content clause with ὑποκρινομένους *pretending*; **3.** better translation: "pretending that they themselves were righteous"

> παραδοῦναι = **1.** AAN; **2.** conjunction construction with ὥστε, purpose or possibly result-consequence; **3.** better translation: "in order to hand him over" (purpose); "so that they would hand him over" (result).

> **1 Cor 14:39** Ὥστε, ἀδελφοί [μου], ζηλοῦτε τὸ προφητεύειν, καὶ τὸ λαλεῖν μὴ κωλύετε γλώσσαις·
> *So then, my brothers, seek <u>to prophesy</u>, and <u>to speak</u> do not hinder with tongues.*
> προφητεύειν = **1.** PAN; **2.** substantival; **3.** better translation: "seek (to be) prophesying"
> λαλεῖν = **1.** PAN; **2.** substantival; **3.** better translation: "do not hinder (to be) speaking"

> **Acts 14:1** Ἐγένετο δὲ ἐν Ἰκονίῳ ... <u>εἰσελθεῖν</u> αὐτοὺς εἰς τὴν συναγωγὴν τῶν Ἰουδαίων καὶ λαλῆσαι οὕτως ὥστε πιστεῦσαι Ἰουδαίων τε καὶ Ἑλλήνων πολὺ πλῆθος.
> *And it happened in Iconia … <u>to enter</u> them into the synagogue of the Jews and <u>to speak</u> in a manner so that <u>to believe</u> a great multitude both of Jews and Greeks.*
> εἰσελθεῖν = **1.** AAN; **2.** substantival with Ἐγένετο or perhaps better the "content" of what happened; **3.** better translation: "And it happened that they entered into the synagogue of the Jews and spoke in a manner...."
> λαλῆσαι = **1.** AAN; **2.** same as above; **3.** better translation: see above.
> πιστεῦσαι = **1.** AAN; **2.** conjunction construction with ὥστε, result or possibly descriptive; **3.** better translation: "so that a great multitude believed..."

23.6 SPECIAL USES OF THE ACCUSATIVE CASE

A. **Common Uses of the Accusative Case:** So far, you have learned these common uses:

1. <u>Direct Object of the Verb</u>, i.e. what is transferred or created by the action of the verb.
2. <u>Adverbial and Adjectival Uses</u>, with accusative substantives found as objects of prepositions in prepositional phrases and neuter accusative adjective forms functioning as adverbs.
3. <u>Subjects of Infinitives</u>, as has been discussed above.

The special uses described below are extensions of these three uses.

B. **Double Accusatives and Cognate Accusatives:**

1. <u>Definition</u>. Not uncommonly, you will observe that some verbs will sometimes or even regularly take two object complements in the accusative case. Strikingly, too, you may observe a verb that will take a cognate accusative direct object, i.e. an object made from the same verbal root. Consider these examples of sentences that contain two accusative objects and then finally an example that contains cognate accusatives.

> **1 Cor 3:2a** <u>γάλα</u> <u>ὑμᾶς</u> ἐπότισα... *I gave <u>you</u> <u>milk</u> to drink...*

Matt 4:19b ποιήσω <u>ὑμᾶς</u> <u>ἁλιεῖς</u> ἀνθρώπων. *I will make <u>you fishers</u> of people.*

John 14:26 τὸ πνεῦμα τὸ ἅγιον ... <u>ὑμᾶς</u> διδάξει <u>πάντα</u> καὶ ὑπομνήσει <u>ὑμᾶς</u> <u>πάντα</u> ἃ εἶπον ὑμῖν [ἐγώ].
The Holy Spirit ... will teach <u>you</u> <u>all things</u> and will remind <u>you</u> of <u>all things</u> which I [myself] said to you.

1 Tim 6:12a <u>ἀγωνίζου</u> τὸν καλὸν <u>ἀγῶνα</u> ... <u>ὡμολόγησας</u> τὴν καλὴν <u>ὁμολογίαν</u>...
<u>fight</u> the good <u>fight</u>... you <u>confessed</u> the good <u>confession</u>...

2. <u>Types of Double Objects</u>. Wallace (181-89) distinguishes two types of double accusative constructions, which can be further supplemented by another from Smyth (§§1619-33).

   a. *Personal/Impersonal*. The first type of object classification entails persons and things, with the person being the object *affected* and the thing being the object *effected*, i.e. produced or construed in the verb. In the examples above, *milk* and *things* are impersonal objects.

   b. *Predicate Complement*. The second classification involves an object and complement relation in which "[t]he direct object usually combines with the verb to form a new verbal idea that has another accusative (the complement) as its object" (Wallace 183). Sometimes the complement is further marked off with a ὡς. Otherwise, the object, in distinction from the complement, is often the pronoun, or articular, or a proper name. "Verbs meaning *to appoint, call, choose, consider, make, name, show*, and the like, may take a second accusative as a predicate [complement] to the direct object" (Smyth §1613). To help identify the predicate complement, one may add the infinitive *to be* or *to become* in the double accusative construction. In Matt 4:19b, the *fishers* is the predicate compliment.

   Matt 4:19b ποιήσω <u>ὑμᾶς</u> <u>ἁλιεῖς</u> ἀνθρώπων.
   I will make <u>you</u> [to become] <u>fishers</u> of people.

   c. *Internal/External*. Another criterion, regardless of person or object, is to consider Smyth's classical grammatical distinction (§1619-33) between the external object (that *affected*) and the internal object complement (that *effected*, i.e. produced or construed in the verb). One object maybe considered "internal" to the verbal action (i.e. internally affected and produced in and through the verb) and the other "external" to the verbal action (i.e. starting outside the verbal action, yet affect by it). In these examples, the internal objects are *milk, fishers,* and *all things*. These are provided by or produced as a result of the verbal actions. The external object in each case is *you*. Cognate accusatives always entail an internal object.

4. <u>Cognate Accusatives are Emphatic Constructions</u>. The redundancy and repetition of lexical root and sound (aural impact) makes this construction more emphatic, despite Wallace's conditional restriction (52): "*If the accusative has a modifier (either adjective or genitive), the overall construction is more emphatic*" (emphasis mine).[9] So, if modifiers are present, then even more attention attends to the cognate accusative, which, however, already attracts attention by the repetition of lexical root. So, consider these examples, with increasing emphasis indicated by the increased modification given to the cognate accusative.

Matt 6:19a Μὴ <u>θησαυρίζετε</u> ὑμῖν <u>θησαυροὺς</u> ἐπὶ τῆς γῆς...
    6:20a <u>θησαυρίζετε</u> δὲ ὑμῖν <u>θησαυροὺς</u> ἐν οὐρανῷ...
        Do not be treasuring up for yourselves treasures upon earth...
        But be treasuring up for yourselves treasures in heaven...

Matt 2:10 ἰδόντες δὲ τὸν ἀστέρα <u>ἐχάρησαν χαρὰν</u> μεγάλην σφόδρα.
    And after seeing the star, they rejoiced an extremely great joy.

5. <u>Verbs Taking Double Accusatives</u>. Finally, Richard A. Young provides this helpful list of verbs with GNT references as types of verbs that may take two accusative objects:[10]

a. ***verbs of speaking***, such as διδάσκω (John 14:26), ἐρωτάω (Mark 4:10), αἰτέω (Mark 6:22), and ἀναμιμνήσκω (1 Cor 4:17);

b. ***verbs of dressing***, such as ἐνδύω (Matt 27:31), περιβάλλω (John 19:2), and ἐκδύω (Matt 27:31);

c. ***verbs of naming***, such as ὀνομάζω (Luke 6:14), καλέω (Matt 22:43), and λέγω (Mark 10:18);

d. ***verbs of giving***, such as ποτίζω (1 Cor 3:2), and φορτίζω (Luke 11:46, also cognate);

e. ***verbs of thinking***, such as ἡγέομαι (Phil 3:7);

f. ***verbs of sending and presenting***, such as ἀποστέλλω (1 John 4:14), and παρίστημι (Acts 1:3); and

g. ***verbs of making and appointing***, such as ποιέω (Matt 4:19), καθίστημι (Acts 7:10), τίθημι (Heb 1:2), and ἔχω (Acts 13:5).

C. **Adverbial Accusatives:** In this usage, the accusative case noun functions adverbially to further qualify the verb. Two clues to identifying these uses are, first, their forward placement (commonly, but not always; see Eph 4:15 below) and the difficulty to understand the accusative case noun as a direct object. There are several subtypes of adverbial accusatives.

---

[9] Wallace cites BDF 84–85 (§153) and points also to Smyth 355–56 (§§1563–77).

[10] Richard A. Young, *Intermediate New Testament Greek: A Linguistic and Exegetical Approach* (Nashville: Broadman & Holman, 1994), 17, slightly modified in the formatting.

1. Accusative of Extension of Time/Space (*during which*). The accusative with time words indicates duration and extension of time. The decision to use an accusative of time versus a dative of time (*point at which an event occurs*) or a genitive of time (*the quality/kind of time when an event occurs*) is exegetically significant. Compare these different time constructions:

Luke 21:37a ἦν δὲ <u>τὰς ἡμέρας</u> ἐν τῷ ἱερῷ διδάσκων,
   Moreover, he was teaching in the temple <u>during the days</u>,

   21:37b <u>τὰς</u> δὲ <u>νύκτας</u> ἐξερχόμενος ηὐλίζετο εἰς τὸ ὄρος τὸ καλούμενον Ἐλαιῶν·
   But, going out <u>during the nights</u>, he would spend the night at the mountain called 'Olives.'

For a comparison of the dative and gentive cases with ἡ νύξ, νυκτός *night*, consider these examples (compare with other English translations):

Mark 14:30 καὶ λέγει αὐτῷ ὁ Ἰησοῦς· ἀμὴν λέγω σοι ὅτι σὺ σήμερον <u>ταύτῃ τῇ νυκτὶ</u> πρὶν ἢ δὶς ἀλέκτορα φωνῆσαι τρίς με ἀπαρνήσῃ.
   And Jesus says to him, "Amen! I say to you that you yourself today at <u>this very night</u>, before a rooster crows twice, three times you will deny me."

Matt 25:6 <u>μέσης</u> δὲ <u>νυκτὸς</u> κραυγὴ γέγονεν· ἰδοὺ ὁ νυμφίος, ἐξέρχεσθε εἰς ἀπάντησιν αὐτοῦ.
   But <u>in the midst of the night</u> a shout has come, "Behold, the bridegroom! Begin coming out to meet him!"

Although certain examples of accusatives used in statements of time appear to be more *point of time*, which is more customary of the dative case usage, still one can discern a notion of the extension of time (see the discussion in Robertson, 470-71). One debated example occurs in John 4:52.

John 4:52a ἐπύθετο οὖν <u>τὴν ὥραν</u> παρ᾽ αὐτῶν <u>ἐν ᾗ</u> κομψότερον ἔσχεν·
   So, he inquired <u>the hour</u> from them <u>in/at which</u> he had gotten better

   4:52b εἶπαν οὖν αὐτῷ ὅτι ἐχθὲς <u>ὥραν ἑβδόμην</u> ἀφῆκεν αὐτὸν ὁ πυρετός.
   Therefore, they said to him this: "Yesterday <u>during the seventh hour</u> the fever left him."

The initial accusative <u>τὴν ὥραν</u> in 4:52a is simply the direct object, which is then given a dative *point of time* in the relative pronoun clause initiated within a prepositional phrase <u>ἐν ᾗ</u> *at which*. The second accusative <u>ὥραν ἑβδόμην</u> at first appears to be a point of time; yet, equally valid, it seems to me, is to understand duration over the seventh hour: the fever left (sometime) *during the seventh hour*; it is both a point of time and during a period of time.

Why? Perhaps because the patient was checked each hour and between the sixth and seventh hour the fever had left. Another debated accusative of time appears in Acts 20:16 and Paul's desire to be in Jerusalem *at* or *during the day of Pentecost* (τὴν ἡμέραν τῆς πεντηκοστῆς).

For other examples of accustive of time, see Mark 1:13; 4:27; Matt 20:6; Luke 2:37; 15:29; John 1:39; 2:12; 11:6; Acts 27:33; 1 Cor 15:30; Rev 3:3.

2. Accusative of Respect or Reference (*with reference to* or *with respect to*). The accusative case noun qualifies and delimits the sentence by reference to an entity or circumstance:

Eph 4:15 ἀληθεύοντες δὲ ἐν ἀγάπῃ αὐξήσωμεν εἰς αὐτὸν <u>τὰ πάντα</u>, ὅς ἐστιν ἡ κεφαλή, Χριστός,
But by being truthful in love, let us grow <u>with respect to everything</u> into him, who is the Head, the Annointed One,

2 Cor 12:13 τί γάρ ἐστιν ὃ ἡσσώθητε ὑπὲρ τὰς λοιπὰς ἐκκλησίας,...;
For what is that [with reference to] which you were inferior to the remaining churches...?

2 Cor 6:13 <u>τὴν δὲ αὐτὴν ἀντιμισθίαν</u>, ὡς τέκνοις λέγω, πλατύνθητε καὶ ὑμεῖς.
Now <u>in a like exchange</u> (I speak as to children) you yourselves open wide also.

This last example may possibly be an accusative of manner (*in the manner of a like exchange*). It is sometimes difficult to decide or distinguish between adverbial uses. If Paul is making reference to his mutual relationship with the Corinthians, as he has done up to this point in the epistle (1:7, 13-14; 2:3-4; 4:15; 6:1, 11-12), then an accusative of reference makes good sense. Alternatively, on the basis of this relationship he may be indicating the manner of mutual cooperation he is working towards between himself and them, since he will be appealing to them to complete their contribution to the collection (2 Cor 8-9).

3. Accusative of Manner (*in such a manner*). An accusative case noun may be used to indicate the manner in which the verbal action is conducted. This usage overlaps with adjectives functioning as adverbs.

Mark 12:27 οὐκ ἔστιν θεὸς νεκρῶν ἀλλὰ ζώντων· <u>πολὺ</u> πλανᾶσθε.
He is not God of the dead but of the living; <u>greatly</u> you are being deceived.

4. Accusative in Oaths. The person whose name is used to make an oath is given in the accusative case. This usage is somewhat rare.

1 Thess 5:27 Ἐνορκίζω ὑμᾶς <u>τὸν κύριον</u> ἀναγνωσθῆναι τὴν ἐπιστολὴν πᾶσιν τοῖς ἀδελφοῖς.
I adjure you <u>by the Lord</u> that the epistle be read to all the brethren.

D. **Accusative of Retained Object in Passive Voice:** "Some verbs which have *only one accusative* in the active or middle yet retain the accusative of the thing in the passive with the person in the nominative" (Robertson 485, emphasis original). What this means is that you may encounter a passive voice verb that has an accusative case object as the thing received or imparted in the action of the verb. Consider these examples, which in the active voice presentation would have had two accusatives, the person as recipient and the thing as given.

1 Thess 2:4b πιστευθῆναι τὸ εὐαγγέλιον *to be entrusted (with) the gospel*

Gal 6:6b ὁ κατηχούμενος τὸν λόγον *the one instructed (with) the word*

2 Cor 3:18b τὴν αὐτὴν εἰκόνα μεταμορφούμεθα *we are transformed into the same image*

Complete WORKBOOK EXERCISES 23 and consult the ANSWER KEY & GUIDE as needed.

CASE IN POINT 23: INFINITIVES IN 1 THESS 4:9-12

In 1 Thessalonians 4, Paul initiates a series of arguments advancing holiness, brotherly love, and hope in Christ's return. In 1 Thess 4:9-12 Paul turns to the matter of brotherly love, *Now concerning brotherly love….* He begins by indicating that he has no need *to write* them; such a statement involves a complementary infinitive with the noun *need*. Paul's statement is very encouraging. Emphatically, Paul explains why with a supporting γὰρ: *For you yourselves are taught of God in order to love one another*. Throughout this passage, Paul deploys several infinitives that are worth a closer look.

1 Thess 4:9-12 *Now as to the love of the brethren, you have no need for anyone **to write** to you, for you yourselves are taught by God **to love** one another; [10] for indeed you do practice it toward all the brethren who are in all Macedonia. But we urge you, brethren, **to excel** still more, [11] and **to make it your ambition to lead a quiet life** and **attend** to your own business and **work** with your hands, just as we commanded you, [12] so that you will behave properly toward outsiders and not be in any need.* [NASB95]

1 Thess 4:9-12 Περὶ δὲ τῆς φιλαδελφίας οὐ χρείαν ἔχετε γράφειν ὑμῖν, αὐτοὶ γὰρ ὑμεῖς θεοδίδακτοί ἐστε εἰς τὸ ἀγαπᾶν ἀλλήλους, [10] καὶ γὰρ ποιεῖτε αὐτὸ εἰς πάντας τοὺς ἀδελφοὺς [τοὺς] ἐν ὅλῃ τῇ Μακεδονίᾳ. Παρακαλοῦμεν δὲ ὑμᾶς, ἀδελφοί, περισσεύειν μᾶλλον [11] καὶ φιλοτιμεῖσθαι ἡσυχάζειν καὶ πράσσειν τὰ ἴδια καὶ ἐργάζεσθαι ταῖς [ἰδίαις] χερσὶν ὑμῶν, καθὼς ὑμῖν παρηγγείλαμεν, [12] ἵνα περιπατῆτε εὐσχημόνως πρὸς τοὺς ἔξω καὶ μηδενὸς χρείαν ἔχητε.

There are several very interesting Greek constructions in 4:9. Notice the doubly emphatic subject (αὐτοὶ ὑμεῖς). Then there is the unique predicate adjective θεο-δίδακτοί, *taught of God* literally, *God-taught*. Notice that Greek is able to combine words into new ones. What significance is it that God has taught us something? What is the goal of God's curriculum for us? Paul answers such a question using a preposition with the infinitive construction expressing purpose: *to love one another* (εἰς τὸ ἀγαπᾶν ἀλλήλους). The verbal aspect of the present tense indicates continual action. We ought to ponder how God is teaching us to love on and on; indeed, arguably, to love like God loves is the main purpose of God's instructional pedagogy in Christ (see Matt 5:48; John 13:34; 1 Pet 1:22).

In 4:10, Paul next congratulates the Thessalonians for their love for fellow believers in the broader region of Macedonia. And in 4:11 Paul uses a metacomment (*I exhort you*) to communicate his desire for them *to abound* more and more in love, which is expressed with an infinitive of indirect discourse. Rather than using the metacomment, we could instead imagine Paul simply commanding them: "*Abound more and more in this sort of activity.*" To think through Paul's exhortation like this helps to identify περισσεύειν *to abound* as an infinitive of indirect discourse. This Present Tense is also significant, since the imperfective aspect suggests ongoing, progressive action.

The indirect discourse begun in 4:10 continues through 4:11 (we'll return to this) all the way into 4:12, which concludes with a purpose statement, where Paul directs the Thessalonians' efforts to a particular manifestation of love as it may be observed by outsiders (τοὺς ἔξω—4:12), i.e. unbelievers. *Those outside* are people living closer to them than the fellow believers in Macedonia. Why is it sometimes harder to love those closer than those further away? And, how should we show our love to our unbelieving neighbors?

Here we face an exegetical decision. There are four infinitives in 4:11 with the latter two each introduced with a καί (καὶ πράσσειν τὰ ἴδια καὶ ἐργάζεσθαι... *and to do your own things and to work...*). The first two infinitives (φιλοτιμεῖσθαι ἡσυχάζειν) are in a complementary relationship since the initial infinitive φιλοτιμεῖσθαι (meaning *consider it an honor to* [BDAG]) takes a complementary infinitive to complete its meaning: *Consider it an honor ... to live quietly*. The question is whether the latter two infinitives (πράσσειν and ἐργάζεσθαι, *to do/attend* and *to work*, respectively) are also infinitive complements of φιλοτιμεῖσθαι <u>or</u> infinitives of indirect discourse like περισσεύειν in 4:10. Each option is depicted in translation below.

> **Option 1:** *We exhort you to abound more [περισσεύειν] in this <u>and</u> [we exhort you] to consider it an honor [φιλοτιμεῖσθαι] (1) to live quietly, and (2) to do your own things, and (3) to work with your hands.*

> **Option 2:** *We exhort you (1) to abound more in this, (2) to consider it an honor to live quietly, (3) to do your own things, <u>and</u> (4) to work with your hands.*

How do we decide between these options? It is very difficult. The nearness of φιλοτιμεῖσθαι to the latter two infinitives would suggest to the readers/hearers that they are complementing φιλο-τιμεῖσθαι (so, Option 1). More research would be necessary, but the evidence leans in favor of Option 1.

So then, according to Option 1, after exhorting the Thessalonians to *abound more* in their current behavior of love towards believers, Paul then attaches three actions to the verb φιλοτιμεῖσθαι (*to consider as honorable*) as infinitive complements for the purpose of "behaving properly toward outsiders" (4:12). In other words, acting "honorably" indicates outward behavior for the purpose of witness before unbelievers. Ancient Mediterranean culture was an honor-driven culture. For Paul to highlight certain actions as *honorable* indicates a very strong desire on his part for the Thessalonians to do them. Paul thus encouraged the Thessalonians to *continually* do these actions (present tense), and such actions are *according to Paul's previous instruction* and *for the purpose of living properly in relation to outsiders*. This is how we show love to outsiders: by being honorable in terms of living quietly (not causing disturbances), minding our own business, and working with our own hands (i.e. not expecting others to meet our financial needs). Further insight would be gained by studying the meaning of each of these infinitive verbs that describe these behaviors within the Mediterranean culture of Paul's day.

Below is a reproduction of an inscribed stone, called the Siloam Inscription found in 1871, which was located at the various entrances around the balustrade that surrounded the Jerusalem temple proper in Jesus' day.[11] It marked the point at which Gentiles were not allowed to pass upon the consequence of death. The text was dyed red, as found elsewhere on inscribed stones. The Jewish historian, Josephus, provides more information about the inscriptions:

> Proceeding through this [first courtyard] towards the second court of the temple, a stone balustrade had been placed around it, three cubits high and having been very beautifully crafted; in this at regular intervals stood stones giving announcement of the law of purification, some in Greek others in Latin characters [αἱ μὲν Ἑλληνικοῖς αἱ δὲ Ῥωμαϊκοῖς γράμμασιν] that no foreigner was permitted to pass by inside the holy place [μηδένα ἀλλόφυλον ἐντὸς τοῦ ἁγίου παριέναι], for so the second enclosure of the temple was called (*Wars* 5.193-194; cf. *Against Apion* 2.103).

The Jewish Philosopher and theologian Philo (c. 30 BC to AD 50) explained the eagerness of the whole Jewish to preserve the purity of the temple space by penalty of death (*Embassy* 212). This concern is seen also with the charges brought against the apostle Paul, that he had brought Greeks into the temple and defiled it (Acts 21:27-30). A central truth of Jesus' teaching was that Jesus himself became the cornerstone of the new temple (Mark 12:1-11), and so members of his body were the temple of God (1 Cor 3:16; 1 Cor 6:19; 2 Cor 6:16; Rom 8:9; Eph 2:21-22; 1 Pet 2:4-10).

---

[11] Photo, slightly enhanced, by Giovanni Dall'Orto (Own work) [Attribution], via Wikimedia Commons. Used by permission. This reconstruction and the original are located at the Museum Tschinili-Kirschk, Istanbul.

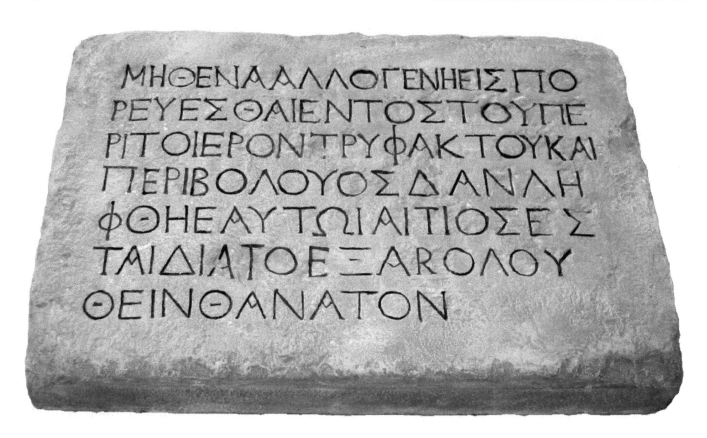

The text written with minuscules and accented is translated below.

μηθένα ἀλλογενῆ <u>εἰσπο- ρεύεσθαι</u> ἐντὸς τοῦ πε- ρὶ τὸ ἱερὸν τρυφάκτου καὶ περιβόλου· ὃς δ' ἂν λη- φθῇ, ἑαυτῷ αἴτιος ἔσ- ται διὰ τὸ <u>ἐξακολου- θεῖν</u> θάνατον.	*No foreigner shall enter* *inside the balustrade* *around the temple* *and enclosure; and whoever* *is caught will have the blame* *in himself because of* *the death resulting.*

Notice the two infinitives (underlined). What infinitival uses are present? The first, <u>εἰσπορεύ-
εσθαι</u>, is imperatival (see §23.4.F above). The second, <u>ἐξακολουθεῖν</u>, belongs to a adverbial clause formed with the preposition διά (see §23.5.C above).

CHAPTER 24

24.0 VOCABULARY
24.1 IMPORTANT CHARACTERISTICS OF THE Μι CONJUGATION
24.2 ENDINGS AND FORMATION OF THE Μι CONJUGATION
24.3 Μι VERBS IN THE NON-INDICATIVE MOODS
24.4 PRINCIPAL PARTS OF Μι VERBS IN THE GNT
      CHECK POINT 24.1-4 Μι VERBS
24.5 THE OPTATIVE MOOD (ἡ Εὐκτικὴ Ἔγκλισις)
24.6 SPECIAL GRAMMATICAL CONSTRUCTIONS WITH THE ARTICLE
CASE IN POINT 24: INFINITIVES IN EPH 4:20-24

What does it mean to "put on the new self" in the likeness of God? What one wore in antiquity told a story—it conveyed your social status and legal attachments. In Eph 4:20-24 Paul described what it means to "Learn Christ"; the first step is "putting off" the old self. He here uses a verb ἀποτίθημι, a Μι verb, which is worth looking at more closely.

This chapter covers **Μι Verbs**, which is the -μι conjugation of verbs. This conjugation is related to the common irregular verb already learned, εἰμί *I am*, but uses somewhat unique endings. These verbs are very regular in formation. Then we take a brief look at the **Optative Mood** before looking once again at **Special Constructions of the Article**.

VOCABULARY 24　Μι VERBS

Μι Verbs:		ἀνίστημι [108]	I raise up; I resurrect
ἀφίημι [143]	I send off, release; I permit; I forgive (+ *dat.*)	παρίστημι [41]	I place near; I stand before/with
δίδωμι [415]	I give, entrust	τίθημι [100]	I set, put, place
ἀποδίδωμι [48]	I deliver; I pay	φημί [65]	I say, declare
παραδίδωμι [119]	I hand over, deliver; I betray	Slightly Irregular Μι verb:	
ἵστημι [154]	I cause to stand; I set up (*1st Aorist*); I stand (*2nd Aorist*)	ἀπόλλυμι [90]	I destroy (*active*); I perish (*middle*)

After learning this vocabulary, you will know 81.2% of the words in the GNT. If you are able, listen to audio recordings of VOCABULARY 24 and do the CROSSWORD PUZZLE in the WORKBOOK.

NOTES ON VOCABULARY 24:

There are no English cognates that will help the student memorize the vocabulary words in this lesson. However, one should notice that there are several roots used to form many Μι Verbs, including those with a much less frequency that are not included here. The most common root δο- is used to make δί-δω-μι *I give* and many compound forms, such as ἀποδίδωμι *I deliver* and παραδίδωμι *I hand over*. See the discussion of the other common Μι Verb stems below.

Several Μι Verbs deserve special comment. First, ἀφίημι, which can mean *I forgive*, commonly has the person who is forgiven in the dative case. Second, ἵστημι has two Aorist Tense formations. When formed as a 1st Aorist, this verb is transitive and takes a <u>direct object</u>: *I cause <u>something</u> to stand* or *I set up <u>something</u>*. When formed as a 2nd Aorist, ἵστημι is intransitive and means *I stand up*. Third, the verb παρίστημι is similar. It is transitive in the 1st and 2nd Principal Parts and 1st Aorist (*I place <u>something</u> for someone*); but it is intransitive with the 2nd Aorist and 4th, 5th, and 6th Principal Parts (*I stand before/with*; *I assist*). The person for whom or with whom one is standing or assisting is put into the dative case. Finally, φημί *I say* is most commonly found in the Imperfect 3rd singular form ἔφη *he was saying* and the Present 3rd singular form φησίν *he says*, which in the GNT is often used as an Historic Present (see §6.6 HISTORIC PRESENT (HP) AND DISCOURSE PRAGMATICS).

Below is an artist's rendition of the Theater of Dionysus on the southern slopes of the Acropolis in Athens.[1] Initially able to seat 30,000 people (all Athens), the wooden theater was reconstructed with marble so that in the 4th century BC the theater held 17,000 spectators. The men sat in the closest rows. The front seats (with backs) were for honored guests, the central seat reserved for the priest of Dionysus. The male actor (ὁ ὑποκριτής) sometimes wore masks (see next pages) to play parts in tragedies, comedies, and satirical dramas. The semi-circular *orchestra* (ἡ ὀρχήστρα) consisted of men and boys singing and dancing to reflect the unfolding drama.

---

[1] The slightly edited images here and on the next two pages are from William Carey Morey, *Outlines of Greek History: With a Survey of Ancient Oriental Nations* (New York: American Book Company, 1903), 243 and 294.

24.1 IMPORTANT CHARACTERISTICS OF THE Mι CONJUGATION

A. **Two Conjugations: The -Ω and the -Mι Conjugations:** Thus far we have learned the verb endings for the ὦ μέγα (-ω) Conjugation. There is another grouping of verbs called Mι Verbs. This conjugation is called the Mι Conjugation since the lexical form ends in -μι. At the outset, if one learns the next three things, Mι Verbs will be more easily mastered.

B. **False Reduplication in the Present and Imperfect Tenses:** Most Mι Verbs display a **false reduplication** in the Present and Imperfect Tenses (although φημί does not). This false reduplication consists of a doubling of the first consonant (if possible) and the addition of an ἰῶτα. Study the examples below.

Verb Stem Beginning with a Consonant	Verb Stem Beginning with a Vowel or Consonant Cluster
δί-δωμι	ἀφ-ί-ημι
ἀπο-δί-δωμι	ἵ-στημι
παρα-δί-δωμι	ἀν-ί-στημι
τί-θημι	παρ-ί-στημι

The identification of this "false reduplication" will greatly help you parse Mι Verbs, *since it occurs only in the First Principal Part, i.e. the Present and Imperfect Tenses.*

C. **Mι Verbs are Basically Contract Verbs:** Most Mι Verbs are contract verbs. That is to say, their verb stem ends in a vowel, either ε, α, or ο.

Verb Stem

δί-δω-μι → δο-   Notice that the contract vowel <u>lengthens</u> when
τί-θη-μι → θε-   forming the Present Tense *singular*. However, the
ἀφί-η-μι → ἑ-   contract vowel <u>does not lengthen</u> in the *plural*.
ἵ-στη-μι → στα-   See the paradigms below.
φη-μί → φα-

D. **Present and Imperfect Forms Lack a Coupling Vowel:** In the Present and Imperfect Tenses, Mι Verbs lack a coupling vowel. Thus, the endings are added *directly* to the verb stem and look different from what you have already learned. However, in the other tenses the Mι Verb endings are essentially the same as what you have already learned.

MASKS USED IN TRAGEDY

24.2 ENDINGS AND FORMATION OF THE **Mι** CONJUGATION

A. The endings for the Mι Verbs are fairly regular outside the First Principal Part. Therefore, special attention must be given to the endings used within the First Principal Part, that is, the Present and Imperfect Tenses. For an overview, see APPENDIX §23.

B. Present and Imperfect Indicative of Mι Verbs:

1. <u>Endings</u>. The endings for the Present Active Indicative will be partially recognizable from the verb εἰμί. Also, you should easily recognize all the other endings.

		PRESENT TENSE				IMPERFECT TENSE	
		A	**M/P**			**A**	**M/P**
sg.	1	-μι	-μαι		**sg.** 1	-ν	-μην
	2	-ς	-σαι		2	-ς	-σο
	3	-σι(ν)	-ται		3	-	-το
pl.	1	-μεν	-μεθα		**pl.** 1	-μεν	-μεθα
	2	-τε	-σθε		2	-τε	-σθε
	3	-ασι(ν)	-νται		3	-ν or -σαν	-ντο

<u>Notice</u>: (1) There is no coupling vowel for these endings; earlier in the language the –ασι(ν) ending was -νσι. (2) With the Present endings, only the third person singular active endings are new; it may help to consider -ασιν to be similar to -ουσιν. (3) The Imperfect endings are endings that you have already learned. These are the Secondary Tense Endings and are used also for the Aorist **Mι** Verbs.

2. <u>The Present and Imperfect of δίδωμι, τίθημι, ἀφίημι, ἵστημι.</u>

These paradigms should **not** be memorized in rote. They are given here for you to study and analyze, to compare and contrast.

		PRESENT A				PRESENT M/P			
sg.	1	δίδωμι	τίθημι	ἀφίημι	ἵστημι	δίδομαι	τίθεμαι	ἀφίεμαι	ἵσταμαι
	2	δίδως	τίθης	ἀφίης	ἵστης	δίδοσαι	τίθεσαι	ἀφίεσαι	ἵστασαι
	3	δίδωσι(ν)	τίθησι(ν)	ἀφίησι(ν)	ἵστησι(ν)	δίδοται	τίθεται	ἀφίεται	ἵσταται
pl.	1	δίδομεν	τίθεμεν	ἀφίεμεν	ἵσταμεν	διδόμεθα	τιθέμεθα	ἀφιέμεθα	ἱστάμεθα
	2	δίδοτε	τίθετε	ἀφίετε	ἵστατε	δίδοσθε	τίθεσθε	ἀφίεσθε	ἵστασθε
	3	διδόασι(ν)	τιθέασι(ν)	ἀφιᾶσι(ν)	ἱστᾶσι(ν)	δίδονται	τίθενται	ἀφίενται	ἵστανται

MASKS USED IN COMEDY

		IMPERFECT A				IMPERFECT M/P		
sg. 1	ἐδίδουν	ἐτίθην	ἀφίην	ἵστην	ἐδιδόμην	ἐτιθέμην	ἀφιέμην	ἱστάμην
2	ἐδίδους	ἐτίθεις	ἀφίεις	ἵστης	ἐδίδοσο	ἐτίθεσο	ἀφίεσο	ἵστασο
3	ἐδίδου	ἐτίθει	ἀφίηει	ἵστη	ἐδίδοτο	ἐτίθετο	ἀφίετο	ἵστατο
pl. 1	ἐδίδομεν	ἐτίθεμεν	ἀφίεμεν	ἵσταμεν	ἐδιδόμεθα	ἐτιθέμεθα	ἀφιέμεθα	ἱστάμεθα
2	ἐδίδοτε	ἐτίθετε	ἀφίετε	ἵστατε	ἐδίδοσθε	ἐτίθεσθε	ἀφίεσθε	ἵστασθε
3	ἐδίδοσαν	ἐτίθεσαν	ἀφίεσαν	ἵστασαν	ἐδίδοντο	ἐτίθεντο	ἀφίεντο	ἵσταντο

<u>Notice</u>: (1) A false reduplication with ἰῶτα is seen throughout this First Principal Part. (2) The contract vowel <u>lengthens</u> in the Present Active singular endings. (3) In all other forms, the contract vowel remains <u>or</u> becomes a monophthong (ου or ει). (4) No augment is seen on ἀφίημι and ἵστημι due to the initial ἰῶτα of the false reduplication.

C. **Tenses Outside the First Principal Part:** The endings used outside the First Principal Part are essentially the same as the ὦ μέγα (-Ω) Conjugation. One notable difference is with the Aorist Tense: A κάππα is often used instead of a σίγμα. Also, the false reduplication is no longer seen in the other principal parts, only the standard reduplication of the Perfect tense in the Four and Fifth Principal Parts.

SUMMARY OF Mι VERBS IN THE INDICATIVE MOOD

STEM	**FIRST**	**SECOND**	**THIRD**	**FOURTH**	**FIFTH**	**SIXTH**
δο	δίδωμι	δώσω	ἔδωκα	δέδωκα	δέδομαι	ἐδόθην
θε	τίθημι	θήσω	ἔθηκα	τέθεικα	τεθεῖμαι	ἐτέθην
ε	ἀφ-ίημι	ἀφ-ήσω	ἀφ-ηκα	ἀφ-εῖκα	ἀφ-εῖμαι	ἀφ-είθην
στα	ἵστημι	στήσω	ἔστησα (1st A)	ἔστηκα	ἔσταμαι	ἐστάθην
			ἔστην (2nd A)			

Notes:	*-false reduplication*	*-no false reduplication*	*-no false reduplication*	*-regular reduplication*		*-no false reduplication*
	-some new endings	*-regular endings*	*-some kappa endings*	*-regular endings*		*-regular endings*

D. **Closer Look at the Aorist Forms of ἵστημι in the Indicative:**

		1ST AORIST	**2ND AORIST**
sg.	1	ἔστησα	ἔστην
	2	ἔστησας	ἔστης
	3	ἔστησε(ν)	ἔστη
pl.	1	ἐστήσαμεν	ἔστημεν
	2	ἐστήσατε	ἔστητε
	3	ἔστησαν	ἔστησαν

24.3 Μι VERBS IN THE NON-INDICATIVE MOODS

A. **Participles:** The Present Participle is going to continue to have its false reduplication. This *alone* distinguishes between the Present and the Aorist Participles in Μι Verbs. Below are given the nominative and genitive participle forms in all genders for δίδωμι, τίθημι, and ἵστημι (with the 2nd Aorist). For full paradigms, see the APPENDIX §23.

		PRESENT A nom., gen….	**AORIST A** nom., gen….	**AORIST P** nom., gen….
	masc.	διδούς, διδόντος...	δούς, δόντος...	δοθείς, δοθέντος...
δίδωμι	fem.	διδοῦσα, διδούσης...	δοῦσα, δούσης...	δοθεῖσα, δοθείσης...
	neut.	διδόν, διδόντος...	δόν, δόντος...	δοθέν, δοθέντος...
	masc.	τιθείς, τιθέντος...	θείς, θέντος...	τεθείς, τεθέντος...
τίθημι	fem.	τιθεῖσα, τιθείσης...	θεῖσα, θείσης...	τεθεῖσα, τεθείσης...
	neut.	τιθέν, τιθέντος...	θέν, θέντος...	τεθέν, τεθέντος...
	masc.	ἱστάς, ἱστάντος...	στάς, στάντος...	σταθείς, σταθέντος...
ἵστημι	fem.	ἱστᾶσα, ἱστάσης...	στᾶσα, στάσης...	σταθεῖσα, σταθείσης...
(2nd Aorist)	neut.	ἱστάν, ἱστάντος...	στάν, στάντος...	σταθέν, σταθέντος...

Notice that a τε- is added to distinguish the Aorist Passive from the Aorist Active for τίθημι. The middle/passive participles follow the same patterns.

B. **Subjunctive Mood:** Μι Verbs use exactly the same Subjunctive endings as do other verbs. To refresh your memory here are the Subjunctive endings:

	ACTIVE SUBJUNCTIVE			**M OR M/P SUBJUNCTIVE**	
	sg.	pl.		sg.	pl.
1	-ω	-ωμεν	1	-ωμαι	-ωμεθα
2	-ῃς	-ητε	2	-ῃ	-ησθε
3	-ῃ	-ωσι(ν)	3	-ηται	-ωνται

These endings are added to the appropriate stem of the Μι Verb. With the Subjunctive Mood, the contract vowel of the Μι Verb joins with the long vowel of the Subjunctive ending and disappears (except in δίδωμι where an ὦ μέγα results—see below). Here are the Active and Middle/Passive Subjunctive endings on τίθημι:

		ACTIVE SUBJUNCTIVE			**MIDDLE/PASSIVE SUBJUNCTIVE**	
		PRESENT A	AORIST A	AORIST P	PRESENT M/P	AORIST M
sg.	1	τιθῶ	θῶ	τεθῶ	τιθῶμαι	θῶμαι
	2	τιθῇς	θῇς	τεθῇς	τιθῇ	θῇ
	3	τιθῇ	θῇ	τεθῇ	τιθῆται	θῆται
pl.	1	τιθῶμεν	θῶμεν	τεθῶμεν	τιθώμεθα	θώμεθα
	2	τιθῆτε	θῆτε	τεθῆτε	τιθῆσθε	θῆσθε
	3	τιθῶσι(ν)	θῶσι(ν)	τεθῶσι(ν)	τιθῶνται	θῶνται

With δίδωμι a contraction with ὁ μικρόν in the Present and Aorist forms results in an ῶ μέγα in the endings. This does not happen in the Aorist Passive forms, however.

	PRESENT A	AORIST A	AORIST P	PRESENT M/P	AORIST M
sg. 1	διδῶ	δῶ	δοθῶ	διδῶμαι	δῶμαι
2	διδῶς	δῷς	δοθῇς	διδῷ	δῷ
3	διδῷ	δῷ	δοθῇ	διδῶται	δῶται
pl. 1	διδῶμεν	δῶμεν	δοθῶμεν	διδώμεθα	δώμεθα
2	διδῶτε	δῶτε	δοθῆτε	διδῶσθε	δῶσθε
3	διδῶσι(ν)	δῶσι(ν)	δοθῶσι(ν)	διδῶνται	δῶνται

C. **Infinitives:** Here are the Infinitive endings. The contract vowel does not contract.

Μι Verb	PRESENT A	PRESENT M/P	AORIST A	AORIST M	AORIST P
δίδωμι	διδόναι	δίδοσθαι	δοῦναι	δόσθαι	δοθῆναι
τίθημι	τιθέναι	τίθεσθαι	θεῖναι	θέσθαι	τεθῆναι
ἀφίημι	ἀφιέναι	ἀφίεσθαι	ἀφεῖναι	ἀφέσθαι	–
ἵστημι	ἱστάναι	ἵστασθαι	στῆσαι (1st A)	–	σταθῆναι
			στῆναι (2nd A)		

D. **Imperative Mood:** The Imperative Mood, the mood of command, request, and petition, is covered in CHAPTER 25. Here are the endings now in order to be complete.

		δίδωμι		τίθημι		ἵστημι	
		sg.	pl.	sg.	pl.	sg.	pl.
PRESENT A	2	δίδου	δίδοτε	τίθει	τίθετε	ἵστη	ἵστατε
	3	διδότω	διδότωσαν	τιθέτω	τιθέτωσαν	ἱστάτω	ἱστάτωσαν
PRESENT M/P	2	δίδοσο	δίδοσθω	τίθεσο	τίθεσθε	ἵστασο	ἵστασθε
	3	διδόσθω	διδόσθωσαν	τιθέσθω	τιθέσθωσαν	ἱστάσθω	ἱστάσθωσαν
AORIST A	2	δός	δότε	θές	θέτε	στῆσον	στήσατε
	3	δότω	δότωσαν	θέτω	θέτωσαν	στησάτω	στησάτωσαν
AORIST M	2	δοῦ	δόσθε	θοῦ	θέσθε	στῆθι*	στῆτε*
	3	δόσθω	δόσθωσαν	θέσθω	θέσθωσαν	στήτω*	στήτωσαν*
AORIST P	2	δόθητι	δόθητε	τέθητι	τέθητε	στάθητι	στάθητε
	3	δοθήτω	δοθήτωσαν	τεθήτω	τεθήτωναν	σταθήτω	σταθήτωσαν

* 2nd Aorist Active forms
of ἵστημι

E. Ἵστημι: Since this verb shows a 1st and 2nd Aorist formation, here are the Subjunctive and Participle Forms of ἵστημι in the Aorist tense.

SUBJUNCTIVE

		1ST AORIST	2ND AORIST			1ST AORIST	2ND AORIST
sg.	1	στήσω	στῶ	pl.	1	στήσωμεν	στῶμεν
	2	στήσῃς	στῇς		2	στήσητε	στῆτε
	3	στήσῃ	στῇ		3	στήσωσι(ν)	στῶσι(ν)

PARTICIPLE

		1ST AORIST			2ND AORIST		
		Masculine	Feminine	Neuter	Masculine	Feminine	Neuter
sg.	nom.	στήσας	στήσασα	στῆσαν	στάς	στᾶσα	στάν
	gen.	στήσαντος	στησάσης	στήσαντος	στάντος	στάσης	στάντος
	dat.	στήσαντι	στησάσῃ	στήσαντι	στάντι	στάσῃ	στάντι
	acc.	στήσαντα	στήσασαν	στῆσαν	στάντα	στᾶσαν	στάν
pl.	nom.	στήσαντες	στήσασαι	στήσαντα	στάντες	στᾶσαι	στάντα
	gen.	στησάντων	στησασῶν	στησάντων	στάντων	στασῶν	στάντων
	dat.	στήσασι(ν)	στησάσαις	στήσασι(ν)	στᾶσι(ν)	στάσαις	στᾶσι(ν)
	acc.	στήσαντας	στησάσας	στήσαντα	στάντας	στάσας	στάντα

24.4 PRINCIPAL PARTS OF Mι VERBS IN THE GNT

A. **Overview:** Here are the Principal Parts of the Mι Verbs covered in this handbook. The cognates are included below the main verb stem and indented.

FIRST	SECOND	THIRD	FOURTH	FIFTH	SIXTH
ἀπόλλυμι	ἀπολέσω	ἀπώλεσα	ἀπολώλεκα	–	–
	ἀπολῶ		ἀπόλωλα		
ἀφίημι	ἀφήσω	ἀφῆκα	–	ἀφέωμαι	ἀφέθην
δίδωμι	δώσω	ἔδωκα	δέδωκα	δέδομαι	ἐδόθην
ἀποδίδωμι (P,F,A,–,–,Ap)					
παραδίδωμι (P,F,A,Ra,Rp,Ap)					
ἵστημι	στήσω	ἔστησα (1 Aor.)	ἕστηκα	–	ἐστάθην
		ἔστην (2 Aor.)			
ἀνίστημι (P,F,A,–,–,–)					
παρίστημι (P,F,A,Ra,–,–)					
τίθημι	θήσω	ἔθηκα	τέθεικα	τέθειμαι	ἐτέθην
φημί	–	ἔφην	–	–	–

B. **Cognate Forms:** Actually, many additional words may be learned, since they are built from Mι verb stems, just like other verbs. To illustrate this, below are words built from δίδωμι and τίθημι.[2] It is helpful first to see the significance of the prefixes and the suffixes, *although we must remember that words are not necessarily the sum of the meaning of their compnent parts.*

1. Prefixes and Suffixes on Cognates of δίδωμι and τίθημι.

PREFIXES		SUFFIXES
ἀ or ἀν- *lacking* (a privative ἄλφα)	μετα- *with,* or an intensifier	-μι, Mι verb ending
ἀνα- *above, again*	μισθ(ος)-*reward*	-μα, resultant thing or entity
ἀντ(ι)- *in stead of*	νομο(ς)- *law*	-σις, process
απο- *from, back*	παρα- *along, beside*	-της, a person, agent
δια- *through,* or an intensifier	πατρο(ς)- *of father*	-α, -ον, noun endings
ἐκ- *from,* or an intensifier	περί- *around*	-ομαι, verb ending
ἐπι- *upon, on*	προ- *before*	-τος, past passive participle
εὐ- *well, good*	προσ- *to*	-σια, noun ending
κατά- *against, down*	συν-/συγ- *with*	-ω, verb ending

2. Cognates from δίδωμι with basic gloss.

ἀνα-δίδωμι, *I deliver up*	δωρεά, *gift*	μετα-δίδωμι, *I give, impart*
ἀντ-απο-δίδωμι, *I repay*	δωρεάν, *freely given*	μισθ-απο-δοσία, *recompense*
ἀντ-από-δομα, *repayment*	δωρέομαι, *I bestow*	μισθ-απο-δότης, *rewarder*
ἀντ-από-δοσις, *repaying*	δώρημα, *gift, present*	παρα-δίδωμι, *I deliver*
ἀπο-δίδωμι, *I give (back)*	δῶρον, *gift, present*	παρά-δοσις, *tradition*
δια-δίδωμι, *I distribute*	ἐκ-δίδωμι, *I tease*	πατρο-παρά-δοτος, *(father-) inherited*
δόμα, *gift*	ἔκ-δοτος, *delivered up*	προ-δίδωμι, *I give in advance; I betray*
δόσις, *giving*	ἐπι-δίδωμι, *I give over*	προ-δότης, *betrayer*
δότης, *giver*	εὐ-μετά-δοτος, *generous*	

3. Cognates from τίθημι with basic gloss.

ἄ-θεσμος, *lawless*	δια-τίθημι, *I decree*	παρα-θήκη, *deposit*
ἀ-θετέω, *I nullify*	ἔκ-θετος, *cast out, exposed*	παρα-τίθημι, *I set before*
ἀ-θέτησις, *annulment*	ἐκ-τίθημι, *I cast out, expose*	περί-θεσις, *putting on/around*
ἀ-θῷος, *without penalty*	ἐπί-θεσις, *laying upon*	περι-τίθημι, *I put on/around*
ἀ-μετά-θετος, *unalterable*	ἐπι-τίθημι, *I lay upon*	πρό-θεσις, *plan, setting forth*
ἀνά-θεμα, *curse*	εὔ-θετος, *fit, suitable*	προ-θεσμία, *fixed time*
ἀνα-θεματίζω, *I curse*	κατά-θεμα, *accursed thing*	προσ-ανα-τίθημι, *I add up to*
ἀνά-θημα, *votive offering*	κατα-θεματίζω, *I curse*	προσ-τίθημι, *I add to*

---

[2] As found in *The Lexham Analytical Lexicon to the Greek New Testament* (Bellingham, WA: Logos Bible Software, 2011). Many of the glosses are from this lexicon.

ἀνα-τίθημι, I lay/set up	κατα-τίθημι, I lay down	προ-τίθημι, I set/plan forth
ἀν-εύ-θετος, unsuitable	μετά-θεσις, change	συγ-κατά-θεσις, agreement
ἀντι-δια-τίθημι, I oppose	μετα-τίθημι, I change	συγ-κατα-τίθημι, I agree w/
ἀντί-θεσις, contradiction	νομο-θετέω, I make laws	συν-επι-τίθημι, I join against
ἀπό-θεσις, removal	νομο-θέτης, lawgiver	συν-τίθημι, I place with, agree
ἀπο-θήκη, storehouse	νου-θεσία, admonition	υἱο-θεσία, adoption, set as son
ἀπο-τίθημι, I take off	νου-θετέω, I admonish	ὑπο-τίθημι, I lay down, teach
ἀ-σύν-θετος, faithless	ὁρο-θεσία, fixed boundary	

CHECK POINT 24.1-4 Mι VERBS

Parse these common verb forms. Be sure to look for false reduplication and other indicators.

1. παραδώσουσιν		9. δώσω	
2. τίθησιν		10. δέδωκεν	
6. ἔδωκεν		11. ἀναστὰς	
4. ἀποδοῦναι		12. δώσει	
5. ἀφεθήσεται		13. ἀφῆκεν	
3. εἱστήκεισαν		14. ἐδόθη	
7. παρέδωκεν		15. ἔφη	
8. ἀπολέσει		16. δίδωσιν	

ANSWERS

1. παραδώσουσιν	FAI3P παραδίδωμι	9. δώσω	FAI1S δίδωμι
2. τίθησιν	PAI3S τίθημι	10. δέδωκεν	RAI3S δίδωμι
6. ἔδωκεν	AAI3S δίδωμι	11. ἀναστὰς	AAP-MNS ἀνίστημι
4. ἀποδοῦναι	AAN ἀποδίδωμι	12. δώσει	FAI3S δίδωμι
5. ἀφεθήσεται	FPI3S ἀφίημι	13. ἀφῆκεν	AAI3S ἀφίημι
3. εἱστήκεισαν	LAI3P ἵστημι	14. ἐδόθη	API3S δίδωμι
7. παρέδωκεν	AAI3S παραδίδωμι	15. ἔφη	IAI3S or AAI3S φημί
8. ἀπολέσει	FAI3S ἀπόλλυμι	16. δίδωσιν	PAI3S δίδωμι

24.5 THE OPTATIVE MOOD (ἡ Εὐκτικὴ Ἔγκλισις)

A. **Introduction and Frequency:** The Optative Mood *expressed wish* (the meaning of the adjective εὐκτικός, -ή, -όν), although its usage overlapped considerably with the Subjunctive Mood (see C. below). In the NT era it is being replaced by the Subjunctive Mood and the Future Indicative. In the GNT, it occurs 68 times and, of these, 15 times mainly in Paul's letters as the conventional negative exclamatory expression Μὴ γένοιτο, *May it not be!*

B. **Endings:** In the GNT, the Optative Mood is limited in the Present and Aorist Tenses. For specialized verbs in the Optative Mood, see APPENDICES §21 CONTRACT VERBS and §23 Μι VERBS.

	PRESENT A	PRESENT M/P	1ST AORIST A	1ST AORIST M	AORIST P
sg. 1	πιστεύοιμι	πιστευοίμην	πιστεύσαιμι	πιστευσαίμην	πιστευθείην
2	πιστεύοις	πιστεύοιο	πιστεύσαις	πιστεύσαιο	πιστευθείης
3	πιστεύοι	πιστεύοιτο	πίστευσαι	πιστεύσαιτο	πιστευθείη
pl. 1	πιστεύοιμεν	πιστευοίμεθα	πιστεύσαιμεν	πιστευσαίμεθα	πιστευθείημεν
2	πιστεύοιτε	πιστεύοισθε	πιστεύσαιτε	πιστεύσαισθε	πιοστευθείητε
3	πιστεύοιεν	πιστεύοινται	πιστεύσαιεν	πιστεύσαιντο	πιστευθείησαν

C. **Functions of the Optative Mood:** Robertson (937) summarizes the functions of the Optative as "the futuristic (potential), the volitive (wishes) and the deliberative." Sometimes accompanying an optative mood verb is the particle ἄν (formally introduced in CH.26), the presence of which may help identify the particular use of the Optative.

1. Futuristic, Potential, or Conditional Optative (sometimes with ἄν). This usage occurs in conditional sentences that are treated in CH.26. The Optative Mood verb may occur in a conditional sentence's supposition with εἰ *if* and without ἄν or in its conclusion with ἄν. In this usage, the Optative Mood verb portrays the conditional thought of the supposition or conclusion "less vividly" in order to "soften" the reality or possibility referred to.

Acts 17:27 ζητεῖν τὸν θεόν, εἰ ἄρα γε ψηλαφήσειαν αὐτὸν καὶ εὕροιεν, καί γε οὐ μακρὰν ἀπὸ ἑνὸς ἑκάστου ἡμῶν ὑπάρχοντα.

that they would be seeking God, if then indeed they would grope for him and find him, indeed also being not far from each one of us.

Acts 17:18a τινὲς δὲ καὶ τῶν Ἐπικουρείων καὶ Στοϊκῶν φιλοσόφων συνέβαλλον αὐτῷ, καί τινες ἔλεγον· τί ἂν θέλοι ὁ σπερμολόγος οὗτος λέγειν;

And some both of the Epicurean and the Stoic Philosophers were conversing with him [Paul], and some were saying, "What would this babbler want to say?"

Wallace suggests that the implicit supposition in Acts 17:18 is, "If he could say anything that made sense!" (484).

2. <u>Volitive Optative in Wishes (no ἄν)</u>. This usage occurs 38 times in the GNT, depending on classification. In addition to the expression Μὴ γένοιτο, *May it not be!*, here is another example:

Mark 11:14 καὶ ἀποκριθεὶς εἶπεν αὐτῇ· μηκέτι εἰς τὸν αἰῶνα ἐκ σοῦ μηδεὶς καρπὸν φάγοι.
And replying, he said to it [*the barren fig tree*], *"No longer for ever from you <u>may</u> anyone <u>eat</u> fruit!"*

3. <u>Deliberative Optative in Questions</u>. Within indirect questions within historical narrative description, the optative may substitute for a deliberative subjunctive or a simple question with an indicative mood verb. Such usage marks elevated literary style. This occurs 12 times in the GNT in Luke-Acts.

Luke 3:15b-16 καὶ διαλογιζομένων πάντων ἐν ταῖς καρδίαις αὐτῶν περὶ τοῦ Ἰωάννου, μήποτε αὐτὸς <u>εἴη</u> ὁ χριστός, ¹⁶ ἀπεκρίνατο λέγων πᾶσιν ὁ Ἰωάννης·...
and as all were considering in their hers concerning John, whether perchance he himself <u>might be</u> the Messiah, ¹⁶ *John answered back to them all saying, ...*

Here in 3:16, the historical narrative involves John's "answer back" (ἀπεκρίνατο). Before this in 3:15b, a genitive absolute construction has an indirect question using the Optative Mood. The direct form of the question would be, "Might he himself be the Messiah?"

24.6 SPECIAL GRAMMATICAL CONSTRUCTIONS WITH THE ARTICLE

A. **Introduction:** The Greek article accounts for nearly one-fifth of the words occurring in the GNT. The article has been treated in distinct sections throughout this handbook, not the mention numerous constructions that have the article (e.g., 2nd attributive position).

§4.4 FEMININE ARTICLE FORMS
§4.5 THE ARTICLE (τὸ Ἄρθρον) AND LACK OF AN ARTICLE (Ἄναρθρος)
§5.2 MASCULINE AND NEUTER ARTICLE ENDINGS
§7.4 COMMON USES OF THE ARTICLE
§21.4 DISCOURSE PRAGMATIC USE OF THE ARTICLE OR ITS ABSENCE

Three article constructions deserve treatment here: Apollonius' Canon and its Corollary, Colwell's Rule, and Granville Sharp's Rule.

B. **Apollonius' Canon and Its Corollary:** The Greek Grammarian Apollonius Dyscolus (2nd century AD) articulated a canon/rule and a corollary regarding the article with two nouns in a modifying (genitive) relationship (see Wallace 239-40).

1. <u>The Canon</u>. Genitive modifiers and their head noun will normally both have the article.

Acts 17:30a τοὺς ... χρόνους τῆς ἀγνοίας *the times of ignorance*

Gal 2:14 πρὸς τὴν ἀλήθειαν τοῦ εὐαγγελίου *to the truth of the Gospel*

2. <u>Its Corollary</u>. If the head noun is anarthrous, the genitive modifier will tend to be anarthrous.
John 1:12 τέκνα θεοῦ *children of God*

Gal 2:16 ἐκ πίστεως Χριστοῦ *from (the) faith(fulness) of Christ*

3. <u>Exceptions to the Canon and its Corollary</u>. After studying the exceptions to Apollonius' Canon, Sanford D. Hull articulated seven conditions that helped explain all but 32 of the 461 exceptions.[3]

   a. *Anarthrous Proper Names.*

   Mark 10:35 οἱ υἱοὶ Ζεβεδαίου *the sons of Zebedee*

   b. *Anarthrous head noun as the object of a prepositional phrase.*

   1 Cor 1:9 εἰς <u>κοινωνίαν</u> τοῦ <u>υἱοῦ</u> αὐτοῦ Ἰησοῦ Χριστοῦ
   for <u>fellowship</u> <u>of</u> his <u>Son</u> Jesus Christ

   c. *The head noun is a predicate nominative.*

   Eph 5:1 Γίνεσθε οὖν μιμηταὶ τοῦ θεοῦ *Therefore, be imitators of God*

   d. *The genitive modifying noun is κύριος.*

   John 1:23 (Isa 40:3) τὴν ὁδὸν κυρίου *the way of the Lord*

   e. *Anarthrous head noun is in the vocative case.*

   Mark 5:7 Ἰησοῦ <u>υἱὲ</u> <u>τοῦ</u> <u>θεοῦ</u> τοῦ ὑψίστου *Jesus <u>Son</u> <u>of</u> <u>the God</u> Most High*

---

[3] Sanford D. Hull, "Exceptions to Apollonius' Canon in the New Testament: A Grammatical Study," *Trinity Journal* 7 1 (1986): 3–16.

f. *Anarthrous head noun is modified by an adjective of quantity that resists taking an article*, such as τις *someone*; numbers; πᾶς *all, every*; πολύς *many*; ἱκανός *sufficient*; πόσος *how many.*

Luke 7:12 ὄχλος τῆς πόλεως ἱκανὸς *a suffient crowd* of the city

g. *Anarthrous head noun is in apposition to another substantive.*

Rom 4:11a καὶ σημεῖον ἔλαβεν περιτομῆς σφραγῖδα τῆς δικαιοσύνης
and he received a sign of circumcision (as) a seal of righteousness

C. **Colwell's Rule:** E. C. Colwell's study was summarized and discussed with some examples in CASE IN POINT 5: MORE ABOUT PREDICATE NOMINATIVES IN JOHN 1. To summarize, Colwell stated his rule as follows: "Definite predicate nouns which precede the verb usually lack the article … a predicate nominative which precedes the verb cannot be translated as an indefinite or a 'qualitative' noun solely because of the absence of the article; if the context suggests that the predicate is definite, it should be translated as a definite noun…."[4] One refinement of the rule was that preverbal predicate nominatives are usually qualitative, not definitive or indefinite.[5] Philip B. Harner found that in such cases of preverbal anarthrous predicate nominatives, approximately 80% were qualitative in significance and 20% remained definite. Importantly, none are indefinite.[6] For an extended discussion, see Wallace 256-70.

D. **Granville Sharp's Rule:** From his treatise in 1798, Sharp expressed six rules, but the first is the one under consideration here:

> *When the copulative καὶ connects two nouns of the same case, [viz. nouns (either substantive or adjective, or participles) of personal description, respecting office, dignity, affinity, or connexion, and attributes, properties, or qualities, good or ill], if the article ὁ, or any of its cases, precedes the first of the said nouns or participles, and is not repeated before the second noun or participle, the latter always relates to the same person that is expressed or described by the first noun or participle: i.e. it denotes a farther description of the first-named person ….*[7]

Porter summarizes the rule: "Granville Sharp's rule states simply that *if a single article links*

---

[4] E. C. Colwell, "A Definite Rule for the Use of the Article in the Greek New Testament," *Journal of Biblical Literature* 52 (1933): 12-21; as quoted by Wallace 257.

[5] For a discussion of the subsequent research and qualification of Colwell's Rule, see Wallace 256-69, on whom I am dependent here.

[6] Philip B. Harner, "Qualitative Anarthrous Predicate Nouns: Mark 15:39 and John 1:1," *Journal of Biblical Literature* 92 (1973): 75–87; cited and summarized by Wallace.

[7] Granville Sharp, *Remarks on the Definitive Article in the Greek Text of the New Testament, Containing Many New Proofs of the Divinity of Christ, from Passages Which Are Wrongly Translated in the Common English Version* (Durham: L. Pennington, 1798), 3 (italics original); as quoted by Wallace (271).

two or more singular substantives (excluding personal names), the second and subsequent substantives are related to or further describe the first" (110, emphasis original).[8] Wallace adds importantly, "a perusal of his monograph reveals that he felt the rule could be applied absolutely only to personal, singular, non-proper nouns" (271).

1. <u>Examples</u>. Wallace has catalogued the construction by type of substantive.

a. *With Nouns.*

Mark 6:3 <u>ὁ υἱὸς</u> τῆς Μαρίας <u>καὶ ἀδελφὸς</u> Ἰακώβου καὶ Ἰωσῆτος καὶ Ἰούδα καὶ Σίμωνος
the <u>son</u> of Mary <u>and brother</u> of Jacob and Justus and Judah and Simon.

Eph 1:3 <u>ὁ θεὸς καὶ πατὴρ</u> τοῦ κυρίου ἡμῶν Ἰησοῦ Χριστοῦ
<u>The God</u> and <u>Father</u> of our Lord Jesus Christ...

Wallace supplies these other instances: Luke 20:37; John 20:17; Rom 15:6; 2 Cor 1:3; 11:31; Gal 1:4; Eph 1:3; 5:20; 6:21; Phil 4:20; Col 4:7; 1 Thess 1:3; 3:11, 13; 1 Tim 6:15; Heb 3:1; 12:2; Jas 1:27; 3:9; 1 Pet 1:3; 2:25; 5:1; 2 Pet 1:11; 2:20; 3:2, 18; Rev 1:6, 9.

b. *With Participles.*

John 6:33 ὁ γὰρ ἄρτος τοῦ θεοῦ ἐστιν <u>ὁ καταβαίνων</u> ἐκ τοῦ οὐρανοῦ <u>καὶ ζωὴν διδοὺς</u> τῷ κόσμῳ.
For the bread of God is <u>the One that comes</u> from heaven <u>and is giving</u> life to the world.

Wallace supplies these other instances: Matt 7:26; 13:20; 27:40; Mark 15:29; Luke 6:47; 16:18; John 5:24; 6:54; 9:8; Acts 10:35;15:38; 1 Cor 11:29; 2 Cor 1:21, 22; Gal 1:15; Eph 2:14; 2 Thess 2:4; Heb 7:1; Jas 1:25; 1 John 2:4, 9; 2 John 9; Rev 1:5; 16:15.

c. *With Adjectives.* See also Phlm 1 and Rev 3:17.

Acts 3:14a ὑμεῖς δὲ <u>τὸν ἅγιον καὶ δίκαιον</u> ἠρνήσασθε
And you denied <u>the Holy (One)</u> and <u>Righteous One</u>

d. *With Mixed Substantives.* See also Phil 2:25 and 1 Thess 3:2.

1 Tim 5:5a <u>ἡ</u> δὲ ὄντως <u>χήρα καὶ μεμονωμένη</u> ἤλπικεν ἐπὶ θεόν...
Now <u>the</u> true <u>widow</u> and <u>having become solitary</u> has hoped in God

In 1 Tim 5:5a a noun is combined with a participle governed by the single article.

---

[8] In the following discussion, I am dependent on Porter (110-11) and Wallace (270-90).

2. <u>Clarifications</u>.

a. *This rule does <u>not</u> apply to proper names*. Compare these parallel passages.

Mark 9:2b παραλαμβάνει ὁ Ἰησοῦς τὸν Πέτρον καὶ τὸν Ἰάκωβον καὶ τὸν Ἰωάννην
Jesus takes along Peter and Jacob and John.

Matt 17:1b παραλαμβάνει ὁ Ἰησοῦς τὸν Πέτρον καὶ Ἰάκωβον καὶ Ἰωάννην
Jesus takes along Peter and Jacob and John.

The difference between the two parallel passages is that Mark emphasizes the distinctness of each disciple, whereas Matthew treats them as a group.

b. *The article may in fact be repeated for the same individual.*

John 20:28 ἀπεκρίθη Θωμᾶς καὶ εἶπεν αὐτῷ· ὁ κύριός μου καὶ ὁ θεός μου.
Thomas answered back and said to him, "My Lord and my God!"

Here Thomas is speaking of Jesus as *Lord* and *God*.

c. *The rule does not apply to impersonal entities.* See Titus 2:13a immediately below. Notice that, even though *the hope* and *appearing* share an article and are singular, yet they are impersonal and so the rule does not apply.

3. <u>Notable Example</u>.

Titus 2:13 προσδεχόμενοι τὴν μακαρίαν ἐλπίδα καὶ ἐπιφάνειαν τῆς δόξης τοῦ μεγάλου θεοῦ καὶ σωτῆρος ἡμῶν Ἰησοῦ Χριστοῦ,

awaiting the blessed hope and appearing of the glory of our great <u>God</u> and <u>Savior</u>, Jesus Christ

This verse contains one instance of the rule. *God* and *Savior* share an article. Since the *Savior* is clearly *Jesus Christ* (appositional) thus Jesus Christ is also here affirmed as *God*. For other noteworthy passages, see Eph 5:20; 2 Pet 1:1, 11; 2:20; 3:18.

4. <u>Debatable Example</u>. The following is contested or even rejected because it is thought to contain a proper name by the inclusion of Χριστός *Christ*. But, was this word considered a proper name or a title like βασιλεύς *king* or κύριος *lord*? I would maintain that the latter was true. If so, there would be other passages (in addition to Eph 5:5) for which Sharp's rule would apply such as 2 Thess 1:12; 1 Tim 5:21; 2 Tim 4:1 (*pace* Wallace 276).

Eph 5:5 πᾶς πόρνος ἢ ἀκάθαρτος ἢ πλεονέκτης, ὅ ἐστιν εἰδωλολάτρης, οὐκ ἔχει κληρονομίαν ἐν τῇ βασιλείᾳ <u>τοῦ Χριστοῦ</u> καὶ <u>θεοῦ</u>.

Every sexually immoral person or unclean person or thief, which is an idolater, has no inheritance in the kingdom of <u>the Christ</u> and <u>God</u>.

5. <u>Sharp's Rule Applied to Plural Personal Nouns</u>. Wallace has extended the rule for plural personal nouns (**not** proper nouns or names) under various possibilities: *distinct, overlapping, subsets of one another,* or *identical*. There are 73 instances with 62 being unambiguous.

a. *Distinct but united groups.* See also Matt 2:4; 16:21; Mark 15:1; Luke 9:22; Acts 17:12.

Matt 3:7 πολλοὺς <u>τῶν</u> <u>Φαρισαίων</u> καὶ <u>Σαδδουκαίων</u>
many of <u>the</u> <u>Pharisees</u> and <u>Sadducees</u>

b. *Overlapping Groups.* See also Matt 4:24; Rev 21:8.

Luke 14:21 <u>τοὺς</u> <u>πτωχοὺς</u> καὶ <u>ἀναπείρους</u> καὶ <u>τυφλοὺς</u> καὶ <u>χωλούς</u>
<u>the</u> <u>poor</u> and <u>crippled</u> and <u>blind</u> and <u>lame</u>

c. *The first group is a subset of the second group.* See also Matt 5:20; 9:11; Mark 2:16; Luke 5:30; 6:35; 14:3.

Matt 12:38 τινες <u>τῶν</u> <u>γραμματέων</u> καὶ <u>Φαρισαίων</u>
certain ones of <u>the</u> <u>scribes</u> and <u>Pharisees</u>

d. *The second group is a subset of the first group.* See also Mark 2:16; 1 Tim 5:8; 3 John 5.

1 Cor 5:10 <u>τοῖς</u> <u>πλεονέκταις</u> καὶ <u>ἅρπαξιν</u>
with <u>the</u> <u>greedy</u> and <u>swindlers</u>

e. *The two groups are identical.* See also Mark 12:40; Luke 7:32; John 1:20; 20:29; 2 Cor 12:21; Eph 1:1; Phil 3:3; 1 Thess 5:12; 2 Pet 2:10; 2 John 9; Rev 1:1; 18:9.

Matt 5:6 <u>οἱ</u> <u>πεινῶντες</u> καὶ <u>διψῶντες</u> τὴν δικαιοσύνην
<u>the ones</u> <u>hungering</u> and <u>thirsting</u> for justice/righteousness

f. *Ambiguous.* See Eph 2:20; 4:11.

John 1:40 εἷς ἐκ <u>τῶν</u> δύο <u>τῶν</u> <u>ἀκουσάντων</u> παρὰ Ἰωάννου καὶ <u>ἀκολουθησάντων</u> αὐτῷ
one of <u>the</u> two <u>hearing</u> John and <u>following</u> him

6. <u>Sharp's Rule Applied to Plural Impersonal Nouns.</u> Wallace counts nearly 50 examples that fit into this category. The references are collected here for further study.

    a. *Distinct but united groups.* See Luke 21:12; 24:44; Acts 10:12; 21:25; 2 Cor 6:7; Eph 3:12, 18; Col 2:19; Rev 1:9; 20:10.

    b. *Overlapping Groups.* See 2 Cor 12:21.

    c. *The first group is a subset of the second group.* See Mark 12:33; Luke 1:6; 9:12; Rom 1:20; 16:18; Col 2:22; Phil 1:7; Rev 9:15.

    d. *The second group is a subset of the first group.* See Matt 24:36; Mark 6:36; Luke 5:17; 6:17; Heb 13:16; Rev 14:7.

    e. *The two groups are identical.* See Acts 1:25.

    f. *Ambiguous.* See Acts 2:23; 20:21; 2 Thess 2:1.

7. <u>Finally, the type of Plural Personal Substantive also delimits which possibilities may apply.</u>

    a. *article* + *substantive participle* + καί + *substantive participle* = *identical*

    b. *article* + *noun* + καί + *noun* = *distinct* or *overlap* (see Eph 2:20; 4:11)

    c. *article* + *adjective* + καί + *adjective* = *identical* or *overlap*

    d. *mixed constructions* = *mixed semantic values*

    e. The same possibilities apply also for plural impersonal nouns, although the identical possible relationship is rare. See Acts 2:23; 20:21; 2 Thess 2:1.

Complete WORKBOOK EXERCISES 24 and consult the ANSWER KEY & GUIDE as needed.

CASE IN POINT 24: INFINITIVES IN EPHESIANS 4:20-24

Eph 4:20-24 But you did not learn Christ in this way, [21] if indeed you have heard Him and have been taught in Him, just as truth is in Jesus, [22] that, in reference to your former manner of life, you <u>lay aside</u> the old self, which is being corrupted in accordance with the lusts of deceit, [23] and that you <u>be renewed</u> in the spirit of your mind, [24] and <u>put on</u> the new self, which in *the likeness of* God has been created in righteousness and holiness of the truth. (NASB95)

Eph 4:20-24 ὑμεῖς δὲ οὐχ οὕτως ἐμάθετε τὸν Χριστόν, [21] εἴ γε αὐτὸν ἠκούσατε καὶ ἐν αὐτῷ ἐδιδάχθητε, καθώς ἐστιν ἀλήθεια ἐν τῷ Ἰησοῦ, [22] <u>ἀποθέσθαι</u> ὑμᾶς κατὰ τὴν προτέραν ἀναστροφὴν τὸν παλαιὸν ἄνθρωπον τὸν φθειρόμενον κατὰ τὰς ἐπιθυμίας τῆς ἀπάτης, [23] <u>ἀνανεοῦσθαι</u> δὲ τῷ πνεύματι τοῦ νοὸς ὑμῶν [24] καὶ <u>ἐνδύσασθαι</u> τὸν καινὸν ἄνθρωπον τὸν κατὰ θεὸν κτισθέντα ἐν δικαιοσύνῃ καὶ ὁσιότητι τῆς ἀληθείας.

In the course of encouraging the Ephesians to live properly within a communal context (Eph 4:1-16), Paul turns to encourage them to live differently than the peoples around them. He then links such a different behavior to how they *were taught the Christ* (ἐμάθετε τὸν Χριστόν) in 4:20. The content of that teaching is given in a series of infinitives of indirect discourse in 4:22-24. Upon closer inspection, these infinitives disclose a process of spiritual/moral transformation. Paul's instructions here have fundamental similarities to other NT texts describing moral transformation. One simply needs to perform a word study on the Μι Verb ἀποτίθημι to see the connections (e.g. Rom 13:12; Col 3:8; Heb 12:1; Jas 1:21; 1 Pet 2:1; cf. Matt 16:24).

This is the content of what it means to be "taught the Christ" in 4:22-24:

(1) to put off the old self according to the former lifestyle, which is constantly being destroyed by the desires/lusts of deceitfulness;

(2) to be continually renewed with respect to the spirit of your mind; and

(3) to put on the new self which is created according to God in righteousness and holiness of the truth.

There are several notable grammatical features and exegetical nuances and issues to delve into.

Let's start with some observations. *The old self* (τὸν παλαιὸν ἄνθρωπον) is thoroughly contrasted with *the new self* (τὸν καινὸν ἄνθρωπον) in a variety of expressions.

THE OLD SELF (τὸν παλαιὸν ἄνθρωπον)	THE NEW SELF (τὸν καινὸν ἄνθρωπον)
o *to be put off* like clothing (ἀποτίθημι)	o *to be put on* like clothing (ἐνδύω)
o *according to former lifestyle* (κατὰ τὴν προτέραν ἀναστροφὴν)	o *according to God* (κατὰ θεὸν)
o *being destroyed* (τὸν φθειρόμενον)	o *created* (τὸν...κτισθέντα)
o *according desires/lusts* (κατὰ τὰς ἐπιθυμίας)	o *in righteousness and holiness* (ἐν δικαιοσύνῃ καὶ ὁσιότητι)
o *of the deceitfulness* (τῆς ἀπάτης)	o *of the truth* (τῆς ἀληθείας)

There is much grammar to ponder in this series of contrasts. The infinitives are in the aorist tense; but are they ingressive (*begin* to do these things), consummative (completed action), or merely constantive (unspecified action)? I think the latter.

The expressions *being corrupted* (τὸν φθειρόμενον) and *created* (τὸν...κτισθέντα) both involve articles used like relative pronouns pointing to the realities of each *self*. The old self is *continually being destroyed* (present tense participle) as a result of desires/lusts. This is a very sad, but graphic, depiction of what happens to persons who are consumed with addictions and lusts—their God-designed humanity undergoes a critical reduction in stature.

Deceitfulness (τῆς ἀπάτης) has an article as does the *Truth* (τῆς ἀληθείας). This is a particular use of the article with abstract nouns (see Wallace 226). It functions in this context to point to and contrast these two basic orientations to reality. It forces persons to ask whether they are influenced primarily by Deceitfulness or the Truth.

This brings us to a brief consideration of the central infinitive in 4:23: *to be continually renewed by* or *with reference to the spirit of your mind*. It is introduced with δέ indicating a contrast with *the Deceitfulness* that concludes 4:22. First, the infinitive is passive/middle and present in tense. The present tense is either progressive (continuous process; see Wallace 518) or habitual (something that regularly occurs or an ongoing state; see Wallace 521). In either case, it would seem that this continuous reality of being renewed is pivotal in the process of transformation.

Just how this transformation occurs, or its manner or location, is described by the dative case construction *by* or *with reference to the spirit of your mind* (τῷ πνεύματι τοῦ νοὸς ὑμῶν). We face the question of how the dative case is used here. A part of the answer may depend on whether we take spirit as *the (Holy) Spirit of our mind* (not likely, it seems to me) or simply as *the orientation* or *disposition of our mind* (as does BDAG). If it is the latter, then we likely have a dative of reference or respect. In other words, the dative of reference indicates that portion of us that must be renewed—*we are renewed with reference to the spirit/orientation of our mind*.

The *mind* is to be understood either as our faculty of thinking, a way of thinking, or the result of our thinking (BDAG). Given the context of transformation and the use of πνεῦμα, Paul would likely have in mind that our *way of thinking* needs renewing constantly. When this renewing takes place, then we are able to put off the old self and put on the new. The key is *renewal of our thinking*. Paul explains something quite similarly in Rom 12:1-2. Check it out!

Below is an image of a dedicatory marble base and inscription found near the Theater of Dionysus dating to the 2nd century BC.[9] Originally, there were four faces of the debauched god Silenus, who was the friend of Dionysus. The Greek text commemorates the election of two men as leaders (ἄρχοντες) of the family clan (γενός) of the Bakchidiai, an ancient family of Corinth. These men had received the honor "with pomp and circumstance" to lead the πομπή (the religious procession). The two brothers "consecrated" (ἀνέθηκαν) this piece; can you parse the verb ἀνέθηκαν (from ἀνατίθημι)? (See end of the footnote below.)

Πιστοκράτης καὶ Ἀπολλόδωρος Σατύρου Αὐρίδαι πομποστολήσαντες καὶ ἄρχοντες γενόμενοι τοῦ γένους τοῦ Βακχιαδῶν ἀνέθηκαν.	Pistokrates and Apollodoros, sons of Satyros, of the demos Auridai, having been the leaders of the πομπή (or religious procession), and having been elected archons of the γενός of the Bakchiadai, consecrated.

---

[9] The image (slightly enhanced) and translation is from Victor Duruy, *History of Greece, and of the Greek People: From the Earliest Times to the Roman Conquest*, trans. M. M. Ripley, vol. Vol. 1, Sect. 2 (Boston: Estes and Lauriat, 1890), 553. The inscriptional text is referenced IG II² 2949 and may be found at the PHI inscriptional database http://epigraphy. packhum.org/inscriptions/main. The verb ἀνέθηκαν is AAI-3P.

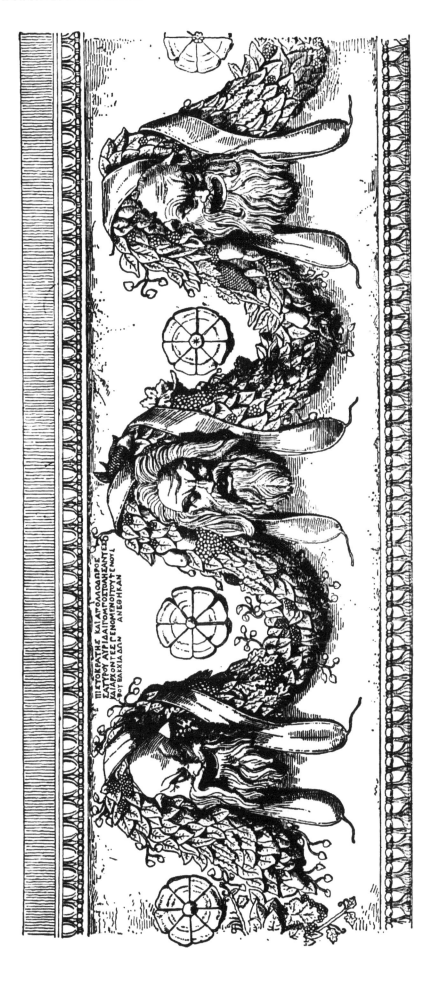

CHAPTER 25

Jesus has much to say about material goods. Two-thirds of his parables speak to matters of wealth. One passage in particular is Luke 12. After telling the parable of the rich man building bigger barns to store his stuff (12:16-21), Jesus then gives detailed instructions with commands and prohibitions (12:22-40). We need to hear what he said.

This chapter will introduce the **Imperative Mood** that is used for commands, prohibitions, requests, and petitions. Importantly, commands and the like may be mitigated, and so we will also look at the **Pragmatics of the Potency of Commands**. This leads in to a discussion of **Periphrastic Participles formed with Non-Indicative Moods**. Finally, we will look at the formation and the uses of **Adverbial**, **Comparative**, and **Superlative Adjectives** before then considering the possibility of **Comparative Emphasis**.

VOCABULARY 25 MIDDLE-FORMED VERBS, COMPARATIVES, AND CONJUNCTIONS

Middle-Formed Verbs:

ἀσπάζομαι [59]	I greet, welcome; I embrace
δέχομαι [56]	I receive, welcome; I take

Adverb sometimes used in Comparisons:

μᾶλλον [81]	rather; more

Comparative Adjectives:

μείζων, -ον [48]	larger, greater (from μέγας)
πλείω, -ον [57]	more, greater (from πολύς)

Conjunctions:

ἄρα [53]	therefore
διό [53]	wherefore, therefore
εἴτε [65]	whether, if; or
εἴτε ... εἴτε	whether ... or
ἤ [346]	or; than (*with comparitives*)

After learning vocabulary to this point, you will know 81.7% of the words in the GNT. If you are able, listen to audio recordings of VOCABULARY 25 and complete the CROSSWORD PUZZLE in the WORKBOOK EXERCISES.

NOTES ON VOCABULARY 25:

There are no English cognates that will help the student memorize the vocabulary. But, the comparative forms of μείζων,-ον and πλείω,-ον should be recognizable from the adjectives already learned.

Ἄρα and διό are important inferential conjunctions that generally indicate a move from cause to effect (causation). These conjunctions signal the logical development of thought. More specifically, ἄρα is marked +consequence and tends to be used to support inter-clausal connections (near contexts) rather inter-sentential ones (extended contexts). For example, ἄρα connects conditional sentence parts: "if this, *then* (ἄρα) that." Regarding Διό, which is derived from δι' ὅ (διά and the neuter relative pronoun ὅ; BDAG 250), Levinsohn helpfully summarizes his views: "it typically introduces an expository or hortatory THESIS that is inferred from what has already been stated. I therefore classify the constraint that the presence of διό imposes as **+Inferential +Continuative**. It contrasts with οὖν in that it does not move the argument on to a new point."[1]

The remaining conjunctions, εἴτε and ἤ, may be used alone or in combination with other conjunctions and adverbs, thus forming correlative emphasis (see §15.6 CORRELATIVE EMPHASIS: LISTS AND COORDINATED CONNECTIVES). Εἴτε combines εἰ and τε and has the significance of each: εἰ is used for conditions and questions (direct or indirect; see NOTES ON VOCABULARY 8) and τε is marked for +addition and +sameness (not of identity, but function; see NOTES ON VOCABULARY 15). Ἤ marks +alternative and may be used to form comparative statements (see §25.5.C.3.b below).

25.1 THE IMPERATIVE MOOD (ἡ Προστατικὴ Ἔγκλισις): FORMATION AND TRANSLATION

A. **Introduction:** The Imperative Mood is a mood of command, request, or volition. As such, an Imperative verb will be naturally prominent within the discourse. In the GNT, the mood has a frequency of 1,820 occurrences, just lower than the Subjunctive Mood with 1,870 occurrences. The Imperative Mood is found only in the Present and Aorist Tenses. Like other non-Indicative moods, it is not marked for time, but retains verbal aspect. (See Wallace 485-93.) The parsing abbreviation is M.

B. **Negation and Prohibition:** To negate an Imperative Mood verb, μή is used. Such a negated command is called a prohibition. Remember that one use of the Subjunctive Mood was to create prohibitions with the Aorist Tense (see §22.4.B).

C. **Present Imperative Formation and Translation:** The Imperative Mood is found mainly in the 2nd person singular and plural. However, it does occur in the 3rd person, which may seem rather odd: e.g., _Let_ him _do_ this or that.

---

[1] Stephen H. Levinsohn, "'Therefore' or 'Wherefore': What's the Difference?" (presented at the SBL Greek Language and Linguistics Section, San Francisco, CA, 2011), 3. Emphasis original.

1. <u>Present Tense</u>. Here are the Imperative Endings for the Present Tense.

	PRESENT ACTIVE				**PRESENT MIDDLE/PASSIVE**	
	sg.	pl.			sg.	pl.
2	-ε	-ετε		2	-ου	-εσθε
3	-ετω	-έτωσαν		3	-εσθω	-έσθωσαν

2. <u>Translation of Present Imperatives</u>. The verbal aspect conveyed by the Present Tense in the Imperative Mood is imperfective: "Action as viewed internally as in progress or incomplete." As such, using the Present Tense indicates that the action commanded is understood as *an ongoing process*, or *customary activity*, or involves *repeated actions* (see Wallace 721-22). Thus, the Present Imperative could be translated *Continue doing such and such...!* or, *Be sure (not) to be doing such and such...!* It is sometimes difficult to translate the significance of a Present Tense Imperative.

   a. **Active:**

sg.	2	πιστεύε	Continue believing! (sg.)
	3	πιστευέτω	*Let him* continue believing!
pl.	2	πιστεύετε	Continue believing! (pl.)
	3	πιστευέτωσαν	Let *them* continue believing!

   b. **Middle/Passive:** (Here translated passively)

sg.	2	πιστεύου	Continue to be entrusted!
	3	πιστευέσθω	*Let him* continue to be entrusted!
pl.	2	πιστεύεσθε	Continue to be entrusted!
	3	πιστευέσθωσαν	*Let them* continue to be entrusted!

D. Aorist Imperative: Formation and Translation:

1. <u>Aorist Tense</u>. Here are the Imperative endings for the Aorist Tense.

	AORIST A				**AORIST M**				**AORIST P**	
	sg.	pl.			sg.	pl.			sg.	pl.
2	-σον	-σατε		2	-σαι	-σασθε		2	-θητι	-θητε
3	-σάτω	-σάτωσαν		3	-σάσθω	-σάσθωσαν		3	-θήτω	-θήτωσαν

2. <u>Translation of Aorist Imperatives</u>. The verbal aspect conveyed by the Aorist Tense in the Imperative Mood is perfective: "Action as viewed as a whole externally or as complete (but not necessarily completed)." As such, using the Aorist Tense indicates that the action commanded or prohibited remains *general* or is *simply undefined*, with no indication of what is involved in the action. Thus, the Aorist Imperative could be translated *Do such and such...!*

a. *Active.*

sg.	2	πίστευσον	Believe! (sg.)
	3	πιστευσάτω	*Let him* believe!
pl.	2	πιστεύσατε	Believe! (pl.)
	3	πιστευσάτωσαν	*Let them* believe!

b. *Passive.*

sg.	2	πιστεύθητι	Be entrusted! (sg.)
	3	πιστευθήτω	*Let him* be entrusted!
pl.	2	πιστεύθητε	Be entrusted! (pl.)
	3	πιστευθήτωσαν	*Let them* be entrusted!

3. <u>Mι Verbs</u>. The Imperative endings for Mι Verbs are virtually identical to the above. One exception is the Aorist 2nd person singular. Since this form is very common, it is given below for δίδωμι, ἵστημι, and τίθημι:

<u>Aorist second person sg.</u>
δός	*Give!*
στῆθι	*Stand!* (2nd Aorist of ἵστημι)
θές	*Set!*

For the forms of the Imperative Mood of Mι Verbs, see APPENDIX §23.

4. <u>Contract and Liquid Verbs</u>. For the formation of Imperatives from Contract and Liquid Verbs, see APPENDIX §21 and APPENDIX §22 respectively.

25.2 THE IMPERATIVE MOOD: USES AND SIGNIFICANCE

A. **Functions:** Commands are always prominent within a discourse. Additionally, the Imperative Mood has a variety of functions. It is important also to carefully consider the verbal aspect distinctives of the Aorist (perfective) or Present (imperfective). Wallace summarizes as follows:

> With the *aorist*, the force generally is to *command the action as a whole*, without focusing on duration, repetition, etc. In keeping with its aspectual force, the aorist puts forth a *summary command*. With the *present*, the force generally is to *command the action as an ongoing process*. This is in keeping with the present's aspect, which portrays an *internal* perspective (485, emphasis original).

1. <u>Command</u>. This mood is mainly used for **commands** or **positive exhortations** (see Wallace 485-86, 718-22).

a. *Present Tense.*

Eph 6:21 <u>τίμα</u> τὸν πατέρα σου καὶ τὴν μητέρα.
(Continuously) Honor your father and your mother.
Or, *Be honoring your father and your mother.*

b. *Aorist Tense.*

> **Luke 11:1** κύριε, <u>δίδαξον</u> ἡμᾶς προσεύχεσθαι, *Lord, <u>teach</u> us how to pray.*

c. *Aorist and Present Tense together.*

> **Mark 8:34b** Εἴ τις θέλει ὀπίσω μου ἀκολουθεῖν, <u>ἀπαρνησάσθω</u> ἑαυτὸν καὶ <u>ἀράτω</u> τὸν σταυπὸν αὐτοῦ καὶ <u>ἀκολουθείτω</u> μοι.
>
> *If someone wishes to follow after me, <u>let</u> him <u>deny</u> himself and <u>take up</u> his cross and <u>continue following</u> me.*

2. <u>Prohibition</u>. Less often the Imperative mood is employed for negative commands (see Wallace 487, 723-25). Remember that prohibitions may also be formed with μή and the Aorist Subjunctive (see §22.4.B). Thus, the choice to use a prohibition with the Present Tense Imperative verb is significant, because of the imperfective aspect. The first example is with a 2nd aorist imperative form.

> **Matt 6:3** σοῦ δὲ ποιοῦντος ἐλεημοσύνην <u>μὴ γνώτω</u> ἡ ἀριστερά σου τί ποιεῖ ἡ δεξιά σου,
> *But as you are making an act of mercy (almsgiving), <u>do not let</u> your left hand <u>know</u> what your right hand is doing.*

> **Eph 5:11** καὶ <u>μὴ συγκοινωνεῖτε</u> τοῖς ἔργοις τοῖς ἀκάρποις τοῦ σκότους, μᾶλλον δὲ καὶ <u>ἐλέγχετε</u>.
>
> *And <u>do not be associated with</u> the fruitless deeds of darkness, but rather instead also <u>be refuting</u> [them].*

3. <u>Requests and Petitions</u>. Additionally, the Imperative Mood may be used in **requests** and **petitions**, especially when inferiors are addressing superiors (see Wallace 487-88). For example, the Lord's Prayer is full of requests and not commands! Here is one of them:

> **Matt 6:11** Τὸν ἄρτον ἡμῶν τὸν ἐπιούσιον <u>δὸς</u> ἡμῖν σήμερον.
> *<u>Give</u> to us our daily bread today.*

It would be entirely wrong to take this as a command to God. It is a petition in a prayer.

B. **A Note of Caution:** You can begin to see the importance of whether or not the Aorist or Present Tense is used with the Imperative Mood. The presentation in this textbook is based on the most recent research that maintains that the Present Imperatives point to the continuous action involved in the commanded action and that Aorist Imperatives simply refer to the action commanded as a whole or as undefined. Older grammars (both at the intermediate and advanced levels) and commentators may argue for more nuanced meanings of the tenses in the Imperative Mood. However, be sure to consult more recent reference Greek grammars (since 1990) for further explanation of the significance of the Imperative Mood in the Greek NT. On further uses of the Imperative mood, see Wallace 713-25.

CHECK POINT 25.1-2 IMPERATIVES

Given these three passages containing imperative verbs with a basic translation, **first**, parse the verb form. **Second**, consider the verbal aspect significance of each verb. **Third**, provide a translation that might better reflect the verbal aspect.

Luke 18:16 ὁ δὲ Ἰησοῦς προσεκαλέσατο αὐτὰ λέγων· ἄφετε τὰ παιδία ἔρχεσθαι πρός με καὶ μὴ κωλύετε αὐτά, τῶν γὰρ τοιούτων ἐστὶν ἡ βασιλεία τοῦ θεοῦ.
And Jesus called to them saying, "Allow the little children to come to me and do not hinder them, for the Kingdom of God belongs to such as these.

ἄφετε = (hint: a Μι verb.)

κωλύετε =

---

1 Thess 5:25-26 Ἀδελφοί, προσεύχεσθε [καὶ] περὶ ἡμῶν. 26 Ἀσπάσασθε τοὺς ἀδελφοὺς πάντας ἐν φιλήματι ἁγίῳ.
25 Brothers, pray also for us. 26 Greet all the brothers with a holy kiss.

προσεύχεσθε =

Ἀσπάσασθε =

Luke 3:11 ἀποκριθεὶς δὲ ἔλεγεν αὐτοῖς· ὁ ἔχων δύο χιτῶνας μεταδότω τῷ μὴ ἔχοντι, καὶ ὁ ἔχων βρώματα ὁμοίως ποιείτω.
And responding back, he was saying to them, "The one that is having two tunics impart to the one not having, and the one that is having food rations do likewise."

μεταδότω =

ποιείτω =

SUGGESTED ANSWERS

Luke 18:16 ὁ δὲ Ἰησοῦς προσεκαλέσατο αὐτὰ λέγων· <u>ἄφετε</u> τὰ παιδία ἔρχεσθαι πρός με καὶ μὴ <u>κωλύετε</u> αὐτά, τῶν γὰρ τοιούτων ἐστὶν ἡ βασιλεία τοῦ θεοῦ.
And Jesus called to them saying, "<u>Allow</u> the little children to come to me and <u>do not hinder</u> them, for the Kingdom of God belongs to such as these.

ἄφετε = **1.** AAM-2P; for parsing help, see CH. 24 and APPENDIX §23. **2.** Perfective aspect: "Action as viewed as a whole externally or as complete (but not necessarily completed)." **3.** Translation is fine.

κωλύετε = **1.** PAM-2P; **2.** Imperfective aspect: "Action as viewed internally as in progress or incomplete." **3.** "Don't be hindering…"

1 Thess 5:25-26 Ἀδελφοί, <u>προσεύχεσθε</u> [καὶ] περὶ ἡμῶν. [26] <u>Ἀσπάσασθε</u> τοὺς ἀδελφοὺς πάντας ἐν φιλήματι ἁγίῳ.
[25] *Brothers, <u>pray</u> also for us.* [26] *Greet all the brothers with a holy kiss.*

προσεύχεσθε = **1.** PDM-2P; **2.** Imperfective aspect: "Action as viewed internally as in progress or incomplete." **3.** "Be (repeatedly) praying for us." or "Keep praying for us."

Ἀσπάσασθε = **1.** ADM-2P; **2.** Perfective Aspect: "Action as viewed as a whole externally or as complete (but not necessarily completed)." **3.** Translation is fine. If this were imperfective aspect, the envisioned kissing would be repeated or continuous(!).

Luke 3:11 ἀποκριθεὶς δὲ ἔλεγεν αὐτοῖς· ὁ ἔχων δύο χιτῶνας <u>μεταδότω</u> τῷ μὴ ἔχοντι, καὶ ὁ ἔχων βρώματα ὁμοίως <u>ποιείτω</u>.
And responding back, he was saying to them, "The one that is having two tunics <u>impart</u> to the one not having, and the one that is having food rations <u>do</u> likewise."

μεταδότω = **1.** ADM-2P; **2.** Perfective Aspect: "Action as viewed as a whole externally or as complete (but not necessarily completed)." **3.** Better translation: *Let the one that is having two tunics <u>impart</u>* ... since this is 3rd person.

ποιείτω = **1.** PAM-3S; **2.** Imperfective aspect: "Action as viewed internally as in progress or incomplete." **3.** better translation: *Let the one that is having food rations <u>be (repeatedly) doing</u> likewise*... since this is 3rd person and has imperfective. It would seem that the difference between the aorist imperative versus the present is that, once you have an extra tunic, you give it away (Aorist/perfective). However, food is a daily and repeated and recurring need (Present/imperfective).

25.3 POTENCY OF EXHORTATIONS: PRAGMATIC CONSIDERATIONS

A. **Introduction to the Potency and Mitigation of Exhortations:** We recognize that certain commands or requests carry different weight and are appropriate for certain situations. Consider these two lists: On the left, I have arranged the statements (as best as I could) from least to most forceful, assuming the same person speaking (whoever this may be).[2] This depends, of course, on stress on the words (indicated by italics) and the situation envisioned. You may or may not agree with my order. Also, it is important to understand that a mitigated exhortation does not mean necessarily that the exhortation is less important, but only that it was presented with less force. One must carefully consider contextual indicators of the situation and argumentation to assess the (relative) importance of this or that exhortation.

For the list of statements on the right, how would you rank the statements from least to most forceful assuming the same person speaking? See this footnote for my proposed order.[3]

"Marcy, time to get up."	1. "You *must* clean up your room!"
"Let's get up, sweetie."	2. "You *need* to clean up your room."
"Hey, let's get Jonathan up, too."	3. "I…need…you…to…clean…up…your…room!"
"Time to get up."	4. "I would like you to clean up your room."
"*Mom* said to get up."	5. "You can clean up your room."
"Please get up."	6. "You *will* clean up your room!"
"Okay, *I'm asking you* to get up."	7. "Let's clean up your room."
"Get up!"	8. "Jonathan Thomas, clean up your room *right now*!"
"Get up *now*!"	9. "*Dad said* to clean up your room.
"Get *yourself* up *now*!"	10. "Clean up your room!"
"*Marcy Marie Smith*, get up now!"	11. "I would suggest that you clean up your room."

Now, we likely disagreed on the order of some of these. This may be due to (sub)cultural differences of word usage, conventions of stressing words with such statements, imagining a parent or a sibling speaking, and/or envisioning different communication situations that would accompany the statements. For example, the two statements "You can clean up your room" and "I would suggest that you clean up your room" may both be responses to a question asked of the person making the statements: "What should I do now?" In this case, the two statements are suggestions, but the one beginning with "I would suggest" (which is a metacomment; see §10.8 METACOMMENTS AND PRAGMATICS) carries more gravitas by appealing to the authority of "I," especially if a parent is making the statements.

---

[2] This expands what I have presented in *2 Corinthians: A Handbook on the Greek Text*, Baylor Handbook on the Greek New Testament (Waco, TX: Baylor University Press, 2015), xxvi.

[3] From least to most forceful: 5, 11, 7, 4, 2, 9, 10, 1, 3, 6, 8. Levinsohn begins his treatment of potency by having readers in an exercise consider the relative potency of a different list of commands (see the following footnote).

To help understand the relative "weighting" of these statements, Levinsohn applies two terms, **potency** and **mitigation**: "One way to distinguish different forms of exhortation is on the basis of their relative potency. Wendland (2000:58) defines the potency of an exhortation as 'its relative directness, urgency, or degree of mitigation'. 'Mitigate' means 'make less severe' (*OED*)."[4] I am using (and developing at places) Levinsohn's treatment of factors affecting potency and influencing the choice of the type of exhortation.[5]

B. **Factors Affecting Potency:** There are many factors that can be considered when studying the potency of exhortations. These provide a good place to begin. Moreover, there will always be specific contextual considerations that must be weighed.

1. Verbal Mood.

   a. ***Imperative Mood Verbs*** are usually more potent than exhortations formed with ***Subjunctive Mood Verbs***, i.e. prohibition and hortatory subjunctives. But Imperatives and Subjunctive mood exhortations are more potent than ***Indicative Mood Verbs*** and ***Infinitives*** (used in indirect exhortations). For example, the use of infinitives in Rom 12:15 mitigates their potency as exhortations in contrast to the 2nd person imperatives of 12:14.

     Rom 12:14-15 εὐλογεῖτε τοὺς διώκοντας [ὑμᾶς], εὐλογεῖτε καὶ μὴ καταρᾶσθε. [15] <u>χαίρειν</u> μετὰ χαιρόντων, <u>κλαίειν</u> μετὰ κλαιόντων.

       Bless the ones that are persecuting you, bless and do not curse. [15] *<u>Rejoice</u> with the ones that are rejoicing, <u>weep</u> with the ones that are weeping.*

   b. ***Circumstantial Participles***, if they follow and explicate the nuclear clause with an exhortation, have the same potency. If they precede the exhortation, circumstantial participles provide a back grounded attendant circumstance to the nuclear clause. These prenuclear participles will provide an important framework for the exhortation and/or describe procedural action prior to the exhortation (see §17.4.D).

     1 Thess 5:8 ἡμεῖς δὲ ἡμέρας <u>ὄντες</u> <u>νήφωμεν</u> <u>ἐνδυσάμενοι</u> θώρακα πίστεως καὶ ἀγάπης καὶ περικεφαλαίαν ἐλπίδα σωτηρίας·

       But <u>let us</u> ourselves, <u>being</u> of the day, <u>be sober minded</u>, putting on a breastplate of faithfulness and love and a helmet, the hope of salvation.

---

    [4] Stephen H. Levinsohn, *Self-Instruction Materials on Narrative Discourse Analysis* (Dallas: SIL International, 2012), 73-81. He cites Ernst R. Wendland, "'Stand fast in the true grace of God!' A Study of 1 Peter," *Journal of Translation and Textlinguistics* 13 (2000): 25-102 and the *Oxford English Dictionary* (OED).
    [5] Levinsohn's treatment was initially summarized by my teaching intern Andrew Coutras.

The prenuclear circumstantial participle clause ἡμέρας ὄντες *being of the day* provides a critical framework and basis (the adverbial translation of "since" may be appropriate) within which the exhortation is given, here, a hortatory subjunctive νήφωμεν *let us be sober minded*. The postnuclear circumstantial participle ἐνδυσάμενοι *putting on* explicates the exhortation (*let us be sober minded*) and hence has a concomitant potency. This explication may be translated with the adverbial sense of *means* ("by means of").

2. Person. **2nd Person** (*You*) is more potent than **1st Person** (*We*, as in *Let us*....). Both are more potent than **3rd Person**. In this later case, the exhortation is often mitigated by being passed along from one party to another. So, in this regard, in Rom 12:14 above, we observe the most potent exhortation, a 2nd Person imperative form. In 1 Thess 5:8 we see a less potent 1st Person plural hortatory subjunctive. Below is a mitigated 3rd person imperative form.

> **1 Tim 3:12a** διάκονοι ἔστωσαν μιᾶς γυναικὸς ἄνδρες,
> *Let deacons be husbands of one wife,*

3. Independent versus Dependent Clauses. Exhortations in independent clauses are generally more potent than those in dependent clauses. Exhortations in dependent clauses are indirect and, because of this, may be mitigated.

> **1 Thess 4:13** *We do not want you* (Οὐ θέλομεν), *brothers, to be ignorant about those who fall asleep, in order that* (ἵνα) *you would not grieve like the rest that have no hope.*

However, we must remember that decreased potency does not mean decreased importance. Some dependent exhortative clauses are introduced with intensifying metacomments, such παρακαλῶ ὑμᾶς *I exhort you* as in this example.

> **Rom 12:1** Παρακαλῶ οὖν ὑμᾶς, ἀδελφοί, διὰ τῶν οἰκτιρμῶν τοῦ θεοῦ παραστῆσαι τὰ σώματα ὑμῶν θυσίαν ζῶσαν ἁγίαν εὐάρεστον τῷ θεῷ, τὴν λογικὴν λατρείαν ὑμῶν·
> *Therefore, I exhort that you, brothers, through the compassions of God present your bodies as a sacrifice, living, holy, pleasing to God, your reasonable worship.*

Many other important factors are at play here, such as the presence of intensifying orienting expressions: the direct address, appeal to God's compassions, and the appositional elaboration of what it means to offer bodies as a sacrifice. So, such metacomments as παρακαλῶ increase the prominence and potency of the exhortations that are found in the dependent clauses. See, e.g., 1 Tim 6:13-14 and the example below involving dependent infinitives in Eph 4:22-24.

4. <u>Mitigating or Intensifying Expressions/Orienters.</u> Adding words like "Please, …" will mitigate the command and make it less potent. Conversely, adding a qualifier like ἐν τῷ
ὀνόματι 'Ιησοῦ Χριστοῦ *in the name of Jesus* (Acts 3:6) intensifies the command. A
worthwhile study would investigate and attempt to classify expressions and orienteers used
with exhortations to assess their contribution to mitigate or intensify commands. For example, the use of vocatives of direct address intensifies exhortations by making explicit
reference to identity, social relationships, and their concomitant responsibilities. So, the
vocative ἀδελφοί *brothers* not only identifies and affirms social identity and relationship,
but also implies the obligation to act fittingly.

5. <u>Chart Summarizing These Factors along a Relative Scale of Most to Less Potency.</u>

EXHORTATION MOOD	PERSON	POTENCY	CLAUSE TYPE	QUALIFIERS
Imperative	2nd	MOST	Independent (direct)	Intensifying
Subjunctive	1st	↑		
Indicative		↓		
Infinitive	3rd	LESS	Dependent (Indirect)	Mitigating

C. Factors Influencing Choice of Type of Exhortation:

1. <u>Social relationship Involved.</u> One should think of power, authority, eldership, knowledge,
wisdom and the like and how these will affect the form of the exhortation.

2. <u>Type of Hortatory Discourse.</u>

   a. *Instruction versus Persuasion.* Imperatives are the default exhortation for instruction.
   Conversely, subjunctives, as a mitigated form of exhortation, are more fitting in con-
   texts of persuasion (e.g., *Let us do this…* or *let him do that…*). See, e.g., the Book of
   Hebrews that uses many hortatory subjunctives throughout.

   b. *Rebuke verses Advising.* Tone and the use of rhetorical questions interspersed among
   commands will likely demarcate rebuke or censor from giving friendly advice. Also,
   when one gives advice, there is more often appeal to opinion through using metacomments and indirect commands, such as "I would want you to do this …."

3. <u>Position of Exhortation.</u> The location of exhortations helps one consider their potency in relation to the type of discourse.

   a. ***Advisement.*** Such discourse usually begins with *less potent exhortations* and then ends
   with *more potent exhortations*. First Thessalonians exemplifies such discourse. An indi-

rect exhortation occurs at 4:13; the first direct exhortation uses an affirming 2nd person form at 4:18; then one finds two less potent 1st person exhortations in 5:6, 8 before indirect exhortations at 5:12-13. Then we observe an intensifying orienter followed by several 2nd person imperatives in 5:14-26 and finally a very strong, although indirect, exhortation as the object of Paul's intensifying statement at 5:27: "I adjure you in the Lord to read the letter to all the brethren" (Ἐνορκίζω ὑμᾶς τὸν κύριον ἀναγνωσθῆναι τὴν ἐπιστολὴν πᾶσιν τοῖς ἀδελφοῖς).

b. ***Rebuke***. Such discourse will likely begin with potent exhortations. Galatians exemplifies this in many respects, since the first commands in 1:8-9 are "Let him be accursed!" (ἀνάθεμα ἔστω) followed by two rhetorical questions in 1:10a. See also 3:1-5 and the tone expressed in the epistle, which Paul explicitly wants to change (4:19-20).

4. <u>Emphasis and Prominence</u>. Emphatic constructions will affect the potency of exhortations, making them less or more potent. Here, I have in mind redundant personal pronouns (see above 1 Thess 5:8 ἡμεῖς), repetitions (see above Rom 12:14 εὐλογεῖτε), and fronted genitives and quantitative specifiers (see above 1 Tim 3:12a μιᾶς γυναικὸς), etc. One must study which constituents are emphasized and consider why they are so in the discursive context.

5. <u>Scope and Timing of Exhortation</u>. One should also consider whether the exhortation is simple or more complex action, entails a single act or multiple continuous ones, has immediacy or urgency or not. Levinsohn comments on verbal aspect in this regard: "In Greek, forms with perfective aspect ("aorists") are used for exhortations that call for a single, usually immediate response. Forms with imperfective aspect ("presents") are used for those of a more general or indefinite nature."[6] See the examples given above under §25.2.A and elsewhere.

D. **Relative Importance of Exhortations and Weighing Exegetical Determinants:** I should reiterate here that a less potent or a mitigated exhortation does not necessarily mean that it is less important. Contextual and situational considerations must help to determine that. For example, in Eph 4:22-24 Paul uses infinitives to summarize teaching on the moral transformation in the Christian life (see my fuller treatment in CASE IN POINT 24: INFINITIVES IN EPH 4:20-24).

> 4:22 *to put off the old self according to the former lifestyle, which is constantly being destroyed by the desires/lusts of deceitfulness;*
>
> 4:23 *to be continually renewed with respect to the spirit of your mind; and*
>
> 4:24 *to put on the new self which is created according to God in righteousness and holiness of the truth.*

---

[6] Levinsohn, *Self-Instruction Materials on Narrative Discourse Analysis*, 75.

Since infinitives have the lowest exhortative potency of the verbal Moods and form dependent clauses that are less potent, one might consider (wrongly) that, therefore, Paul's exhortative statements in 4:22-24 are relatively unimportant. However, Paul used a number of important intensifying qualifiers with them (*being destroyed* vs. *created according to God*, etc.), created a list (see §15.6 CORRELATIVE EMPHASIS: LISTS AND COORDINATED CONNECTIVES), and framed these statements as being "taught in Christ" (4:20-21) that provide a foundation for all the following exhortations in the rest of the book (through 6:20).

25.4 PERIPHRASTIC PARTICIPLE WITH NON-INDICATIVE MOODS

A. **Introduction:** Periphrastic Participles are found with a verb of being like εἰμί or γίνομαι ascribing a verbal attribute to the subject. Although often treated and translated like finite verbs, periphrastic participles are different because they require two verbal components, allow for flexibility of word order, are able to represent a complexity of verbal aspect (e.g. imperfective with stative), and generally draw more attention to the verbal affirmation. See §19.5 PERIPHRASTIC USE OF THE PARTICIPLE. Interestingly, periphrastic participles occur with forms of εἰμί or γίνομαι in different moods, which impacts the case of the participle, thus making the construction sometimes hard to identify. However, it is worth noticing the construction to consider the exegetical significance.

B. **With Non-Indicative Moods:**

1. *Imperatives.* The forcefulness of the periphrastic participles is augmented by their being part of a command. In 2 Cor 6:14, Paul is ramping up his admonitions for the Corinthians to differentiate themselves from idolatrous involvements (see 6:15–7:1).

   2 Cor 6:14a Μὴ <u>γίνεσθε ἑτεροζυγοῦντες</u> ἀπίστοις·
   Do not <u>be becoming unequally yoked</u> with unbelievers!

   Luke 12:35 <u>Ἔστωσαν</u> ὑμῶν αἱ ὀσφύες <u>περιεζωσμέναι</u> καὶ οἱ λύχνοι <u>καιόμενοι</u>·
   <u>Let</u> your loins <u>be covered</u> and your lamps <u>burning</u>.

2. *Subjunctives.* In the following two examples, the periphrastic participles occur within constructions taking the subjunctive mood. See also 1 Cor 7:29-31.

   John 16:24b αἰτεῖτε καὶ λήμψεσθε, ἵνα ἡ χαρὰ ὑμῶν <u>ᾖ πεπληρωμένη</u>.
   Ask and you will receive, in order that your joy <u>would be fulfilled</u>.

   Jas 5:15b κἂν ἁμαρτίας <u>ᾖ πεποιηκώς</u>, ἀφεθήσεται αὐτῷ.
   If he <u>has committed</u> sins, it will be forgiven him.

3. *Participles.* When occurring with participles, the case of the periphrastic participle will depend on the case of the head participle form of εἰμί or γίνομαι. In Col 1:21 below, the second periphrastic participle is accusative to agree with ὄντας.

Eph 4:18a ἐσκοτωμένοι τῇ διανοίᾳ <u>ὄντες</u>...
   since they <u>are</u> <u>(having been) darkened</u> in (their) understanding...

Col 1:21-22a Καὶ ὑμᾶς ποτε <u>ὄντας</u> <u>ἀπηλλοτριωμένους</u> καὶ ἐχθροὺς τῇ διανοίᾳ ἐν τοῖς ἔργοις τοῖς πονηροῖς, νυνὶ δὲ ἀποκατήλλαξεν ἐν τῷ σώματι τῆς σαρκὸς αὐτοῦ
   And <u>as</u> you at that time <u>were</u> <u>being alienated</u> and enemies in thinking with evil actions, but now he reconciled [you] in the body of his flesh.

4. *Infinitives.* When occurring with infinitives, the case of the periphrastic participle will be accusative. In the first example, the verb of being is ὑπάρχω and occurs within an impersonal verbal construction with the participle δέον from δεῖ *it is necessary, one must.* In Luke 9:18a, the participle occurs within a preposition with infinitive construction (see §23.5 ADVERBIAL INFINITIVES). To use the periphrastic construction here seems quite unnecessary, unless to stress Jesus' praying as a contextually important verbal attribute.

Acts 19:36b δέον ἐστὶν ὑμᾶς <u>κατεσταλμένους</u> <u>ὑπάρχειν</u> καὶ μηδὲν προπετὲς πράσσειν.
   It is necessary that you <u>be</u> <u>calm</u> and do nothing rash.

Luke 9:18a Καὶ ἐγένετο ἐν τῷ <u>εἶναι</u> αὐτὸν <u>προσευχόμενον</u> κατὰ μόνας συνῆσαν αὐτῷ οἱ μαθηταί,
   And it happened, as he <u>was</u> <u>praying</u> alone [that] his disciples were with him,

25.5 COMPARATIVE AND SUPERLATIVE ADJECTIVES AND ADVERBS (Συγκριτικὰ καὶ Ὑπερθετικὰ Ὀνόματα καὶ Ἐπιρρήματα)

A. **General Information:** Already we have briefly considered how to create adverbs from adjectives (§22.5). There are two other forms created from the adjectives. Technically, these are called further **degrees** of the adjective, namely, the **comparative** and **superlative** degrees. (The normal adjective meaning is called the **positive** degree.)

   A **comparative adjective** in English is one that generally ends in –*er*: *nicer, greater, larger.* Sometimes, however, we use the helping word *more* to create a comparison (*this ride is more fun than that one*). These constructions serve to relate two items to some set standard of comparison or contrast (*this seed is <u>smaller</u> than other seeds*).

   A **superlative adjective** in English normally ends in –*est*: *nicest, greatest, largest.* Sometimes, however, we use the helping word *most* (*this ride is the <u>most</u> exhilarating one*). Greek superlatives function either to indicate that one item surpasses all others in some way (*he was the best athlete*) or to indicate emphasis (*he was a very good athlete*). This latter use is called **elative**. See Wallace 298-305.

B. **Formation of Comparatives and Superlative Adjectives:** There are two formations of the comparative and superlative adjectives.

1. <u>1st and 2nd Declension Formation</u>. In the this formation, the positive, comparative, and superlative forms use 1st and 2nd declension endings.

<table>
<tr><td></td><td>COMPARATIVE ENDING</td><td>SUPERLATIVES ENDINGS</td></tr>
<tr><td></td><td>-τερος, -α, -ον</td><td>-τατος, -η, -ον
-ιστος, η, ον</td></tr>
</table>

Examples:

POSITIVE Adjective	COMPARATIVE Form	SUPERLATIVE Form
μικρός, -ά, -όν *small*	μικρότερος, -α, -ον *smaller*	μικρότατος, -η, -ον *smallest*
πονηρός, -ά, -όν *evil*	πονηρότερος, -α, -ον *more evil*	(*no form attested in Greek*)

2. <u>1st, 2nd, and 3rd Declension Formation</u>. In this formation, the positive and superlative forms use the 1st and 2nd declension endings, whereas the comparative forms use 3rd declension endings. Additionally, the adjective stems may show variation in form. Something similar can also occur in English; for example, *good, better, best*. Here are the more frequently occurring adjectives and their positive, comparative, and superlative forms:

POSITIVE ADJECTIVE	COMPARATIVE DEGREE	SUPERLATIVE DEGREE
πολύς *many*	πλείων, -ονος *more*	πλεῖστος,-η,-ον *most*
μέγας *great*	μείζων, -ονος *greater*	μέγιστος,-η,-ον *greatest*
ἀγαθός *good*	κρείσσων, -ονος *better* or κρείττων, -ονος	κράτιστος,-η,-ον *best*
μικρός *small*	ἐλάσσων, -ονος *smaller* or ἐλάττων, -ονος	ἐλάχιστος,-η,-ον *smallest*

<u>Notice</u> that the comparative forms have 3rd Declension endings. Notice also that for μικρός and ἀγαθός two sets of comparative forms are found, one with double σίγμα and the other with double ταῦ. These differences are due to the difference between the Doric and Attic Greek dialects, respectively. Also, the comparative stem is completely different. This is, for example, because another adjective, ἐλαχύς, has dropped completely out of use and its comparative and superlative forms are still used and classified under μικρός.

C. Constructions and Translation of Comparatives and Superlatives:

1. <u>Genitive Construction</u>. The common Greek comparative construction is as follows:

comparative adjective + genitive case noun = _____ -er than _____

μείζων <u>αὐτοῦ</u> *greater* <u>*than him/it*</u> (cf. Matt 11:11)

πνεύματα πονηρότερα <u>ἑαυτοῦ</u> *spirits more evil* <u>*than itself*</u> (cf. Matt 12:45)

The word *than* comes from the construction of the genitive case. In fact, this use of the genitive case is called the **genitive of comparison** (see Wallace 110-12).

2. <u>With the Conjunction ἤ *than*</u>.

Luke 10:14 πλὴν Τύρῳ καὶ Σιδῶνι <u>ἀνεκτότερον</u> ἔσται ἐν τῇ κρίσει <u>ἤ</u> ὑμῖν.
> *But it will be* <u>*more bearable*</u> *for Tyre and Sidon in the judgement* <u>*than*</u> *for you.*

3. <u>With a Preposition to mark Compared Items</u>. Such prepositions include παρά and ὑπέρ.

Luke 3:13 ὁ δὲ εἶπεν πρὸς αὐτούς· μηδὲν <u>πλέον</u> <u>παρὰ</u> τὸ διατεταγμένον ὑμῖν πράσσετε.
> *And he said to them, "Collect nothing* <u>*more*</u> <u>*than*</u> *that commanded to you."*

4. <u>The Versatile Use of Μᾶλλον</u>. The comparative word μᾶλλον *more* is from the intensifying adverb μάλα *very, very much, exceedingly*. Μᾶλλον may be used in many ways.

a. *Create a Comparison with a Positive Degree Adjective.*

Acts 20:35c αὐτὸς εἶπεν· <u>μακάριόν</u> ἐστιν <u>μᾶλλον</u> διδόναι ἤ λαμβάνειν.
> *He himself said, "It is* <u>*more*</u> <u>*blessed*</u> *to give than to receive."*

b. *Create a Comparative Statement with ἤ (meaning* than*) or Genitive of Comparison.*

Acts 5:29b πειθαρχεῖν δεῖ θεῷ <u>μᾶλλον</u> <u>ἤ</u> ἀνθρώποις.
> *It is necessary to please God* <u>*more*</u> <u>*than*</u> *humans.*

Matt 6:26c οὐχ ὑμεῖς <u>μᾶλλον</u> διαφέρετε <u>αὐτῶν</u>;
> *Aren't you yourselves worth* <u>*more*</u> <u>*than*</u> <u>*them*</u>?

c. *Strengthen a Comparative/Superlative Statement.* See also §25.6.C.

2 Cor 7:13b Ἐπὶ δὲ τῇ παρακλήσει ἡμῶν <u>περισσοτέρως</u> <u>μᾶλλον</u> ἐχάρημεν ἐπὶ τῇ χαρᾷ Τίτου,
> *And upon our encouragement we rejoiced* <u>*more abundantly*</u> <u>*more*</u> *at Titus's joy.*

d. *Strengthen Adverbial Modifications.* See also §25.6.C. In the first example, μᾶλλον is repeated; in the second, μᾶλλον works with a dative of degree, in this case with πολλῷ *by how much more* (in 12 instances).

> **Phil 1:9a** Καὶ τοῦτο προσεύχομαι, ἵνα ἡ ἀγάπη ὑμῶν ἔτι <u>μᾶλλον</u> καὶ <u>μᾶλλον</u> περισσεύῃ...
> *And I pray this, that your love would increase yet <u>more</u> and <u>more</u>...*

> **Mark 10:48b** ὁ δὲ πολλῷ <u>μᾶλλον</u> ἔκραζεν· υἱὲ Δαυίδ, ἐλέησόν με.
> *But he kept crying out that much <u>more</u>: "Son of David, have mercy on me!"*

e. *Make an Intensified Contrastive Alternative Statement.*

> **Eph 5:11** καὶ μὴ συγκοινωνεῖτε τοῖς ἔργοις τοῖς ἀκάρποις τοῦ σκότους, <u>μᾶλλον</u> δὲ καὶ ἐλέγχετε.
> *And do not be associated with the fruitless deeds of darkness, but <u>rather instead</u> also be refuting [them].*

Here the alternative to being associated with the fruitless deeds of darkness is <u>rather instead</u> to be refuting them.

5. <u>Implied Counterparts</u>. Sometimes the comparison or superlative has no explicit counter part, but such counterpart may be implied from the context.

> **Matt 8:12a** οἱ δὲ υἱοὶ τῆς βασιλείας ἐκβληθήσονται εἰς <u>τὸ σκότος τὸ ἐξώτερον</u>·
> *And the sons of the kingdom will be cast into <u>the outer darkness</u>.*

The comparative adjective ἐξώτερον *outer* does not have an explicit counterpart, but an implicit one from the preceding verse, where the counterpart *inner* would pertain to feasting with Abraham, Isaac, and Jacob.

6. <u>Elative/Intensive Use</u>. Not infrequently, comparative and superlative forms have no explicit or implied counterparts and thus make no comparisons, etc. Instead, they function to make elative statements denoting intensity, which is important to notice for interpretation. For comparative forms, this may be translated with *rather* or *very*; for superlatives, use *very*.

> **Acts 17:22b** κατὰ πάντα ὡς <u>δεισιδαιμονεστέρους</u> ὑμᾶς θεωρῶ
> *In all respects, I see you as <u>rather religious</u>* [in a pagan sense]

> **Jas 3:4** ἰδοὺ καὶ τὰ πλοῖα ... μετάγεται ὑπὸ <u>ἐλαχίστου</u> πηδαλίου.
> *Behold also the boats ... are guided by the <u>very small</u> rudder.*

C. **Comparative and Superlative Adverbs:** Adverbs may be formed based upon the comparative and superlative formations above by adding the common adverbial ending –ως or using the neuter plural ending.

2 Cor 2:4c … ἀλλὰ τὴν ἀγάπην ἵνα γνῶτε ἣν ἔχω <u>περισσοτέρως</u> εἰς ὑμᾶς.

> … *but that you would know the love, which I have <u>rather exceedingly</u> for you.*

The comparative adverb <u>περισσοτέρως</u> is from the adjective περισσός, -ή, -όν *abundant.*

Phil 4:22 ἀσπάζονται ὑμᾶς πάντες οἱ ἅγιοι, <u>μάλιστα</u> δὲ οἱ ἐκ τῆς Καίσαρος οἰκίας.

> *All the saints greet you, but <u>most especially</u> the ones from the household of Caesar.*

Here, μάλιστα is superlative adverb derived from the comparative form μᾶλλον.

25.6 COMPARATIVE AND SUPERLATIVE EMPHASIS

A. **Introduction:** When one chooses to compare on contrast two or more items, an important rhetorical point is being made. Indeed, the elative/intensive use of the comparative and superlative forms of the adjectives stresses the adjectival attributive. However, Robert E. Smith is correct to indicate, "In adjectives and adverbs the comparative forms and especially any superlative forms put prominence on the idea in the adjective or adverb."[7] Robertson discussed the growing use of double comparison forms and "other means of strengthening the comparative" because of "the desire for emphasis" (663-64).[8] ***Comparative emphasis*** *is the stress placed upon adjective modifiers and their qualified sentence elements through the use of comparative and superlative forms and constructions.* One must gather evidence from context to understand the exact nature of the emphasis.

B. **Inscription with Superlative Adjectives:** The image below shows an inscription dating to c. 100 BC that was double-sided and repeats the desperate prayer showing hands lifted up.[9] It was found on the Island Rheneia near Delos in the Aegean Sea. The petition is most likely Jewish in origin, since it alludes extensively to the LXX. The inscription calls for vengeance on the murderer of two Jewish young ladies. The marble stele remarkably depicts raised hands calling upon God's assistance to avenge. The Greek text shows superlative adjectives (underlined), the last being elative intensive, helping to express the intense cause of justice.

---

[7] Robert E. Smith, "Recognizing Prominence Features in the Greek New Testament," *Selected Technical Articles Related to Translation* 14 (1985): 16–25 at 20.

[8] This material borrows from and extends my statements in *2 Corinthians: A Handbook on the Greek Text*, Baylor Handbook on the Greek New Testament (Waco, TX: Baylor University Press, 2015), 67.

[9] For a through discussion of dating and origins, see Adolf Deissmann, *Light from the Ancient East the New Testament Illustrated by Recently Discovered Texts of the Graeco-Roman World*, 2nd ed., trans. Lionel Richard Mortimer Strachan, (London: Hodder & Stoughton, 1910), 423-35. The image, text, and translation is from 424-25.

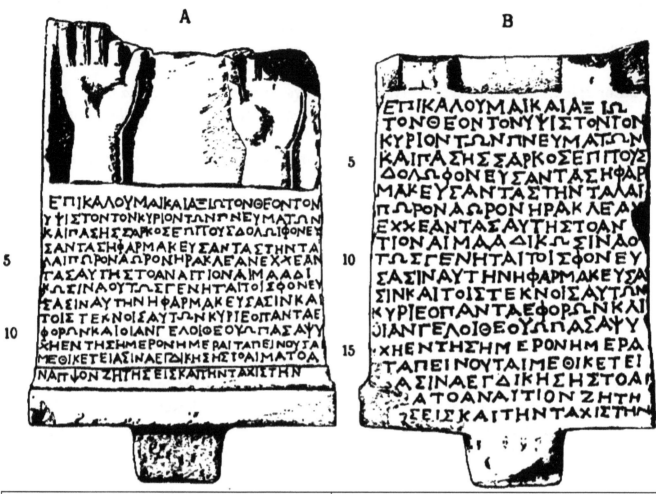

1 Ἐπικαλοῦμαι καὶ ἀξιῶ τὸν θεὸν τὸν <u>ὕψιστον</u>, τὸν κύριον τῶν πνευμάτων καὶ πάσης σαρκός, ἐπὶ τοὺς δόλωι φονεύ-σαντας ἢ φαρμακεύσαντας τὴν τα- 5 λαίπωρον ἄωρον Ἡράκλεαν ἐχχέαν-τας αὐτῆς τὸ ἀναίτιον αἷμα ἀδί-κως, ἵνα οὕτως γένηται τοῖς φονεύ-σασιν αὐτὴν ἢ φαρμακεύσασιν καὶ τοῖς τέκνοις αὐτῶν, κύριε ὁ πάντα ἐ- 10 φορῶν καὶ οἱ ἄγγελοι θεοῦ, ὧ πᾶσα ψυ-χὴ ἐν τῇ σήμερον ἡμέραι ταπεινοῦται μεθ᾽ ἱκετείας, ἵνα ἐγδικήσῃς τὸ αἷμα τὸ ἀ-ναίτιον ζητήσεις καὶ τὴν <u>ταχίστην</u>.	"I call upon and pray <u>the Most High</u> God, the Lord of the spirits and of all flesh, against those who with guile murdered or poisoned the wretched, untimely lost Heraclea, shedding her innocent blood wickedly: that it may be so with them that murdered or poisoned her, and with their children; O Lord that seeth all things, and ye angels of God, Thou before whom every soul is afflicted this same day with supplication: that Thou mayst avenge the in-nocent blood and require it again <u>right speedily</u>!"

Each superlative makes an important point. In the appellative τὸν θεὸν τὸν <u>ὕψιστον</u> *the God Most High*, the inscription affirms the supremacy and authority of God, which is further highlighted through the following appositional statement. The last superaltive ταχίστην *right speedily* sounds the final note of the prayer and texpresses confidence in the efficacy of God's retribtuion.

C. **Extra Words Convey Greater Marking:** Greater comparative emphasis occurs when additional modifiers are added to assist in the comparison. Thus, we have μᾶλλον being used with comparative forms, which should be sufficient.

Mark 7:36 καὶ διεστείλατο αὐτοῖς ἵνα μηδενὶ λέγωσιν· ὅσον δὲ αὐτοῖς διεστέλλετο, αὐτοὶ <u>μᾶλλον περισσότερον</u> ἐκήρυσσον.
   And he commanded to them that they speak to no one. Yet, to the degree he was commanding them, they themselves even more abundantly were proclaiming it!"

Robertson indicates, "Other means of strengthening the comparative were the accusative adverb πολύ, as in Heb. 12:9, 25 (cf. 2 Cor. 8:22), and in particular the instrumental πολλῷ, as in Lu. 18:39"; Robertson concludes, "The ancient Greek used all these devices very often" and "The older Greek used also μέγα and μακρῷ to strengthen the comparison" (664).

D. **Extra Morphological Marking:** Greek writers could pile morphological indicators upon one another. For example, in μειζο-τέραν (3 John 4) we have the comparative ending (-τερος) added onto the (already) comparative adjective μείζων *greater*; in the word ἐλαχ-ιστο-τέρῳ (Eph 3:8) we have the comparative ending (-τερος) added onto a superlative ending (-ιστος). Robertson says of the use of double comparative endings: "All this is due to the fading of the force of the comparative suffix and the desire for emphasis" (664).

E. **Further Examples:**

2 Cor 12:15 ἐγὼ δὲ <u>ἥδιστα</u> δαπανήσω καὶ ἐκδαπανηθήσομαι ὑπὲρ τῶν ψυχῶν ὑμῶν. εἰ <u>περισσοτέρως</u> ὑμᾶς ἀγαπῶ[ν], <u>ἧσσον</u> ἀγαπῶμαι;
   But I myself will <u>very gladly</u> spend and will be completely spent for your souls. If I love you <u>more exceedingly</u>, am I loved <u>less</u>?

The force of the superlative adverb ἥδιστα is elative. Comparative emphasis occurs extensively throughout 2 Corinthians at 1:12; 2:4, 6, 7²; 4:15; 7:15; 8:17; 9:2; 10:8; 11:23. Instances of greater comparative emphasis occur at 3:7, 9, 11; 7:13; 8:22; and 12:9, 15.

Phil 1:23 συνέχομαι δὲ ἐκ τῶν δύο, τὴν ἐπιθυμίαν ἔχων εἰς τὸ ἀναλῦσαι καὶ σὺν Χριστῷ εἶναι, <u>πολλῷ</u> [γὰρ] <u>μᾶλλον κρεῖσσον</u>.
   And I am hard pressed from the two (options), having the desire to depart and to be with Christ, for <u>by much</u> more [it would be] <u>better</u>.

All that is needed grammatically is the adjective κρεῖσσον *better* that is in the comparative degree. However, to this was added πολλῷ μᾶλλον *by much more*. Robertson explains "all this emphasis is due to Paul's struggling emotion" (664).

Complete WORKBOOK EXERCISES 25 and consult the ANSWER KEY & GUIDE as needed.

CASE IN POINT 25: COMMAND FORMS IN LUKE 12:22-40

After Jesus tells the story of a man tearing down his barns to build bigger ones in order to store all his belongings (Luke 12:16-21), he turns to issue a series of instructions to the crowds and disciples. Throughout his teaching, Jesus commands his hearers to do and to avoid certain attitudes and behaviors. Let's look at the significance of the verb tense to understand these commands and prohibitions in context.

Here are the relevant verses of Luke 12:22-40 in the NASB95 with the English commands in bold and the Greek command forms and basic parsing imbedded in brackets.

[22] And He said to His disciples, "For this reason I say to you, **do not** worry [μὴ μεριμνᾶτε—Present Imperative] about *your* life, *as to* what you will eat; nor for your body, *as to* what you will put on. [23] "For life is more than food, and the body more than clothing. [24] "**Consider** [κατανοήσατε—Aorist Imperative] the ravens, for they neither sow nor reap; they have no storeroom nor barn, and *yet* God feeds them; how much more valuable you are than the birds! [25] "And which of you by worrying can add a *single* hour to his life's span? [26] "If then you cannot do even a very little thing, why do you worry about other matters? [27] "**Consider** [κατανοήσατε—Aorist Imperative] the lilies, how they grow: they neither toil nor spin; but I tell you, not even Solomon in all his glory clothed himself like one of these. [28] "But if God so clothes the grass in the field, which is *alive* today and tomorrow is thrown into the furnace, how much more *will He clothe* you? You men of little faith! [29] "**And do not seek** [ὑμεῖς μὴ ζητεῖτε—Present Imperative] what you will eat and what you will drink, and **do not keep worrying** [μὴ μετεωρίζεσθε—Present Imperative]. [30] "For all these things the nations of the world eagerly seek; but your Father knows that you need these things. [31] "But **seek** [ζητεῖτε—Present Imperative] His kingdom, and these things will be added to you. [32] "**Do not be afraid** [Μὴ φοβοῦ—Present Imperative], little flock, for your Father has chosen gladly to give you the kingdom. [33] "**Sell** [Πωλήσατε—Aorist Imperative] your possessions and **give** [δότε—Aorist Imperative] to charity; **make yourselves** [ποιήσατε ἑαυτοῖς—Aorist Imperative] money belts which do not wear out, an unfailing treasure in heaven, where no thief comes near nor moth destroys. [34] "For where your treasure is, there your heart will be also. [35] "**Be dressed** [Ἔστωσαν—Present Imperative] in readiness, and *keep* your lamps lit. [36] "Be like men who are waiting for their master when he returns from the wedding feast, so that they may immediately open *the door* to him when he comes and knocks. [37] "Blessed are those slaves whom the master will find on the alert when he comes; truly I say to you, that he will gird himself *to serve*, and have them recline *at the table*, and will come up and wait on them. [38] "Whether he comes in the second watch, or even in the third, and finds *them* so, blessed are those *slaves*. [39] "But **be sure** [γινώσκετε—Present Imperative] of this, that if the head of the house had known at what hour the thief was coming, he would not have allowed his house to be broken into. [40] "**You** too, **be ready** [ὑμεῖς γίνεσθε—Present Imperative]; for the Son of Man is coming at an hour that you do not expect."

When addressing emotional states or attitudes, the present tense is used:

> 12:22 *do not worry* (μὴ μεριμνᾶτε)
> 12:29 *do not keep worrying* (μὴ μετεωρίζεσθε)
> 12:32 *Do not be afraid* (Μὴ φοβοῦ)

Likewise, commands relating to the pursuits of the disciples are in the present tense, first stated negatively in terms of what not to seek, then positively of what to seek:

> 12:29 *do not seek* (ὑμεῖς μὴ ζητεῖτε)
> 12:31 *seek* (ζητεῖτε)

The clear thrust of these present tense commands is that the disciples should continuously not worry about material matters or pursuits. Rather, disciples are positively exhorted to seek the kingdom; consequently, something better than material things awaits them (12:31-32).

In the midst of these present imperatives are two aorist tense imperatives in 12:24, 27: *Consider* (κατανοήσατε). The aorist tense is gnomic, relating general considerations for the disciples to ponder. There is also a present imperative at 12:39 (*be sure* or *know* [γινώσκετε]), which is probably also gnomic. In each of these instances, there is no call to ponder *continuously*, but to consider (*timelessly*) the significance of *ravens* and *lilies* for discerning God's provision for humans (12:24, 27) and how house owners prevent thieves from breaking in, if they know when they will do so (12:39).

The next commands to investigate are stated positively using the aorist tense in 12:33: *Sell... Give...Make for yourselves unfailing treasure in heaven....* (What type of dative use is ἑαυτοῖς with ποιήσατε?) The aorist tenses here are probably constantive (undefined action). These commands are not continuous actions that the disciples are to follow. Rather, they are examples of how to implement both the call not to worry about material possessions and the command to seek the kingdom. Essentially these commands relativize *perishable, physical* wealth to *imperishable* Kingdom realities.

The final set of imperatives is in the present tense and contributes to the continuous activity of being *ready*.

> 12:35 *Be dressed* (Ἔστωσαν) *in readiness*
> 12:40 *You too, be ready* (ὑμεῖς γίνεσθε)

The readiness is for the coming of the Master, the Lord, to check whether the servants are ready to open the door for him. The imperative form in 12:35 involves the verb of being εἰμί in third person with two periphrastic participles, one perfect tense and the other present. Knowing the Greek text allows us to translate it more literally: *Let your loins be covered and your lamps continuously be burning.* (Ἔστωσαν ὑμῶν αἱ ὀσφύες περιεζωσμέναι καὶ οἱ λύχνοι καιόμενοι·). Both speak to ancient cultural practices concerning dressing and lighting. Additionally, we can see in the final command at 12:40 added emphasis by the addition of an emphatic personal pronoun (ὑμεῖς).

In conclusion, a closer look at the imperatives allows us to see a movement from addressing emotional issues of fear and material pursuits through timeless illustrations that permit us to see God's concern for humans. Then, we find a series of general commands as illustrations of how *not to fear* and how *to seek the kingdom*. Finally, there are commands calling disciples to be *continuously ready* in their service for the coming of the Master.

Below is funeral scene from a terra-cotta plaque found in Attica Greece.[10]

Victor Duruy explains: "The painter represents the πρόθεσις, or lying in state of a corpse, which takes place in the interior of the house, as appears from a column at the left. Around the body are grouped the members of the family, the women on one side, the men on the other. Near the bed are the mother (ΜΕΤΕΡ) and the grandmother (ΘΕΤΕ); then the aunts (ΘΕΤΙΣ), of whom one, immediately behind the mother, is perhaps the paternal aunt (ΘΕΤΙΣ ΠΡΟΣ ΠΑΤΡ[ός]); in front are the young sisters (ΑΔΕΛΦΕ) of the dead. All express their grief with violent gestures; either they raise one hand, as if about to tear their hair, and stretch the other hand towards the dead, or else they grasp the head with both hands. Farther off, at the left, is the chorus of men, the father (ΠΑΤΕΡ), and brothers (ΑΔΕΛΦΕ). All extend the right arm, and with head thrown back chant 'the lamentable hymn,' which the father has begun and leads, turning towards the others. One of the women looks at them, waiting apparently until they have finished, to give the signal for her companions to begin. Thus the sad day is spent …. Among the inscriptions on the background, some are translated as exclamations of grief, like οἴμοι, 'alas!' twice repeated; others, ΥΟΝΝΤΟΣ, Ο. ΕΛΟΣΛ, are not satisfactorily explained."

---

[10] Explanation and image (slightly enhanced) is from Victor Duruy, *History of Greece, and of the Greek People: From the Earliest Times to the Roman Conquest*, trans. M. M. Ripley, Vol. 1, Sect. 2 (Boston: Estes and Lauriat, 1890), 306-8 n.2

CHAPTER 26

How well do you know the Golden Rule? It may be that the English Translations may disappoint you. What is stressed there?

This chapter covers the major types of **conditional sentences** (*If … , then…*). Also in the Vocabulary are featured four pronouns: the **Relative and Interrogative Pronouns of Quantity** and the **Interrogative and Demonstrative Pronouns of Quality**. These latter two pronouns participate more broadly in what maybe called **Qualitative Emphasis**.

VOCABULARY 26   SPECIAL PRONOUNS AND CONDITIONAL WORDS

Relative Pronoun of Quantity:

ὅσος, -η, -ον [111]   how many, as much as

Interrogative Pronoun of Quality:

ποῖος, -α, -ον [33]   of what kind? which?

Interrogative Pronoun of Quantity:

πόσος, -η, -ον [27]   of what quantity?
how many?

Demonstrative Pronoun of Quality:

τοιοῦτος, τοιαύτη, τοιοῦτον [57]
such as this, of such a kind

Conditional Particle:

ἄν [170]   *a particle marking potential circumstance or condition*

Conditional Combinations:

ἐάν [330] (εἰ + ἄν)	if (introduced in CH.22)
ἐάν μή [48]	unless; if not
εἰ μή [92]	except; if not
ἕως ἄν [20]	until (ever)
ὃς ἄν [67] or ὃς ἐάν [44]	who(ever)
ὅσος ἄν [6] or ὅσος ἐάν [7]	however so many
ὅπου ἐάν [8] or ὅπου ἄν [2]	where(ever)
ὅταν [123] (ὅτε + ἄν)	when(ever)

After learning vocabulary to this point, you will know 82% of the words in the GNT. Congratulations! What this means is that, on average, you should be able recognize over 8 out of 10 words while reading the GNT. When one factors in recognizable names and cognate forms with similar meanings, this percentage is probably closer to 85% or even 90%. If you are able, listen to audio recordings of VOCABULARY 26 and complete the CROSSWORD PUZZLE in the WORKBOOK EXERCISES.

NOTES ON VOCABULARY 26:

Many important conjunctions, particles, and their combinations are introduced here. Let's start with ἄν. As an independent particle, ἄν marks +potential circumstance or condition. Smyth (§1762) indicates, "No separate word can be used to translate ἄν by itself; its force varies as it modifies the meaning of the moods. In general ἄν limits the force of the verb to particular conditions or circumstances ('under the circumstances,' 'in that case,' 'then')." The particle may occur more than once in a sentence for effect. Smyth (§1765.b) indicates, "For rhetorical emphasis ἄν is added to give prominence to particular words." An example of doubling of the ἄν is seen with the hemorrhaging women's rationale for touching Jesus's garments in Mark 5:28:

Mark 5:28 ἔλεγεν γὰρ ὅτι <u>ἐὰν</u> ἅψωμαι <u>κἂν</u> τῶν ἱματίων αὐτοῦ σωθήσομαι.
> *For she kept saying this: "If I would touch even <u>indeed</u> his garments, I will be healed."*

The second ἄν in the contraction <u>κἂν</u> (καὶ ἄν *even indeed*) places focus on Jesus' garments.

Εἰ and ἐάν are both used to introduce a subordinate conditional clause. Εἰ will take an Indicative Mood verb or rarely in the GNT an Optative, whereas ἐάν will typically take a Subjunctive Mood verb. Ἐάν results from the contraction of εἰ and ἄν.

Ἐάν μή and εἰ μή form **exception clauses**. Ἐάν μή will be used with the Subjunctive Mood, whereas εἰ μή will be used with the Indicative Mood. These subordinate clauses are conditional and generally occur with a main clause that makes a totalizing claim to which the exception clause identifies an important and highlighted exception (Runge 85-86).

Ὅταν, ὃς ἄν, ὅσος ἄν, ἕως ἄν, ὅπου ἄν, and ὅπου ἐάν form various types of conditional statements: **relative conditional sentences** (ὃς ἄν; ὅσος ἄν), **locative conditional sentences** (ὅπου ἄν, ὅπου ἐάν), and **temporal conditional sentences** (ὅταν). Each of these combinations will generally be found with the Subjunctive Mood. *The most frequent are* ὅταν *and* ὃς ἄν.

The four new pronouns are classified under **correlative pronouns** because they were used *in tandem* with other corresponding pronouns in Attic Greek. This *balancing of ideas* through pronoun combinations is somewhat rare in the GNT. Ὅσος, -η, -ον *how many, as much as* is difficult to translate at times, as is its interrogative counterpart πόσος, -η, -ον *of what quantity? how many?* Feel free to render them differently, although somehow try to maintain the notion of **quantity**. See also the archaic pronoun of quantity ἡλίκος[3] *how great*.

LSJ (Int.) defines τοιοῦτος, τοιαύτη, τοιοῦτον *such as this, of such a kind* as "stronger form of τοῖος." This pronoun would often accompany its corresponding correlative counterpart also stressing quality οἷος[13] *what sort of, what quality of.* Other pronouns stressing quality are ὁποῖος[5] *of what sort* or *quality* and the interrogative ποῖος, -α, -ον *of what kind? which?*

Have fun with *such kinds* of pronouns! Unfortunately, *these kinds* of words are not that *frequent* (ironic!), but when they are found, correlative pronouns are usually exegetically significant. One should understand that these words stress the **quantity** of items (see §12.4 QUANTITATIVE EMPHASIS) or the **quality** of them, creating **qualitative emphasis** (see §26.4 below).

26.1 An Introduction to Conditional Sentences

A. **Definition:** A **conditional sentence** is a sentence in which a **supposition** is given as a subordinate clause in relation to the main clause which is the **conclusion**. In English, this supposition is often introduced by the subordinating conjunction *if*; the conclusion (the main clause) may or may not be marked with a *then*, which is otherwise implied. A conditional sentence may also be called a syllogism (which is a philosophical term) that entails "if... , (then) ..." logical argumentation or a movement from cause (*if*) to effect (*then*).

If it rains tomorrow,	*(then) my plants will grow.*
Supposition	**Conclusion**

In the example above, the first clause is the supposition (the subordinate clause); the second clause is the conclusion (the main sentence). The supposition cannot stand alone, since it is a dependent clause. Notice also that the conclusion in English may or may not be introduced by the word *then*. In English *then* is optional; but, if present, it stresses the resultant effect of the conditional sentence. This additional marking of the logic is very similar in Greek where the *then* may be expressed with a conjunction ἄρα for extra emphasis; in such a case, the "if (εἰ, ἐάν, etc.) and the "then" (ἄρα) participate in **correlative emphasis** (see §15.6 Correlative Emphasis: Lists and Coordinated Connectives).

B. **Terminology of Protasis and Apodosis:** Within Greek grammars and commentaries, the supposition (*if...,*) is called the **protasis** (pronounced *praw-tah-sis*), which is from a Greek verb meaning *to put forward*. The conclusion (*then...*) is called the **apodosis** (pronounced *ah-pah-dah-sis*), which is from the Greek verb *to deliver*. These terms are the standard terminology used in most Greek grammars. See Wallace 679-87 for a general overview of conditions.

Protasis	Apodosis
John 10:24c εἰ σὺ εἶ ὁ χριστός,	εἰπὲ ἡμῖν παρρησίᾳ.

If you yourself are the Christ, (then) speak to us in the open.

C. **Unmarked and Marked Order of Protasis and Apodosis:** In the vast majority of cases, the supposition or protasis will be placed first and then will be followed by the conclusion or apodosis. This is the unmarked construction. *However, if the supposition follows the conclusion, this is a marked ordering.* Therefore, one should consider the pragmatic intention for such a departure from the default ordering. Exception clauses will often show this marked word order (see §26.3). Consider these examples in Rom 8:9a and 9b.

Rom 8:9a Ὑμεῖς δὲ οὐκ ἐστὲ ἐν σαρκὶ ἀλλ' ἐν πνεύματι, εἴπερ πνεῦμα θεοῦ οἰκεῖ ἐν ὑμῖν.

But you yourselves are not in the flesh, but in the Spirit, if indeed the Spirit of God is dwelling within you.

Rom 8:9b εἰ δέ τις πνεῦμα Χριστοῦ οὐκ ἔχει, οὗτος οὐκ ἔστιν αὐτοῦ.

> *But if someone does not have the Spirit of Christ, this one is not his.*

In 8:9a, the protasis is placed after the apodosis and is thus marked. So, Paul is making a very important point here; what additional emphatic features of this sentence help increase its prominence?[1] In 8:9b, we observe an unmarked order of conditional components, although there appears to be a left (dis)located topic (LDT) within a conditional frame, since the pronoun τις in the protasis is referred back to explicitly by the trace of the demonstrative pronoun οὗτος. This pronoun is marked +proximity, and here provides focused contrast with 8:9a. Remember that LDTs mark discontinuity (see §21.3 LEFT (DIS)LOCATED TOPICS & FRAMES WITH A TRACE).

D. **Truthfulness or Not of Conditions:** There is a logical connection between the supposition and its conclusion. The truthfulness or likelihood of the conclusion is based upon how true the supposition is. In most conditions for the sake of argumentation, the author puts forth the supposition in relation to the conclusion *in order to show the logical connection between them*. The author may or may not be assuming the reality of the supposition; however, **what is stressed often is that, if the supposition were true, then the conclusion would be true**. Contextual considerations must come into play when considering how true the NT author thought the supposition to be. For example, consider what Jesus says about himself for the sake of argument.

Matt 12:27a καὶ εἰ ἐγὼ ἐν Βεελζεβοὺλ ἐκβάλλω τὰ δαιμόνια, οἱ υἱοὶ ὑμῶν ἐν τίνι ἐκβάλλουσιν;

> *And if I myself by Beelzebul am casting out demons, your sons, by whom are they casting [them] out?*

Jesus advances an argument by setting forth a supposition that is not true. See the more detailed explanation in Wallace 682-87.

Greek conditional sentences work basically the same way as English conditions. Perhaps not surprisingly, Greek displays a variety of types of conditional sentences, which are both rather interesting and often exegetically significant.

E. **Negation in Conditions:** One will see both οὐ and μή used in conditional sentences, however οὐ will be used in the protases of First Class Conditions (see chart below).

---

[1] In addition to the marked order of the condition, we see an emphatic subject pronoun Ὑμεῖς; a point/counter point construction (οὐκ ... ἀλλʼ); the morphological emphasis with –περ being added to εἰ; and prominent subject matter that contrasts σάρξ and τὸ πνεῦμα τοῦ θεοῦ, which dwells within humans.

26.2 Types of Greek Conditions

A. **Introduction to Greek Conditional Classifications:** Greek conditions are very dynamic. Robertson has rightly said, "No hypotactic clause is more important than this. For some reason the Greek conditional sentence has been very difficult for students to understand. In truth the doctors have disagreed themselves and the rest have not known how to go" (1004). When entering into a discussion of Greek conditions, one must choose the classification system one will use. Currently in NT Grammars, the *First, Second, Third, Fourth Class* approach is the most common. However, in my estimation, using this classification system simply obscures important dimensions of the semantics of conditional constructions. So, I will supplement this "Class System" with a classical Greek grammatical Temporal-Functional System as described in Smyth's *Greek Grammar*.

B. **Pragmatic Benefits of a Temporal-Functional Classification System:** For Conditional Sentences, Smyth provides a classical Greek "Classification according to Function" (§§2290–2342) and specifically "According to Time" (see his chart in §2297). There are several benefits to do so. First, a temporal-functional classification moves us away from the obscurity of *First Class, Second Class, Third Class*, etc., which in fact subsume different types of conditions under the same class (see this depicted in the charts below).[2] Second, a temporal-functional description more accurately distinguishes marked semantic features of conditions, which may include *time, reality,* and *generality/specificity*. And, third, this accuracy consequently provides a better descriptive framework to understand and explain the semantics of commonly occurring **Mixed Conditions** (see E. below) and **Subtypes of Conditions** (see F. below). In the two charts provided immediately below, one will see how the *First, Second, Third, Fourth, Fifth, (Sixth) Class* conditional system as described by NT grammarians (such as Wallace) relates to Smyth's classical taxonomy.

This first chart (I.) more generally describes the classification systems and where one could go to read more about them. This second chart (II.) describes the basic constructions of conditions as understood by Class with the name of the corresponding temporal-functional classification. Particularly problematic are the Third and Fifth Classes (since the Present General Condition is included in both) and the Sixth Class (since it is not treated in Wallace). The specific constructions will be summarized in C. and described more fully in D. below.

---

[2] Wallace also shows ambivalence towards conditional classifications when discussing *Third Class* and *Fifth Class* Conditions, and specifically, the Present General Conditions, which he believes should be considered a "simple condition" (470, 697). In this regard, Boyer has argued that Present General Conditions really should be classified as Future oriented in the Third Class (i.e. Future More Vivid), because apparently he [a Greek author] did not see these as diverse types; there must be some common characteristic which in his mind linked them in the same manner of expression. His choice to use the subjunctive points to the common element. They are both undetermined, contingent suppositions, future in time reference" ("Third (and Fourth) Class Conditions," *Grace Theological Journal* 3.2 [1982]: 163–75 at 173).

I. GENERAL CLASSIFICATION SCHEMA FOR CONDITIONAL SENTENCES	
"CLASSES" OF CONDITIONALS (WALLACE)	FUNCTIONAL-TEMPORAL CLASSIFICATION (SMYTH)
First ("Assumed True for Argument Sake"; Wallace 69–94)	Future Most Vivid/Emotional (§2328) Present Simple (§2298) Past Simple (§§2297–98)
Second ("Contrary to Fact"; Wallace 694–96)	Present Contrary-to-Fact (§§2302–20) Past Contrary-to-Fact (§§2302-20)
Third (no label given, but described; Wallace 696–99)	Future More Vivid (§§2323–26) [*Present General (§§2335–37)]
Fourth ("Less Probable Future"; Wallace 699-701)	Future Less Vivid (§§2329–34)
Fifth (no label given, but described; Wallace 470, 696–97, 712)	*Present General (§§2335–37)
Sixth (not mentioned by Wallace)	Past General (§§2340-41)

II. CONSTRUCTIONS OF THE CLASS SYSTEM AND TEMPORAL-FUNCTIONAL CLASSIFICATION			
TYPE	PROTASIS ("IF")	APODOSIS ("THEN")	TEMPORAL-FUNCTIONAL CLASSIFICATION
First Class	εἰ + indicative mood any tense negative οὐ	any mood any tense	Future Most Vivid Present Simple Past Simple
Second Class	εἰ + indicative mood past tense: aorist or imperfect negative μή	(ἄν) + indicative past tense: aorist (past) or imperfect (present)	Present Contrary-to-Fact Past Contrary-to-Fact
Third Class	ἐάν + subjunctive mood any tense negative μή	any mood ***any tense**	Future More Vivid
Fourth Class	εἰ + optative mood present or aorist tense	ἄν + optative mood present or aorist tense	Future Less Vivid
[Fifth Class] (Ambiguous Category)	ἐάν + subjunctive mood any tense negative μή	***Present tense**	Present General
[Sixth Class] (not discussed)			Past General

C. **Temporal-Functional Classification of Conditions:** These conditions are most easily categorized under their time frame (Future, Present, and Past) and functions. The specific name of each type should help one understand its corresponding significance. Remember that the Greek conditional sentence *does not need to be in the order of supposition first, then conclusion*, although this is the default ordering (see §26.1.B above). This ordering of the protasis first followed by the apodosis is for clarity of the elements of the construction.

TYPE AND NAME OF CONDITION		GREEK CONSTRUCTION	
		Supposition	**Conclusion**
Future:	a) Future Most Vivid/Emotional	εἰ + Future Ind.	Future Ind.
	b) Future More Vivid	ἐάν + Subjunctive	Future Ind.
	c) Future Less Vivid	εἰ + Optative	Optative + ἄν
Present:	d) Present General	ἐάν + Subjunctive	Present Ind.
	e) Present Simple	εἰ + Present Ind.	Present Ind.
	f) Present Contrary-to-Fact	εἰ + Imperfect Ind.	Imperfect + ἄν
Past:	g) Past Simple	εἰ + Past Ind.	Past tense
	h) Past Contrary-to-Fact	εἰ + Past Ind.	Past tense + ἄν
	i) Past General *Indicative Form:*	εἰ + Imperfect Ind.	Imperfect Ind.
	Optative Form:	εἰ + Optative	Imperfect Ind.

Essentially, conditions may be translated without any knowledge of the type or significance of the condition construction, except for the **Present Contrary-to-Fact** and **Past Contrary-to-Fact** conditions, which should be studied carefully below. Of these nine types of conditional constructions, only seven occur with any sort of frequency in the GNT; the Past General is very rare (Mark 6:56[2]) and Future Less Vivid is often partial in form (see, e.g., 1 Pet 3:14, 17).

D. Discussion of Constructions with Examples:

1. <u>Future Conditions</u>. These conditions are cast in future time, so their fulfillment remains to be seen from the perspective of the writer. However, since these types of conditions are often used in reference to God's future activity and are spoken by reliable and trustworthy persons, then we can be confident in their future fulfillment. The three types of Future conditions vary in terms of their *vividness*, that is, how *vividly* the conditional idea is portrayed or how clearly or graphically the idea or situation is "painted"; the more vivid, the more emotional impact is intended.

   a. *Future Most Vivid* or **Emotional** *Condition*. The Future Most Vivid Condition is often used to depict *unfavorable circumstances*. Smyth considers this usage "Emotional Future Conditions" indicating, "When the protasis expresses strong feeling, the future indicative with εἰ is commonly used instead of ἐάν with the subjunctive…. The protasis commonly suggests something undesired, or feared, or intended independently of the speaker's will; the apodosis commonly conveys a threat, a warning, or an earnest appeal to the feelings" (525). It is not common in the GNT.

FUTURE MOST VIVID	
Supposition	**Conclusion**
εἰ + Future Indicative	Future Indicative

2 Tim 2:12b εἰ ἀρνησόμεθα, κἀκεῖνος ἀρνήσεται ἡμᾶς.
If we will deny (him), then also that one will deny us.

Notice the tone of warning; this is very unfavorable. Look how the additive καί (in κἀκεῖνος) emphasizes reciprocity of treatment, in addition to the repetition of the verb. Notice, too, the distal referent to Christ as "that one" (κἀκεῖνος), further pointing to alienation. Consider this next example, in which Peter speaks of unfavorable circumstances and insists emphatically on his future singular heroic faithfulness:

Matt 26:33 ἀποκριθεὶς δὲ ὁ Πέτρος εἶπεν αὐτῷ· εἰ πάντες <u>σκανδαλισθήσονται</u> ἐν σοί, ἐγὼ οὐδέποτε <u>σκανδαλισθήσομαι</u>.
And Peter, answering back, said to him: "If all <u>will be scandalized</u> by you, I myself <u>will</u> never ever <u>be scandalized</u>."

b. *Future More Vivid Condition.* The Future More Vivid Condition relates *future events* that may entail either *favorable* or *unfavorable circumstances.* The Future More Vivid Condition is the most common (the default) future-time condition (cf. Wallace 696-99).

FUTURE MORE VIVID	
Supposition	**Conclusion**
ἐάν + Subjunctive	Future Indicative

John 11:40b <u>ἐὰν</u> πιστεύσῃς, ὄψῃ τὴν δόξαν τοῦ θεοῦ.
<u>If</u> you believe, you will see the glory of God.

c. *Future Less Vivid Condition.* This condition is classified as a Fourth Class Condition. According to Wallace, "It is used to indicate a *possible* condition in the future, usually a remote possibility (such as, *if he could do something, if perhaps this should occur*)" (484). The remoteness of presentation is a decision of the author.

FUTURE LESS VIVID	
Supposition	**Conclusion**
εἰ + Optative	Optative + ἄν

There may be only one complete example of this, but it has an implied verb in the conclusion.

1 Pet 3:14a ἀλλ᾽ εἰ καὶ πάσχοιτε διὰ δικαιοσύνην, μακάριοι.

But if even you would suffer because of righteousness, you [would be] blessed.

For other examples of partial or mixed Future Less Vivid Conditions, see Acts 17:27; 20:16; 24:19; 27:12, 39; 1 Cor 14:10; 15:37; 1 Pet 3:17.

2. Present Conditions. There are three types of conditions that are cast in the present time. The **Present General** is used when an author wanted to make a statement about a general truth or about repeated or habitual action. More specifically, a present general condition makes a generalized truth claim: "The conclusion holds true of any time or of all time" (Smyth §2337). The **Present Simple** is used for normal conditions about specific events and happenings. The **Present Contrary-to-Fact** is especially used for rhetorical purposes. By using this last construction, *the author is readily admitting that the conclusion is not true.* Thus, the supposition upon which the conclusion is logically based is therefore *dubious.* The construction is used to make some particular argumentative point.

d. *Present General* (cf. Wallace 696-99).

PRESENT GENERAL	
Supposition	**Conclusion**
ἐάν + Subjunctive	Present Indicative

John 3:2b οὐδεὶς γὰρ δύναται ταῦτα τὰ σημεῖα ποιεῖν ἃ σὺ ποιεῖς, ἐὰν μὴ ᾖ ὁ θεὸς μετ᾽ αὐτοῦ.

For, no one is able to do these things, which you are doing, if God were not with him. (or unless God were with him.)

2 Cor 3:16 ἡνίκα δὲ ἐὰν ἐπιστρέψῃ πρὸς κύριον, περιαιρεῖται τὸ κάλυμμα.

Moreover, whenever one turns to the Lord, the veil is removed.

e. *Present Simple* (cf. Wallace 690-94).

PRESENT SIMPLE	
Supposition	**Conclusion**
εἰ + Present Indicative	Present Indicative

John 8:46b εἰ ἀλήθειαν λέγω, διὰ τί ὑμεῖς οὐ πιστεύετέ μοι;
If I speak the truth, (then) why do you not believe me?

f. *Present Contrary-to-Fact* (cf. Wallace 694-96).

PRESENT CONTRARY-TO-FACT	
Supposition	**Conclusion**
εἰ + Imperfect Indicative	Imperfect + ἄν

Smyth explains why the past Indicative is used here: "In the *form* of the protasis and the apodosis of unreal conditions there is nothing that denotes unreality, but, in the combination, the unreality of the protasis is always, and that of the apodosis generally, implied. The past tenses of the indicative are used in unreal conditions referring to present time, because the speaker's thought goes back to the past, when the realization of the condition was still possible, though at the time of speaking that realization is impossible" (§2308).

John 5:46a εἰ γὰρ ἐπιστεύετε Μωϋσεῖ, ἐπιστεύετε ἄν ἐμοί.
For, if you <u>were (actually presently) believing</u> Moses, (then) you <u>would (now) believe</u> me.

Notice: Using *were (actually presently)* and *would (now)* helps to communicate both the present time and the contrary-to-fact conclusion (and thus, the contrary-to-fact supposition). Jesus' point is that, since the religious leaders don't believe Him, in fact they don't *really* believe Moses. They are as good as infidels; Jesus was pulling the rug out from their self-understanding in relation to their claim to know and understand God's Word through Moses.

3. <u>Past Conditions.</u> There are two main conditions within a past time framework: **Past Simple** and **Past Contrary-to-Fact.** A third kind, the **Past General**, is very rare. These types of conditions are analogous to the Present Simple, Present Contrary-to-Fact, and Present General conditions.

g. ***Past Simple*** (cf. Wallace 690-94).

PAST SIMPLE	
Supposition	**Conclusion**
εἰ + Past Indicative (Aorist or Imperfect)	Past Indicative (Aorist or Imperfect)

Rev 20:15 καὶ εἴ τις οὐχ εὑρέθη ἐν τῇ βίβλῳ τῆς ζωῆς γεγραμμένος, ἐβλήθη εἰς τὴν λίμνην τοῦ πυρός.
> And *if* someone <u>was</u> not <u>found</u> written in the Book of Life, he <u>was cast out</u> into the lake of fire.

h. ***Past Contrary-to-Fact*** (cf. Wallace 694-96).

PAST CONTRARY-TO-FACT	
Supposition	**Conclusion**
εἰ + Past Indicative (Aorist or Imperfect)	Past Indicative + ἄν (Aorist or Imperfect)

1 Cor 2:8b εἰ γὰρ ἔγνωσαν, οὐκ ἂν τὸν κύριον τῆς δόξης ἐσταύρωσαν.
> For, if they <u>had then</u> known, (then) they <u>would</u> not <u>have</u> crucified the Lord of glory.

John 9:33 εἰ μὴ ἦν οὗτος παρὰ θεοῦ, οὐκ ἠδύνατο ποιεῖν οὐδέν.
> If he <u>were</u> not from God, (then) he <u>would not have</u> been able to do anything. [Note that there is no ἄν; both verbs are Imperfect Tense]

This latter example is also instructive of the ambiguity with Imperfect Tense verbs within Contrary-to-Fact conditions: One must choose whether the time frame is present or past. John 9:33 might just as well be a Present Contrary-to-Fact condition.

Notice: Using *had then* and *would have* helps to communicate both the past time and the contrary-to-fact conclusion (and thus, the Contrary-to-Fact supposition).

i. ***Past General (very rare)***. This type of condition had two forms depending on the particular semantics involved. In the protasis, an Optative was used, unless there was need for an indefinite pronoun τις *someone, anyone*, in which case an Indicative was used (Smyth §2342). In the two GNT examples below, instead of an indefinite pronoun (which generalized the construction), we have very similar semantics of generalization; the relative pronouns of place (ὅπου) and person (ὅσοι) are followed immediately by ἄν and a Past Indicative verb. These are the protases. The apodosis then has an Imperfect Indicative. This usage is very rare; these two instances may be the only occurrences in the GNT.

Past General	
Supposition	**Conclusion**
(ἄν) + Imperfect Indicative	Imperfect Indicative

Mark 6:56a καὶ <u>ὅπου</u> <u>ἂν</u> εἰσεπορεύετο εἰς κώμας ἢ εἰς πόλεις ἢ εἰς ἀγρούς, ἐν ταῖς ἀγοραῖς <u>ἐτίθεσαν</u> τοὺς ἀσθενοῦντας καὶ <u>παρεκάλουν</u> αὐτὸν ἵνα <u>κἂν</u> τοῦ κρασπέδου τοῦ ἱματίου αὐτοῦ ἅψωνται·
And <u>wherever</u> he would go into villages or into cities or into fields, in the open spaces <u>they would set out</u> the weak and <u>they would be pleading</u> him that they would touch even the edge of his garment.

Mark 6:56b καὶ <u>ὅσοι</u> <u>ἂν</u> ἥψαντο αὐτοῦ ἐσῴζοντο.
And <u>as many as</u> would touch him were being healed.

Mark portrays a generalized set of circumstances surrounding Jesus's practices and the people's stratagems as a response. The time frame for these generalized practices and responses is depicted as happening in the past.

E. **Mixed Conditions:** Conditional types may be mixed. That is, a conditional sentence will have the **protasis** of one type and the **apodosis** of another type. This especially happens in argumentative discourse where past, present, future realities come to bear on human volition and persuasion. Mixed conditions occur much more frequently with the protasis formed with εἰ than with ἐάν. One may or may not be able to identify the supposition (protasis) as belonging to one type of condition and the conclusion (apodosis) to another. Musing between options is often helpful for thinking more deeply about the condition in context. *It is often exegetically significant why the author chose to "mix" condition types.* Below are some examples of mixed conditions along with some brief comments.

Rom 6:8 <u>εἰ</u> δὲ <u>ἀπεθάνομεν</u> σὺν Χριστῷ, <u>πιστεύομεν</u> ὅτι καὶ συζήσομεν αὐτῷ.
<u>If</u> we <u>died</u> with Christ, we <u>believe</u> that we will also live with him.
(Simple Past supposition, a Simple Present conclusion with a future view)

The protasis is for a Simple Past Condition and the apodosis is for a Simple Present Condition, although with a future view in the content of believing. The implication of this construction is that Paul affirms that the concurrent Christian faith and hope (the conclusion) is based upon certain historical realities (the supposition), namely, Christian participation in Christ's death.

Mark 9:35b εἴ τις θέλει πρῶτος εἶναι, ἔσται πάντων ἔσχατος καὶ πάντων διάκονος.

If someone wants to be first [Present Simple], *he will be last of all and servant of all* [Future Most Vivid or More Vivid]

In Mark 9:35, Jesus is teaching the disciples after they had been arguing who would be the greatest. In this persuasive/argumentative context, the condition is mixed. The condition is a bit ambiguous, since it is unclear who is responsible for the final state of being last and a servant of all. If this is seen as a punishment for someone putting themselves first, then this may be seen as a Future Most Vivid conclusion describing a negative outcome: *if you want to be first, then you will be made to be last and a servant of all.* If, however, Jesus intends for someone who wants to be "first" or "greatest" in his Kingdom to do so by becoming last and a servant of all, then the conclusion may be a Future More Vivid. By considering the possible construction, however, we have become alerted to the possibility that Jesus issues here a warning (Future Most Vivid) or a call to adjust one's understanding of becoming the greatest by becoming a Servant of all (Future More Vivid).

Luke 11:18a εἰ δὲ καὶ ὁ σατανᾶς ἐφ᾽ ἑαυτὸν <u>διεμερίσθη</u>, <u>πῶς</u> σταθήσεται ἡ βασιλεία αὐτοῦ;

But <u>if</u> also Satan <u>were divided</u> against himself, <u>how</u> will his kingdom stand?

What type of supposition do we have? The options are Past Simple and Past Contrary-to-Fact, since both use εἰ + past indicative (here Aorist, so, it cannot be Present Contrary-to-Fact). However, Jesus' argument hinges on the unreality of Satan being divided against himself; thus, the protasis more likely is Past Contrary-to-Fact. If so, a better translation would be: *But if also Satan <u>had been divided</u> against himself* [which he was not!], *<u>how</u> would his kingdom stand?* Jesus' point is not to argue that Satan's kingdom will not falter, but that, He himself is not a part of Satan's work.

F. **Sub-Types of Conditional Clauses:** There are other types of clauses that involve some form of ἄν. This word often signals some sort of conditional supposition, the protasis. Below are the most common introductory words used with these constructions:

WORD	MEANING	SUBTYPE OF CONDITION
ὅταν	*when(ever)*	**Temporal**
ὃς ἄν or ἐάν	*who(ever)*	**Relative** (see Smyth §2560)
ἕως ἄν	*until*	**Temporal**
ὅπου ἐάν or ἄν	*where(ever)*	**Locative**
ὅσος ἄν or ἐάν	*however so many*	**Quantitative Relative**

Study these examples below:

Matt 5:11 μακάριοί ἐστε <u>ὅταν</u>. . . ὑμᾶς διώξωσιν . . .
　　　Blessed are you <u>whenever</u> they persecute you. . . [Temporal Condition]

Matt 5:21b <u>ὅς</u> δ᾽ <u>ἂν</u> φονεύσῃ, ἔνοχος ἔσται τῇ κρίσει.
　　　And <u>whoever</u> murders, will be liable to judgment. [Relative Condition]

Luke 21:32b οὐ μὴ παρέλθῃ ἡ γενεὰ αὕτη <u>ἕως ἂν</u> πάντα γένηται.
　　　This generation will never ever pass away <u>until</u> all things have come to pass.
　　　[Temporal Condition]

Mark 6:56b καὶ <u>ὅσοι ἂν</u> ἥψαντο αὐτοῦ ἐσῴζοντο.
　　　And <u>however so many</u> touched him, they were being healed. [Quantitative Relative Condition]

Matt 8:19b ἀκολουθήσω σοι <u>ὅπου ἐὰν</u> ἀπέρχῃ.
　　　I will follow you <u>wherever</u> you go. [Locative Condition]

G. **Miscellany Concerning Conditional Sentences:** Students will encounter some "odd" constructions in actual use; so it will be helpful anticipate questions and to reiterate some things discussed already.

1. <u>Correlative Emphasis by Marking the Apodosis.</u> Additional force may be given to the apodosis by explicating the "then" (ἄρα).

Gal 3:29 εἰ δὲ ὑμεῖς Χριστοῦ, <u>ἄρα</u> τοῦ Ἀβραὰμ σπέρμα ἐστέ,
　　　Moreover, if you are Christ's, <u>then</u> you are Abraham's offspring.

See also §15.6 CORRELATIVE EMPHASIS: LISTS AND COORDINATED CONNECTIVES.

2. <u>A Double Protasis Possible.</u> A conditional sentence may be formed with two protases (cf. Smyth §§2366–67):

2 Tim 2:5 ἐὰν δὲ καὶ ἀθλῇ τις, οὐ στεφανοῦται <u>ἐὰν μὴ</u> νομίμως ἀθλήσῃ.
　　　And also if someone competes, he is not crowned <u>unless</u> he competes lawfully.

In 2 Tim 2:5, each protasis contributes to form a Present General Condition and describes a generalized condition of competition that is necessary before being crowned: First, one must enter the competition; second, one must compete lawfully. In the next example, the protases are of two different types:

2 Cor 8:12 εἰ γὰρ ἡ προθυμία πρόκειται, <u>καθὸ ἐὰν</u> ἔχῃ εὐπρόσδεκτος, οὐ καθὸ οὐκ ἔχει.

For if the eagerness is present (for finishing) [present simple protasis], *it is acceptable* [apodosis for both] <u>to whatever degree that</u> *one might ever have something* [present general protasis], *not to the degree that one has nothing.*

I have explained this verses as follows: "the first [clause] with εἰ is a present simple protasis (see 2:2 on εἰ) and the second with ἐὰν is a present general (see 3:15 on ἡνίκα ἂν). For both protases, the verb of the apodosis is an implied present indicative.… The implication is that, in the case of the Corinthians, and giving in general, it is acceptable to give if the desire is present, but only under the general truth condition that one has something to give (this is the general truth)."[3]

3. <u>Imperatives and Emphatic Negations in the Conclusion.</u> Not infrequently, one observes an Imperative Mood verb in the conclusion. But, how does one classify the type of condition? Often the imperative mood verb seems equivalent to a Present Tense Indicative since the force of the command is received concurrently in the present time in the utterance itself.

1 Cor 14:28a ἐὰν δὲ μὴ ᾖ διερμηνευτής, <u>σιγάτω</u> ἐν ἐκκλησίᾳ,

But if he is not an interpreter, <u>let him keep silent</u> in a church assembly,

Here Paul is establishing a general rule, using a Present General condition with the main verb being a Present Tense Imperative that is equivalent to a Present Tense verb. Alternatively, emphatic negation (οὐ μή + Subjunctive) is equivalent to a Future Tense verb.

4. <u>The Participle with or without ὡς.</u> One will sometimes find a circumstantial participle with or without ὡς that may function as a protasis (see Smyth §2344).

2 Cor 10:12b ἀλλὰ αὐτοὶ, ἐν ἑαυτοῖς ἑαυτοὺς <u>μετροῦντες</u> καὶ <u>συγκρίνοντες</u> ἑαυτοὺς ἑαυτοῖς, οὐ συνιᾶσιν. [commas added]

But they themselves, if <u>measuring</u> themselves among themselves and <u>judging</u> themselves by themselves, do not understand.

2 Cor 10:14 οὐ γὰρ, ὡς μὴ <u>ἐφικνούμενοι</u> εἰς ὑμᾶς, ὑπερεκτείνομεν ἑαυτούς. [commas added]

For we did not overstep ourselves, as (if) not <u>reaching</u> unto you.

5. <u>Two Verbs may be Found.</u> In a supposition (e.g. John 15:7); in a conclusion (e.g. Jas 1:5).

---

[3] Fredrick J. Long, *2 Corinthians: A Handbook on the Greek Text*, Baylor Handbook on the Greek New Testament (Waco, TX: Baylor University Press, 2015), 154.

6. <u>Implied Verbs in the Protasis</u>. It is not uncommon for the protasis to have its verb implied, especially when it is the same as in the main clause (Smyth §2345); see Gal 3:29 in 1. above. Such ellipsis is the norm in the conditional pairing εἰ μή *except*, which introduces exception clauses; see §26.3 below.

26.3 EXCEPTION CLAUSES

A. **Introduction:** One may be surprised to see the conjunction εἰ immediately before the negative adverb μή, especially since you would expect οὐ. The εἰ μή combination reflects an archaic Greek construction, when μή was the default negative for the protasis in conditional sentences. However, the construction persists into the Koine era. Εἰ μή is a special type of protasis in a conditional sentence that is marked +*exception* and forms exception clauses; other names given include exceptive, exclusion, restriction, or limitative clauses.[4] Consider this example:

Mark 5:37 καὶ οὐκ ἀφῆκεν οὐδένα μετ᾿ αὐτοῦ συνακολουθῆσαι <u>εἰ μή</u> τὸν Πέτρον καὶ Ἰάκωβον καὶ Ἰωάννην τὸν ἀδελφὸν Ἰακώβου.

> *And he did not permit anyone to follow along with him, <u>except</u> Peter and Jacob and John, the brother of Jacob.*

Often a denial is stated that is followed by the exception clause. Runge explains the basic features of this construction:

> This rhetorical process is analogous to having a table full of items, sweeping all of them onto the floor, and then placing the one item you are interested in back onto the table all by itself. You could have simply pointed to the item and said, "This is the one I am interested in." But sweeping every item onto the floor has a dramatic effect, on top of making a mess! Removing everything and then adding back the important item that was already there attracts far more attention to it than just pointing to it on the table. The same holds for negation + exception/restriction (84).

Runge discusses exception or restriction under his consideration of point/counter point sets (ch.4; cf. my earlier discussion of ἀλλά in §4.8.D), although his description focuses on οὐ … εἰ μή or question followed by εἰ μή. Only one example with ἐὰν μή is given (2 Tim 2:5), but indeed exception clauses may also be formed with ἐὰν μή.

---

[4] While summarizing the uses of ἐάν, Richard A. Young includes last "exclusion" (*Intermediate New Testament Greek: A Linguistic and Exegetical Approach* [Nashville: Broadman & Holman, 1994], 185); when discussing εἰ, Young does not mention "exclusion." "Limitative" is used to describe exceptive clauses in, e.g., Ronald J. Williams, *Williams Hebrew Syntax*, 3rd ed., expanded by John C. Beckman (Toronto: University of Toronto Press, 2007), §§556-57.

B. **Semantics:** The two main functions of exception clauses, according to Runge, depend on their sentence location with respect to the main clause (the apodosis). In a pre-position, they provide a framework for what follows; in a post-position, they emphasize the constituent in the clause. He summarizes,

> In cases where the exceptive clause *precedes* the main clause (i.e., protasis), it functions to establish a specific 'frame of reference' for the clause that follows.... In cases where the exceptive clause *follows* the main clause (i.e., apodosis) and is preceded by either a negated main clause or an interrogative clause, the exceptive clause receives emphasis with respect to the main clause (85, emphasis original).

In what follows, I offer an intermediate-advanced discussion of the constructions and pragmatics with further examples.

C. **Constructions:** Grammarians have not given exception clauses much treatment,[5] except for Runge.[6] Exception clauses may involve the constructions εἰ μή, ἐὰν μή, and sometimes the conjunction πλήν (32 occurences in the GNT), although there are differences with each construction and individual cases are debated.

James L. Boyer identified three characteristic features of the construction: "First, there is an ellipsis of the verb in the protasis which is supplied from the principal clause, often the same verb. Second, there is a negative comparison between the two clauses. And third, the protasis always follows the apodosis."[7] However, Boyer's first feature only applies to εἰ μή constructions, and not to ἐὰν μή; consequently, Boyer did not consider ἐὰν μή as forming exceptive clauses. Yet, since the same semantics are involved (a negation/question accompanied by a clause indicating exception), there is good reason to think that ἐὰν μή can form exception clauses (see examples below). Boyer's third feature is also debatable, since there may be counter examples (see Mark 8:14).

Runge explains that exception constructions will normally entail two elements: 1) a negation or rhetorical question (implying "nothing" as the answer) and 2) the exception clause. Also, the relative positioning respective to each element will vary, one occurring before the other. This differs from Boyer, who uses this criterion of position to exclude certain cases as

---

[5] So, Runge 85-86. Yet, James L. Boyer offers a good treatment, although I disagree with some of his analysis ("Other Conditional Elements in New Testament Greek," *Grace Theological Journal* 4.2 [1983]: 173–88 at 178-83). Young indicates that "exclusion" is one use of ἐὰν (*Intermediate New Testament Greek*, 185). Robertson treats εἰ μή under a discussion of adversative conjunctions: "Εἰ μή. This phrase marks an exception, as in Mt. 12:4; Jo. 17:12. We even have ἐκτὸς εἰ μή (1 Cor. 14:5; 15:2; 1 Tim. 5:19)" (1188). See also his more substantive discussion in a paragraph when treating conditional sentences (1024-25). Also, Wesley J. Perschbacher identifies ἐὰν μή as forming exceptive clauses, with no discussion (*New Testament Greek Syntax: An Illustrated Manual* [Chicago: Moody, 1995], 106, 334).

[6] In addition to the section within Runge (§4.2; pp. 83-91), he himself points readers to his paper, "Teaching Them What NOT to Do: The Nuances of Negation in the Greek New Testament" (paper presented at the annual meeting of the Evangelical Theology Society, San Diego, CA, November 13–16, 2007).

[7] Boyer, "Other Conditional Elements," 178.

being exception clauses. Remember also for Boyer that one criterion for exception clauses is the need to supply an implied verb (i.e. they are elliptical clauses).

1. <u>Basic Constituents in the Construction.</u>

    a. **negation** (with οὐ, etc.) + **exception/restriction** (with εἰ μή or ἐὰν μή)

    b. **rhetorical questions** ("nothing" as the answer) + **exception/restriction** (with εἰ μή or ἐὰν μή).

    c. Variation from these would be "exceptional" (pun intended) and worthy of careful study.

2. <u>Position.</u>

    a. *Post-Negation/Question.* It is most common for the exceptive clause to come **after** the negation or at the end of the rhetorical question; and thus, this post-position is the default or unmarked construction.

    b. *Pre-Negation/Question.* Since this pre-position is less common, it is more marked.

3. <u>Verb Implied or Explicit in the Exceptive Clause.</u>

    a. *Implied.* As we will see with exceptive clauses formed with εἰ μή, the majority have implied verbs. So, when an exception clause with εἰ μή has a verb, this marks a departure from the default construction. For Boyer, this was one signal that we do not have the construction, in addition to its location.

    b. *Explicit.* As we will see, with exceptive clauses formed with ἐὰν μή, all instances have an explicit verb. For Boyer, this would exclude them.

4. <u>Additional Emphatic and Pragmatic Markers.</u> One should pay attention to additional constituents that additionally mark the construction for emphasis or for other constraints. For instance, we observe the adverb ἐκτός *outside* added three times to εἰ μή to provide addition emphasis to the exception: ἐκτὸς εἰ μή (1 Cor 14:5; 15:2; 1 Tim 5:19). Also, we observe the conjunction δέ marking +*new development*, and in such cases, we observe explicit verbs, rather than ellipsis.

D. **Pragmatics:** Having myself looked at every construction with εἰ μή and ἐὰν μή, let me offer the following summary and description of my findings concerning usage, and whether each of these may be considered to be forming exception clauses.

1. <u>Εἰ Μή</u> (*Except*). Exclusion clauses formed with this εἰ μή combination occur as many as ninety-two times, inclusive of four instances of εἰ δὲ μή (but not all instances; cf. Rev 2:5, 16) and two of the three instances of εἰ μήτι (but not at 2 Cor 13:5). Exception clauses with εἰ μή are very often elliptical; one must supply an implied verb from the main clause.

CHART OF Εἰ Μή USAGE	
PRE-POSITION (7 times)	**POST-POSITION (85 times)**
<u>Before a Negation/Denial (6 times):</u> Matt 24:22 (NOT elliptical; ἄν in apodosis) Mark 8:14; 13:20 (NOT elliptical; ἄν in apodosis) John 9:33 (NOT elliptical; ἄν is likely implied in apodosis); 15:22 (NOT elliptical; ἄν is likely implied in apodosis); 18:30 (NOT elliptical; ἄν in apodosis) <u>Before a Warning:</u> Rom 9:29 (NOT elliptical; quoting Isa 1:9; condition has ἄν in apodosis)	<u>After a Negation/Denial (71 times):</u> Matt 5:13; 11:27[2]; 12:4, 24, 39; 13:57; 14:17; 15:24; 16:4; 17:8; 21:19; 24:36 Mark 2:21 (εἰ δὲ μή NOT elliptical), 22 (εἰ δὲ μή NOT elliptical); 5:37; 6:4, 5, 8; 9:9, 29; 10:18; 11:13; 13:32 Luke 4:26, 27; 5:36 (εἰ δὲ μή γε NOT elliptical), 37 (εἰ δὲ μή γε NOT elliptical); 6:4; 8:51; 9:13 (with εἰ μήτι NOT elliptical); 10:22[2]; 11:29; 17:18 (in rhetorical question); 18:19 John 3:13; 6:22; 6:46; 10:10; 13:10; 14:6; 17:12; 19:11 (NOT elliptical), 15 Acts 11:19 Rom 7:7; 13:8; 14:14; 1 Cor 1:14; 2:2; 2:11; 7:5 (εἰ μήτι ἄν); 8:4; 10:13; 12:3; 2 Cor 2:2; 12:5; Gal 1:7, 19; 6:14; Phil 4:15; 1 Tim 5:19 Rev 2:17; 9:4; 13:17; 14:3; 19:12; 21:27 (after οὐ μὴ) <u>After or at the End of a Question (12 times):</u> Mark 2:7, 26 Luke 5:21 Rom 11:15 (favorable outcome); 1 Cor 2:11; 7:17 (two questions are in 7:16); 1 Cor 15:2 (after indirect question); 2 Cor 12:13; Eph 4:9 Heb 3:18 1 John 2:22; 5:5 <u>After a Favorable Scenario:</u> Acts 26:32 (NOT Elliptical) <u>After Comparison/Contrast:</u> 1 Cor 14:5

The εἰ μή construction is broadly distributed across the GNT. It occurs 85 times in a post-position after the main clause, providing stress on the exceptional elements. In seventy-six instances the exception clause was related to a negation or denial involving οὐ or cognates.

Mark 6:4b <u>οὐκ</u> ἔστιν προφήτης ἄτιμος <u>εἰ μὴ</u> ἐν τῇ πατρίδι αὐτοῦ καὶ ἐν τοῖς συγγενεῦσιν αὐτοῦ καὶ ἐν τῇ οἰκίᾳ αὐτοῦ.

A prophet is <u>not</u> without honor, <u>except</u> in his home country and among his relatives and in his house.

In twelve instances, the exception clause comes after or at the end of a question. Sometimes these questions are rhetorical (expecting a no answer), and other times more open ended, although containing an implicit warning.

Mark 2:7c τίς δύναται ἀφιέναι ἁμαρτίας <u>εἰ μὴ</u> εἷς ὁ θεός;
      Who is able to forgive sins, <u>except</u> one, namely, God?

Romans 11:15 is particularly interesting, since it involves not a negation or a warning, but expects a positive response and favorable outcome:

Rom 11:15 εἰ γὰρ ἡ ἀποβολὴ αὐτῶν καταλλαγὴ κόσμου, τίς ἡ πρόσλημψις <u>εἰ μὴ</u> ζωὴ ἐκ νεκρῶν;
      For if their rejection is the reconciliation of the world, what is their acceptance, <u>except</u> life from the dead?

The εἰ μή combination was NOT elliptical twelve times; of these, almost all of the examples of a pre-position are NOT elliptical, which may support Boyer's denial of these being exception clauses. Additionally, all the pre-position examples, except for Mark 8:14, have features that would indicate they are contrary-to-fact conditions, since there is an explicit ἄν or an implied ἄν (in John's usage). Below is John 9:33 first translated (assuming an ἄν) to form a Present Contrary-to-Fact condition, and then followed by translating it as an exception clause.

John 9:33 εἰ μὴ ἦν οὗτος παρὰ θεοῦ, οὐκ ἠδύνατο ποιεῖν οὐδέν.
      If this guy were not from God, (then) he would not be able to do anything.

So, three factors mitigate against εἰ μή in pre-position being exception clauses: their position, their NON-elliptical form, and their use of ἄν or an implied ἄν. Only Mark 8:14 may be truly an exception clause:

Mark 8:14 Καὶ ἐπελάθοντο λαβεῖν ἄρτους καὶ <u>εἰ μὴ</u> ἕνα ἄρτον οὐκ εἶχον μεθ' ἑαυτῶν ἐν τῷ πλοίῳ.
      And they forgot to take along bread and, <u>except</u> one loaf, they were not having (anything) with themselves in the boat.

Of the remaining NOT elliptical instances, five involve a slightly altered construction with more conjunctive or morphological marking: εἰ μήτι (Luke 9:31) and εἰ δὲ μή (Mark 2:21, 22) and in the Gospel parallel text εἰ δὲ μή γε (Luke 5:36, 37). It is likely that the presence of the conjunction δέ (marked +*new development*) helps signal the presence of a different explicit verb, rather than implying the verb from the main clause.

2. Ἐὰν Μή (*Unless*). This combination occurs 48 times.[8]

<table>
<tr><td colspan="2" align="center">CHART OF Ἐὰν Μή USAGE</td></tr>
<tr><td align="center">PRE-POSITION (21 times)</td><td align="center">POST-POSITION (27 times)</td></tr>
<tr><td>Before a Negation/Denial (13 times):
  Matt 5:20 (οὐ μὴ); Matt 18:3 (οὐ μὴ)
  Mark 7:3, 4
  John 3:3, 5 (both strong thematic denials);
    4:48 (οὐ μὴ); 6:53; 13:8 [responding to
    prior emphatic negation]; 20:25 (οὐ μὴ)
  Acts 15:1; 27:31
  1 Cor 8:8
Before a Warning: John 15:6
Before Neutral Scenario: John 12:24
Before Favorable Scenario: Rom 11:23
Beginning of Question: 1 Cor 14:9
Forming Relative Conditionals:
  Matt 11:6 (ὃς ἐὰν μὴ//Luke 7:23)
  Acts 3:23 (ἥτις ἐὰν μὴ)
  Rev 13:15 (ὅσοι ἐὰν μὴ)</td><td>After a Negation/Denial (18 times):
  Matt 26:42
  Mark 3:27; 4:22; 10:30
  Luke 13:3, 5 [both after οὐχί response]
  John 3:2, 27; 5:19; 6:44, 65; 7:51 [denial in
    form of rhetorical question]; 15:4[2]
  1 Cor 15:36; Gal 2:16; 2 Thess 2:3; 2 Tim
    2:5
After Warning/Negative Outcome (5 times):
  Matt 18:35
  1 Cor 9:16
  Jas 2:17
  Rev 2:5, 22
After or at the End of a Question (4 times):
  Matt 12:29; Acts 8:31 (implies negative
    scenario); Rom 10:15; 1 Cor 14:6</td></tr>
</table>

In general, the translation "unless" works well for ἐὰν μή. A few additional comments are worth making. First, the ἐὰν μή construction is broadly distributed across the GNT (like εἰ μή). Second, the clauses formed by ἐὰν μή are never elliptical (unlike εἰ μή). Third, a large majority are in relationship with (strong) negation/denials (31 times) or warnings (6 times), which occur almost twice as often in post-position (23 times) and in pre-position (14 times); an example of each is given below:

Mark 7:4b καὶ ἀπ᾽ ἀγορᾶς <u>ἐὰν μὴ</u> βαπτίσωνται, οὐκ ἐσθίουσιν, [pre-position]
    And (coming) from the market, <u>unless</u> they wash themselves, they do not eat.

2 Tim 2:5 ἐὰν δὲ καὶ ἀθλῇ τις, οὐ στεφανοῦται <u>ἐὰν μὴ</u> νομίμως ἀθλήσῃ.
    And also if someone compete, he is not crowned <u>unless</u> he competes lawfully.

Fourth, only a handful of ἐὰν μή clauses work with questions.

1 Cor 14:9 οὕτως καὶ ὑμεῖς διὰ τῆς γλώσσης <u>ἐὰν μὴ</u> εὔσημον λόγον δῶτε, <u>πῶς</u>
    γνωσθήσεται τὸ λαλούμενον;
    Thus also you yourselves through the language, <u>unless</u> you give a distinct word, <u>how</u> will the matter that is being spoken be known?

---

[8] This excludes four instances of ἐὰν δὲ μή.

Fifth, not indicated in the chart above, many of these clauses are found with proleptic (fronted) word order. In Mark 7:4b above, the prepositional phrase ἀπ' ἀγορᾶς *from the market* is pulled out of its subordinate clause for extra focus. Also, in 1 Cor 14:9 above, consider how ὑμεῖς and διὰ τῆς γλώσσης are pulled forward for emphasis. Finally, four instances of ἐὰν μή worked to form a relative-conditional clause; one wonders whether these instances should be classified as exception clauses, even though one may translate it as such.

Matt 11:6 καὶ μακάριός ἐστιν <u>ὃς ἐὰν μὴ</u> σκανδαλισθῇ ἐν ἐμοί.
> *And he is blessed <u>whoever</u> is <u>not</u> scandalized by me.*
> *And he is blessed, <u>unless</u> he is scandalized by me.*

3. <u>Πλήν</u>. Historically in the Greek language πλήν was a preposition, and this usage persists in the NT (Mark 12:32 quoting Deut 4:35; Acts 8:1). But as a preposition, it follows a denial sweeping all away, and then provides the exception.

Mark 12:32b εἷς ἐστιν καὶ οὐκ ἔστιν ἄλλος πλὴν αὐτοῦ·
> *He is one and there is no other [god] except Him.*

However, πλήν also functions as a conjunction to mark a rather strong contrast of expectation (Matt 11:22, 24, etc.). In the example below, we observe the initial denial of knowledge followed by the exception of what has been revealed.

Acts 20:22-23 Καὶ νῦν ἰδοὺ δεδεμένος ἐγὼ τῷ πνεύματι πορεύομαι εἰς Ἰερουσαλὴμ τὰ ἐν αὐτῇ συναντήσοντά μοι μὴ εἰδώς, ²³ πλὴν ὅτι τὸ πνεῦμα τὸ ἅγιον κατὰ πόλιν διαμαρτύρεταί μοι λέγον ὅτι δεσμὰ καὶ θλίψεις με μένουσιν.
> ²² *And now behold, having been bound by the Spirit, I myself am going to Jerusalem, not knowing that which will happen to me in it,* ²³ <u>except</u> *that the Holy Spirit solemnly testifies to me in every city, saying that bonds and afflictions await me.*

Significantly, Friedrich Blass noted "that Paul uses it [πλήν] at the end of an argument to single out the main point. Cf. 1 Cor. 11:11; Eph. 5:33; Ph. 3:16; 4:14" (Robertson 1187). So, in Eph 5:33 see how Paul summarily concludes his argument.

Eph 5:32 τὸ μυστήριον τοῦτο μέγα ἐστίν· ἐγὼ δὲ λέγω εἰς Χριστὸν καὶ εἰς τὴν ἐκκλησίαν. ³³ πλὴν καὶ ὑμεῖς οἱ καθ' ἕνα, ἕκαστος τὴν ἑαυτοῦ γυναῖκα οὕτως ἀγαπάτω ὡς ἑαυτόν, ἡ δὲ γυνὴ ἵνα φοβῆται τὸν ἄνδρα.
> ³² *This mystery is great; moreover, I myself am speaking regarding Christ and regarding the church assembly.* ³³ <u>Nevertheless</u>, *also you, one by one, let each one thus love his own wife as himself, and the wife [look] that she give reverence to her husband.*

26.4 QUALITATIVE EMPHASIS

A. **Modifiers May Signify Quality and Significance:** The choice to use modifiers that indicate *quality* is exegetically significant. Such qualitative modification will stress some attribute of a sentence constituent. Qualitative Emphasis is, "The use of qualitative demonstratives (e.g., τοιοῦτος), relative pronouns (e.g., οἷος), and other modifying words that inherently entail and stress the quality of the entity modified or described. The modification of sentence elements by reference to quality is strategic and contextually significant."[9] One must ask, Why? Does this clarify identity? Does this add vividness to the description? Does it augment a contrast that is already explicit or implicit in the discourse? Does it provide recurring focus in the discourse? More than likely, the qualitative emphasis contributes to larger discursive meaning.

B. **Words Denoting Quality:** It might surprise you to learn that Greek would encode qualitative stress. In other words, Greek has modifiers that are marked +*quality*.

WORDS DENOTING QUALITY	
τοιοῦτος, τοιαύτη, τοιοῦτον [57]	*such as this, of such a kind*
ποῖος, -α, -ον [33]	*of what kind? which?*
οἷος [13]	*what sort of, what quality of*
ὁποῖος [5]	*of what sort or quality*
τοιόσδε, τοιάδε, τοιόνδε [1]	*such as this, of this kind* (2 Pet 1:17)

Unfortunately, English Translations often may not translate the qualitative sense. For a corresponding discussion on quantitative emphasis, see §12.4 QUANTITATIVE EMPHASIS.

C. **Examples of Qualitative Emphasis:**

1 Cor 15:48 <u>οἷος</u> ὁ χοϊκός, <u>τοιοῦτοι</u> καὶ οἱ χοϊκοί, καὶ <u>οἷος</u> ὁ ἐπουράνιος, <u>τοιοῦτοι</u> καὶ οἱ ἐπουράνιοι·

> *<u>As</u> is <u>the quality of</u> the earthly one, <u>such</u> also are the earthly ones; and <u>as</u> is <u>the quality of</u> the heavenly one, <u>such</u> also are the heavenly ones.*

It is difficult to translate in such a way to convey quality. The NASB95, ESV, RSV, NRSV, etc. use *as ... so are those*; the NET *Like ... so*. Paul is wanting to show the corresponding natures of those in Adam as like Adam and those belonging to Christ as like Christ, in order to speak to the heavenly, resurrection destiny of those in Christ.

---

[9] Fredrick J. Long, *2 Corinthians: A Handbook on the Greek Text*, Baylor Handbook on the Greek New Testament (Waco, TX: Baylor University Press, 2015), 274-75.

2 Cor 12:20 φοβοῦμαι γὰρ μή πως ἐλθὼν οὐχ <u>οἴους</u> θέλω εὕρω ὑμᾶς κἀγὼ εὑρεθῶ ὑμῖν <u>οἷον</u> οὐ θέλετε· μή πως ἔρις, ζῆλος, θυμοί, ἐριθεῖαι, καταλαλιαί, ψιθυρισμοί, φυσιώσεις, ἀκαταστασίαι·

> *For I am afraid that somehow, after coming, I will find you not <u>how (as in what qualitative state)</u> I want and I will be found by you not <u>how (as in what kind of disposition)</u> you want—that somehow [there will be] strife, envy, displays of anger, selfish ambitions, slanders, gossiping, conceit, disruptions.*

In this first example, Paul is warning the Corinthians about his impending visit and how he and the Corinthians would qualitatively relate to each other. The problem is that the Corinthians are engaged in sinful, hurtful behavior; and Paul will not be sparing anyone (13:2), even if it means tearing down so as to build up (13:10; cf. 10:3-6, where Paul uses technical staged siege imagery for a battle).

Complete WORKBOOK EXERCISES 26 and consult the ANSWER KEY & GUIDE as needed.

CASE IN POINT 26: CORRELATIVE PRONOUNS AND THE GOLDEN RULE

The correlative pronouns such as ὅσος, -η, -ον and τοιοῦτος, τοιαύτη, τοιοῦτον draw our attention to the **quantity** of or to the **quality** of persons or things, respectively. Let me have you consider some verses in English to ponder what exactly is stressed by the underlying Greek correlative pronoun. We start with Gal 5:19-21 and 1 Cor 5:11 (NASB95, placed into italics):

Gal 5:19-21 *Now the deeds of the flesh are evident, which are: immorality, impurity, sensuality, [20] idolatry, sorcery, enmities, strife, jealousy, outbursts of anger, disputes, dissensions, factions, [21] envying, drunkenness, carousing, and things like these, of which I forewarn you, just as I have forewarned you, that those who practice **<u>such things</u>** will not inherit the kingdom of God.*

1 Cor 5:11 *But actually, I wrote to you not to associate with any so-called brother if he is an immoral person, or covetous, or an idolater, or a reviler, or a drunkard, or a swindler-- not even to eat with **<u>such a one</u>**.*

What is stressed by the use of the correlative pronoun of quality τοιοῦτος, τοιαύτη, τοιοῦτον? A similar (although opposite) stress is found in the following verse:

Heb 13:16 *And do not neglect doing good and sharing, for with **<u>such</u>** sacrifices God is pleased.*

The correlative pronoun of quantity ὅσος, -η, -ον is often harder to detect in English translations. Are you able to find it below in the NASB95 (a fairly literal translation) in the following verse?

Phil 4:8 *Finally, brethren, whatever is true, whatever is honorable, whatever is right, whatever is pure, whatever is lovely, whatever is of good repute, if there is any excellence and if anything worthy of praise, dwell on these things.*

Now look at the underlying Greek:

Phil 4:8 Τὸ λοιπόν, ἀδελφοί, <u>ὅσα</u> ἐστὶν ἀληθῆ, <u>ὅσα</u> σεμνά, <u>ὅσα</u> δίκαια, <u>ὅσα</u> ἁγνά, <u>ὅσα</u> προσφιλῆ, <u>ὅσα</u> εὔφημα, εἴ τις ἀρετὴ καὶ εἴ τις ἔπαινος, ταῦτα λογίζεσθε·

In fact, ὅσος, -η, -ον is used six times and is here translated unfortunately simply like an indefinite relative pronoun *whatever*. This English rendering may actually mislead the reader into thinking that Paul speaks of a singular entity. The text, however, stresses just the opposite. In Greek, the pronouns are plural. A more accurate, but cumbersome, translation would be, *however so many things are true, however so many things are honorable...* There are many true, honorable, righteous, holy things, and things of good repute to dwell on within the scope of God's creative and redemptive purposes.

Consider also the following verse also with the NASB95. Once again, are you able to identify the correlative pronoun? Below it is the Greek text.

Matt 7:12 *In everything, therefore, treat people the same way you want them to treat you, for this is the Law and the Prophets.*
Matt 7:12 Πάντα οὖν <u>ὅσα</u> ἐὰν θέλητε ἵνα ποιῶσιν ὑμῖν οἱ ἄνθρωποι, οὕτως καὶ ὑμεῖς ποιεῖτε αὐτοῖς· οὗτος γάρ ἐστιν ὁ νόμος καὶ οἱ προφῆται.

We can see in the Greek text that there is a correlative conditional sentence of a Present General variety since the Imperative verb is equivalent to the Present Tense.

Protasis: <u>ὅσα</u> ἐὰν θέλητε ...   *However much you want...,*
Apodosis: ὑμεῖς ποιεῖτε αὐτοῖς.   (then) *you yourselves be doing to them.*

Jesus is issuing a general command of continuous applicability using a Present Tense Imperative. Notice too the emphatic subject pronoun ὑμεῖς *yourselves* that goes untranslated. More critically, the NASB95 misses the emphasis of word order by placing the conclusion (or apodosis) first, and not translating the protasis <u>as a supposition</u>. The sentence is better translated:

Therefore, all things, however much you are wanting that people do for you, also in this way you yourselves be doing for them. For this is the Law and the Prophets.

There is quantitative emphasis here (see §12.4 QUANTITATIVE EMPHASIS). The correlative pronoun of quantity works in conjunction with the initially emphatic πάντα, which is inclusive in scope. Together πάντα ... ὅσα *all things... as much as* stresses the inclusive nature of the supposition—in every respect *quantitatively* possible—what you would want done for you, thus be doing to others. The main sentence is the conclusion: *Do all things for them.* The *all* is quantified by the correlative-quantitative-conditional clause.

Well, this marks the final CASE IN POINT in Κοινὴ Γραμματική. Quite frankly, there is no better way to conclude than with Matt 7:12, the Golden Rule. I hope you will continue to strive to better understand the Greek language, its grammar, pragmatics, and emphases. By your study of God's Word, my prayer is that you would draw nearer to God in Christ to love God and neighbor.

Below is Papyrus 1 (𝔓[1]), a fragment of Matthew 1 at the very beginning of the Gospel.[10] It is the verso (i.e., the back side of a page). How much of the Greek are you able to make out?

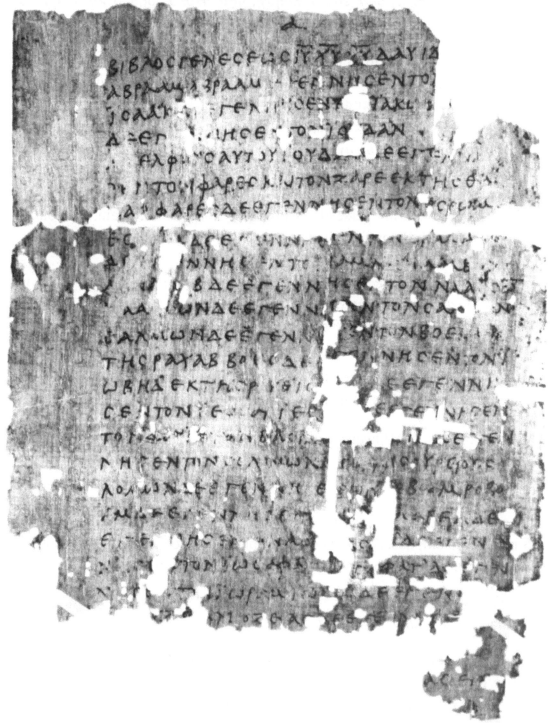

---

[10] Image slightly edited from Bernard Pyne Grenfell and Arthur Surridge Hunt, *The Oxyrhynchus Papyri*, vol. 1 (London: Egypt Exploration Fund, 1898), Plate I. This papyrus is also identified as *P. Oxy.* 2.

CHAPTER 27

Paul disparages *boasting* among the Corinthians (1 Cor 3:32; 4:7) but yet boasts himself, although he would rather not (2 Cor 10:8; 11:18, 30). Paul later used the same verb καυχάομαι positively in Rom 5:3, which is translated *exult* (NASB95) or *rejoice* (NIV, ESV, NLT). On what basis did Paul *exult* or *boast* in Rom 5:3?

The building blocks of any discourse are morphemes and the words they form. **How to study words** is the major topic of this lesson. To help illustrate how to perform a word study, included is one undergraduate student's word study on βοάω *I cry*. The chapter concludes with my word study on καυχάομαι *I boast*.

27.1 INTRODUCTION TO WORD STUDY

A. Priorities in Word Study:

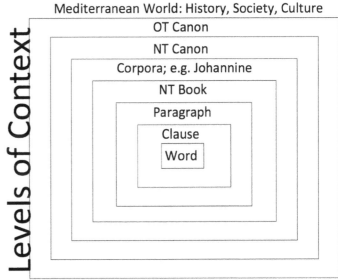

1. <u>Words are the Building Blocks of Discourse</u>. God's Word has been communicated through individual words. While every word contributes to the message of God's Word, certain words are more pivotal for exploration given our own cultural, ecclesial, and personal limitations of knowledge. One purpose in learning Greek is to be able to study key words.

2. <u>Context is Everything (CIE)</u>. *Word studies should be done in context, i.e. the meaning of a word in a passage should be determined by its immediate contexts.* The levels of context may be conceptualized from the word occurring within a main clause (with or without modifiers), which occurs within a paragraph and successively higher levels of book structure. That book belongs to a corpus within the NT Canon within the Biblical Canon.

3. <u>Words Cohere within a Network of Concepts</u>. In addition to literary contexts, recent research into mental conception (i.e. how humans conceptualize thought) and the rhetoric of communication indicates that words are used in relation to other words to form networks of

meaning. When one word is used, other ideas/words are assumed and/or more likely to be used. In other words, ideas and words travel together. For example, consider this opening sentence: *Farms are really smelly.* In your mind you may begin to envision why this is true. You think of cattle, pigs, horses, and manure. What this means is that when studying words, students need to try to re-conceptualize what networks of ideas existed around them. Such networks are not static, but are often linked to real, lived-in human experience within time, space, cultures, and society. Words are very dynamic and networks of relations develop. Paying attention to modifications, relationships, and development is a major skill for word study.

4. Study Important Words. One should particularly study words that are critical for a proper interpretation of any given passage. Consider especially, however, morally, socially, or theologically significant words.

5. Consider Studying Closely Related Cognates, Synonyms, or even Antonyms.
   a. *Cognates.* Meaning across a discourse can be constructed through the use of semantically related words that are derived from the same Greek root. Such words are called **cognates.** *Cognates* are words that are built from the same Greek root: e.g., δικαιοσύνη is a cognate noun related to the verb δικαιόω. The search for cognates might on occasion uncover a broader association of meanings in a passage. Consider, for example, the οικ- Greek root in Eph 2:19-22, in which the stem is found six times in six different words with a variety of meanings. The root conveys generally the idea of "house(hold)" and these six words help communicate powerfully the Gentiles' changed social status of once being "aliens" (πάροικοι) but who are now in Christ "household members" (οἰκεῖοι) who are being built (ἐποικοδομηθέντες and συνοικοδομεῖσθε) into a structure (οἰκοδομὴ) which is a temple (κατοικητήριον) of God. *However, importantly not all cognates will carry a similar range of meaning*; so one must be careful in selecting which cognate word are worthy for further investigation. See §27.4.D. below.
   b. *Synonyms.* Words that have overlapping meanings are called **synonyms.** In order to study the broader concept, a look at synonyms may be necessary.
   c. *Antonyms.* Additionally, **antonyms** are words that have an opposite meaning. Some of these may be cognates, built with the same root but with an ἄλφα *privative* prefix that negates the Greek root. For example, ἀ-δίκως means *unjustly.* Antonyms and synonyms may or may not help your study—but they will increase your work.

B. **Types of Word Study:** There are at least two ways of conducting word studies, each with benefits and weaknesses.

1. Passage Word Study. Choose a passage and a key word in that passage. The **benefit** of this approach is that one is working primarily with one context, and the focus of the study is more manageable (one literary context primarily). On the other hand, a **weakness** may be that your investigation of the other occurrences of the word outside that one passage may be influenced by the "interpretive view" of that one passage. Also, the results of your study

will pertain primarily to the meaning of the word in that one passage. For an example of a passage word study by a college student, see below §27.5 A WORD STUDY ON Βοάω *I CRY OUT* FROM MARK 15:34 by Gregory Neumayer (used by permission).

2. Thematic Word Study. Choose a morally or theologically significant word to study across the NT. The **benefit** is that, after a careful investigation of the word's many contexts, you will have a significant understanding of that word. This requires a lot of work. A **weakness** is *that one may not adequately study each specific context where the word is found*. Thus, one's word study may not be very accurate and/or may be superficial.

27.2 BASIC TOOLS OF WORD STUDY

A. **Concordances:** The most essential tool for doing a word study is not a dictionary or lexicon (surprisingly!), but a concordance. A concordance provides all the occurrences of a word in the NT by giving references and sometimes even the portion of a verse in which the word is found. These are massive resources. There are English-based concordances and Greek-based concordances. There are even concordances with English text based on Greek words (see Wigram below). There are print, web, and electronic software concordances. The types and relative dangers of using concordances are described below.

1. *Print Concordances and Numbering Systems*. The classic combination of English concordance based upon the Greek text is Strong's Exhaustive Concordance, which employed a numbering system for each Hebrew and Greek word that one could use to study a Greek word without knowing Greek! It is still being updated in print. Alternatively, Zondervan published its own concordance and numbering system edited by Kohlenberger-Goodrick based upon the NIV text and its underlying Hebrew and Greek text. Hence, the numbering system is called the G/K system. What this means, however, is that there are competing numbering systems, editions, and versions.

   a. Goodrick, Edward W. and John R. Kohlenberger III, *The Strongest NIV Exhaustive Concordance* (Grand Rapids: Zondervan, 2004).

   b. Kohlenberger III, John R. *The Greek-English Concordance of the New Testament.* Grand Rapids: Zondervan, 1993.

   c. Moulton, W. F., A. S. Geden, H. K. Moulton, and I. Howard Marshall. *A Concordance to the Greek Testament.* 6th ed. Edinburgh: Clark, 2002.

   d. Strong, James. *The New Strong's Expanded Exhaustive Concordance of the Bible.* Expanded ed.; Thomas Nelson, 2010.

   e. Wigram, George V. *The Englishman's Greek Concordance of New Testament: Coded with Strong's Concordance Numbers.* Reprinted.; Peabody, Mass.: Hendrickson, 1996.

2. *Web-based Concordances*. Now, with the advent of electronic media, print editions of concordances are not needed. On the web, one can find search engines that contain English

concordances based upon the underlying Greek word. These may be limited to the KJV and the NASB (1971). One website boasts searches in 100 languages and versions, among which is included Greek New Testaments by Stephanus, Scrivener, Westcott-Hort, and the SBLGNT. One must type in the exact Greek word "form" with breathing and accent marks. One is thus searching for one particular form of a Greek word rather than all the occurrences of the word itself. For example (using an English example), if one wanted to search for all occurrences of the verb "to sing," one would have to search for "sing," "sings," "sang," "sung," etc. Thus, to search properly, one must know alternative forms of a Greek word—but such knowledge is beyond the learning of the average person. Another website, Biblios, has a multiple version concordance search, and also provides Strong's and Englishman's searches for Greek and Hebrew. It contains an interlinear version with active links directly to the Englishman's concordance, providing one with results showing all the occurrences of that particular word form (not all the forms of the word), but then shows a link to a complete listing based on Strong's numbering that then shows all forms of the word.

   a. Find concordances on http://www.biblestudytools.com/concordances/
   b. See Biblios.com at http://concordances.org/

3. *Software Based Concordances*. Computer software offers more robust searching options on the most recent English versions and the most recent critical Greek editions, such as the UBS^{3-4-5}, NA$^{27-28}$, and SBLGNT. In addition to the broadly available KJV and NASB95 versions, the NIV, RSV, NRSV, ESV among others are tagged to the underlying modern-critical Greek NT editions. There are a number of software options for accessing and searching the Greek NT. The top three in alphabetical order are Accordance, BibleWorks, and Logos. The searching interface varies considerably between the three, and each has its respective searching strengths and access to results data, apart from considering the complete software package. *However, whichever platform you choose, it is incumbent for you to learn how best to use your software.* These companies have video tutorials available online or on DVD, as well as user blogs and live help options. These companies are eager to teach you how to use their software. Also, fellow students and professors can be excellent resources to learn how to use Bible software. Ask them!

4. *Dangers with English Concordances and Other Concordances.* One serious problem can be identified quite simply: What is the underlying base Greek text upon which the concordance is based? Is it the more recently established critical text that has considered *every* Greek manuscript found, every quotation in the Church Fathers, all the early versions, etc., or not? Or, is the concordance based on the old KJV-based Greek text or the Majority or Byzantine text? The problem with these freely available online concordances is that *they do not allow direct access to the most critical editions of the Greek NT.* Instead, one is searching older, inferior Greek testaments.

B. **Essential Lexicons:** After concordances, the most important tools for lexical study are dictionaries or lexicons. These will provide an essential range of meanings for a word, which is a
word's **semantic range**. The problem, however, is that interpreters are too often tempted to
use the lexicon as if it were a random smorgasbord from which to select a word meaning for
the passage they are interpreting. They may feel quite justified to do this, since one word
meaning may support the interpretation they have of the passage. However, lexicons are by nature limited in their ability to represent fully the nuances, meanings, and contextual significance of words as deployed by authors. Daniel P. Fuller has articulated this point so well:

> It is obvious, then, that a dictionary or lexicon can provide only partial assistance in
> coming to terms with words. Their only service is to show the various possible mean-
> ings that a word may have. Even then they do not always show the process meaning a
> word has in a particular context, for authors (and Biblical authors are no exception!) of-
> ten impart a unique emphasis to a word so that it can become the means whereby they
> can communicate the new concept which they have in their minds.[1]

In §3.1 GREEK WORDS AND LEXICAL MEANINGS, students were given a basic description of
types of lexicons. In §6.7 A LOOK AT MAJOR LEXICONS: BDAG, L&N, AND LSJ, students
were given a peek at lexical entries. Then, a detailed explanation of full entries of BDAG,
L&N, and LSJ was provided in §12.6 NAVIGATING MAJOR LEXICONS. A discussion of verbal
objects with BDAG and LSJ occured in §14.7 LEXICAL INFORMATION ON THE CASE OF VER-
BAL OBJECTS. Below are listed important lexicons for consultation.

1. Bauer, Walter and F. W. Danker, W. F. Arndt, and F. W. Gingrich (BDAG). *Greek-English
   Lexicon of the New Testament and Other Early Christian Literature*. 3rd ed. Revised. Chicago: The University of Chicago Press, 2000. This is the standard scholarly GNT lexicon.
2. Friberg, Barbara and Timothy Friberg (Friberg). *Analytical Lexicon to the Greek New Testament*. Grand Rapids: Baker, 2000.
3. Liddell, H. G., R. Scott and H. S. Jones (LSJ). *A Greek-English Lexicon*. 9th ed., revised.
   Oxford: Clarendon, 1996. This is the standard Classical Greek lexicon, including coverage
   of the NT. The previous edition, missing only a supplement, is found at http://www. per-
   seus.tufts.edu/cgi-bin/resolveform.
4. Liddell, H. G. *A Lexicon: Abridged from Liddell and Scott's Greek-English Lexicon*. Oxford: Clarendon, 1963 (LSJInt). An abridgment of the 7th edition that importantly still contains word derivation information in parentheses.
5. Louw, Johannes and Eugene Nida (L&N). *Greek-English Lexicon of the New Testament
   Based on Semantic Domains*. 2 Vols. 2nd ed. New York: United Bible Societies, 1988. A

---

[1] Daniel P. Fuller, *The Inductive Method of Bible Study*, 3rd ed. (Pasadena, CA: Fuller Theological Seminary, 1959),
V-11-12.

very valuable lexicon which allows one to find synonyms and antonyms; has its own numbering system based upon semantic domains.

6. Swanson, James. *Dictionary of Biblical Languages With Semantic Domains: Greek (New Testament)*. Electronic ed. Oak Harbor: Logos Research Systems, 1997. Very accessible lexicon using Strong's numbering and referencing other lexicons and theological dictionaries.

7. Thayer, Joseph Henry. *Thayer's Greek-English Lexicon of the New Testament*. Electronic ed. International Bible Translators (IBT), Inc., 1998-2000. Prior to BDAG, Thayer's was the standard lexicon for the GNT. It is dated, but still contains some insightful information, e.g., for some words the underlying roots are given in the formation of the word.

8. Zodhiates, Spiros. *The Complete Word Study Dictionary: New Testament*. Chattanooga, TN: AMG, 1992. Not recognized as an academic lexicon, but Zodhiates often provides an insight perspective on the possible meanings of a word, as well as listing valuable data on synonyms and antonyms and often the roots used in the formation of words, linked also to Strong's data.

27.3 PROBLEMATIC ASSUMPTIONS AND PRACTICES OF WORD STUDY

A. **Introduction**: With the increased ease of access to the Greek, anyone can begin to study words. From the start, however, one must understand and avoid common problematic assumptions and questionable practices when doing word studies. Before I provide a step-by-step approach for word studies, it will be instructive to think about common types of problematic assumptions and mistakes when doing word studies.[2]

1. Part-Whole Fallacy. *It is problematic to assume that by studying one particular word, a whole concept has been studied.* In reality, a single theme may be represented by several different words or phrases, and the totality of a certain truth/theme is usually not represented in one word. To study a theme may also involve studying **cognates** (words built from the same Greek root), **synonyms** (other words having similar or overlapping meanings and uses), and even **antonyms** (words with the opposite meaning). Lexicons will often be helpful in identifying cognates and related forms. A particular helpful resource for identifying synonyms and antonyms is Louw and Nida's Greek-English lexicon (L&N) (see bibliography below). To illustrate this point, consider this chart generated by Logos Bible Software (Version 4) on the word "body" from the NASB95—the one English word in the NT can be a translation of eight different Greek words, even though the largest pie portion is from only one word σῶμα *body*.

---

[2] For a thorough discussion on this topic, see D. A. Carson, *Exegetical Fallacies*, 2nd ed. (Grand Rapids: Baker, 1996), 27-64. The names of the fallacies here do not necessarily come from Carson.

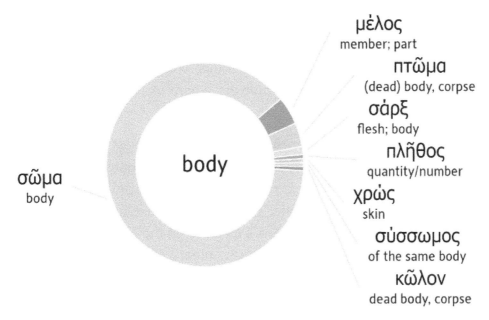

μέλος
member; part

πτῶμα
(dead) body, corpse

σάρξ
flesh; body

πλῆθος
quantity/number

χρώς
skin

σύσσωμος
of the same body

κῶλον
dead body, corpse

σῶμα
body

body

2. <u>One Meaning Fallacy</u>. *It is erroneous to assume that a word has only one meaning in all its occurrences*. In other words, some will argue that a Greek word, whenever it is used, must carry the same meaning. However, this view involves a naïve understanding of how communication takes place. We use words all the time in different ways and meanings, even within the same sentence or document. Even under divine inspiration, Greek words may have various meanings when used within the same book. For example, the word *spirit* (πνεῦμα) by itself (i.e. with no adjectival or other modifiers) is found meaning God's Spirit (1 Cor 2:10; 12:4, 8, 11, 13), a person's spirit (1 Cor 5:5), and the prophets' spirits (1 Cor 14:32), all within 1 Corinthians. So, be careful to consider alternative meanings when looking at each occurrence of a word.

3. <u>Lexicon Fallacy</u>. *It is not always true that a lexicon provides the definitive list of word meanings/uses*. Lexicons may not provide enough definitions or nuanced definitions or they may be too interpretive in these definitions. Indeed, calling for a new lexicon for the NT a century earlier, the gifted philologist Adolf Deissmann said,

> The scientific attitude towards lexicography begins the minute we learn that the meaning of a given word cannot always be got straight from the dictionary, that every word presents a problem in itself, and that we have no right to speak scientifically about a word until we know its history, *i.e.* its origin, its meaning, and how meanings have been multiplied by division or modification.[3]

The lexicon fallacy will depend in large part on the quality and thoroughness of the lexicon consulted. Actually, lexicons normally attempt to provide a listing of *the basic range of meanings*. But some lexicons provide only glosses (basic definitions). So, know the limitations of your lexicons. It is possible that there are special word "nuances" that are not listed

---

[3] G. Adolf Deissmann, *Light from the Ancient East: The New Testament Illustrated by Recently Discovered Texts of the Graeco-Roman World*, trans. L. R. M. Strachan, 2nd ed. (London: Hodder & Stoughton, 1910), 412.

in a lexicon; or, conversely, a special meaning is assigned to explain/interpret(!) a unique use in a difficult passage (e.g. σῶμα in BDAG def. 4 "substantive reality" with only one reference Col 2:17). However, one must be very cautious, when arriving at a "new" word meaning, to establish such a nuance by actual usage elsewhere. A listing of lexicons is provided further below.

4. Etymological Fallacy. *A word's meaning in the NT is determined by its etymology of its component parts and its previous meaning.* In other words, it is questionable whether a word's root or the history of use of a Greek word provides the definitive insight into the Greek word's meaning in the NT. For example, a Greek word's use in Homer (8th century BC) **may** or **may not** have any bearing on a word's meaning in the NT. The problem is that Greek words were used over centuries and in various contexts. Remember that the NT represents one corpus of Koine Greek—it represents a thin slice of Greek usage across time (see CHART 2.1 in CHAPTER 2). NT authors likely were not intimately familiar with a word's root or how a word was used historically. Therefore, while a word's root or history of use may be valuable evidences for what a word in the NT may mean, either its root or its history does not automatically determine a word's meaning. The word's meaning is most fundamentally to be determined by its use in context.

5. Anachronistic Fallacy. *It is problematic to think that a word's meaning can be transported back from our current English use of a cognate form to determine or illuminate a Greek word's meaning.* For example, the English word *dynamite* denotes something very *powerful* and *explosive.* It would be wrong to conclude necessarily that the Greek word δύναμις carries an *explosive* meaning.

6. Overload Fallacy. *It is a common mistake to think that all the possible meanings of a particular word given in a lexicon are found in each and every occurrence of that word.* This reflects, again, a very poor understanding of how communication normally occurs. Every word spoken does not mean three, four, or five things *simultaneously*. Normally, an author communicates a singular meaning with a word. Conversely, arguably the NT authors understood that their audiences were diverse, and that words may communicate richly to different perspectives of an audience. Ultimately, then, in order to understand the meaning of a word, we must consider two things: (1) whether a word's meaning would reasonably be in the original author's repertoire of understanding; and (2) whether the original receptor audience(s) would have been able to understand this meaning from the literary and historical context.

B. **Conclusion:** Be diligent and careful when performing word study. Allow the evidence to guide your conclusions, and keep thinking about the original context and audiences. A word should not mean now what it never meant.

To the left is an Athenian youth looking at and reading (?) from a scroll. This image was on a marble funeral stele c. 4th century BC.[4] Under his seat is lying a dog. What was the boy reading? It is hard to say. Estimates of ancient literacy (the ability to read) are between 5% and 10%. This boy may represent a type-scene of a youth reading the religious "mysteries" upon death, e.g. compare with the painted frieze in the Villa of the Mysteries that shows a youth with mouth closed looking intently at a scroll.

In my view, the ability to read was more widespread than is generally thought. For instance, the drama competitions at Athens held each year involved 7,000 participants (5,000 were boys) who would have to memorize long lyric choruses to sing while dancing. Also, there were numerous speech writers (λογογράφοι) who would prepare speeches for their clients to memorize and perform in various settings. Libraries existed, too, that began cataloguing rhetorical speeches (ῥητορικοὶ πίνακες). At Alexandria, the famous librarian Callimachos of Cyren, in the 3rd century BC produced a massive historical catalogue of Greek literature, Πίνακες *Tablets*, that contained 120 scroll rolls organized by subject and genre with notes on the author and the opening line of the work. If the scrolls were 133 feet long (a maximum length) with four entries per page (a modest figure), the number of literary works listed would be around 17,000. It is also estimated that the Alexandrian Library held between 100,000 and 700,000 books! Moreover, a considerable book trade existed in the Roman empire. One stash of 1,700 scrolls (now "carbonized") was buried at Pompei by the volcanic eruption of Vesuvius; the private library may have belonged to the Philosopher Philodemus (see also p. 235). Currently, progress is being made to perform careful scans of these fragile rolled up scrolls to recover their contents.

27.4 A PROCEDURE FOR PERFORMING A WORD STUDY

A. **Choose an Important Word or Words to Study:** Starting with a specific passage or as part of a theme you want to study, choose an important word to study.

B. **Identify Cognates; also consider Synonyms or Antonyms:** Focus on Cognates, that is, words built from the same stem, since these may have more relevance for your study. This will de-

---

[4] Image (slightly edited) from Victor Duruy, *History of Greece, and of the Greek People: From the Earliest Times to the Roman Conquest*, trans. M. M. Ripley, Vol. 4, Sect. 2 (Boston: Estes and Lauriat, 1892), 419.

pend, of course. But start here. To identify such words is not to enter into a full study of them, but to perform an initial assessment as to their potential relationship to your chosen important word. You must be judicious here, since you have limited time.

C. **Determine the Semantic Range of Words:** Using two or three high quality Greek Lexicons, find the possible meanings for the word (and any cognates you choose to study). Record these clearly and succinctly.

D. **Decide whether to Perform Cognate, Synonym, Antonym, or Compound Study:** Although potentially quite significant, in a good number of cases, cognates and compounds will not significantly enough overlap with the semantic range of meanings of your main word to warrant further study. In other words, such words *might have quite a different semantic meaning/field*, and if this is the case, they have limited relevance to the study. For example, υἱοθεσία *adoption* is derived from υἱός *son* and the verb τίθημι *I set, place*. This verb, however, has quite a different basic meaning and is very common; thus, it is unlikely that it would be helpful in a study on υἱοθεσία.

E. **Find All Occurrences of the Words and Chart Them by Author/Corpus:** Find all the occurrences of this word (and its cognate[s]) in the NT using print or electronic concordances. Record them by creating a chart that breaks down occurrences by Author and/or by Gospels-Acts, Pauline Literature, and the latter NT (Hebrews through Revelation). Be sure that you are searching for the lemma or lexical form rather than a specific verb form or noun form.

F. **Study Carefully Each Occurrence of the Word(s) in Context:** This can be performed in two stages. First, study and take notes. Second, if possible, organize your findings into a taxonomy for clear presentation. To study, look at each word in context to "inform" or "broaden" your understanding of the use of this word. As you study these occurrences, record what you are learning about the word. Here are some particular considerations to keep in mind:

1. "Seek for any definition, explanation, or description the author may give to the word in question."[5] For example, consider how "eternal life" is defined in John 17:3 or "God's will" as "your sanctification" in 1 Thess 4:3.
2. Notice the surrounding structure of each passage where the word is found. For example, is the word involved in a parallel structure that helps define the word? Is it being contrasted or compared with other words? Is the word a part of a command or the conclusion of an argument, so that it summarizes the previous discussion? Or, is the word part of a preparatory statement that may provide a general idea that is elaborated upon in what follows?

---

[5] This is the first step of Daniel Fuller's description of how to study a word (*Inductive Method*, V-12). His subsequent steps, which correspond with some of mine, are presented in this order: 2. Note the word's syntactical relationships; 3. Note the words used in parallel or antithesis to the word in question; 4. See how the word is used in the immediate context; 5. Note the way a word is used in parallel passages; 6. Note the way the word is used in other passages in the Bible; and 7. Investigate the roots of a word that may be found in parent or cognate languages (V-12 – V-14).

3. Notice how the word functions and relates to other words grammatically.

4. Notice how the word is being modified. Is it being defined or nuanced in some way?

5. Ask questions like, Are there synonyms or antonyms used in the context? And, should these synonyms and/or antonyms be studied also?

6. Consider how a word's meaning may be developed and carried through any particular NT book. For example, if you are doing a Passage Word Study, consider how the *previous occurrences* of a word contribute to the word's meaning in a later portion of the NT book. Then also, consider how the word's meaning is developed progressively in the individual occurrences throughout the book.

7. Generally, **be analytical and be discerning of patterns of usage across the NT canon.** For example, one of my students noted that the term "temple" ναός through the NT canon is at first a referent to the physical temple structure in Jerusalem in the Synoptic Gospels, then applied to Jesus' own person in John 2:21; next in Acts 17:24 "God needs no temple to dwell in." In Paul, God's People are God's temple; Revelation ends with "And I did not see a temple in the city, for the Lord God Almighty and the Lamb are its temple" (21:22).

G. **Record and Summarize your General Findings:** Provide a summary of your most significant findings as well as any pivotal interpretive questions that resulted from your work. Consider using a chart to represent your findings. Include observations and insights from the following questions and considerations:

1. Which meanings are most common? And in which NT author are they found? Consider why. Systematize or categorize the uses of this word.

2. Also, notice any patterns you might observe. Are there other ideas or words that are used often with your particular word? What are the implications?

3. What passages seem to be most helpful or important for understanding the word or its importance?

4. On a larger scale, how does your word study change your understanding of God, the nature of people, the world, or your living and relating to God, people, and the world?

H. **Determine the Best Meaning/interpretation of the Word in the Context of your Pericope:** If studying a particular passage, how does your word study work bear on the particular meaning of the word(s) for that passage?

I. **Significance of Findings and Considerations of Places of Application:** Having just canvassed all the usages of a word or words in the GNT, you are in a unique position to consider points of contact between the ancient world and with your world. What new understandings of God, Jesus, the Holy Spirit, or the early Christian movement in its mission and life in the world emerge from your study? How are you challenged to live differently as a result of your word study work?

27.5 A Word Study on **Βοάω** *I Cry out* from Mark 15:34

The following word study was conducted and written up by a student of mine, Gregory Neumayer (February 23, 2007); it is provided here with slight modifications and is used with his permission.

A. **Passage Instigating Investigation:**

Mark 15:34 καὶ τῇ ἐνάτῃ ὥρᾳ **ἐβόησεν** ὁ Ἰησοῦς φωνῇ μεγάλῃ· ελωι ελωι λεμα σαβαχθανι; ὅ ἐστιν μεθερμηνευόμενον· ὁ θεός μου ὁ θεός μου, εἰς τί ἐγκατέλιπές με;

> [34]At the ninth hour Jesus **cried out** with a loud voice, "ELOI, ELOI, LAMA SABACHTHANI?" which is translated, "MY GOD, MY GOD, WHY HAVE YOU FORSAKEN ME?" (NASB95)

What is the meaning of Jesus' crying out to God? What is implied in such a crying out? Desperation? Confidence? Something else?

B. **Identify Cognates; also Consider Synonyms or Antonyms:** There is one cognate noun βοή. There is cognate verb: ἀναβοάω. Another verb, ἐπιβοάω, is only found within textual variants.

C. **Determine the Semantic Range for βοάω, ἀναβοάω, and Cognate βοή:**

1. βοάω
   a. BDAG:
      i. Call, shout out
      ii. Abs. Break forth and shout
      iii. Of solemn proclamation
      iv. Of cries of anguish for help
      v. Of prayer as calling for God
   b. Friberg and Friberg, *Analytical Lexicon to the Greek New Testament.* Grand Rapids: Baker, 2000.
      i. Absolutely exult, shout for joy
      ii. Solemn proclaiming cry, call out, shout
      iii. As a crowd rousing an outcry
      iv. As crying for help, call to, call out
      v. As crying out in anguish, shout, cry
2. ἀναβοάω.
   a. BDAG: Cry out
   b. Friberg: cry out, cry aloud, shout
3. βοή
   a. BDAG: Cry, shout
   b. Friberg: Cry, shout (as workers for compensation), outcry

D. **Consider Studying Cognates:** While searching for cognates for these verbs, I came across a few compounded forms: βοήθεια, βοηθέω, and βοήθος. These forms I have determined to be unrelated to this study on the grounds that with the merging of a cognate of the original stem (βοή: *cry, shout*) with another stem (θέω: *to run*) and thus forming an entirely new word, it is removed from the semantic range of either βοάω or βοή. I find this situation comparable to that of the English word "philosophy," the root of which is the combination of "phil" that is, "love" and "soph" that is, "wisdom." Apart, these roots have nothing in common, but when joined together, they create a word that is different than either of them originally. I believe the same is true of βοήθεια, βοηθέω, and βοήθος. When βοή is joined to θέω, it becomes something close to the roots, but containing a definition that is unrelated to the original range of one of the roots.

E. **Chart of Occurrences in the GNT:**

	Βοάω	ἀναβοάω	Βοή
Synoptic Gospels and Acts	Matt 3:3; 27:46 Mark 1:3; 15:34 Luke 3:4; 9:38; 18:7, 38 Acts 8:7; 17:6; 21:34; 25:24	Matt 27:46	
John	John 1:23		
Paul	Gal 4:27		
James			Jas 5:4

F. **Study Carefully Each Occurrence of the Word(s) in Context:**

1. <u>Verses of Occurrences (all verses provided from the ESV)</u>.

Matthew 3:3 For this is he who was spoken of by the prophet Isaiah when he said, "The voice of one *crying* in the wilderness: 'Prepare the way of the Lord; make his paths straight.'"

Matthew 27:46 And about the ninth hour Jesus *cried* out with a loud voice, saying, "*Eli, Eli, lema sabachthani?*" that is, "My God, my God, why have you forsaken me?"

Mark 1:3 the voice of one *crying* in the wilderness: 'Prepare the way of the Lord, make his paths straight,'"

Mark 15:34 And at the ninth hour Jesus *cried* with a loud voice, "Eloi, Eloi, lema sabachthani?" which means, "My God, my God, why have you forsaken me?"

Luke 3:4 As it is written in the book of the words of Isaiah the prophet, "The voice of one *crying* in the wilderness: 'Prepare the way of the Lord, make his paths straight.'

Luke 9:38 And behold, a man from the crowd *cried out*, "Teacher, I beg you to look at my son, for he is my only child.

Luke 18:7 And will not God give justice to his elect, who *cry* to him day and night? Will he delay long over them?

Luke 18:38 And he *cried out*, "Jesus, Son of David, have mercy on me!"

Acts 8:7 For unclean spirits came out of many who were possessed, *crying* with a loud voice, and many who were paralyzed or lame were healed.

Acts 17:6 And when they could not find them, they dragged Jason and some of the brothers before the city authorities, *shouting*, "These men who have turned the world upside down have come here also,

Acts 21:34 Some in the crowd were *shouting* one thing, some another. And as he could not learn the facts because of the uproar, he ordered him to be brought into the barracks.

Acts 25:24 And Festus said, "King Agrippa and all who are present with us, you see this man about whom the whole Jewish people petitioned me, both in Jerusalem and here, *shouting* that he ought not to live any longer.

John 1:23 He said, "I am the voice of one *crying* out in the wilderness, 'Make straight the way of the Lord,' as the prophet Isaiah said."

Galatians 4:27 For it is written, "Rejoice, O barren one who does not bear; break forth and *cry aloud*, you who are not in labor! For the children of the desolate one will be more than those of the one who has a husband."

James 5:4 Behold, the wages of the laborers who mowed your fields, which you kept back by fraud, are *crying out* against you, and the cries of the harvesters have reached the ears of the Lord of hosts.

2. <u>Observations based on Occurrences.</u>

   o Apart from the quotations from Isa 40:3 in Matt 3:3, Mark 1:3, Luke 3:4 and John 1:23, the cry represented in each case is one of a person/group of people to someone who is in **direct authority** over them and the situation. Whether it is to governing bodies or figureheads, or to **God Himself**, we see in each of these passages that recognition **of their own limitations is evident.**

   o The cry is one of desperation. In each passage, the situation can be considered **desperate.** Not only is the acting individual crying out, but they are crying out because there is nothing else they could truly do themselves and they must appeal to those above them (Acts 17:6; Jas 5:4) or cry out in obedience to God (Matt 3:3; Mark 1:3; Luke 3:4; John 1:23).

   o It is seen especially in those cases within the gospels where it is **a direct cry to God** from someone experiencing a pain of some kind (Matt 27:46; Luke 9:38) or in a **spiritual situation of desperation.**

   o Within the gospels, this act of crying is implied to be much more adamant than other forms of crying (i.e. κράζω). It implies more than just a vocal scream or shout, but indicates **a plea from the desperate spirit of a person to God, the Maker**, who is the ultimate authority over all. Luke 9:38 gives a good example of the desperation of the cry itself, as the man's only son is in spiritual bondage to an evil spirit. The man can do nothing but cry to Jesus as a representative of God's authority on earth.

   o In the Septuagint which is quoted from Isa 40:3 in each Gospel (Matt 3:3; Mark 1:3; Luke 3:4; John 1:23), the usage indicates once more a **cry to God**, though it is not in the sense of desperation, but (as in Isaiah) a **plea to the people on behalf of God to be ready for God's saving activity.** Also in Paul's use of Isaiah in Galatians, the cry is an instance of the prophet imploring the barren women to rejoice in their future blessings, which **God will give them** in their patience and faith.

G. **Summarize your General Findings:** I find it very intriguing to see how the situations of each passage influenced the type of cry. Whether there be a spiritual pain occurring, or a physical suffering or even social injustice (Jas 5:4), the cry indicates a **last desperate plea.** It seems to me that the cry emphasizes not the volume of the voice, but the **pleading of the heart.** It is especially noted that, except in Acts, the cries of the individual ultimately reach the ear of God.

I see a problem in the contexts of the Acts passages, where the Jews of the region (17:6; 21:34; etc.) are persecuting Paul. Why would this cry be considered desperate as I have seen in the rest of the passages? I submit the theory that the use of βοάω in these passages is, in fact, the same desperate cry that is seen in other passages. Not only do the Jews recognize God as their support and authority, but the blasphemies that Paul was preaching in proclaiming Jesus as Messiah would be, in my opinion, a situation that the Jews could recognize as worthy of βοάω, or a desperate cry to God. The proclamation of Messiah would mean the fulfillment of Judaism, but in a way that was not expected, and the Jews could be desperate to have this blasphemy and heretical teaching ended. However, given my lack of New Testament cultural knowledge, I can only theorize this and thus, mention it as theory, not claiming it as even insight, but as speculation. In other passages, the use of βοάω involves the recognition of God's ultimate control over the situations that we find hopeless and desolate.

H. **Determine the Best Meaning/interpretation of the Word in the Context of your Pericope:** When I was originally reading Mark 15:34, I had wondered if, when looking at the original lexical entries, the cry of Christ was one of grief, suffering, anger, anguish, joy, or another emotion that He could have been experiencing. However, on looking at the contexts of other occurrences of the word, especially in the Gospels, it seems more probable that Jesus was, just as in the case of the man in Luke 9:38, recognizing the only One who had any control over the situation in desperation.

I. **Significance of Findings and Considerations of Places of Application:** The act of this cry from the mouth of a human restores God to His rightful place in life, the highest of all. I believe that, when humans are the ones who are crying out, this cry, βοάω, shows God's power and glory, for, in each situation, God hears each one of these cries. The desperation of each individual recorded crying out to God in this way does not escape God's attention or notice. I find it incredibly encouraging to know that the God who is the Highest of high, the Authority over all, the Ruler and Governor over everything, notices when I am at my most despairing moment, and He hears. The use of this word βοάω reveals a desperate situation where all reliance on humanity has been forgotten, and only God remains able.

If you are able, complete the CROSSWORD PUZZLES in the WORKBOOK EXERCISES 27.

CASE IN POINT 27: WORD STUDY ON **Καυχάομαι** *I BOAST* FROM ROM 5:3

I. CHOOSE AN IMPORTANT WORD OR WORDS TO STUDY.

Rom 5:3 And not only this, but we also **exult** in our tribulations, knowing that tribulation brings about perseverance; (NASB95)

What is the meaning of καυχάομαι (*I exult; I boast*) in Rom 5:3?

II. IDENTIFY COGNATES, SYNONYMS, OR ANTONYMS.

Cognates: two nouns, καύχησις and καύχημα; one verb ἐγκαυχάομαι

III. DETERMINE THE SEMANTIC RANGE OF WORDS.

A. Verb **Καυχάομαι**:
1. BDAG
   a. to take pride in someth., *boast, glory, pride oneself, brag*, intransitive
   b. to make a boast about someth., *boast about, mention in order to boast of, be proud of*, transitive; τὶ *someth.*
2. L&N: 33.368: to express an unusually high degree of confidence in someone or something being exceptionally noteworthy—'to boast.'…Whether in any particular context the boasting is legitimate or not depends upon what is boasted about.
3. Friberg
   a. intransitively;
      i. in a bad sense of self-glorying *boast, pride oneself on*;
      ii. in a good sense of an attitude of confidence in God *rejoice in, glory in, boast in*;
   b. transitively, of achievements through divine help *boast about, glory in*

B. VERB **Ἐγκαυχάομαι**:
1. BDAG: to be proud of someone or someth. and express oneself accordingly, *boast*
2. L&N: 33.368: to express an unusually high degree of confidence in someone or something being exceptionally noteworthy—'to boast.'…Whether in any particular context the boasting is legitimate or not depends upon what is boasted about.
3. Friberg: *boast about* someone or something; *take pride in*

C. VERB **Κατακαυχάομαι**:
1. BDAG:
   a. to boast at the expense of another, *boast against, exult over* τινός *someone* or *someth.*
   b. to have a cause for boasting because of advantage in power, *triumph over* τινός

2. L&N:

    a. 33.370: to boast about something by downgrading something else—'to boast against, to degrade.'

    b. 74.11: to have greater power or potential than—'to be more powerful than, to triumph over.'

3. Friberg:

    a. as expressing a feeling of one's comparative superiority *boast against, exult over…* absolutely *boast, brag, look down on*

    b. as expressing what is better or victorious *triumph over, win out over, be more powerful than*

D. Noun **Καύχησις**:

1. BDAG

    a. act of taking pride in someth., *boasting*

    b. that which constitutes a source of pride, *object of boasting, reason for boasting*

2. L&N

    a boasting: 33.368

    b what one boasts about: 33.371

    c pride: 25.204

3. Friberg

    a. as an action *boasting, glorying, pride*; in a good sense (Rom 15:17); in a bad sense (Rom 3:27);

    b. as an object, of boasting, equivalent to **καύχημα** *boast*

    c. as an attitude *pride*; in a good sense

E. Noun **Καύχημα**:

1. BDAG

    a. act of taking pride in someth. or that which constitutes a source of pride, boast

    b. expression of pride, boast, what is said in boasting

2. L&N

    a boast: 33.368

    b what one boasts about: 33.371

    c the right to boast: 33.372

    d basis of pride: 25.203

3. Friberg

    a. what one is proud of *pride, boast, something to boast about*;

    b. what is said in boasting *boast, praise* (2 Cor 9:3); *justification for boasting, right to boast* (1 Cor 9:16)

IV. Decide whether to Perform Cognate, Synonym, Antonym, or Compound Study.

Since these cognates are so close in meaning with the verb, and because they do not have a high frequency of occurrence, I will study all of them.

V. FIND ALL OCCURRENCES OF THE WORDS AND CHART THEM BY AUTHOR/CORPUS.

καυχάομαι	ἐγκαυχάομαι	κατακαυχάομαι	καύχησις	καύχημα
Rom 2:17, 23; 5:2-3, 11	2 Thess 2:4	Rom 11:18²	Rom 3:27; 15:17	Rom 4:2
1 Cor 1:29, 31; 3:21;			1 Cor 15:31	1 Cor 5:6;
4:7; 13:3			2 Cor 1:12; 7:4,	9:15-16
2 Cor 5:12; 7:14; 9:2;			14; 8:24;	2 Cor 1:14;
10:8, 13, 15-18;			11:10, 17	5:12; 9:3
11:12, 16, 18, 30;			1 Thess 2:19	Gal 6:4
12:1, 5-6, 9				Phil 1:26; 2:16
Gal 6:13-14				
Eph 2:9				
Phil 3:3				Heb 3:6
Jas 1:9; 4:16		Jas 2:3; 3:14	Jas 4:16	

This charting reveals that the word group was important for Paul and James. These texts are very argumentative. But probably more important that this, James and Paul were writing to people of varying social status, confronting matters of their relationships; in the Mediterranean context, "boasting" would entail honor and shame, and exchanges would get ugly. At issue was trying to maintain one's status through one's speech, especially boasting.

VI. CAREFUL STUDY OF EACH OCCURRENCE OF καυχάομαι, καύχησις, AND καύχημα.

Notice: Below I have created a taxonomy of meanings based upon my study. I have only included the full English text of all the verses containing the verb καυχάομαι. To include the English or Greek verses is optional; it may help in your presentation of findings to have the verses readily accessible to others. Or, you could include only the most significant verses. However, don't just quote verses—notice that I have analyzed and categorized uses of the verb for presentation below.

A. Inappropriate Behavior ("Boasting"):

1. <u>in the Law and through the Law boasting in God</u> (Rom 2:17, 23; see also the noun forms in Rom 4:2)
   Rom 2:17 But if you bear the name "Jew " and rely upon the Law and boast in God,
   Rom 2:23 You who boast in the Law, by your breaking the Law, do you dishonor God?

2. <u>in (the work of other) people (for our own credit)</u> (1 Cor 3:21; Gal 6:13)
   1 Cor 3:21 So then let no one boast in men. For all things belong to you,
   Gal 6:13 For those who are circumcised do not even keep the Law themselves, but they desire to have you circumcised so that they may boast in your flesh.

3. <u>in oneself</u> (1 Cor 4:7; [13:3]; 2 Cor 11:12, 16-18; Jas 4:16)
   1 Cor 4:7 For who regards you as superior? What do you have that you did not receive? And if you did receive it, why do you boast as if you had not received it?
   1 Cor 13:3 And if I give all my possessions to feed *the poor*, and if I surrender my body to be burned [or in order to boast—textual variant], but do not have love, it profits me nothing.

Jas 4:16 But as it is, you boast in your arrogance; all such boasting is evil.

4. <u>taking credit for the work of others</u> (2 Cor 10:15-16)
>   2 Cor 10:15 not boasting beyond *our* measure, *that is*, in other men's labors, but with the hope that as your faith grows, we will be, within our sphere, enlarged even more by you,
>   2 Cor 10:16 so as to preach the gospel even to the regions beyond you, *and* not to boast in what has been accomplished in the sphere of another.

5. <u>in immorality</u> (καύχημα; 1 Cor 5:6)

6. <u>arrogance arising out of jealousy and selfishness</u> (κατακαυχάομαι Jas 3:14)
>   Jas 3:14 But if you have bitter jealousy and selfish ambition in your heart, do not be arrogant and *so* lie against the truth.

7. <u>acting arrogantly against others</u> (κατακαυχάομαι; Rom 11:18[2])
>   Rom 11:18 do not be arrogant toward the branches; but if you are arrogant, *remember that* it is not you who supports the root, but the root *supports* you.

B. Appropriate Behavior ("Boasting"):

1. <u>in God through Christ and God's future for us</u> (Rom 5:2, 11; 1 Cor 1:31; 2 Cor 10:17; Gal 6:14; Phil 3:3; see the noun in Heb 3:6)
>   Rom 5:2 through whom also we have obtained our introduction by faith into this grace in which we stand; and we <u>exult</u> in hope of the glory of God.
>   Rom 5:11 And not only this, but we also <u>exult</u> in God through our Lord Jesus Christ, through whom we have now received the reconciliation.
>   1 Cor 1:31 so that, just as it is written, "LET HIM WHO BOASTS, BOAST IN THE LORD."
>   2 Cor 10:17 But HE WHO BOASTS IS TO BOAST IN THE LORD.
>   Gal 6:14 But may it never be that I would boast, except in the cross of our Lord Jesus Christ, through which the world has been crucified to me, and I to the world.
>   Phil 3:3 for we are the *true* circumcision, who worship in the Spirit of God and <u>glory</u> in Christ Jesus and put no confidence in the flesh,

2. <u>in our sufferings and weakness in view of God's strength</u> (Rom 5:3; 2 Cor 11:30; 12:5-6, 9; Jas 1:9)
>   Rom 5:3 And not only this, but we also <u>exult</u> in our tribulations, knowing that tribulation brings about perseverance;
>   2 Cor 11:30 If I have to boast, I will boast of what pertains to my weakness.
>   Jas 1:9 But the brother of humble circumstances is to glory in his high position;

3. <u>in the work of others for their credit</u> (2 Cor 5:12; 7:14; 9:2; see the noun uses in 1 Cor 15:31; 2 Cor 1:14; 5:12; 7:4, 14; 8:24; 9:3; Phil 1:26; 1 Thess 2:19)
>   2 Cor 5:12 We are not again commending ourselves to you but *are* giving you an occasion to be proud of us, so that you will have *an answer* for those who take pride in appearance and not in heart.
>   2 Cor 7:14 For if in anything I have boasted to him about you, I was not put to shame; but as

we spoke all things to you in truth, so also our boasting before Titus proved to be *the* truth.

2 Cor 9:2 for I know your readiness, of which I boast about you to the Macedonians, *namely*, that Achaia has been prepared since last year, and your zeal has stirred up most of them.

4. <u>in oneself (as a minister of God)</u> (2 Cor 10:8, 13; see the noun uses in Rom 15:17; 1 Cor 9:15-16; 2 Cor 1:12; 11:10,17; Gal 6:4; Phil 2:16)

2 Cor 10:8 For even if I boast somewhat further about our authority, which the Lord gave for building you up and not for destroying you, I will not be put to shame,

2 Cor 10:13 But we will not boast beyond *our* measure, but within the measure of the sphere which God apportioned to us as a measure, to reach even as far as you.

5. <u>in others because of their enduring suffering</u> (ἐγκαυχάομαι 2 Thess 1:4)

2 Thess 1:4 therefore, we ourselves speak proudly of you among the churches of God for your perseverance and faith in the midst of all your persecutions and afflictions which you endure.

6. <u>mercy triumphing over judgment</u> (κατακαυχάομαι Jas 2:13)

Jas 2:13 For judgment *will be* merciless to one who has shown no mercy; mercy triumphs over judgment.

C. Boasting Excluded (1 Cor 1:29; Eph 2:9; see the noun in Rom 3:27):

1 Cor 1:29 [God chose weak and foolish things/people] so that no man may boast before God.

Eph 2:9 not as a result of works, so that no one may boast.

VII. RECORD AND SUMMARIZE YOUR GENERAL FINDINGS.

The idea of boasting in Paul is complex. Each particular instance must be determined by the immediate argumentative context.

The verb κατακαυχάομαι (with the meaning "against" in the prepositional prefix κατά) has a very negative connotation, "arrogance against others" (Rom 11:18[2]; Jas 3:14) except when mercy "triumphs over judgment" (Jas 2:13).

Thus, boasting in others can be done in a negative fashion (1 Cor 3:21; Gal 6:13) or in a positive fashion (2 Cor 5:12; 7:14; 9:2; 2 Thess 1:4). What distinguishes these is the moral basis or "substance" of the boasting. It is possible to boast rightly in the upright ministry work of others, if the boasting is for their glory and not our own (2 Cor 7:14; 9:2) and in view of their enduring suffering (2 Thess 1:4) Also, Paul wants the Corinthians to "boast in him" in view of rival (and erroneously boastful) missionary opponents (2 Cor 5:12; cf. 10:15-16).

Likewise, one may boast of oneself wrongly (1 Cor 4:7; [13:3]; 2 Cor 11:12, 16-18; Jas 4:16) or boast of oneself rightly (Rom 15:17; 1 Cor 9:15-16; 2 Cor 1:12; 10:8, 13; 11:10, 17; Gal 6:4; Phil 2:16).What distinguishes these two extremes is one's relationship to the Gospel of Christ. If one boasts in one's own abilities apart from Christ, it is wrong. However, if one boasts in God's ministry through people as weak vessels, this is acceptable. Boasting in one's weakness or deficiencies is what Paul models for the Corinthians (2 Cor 11:30; 12:5, 6, 9). In this situation, God's power needs to be fully relied upon.

VIII. DETERMINE THE BEST MEANING/INTERPRETATION OF THE WORD IN THE CONTEXT OF YOUR PERICOPE.

This last idea is closest to Paul's in Rom 5:3: We boast in our weaknesses, because this magnifies God's work in us to bring about our moral character (5:4). Rather than boasting in the possession of the Law (Rom 2:17, 23), one ought to boast in what the Lord God has accomplished through the work of Christ and in our glorious future (5:2, 11). In an ultimate sense, only God is the correct object of boasting (1 Cor 1:31; 2 Cor 10:17; Gal 6:14; Phil 3:3).

IX. SIGNIFICANCE OF FINDINGS AND CONSIDERATIONS OF PLACES OF APPLICATION.

The notion of boasting is instructive for ministry. It is tempting to take credit for what good results or even happens. Paul reminds us that God is truly the one to be given credit. I may boast in what others are doing *in the Lord*; this gives due credit to God. It also reminds us of the responsibility that we as persons have as co-participants with God in carrying out His work. At the same time, we ought to have a godly respect and confidence in the work that God is carrying out through us. This is not to be done boastfully, but our confidence is to remain in God and in what God is able to accomplish through us. In other words, we ought to esteem appropriately the work God accomplishes as we are faithful to God's calling.

It would seem that Paul was often under pressure to convey such boasting of his ministry for the missionary outreach to the Gentiles. In the Corinthian correspondence, he must ward off missionary rivals to maintain proper relationship with the Corinthians. Our situation and need to boast in what God is doing in us will probably not parallel Paul's particular needs. However, from this somewhat unique situation, we learn that Paul's boast in his ministry involves his *moral integrity* and *faithfulness* to others. We ought to value these characteristics in our own ministries.

From a different perspective, Rom 5:3 helps provide a broader context within which to view our suffering in Christ. Suffering produces a divine effect in our lives: moral character formation to the likeness of Christ. When I identify with Christ and am morally reformed, I may boast in the hope of God's restoration of my body (Rom 5:11; 8:18). We ought to glory and exult in what transformation God is bringing about in our lives as a result of the power of the Holy Spirit. Suffering in the Gospel may be the primary way this transformation takes place.

APPENDICES §§0-30

§0 THE FORMS OF THE ARTICLE (τὸ Ἄρθρον)

	F	M	N		F	M	N
sg. nom.	ἡ	ὁ	τό	pl. nom.	αἱ	οἱ	τά
gen.	τῆς	τοῦ	τοῦ	gen.	τῶν	τῶν	τῶν
dat.	τῇ	τῷ	τῷ	dat.	ταῖς	τοῖς	τοῖς
acc.	τήν	τόν	τό	acc.	τάς	τούς	τά

§1 FIRST DECLENSION OR "A" CLASS DECLENSION (Πρώτη Κλίσις)

	Regular Stem	ε, ι, ρ Stems	σ, ξ, ζ, ψ Stems	Masculine Stems	Regular Stems	ε, ι, ρ Stems	σ, ξ, ζ, ψ Stems	Masculine Stems
sg. nom.	-η	-α	-α	-ης	ἐντολή	ἡμέρα	δόξα	μαθητής
gen.	-ης	-ας*	-ης	-ου	ἐντολῆς	ἡμέρας	δόξης	μαθητοῦ
dat.	-ῃ	-ᾳ	-ῃ	-ῃ	ἐντολῇ	ἡμέρᾳ	δόξῃ	μαθητῇ
acc.	-ην	-αν	-αν	-ην	ἐντολήν	ἡμέραν	δόξαν	μαθητήν
pl. nom.	-αι				ἐντολαί	ἡμέραι	δόξαι	μαθηταί
gen.	-ων				ἐντολῶν	ἡμέρων	δόξων	μαθητῶν
dat.	-αις				ἐντολαῖς	ἡμέραις	δόξαις	μαθηταῖς
acc.	-ας*				ἐντολάς	ἡμέρας	δόξας	μαθητάς

§2 SECOND DECLENSION OR "O" CLASS DECLENSION (Δευτέρη Κλίσις)

	Masculine		Neuter	Examples:	Masculine	Neuter
sg. nom.	-ος		-ον*		λόγος	τέκνον
gen.	-ου	→	-ου		λόγου	τέκνου
dat.	-ῳ	→	-ῳ		λόγῳ	τέκνῳ
acc.	-ον		-ον*		λόγον	τέκνον
pl. nom.	-οι		-α*		λόγοι	τέκνα
gen.	-ων	→	-ων		λόγων	τέκνων
dat.	-οις	→	-οις		λόγοις	τέκνοις
acc.	-ους		-α*		λόγους	τέκνα

§3 THIRD DECLENSION (Τρίτη Κλίσις)

	PURE ENDINGS			CONSONANT STEMS		VOWEL STEMS		
	Masc./Fem.		Neuter	Masc./Fem.	Neuter	Masculine	Feminine	Neuter
sg. nom.	-ς		- or -ς	ἀνήρ	ῥῆμα	βασιλεύς	πίστις	ἔθνος
gen.	-ος	→	-ος	ἀνδρός	ῥήματος	βασιλέως	πίστεως	ἔθνους
dat.	-ι	→	-ι	ἀνδρί	ῥήματι	βασιλεῖ	πίστει	ἔθνει
acc.	-α or ν		- or -ς	ἄνδρα	ῥῆμα	βασιλέα	πίστιν	ἔθνος
pl. nom.	-ες		-α	ἄνδρες	ῥήματα	βασιλεῖς	πίστεις	ἔθνη
gen.	-ων	→	-ων	ἀνδρῶν	ῥημάτων	βασιλέων	πίστεων	ἐθνῶν
dat.	-σι(ν)	→	-σι(ν)	ἀνδράσι	ῥήμασιν	βασιλεῦσιν	πίστεσιν	ἔθνεσιν
acc.	-ας		-α	ἄνδρας	ῥήματα	βασιλεῖς	πίστεις	ἔθνη
Stems:				ἀνδρ-	ῥήματ-	βασιλεύ/έ-	πίστι/ε-	ἐθνε-

§4 FORMATION OF THE VOCATIVE CASE (Κλητικὴ Πτῶσις)

The vocative in the plural for all genders are the same as the nominative endings. In the singular, the vocative form is different.

FEMININE SG.			MASCULINE SG.			NEUTER SG.	
1st decl.	2nd decl.	3rd decl.	1st decl.	2nd decl.	3rd decl.	2nd decl.	3rd decl.
-α or -η	-ε	none	-α or -η	-ε	none	-ον	-ν or none

Note: In the singular, for 3rd declension nouns with the final syllable ἦτα, the final vowel will change to ἒ ψιλόν. Thus, πατήρ "father," μήτηρ "mother," θυγάτηρ "daughter," and ἀνήρ "husband" become in the vocative singular πάτερ, μῆτερ, θύγατερ, and ἄνερ (notice, too, the change of accents). For vowel stem 3rd Declension, the pure stem is seen after removing the final σίγμα; thus, βασιλεύς becomes βασιλεῦ to form the vocative (notice the change in accent).

§5 FIRST AND SECOND DECLENSION ADJECTIVES

For example, ὅλος, -η, -ον *whole, entire.* These use First/Second Declension Endings. See APPENDIX §1 and APPENDIX §2.

§6 PURE THIRD DECLENSION ADJECTIVES

	Consonant Stem			Vowel Stem (contracted form shown with →)		
	Masc./Fem.	Neuter		Masc./Fem.		Neuter
sg. nom.	μείζων	μεῖζον	sg. nom.	ἀληθέ + ς	→ ἀληθής	ἀληθές
gen.	μείζονος	μείζονος	gen.	ἀληθέ + ος	→ ἀληθοῦς	ἀληθοῦς
dat.	μείζονι	μείζονι	dat.	ἀληθέ + ι	→ ἀληθεῖ	ἀληθεῖ
acc.	μείζονα	μεῖζον	acc.	ἀληθέ + α	→ ἀληθῆ	ἀληθές
pl. nom.	μείζονες	μείζονα	pl. nom.	ἀληθέ + ες	→ ἀληθεῖς	ἀληθέ + α → ἀληθῆ
gen.	μειζόνων	μειζόνων	gen.	ἀληθέ + ων	→ ἀληθῶν	ἀληθῶν
dat.	μείζοσι(ν)	μείζοσι(ν)	dat.	ἀληθέ + σι(ν) → ἀληθέσι(ν)		ἀληθέσι(ν)
acc.	μείζονας	μείζονα	acc.	ἀληθέ + ες	→ ἀληθεῖς	ἀληθέ + α → ἀληθῆ

§7 MIXED DECLENSION: THIRD AND FIRST DECLENSION ADJECTIVES

	πᾶς, πᾶσα, πᾶν *every, all*			εἷς, μία, ἕν *one*		
Gender:	Masculine	Feminine	Neuter	Masculine	Feminine	Neuter
Declension:	3rd	1st	3rd	3rd	1st	3rd
sg. nom.	πᾶς	πᾶσα	πᾶν	εἷς	μία	ἕν
gen.	παντός	πάσης	παντός	ἑνός	μιᾶς	ἑνός
dat.	παντί	πάσῃ	παντί	ἑνί	μιᾷ	ἑνί
acc.	πάντα	πᾶσαν	πᾶν	ἕνα	μίαν	ἕν
pl. nom.	πάντες	πᾶσαι	πάντα	The same endings are also used for οὐδείς, οὐδεμία, οὐδέν and μηδείς, μηδεμία, μηδέν. There are no plural forms, since *one* cannot be plural.		
gen.	πάντων	πασῶν	πάντων			
dat.	πᾶσι(ν)	πάσαις	πᾶσι(ν)			
acc.	πάντας	πάσας	πάντα			

§8 SLIGHTLY IRREGULAR ADJECTIVE FORMATIONS (see especially *)

	μέγας, μεγάλη, μέγα *great*			πολύς, πολλή, πολύ *much, many*		
	Masculine	Feminine	Neuter	Masculine	Feminine	Neuter
sg. nom.	μέγας*	μεγάλη	μέγα*	πολύς*	πολλή	πολύ*
gen.	μεγάλου	μεγάλης	μεγάλου	πολλοῦ	πολλῆς	πολλοῦ
dat.	μεγάλῳ	μεγάλῃ	μεγάλῳ	πολλῷ	πολλῇ	πολλῷ
acc.	μέγαν*	μεγάλην	μέγα*	πολύν*	πολλήν	πολύ*
pl. nom.	μεγάλοι	μεγάλαι	μεγάλα	πολλοί	πολλαί	πολλά
gen.	μεγάλων	μεγάλων	μεγάλων	πολλῶν	πολλῶν	πολλῶν
dat.	μεγάλοις	μεγάλαις	μεγάλοις	πολλοῖς	πολλοῖς	πολλοῖς
acc.	μεγάλους	μεγάλας	μεγάλα	πολλούς	πολλάς	πολλά

§9 NUMERALS

1. 3rd Declension Plural: τρεῖς, τρία and τέσσαρες, τέσσαρα. See APPENDIX §6 for 3rd declension endings.
2. Non-Declinable: δύο (δυσί *dat. pl.*), ἑπτά, δώδεκα

You should recognize all the letters below but the numbers 6 (F a *digamma*, ς a later form called *stigma*), 90 (Ϙ a *koppa*), and 900 (ϡ a *sampi*). If the number appears written out in the GNT, it is included in the table below.	GREEK ALPHABET FOR NUMBERS AND WRITTEN OUT								
	1	A	εἷς, μία, ἕν	10	I	δέκα	100	Ρ	
	2	B	δύο	20	K		200	Σ	διακόσιοι, -αι, -α
	3	Γ	τρεῖς, τρία	30	Λ	τριάκοντα	300	Τ	
	4	Δ	τέσσαρες	40	Μ	τεσσαράκοντα	400	Υ	
	5	E	πέντε	50	N	πεντήκοντα	500	Φ	
	6	F, ς	ἕξ	60	Ξ	ἑξήκοντα	600	Χ	
	7	Z	ἑπτά	70	O		700	Ψ	
	8	H	ὀκτώ	80	Π		800	Ω	
	9	Θ		90	Ϙ		900	ϡ	

Additional numbers occurring in the GNT are written out as follows:

11 = ἕνδεκα, 12 = δώδεκα, 14 = δεκατέσσαρες, 24 = εἰκοσιτέσσαρες
1000 = ἡ χιλιάς, -άδος, 1000s = χίλιοι, -αι, -α
4000 = τετρακισχίλιοι, 5000 = πεντακισχίλιοι, 6000 = ἑξακόσιοι

§10 PRONOUNS (Ἀντωνυμίαι) (Frequency in the GNT)

1 Personal (8468)

	1st (1804)	2nd (1067)	3rd (5597) M	F	N
sg. nom.	ἐγώ	σύ	αὐτός	αὐτή	αὐτό
gen.	ἐμοῦ, μου	σοῦ, σου	αὐτοῦ	αὐτῆς	αὐτοῦ
dat.	ἐμοί, μοι	σοί, σοι	αὐτῷ	αὐτῇ	αὐτῷ
acc.	ἐμέ, με	σέ, σε	αὐτόν	αὐτήν	αὐτό
pl. nom.	ἡμεῖς	ὑμεῖς	αὐτοί	αὐταῖ	αὐτά
gen.	ἡμῶν	ὑμῶν	αὐτῶν	αὐτῶν	αὐτῶν
dat.	ἡμῖν	ὑμῖν	αὐτοῖς	αὐταῖς	αὐτοῖς
acc.	ἡμᾶς	ὑμᾶς	αὐτούς	αὐτάς	αὐτά

2 Possessive (116)

1st	"my, our"	M	F	N
sg. (73) nom.		ἐμός	ἐμή	ἐμόν
pl. (7) nom.		ἡμέτερος	-α	-ον

2nd	"your"	M	F	N
sg. (25) nom.		σός	σή	σον
pl. (11) nom.		ὑμέτερος	-α	-ον

3 Relative (1406)

	M	F	N
sg. nom.	ὅς	ἥ	ὅ
gen.	οὗ	ἧς	οὗ
dat.	ᾧ	ᾗ	ᾧ
acc.	ὅν	ἥν	ὅ
pl. nom.	οἵ	αἵ	ἅ
gen.	ὧν	ὧν	ὧν
dat.	οἷς	αἷς	οἷς
acc.	οὕς	ἅς	ἅ

4 Indefinite Relative (144)

	M	F	N
sg. nom.	ὅστις	ἥτις	ὅτι
gen.	οὗτινος	ἧστινος	ὅστινος
dat.	ᾧτινι	ᾗτινι	ᾧτινι
acc.	ὅντινα	ἥντινα	ὅτι
pl. nom.	οἵτινες	αἵτινες	ἅτινα
gen.	ὧντινων	ὧντινων	ὧτινων
dat.	οἵστισι	αἵστισιν	οἵστισιν
acc.	οὕστινας	ἅστινας	ἅτινα

5 Interrogative (579)

	M/F	N
sg. nom.	τίς	τί
gen.	τίνος	τίνος
dat.	τίνι	τίνι
acc.	τίνα	τί
pl. nom.	τίνες	τίνα
gen.	τίνων	τίνων
dat.	τίσι	τίσι
acc.	τίνας	τινα

6 Indefinite (510)

	M/F	N
sg. nom.	τις	τι
gen.	τινός	τινός
dat.	τινί	τινί
acc.	τινά	τι
pl. nom.	τινές	τινά
gen.	τινῶν	τινῶν
dat.	τισί	τισί
acc.	τινάς	τινά

7 Demonstrative (1662)

	"this, these" (1387) M	F	N	"that, those" (265) M	F	N	"this, such and such" (10) M	F	N
sg. nom.	οὗτος	αὕτη	τοῦτο	ἐκεῖνος	ἐκείνη	ἐκεῖνο	ὅδε	ἥδε	τόδε
gen.	τούτου	ταύτης	τούτου	ἐκείνου	ἐκείνης	ἐκείνου	τοῦδε	τῆσδε	τοῦδε
dat.	τούτῳ	ταύτῃ	τούτῳ	ἐκείνῳ	ἐκείνη	ἐκείνῳ	τῷδε	τῇδε	τῷδε
acc.	τοῦτον	ταύτην	τοῦτο	ἐκεῖνον	ἐκείνην	ἐκεῖνο	τόνδε	τήνδε	τόδε
pl. nom.	οὗτοι	αὗται	ταῦτα	ἐκεῖνοι	ἐκεῖναι	ἐκεῖνα	αἵδε	αἵδε	τάδε
gen.	τούτων	τούτων	τούτων	ἐκείνων	ἐκείνων	ἐκείνων	τῶνδε	τῶνδε	τῶνδε
dat.	τούτοις	ταύταις	τούτοις	ἐκείνοις	ἐκείναις	ἐκείνοις	τοῖσδε	ταῖσδε	τοῖσδε
acc.	τούτους	ταύτας	ταῦτα	ἐκείνους	ἐκείνας	ἐκεῖνα	τούσδε	τάσδε	τάδε

8 Reflexive Personal (399)									9 Reciprocal (100)		
	1st "myself" (37)		**2nd** "yourself" (43)		**3rd** "himself; herself" (319)				ἀλλήλων, -οις, etc.		
	M	**F**	**M**	**F**	**M**	**F**	**N**		(plural only)		
sg. gen.	ἐμαυτοῦ	ἐμαυτῆς	σεαυτοῦ	σεαυτῆς	ἑαυτοῦ	ἑαυτῆς	ἑαυτοῦ				
dat.	ἐμαυτῷ	ἐμαυτῇ	σεαυτῷ	σεαυτῇ	ἑαυτῷ	ἑαυτῇ	ἑαυτῷ			**M**	**F**	**N**
acc.	ἐμαυτόν	ἐμαυτήν	σεαυτόν	σεαυτήν	ἑαυτόν	ἑαυτήν	ἑαυτό	pl. gen.	-ων	-ων	-ων
	M	**F**	**N**					dat.	-οις	-αις	-οις
pl. gen.	ἑαυτῶν	ἑαυτῶν	ἑαυτῶν	Note: Plural forms are the same				acc.	-ους	-ας	-α
dat.	ἑαυτοῖς	ἑαυταῖς	ἑαυτοῖς	for 1st, 2nd, and 3rd persons.							
acc.	ἑαυτούς	ἑαυτάς	ἑαυτά								

§11 PREPOSITIONS (Προθέσεις) (Frequency in the GNT)

A. Proper Prepositions: These take substantive objects in specific cases to form prepositional phrases. For a spatial representation of prepositional meanings, see Wallace 358.

	GENITIVE	**DATIVE**	**ACCUSATIVE**
ἐκ	out of, from (914)		
ἀπό	from (646)		
ἐνώπιον	before, in front of (94)		
πρό	before (47)		
ἄρχι(ς)	as far as, until (49)		
ἀντί	in stead of (22)		
ἐν		in (2752)	
σύν		with (128)	
εἰς			into (1767)
πρός			towards, with (700)
ἀνά			each, in the midst (13)
διά	through (387)		on account of (280)
κατά	against (74)		according to (399)
μετά	with (366)		after (105)
περί	about (294)		around (39)
ὑπό	by (169)		under (51)
ὑπέρ	in behalf of (130)		above (19)
ἐπί	on, over (220)	at, on the basis of (187)	on, to, against (483)
παρά	from (82)	beside (53)	alongside (59)

B. Improper Prepositions: These improper prepositions also typically use only the genitive case for their object. In this handbook, two such prepositions are presented: ἕως (CH.11). There are about two dozen such words.

ἕως (in ch.11)	*until, as far as, up to; while (conj.)*
ἀντί (compounded)	*instead of, for*
ἕνεκα or ἕνεκεν	*on account of*
χωρίς	*without, apart from*
πέραν	*beyond*

C. Basic Function and Uses of Prepositions: Prepositions form prepositional phrases (which are qualifying expressions) that indicate certain relationships between verbs or nouns within a sentence. Additionally, prepositions may be used to form words. There are four basic uses:

1. Adjectival. when the prepositional phrase modifies a noun or substantive.
2. Adverbial. (*more common*); when the prepositional phrase modifies the action of the verb.
3. Compounded. (*most common*); when prepositional forms help to form words.
4. Conjunctions. (*not common*); prepositions may be used as conjunctions or in special constructions to form subordinate clauses.

§12 Paradigm Verb Πιστεύω in the Indicative Mood

	1st	2nd	3rd	4th	5th	6th
Primary A Endings sg. 1	PRESENT A πιστεύω	FUTURE A πιστεύσω				
2	πιστεύεις	πιστεύσεις				
3	πιστεύει	πιστεύσει				
pl. 1	πιστεύομεν	πιστεύσομεν				
2	πιστεύετε	πιστεύσετε				
3	πιστεύουσι(ν)	πιστεύσουσι(ν)				
Primary M/P Endings sg. 1	PRESENT M/P πιστεύομαι	FUTURE M πιστεύσομαι			PERFECT M/P πεπίστευμαι	FUTURE P πιστευθήσομαι
2	πιστεύῃ	πιστεύσῃ			πεπίστευσαι	πιστευθήσῃ
3	πιστεύεται	πιστεύσεται			πεπίστευται	πιστευθήσεται
pl. 1	πιστευόμεθα	πιστευσόμεθα			πεπιστεύμεθα	πιστευθησόμεθα
2	πιστεύεσθε	πιστεύσεσθε			πεπίστευσθε	πιστευθήσεσθε
3	πιστεύονται	πιστεύσονται			πεπίστευνται	πιστευθήσονται
Secondary A Endings sg. 1	IMPERFECT A ἐπίστευον		AORIST A ἐπίστευσα	PERFECT A πεπίστευκα		AORIST P ἐπιστεύθην
2	ἐπίστευες		ἐπίστευσας	πεπίστευκας		ἐπιστεύθης
3	ἐπίστευε(ν)		ἐπίστευσε(ν)	πεπίστευκε(ν)		ἐπιστεύθη
pl. 1	ἐπιστεύομεν		ἐπιστεύσαμεν	πεπιστεύκαμεν		ἐπιστεύθημεν
2	ἐπιστεύετε		ἐπιστεύσατε	πεπιστεύκατε		ἐπιστεύθητε
3	ἐπίστευον		ἐπίστευσαν	πεπιστεύκασι(ν)		ἐπιστεύθησαν
				PLUPERFECT A ἐπεπιστεύκειν		
				ἐπεπιστεύκεις		
				ἐπεπιστεύκει		
				ἐπεπιστεύκειμεν		
				ἐπεπιστεύκειτε		
				ἐπεπιστεύκεισαν		
Secondary M/P Endings sg. 1	IMPERFECT M/P ἐπιστευόμην		AORIST M ἐπιστευσάμην		PLUPERFECT M/P ἐπεπιστεύμην	
2	ἐπιστεύῃ		ἐπιστεύσω		ἐπεπίστευσο	
3	ἐπιστεύετο		ἐπιστεύσατο		ἐπεπίστευτο	
pl. 1	ἐπιστευόμεθα		ἐπιστευσάμεθα		ἐπεπιστεύμεθα	
2	ἐπιστεύεσθε		ἐπιστεύσασθε		ἐπεπίστευσθε	
3	ἐπιστεύοντο		ἐπιστεύσαντο		ἐπεπίστευντο	

§13 Indicative Mood Formation Sheet by Principal Parts

Easy Identification	PRESENT A		IMPERFECT A	
1 Present A M/P **Imperfect A M/P** *Present: no augment, no stem change, no σίγμα, no κάππα* *Imperfect: augment, no σίγμα, no stem change*	verb stem + -ω -ομεν -εις -ετε -ει -ουσι(ν)		"ε" + verb stem + -ον -ομεν -ες -ετε -ε(ν) -ον	
	PRESENT M/P		IMPERFECT M/P	
	verb stem + -ομαι -όμεθα -ῃ -εσθε -εται -ονται		"ε" + verb stem + -όμην -όμεθα -ου -εσθε -ετο -οντο	
2 Future A M *no augment + σίγμα*	FUTURE A			
	verb stem + σ + -ω -ομεν -εις -ετε -ει -ουσι(ν)			

	Future M		
	verb stem + σ + -ομαι	-όμεθα	
	-ῃ	-εσθε	
	-εται	-ονται	
3 Aorist A M *1st Aorist: augment* *σίγμα–ἄλφα* *2nd Aorist: augment* *different stem*	**1st Aorist A** "ε" + verb stem + σ + -α -αμεν -ας -ατε -ε(ν) -αν		**2nd Aorist A** "ε" + changed stem + -ον -ομεν -ες -ετε -ε(ν) -ον
	1st Aorist M "ε" + verb stem + σ + -άμην -άμεθα -ω -ασθε -ατο -αντο		**2nd Aorist M** "ε" + changed stem + -όμην -όμεθα -ου -εσθε -ετο -οντο
4 Perfect/Pluperfect A *Perfect: reduplication* *κάππα–ἄλφα* *Pluperfect: "ε" + redupli-* *cation; ἒ ψιλόν–ἰῶτα*	**Perfect A** redup. + verb stem + κ + -α -αμεν -ας -ατε -ε(ν) -αν		**Pluperfect A** "ε" + redup. + verb stem + κ + -ειν -ειμεν -εις -ειτε <u>note</u>: the augment is optional -ει -εισαν
5 Perfect/Pluperfect M/P *reduplication, no κάππα* *no coupling vowel*	**Perfect M/P** redup. + verb stem + -μαι -μεθα -σαι -σθε -ται -νται		**Pluperfect M/P** "ε" + redup. + verb stem + -μην -μεθα -σο -σθε <u>note</u>: the augment is optional -το -ντο
6 Future P & Aorist P *θῆτα–ἦτα, Fut P also has* *σίγμα; Aor P has augment*	**Future P** verb stem + θησ + -ομαι -όμεθα -ῃ -εσθε -εται -ονται		**Aorist P** "ε" + verb stem + θη + -ν -μεν -ς -τε - -σαν

§14 Indicative Mood Principal Parts Easy Identification

1 Present A & M/P **Imperfect A & M/P**	**Easy Identification Markers:** The Present Tense has no augment, no reduplication, no stem changes, no stem indicator, and uses the PRIMARY ENDINGS. The Imperfect Tense has an augment, no stem indicator, and uses the SECONDARY ENDINGS. The Present Tense and the Imperfect Tense are placed together because they *always share the same verb stem*. Remember, *verb stems may change <u>between</u> Principal Parts, but never <u>within</u> the same Principal Part.*
2 Future A & M	**Easy Identification Markers:** The Future Tense has no augment, but does have a stem indicator, a σίγμα (σ). The Future Tense like the Present Tense uses the PRIMARY ENDINGS. The only difference between the Present and the Future is the Future's σίγμα (σ). Only the Active and Middle Voices of the Future are found here. *For the Passive Voice, one goes the 6th Principal Part (see below).* <u>Note</u>: *Verbs may have a different verb stem in the Future Tense,* e.g., λέγω in the Present, but ἐρῶ in the Future; ἐσθίω is Present, but in the Future is φάγομαι.
3 Aorist A & M	**Easy Identification Markers:** The 1st Aorist has an augment, a stem indicator, a σίγμα (σ), and uses the SECONDARY ENDINGS. The 2nd Aorist also has an augment, but uses a different stem, and likewise uses the SECONDARY ENDINGS. What makes the 1st Aorist easy to spot is the σίγμα–ἄλφα (σα) along with the augment. What makes the 2nd Aorist easy to spot is the (usually) obvious stem change along with the augment. Although the 1st and 2nd Aorists are formed differently, they are translated the same and have the same Verbal Aspect.
4 Perfect A **Pluperfect A**	**Easy Identification Markers:** The Perfect Tense (Active Voice) has reduplication, the κάππα (κ) stem indicator plus the SECONDARY ACTIVE ENDINGS. The Pluperfect has reduplication with an augment (which is optional) and also uses the SECONDARY ACTIVE ENDINGS. Occasionally, when a verb stem begins with a vowel, the reduplication will look like an augment and might be confused with the Aorist Tense. But, look for the distinctive κάππα–ἄλφα (κα) endings, which distinguish of the Active Voice of the Perfect Tense. <u>Note</u>: There is a 2nd Perfect that drops the κάππα. This 2nd Perfect can still be identified by the reduplication and SECONDARY ENDINGS.

5 Perfect M/P Pluperfect M/P	**Easy Identification Markers:** The Perfect M/P Tense has reduplication and uses the PRIMARY M/P ENDINGS. The Pluperfect M/P has reduplication with an augment (optional) and uses the SECONDARY M/P ENDINGS. What is unique about the Perfect and Pluperfect M/P (even in the Participle) is the *lack of coupling vowel before the endings*. Noticing this, along with the reduplication, makes parsing the Perfect M/P a breeze.
6 Aorist P Future P	**Easy Identification Markers:** These are perhaps the easiest forms to parse. The give away is the θῆτα–ῆτα (θη). The Future Passive has the same easy identification markers as the Future Middle, i.e., the σίγμα (σ) stem indicator and the PRIMARY M/P ENDINGS. The Aorist Passive has the easy identification markers as the 1st Aorist (augment, endings), but has no σίγμα (σ). The Aorist Passive uses the SECONDARY ACTIVE ENDINGS.

	PRIMARY ENDINGS		**Tenses →**	**Coupling Vowel**		**SECONDARY ENDINGS**		**Tenses →**	**Coupling Vowel**
A	-ω	-ομεν	PRESENT →	-	**A**	-ν	-μεν	Imperfect →	ο, ε
	-εις	-ετε	FUTURE →	-		-ς	-τε	Aorist →	α
	-ει	-ουσι(ν)				-	-ν or (σαν)	Perfect →	α
								Pluperfect →	ει
M/P	-μαι	-μεθα	PRESENT →	ο, ε	**M/P**	-μην	-μεθα	Aorist Pass →	η
	-σαι	-σθε	FUTURE →	ο, ε		-σο	-σθε	Same Tenses as above,	
	-ται	-νται	PERFECT →	none		-το	-ντο	except for the Perfect M/P.	

§15 PARTICIPLE FORMS (ἡ Μετοχή)

PRESENT	**ACTIVE**			**MIDDLE/PASSIVE**
	Masculine	**Feminine**	**Neuter**	**M,-F,-N**
sg. nom.	πιστεύων	πιστεύουσα	πίστευον	πιστευόμενος,-η,-ον
gen.	πιστεύοντος	πιστευούσης	πιστεύοντος	πιστευομένου,-ης,-ου
dat.	πιστεύοντι	πιστευούσῃ	πιστεύοντι	πιστευομένῳ,-η,-ῳ
acc.	πιστεύοντα	πιστεύουσαν	πίστευον	πιστευόμενον,-ην,-ον
pl. nom.	πιστεύοντες	πιστεύουσαι	πιστεύοντα	πιστευόμενοι,-αι,-α
gen.	πιστευόντων	πιστευουσῶν	πιστευόντων	πιστευομένων
dat.	πιστεύουσι(ν)	πιστευούσαις	πιστεύουσι(ν)	πιστευομένοις,-αις,-οις
acc.	πιστεύοντας	πιστευούσας	πιστεύοντα	πιστευομένους,-ας,-α

AORIST	**ACTIVE**			**MIDDLE**
	Masculine	**Feminine**	**Neuter**	**M,-F,-N**
sg. nom.	πιστεύσας	πιστεύσασα	πίστευσαν	πιστευσάμενος,-η,-ον
gen.	πιστεύσαντος	πιστευσάσης	πιστεύσαντος	πιστευσαμένου,-ης,-ου
dat.	πιστεύσαντι	πιστευσάσῃ	πιστεύσαντι	πιστευσαμένῳ,-η,-ῳ
acc.	πιστεύσαντα	πιστευσάσαν	πίστευσαν	πιστευσάμενον,-ην,-ον
pl. nom.	πιστεύσαντες	πιστεύσασαι	πιστεύσαντα	πιστευσάμενοι,-αι,-α
gen.	πιστευσάντων	πιστευσάσων	πιστευσάντων	πιστευσαμένων
dat.	πιστεύσασι(ν)	πιστευσάσαις	πιστεύσασι(ν)	πιστευσαμένοις,-αις,-οις
acc.	πιστεύσαντας	πιστευσάσας	πιστεύσαντα	πιστευσαμένους,-ας,-α

PASSIVE	**Masculine**	**Feminine**	**Neuter**
sg. nom.	πιστευθείς	πιστευθεῖσα	πιστευθέν
gen.	πιστευθέντος	πιστευθείσης	πιστευθέντος
dat.	πιστευθέντι	πιστευθείσῃ	πιστευθέντι
acc.	πιστευθέντα	πιστευθεῖσαν	πιστευθέν
pl. nom.	πιστευθέντες	πιστευθεῖσαι	πιστευθέντα
gen.	πιστευθέντων	πιστευθεισῶν	πιστευθέντων
dat.	πιστευθεῖσι(ν)	πιστευθείσαις	πιστευθεῖσι(ν)
acc.	πιστευθέντας	πιστευθείσας	πιστευθέντα

PERFECT	ACTIVE			MIDDLE/PASSIVE
	Masculine	**Feminine**	**Neuter**	**M,-F,-N**
sg. nom.	πεπιστευκώς	πεπιστευκυῖα	πεπιστευκός	πεπιστευμένος,-η,-ον
gen.	πεπιστευκότος	πεπιστευκυίας	πεπιστευκότος	πεπιστευμένου,-ης,-ου
dat.	πεπιστευκότι	πεπιστευκυίᾳ	πεπιστευκότι	πεπιστευμένῳ,-η,-ῳ
acc.	πεπιστευκότα	πεπιστευκυῖαν	πεπιστευκός	πεπιστευμένον,-ην,-ον
pl. nom.	πεπιστευκότες	πεπιστευκυῖαι	πεπιστευκότα	πεπιστευμένοι,-αι,-α
gen.	πεπιστευκότων	πεπιστευκυιῶν	πεπιστευκότων	πεπιστευμένων,-ων,-ων
dat.	πεπιστευκόσι(ν)	πεπιστευκυίαις	πεπιστευκόσι(ν)	πεπιστευμένοις,-αις,-οις
acc.	πεπιστευκότας	πεπιστευκυίας	πεπιστευκότα	πεπιστευμένους,-ας,-α

§16 INFINITIVE FORMS (ἡ Ἀπαρέμφατος Ἔγκλισις)

PRESENT	AORIST	PERFECT
A πιστεύειν	A πιστεῦσαι	A πεπιστευκέναι
M/P πιστεύεσθαι	M πιστεύσασθαι	M/P πεπιστεῦσθαι
	P πιστευθῆναι	

§17 SUBJUNCTIVE FORMS (ἡ Ὑποτακτικὴ Ἔγκλισις)

		PRESENT A	PRESENT M/P	1ST AORIST A	1ST AORIST M	AORIST P
sg.	1	πιστεύω	πιστεύωμαι	πιστεύσω	πιστεύσωμαι	πιστευθῶ
	2	πιστεύῃς	πιστεύῃ	πιστεύσῃς	πιστεύσῃ	πιστευθῇς
	3	πιστεύῃ	πιστεύηται	πιστεύσῃ	πιστεύσηται	πιστευθῇ
pl.	1	πιστεύωμεν	πιστευώμεθα	πιστεύσωμεν	πιστευσώμεθα	πιστευθῶμεν
	2	πιστεύητε	πιστεύησθε	πιστεύσητε	πιστεύσησθε	πιοστευθῆτε
	3	πιστεύωσιν	πιστεύωνται	πιστεύσωσι	πιστεύσωνται	πιστευθῶσι(ν)

§18 IMPERATIVE FORMS (ἡ Προστατικὴ Ἔγκλισις)

		PRESENT A	PRESENT M/P	AORIST A	AORIST M	AORIST P
sg.	2	πίστευε	πιστεύου	πίστευσον	πίστευσαι	πιστεύθητι
	3	πιστευέτω	πιστευέσθω	πιστευσάτω	πιστευσάσθω	πιστευθήτω
pl.	2	πιστεύετε	πιστεύεσθε	πιστεύσατε	πιστεύσασθε	πιστεύθητε
	3	πιστευέτωσαν	πιστευέσθωσαν	πιστευσάτωσαν	πιστευσάσθωσαν	πιστευθήτωσαν

§19 OPTATIVE FORMS (ἡ Εὐκτικὴ Ἔγκλισις)

		PRESENT A	PRESENT M/P	1ST AORIST A	1ST AORIST M	AORIST P
sg.	1	πιστεύοιμι	πιστευοίμην	πιστεύσαιμι	πιστευσαίμην	πιστευθείην
	2	πιστεύοις	πιστεύοιο	πιστεύσαις	πιστεύσαιο	πιστευθείης
	3	πιστεύοι	πιστεύοιτο	πίστευσαι	πιστεύσαιτο	πιστευθείη
pl.	1	πιστεύοιμεν	πιστευοίμεθα	πιστεύσαιμεν	πιστευσαίμεθα	πιστευθείημεν
	2	πιστεύοιτε	πιστεύοισθε	πιστεύσαιτε	πιστεύσαισθε	πιοστευθείητε
	3	πιστεύοιεν	πιστεύοιντο	πιστεύσαιεν	πιστεύσαιντο	πιστευθείησαν

§20 FORMS OF Εἰμί AND Οἶδα

		INDICATIVE					INDICATIVE	
		PRESENT	IMPERFECT	FUTURE			PERFECT	PLUPERFECT
sg.	1	εἰμί	ἤμην	ἔσομαι		sg. 1	οἶδα	ᾔδειν
	2	εἶ	ἦς	ἔσῃ		2	οἶδας	ᾔδεις
	3	ἐστί(ν)	ἦν	ἔσται		3	οἶδε(ν)	ᾔδει
pl.	1	ἐσμέν	ἦμεν, ἤμεθα	ἐσόμεθα		pl. 1	οἴδαμεν	ᾔδειμεν
	2	ἐστέ	ἦτε	ἔσεσθε		2	οἴδατε	ᾔδειτε
	3	εἰσί(ν)	ἦσαν	ἔσονται		3	οἴδασι(ν)	ᾔδεισαν

SUBJUNCTIVE

sg. 1 ὦ
   2 ῇς
   3 ῇ
pl. 1 ὦμεν
   2 ῆτε
   3 ὦσι(ν)

IMPERATIVE

sg. 2 ἴσθι
   3 ἔστω
pl. 2 ἔστε
   3 ἔστωσαν

INFINITIVE

   εἶναι

PARTICIPLE

	M	F	N
sg. nom.	ὤν	oὔσα	ὄν
gen.	ὄντοσ	oὔσησ	ὄντοσ
dat.	ὄντι	oὔση	ὄντι
acc.	ὄντα	oὔσαν	ὄν
pl. nom.	ὄντεσ	oὔσαι	ὄντα
gen.	ὄντων	oὔσῶν	ὄντων
dat.	oὔσι(ν)	oὔσαισ	oὔσι(ν)
acc.	ὄντασ	oὔσασ	ὄντα

SUBJUNCTIVE

sg. 1 εἰδὦ
   2 εἰδῇσ
   3 εἰδῇ
pl. 1 εἰδὦμεν
   2 εἰδῆτε
   3 εἰδὦσι(ν)

IMPERATIVE

sg. 2 ἴσθι
   3 ἴστω
pl. 2 ἴσθε
   3 ἴστωσαν

INFINITIVE

   εἰδέναι

PARTICIPLE

	M	F	N
sg. nom.	εἰδώσ	εἰδῖα	εἰδόσ
gen.	εἰδόντοσ	εἰδήασ	εἰδόντοσ
dat.	εἰδόντι	εἰδήᾳ	εἰδόντι
acc.	εἰδόντα	εἰδῖαν	εἰδόσ
pl. nom.	εἰδόντεσ	εἰδῖαι	εἰδόντα
gen.	εἰδόντων	εἰδών	εἰδόντων
dat.	εἰδοώσι(ν)	εἰδήαισ	εἰδοώσι(ν)
acc.	εἰδόντασ	εἰδῖασ	εἰδόντα

§21 CONTRACT VERB FORMS

Contract Verbs have regular endings outside the First Principal Part, since the lengthened contract vowel "will put on display" the endings.

	FIRST	SECOND	THIRD	FOURTH	FIFTH	SIXTH
᾿Ε ψιλόν	λαλέω*	λαλήσω	ἐλάλησα	λελάληκα	λελάλημαι	ἐλαλήθην
᾿Αλφα	ἀγαπάω*	ἀγαπήσω	ἠγάπησα	ἠγάπηκα	ἠγάπημαι	ἠγαπήθην
᾿Ο μικρόν	πληρόω*	πληρώσω	ἐπλήρωσα	πεπλήρωκα	πεπλήρωμαι	ἐπληρώθην

It is only with the First Principal Part (Present and Imperfect Tenses) that there will likely be difficulty in parsing. So, students should understand the principles of this Contraction Chart.

CONTRACTION CHART

Contract	Initial Vowel or Monophthong of Ending						
Vowel +	ε	ει	η	ῃ	o	oυ	ω
-ε	ει	ει	η	ῃ	oυ	oυ	ω
-α	α	ᾳ	α	ᾳ	ω	ω	ω
-o	oυ	oι	ω	oι	oυ	oυ	ω

"Ε ψιλόν Contract: δοκέω *I seem* (pre-contracted forms)

INDICATIVE MOOD

	PRESENT A		PRESENT M/P	
sg. 1	δοκῶ	(δοκέω)	δοκοῦμαι	(δοκέομαι)
2	δοκεῖς	(δοκέεις)	δοκῇ	(δοκέη)
3	δοκεῖ	(δοκέει)	δοκεῖται	(δοκέεται)
pl. 1	δοκοῦμεν	(δοκέομεν)	δοκούμεθα	(δοκεόμεθα)
2	δοκεῖτε	(δοκέετε)	δοκεῖσθε	(δοκέεσθε)
3	δοκοῦσι(ν)	(δοκέουσιν)	δοκοῦνται	(δοκέονται)

INDICATIVE MOOD

	IMPERFECT A		IMPERFECT M/P	
sg. 1	ἐδόκουν	(ἐδόκεον)	ἐδοκούμην	(ἐδοκεόμην)
2	ἐδόκεις	(ἐδόκεες)	ἐδοκοῦ	(ἐδοκέου)
3	ἐδόκει	(ἐδόκεε)	ἐδόκεῖτο	(ἐδοκέετο)
pl. 1	ἐδοκοῦμεν	(ἐδοκέομεν)	ἐδοκούμεθα	(ἐδοκεόμεθα)
2	ἐδοκεῖτε	(ἐδοκέετε)	ἐδοκεῖσθε	(ἐδοκέεσθε)
3	ἐδόκουν	(ἐδόκεον)	ἐδοκοῦντο	(ἐδοκέοντο)

SUBJUNCTIVE MOOD

	PRESENT A		PRESENT M/P	
sg. 1	δοκῶ	(δοκέω)	δοκῶμαι	(δοκέωμαι)
2	δοκῇς	(δοκέῃς)	δοκῇ	(δοκέη)
3	δοκῇ	(δοκέη)	δοκῆται	(δοκέηται)
pl. 1	δοκῶμεν	(δοκέωμεν)	δοκώμεθα	(δοκεώμεθα)
2	δοκῆτε	(δοκέητε)	δοκῆσθε	(δοκέησθε)
3	δοκῶσι(ν)	(δοκέωσιν)	δοκῶνται	(δοκέωνται)

IMPERATIVE MOOD

	PRESENT A		PRESENT M/P	
sg. 2	δόκει	(δόκεε)	δοκοῦ	(δοκέου)
3	δοκείτω	(δοκέετω)	δοκείσθω	(δοκέεσθω)
pl. 2	δοκεῖτε	(δοκέετε)	δοκεῖσθε	(δοκέεσθε)
3	δόκείτωσαν	(δοκεέτωσαν)	δοκείσθωσαν	(δοκεέσθωσαν)

OPTATIVE MOOD

	PRESENT A		PRESENT M/P	
sg. 1	δοκοῖμι	(δοκέοιμι)	δοκοίμην	(δοκεοίμην)
2	δοκοῖς	(δοκέοις)	δοκοῖο	(δοκέοιο)
3	δοκοῖ	(δοκέοι)	δοκοῖτο	(δοκέοιτο)
pl. 1	δοκοῖμεν	(δοκέοιμεν)	δοκοίμεθα	(δοκεοίμεθα)
2	δοκοῖτε	(δοκέοιτε)	δοκοῖσθε	(δοκέοισθε)
3	δοκοῖεν	(δοκέοιεν)	δοκοῖντο	(δοκέοιντο)

INFINITIVE

PRESENT A	PRESENT M/P
δοκεῖν (δοκέειν)	δοκεῖσθαι (δοκέεσθαι)

PARTICIPLE

PRESENT A (nom., gen.,)			PRESENT M/P
Masculine (sg.)	**Feminine (sg.)**	**Neuter (sg.)**	**Masc., Fem., Neut., (sg.)**
δοκῶν, δοκοῦντος...	δοκοῦσα, δοκούσης...	δοκοῦν, δοκοῦντος...	δοκούμεν-ος, -η, -ον

Ἄλφα Contract: ἀγαπάω *I love* (pre-contracted forms)

INDICATIVE MOOD

	PRESENT A		PRESENT M/P	
sg. 1	ἀγαπῶ	(ἀγαπάω)	ἀγαπῶμαι	(ἀγαπάομαι)
2	ἀγαπᾷς	(ἀγαπάεις)	ἀγαπᾷ	(ἀγαπάῃ)
3	ἀγαπᾷ	(ἀγαπάει)	ἀγαπᾶται	(ἀγαπάεται)
pl. 1	ἀγαπῶμεν	(ἀγαπάομεν)	ἀγαπώμεθα	(ἀγαπαόμεθα)
2	ἀγαπᾶτε	(ἀγαπάετε)	ἀγαπᾶσθε	(ἀγαπάεσθε)
3	ἀγαπῶσι(ν)	(ἀγαπάουσιν)	ἀγαπῶνται	(ἀγαπάονται)

INDICATIVE MOOD

	IMPERFECT A		IMPERFECT M/P	
sg. 1	ἠγάπων	(ἠγάπαον)	ἠγαπώμην	(ἠγαπαόμην)
2	ἠγάπας	(ἠγάπαες)	ἠγαπῶ	(ἠγαπάου)
3	ἠγάπα	(ἠγάπαε)	ἠγαπᾶτο	(ἠγαπάετο)
pl. 1	ἠγαπῶμεν	(ἠγαπάομεν)	ἠγαπώμεθα	(ἠγαπαόμεθα)
2	ἠγαπᾶτε	(ἠγαπάετε)	ἠγαπᾶσθε	(ἠγαπάεσθε)
3	ἠγάπων	(ἠγάπαον)	ἠγαπῶντο	(ἠγαπάοντο)

SUBJUNCTIVE MOOD

	PRESENT A		PRESENT M/P	
sg. 1	ἀγαπῶ	(ἀγαπάω)	ἀγαπῶμαι	(ἀγαπάωμαι)
2	ἀγαπᾷς	(ἀγαπάῃς)	ἀγαπᾷ	(ἀγαπάῃ)
3	ἀγαπᾷ	(ἀγαπάῃ)	ἀγαπᾶται	(ἀγαπάηται)
pl. 1	ἀγαπῶμεν	(ἀγαπάωμεν)	ἀγαπώμεθα	(ἀγαπαώμεθα)
2	ἀγαπᾶτε	(ἀγαπάητε)	ἀγαπᾶσθε	(ἀγαπάησθε)
3	ἀγαπῶσι(ν)	(ἀγαπάωσιν)	ἀγαπῶνται	(ἀγαπάωνται)

IMPERATIVE MOOD

	PRESENT A		PRESENT M/P	
sg. 2	ἀγάπα	(ἀγαπάε)	ἀγαπῶ	(ἀγαπάου)
3	ἀγαπάτω	(ἀγαπάετω)	ἀγαπάσθω	(ἀγαπάεσθω)
pl. 2	ἀγαπᾶτε	(ἀγαπάετε)	ἀγαπᾶσθε	(ἀγαπάεσθε)
3	ἀγαπάτωσαν	(ἀγαπαέτωσαν)	ἀγαπάσθωσαν	(ἀγαπαέσθωσαν)

OPTATIVE MOOD

	PRESENT A		PRESENT M/P	
sg. 1	ἀγαπῷμι	(ἀγαπάοιμι)	ἀγαπῷμην	(ἀγαπαοίμην)
2	ἀγαπῷς	(ἀγαπάοις)	ἀγαπῷο	(ἀγαπάοιο)
3	ἀγαπῷ	(ἀγαπάοι)	ἀγαπῷτο	(ἀγαπάοιτο)
pl. 1	ἀγαπῷμεν	(ἀγαπάοιμεν)	ἀγαπώμεθα	(ἀγαπαοίμεθα)
2	ἀγαπῷτε	(ἀγαπάοιτε)	ἀγαπῷσθε	(ἀγαπάοισθε)
3	ἀγαπῷεν	(ἀγαπάοιεν)	ἀγαπῷντο	(ἀγαπάοιντο)

INFINITIVE

PRESENT A	PRESENT M/P
ἀγαπᾶν (ἀγαπάεεν)	ἀγαπᾶσθαι (ἀγαπάεσθαι)

PARTICIPLE

PRESENT A (nom., gen., ...)			PRESENT M/P
Masculine (sg.)	Feminine (sg.)	Neuter (sg.)	Masc., Fem., Neut., (sg.)
ἀγαπῶν, ἀγαπῶντος...	ἀγαπῶσα, ἀγαπώσης...	ἀγαπῶν, ἀγαποῦντος...	ἀγαπώμεν-ος, -η, -ον

Ὁ μικρόν Contract: πληρόω *I fulfill* (pre-contracted forms)

INDICATIVE MOOD

		PRESENT A		PRESENT M/P	
sg.	1	πληρῶ	(πληρόω)	πληροῦμαι	(πληρόομαι)
	2	πληροῖς	(πληρόεις)	πληροῖ	(πληρόῃ)
	3	πληροῖ	(πληρόει)	πληροῦται	(πληρόεται)
pl.	1	πληροῦμεν	(πληρόομεν)	πληρούμεθα	(πληροόμεθα)
	2	πληροῦτε	(πληρόετε)	πληροῦσθε	(πληρόεσθε)
	3	πληροῦσιν	(πληρόουσιν)	πληροῦνται	(πληρόονται)

INDICATIVE MOOD

		IMPERFECT A		IMPERFECT M/P	
sg.	1	ἐπλήρουν	(ἐπλήροον)	ἐπληρούμην	(ἐπληροόμην)
	2	ἐπλήρους	(ἐπλήροες)	ἐπληροῦ	(ἐπληρόου)
	3	ἐπλήρου	(ἐπλήροε)	ἐπληροῦτο	(ἐπληρόετο)
pl.	1	ἐπληροῦμεν	(ἐπληρόομεν)	ἐπληρούμεθα	(ἐπληροόμεθα)
	2	ἐπληροῦτε	(ἐπληρόετε)	ἐπληροῦσθε	(ἐπληρόεσθε)
	3	ἐπλήρουν	(ἐπλήροον)	ἐπληροῦντο	(ἐπληρόοντο)

SUBJUNCTIVE MOOD

		PRESENT A		PRESENT M/P	
sg.	1	πληρῶ	(πληρόω)	πληρῶμαι	(πληρόωμαι)
	2	πληροῖς	(πληρόῃς)	πληροῖ	(πληρόῃ)
	3	πληροῖ	(πληρόῃ)	πληρῶται	(πληρόηται)
pl.	1	πληρῶμεν	(πληρόωμεν)	πληρώμεθα	(πληροώμεθα)
	2	πληρῶτε	(πληρόητε)	πληρῶσθε	(πληρόησθε)
	3	πληρῶσιν	(πληρόωσιν)	πληρῶνται	(πληρόωνται)

IMPERATIVE MOOD

		PRESENT A		PRESENT M/P	
sg.	2	πλήρου	(πλήροε)	πληροῦ	(πληρόου)
	3	πληρούτω	(πληροέτω)	πληρούσθω	(πληρόεσθω)
pl.	2	πληροῦτε	(πληρόετε)	πληροῦσθε	(πληρόεσθε)
	3	πληρούτωσαν	(πληροέτωσαν)	πληρούσθωσαν	(πληροέσθωσαν)

OPTATIVE MOOD

		PRESENT A		PRESENT M/P	
sg.	1	πληροῖμι	(πληρόοιμι)	πληροίμην	(πληροοίμην)
	2	πληροῖς	(πληρόοις)	πληροῖο	(πληρόοιο)
	3	πληροῖ	(πληρόοι)	πληροῖτο	(πληρόοιτο)
pl.	1	πληροῖμεν	(πληρόοιμεν)	πληροίμεθα	(πληροοίμεθα)
	2	πληροῖτε	(πληρόοιτε)	πληροῖσθε	(πληρόοισθε)
	3	πληροῖεν	(πληρόοιεν)	πληροῖντο	(πληρόοιντο)

INFINITIVE

PRESENT A	PRESENT M/P
πληροῦν (πληρόεεν)	πληροῦσθαι (πληρόεσθαι)

PARTICIPLE

PRESENT A			PRESENT M/P
(nom., gen., …)			
Masculine (sg.)	**Feminine (sg.)**	**Neuter (sg.)**	**Masc., Fem., Neut., (sg.)**
πληρῶν, πληροῦντος...	πληροῦσα, πληρούσης...	πληροῦν, πληροῦντος...	πληρούμεν-ος, -η, -ον

§22 LIQUID VERB FORMS

Liquid verbs have stems ending in λ, μ, ν, or ρ, which reject the σίγμα of the Future and Aorist endings. Therefore, they are difficult in the Future and Aorist Indicative and in the Aorist Non-Indicative Moods. Here is the verb ἐγείρω *I raise*.

INDICATIVE

	PRESENT ACTIVE		FUTURE ACTIVE		FUTURE MIDDLE	
	sg.	pl.	sg.	pl.	sg.	pl.
1	ἐγείρω	ἐγείρομεν	ἐγερῶ	ἐγεροῦμεν	ἐγεροῦμαι	ἐγερούμεθα
2	ἐγείρεις	ἐγείρετε	ἐγερεῖς	ἐγερεῖτε	ἐγερῇ	ἐγερεῖσθε
3	ἐγείρει	ἐγείρουσιν	ἐγερεῖ	ἐγεροῦσιν	ἐγερεῖται	ἐγεροῦνται

INDICATIVE

	AORIST ACTIVE		AORIST MIDDLE	
	sg.	pl.	sg.	pl.
1	ἤγειρα	ἠγείραμεν	ἠγειράμην	ἠγειράμεθα
2	ἤγειρας	ἠγείρατε	ἠγείρω	ἠγείρασθε
3	ἤγειρε(ν)	ἤγειραν	ἠγείρατο	ἠγείραντο

SUBJUNCTIVE

	AORIST ACTIVE		AORIST MIDDLE	
	sg.	pl.	sg.	pl.
1	ἐγείρω	ἐγείρωμεν	ἐγείρωμαι	ἐγειρώμεθα
2	ἐγείρῃς	ἐγείρητε	ἐγείρῃ	ἐγείρησθε
3	ἐγείρῃ	ἐγείρωσι(ν)	ἐγείρηται	ἐγείρωνται

IMPERATIVE

	AORIST ACTIVE		AORIST MIDDLE	
	sg.	pl.	sg.	pl.
2	ἔγειρον	ἐγείρατε	ἔγειραι	ἐγείρασθε
3	ἐγειράτω	ἐγειράτωσαν	ἐγειράσθω	ἐγειράσθωσαν

PARTICIPLE

AORIST ACTIVE
Masculine, Feminine, Neuter
ἔγειρας, ἐγείρασα, ἔγειραν

INFINITIVE

AORIST ACTIVE	AORIST MIDDLE
ἔγειραι	ἐγείρασθαι

§23 Μι VERB FORMS

INDICATIVE MOOD OF Μι VERBS

		PRESENT A			PRESENT M/P		
sg.	1	δίδωμι	τίθημι	ἵστημι	δίδομαι	τίθεμαι	ἵσταμαι
	2	δίδως	τίθης	ἵστης	δίδοσαι	τίθεσαι	ἵστασαι
	3	δίδωσι(ν)	τίθησι(ν)	ἵστησι(ν)	δίδοται	τίθεται	ἵσταται
pl.	1	δίδομεν	τίθεμεν	ἵσταμεν	διδόμεθα	τιθέμεθα	ἱστάμεθα
	2	δίδοτε	τίθετε	ἵστατε	δίδοσθε	τίθεσθε	ἵστασθε
	3	διδόασι(ν)	τιθέασι(ν)	ἱστᾶσι(ν)	δίδονται	τίθενται	ἵστανται
		IMPERFECT A			IMPERFECT M/P		
sg.	1	ἐδίδουν	ἐτίθην	ἵστην	ἐδιδόμην	ἐτιθέμην	ἱστάμην
	2	ἐδίδους	ἐτίθεις	ἵστης	ἐδίδοσο	ἐτίθεσο	ἵστασο
	3	ἐδίδου	ἐτίθει	ἵστη	ἐδίδοτο	ἐτίθετο	ἵστατο

pl. 1	ἐδίδομεν	ἐτίθεμεν	ἵσταμεν	ἐδιδόμεθα	ἐτιθέμεθα	ἱστάμεθα
2	ἐδίδοτε	ἐτίθετε	ἵστατε	ἐδίδοσθε	ἐτίθεσθε	ἵστασθε
3	ἐδίδοσαν	ἐτίθεσαν	ἵστασαν	ἐδίδοντο	ἐτίθεντο	ἵσταντο

	AORIST A						AORIST M		
	δίδωμι		τίθημι		ἵστημι		δίδωμι	τίθημι	ἵστημι
	1st Aor	2nd Aor	1st Aor	2nd Aor	1st Aor	2nd Aor			
sg. 1	ἔδωκα	ἔδων	ἔθηκα	ἔθην	ἔστησα	ἔστην	ἐδόμην	ἐθέμην	ἐστάμην
2	ἔδωκας	ἔδως	ἔθηκας	ἔθης	ἔστησας	ἔστης	ἔδου	ἔθου	ἔστω
3	ἔδωκε(ν)	ἔδω	ἔθηκε(ν)	ἔθη	ἔστησε(ν)	ἔστη	ἔδοτο	ἔθετο	ἔστατο
pl. 1	ἐδώκαμεν	ἔδομεν	ἐθήκαμεν	ἔθεμεν	ἐστήσαμεν	ἔστημεν	ἐδόμεθα	ἐθέμεθα	ἐστάμεθα
2	ἐδώκατε	ἔδοτε	ἐθήκατε	ἔθετε	ἐστήσατε	ἔστητε	ἔδοσθε	ἔθεσθε	ἔστασθε
3	ἔδωκαν	ἔδοσαν	ἔθηκαν	ἔθεασαν	ἔστησαν	ἔστησαν	ἔδοντο	ἔθεντο	ἔσταντο

SUMMARY OF Mι VERBS IN THE INDICATIVE MOOD

Stem	FIRST	SECOND	THIRD	FOURTH	FIFTH	SIXTH
δο	δίδωμι	δώσω	ἔδωκα	δέδωκα	δέδομαι	ἐδόθην
θε	τίθημι	θήσω	ἔθηκα	τέθεικα	τεθεῖμαι	ἐτέθην
ε	ἀφ-ίημι	ἀφ-ήσω	ἄφ-ηκα	ἀφ-εῖκα	ἀφ-εῖμαι	ἀφ-είθην
στα	ἵστημι	στήσω	ἔστησα (1st A)	ἔστηκα	ἔσταμαι	ἐστάθην
			ἔστην (2nd A)			

Notes:
-*false reduplication* -*no false reduplication* -*no false reduplication* -*regular reduplication* -*no false reduplication*
-*some new endings* -*regular endings* -*some kappa endings* -*regular endings* -*regular endings*

PARTICIPLES OF Mι VERBS

		PRESENT A	1ST AORIST A	2ND AORIST A
		nom., gen....	nom., gen...	nom., gen....
δίδωμι	masc.	διδούς, διδόντος...		δούς, δόντος...
	fem.	διδοῦσα, διδούσης...		δοῦσα, δούσης...
	neut.	διδόν, διδόντος...		δόν, δόντος...
τίθημι	masc.	τιθείς, τιθέντος...	θήκας, θηκάντος...	θείς, θέντος...
	fem.	τιθεῖσα, τιθείσης...	θηκᾶσα, θηκάσης...	θεῖσα, θείσης...
	neut.	τιθέν, τιθέντος...	θήκαν, θηκάντος...	θέν, θέντος...
ἵστημι	masc.	ἱστάς, ἱστάντος...	στήσας, στήσαντος...	στάς, στάντος...
	fem.	ἱστᾶσα, ἱστάσης...	στησᾶσα, στησάσης...	στᾶσα, στάσης...
	neut.	ἱστάν, ἱστάντος...	στήσαν, στήσαντος...	στάν, στάντος...

		PRESENT M/P	1ST AORIST M	2ND AORIST M
		nom., gen....	nom., gen....	nom., gen....
δίδωμι	masc.	διδόμενος, διδομένου...		δόμενος, δομένου...
	fem.	διδομένη, διδομένης...		δομένη, δομένης...
	neut.	διδόμενον, διδομένου...		δόμενον, δομένου...
τίθημι	masc.	τιθέμενος, τιθεμένου...	θηκάμενος, θηκαμένου...	θέμενος, θεμένου...
	fem.	τιθεμένη, τιθεμένης...	θηκαμένη, θηκαμένης...	θεμένη, θεμένης...
	neut.	τιθέμενον, τιθεμένου...	θηκάμενον, θηκαμένου...	θέμενον, θεμένου...
ἵστημι	masc.	ἱστάμενος, ἱσταμένου...	στησάμενος, στησαμένου...	στάμενος, σταμένου...
	fem.	ἱσταμένη, ἱσταμένης...	στησαμένη, στησαμένης...	σταμένη, σταμένης...
	neut.	ἱστάμενον, ἱσταμένου...	στησάμενον, στησαμένου...	στάμενον, σταμένου...

		(1ST) AORIST P	PERFECT A	PERFECT M/P
		nom., gen....	nom., gen....	nom., gen....
δίδωμι	masc.	δοθείς, δοθέντος...	δεδωκώς, δεδωκότος...	δεδομένος, δεδομένου...
	fem.	δοθεῖσα, δοθείσης...	δεδωκυῖα, δεδωκυίας...	δεδομένη, δεδομένης...
	neut.	δοθέν, δοθέντος...	δεδωκός, δεδωκότος...	δεδομένον, δεδομένου...

τίθημι	masc.	τεθείς, τεθέντος...	τεθεικώς, τεθεικότος...	τεθειμένος, τεθειμένου...
	fem.	τεθεῖσα, τεθείσης...	τεθεικυῖα, τεθεικυίας...	τεθειμένη, τεθειμένης...
	neut.	τεθέν, τεθέντος...	τεθεικός, τεθεικότος...	τεθειμένον, τεθειμένου...

ἵστημι	masc.	σταθείς, σταθέντος...	ἑστηκώς, ἑστηκότος...	
	fem.	σταθεῖσα, σταθείσης...	ἑστηκυῖα, ἑστηκυίας...	
	neut.	σταθέν, σταθέντος...	ἑστηκός, ἑστηκότος...	

SUBJUNCTIVE MOOD OF Mι VERBS

SUBJUNCTIVE FORMS OF τίθημι

		ACTIVE SUBJUNCTIVE			MIDDLE/PASSIVE SUBJUNCTIVE	
		PRESENT A	AORIST A	AORIST P	PRESENT M/P	AORIST M
sg.	1	τιθῶ	θῶ	τεθῶ	τιθῶμαι	θῶμαι
	2	τιθῇς	θῇς	τεθῇς	τιθῇ	θῇ
	3	τιθῇ	θῇ	τεθῇ	τιθῆται	θῆται
pl.	1	τιθῶμεν	θῶμεν	τεθῶμεν	τιθώμεθα	θώμεθα
	2	τιθῆτε	θῆτε	τεθῆτε	τιθῆσθε	θῆσθε
	3	τιθῶσι(ν)	θῶσι(ν)	τεθῶσι(ν)	τιθῶνται	θῶνται

SUBJUNCTIVE FORMS OF δίδωμι

		ACTIVE SUBJUNCTIVE			MIDDLE/PASSIVE SUBJUNCTIVE	
		PRESENT A	AORIST A	AORIST P	PRESENT M/P	AORIST M
sg.	1	διδῶ	δῶ	δοθῶ	διδῶμαι	δῶμαι
	2	διδῷς	δῷς	δοθῇς	διδῷ	δῷ
	3	διδῷ	δῷ	δοθῇ	διδῶται	δῶται
pl.	1	διδῶμεν	δῶμεν	δοθῶμεν	διδώμεθα	δώμεθα
	2	διδῶτε	δῶτε	δοθῆτε	διδῶσθε	δῶσθε
	3	διδῶσι(ν)	δῶσι(ν)	δοθῶσι(ν)	διδῶνται	δῶνται

SUBJUNCTIVE FORMS OF ἵστημι

		ACTIVE SUBJUNCTIVE				MIDDLE/PASSIVE SUBJUNCTIVE		
		PRES A	1ST AOR A	2ND AOR A	1ST AOR P	PRES M/P	1ST AOR M	2ND AOR M
sg.	1	ἱστῶ	στήσω	στῶ	σταθῶ	ἱστῶμαι	στήσωμαι	στῶμαι
	2	ἱστῇς	στήσῃς	στῇς	σταθῇς	ἱστῇ	στήσῃ	στῇ
	3	ἱστῇ	στήσῃ	στῇ	σταθῇ	ἱστῆται	στήσηται	στῆται
pl.	1	ἱστῶμεν	στήσωμεν	στῶμεν	σταθῶμεν	ἱστώμεθα	στησώμεθα	στώμεθα
	2	ἱστῆτε	στήσητε	στῆτε	σταθῆτε	ἱστῆσθε	στήσησθε	στῆσθε
	3	ἱστῶσι(ν)	στήσωσι(ν)	στῶσι(ν)	σταθῶσι(ν)	ἱστῶνται	στήωντο	στῶνται

IMPERATIVE MOOD OF Mι VERBS

		δίδωμι		τίθημι		ἵστημι	
		sg.	pl.	sg.	pl.	sg.	pl.
PRESENT A	2	δίδου	δίδοτε	τίθει	τίθετε	ἵστη	ἵστατε
	3	διδότω	διδότωσαν	τιθέτω	τιθέτωσαν	ἱστάτω	ἱστάτωσαν
PRESENT M/P	2	δίδοσο	δίδοσθω	τίθεσο	τίθεσθε	ἵστασο	ἵστασθε
	3	διδόσθω	διδόσθωσαν	τιθέσθω	τιθέσθωσαν	ἱστάσθω	ἱστάσθωσαν
AORIST A	2	δός	δότε	θές	θέτε	στῆσον	στήσατε
	3	δότω	δότωσαν	θέτω	θέτωσαν	στησάτω	στησάτωσαν
AORIST M	2	δοῦ	δόσθε	θοῦ	θέσθε	στῆθι*	στῆτε*
	3	δόσθω	δόσθωσαν	θέσθω	θέσθωσαν	στήτω*	στήτωσαν*
AORIST P	2	δόθητι	δόθητε	τέθητι	τέθητε	στάθητι	στάθητε
	3	δοθήτω	δοθήτωσαν	τεθήτω	τεθήτωναν	σταθήτω	σταθήτωσαν

* 2nd Aorist Active forms of ἵστημι

PRESENT TENSE OPTATIVE MOOD

		FOR Δίδωμι				FOR ἵστημι	FOR τίθημι
		PRESENT A		**PRESENT M/P**		**PRESENT A**	**PRESENT A**
sg.	1	διδοίην	(διδοοίην)	διδοίμην	(διδοοίμην)	ἱσταίην	τιθείην
	2	διδοίης	(διδοοίης)	διδοῖο	(διδόοιο)	ἱσταίης	τιθείης
	3	διδοίη	(διδοοίη)	διδοῖτο	(διδόοιτο)	ἱσταίη	τιθείη
pl.	1	διδοῖμεν	(διδόοιμεν)	διδοίμεθα	(διδοοίμεθα)	ἱσταῖμεν	τιθεῖ-μεν
	2	διδοῖτε	(διδόοιτε)	διδοῖσθε	(διδόοισθε)	ἱσταῖτε	τιθεῖ-τε
	3	διδοῖεν	(διδόοιεν)	διδοῖντο	(διδόοιντο)	ἱσταῖεν	τιθεῖε-ν

INFINITIVES OF Μι VERBS

Μι VERB	**PRESENT A**	**PRESENT M/P**	**AORIST A**	**AORIST M**	**AORIST P**
δίδωμι	διδόναι	δίδοσθαι	δοῦναι	δόσθαι	δοθῆναι
τίθημι	τιθέναι	τίθεσθαι	θεῖναι	θέσθαι	τεθῆναι
ἀφίημι	ἀφιέναι	ἀφίεσθαι	ἀφεῖναι	ἀφέσθαι	-
ἵστημι	ἱστάναι	ἵστασθαι	στῆσαι (1st A)	-	σταθῆναι
			στῆναι (2nd A)		

§24 SYNOPSIS OF RULES FOR THE GREEK ACCENT (ὁ Τόνος)

Resources: For a comprehensive treatment of Greek accents, see D. A. Carson, *A Student's Manual of New Testament Greek Accents* (Grand Rapids: Baker, 1996). I have primarily drawn explanations and examples from M. A. North and A. E. Hillard, *Greek Prose Composition* (Durango, CO: Hollowbrook, 1993). The synopsis of the Heavy and Light Ultima Rules is from W. H. Harper and R. F. Weidner, *An Introductory New Testament Greek Method*, 7th ed. (New York: Scribners, 1895), 399.

A. **There are three accents:** acute (´), grave (`), and circumflex (˜).

B. **Names of Accent Positions:** Before proceeding, one must learn the names of the last three syllables of words. The last syllable is called the *ultima*, the one just before the ultima is the *penult*, and the one before the penult is the *antepenult*. Thus,

	antepenult	penult	ultima
ποταμός *river*	πο-	-τα-	-μός

C. **Restricted Location of Accents:** The acute accent (´) may be found on any of these syllables. The circumflex (˜) may be found <u>only</u> on heavy vowels, monophthongs, and diphthongs and <u>only</u> in the last two syllables (penult and ultima). The grave (`) may be found <u>only</u> on the last syllable (ultima).

D. **What Determines Accent Location:** Where the accents fall depends on the type of word and weight of the last syllable.

E. **Weight of Syllables:** Since the placement of accents depends on the respective weight of syllables (particularly the ultima), it is important to understand the weight of these vowels, monophthongs, and diphthongs.

ALWAYS LIGHT	**ALWAYS HEAVY**	**LIGHT OR HEAVY**
Vowels	**Vowels**	**Vowels**
ἒ ψιλόν ε and ὂ μικρόν ο	ἦτα η and ὦ μέγα ω	ἄλφα α, ἰῶτα ι, and ὖ ψιλόν υ
Mono- & Di-phthongs	**Mono- & Di-phthongs**	
ἄλφα-ἰῶτα -αι (except dative plural –αις)	*all others*	
ὂ μικρόν-ἰῶτα -οι (except dative plural –οις)	–αις and –οις forms	
Exception: -αι and -οι are considered heavy in the Optative Mood, which is rare in the Greek NT.		

F. **The Heavy Ultima Rule:** A word with a *heavy ultima*, if accented
  1. on the penult, has an acute accent; (ἀνθρώπου)
  2. on the ultima, has either a circumflex or an acute. (ἀκολουθεῖν; γυνή)

G. **The Light Ultima Rule:** A word with a *light ultima*, if accented
  1. on the antepenult, has an acute accent; (συνείδησις; διάκονος)
  2. on a light penult, has an acute accent; (εἰρημένον)
  3. on a heavy penult, has a circumflex accent; (ἀγαπᾶτε; μεῖζον)
  4. on the ultima, has an acute accent. (ἐθνικοί)

H. **The Grave Rule:** If a word is to be accented with an acute on the ultima, and that word is followed by another non-enclitic word (for enclitics, see below), then the acute is changed to a grave. For example, αὐτοὶ οὐκ; but note that this does not apply with an intervening punctuation mark: αὐτόν. εἶπον...

I. **Verb Accent Rules:** In verbs the accent normally tries to go as far towards the front of the verb as possible (i.e., away from the ultima) according to the rules of F. and G. above. This is called *recessive accentuation*. Here are the basic verb recessive accent rules:

    1. A verb form with a *heavy ultima* will generally be accented on the penult with an acute accent (πιστεύω).

    2. A verb form with a *light ultima* will generally be accented on the antepenult with an acute accent (πιστεύομεν); or if the verb only has only two syllables, a light ultima and a heavy penult, then it will be accented with a circumflex on the penult (ἦλθον).

    Note, however, that there are additional rules and exceptions for accenting verbs. These are:

    3. *Contracted syllables* retain their accented status, but must finally conform to the Light or Heavy Ultima Rules.

        a. For example, φιλέ+ω contracts to φιλῶ. For example, φιλε+έτω contracts to φιλείτω. This can be stated thus: when the first of the two contracting syllables is to be accented, a circumflex results; but when the second, then an acute. If neither contracted syllables would have received the accent, then the accent is an acute: φίλε+ε→ φίλει.

        b. The following verb forms are considered to be "contracted" forms (and thus has a circumflex):

            i. The subjunctive of all Aorist Passives: λυθῶ

            ii. The Subjunctive and Optative Present and 2nd Aorist Tenses for Μι Verbs (excluding verbs ending in -νυμι): τιθῶ and τιθεῖμεν (from τίθημι).

    4. The 2nd Aorist is accented on the ultima in the Active Infinitive (λαβεῖν) and Participle (λαβών) and 2nd singular Imperative (λαβοῦ) and on the penult in the Middle Infinitive forms (λαβέσθαι).

    5. An *acute* accent is found on the *ultima* in

        a. the following 2nd Aorists in the Imperative: εἰπέ, ἐλθέ, εὑρέ, ἰδέ, λαβέ.

        b. all active participles of Μι Verbs and all other participles ending in -ως or -εις: τιθείς, λυθείς, λελυκώς.

    6. The **recessive accent** is **retained** ("held back") on the penult in the following verb forms:

        a. 1st Aorist Active Infinitive (καταλῦσαι)

        b. all infinitives ending in -ναι (λελυκέναι)

        c. all Infinitives and Participles of the Perfect Middle/Passive (λελυμένος; ἀπολελύσθαι)

    7. In **Compound Verbs** the accent may not go back

        a. beyond the augment (παρέσχον, κατῆγον)

        b. beyond the last syllable of the preposition (ἀπόδος, ἐπίσχες)

        c. beyond the verbal part in Mi Verb Infinitives and Participles (ἀποδούς, ἀποδόσθαι)

        d. beyond the verbal part of 2nd singular Middle Imperatives on Mi Verbs compounded with a preposition of <u>one</u> syllable (προθοῦ; <u>but</u> μετάθου).

J. **Noun and Adjective Accent Rules:** Generally, in nouns accents are **retained** on the lexical form, but necessarily change when the form changes (e.g., the weight of the ultima).

    1. The accent on a noun must be observed in its nominative form. Patterns exist, however.

        a. Nouns with these nominative case endings have an acute on the ultima: -εύς, -ώ, -άς, -ίς (βασιλεύς). The same is true for adjectives that have these nominative singular endings: -ρός, -νός, -ής, -ύς, -ικός, -τός.

        b. These nouns and adjectives have an acute on the penult: most nouns ending in -ία and -τωρ (ῥήτωρ).

        c. The accent is **recessive** in the following words: neuter nouns ending in -μα and -ος (γράμμα→γράμμασιν), comparatives and superlatives (πονηρός,-ά,-όν → πονηρότερος,-α,-ον), and adjectives ending in -ιμος (φρόνιμος).

    2. In the First and Second Declension words with acute ultima, all genitives and datives receive a circumflex (ὁδός→ὁδοῦ, ὁδῷ).

    3. The genitive plural of all First Declension words have a circumflex on the ultima: -ῶν.

    4. The genitives and datives of Third Declension monosyllabic words (excluding participles) are accented on the ultima (χείρ→ χειρός, χεῖρες, χειρῶν)

    5. In words like πόλις and πῆχυς. the endings -εως, -εων are treated as one syllable.

K. **Proclitics** ("leaning forward") are words that have no accent and should be pronounced as if part of the next word. These include ἐν, ἐκ, ἐξ, ὡς, εἰ, οὐ, οὐκ, οὐχ and some forms of the definite article, namely, ὁ, ἡ, οἱ, αἱ. These may take an accent if followed by an **enclitic**.

L. **Enclitics** ("leaning on") are words that lose their own accent and should be pronounced with the preceding word. These include some forms of the 1st and 2nd personal pronoun (μου, μοι, με, σου, σοι, σε), the indefinite pronoun (τις, τι), the indefinite adverbs (που, ποτε, πω, πως), the particles γε, τε, τοι, περ and the indicative forms of εἰμί and φημί (except 2nd singular εἶ and φῇς). Words before enclitics either (1) retain an acute in the ultima (rather than switching to a grave), (2) add an acute to the ultima, if accented on the penult or antepenult, or (3) if a proclitic, receive an acute accent. (There are some exceptions to these rules!)

§25 Principal Parts of Verbs in Chapters 1-15

Regular Verbs throughout the Principal Parts (if they exist in the GNT)

Chapter	First	Second	Third	Fourth	Fifth	Sixth
3	βαπτίζω	βαπτίσω	ἐβάπτισα	-	βεβάπτισμαι	ἐβαπτίσθην
3	βλέπω	βλέψω	ἔβλεψα	-	-	-
3	γράφω	γράψω	ἔγραψα	γέγραφα	γέγραμμαι	ἐγραφην
3	διδάσκω	διδάξω	ἐδίδαξα	-	-	ἐδιδάχθην
10	διώκω	διώξω	ἐδίωξα	-	δεδίωγμαι	ἐδιώχθην
3	δοξάζω	δοξάσω	ἐδόξασα	-	δεδόξασμαι	ἐδοξάσθην
10	ἑτοιμάζω	-	ἡτοίμασα	ἡτοίμακα	ἡτοίμασμαι	ἡτοιμάσθην
3	εὐαγγελίζω	-	εὐηγγέλισα	-	εὐηγγέλισμαι	εὐηγγελίσθην
10	θαυμάζω	-	ἐθαύμασα	-	-	ἐθαυμάσθην
10	θεραπεύω	θεραπεύσω	ἐθεράπευσα	-	τεθεράπευμαι	ἐθεραπεύθην
10	καθίζω	καθίσω	ἐκάθισα	κεκάθικα	-	-
10	κηρύσσω	-	ἐκήρυξα	-	-	ἐκηρύχθην
10	κράζω	κράξω	ἔκραξα	κέκραγα	-	-
10	λύω	(λύσω)	ἔλυσα	(λέλυκα)	λέλυμαι	ἐλύθην
6	ἀπολυω (P, F, A, - Rp, Ap)					
3	πέμπω	πέμψω	ἔπεμψα	-	-	ἐπέμφθην
7	πιστεύω	πιστεύσω	ἐπίστευσα	πεπίστευκα	πεπίστευμαι	ἐπιστεύθην
3	σώζω	σώσω	ἔσωσα	σέσωκα	σέσω(σ)μαι	ἐσώθην

Almost Regular except for one Form

Chapter	First	Second	Third	Fourth	Fifth	Sixth
7	ἀκούω	ἀκούσω	ἤκουσα	ἀκήκοα	-	ἠκούσθην
		(ἀκούσομαι)				
10	ἀνοίγω	ἀνοίξω	ἤνοιξα (ἀνέῳξα) (ἠνέῳξα)	ἀνέῳγα	ἀνέῳγμαι (ἠ᾽νέῳγμαι)	ἠνοίχθην (ἀνεῴχθην) (ἠνεῴχθην)
10	ἐγγίζω	ἐγγίω	ἤγγισα	ἤγγικα	-	-
10	κλαίω	κλαύσω	ἔκλαυσα	-	-	-
10	πείθω	πείσω	ἔπεισα	πέποιθα	πέπεισμαι	ἐπείσθην

Middle-Formed Verbs (See also under 2nd Aorist)

Chapter	First	Second	Third	Fourth	Fifth	Sixth
6	ἀποκρίνομαι	-	ἀπεκρινάμην	-	-	ἀπεκρίθην
3	πορεύομαι	πορεύσομαι		-	πεπόρευμαι	ἐπορεύθην
3	προσεύχομαι	προσεύξομαι	προσηυξάμην	-		

Special Verbs

Chapter			
5	εἰμί (Present)	ἤμην (Imperfect)	ἔσομαι (Future)
10	οἶδα (Perfect, but Present meaning); ᾔδειν (Pluperfect, but Aorist meaning)		

2ND AORIST VERBS

CHAPTER	FIRST	SECOND	THIRD	FOURTH	FIFTH	SIXTH
8	ἄγω	ἄξω	ἤγαγον	-	(ἦγμαι)	ἤχθην
8	συνάγω (P, F, A, -, Rp, Ap)					
8	ὑπάγω (P, -, -, -, -, -)					
11	ἀναβαίνω	ἀναβήσομαι	ἀνέβην	ἀναβέβηκα	-	-
11	καταβαίνω (P, F, A, R, -, -)					
11	ἀποθνήσκω	ἀποθανοῦμαι	ἀπέθανον	-	-	-
8	βάλλω	βαλῶ	ἔβαλον	βέβληκα	βέβλημαι	ἐβλήθην
8	ἐκβάλλω (P, R, A, R, -, Ap)					
11	γίνομαι	γενήσομαι	ἐγενόμην	γέγονα	γεγένημαι	ἐγενήθην
11	γινώσκω	γνώσομαι	ἔγνων	ἔγνωκα	ἔγνωσμαι	ἐγνώσθην
11	ἐπιγινώσκω (R, F, A, R, - Ap)					
3	ἔρχομαι	ἐλεύσομαι	ἦλθον	ἐλήλυθα	-	-
3	ἀπέρχομαι (P, F, A, R, -, -)					
3	διέρχομαι (P, F, A, R, -, -)					
3	εἰσέρχομαι (P, F, A, R, -, -)					
3	ἐξέρχομαι (P, F, A, R, -, -)					
3	προσέρχομαι (P, -, A, R, -, -)					
11	ἐσθίω	φάγομαι	ἔφαγον	-	-	-
3	εὑρίσκω	εὑρήσω	εὗρον (εὗρα)	εὕρηκα	-	εὑρέθην
3	ἔχω	ἕξω	ἔσχον	ἔσχηκα	-	-
11	λαμβάνω	λήμψομαι	ἔλαβον	εἴληφα	-	ἐλήμφθην
11	παραλαμβάνω (P, F, A, -, -, παρελήμφθην)					
3	λέγω	ἐρῶ	εἶπον // εἶπα	εἴρηκα	εἴρημαι	ἐρρέθην
11	ὁράω	ὄψομαι	εἶδον εἶδα ὤψησα	ἑώρακα ἑόρακα	-	ὤφθην
8	πάσχω	-	ἔπαθον*	πέπονθα	-	-
11	πίνω	πίομαι	ἔπιον	πέπωκα	-	-
11	πίπτω	πέσομαι	ἔπεσον	πέπτωκα	-	-
8	φέρω	οἴσω	ἤνεγκα	(ἐνήνοχα)		ἠνέχθην
8	προσφέρω (P, -, A, R, -, Ap)					

§26 PRINCIPAL PARTS OF VERBS IN CHAPTERS 16-21

CHAPTER	FIRST	SECOND	THIRD	FOURTH	FIFTH	SIXTH
17	ὑπάρχω	ὑπάρξω	ὑπῆρξα	-	-	-

CONTRACT VERBS

CHAPTER	FIRST	SECOND	THIRD	FOURTH	FIFTH	SIXTH
20	ἀγαπάω	ἀγαπήσω	ἠγάπησα	ἠγάπηκα	ἠγάπημαι	ἠγαπήθην
20	αἰτέω	αἰτήσω	ᾔτησα	ᾔτηκα	-	-
20	ἀκολουθέω	ἀκολουθήσω	ἠκολούθησα	ἠκολούθηκα	-	-
20	γεννάω	γεννήσω	ἐγέννησα	γεγέννηκα	γεγέννημαι	ἐγεννήθην
20	δοκέω	δόξω	ἔδοξα	-	-	-
20	ἐπερωτάω	ἐπερωτήσω	ἐπηρώτησα	-	-	-
20	ἐρωτάω	ἐρωτήσω	ἠρώτησα	-	-	-
20	ζάω	ζήσω (ζήσομαι)	ἔζησα	-	-	-
20	ζητέω	ζητήσω	ἐζήτησα			ἐζητήθην

20	θεωρέω	θεωρήσω	ἐθεώρησα	-	-	-
20	καλέω	καλέσω	ἐκάλεσα	κέκληκα	κέκλημαι	ἐκλήθην
20	λαλέω	λαλήσω	ἐλάλησα	λελάληκα	λελάλημαι	ἐλαλήθην
20	μαρτυρέω	μαρτυρήσω	ἐμαρτύρησα	μεμαρτύρηκα	μεμαρτύρημαι	ἐμαρτυρήθην
20	παρακαλέω	-	παρεκάλεσα	-	παρακέκλημαι	παρεκλήθην
20	περιπατέω	περιπατήσω	περιεπάτησα	-	-	-
20	πληρόω	πληρώσω	ἐπλήρωσα	πεπλήρωκα	πεπλήρωμαι	ἐπληρώθην
20	ποιέω	ποιήσω	ἐποίησα	πεποίηκα	πεποίημαι	-
20	προσκυνέω	προσκυνήσω	προσκύνησα	-	-	-
20	τηρέω	τηρήσω	ἐτήρησα	τετήρηκα	τετήρημαι	ἐτηρήθην
20	φοβέω					ἐφοβήθην

LIQUID VERBS

CHAPTER	FIRST	SECOND	THIRD	FOURTH	FIFTH	SIXTH
21	αἴρω	ἀρῶ	ἦρα	ἦρκα	ἦρμαι	ἤρθην
21	ἀπαγγέλλω	ἀπαγγελῶ	ἀπήγγειλα	-	-	ἀπηγγέλθην
21	ἀποκτείνω	ἀποκτενῶ	ἀπέκτεινα	-	-	ἀπεκτάνθην
21	ἀποστέλλω	ἀποστελῶ	ἀπέστειλα	ἀπέσταλκα	ἀπέσταλμαι	ἀπεστάλην
21	ἐγείρω	ἐγερῶ	ἤγειρα	-	ἐγήγερμαι	ἠγέρθην
21	κρίνω	κρινῶ	ἔκρινα	κέκρικα	κέκριμαι	ἐκρίθην
21	μένω	μενῶ	ἔμεινα	μεμένηκα		
21	σπείρω	-	ἔσπειρα		ἔσπαρμαι	ἐσπάρην
21	χαίρω	χαιρήσομαι	-	-	-	ἐχάρην

§27 PRINCIPAL PARTS OF VERBS IN CHAPTERS 22-26

MIXED VERBS (MIDDLE-FORMED, LIQUID, IRREGULAR)

CHAPTER	FIRST	SECOND	THIRD	FOURTH	FIFTH	SIXTH
23	ἄρχομαι	ἄρξομαι	ἠρξάμην	-	-	-
25	ἀσπάζομαι	-	ἠσπασάμην	-	-	-
23	δεῖ	-	-	-	-	-
25	δέχομαι	-	ἐδεξάμην	-	δέδεγμαι	ἐδέχθην
23	δύναμαι	δύνησομαι	-	-	-	ἠδυνήθην
23	θέλω	-	ἠθέλησα	-	-	-
23	κάθημαι	καθήσομαι	καθῆκα	-	-	-
23	μέλλω	μελλήσω	-	-	-	-

Μι VERBS

CHAPTER	FIRST	SECOND	THIRD	FOURTH	FIFTH	SIXTH
24	ἀπόλλυμι	ἀπολέσω	ἀπώλεσα	ἀπολώλεκα	-	-
24	ἀπολῶ	ἀπόλωλα				
24	ἀφίημι	ἀφήσω	ἀφῆκα	-	ἀφέωμαι	ἀφέθην
24	δίδωμι	δώσω	ἔδωκα	δέδωκα	δέδομαι	ἐδόθην
24	ἀποδίδωμι (P,F,A,-,-,Ap)					
24	παραδίδωμι (P,F,A,Ra,Rp,Ap)					
24	ἵστημι	στήσω	ἔστησα (1st A) ἔστην (2nd A)	ἕστηκα	-	ἐστάθην
24	ἀνίστημι (P,F,A,-,-,-)					
24	παρίστημι (P,F,A,Ra,-,-)					
24	τίθημι	θήσω	ἔθηκα	τέθεικα	τέθειμαι	ἐτέθην
24	φημί					

§28 ERASMIAN PRONUNCIATION CONVENTION

A. Within the majority of the academic community, the Erasmian pronunciation is still the most common (even in its various forms!), although initially the system was a joke on Erasmus that he latter learned about.[1] See the work of John Schwandt who discusses various pronunciation systems (http://www.biblicalgreek.org/links/pronunciation.php), including the various Erasmian systems. Below is a chart from my earlier *Kairos: A Beginning Greek Grammar* (2005) that presents an Erasmian pronunciation that is followed by a discussion of diphthongs. For transliteration values, which are not pronunciation neutral, since they reproduce Erasmian pronunciation, see APPENDIX §29.

| Letter Name | | Small Letters | Capital Letters | Erasmian Sound Value | | |
In English	In Greek	(Minuscules)	(Uncials)			
alpha	ἄλφα	α	A	a	as in	father
bēta	βῆτα	β	B	b	as in	bark
gamma	γάμμα	γ	Γ	g	as in	get
delta	δέλτα	δ	Δ	d	as in	dog
epsilon	ἒ ψιλόν	ε	E	e	as in	bed
zēta	ζῆτα	ζ	Z	z	as in	zoo
ēta	ἦτα	η	H	ey	as in	prey
thēta	θῆτα	θ	Θ	th	as in	they
iōta	ἰῶτα	ι	I	i	as in	machine
kappa	κάππα	κ	K	k	as in	keen
lambda	λάμβδα	λ	Λ	l	as in	log
mu	μῦ	μ	M	m	as in	mouse
nu	νῦ	ν	N	n	as in	new
xi	ξῖ	ξ	Ξ	x	as in	ox
omicron	ὂ μικρόν	o	O	o	as in	pot
pi	πῖ	π	Π	p	as in	pie
rhō	ῥῶ	ρ	P	r	as in	run
sigma	σίγμα	σ, ς	Σ	s	as in	snake
tau	ταῦ	τ	T	t	as in	tell
upsilon	ὒ ψιλόν	υ	Υ	u	as in	use
phi	φῖ	φ	Φ	ph	as in	phone
chi	χῖ	χ	X	ch	as in	Bach
psi	ψῖ	ψ	Ψ	ps	as in	pseudo
ōmega	ὦ μέγα	ω	Ω	o	as in	obey

B. **Special Rules of Pronunciation**:
   1. The letter ***gamma*** before another *gamma*, *kappa*, *xi*, or *chi* is to be pronounced as an *n*. Thus, γγ is *ng*, γκ is *nk*, γξ is *nx*, and γχ is *nch*.
   2. When *sigma* comes at the end of a word it has a different form (-ς) which looks more like our English *s*. This is called a **final *sigma***. The other *sigma* (σ) is often called a **medial *sigma***.

C. **Vowels and Diphthongs**: Greek has seven vowels, nine proper diphthongs, and three improper diphthongs.
   1. <u>Vowels</u>: The Greek vowels in alphabetical order are α, ε, η, ι, o, υ, and ω. Vowels can be either light or heavy in weight. (Weight concerns how much stress is given). Epsilon (ε) and omicron (o) are always light. *Ēta* (η) and *ōmega* (ω) are always heavy. *Alpha* (α), *iōta* (ι), and *upsilon* (υ) can be either light or heavy.
   2. <u>Diphthongs</u>: A **diphthong** consists of two vowels that occur side-by-side with only one sound. Below are the **proper diphthongs** with pronunciation equivalents:

COMMON				THESE ARE RARE
αι as in *aisle*	ει as in *eight*	οι as in *oil*	υι as in *we*	ηυ as in f*eu*d
αυ as in c*ow*	ευ as in f*eu*d	ου as in f*oo*d		ωυ as in f*oo*d

---

[1] See Chrys C. Caragounis, "The Error of Erasmus and Un-Greek Pronunciations of Greek," *Filología Neotestamentaria* 8 (1995): 151–85.

3. <u>Improper Diphthongs</u>: The **improper diphthongs** are ᾳ, ῃ, and ῳ. Notice the small *iōta* **subscript**. These improper diphthongs arose when, at some point during the development of the language, *iōtas* dropped below the vowel they originally followed. Only these three vowels may have an *iōta* subscript. On the one hand, the *iōta* subscript *does not change* the pronunciation of *alpha* (α), *ēta* (η), and *ōmega* (ω); thus, they are called **improper diphthongs**. On the other hand, the presence or absence of the *iōta* subscript is *always* important grammatically and lexically to distinguish forms and words.

§29 TRANSLITERATION CONVENTION

Bible reference works such as lexicons, commentaries, monographs, and theological dictionaries will not infrequently contain Greek words transliterated into English character values. Such words are conventionally placed into italics. Below are the standard transliteration values of the Greek characters. However, beware that these values generally represent each letter's sound value in the Erasmian pronunciation. Hence, this is why γ *gamma* may need to be represented as a "g" or an "n."

ʽ	= *h* (before vowels)	ζ	= *z* (or *ds*)	ν	= *n*	τ	= *t*
α	= *a*	η	= *ē*	ξ	= *x*	υ	= *y*
β	= *b*	ϑ	= *th*	ο	= *o*	υ	= *u* (in diphthongs)
γ	= *g*	ι	= *i*	π	= *p*	φ	= *ph*
γ	= n (before γ, κ, ξ, or χ)	κ	= *k*	ρ	= *r*	χ	= *ch*
δ	= *d*	λ	= *l*	ῥ	= *rh*	ψ	= *ps*
ε	= *e*	μ	= *m*	σ, ς	= *s*	ω	= *ō*

An initial rough breathing mark (ʽ) over vowels or a *rhō* is transliterated as an *h* (see further below in 2.8). For example, ἡμέρα is transliterated *hēmera*. Notice that the accent mark (´) over the *epsilon* is not transliterated. The word ῥῆμα is transliterated *rhēma*. Furthermore, *gamma* is transliterated *n* before *gamma, kappa, xi,* or *chi*. *Upsilon* may be transliterated as *y* unless it is a part of a diphthong in which it then is transliterated as *u* (υι is transliterated *ui*; ου is transliterated *ou*). Here are some Greek words with their transliterated forms.

ἄγγελος → *angelos*	ϑέος → *theos*
βαπτίζω → *baptizō*	ἱλάσϑητι → *hilasthēti*
υἱός → *huios*	ψυχικός → *psychikos*
ὁμολογία → *homologia*	Χριστός → *Christos*

§30 THE PRONUNCIATION OF KOINE GREEK
by
T. Michael W. Halcomb

In the same way that it is in our best interest to learn the grammatical and syntactical ins and outs of Koine Greek, as this book has helped us do, it is to our benefit to have some understanding of the issues surrounding the matter of pronunciation. Because the majority of English-Greek grammar books employ the so-called Erasmian Pronunciation (I say "so-called" because Erasmus himself did not adopt it), and because professors have been using such textbooks for the last several hundred years, the overwhelming majority of students have accepted this framework without much question. Indeed, many have been taught that recovering any semblance of how Koine originally sounded is beyond possibility. Such a claim, however, simply misses the mark.

The reality is that we can know how Koine sounded. There are a number of resources readily available and at our disposal that can assist us in this regard. Before I mention just a couple of those, however, it will be helpful to understand a bit about the context out of which "Erasmian" took root and grew. For me this historical data is important and should not be divorced from discussions about whether Erasmian should continue to be used. At the same time it is not the "nail in the coffin," so to speak, or the strongest bit of information we have to move away from Erasmian to the Koine Era Pronunciation (KEP).

With regard to context, the 1400s-1600s A.D. in Europe are worthy of note, especially the locales of Greece and England. Given that I cannot provide an in-depth discussion of every significant event or person worthy of mention here, I must be selective. I want to draw our attention first, then, to the fact that in the years preceding the 1400s French and Latin were prominent across Europe but French was the language of power, politics, and social prestige. There came a shift around the 1500s, however, when French began to be replaced by English.

While there were many dialects of English, a standard began to emerge as it was developed at the behest of royalty.

The chancery (the chapel of the king) consisted of scribes and writers who worked at creating an English standard among themselves. Eventually this standard began to proliferate as it was used increasingly outside of the chancery. As English replaced French as the norm and as the chancery's English standard gained momentum, other institutions, especially the academy, began to take note and follow suit. These changes happened quite organically and, relatively speaking, over a period of hundreds of years.

This move toward an English standard also played a role in what is known as The Great Vowel Shift.[2] I cannot explain the shift here at length but it is worth pointing out that basically the vowels *a*, *e*, *i*, *o*, and *u*, along with *ai*, all shifted and took on a different sound. The influence of this change is hard to overestimate because even today's English remains directly affected by it. As it was occurring across the late 1400s to mid 1600s, those living at the time were also dramatically affected by it. We need to realize that Erasmus himself lived during this period, a period when matters pertaining French, Latin, and English, especially the latter, were very socially and politically charged. The pronunciation of English was at the forefront of many debates and discussions.

But this brings us to another matter, namely, the pronunciation of Greek. Following the Turkish invasion and conquering of the Greek-speaking Byzantine Empire in A.D. 1453, for the first time a sharp distinction was beginning to be made between Ancient Greek and Modern Greek. Prior to this point no one had ever really differentiated the two in such a substantive way and in such an aggressive historical manner. In the minds of many, the political misfortunes of the Greeks confirmed that they were weak and intellectually backward; this caused non-Greeks to despise them and avoid their language. This also caused Greeks to strive to "maintain their ethnic identity," which led them to turn in upon themselves, "jealously preserving their language and culture." As one author says, "The use of the Modern Greek pronunciation for the ancient language was only part of this larger phenomenon."[3] Thus, for the Greeks, the pronunciation of the language was a matter of national pride.

Yet, here, for the first time, Ancient Greek—and for our purposes, Koine Greek—was essentially declared dead. What had existed unbroken for thousands of years despite its various permutations and changes was now considered deceased. But the question must be asked: Who declared it a dead language? And the follow-up question: Why? We cannot necessarily pin the event of rendering Koine a dead language on one person. But when we look to figures such as the Spanish humanist Antonio Nebrija, who asserted that Hebrew, Greek, and Latin had ran their courses, and who spoke of "national awakening in all parts of the West," we learn that he may have been an early catalyst for changing the pronunciation of Greek.

Nebrija knew Erasmus and, in fact, Erasmus may have first heard of the non-historical pronunciation from Nebrija. It should be pointed out here that Erasmus himself never adopted what later became known as the "Erasmian Pronunciation." In fact, Erasmus held to a Modern Greek pronunciation. What happened was that Erasmus wrote a fable about a lion and a bear using different Greek pronunciations, one which was based on Modern Greek and the other which was based on English, and this tale became widely popular.

As matters of language change were on the rise and as Greeks were ousted from their academic teaching posts in ancient literature departments and replaced by non-native Greek speakers, the historian and grammarian A. N. Jannaris notes, "The first act ... was to do away with the traditional pronunciation—which reflects perhaps the least changed part of the language—and then to declare Greek a dead tongue."[4] Many jumped on the bandwagon with this thinking. Then, with enough academic elites and social powerhouses on board, the new English-based pronunciation began to spread quickly.

Friedrich Blass, a professor and author living in the 1800s, who, even in his time referred to the Greeks of his day as half-barbarians and their pronunciation as barbaric,[5] along with numerous other leading thinkers such as Martin Luther, "Philipp Melanchthon, Johann Sturm, and their many associates and followers," had "adopted Erasmus' teaching methods and textbooks as the basis of their educational reforms."[6] To be sure, Erasmus talked about pronunciation in some of his works,

---

[2] For an accessible discussion of this see Seth Lerer, *The History of the English Language*, 2nd ed. (Springfield, VA: The Teaching Company, 2008), 37-45.

[3] T. Michael W. Halcomb, "Never Trust A Greek ... Professor: Revisiting the Question of How Koine Was Pronounced," paper presented at the annual meeting of the Stone-Campbell Journal Conference, Knoxville, TN, 14 March 2014.

[4] A. N. Jannaris, *An Historical Greek Grammar Chiefly of the Attic Dialect As Written and Spoken From Classical Antiquity Down to the Present Time: Founded Upon Ancient Texts, Inscriptions, Papyri and Present Popular Greek* (London: Macmillan, 1897), viii.

[5] Attributed to F. Blass in Chrys C. Caragounis, "The Error of Erasmus and Un-Greek Pronunciations of Greek," *Filología Neotestmentaria* 8 (1995), endnote 12. I was unable to gain access to the cited source firsthand.

[6] Judith R. Henderson, "Erasmian Ciceronians: Reformation Teachers of Letter-Writing," *Rhetorica* 10.3 (Summer, 1992): 274.

especially the aforementioned fable. This led people to believe that he himself was an advocate of the pronunciation that be-came attached to his name.

These circumstances reveal that the socio-political climate of the day was ripe for the proliferation of the Erasmian pronunciation. Thus, there was not simply one person responsible for the so-called death of Koine, but rather many in the acad-emy. Declaring Greek dead was a socio-political move; indeed, it allowed the academy to drive a wedge between Ancient and Modern Greek. In doing so, the academics could refer to Ancient Greek as "their Greek," while the Modern Greeks could deal with Modern Greek. This division—a false historical dichotomy between Ancient and Modern Greek—has persisted even until today in the academy; the main progenitors of it have been Western colleges, universities, and seminaries.

In my opinion, it would not only be a just act but also a historically responsible one to move away from Erasmian to the Koine Era Pronunciation (KEP). And in spite of the oft-heard claim that we cannot know it, we surely can. One of the main ways that we can recover the KEP is by comparing "orthographical substitutions," that is, spelling interchanges between docu-ments containing the same text or the same words across different documents. I prefer to call these spelling differences "inter-changes" rather than "mistakes" or "errors" as some like Bart Ehrman do, because they were in fact not always errors. To arrive at such a conclusion one must force modern expectations about reading and writing back on to ancient authors and scribes. Be-fore the rise of modernism, what was written (literary works, letters, documents, etc.) was meant to be read aloud and was composed for the ear. Thus, as long as what was on the page produced the proper sounds and words when spoken, it was con-sidered good, acceptable, and meaningful.

To use a very simple example from English, we might say that when spoken aloud, the word "meen" in the statement "The boy is meen" produces the correct sound to hearers, although it is (mis)spelled "meen" rather than complying with our modern standard of "mean"; yet "meen" would nonetheless have been understood *by hearers*. In fact, if one were to write an entire lecture with words whose spellings were considered atypical, the audience would likely never know about the spelling interchanges. The only way they would know is to look at the manuscript. If they were to view the manuscript, they would then see the non-standard spellings rather than the well-known standard spellings. If listeners were to do this, they would realize that in English "ee" and "ea" make the same sound and are, to the ear, completely interchangeable. This is actually one way that we can reconstruct how Koine sounded, too. If we compare how words were spelled in ancient writings to a more common stand-ard spelling, we can recover which letters sounded alike or different. For instance, one ancient work spells the number three as τρις. When we compare this with the standard spelling τρεις, we learn that Koine ι and ει were often interchanged and thus sounded exactly alike.

In addition to comparing non-standard spellings with standard spellings, we can often just compare words across a single document. For instance, in Papyrus 66 the scribe used both τρις and τρεις; even though they are spelled differently in the document, they made the same sound when read aloud and were thus considered good and acceptable. Beyond this type of analysis, many other ways to recover the KEP exist: We can read, for example, ancient texts that talked about pronunciation; we can look for rhyme and assonance in poetry (this gives us clues as to which letters and syllables sounded alike); we can use tools from the field of historical phonology/linguistics to help chart both synchronic and diachronic sound change.

At the end of the day, it is simply erroneous to claim that we cannot know how Koine sounded. The bald claim that such a task is beyond recovery finally needs to be put to rest. As scholars, researchers, teachers, and learners, our role should not be to regurgitate statements we may have read or heard along the way without checking to see whether or not they can be substantiated. Instead, if we are in the business of teaching truth and doing so in a true manner, then we will let the evidence lead us. I am convinced with regard to the pronunciation of Koine that such evidence abounds; for this reason I have left Erasmian behind and embraced the KEP.

VOCABULARY: WORDS OCCURRING 20 TIMES OR MORE

The following vocabulary includes words occurring 20 words or more, depending on which GNT one consults (UBS or SBLGNT). Occasionally, you will find a bonus word occurring 19 times. The definitions are glosses; they are not comprehensive. The chapter in which the word was formally introduced is given before the word. If a word has no chapter number, it is not formally introduced in the handbook. The gender of the noun is indicated after the noun (m, f, n). The genitive form of Third Declension nouns is always given. Adjectives are distinguished by their endings for each gender (e.g., ος, -η, -ον = m, f, n). If only two endings are given, then the first ending is both masculine and feminine; this is a dual termination adjective. All the verbs presented in this handbook are given below according to their six Principal Parts. If there is a dash (-), this indicates that this particular Principal Part is absent in the GNT. Alternative forms of a Principal Part are put into parentheses immediately after the form. For some compound verbs, the Principal Parts are not all provided, since theses forms may be readily observed on the uncompounded verb forms. Finally, frequencies are given in superscripts.

ἄλφα

2	Ἀβραάμ[78]	Abraham
7	ἀγαθός, -ή, -όν[125]	good, beneficial
20	ἀγαπάω, ἀγαπήσω, ἠγάπησα, ἠγάπηκα, ἠγάπημαι, ἠγαπήθην[143]	I love
15	ἀγάπη[116] f	love
14	ἀγαπητός, -η, -ον[61]	beloved, dearly loved
5	ἄγγελος[175] m	angel, messenger
	ἁγιάζω[28]	I sanctify, consecrate
7	ἅγιος, -α, -ον[233]	holy; devout; οἱ ἅγιοι = saints
	ἀγνοέω[22]	I do not know; I am ignorant
	ἀγοράζω[30]	I buy, purchase
	ἀγρός[36] m	field; countryside; farm
8	ἄγω, ἄξω, ἤγαγον, -, -, ἤχθην[69]	I lead; I bring, carry
	ἀδελφή[26] f	sister; fellow believer
5	ἀδελφός[342] m	brother
	ἀδικέω[28]	I wrong, treat unjustly; I harm
	ἀδικία[25] f	wrongdoing, injustice, unrighteousness
	Αἴγυπτος, -ου[25] f	Egypt
13	αἷμα, -ατος[97] n	blood; bloodshed
21	αἴρω, ἀρῶ, ἦρα, ἦρκα, ἦρμαι, ἤρθην[101]	I raise, lift up; I take away
20	αἰτέω, αἰτήσω, ᾔτησα, ᾔτηκα, -, -[70]	I ask, demand
	αἰτία[20] f	cause, reason; accusation
12	αἰών, αἰῶνος[122] m	age, era; life span; eternity
14	αἰώνιος, -ον[69]	eternal, long-lasting
	ἀκάθαρτος, -ον[32]	unclean(sed), impure; defiled
	ἀκοή[24] f	hearing; report, news
20	ἀκολουθέω, ἀκολουθήσω, ἠκολούθησα, ἠκολούθηκα, -, -[89]	I follow, obey (+ dat.)
7	ἀκούω, ἀκουσω (ἀκούσομαι), ἤκουσα, ἀκήκοα, -, ἠκούσθην[428]	I hear; I obey (+ acc. or gen.)
	ἀκροβυστία[20] f	uncircumcision
4	ἀλήθεια[109] f	truth, reality
22	ἀληθής, -ές[26]	true, truthful
	ἀληθινός, -ή, -όν[28]	true, faithful
4	ἀλλά[638]	but (+ correction); yet, rather
19	ἀλλήλων[100]	one another
7	ἄλλος, -η, -ον[154]	other; another
	ἁμαρτάνω, ἁμαρτήσω, ἡμάρτησα, ἡμάρτηκα, -, -[43]	I miss the mark; I fail, go wrong, sin

15	ἁμαρτία[172] f	sin, failure; guilt
22	ἁμαρτωλός, -όν[47]	sinful; sinner (*noun*)
15	ἀμήν[128]	Amen! Certainly!
	ἀμπελών, -ῶνος[23] m	vineyard
26	ἄν[170]	*particle of potential circumstance or condition*
11	ἀναβαίνω, ἀναβήσομαι, ἀνέβην, ἀναβέβηκα,-,-[81]	I go up, ascend
	ἀναβλέπω[25]	I look up; I receive sight
	ἀναγινώσκω[32]	I read
	ἀνάγω[23]	I lead up; I carry by sea (*mid.*)
	ἀναιρέω[24]	I take up; I destroy, kill
16	ἀνάστασις, -εως[42] f	resurrection
	ἄνεμος[31] m	wind
12	ἀνήρ, ἀνδρός[216] m	man; husband
5	ἄνθρωπος[550] m	person, human; people (*pl.*)
24	ἀνίστημι[108] (P, F, A, -, -, -) (*from* ἵστημι)	I raise up; I resurrect
10	ἀνοίγω, ἀνοίξω, ἤνοιξα, ἀνέῳγα, ἀνέῳγμαι, ἠνοίχθην[77]	I open
	ἀντί[22] (*with genitive*)	over against; in place of; for
22	ἄξιος, -α, -ον[41]	worthy
21	ἀπαγγέλλω, ἀπαγγελῶ, ἀπήγγειλα, -, -, ἀπηγγέλθην[45]	I report, declare
12	ἅπας, -ασα, -αν[34]	(quite) all, every; whole
6	ἀπέρχομαι[117] (P, F, A, Ra, -, -) (*from* ἔρχομαι)	I go away, depart
	ἄπιστος, -ον[23]	unfaithful; incredible; unbeliever (*noun*)
6	ἀπό, ἀπ', ἀφ'[645] (*with genitive*)	from
24	ἀποδίδωμι[48] (P, F, A, -, -, Ap) (*from* δίδωμι)	I deliver; I pay
11	ἀποθνήσκω, ἀποθανοῦμαι, ἀπέθανον, -, -, -[111]	I die
	ἀποκαλύπτω[26]	I uncover, reveal, disclose
6	ἀποκρίνομαι, -, ἀπεκρινάμην, -, -, ἀπεκρίθην[232]	I answer back, reply (+ *dat.*)
21	ἀποκτείνω, ἀποκτενῶ, ἀπέκτεινα, -, -, ἀπεκτάνθην[74]	I kill, slay
24	ἀπόλλυμι, ἀπολέσω (ἀπολῶ), ἀπώλεσα, ἀπολώλεκα (ἀπόλωλα), -, -[90]	I destroy (*active*); I perish (*middle*)
6	ἀπολύω[67] (P, F, A, -, Rp, Ap) (*from* λύω)	I release, send away; I pardon
21	ἀποστέλλω, ἀποστελῶ, ἀπέστειλα, ἀπέσταλκα, ἀπέσταλμαι, ἀπεστάλην[131]	I send (off)
5	ἀπόστολος[79] m	delegate, apostle
	ἅπτω[39]	I fasten; I light; I touch (mid.)
25	ἄρα[53]	therefore
	ἀργύριον[20] n	silver (coin); money
	ἀρνέομαι[33]	I deny, disown; I decline, refuse
	ἀρνίον[30] n	little sheep; lamb
	ἄρτι[36]	just (now); presently
9	ἄρτος[174] m	bread, loaf; food
17	ἀρχή[55] f	beginning; rule, power
16	ἀρχιερεύς, -έως[122] m	high priest, chief priest
23	ἄρχομαι, ἄρξομαι, ἠρξάμην, -, -, -[86]	I begin to; I am
12	ἄρχων, ἄρχοντος[37] m	ruler
	ἀσθένεια[24] f	weakness; sickness
	ἀσθενέω[33]	I am weak, feeble, sick
22	ἀσθενής, -ές[26]	weak; sick
25	ἀσπάζομαι, -, ἠσπασάμην, -, -, -[59]	I greet, welcome; I embrace
	ἀστήρ, ἀστέρος[24] m	(shooting) star; fire

αὐξάνω[23]   I cause to grow; I increase in power

9   αὐτός, -ή, -ό [5569]   he, she, it

9   αὐτοί, -αί, -ά   they

24   ἀφίημι, ἀφήσω, ἀφῆκα, -, ἀφέωμαι, ἀφέθην[143]   I send off, release; I permit; I forgive (+ *dat.*)

22   ἀχρίς[49] (*with genitive*)   as far as; until (*conjunction*)

βῆτα

8   βάλλω, βαλῶ, ἔβαλον, βέβληκα, βέβλημαι, ἐβλήθην[122]   I cast, throw; I place

3   βαπτίζω, βαπτίσω, ἐβάπτισα, -, βεβάπτισμαι, ἐβαπτίσθην[77]   I soak, submerge, wash; I baptize

βάπτισμα, -ατος[19] *n*   baptism

Βαρναβᾶς, -ᾶ[2] *m*   Barnabas

4   βασιλεία[162] *f*   kingdom, reign

16   βασιλεύς, -έως[115] *m*   king

βασιλεύω[21]   I am king; I reign, rule

βαστάζω[27]   I bear, carry (away)

βιβλίον[34] *n*   paper; document, book

βλασφημέω[34]   I revile sacred things, blaspheme; I slander

3   βλέπω, βλέψω, ἔβλεψα, -, -, -[133]   I see, observe

βούλομαι[37]   I wish; I intend

γάμμα

15   Γαλαλία[61] *f*   Galilee

γαμέω[28]   I marry; I give in marriage (mid.)

8   γάρ [1039] (*postpositive*)   For, because

γε[26] (*postpositive*)   indeed, at least; really, even

15   γενεά[43] *f*   generation; age; kind

20   γεννάω, γεννήσω, ἐγέννησα, γεγέννηκα, γεγέννημαι, ἐγεννήθην[97]   I bear, give birth; I parent

γένος, -ους[20] *n*   race; family, descendant; kind

15   γῆ [250] *f*   land; earth

11   γίνομαι, γενήσομαι, ἐψένομην, γέγονα, γεγένημαι, ἐγενήθην[667]   I become, am; I come; I happen

11   γινώσκω, γνώσομαι, ἔγνων, ἔγνωκα, ἔγνωσμαι, ἐγνώσθην[221]   I know, understand

17   γλῶσσα[50] *f*   language; tongue

γνωρίζω[25]   I make known; I know

γνῶσις, -εως[29] *f*   inquiry; knowledge

γονεύς, -έως[20] *m*   parent

16   γραμματεύς, -έως[63] *m*   scribe, law expert

17   γραφή[49] *f*   Scripture; writing

3   γράφω, γράψω, ἔγραψα, γέγραφα, γέγραμμαι, ἐγράφην[192]   I write

γρηγορέω[22]   I am awake, remain alert

13   γυνή, γυναικός[216] *f*   woman; wife

δέλτα

5   δαιμόνιον[63] *n*   demon, spirit, inferior deity

2   Δαυίδ[59]   David

4   δέ [2777] (*postpositive*)   *signifies a new development*; and, but, moreover, additionally

23   δεῖ[101]   it is necessary to

δεικνύω or δείκνυμι[33]   I show, point out, make known

δέκα[25]   ten

δένδρον[25] *n*   tree

14   δεξιός, -ά, -όν[54]   right (*vs. left*)

	δέομαι[22]	I am in need (of); I ask, beg
22	δεύτερος, -α, -ον[43]	second
25	δέχομαι, -, ἐδεξάμην, -, δέδεγμαι, ἐδέχθην[56]	I receive, welcome; I take
	δέω, -, ἔδησα, δέδεκα, δέδεμαι, ἐδέθην[43]	I bind, tie
6	διά, δι᾿ [666] with genitive // accusative	through // on account of, because of
	διάβολος, -ον[37]	slanderous; accuser, the Devil (noun)
	διαθήκη[33] f	will, testament; covenant
	διακονέω[37]	I serve, administer
	διακονία[34] f	service, (ad)ministering
	διάκονος[29] m/f	servant, minister; deacon
	διδασκαλία[21] f	teaching, instruction
5	διδάσκαλος[59] m	teacher, master
3	διδάσκω, διδάξω, ἐδίδαξα, -, -, ἐδιδάχθην[97]	I teach, instruct
	διδαχή[30] f	teaching
24	δίδωμι, δώσω, ἔδωκα, δέδωκα, δέδομαι, ἐδόθην[415]	I give, entrust
6	διέρχομαι[43] (P, F, A, R, -, -) (from ἔρχομαι)	I pass through/over
7	δίκαιος, -α, -ον[79]	righteous, just, fair
4	δικαιοσύνη[91] f	righteousness, justice
	δικαιόω[39]	I set right; I justify, pronounce righteous
25	διό[53]	wherefore, therefore
	διότι[23]	because; wherefore
10	διώκω, διώξω, ἐδίωξα, -, δεδίωγμαι, ἐδιώχθην[45]	I pursue; I persecute
20	δοκέω, δόξω, ἔδοξα, -, -, -[62]	I think; I suppose; I seem
	δοκιμάζω[22]	I examine, test, prove, approve
15	δόξα[165] f	glory, splendor; reputation
3	δοξάζω, δοξάσω, ἐδόξασα, -, δεδόξασμαι, ἐδοξάσθην[61]	I glorify, honor, esteem
	δουλεύω[25]	I am a slave; I am subjected to
9	δοῦλος[126] m	slave; servant
23	δύναμαι, δυνήσομαι, -, -, -, ἠδυνήθην[209]	I am able to
16	δύναμις, -εως[119] f	power; miracle
	δυνατός, -ή, -όν[32]	powerful, able, capable
14	δυό (δυσί dative plural) [135]	two
14	δώδεκα[75]	twelve

ἒ ψιλόν

22	ἐάν [330]	if, (when)ever
26	ἐάν μή [48]	unless; if not
19	ἑαυτοῦ[321]	of himself, herself, itself
10	ἐγγίζω, ἐγγίω, ἤγγισα, ἤγγικα, -, -[42]	I draw near, approach
	ἐγγύς[31]	near, close
21	ἐγείρω, ἐγερῶ, ἤγειρα, -, ἐγήγερμαι, ἠγέρθην[143]	I raise up
	ἔγνων, ἔγνωκα, ἔγνωσμαι, ἐγνώσθην	see γινώσκω
9	ἐγώ [1805]	I
16	ἔθνος, -ους[160] n	nation; Gentile
8	εἰ [502]	if, whether
26	εἰ μή [92]	except; if not
	εἶδον, εἶδα	see ὁράω
	εἰκών, -όνος[23] f	image, likeness; (coin) portrait
	εἴληφα	see λαμβάνω

	Greek	English
5	εἰμί, ἔσομαι, -, -, -, -[2458]	I am, exist
	εἶπον, εἶπα	*see* λέγω
	εἴρηκα, εἴρημαι	*see* λέγω
4	εἰρήνη[91] *f*	peace; well-being
6	εἰς[1857] (*with accusative*)	into, to; for (*may express a purpose*)
12	εἷς, μία, ἕν[344]	one, single
6	εἰσέρχομαι[193] (P, F, A, Ra, -, -) (*from* ἔρχομαι)	I go into, enter
25	εἴτε[65]	whether, if; or
25	εἴτε … εἴτε	whether … or
6	ἐκ, ἐξ[913] (*with genitive*)	from, out of
7	ἕκαστος, -η, -ον[82]	each
	ἑκατοντάρχης (or -αρχος), -ου[20] *m*	centurion
8	ἐκβάλλω[81] (P, F, A, Ra, -, Ap) (*from* βάλλω)	I throw out
	ἐκεῖθεν[27]	from that place; thence, thereafter
12	ἐκεῖνος, -η, -ο[243]	that (one); those (*pl.*)
4	ἐκκλησία[114] *f*	assembly, church
	ἐκλέγομαι[22]	I select, choose
	ἐκλεκτός, -ή, -όν[22]	chosen, elect, select
	ἐκπορεύομαι[33]	I come or go out
	ἐκχέω[27]	I pour out
	ἐλεέω[29]	I have mercy (on), show mercy
	ἔλεος, -ους[27] *n*	pity, mercy, compassion
	ἐλεύθερος, -α, -ον[23]	free
	ἐλεύσομαι, ἐλήλυθα	*see* ἔρχομαι
	Ἕλλην, -ηνος[25] *m*	a Greek (person)
	ἐλπίζω[31]	I hope, expect
13	ἐλπίς, ἐλπίδος[53] *f*	hope
19	ἐμαυτοῦ[37]	of myself
19	ἐμός[68]	my, mine
	ἔμπροσθεν[48] (*with genitive*)	before, in front of, ahead of
6	ἐν[2737] (*with dative*)	in, among, with
	ἐνδύω[27]	I dress; I put on (mid.)
	ἕνεκα or ἕνεκεν[26] (*with genitive*)	on account of, for the sake of
	ἐνεργέω[21]	I work, energize, operate
4	ἐντολή[66] *f*	commandment, order
6	ἐνώπιον[94] (*with genitive*)	before, face to face, in view of
6	ἐξέρχομαι[217] (P, F, A, Ra, -, -) (*from* ἔρχομαι)	I go out, exit
	ἔξεστι(ν)[34] (*impersonal verb*)	it is right, proper, permitted
15	ἐξουσία[102] *f*	authority; power
22	ἔξω[62]	outside
	ἑορτή[25] *f*	feast
17	ἐπαγγελία[52] *f*	promise
	ἐπεί[26]	since, because; when
20	ἐπερωτάω[156] (P, F, A, -, -, -) (*from* ἐρωτάω)	I ask, inquire
10	ἐπί, ἐπ', ἐφ'[887] *with genitive// dative// accusative*	on, over// on, near// on, to, toward
11	ἐπιγινώσκω[44] (P, F, A, R, -, Ap) (*from* γινώσκω)	I know about; I understand
	ἐπίγνωσις, -εως[20] *f*	knowledge, recognition
	ἐπιθυμία[38] *f*	eager desire, passion, lust

	ἐπικαλέω[30]	I call (upon); I invoke
	ἐπιστολή[24] f	letter, epistle
	ἐπιστρέφω[36]	I turn (around)
	ἐπιτίθημι[39]	I lay upon; I impose, inflict
	ἐπιτιμάω[29]	I show honor to; I rebuke, warn
14	ἑπτά[88]	seven
	ἐργάζομαι, -, ἠργασάμην (εἰργασάμην), -, εἴργασμαι, -[41]	I work, perform, accomplish
9	ἔργον[169] n	work, activity; accomplishment
22	ἔρημος, -ον[48]	desolate; desert (noun)
3	ἔρχομαι, ἐλεύσομαι, ἦλθον, ἐλήλυθα, -, -[633]	I come, I go
	ἐρῶ, ἐρρέθην	see λέγω
20	ἐρωτάω, ἐρωτήσω, ἠρώτησα, -, -, -[63]	I ask, inquire
11	ἐσθίω, φάγομαι, ἔφαγον, -, -, -[158]	I eat, consume
	ἔσομαι	Future of εἰμί
	ἔστησα (or ἔστην), ἔστηκα, -, ἐστάθην	see ἵστημι
14	ἔσχατος, -η, -ον[52]	last; end
7	ἕτερος, -α, -ον[97]	different; another
7	ἔτι[93]	yet, still
10	ἑτοιμάζω, -, ἡτοίμασα, ἡτοίμακα, ἡτοίμασμαι, ἡτοιμάσθην[40]	I make ready, prepare
16	ἔτος, -ους[49] n	year
5	εὐαγγέλιον[75] n	good news, gospel
3	εὐαγγελίζομαι, -, εὐηγγέλισα, -, εὐηγγείσμαι, εὐηγγελίσθην[54]	I announce the good news
	εὐδοκέω[21]	I am well pleased or content with
22	εὐθύς/εὐθεώς[59]	immediately, at once; directly
	εὐλογέω, εὐλογήσω, εὐλόγησα, εὐλόγηκα, εὐλόγημαι, -[41]	I speak well of, praise, bless
3	εὑρίσκω, εὑρήσω, εὗρον (or εὗρα), εὕρηκα, -, εὑρέθην[176]	I find, discover
	εὐχαριστέω[38]	I am thankful, give thanks
	ἔφη	Imperfect 3 sg. of φημί
	ἐφίστημι[21]	I come upon; I stand at
	ἐχθρός, -ά, -όν[32]	hated; hostile; an enemy (noun)
3	ἔχω, ἕξω, ἔσχον, ἔσχηκα, -, -[707]	I have; I am
	ἑώρακα (or ἑόρακα)	see ὁράω
11	ἕως[145] (with genitive)	until, as far as, up to; while (as conj.)
26	ἕως ἄν	until

ζῆτα

20	ζάω, ζήσω (ζήσομαι), ἔζησα, -, -, -[140]	I live
20	ζητέω, ζητήσω, ἐζήτησα, -, -, ἐζητήθην[117]	I seek, search; I inquire
4	ζωή[135] f	life; existence
	ζῷον[23] n	living creature, animal

ἦτα

25	ἤ[346]	or; than (with μᾶλλον)
	ἤ … ἤ	either … or
	ἡγεμών, -όνος[20] m	leader; Roman governor
	ἡγέομαι[28]	I lead, guide; I consider
8	ἤδη[60]	already; now
	ἥκω[28]	I have come; I am present
	Ἠλίας, -ου[29] m	Elijah
	ἥλιος[32] m	the sun

9	ἡμεῖς[865]	we
4	ἡμέρα[389] *f*	day
19	ἡμέτερος, -α, -ον[7]	our, ours
	ἤνεγκα, ἠνέχθην	*see* φέρω
	ἦρα, ἦρκα, ἦρμαι, ἤρθην	*see* αἴρω
	ἤτησα, ἤτηκα	*see* αἰτέω
4	Ἡρῴδης, -ου[43] *m*	Herod
	Ἠσαΐας, -ου[22] *m*	Isaiah

θῆτα

15	θάλασσα[91] *f*	lake, sea
9	θάνατος[120] *m*	death
10	θαυμάζω, -, ἐθαύμασα, -, -, ἐθαυμάσθην[43]	I wonder, am amazed
	θεάομαι[22]	I behold
13	θέλημα, -ατος[62] *n*	will, desire
23	θέλω, -, ἠθέλησα, -, -, -[208]	I will, wish, want to
5	θεός[1307] *m*	God; god
10	θεραπεύω, θεραπεύσω, ἐθεράπευσα, -, τεθεράπευμαι, ἐθεραπεύθην[43] I heal; I serve	
	θερίζω[21]	I reap, harvest
20	θεωρέω, θεωρήσω, ἐθεώρησα, -, -, -[58]	I behold, see, view (as spectator)
18	θηρίον[46] *n*	wild beast
16	θλῖψις, -εως[45] *f*	affliction; persecution
18	θρόνος[62] *m*	throne, chair, seat
	θυγάτηρ, -τρός[28] *f*	daughter
	θύρα[39] *f*	door, gate
	θυσία[28] *f*	sacrifice, offering
	θυσιαστήριον[23] *n*	altar, sanctuary

ἰῶτα

	Ἰακώβ[27] *m*	Jacob
2	Ἰάκωβος[42] *m*	Jacob/James
	ἰάομαι[26]	I heal, cure
	ἴδε[28]	See! Behold! (*draws attention*)
7	ἴδιος, -α, -ον[114]	one's own
15	ἰδού[200]	Behold! Look! (*draws attention*)
	ἱερεύς, -έως[31] *m*	priest, sacrificer
18	ἱερόν[72] *n*	temple; holy place
2	Ἰερουσαλήμ[77]/Ἱεροσόλυμα[63] *f/m*	Jerusalem
5	Ἰησοῦς[911] *m*	Jesus; Joshua
	ἱκανός, -ή, -όν[39]	sufficient, considerable; competent
18	ἱμάτιον[60] *n*	garment
22	ἵνα[663]	in order that; that
4	Ἰουδαία[43] *f*	Judea
7	Ἰουδαῖος, -α, -ον[195]	Judean, Jewish; Jew
16	Ἰούδας, -α[49] *m*	Judas, Judah
	Ἰσαάκ[20] *m*	Isaac
2	Ἰσραήλ[68] *m*	Israel
24	ἵστημι, στήσω, ἔστησα (ἔστην), ἕστηκα,-, ἐστάθην[154]	I cause to stand; I set up (*1st Aor*); I stand (*2nd Aor*)
	ἰσχυρός, -ά, -όν[29]	strong
	ἰσχύω[28]	I am strong, able

ἰχθύς, -ύος²⁰ *m*   fish
4   Ἰωάννης, -ου¹³⁵ *m*   John
     Ἰωσήφ³⁵ *m*   Joseph

κάππα

9   κἀγώ⁸³ = καὶ ἐγώ   and I, even I
     καθαρίζω³¹   I make clean, cleanse
     καθαρός, -ά, -όν²⁷   clean, pure; innocent
     καθεύδω²²   I sleep
23   κάθημαι, καθήσομαι, καθῆκα, -, -, -⁹¹   I sit, am sitting
10   καθίζω, καθίσω, ἐκάθισα, κεκάθικα, -, -⁴⁶   I sit; I seat; I stay
     καθίστημι²¹   I set down; I set in order, appoint
16   καθώς¹⁸²   just as, corresponding to
4   καί⁸⁹⁸⁴   and; also, even
4   καί … καί   both … and
22   καινός, -ή, -όν⁴²   new
9   καιρός¹⁷⁴ *m*   season, time; opportunity
     Καῖσαρ, -ος²⁹ *m*   Caesar
14   κακός, -η, -ον⁵⁰   bad; evil
20   καλέω, καλέσω, ἐκάλεσα, κέκληκα, κέκλημαι, ἐκλήθην¹⁴⁸   I call; I name; I invite
7   καλός, -ή, -όν¹⁰¹   good; beautiful; noble
     καλῶς³⁶   well, beautifully
15   καρδία¹⁵⁶ *f*   heart
18   καρπός⁶⁶ *m*   fruit, produce; profit
8   κατά, κατ᾽, καθ᾽ ⁴⁷⁰ *with with genitive // accusative* against; down from // according to
11   καταβαίνω⁸⁰ (P, F, A, R, -, -) (*see* ἀναβαίνω)   I go down, descend
     καταλείπω²⁴   I leave (behind); I forsake
     καταργέω²⁷   I make of no effect, nullify; I annul, abolish
     κατεργάζομαι²²   I accomplish, bring about
     κατηγορέω²³   I accuse
     κατοικέω, -, κατῴκησα, -, -, -⁴⁴   I dwell in, inhabit
     καυχάομαι³⁷   I boast, am proud of
     κεῖμαι²⁴   I lie, recline; I am set up, established
     κέκληκα, κέκλημαι   *see* καλέω
     κελεύω²⁵   I urge, exhort; I command
15   κεφαλή⁷⁵ *f*   head; superior
10   κηρύσσω, -, ἐκήρυξα, -, -, ἐκηρύχθην⁶¹   I proclaim, announce, preach
10   κλαίω, κλαύσω, ἔκλαυσα, -, -, -⁴⁰   I weep (for), lament
     κοιλία²² *f*   the belly; womb
     κοπιάω²³   I work hard, toil; I grow weary
5   κόσμος¹⁸⁵ *m*   world
10   κράζω, κράξω, ἔκραξα, κέκραγα, -, -⁵⁵   I cry out, call out
     κρατέω, κρατήσω, ἐκράτησα, κεκράτηκα, κεκράτημαι, -⁴⁷   I am strong; I hold fast, seize
21   κρίνω, κρινῶ, ἔκρινα, κέκρικα, κέκριμαι, ἐκρίθην¹¹⁵   I judge, decide; I condemn
     κρίμα, -ατος²⁷ *n*   decision, judgment; condemnation
16   κρίσις, -εως⁴⁷ *f*   judging, judgment; trial
5   κύριος⁷¹⁴ *m*   Lord; master, owner
     κωλύω²³   I hinder; I prevent, forbid
     κώμη²⁷ *f*   village

λάμβδα

20	λαλέω, λαλήσω, ἐλάλησα, λελάληκα, λελάλημαι, ἐλαλήθην[297]	I speak
11	λαμβάνω, λήμψομαι, ἔλαβον, εἴληφα, -, ἐλήμφθην[258]	I take; I receive
9	λαός[142] m	people, populace
	λατρεύω[21]	I serve; I worship
3	λέγω, ἐρῶ, εἶπον (or εἶπα), εἴρηκα, εἴρημαι, ἐρρέθην[2352]	I say, speak
	λευκός, -ή, -όν[25]	light, bright; white
18	λίθος[59] m	stone
	λογίζομαι, -, ἐλογισάμην, -, -, ἐλογίσθην[40]	I reckon, consider, think, count
5	λόγος[330] m	word, speech; matter
14	λοιπός, -ή, -όν[55]	rest; remaining
	λυπέω[26]	I grieve, become sad; I offend, insult
10	λύω, (λύσω), ἔλυσα, (λέλυκα), λέλυμαι, ἐλύθην[42]	I loosen, untie; I destroy

μῦ

	Μακεδονία[22] f	Macedonia
4	μαθητής, -οῦ[262] m	disciple, student
7	μακάριος, -α, -ον[50]	blessed, happy, favored
25	μᾶλλον[81]	rather; more
	μανθάνω[25]	I learn; I understand
	μαρτυρία[37] f	testimony, evidence
	μαρτύριον[19] n	testimony, proof
20	μαρτυρέω, μαρτυρήσω, ἐμαρτύρησα, μεμαρτύρηκα, μεμαρτύρημαι, ἐμαρτυρήθην[76]	I testify, witness
	μάρτυς, μάρτυρος[35] m	witness; martyr
13	μάτηρ, μήτρος[83] f	mother
	μάχαιρα[29] f	sword, dagger
12	μέγας, μεγάλη, μέγα[243]	great, large
25	μείζων, -ον[(48)] (comparative of μέγας)	larger, greater
23	μέλλω, μελλήσω, -, -, -, -[109]	I am going to, am about to
	μέλος, -ους[34] n	limb, member, (body) part
15	μέν[178]	indeed, certainly
15	μὲν ... δὲ	on the one hand … on the other hand
21	μένω, μενῶ, ἔμενα, μεμένηκα, -, -[118]	I remain, continue
16	μέρος, μέρους[42] n	part, share
14	μέσος, -η, -ον[58] (with genitive)	middle (of)
8	μετά, μετ', μεθ'[470] with genitive // accusative	with // after, behind
	μετανοέω[34]	I change my mind; I repent
	μετάνοια[22] f	repentance; change of mind
14	μή[1038]	no; (also used in questions expecting a negative answer)
22	μηδέ[56]	and not; not even; neither … nor
22	μηδείς, μηδεμία, μηδέν[91]	no; no one; nothing
	μηκέτι[22]	no longer, no more
22	μήποτε[25]	never; lest ever; whether perhaps
	μήτε[34]	and not; neither … nor
14	μήτι ... ;[18]	no; (expects a negative answer)
22	μικρός, -ά, -όν[46]	small, little
	μιμνήσκομαι[23]	I remember
	μισέω, μισήσω, ἐμίσησα, μεμίσηκα, μεμίσημαι, -[40]	I hate, despise
	μισθός[29] m	wages, reward

18	μνημεῖον[40] *n*	a memorial; grave, tomb
	μνημονεύω[21]	I remember; I call to mind
14	μόνος, -η, -ον[113]	only; alone (*adverb*)
	μυστήριον, -ου[28] *n*	mystery, secret
16	Μωϋσῆς, -έως[80] *m*	Moses

νῦ

	ναί[33]	yes; certainly
18	ναός[45] *m*	temple (edifice); sanctuary
7	νεκρός, -ά, -όν[128]	dead
	νέος, -α, -ον[24]	new, young
	νεφέλη[25] *f*	cloud
	νηστεύω[20]	I fast, abstain from
	νικάω[28]	I conquer, overcome
5	νόμος[194] *m*	law; the Law
	νοῦς, νοός[24] *m*	mind; understanding, way of thinking
7	νῦν[145]	now, currently
	νυνί[20]	now (*emphatic form of* νῦν)
13	νύξ, νυκτός[61] *f*	night

ξῖ

| | ξύλον[20] *n* | wood, tree; post |

ὄ μικρόν

5	ὁ, ἡ, τό[19796]	the (*and other significations*)
5	ὁδός[101] *f*	road, way, path
10	οἶδα, εἰδήσω, ᾔδειν, -, -, -[320]	I know, understand
15	οἰκία[93] *f*	house, dwelling; family
9	οἶκος[113] *m*	house, dwelling; family
	οἰκοδομέω, οἰκοδομήσω, ᾠκοδόμησα, -, οἰκοδόμημαι, οἰκοδομήθην[40] I build (up); I strengthen
	οἶνος[34] *m*	wine
	οἴσω	*see* φέρω
22	ὀλίγος, -η, -ον[40]	little, small; few
12	ὅλος, -η, -ον[108]	whole, entire
	ὀμνύω or ὄμνυμι[26]	I vow, take an oath, swear
22	ὅμοιος, -α, -ον[45]	like, liken to (+ *dat.*)
	ὁμοίως[30]	likewise, in the same way
	ὁμολογέω[26]	I agree with; I confess; I promise
13	ὄνομα, -ατος[229] *n*	name
	ὀπίσω[35] (*with genitive*)	behind, after
16	ὅπου[81]	where
26	ὅπου ἄν or ὅπου ἐάν	wherever
22	ὅπως[53]	in order that; how
11	ὁράω, ὄψομαι, εἶδον (*or* εἶδα *or* ὤψησα), ἑώρακα (*or* ἑόρακα), -, ὤφθην[453] I see; I perceive, understand
	ὀργή[36] *f*	anger, wrath
16	ὄρος, -ους[63] *n*	mountain, hill
9	ὅς, ἥ, ὅ[1407]	who, which, that
26	ὅς ἄν	who(ever)
26	ὅσος, η, -ον[111]	how many, as much as
26	ὅσος ἄν	however so many
19	ὅστις, ἥτις, ὅτι[144]	who(soever), what(soever)

26	ὅταν[123] (*crasis of* ὅτε + ἄν)	when(ever)
16	ὅτε[102]	when, after
8	ὅτι[1294]	that; because
	οὗ[24]	where
3	οὐ, οὐκ, οὐχ[1621]	no, not; (*also used in questions expecting a positive answer*)
15	οὐαί[46]	Woe!
15	οὐδέ[143]	nor; not even; neither
12	οὐδείς, οὐδεμία, οὐδέν[227]	no; no one; nothing
	οὐκέτι[47]	no longer, no further
4	οὖν[495] (*postpositive*)	therefore
	οὔπω[26]	not yet
5	οὐρανός[273] m	heaven, sky
	οὖς, ὠτός[36] n	ear
15	οὔτε[87]	nor; not even; neither
15	οὔτε ... οὔτε	neither ... nor
12	οὗτος, αὕτη, τοῦτο[1387]	this (one); these (pl.)
15	οὕτως[207]	thus, in this manner
14	οὐχί ... ;[54]	no; (*expects a positive answer*)
	ὀφείλω[35]	I owe; I ought
9	ὀφθαλμός[100] m	eye
9	ὄχλος[174] m	crowd, multitude (of people)
	ὄψομαι	*see* ὁράω

πῖ

18	παιδίον[52] n	little child; young servant
	παῖς, παιδός[24] m/f	child (boy or girl); slave
7	πάλιν[141]	again
	πάντοτε[41]	always
10	παρά, παρ'[193] *with genitive// dative// accusative*	from, alongside // beside, near // at, by; out from
4	παραβολή[50] f	parable, illustration
24	παραδίδωμι[119] (P, F, A, Ra, Rp, Ap) (*from* δίδωμι)	I hand over, deliver; I betray
	παραγγέλλω[32]	I transmit a message; I command
	παραγίνομαι[37]	I come, arrive
20	παρακαλέω[109] (P, -, A, -, Rp, Ap) (*from* καλέω)	I exhort; I encourage; I advise
	παράκλησις, -εως[29] f	encouragement, exhortation
11	παραλαμβάνω[49] (P, F, A, -, -, παρελήμφθην) (*from* λαμβάνω)	I take along/with; I receive
	παράπτωμα, -ατος[19] n	false step, transgression, trespass
	πάρειμι[24]	I am present; I have arrived
	παρέρχομαι[29]	I pass by, pass away; I arrive
24	παρίστημι[41] (P, F, A, R, -, -) (*from* ἵστημι)	I place near; I stand before/with
	παρουσία[24] f	presence; arrival, coming
	παρρησία[31] f	boldness, frankness, freedom of speech
12	πᾶς, πᾶσα, πᾶν[1243]	every, all; each
8	πάσχω, -, ἔπαθον, πέπονθα, -, -[42]	I suffer
	πάσχα[29] n (*indeclinable*)	Passover
12	πατήρ, πατρός[413] m	father
2	Παῦλος[158] m	Paul
10	πείθω, πείσω, ἔπεισα, πέποιθα, πέπεισμαι, ἐπείσθην[52]	I persuade; I trust (*+ dat.*); I obey (*middle*)
	πεινάω[23]	I hunger

	πειράζω[38]	I test, tempt; I attempt
	πειρασμός[21] *m*	testing, temptation
3	πέμπω, πέμψω, ἔπεμψα, -, -, ἐπέμφθην[79]	I send, dispatch
	πέντε[38]	five
	πέραν[23] (*with genitive*)	on the other side, beyond
8	περί [332] *with genitive // accusative*	concerning; about // around; about
	περιβάλλω[23]	I put around, clothe
20	περιπατέω, περιπατήσω, περιεπάτησα, -, -, -[95]	I walk; I live, behave
	περισσεύω[39]	I abound, overflow
	περισσός, -ή, -όν[22]	abundant, remarkable; superfluous
	περιτομή[36] *f*	circumcision
2	Πέτρος[156] *m*	Peter
2	Πιλᾶτος[55] *m*	Pilate
	πίμπλημι[24]	I fill (up); I fulfill
11	πίνω, πίομαι, ἔπιον, πέπωκα, -, -[72]	I drink
11	πίπτω, πέσομαι, ἔπεσον, πέπτωκα, -, -[90]	I fall, collapse
7	πιστεύω, πιστεύσω, ἐπίστευσα, πεπίστευκα, πεπίστευμαι, ἐπιστεύθην[241]	I trust; I believe (+ *dat.*)
16	πίστις, -εως[242] *f*	faith; faithfulness
7	πιστός, -ή, -όν[67]	faithful, believing; certain
	πλανάω[39]	I lead astray
25	πλείω, -ον[(57)] (*comparative of* πολύς)	more, greater
	πληγή[22] *f*	blow, strike; wound
	πλῆθος, -ους[31] *n*	a great number, multitude; crowd
	πλήν[31] (*as preposition with genitive*)	but, except, only
20	πληρόω, πληρώσω, ἐπλήρωσα, -, πεπλήρωμαι, ἐπληρώθην[86]	I fill, fulfill
18	πλοῖον[67] *n*	boat
	πλούσιος, -α, -ον[28]	rich, wealthy
	πλοῦτος[22] *m*	wealth, riches
13	πνεῦμα, -ατος[379] *n*	spirit; breath; (Holy) Spirit
	πνευματικός, -ή, -όν[26]	spiritual
	πόθεν[29]	whence? from where?
20	ποιέω, ποιήσω, ἐποίησα, πεποίηκα, πεποίημαι, -[568]	I do; I make
26	ποῖος, -α, -ον[33]	of what kind? which?
16	πόλις, -εως[163] *f*	city
12	πολύς, πολλή, πολύ[415]	much, many
7	πονηρός, -ά, -όν[78]	wicked, evil; sick
3	πορεύομαι, πορεύσομαι, -, -, πεπόρευμαι, ἐπορεύθην[153]	I go, walk
	πορνεία[25] *f*	sexual immorality, prostitution
26	πόσος, -η, -ον[27]	of what quantity? how many?
	ποτέ[29]	at some time, once, ever
14	πότε[19]	when?
	ποτήριον[31] *n*	drinking cup
14	ποῦ [48]	where?
12	πούς, ποδός[93] *m*	foot
	πράσσω[39]	I do, accomplish
14	πρεσβύτερος, -α, -ον[66]	elderly, old; Elder
23	πρό [47] (*with genitive*)	before; in front of

	προάγω[20]	I lead forward, go ahead
	πρόβατον[39] n	a sheep
6	πρός[698] (with accusative)	towards, to; with (may express a purpose)
6	προσέρχομαι[85] (P, -, A, Ra, -, -) (from ἔρχομαι)	I come/ go to (+ dat.)
	προσευχή[36] f	prayer
3	προσεύχομαι, προσεύξομαι, προσηυξάμην, -, -, -[85]	I pray, offer prayer
	προσέχω[24]	I hold to, pay attention to
	προσκαλέω[29]	I summon, call to oneself (mid.)
20	προσκυνέω, προσκυνήσω, προσκύνησα, -, -, -[60]	I worship; I bow down (+ dat.)
8	προσφέρω[47] (P, -, A, R, -, Ap) (from φέρω)	I bring (to); I offer
18	πρόσωπον[76] n	face, appearance; presence
	προφητεία, -ας[19] f	prophecy; expounding Scripture
	προφητεύω[28]	I prophesy; I speak God's word(s)
4	προφήτης, -ου[144] m	prophet
8	πρῶτον (adverb)	first; before
7	πρῶτος, -η, -ον[155]	first; prominent
	πτωχός, -ή, -όν[34]	poor; beggar (noun)
12	πῦρ, πυρός[71] n	fire
	πωλέω[22]	I sell
14	πῶς[105]	how (?); in what way (?)

ῥῶ

13	ῥῆμα, -ατος[67] n	word, saying; thing

σίγμα

18	σάββατον[68] n	Sabbath; rest
13	σάρξ, σαρκός[147] f	flesh
	Σατανᾶς, -ᾶ[36] m	Satan
19	σεαυτοῦ[43]	of yourself
18	σημεῖον[77] n	sign, mark; miracle
	σήμερον[41]	today
12	Σίμων, -ονος[75] m	Simon
	σκανδαλίζω[29]	I cause to stumble, give offence
	σκεῦος, -ους[23] n	vessel or implement of any kind
	σκηνή, -ῆς[20] f	tent, tabernacle
	σκότος, -ους[31] n	darkness; evil world
19	σός, σή, σόν[24]	your, yours (sg.)
17	σοφία[51] f	wisdom
	σοφός, -ή, -όν[20]	skillful, wise
21	σπείρω, -, ἔσπειρα, -, ἔσπαρμαι, ἐσπάρην[52]	I sow seed; I scatter
13	σπέρμα, -ατος[43]	seed; offspring
	σταυρός[27] m	cross
	σταυρόω, σταυρώσω, ἐσταύρωσα, -, ἐσταύρωμαι, ἐσταυρώθην[46]	I crucify
	στέφανος[25] m	crown, wreath
13	στόμα, -ατος[78] n	mouth, opening
	στρατιώτης, -ου[26] m	soldier
	στρέφω[21]	I turn around/back
9	σύ[1067]	you (sg.)
6	σύν[129] (with dative)	with, along with
8	συνάγω[59] (P, F, A, -, συνῆγμαι, Ap) (from ἄγω)	I gather together

17	συναγωγή⁵⁶ f	gathering; synagogue
	συνέδριον²² n	assembled council; the Sanhedrin
	συνείδησις, -εως³⁰ f	conscience; consciousness
	συνέρχομαι³⁰	I come together; I go with
	συνίημι²⁶	I comprehend, understand
	σχῶ	*see* ἔχω
3	σῴζω, σώσω, ἔσωσα, σέσωκα, σέσῳ(σ)μαι, ἐσώθην¹⁰⁶	I save, rescue; I preserve
13	σῶμα, -ατος¹⁴² n	body
	σωτήρ, -ῆρος²⁴ m	rescuer, deliverer, savior
17	σωτηρία⁴⁶ f	deliverance, salvation

ταῦ

15	τέ ²¹³	and; both (*enclitic and postpositive*)
15	τε καί...	both... and
5	τέκνον⁹⁹ n	child
	τέλειος, -α, -ον¹⁹	perfect, complete, mature
	τελειόω²³	I make perfect, complete, mature
	τελέω²⁸	I finish, complete, fulfill
16	τέλος, -ους⁴⁰ n	end, result, purpose
	τελώνης, -ου²¹ m	tax collector
	τεσσαράκοντα²²	forty
14	τέσσαρες, τέσσαρα⁴¹	four
20	τηρέω, τηρήσω, ἐτήρησα, τετήρηκα, τετήρημαι, ἐτηρήθην⁷¹	I keep, guard; I obey
24	τίθημι, θήσω, ἔθηκα, τέθεικα, τέθειμαι, ἐτέθην¹⁰⁰	I set, put, place
	τιμάω²¹	I honor, revere; I set a price on
17	τιμή⁴¹ f	honor, esteem; value, price
	Τιμόθεος²⁴ m	Timothy
14	τίς, τί ⁵⁵¹	Who? What? Why?
14	τις, τι ⁵³⁴	someone, something
26	τοιοῦτος, τοιαύτη, τοιοῦτον⁵⁷	such as this, of such a kind
9	τόπος¹⁷⁴ m	place, position
	τοσοῦτος, τοσαύτη, τοσοῦτον²⁰	so great, so large; so much
8	τότε¹⁵⁹	then, at that time
14	τρεῖς (*m/f*), τρία (*n*) ⁶⁸	three
	τρέχω²⁰	I run; I pursue a course of action
22	τρίτος, -η, -ον⁵⁶	third
14	τυφλός, -ή, -όν⁵⁰	blind

ὖ ψιλόν

12	ὕδωρ, ὕδατος⁷⁶ n	water; rain
5	υἱός³⁷⁵ m	son
9	ὑμεῖς ¹⁸⁴⁰	you (*pl.*)
19	ὑμέτερος, -α, -ον¹¹	your (pl.)
8	ὑπάγω⁷⁹ (P, -, -, -, -, -) (*from* ἄγω)	I depart, go away
	ὑπακούω²¹	I listen to, obey
17	ὑπάρχω, ὑπάρξω, ὑπῆρξα, -, -, -⁶⁰	I exist
8	ὑπέρ¹⁵⁰ *wth genitive // accusative*	on behalf of; over // above; over; superior to
	ὑπηρέτης, -ου²⁰ m	servant, assistant
6	ὑπό, ὑπ᾽, ὑφ᾽ ²²¹ *with genitive // accusative*	by (means of), with // under
	ὑπομονή³² f	patient endurance, perseverance

	ὑποστρέφω[35]	I turn back/around, return
	ὑποτάσσω[38]	I arrange under, put in subjection
	ὑψόω[20]	I lift up, exalt

φῖ

	φάγομαι	*future of* ἐσθίω
	φαίνω[31]	I bring to light, shine; I appear
20	φανερόω, φανερώσω, ἐφανέρωσα, -, πεφανέρωμαι, ἐφανερώθην[49]	I make manifest; I reveal
2	Φαρισαῖος[98] *m*	Pharisee
8	φέρω, οἴσω, ἤνεγκα, (ἐνήνοχα), -, ἠνέχθην[66]	I bear, carry; I bring
	φεύγω, φεύξομαι, ἔφυγον, -, -, -[29]	I flee (from); I escape
24	φημί[65]	I say, declare
	φιλέω[25]	I love; I kiss
	Φίλιππος[36] *m*	Philip
	φίλος, -η, -ον[29]	loved, dear; friend (*noun*)
20	φοβέω, -, -, -, -, ἐφοβήθην[95]	I fear, am afraid; I respect
18	φόβος[47] *m*	fear, reverence; terror
	φρονέω[29]	I think; I am intent on
15	φυλακή[47] *f*	prison; guard; watch (of the night)
	φυλάσσω[31]	I guard, watch; I obey
	φυλή[31] *f*	tribe, nation
	φωνέω, φωνήσω, ἐφώνησα, -, -, ἐφωνήθην[43]	I call (out), speak
15	φωνή[139] *f*	voice; sound
12	φῶς, φωτός[72] *n*	light; torch

χῖ

21	χαίρω, χαιρήσομαι, -, -, -, ἐχάρην[74]	I rejoice, am glad; I welcome
17	χαρά[59] *f*	joy, delight, gladness
	χαρίζομαι[23]	I forgive; I give graciously
13	χάρις, χάριτος[155] *f*	grace; favor; thankfulness
13	χείρ, χειρός[176] *f*	hand
	χήρα[26] *f*	widow
	χιλίαρχος[21] *m*	military tribune; commander
	χιλιάς, -άδος[23] *f*	thousand
17	χρεία[49] *f*	need, what is lacking
2	Χριστός[529] *m*	Christ, Messiah, Anointed
18	χρόνος[53] *m*	time, occasion
	χώρα[28] *f*	country, region
	χωρίς[41] (*with genitive*)	without, apart from

ψῖ

15	ψυχή[102] *f*	soul; life; mind

ῶ μέγα

	ὦ[20]	Oh!
22	ὧδε[61]	here; thus
15	ὥρα[106] *f*	hour
16	ὡς[504]	as, corresponding to; while
	ὡσεί[21]	just as, like; about
	ὥσπερ[36]	just as (*more emphatic than* ὡς)
23	ὥστε[83]	so that, that; therefore
	ὤψησα, ὤφθην	*see* ὁράω

AUTHOR AND SOURCE INDEX

SUBJECT INDEX

Entries marked with asterisk(*) show occurrences in order of appearance.